A History of
SHAKESPEARIAN
CRITICISM

A History of
SHAKESPEARIAN
CRITICISM

By

AUGUSTUS RALLI

VOLUME II

THE HUMANITIES PRESS

NEW YORK
1965

First Published in 1932 by Oxford University Press

Reprinted 1959 by The Humanities Press
by special arrangement with
Oxford University Press
and Mrs. Augustus Ralli

Printed in U.S.A. by
NOBLE OFFSET PRINTERS, INC.
NEW YORK 3, N. Y.

CONTENTS

VOLUME II

Chapter XXIII

ENGLAND 1879–1885

I. COWDEN CLARKES. II. ROSE. III. SWINBURNE. IV. SPEDDING. V. J. A. SYMONDS. VI. HALES. VII. CANNING. VIII. FEIS. IX. MOULTON. X. GRANT WHITE. XI. MINTO. XII. HELEN FAUCIT. XIII. BOYLE. XIV. STOPFORD BROOKE. XV. SHARPE. XVI. CONCLUSION.

I

THE Cowden Clarkes[1] have worked well in the cause of Shakespeare's art. They have discovered meaning and subtle intention in many things which the reader takes for granted. They point out, for instance, how he makes subordinate incidents and inculcated lesson reinforce the main events and precept. The casket scenes of the *Merchant* involve chance and right judgement; and this combined chance and judgement reappears in the legal quirk which saves Antonio's life. At the opening of *Hamlet*, Horatio's incredulity is admirably contrived; it forestalls the reader's, and makes the after-effect on his mind excite an equal impression of reality and awe on theirs.

Their most important section is 'Dramatic Time', where they discover in the plays a system of combined long and short time. As an instance we will give *Hamlet*:

Here the lapses of time before the play are stressed, e.g. allusions to Ghost's previous appearance; to the interval since Hamlet's father died; to the period of Hamlet's attachment to Ophelia, friendship for Horatio, predilection for the players, boyish affection for Yorick. But Shakespeare has counteracted an over-protracted effect by accompanying touches of speed: the embassage to Norway, Laertes' journey to France, Hamlet's to England. He also keeps reiterated tokens of Present Time and Short Time well before the mind, and so contains the incidents of the drama within the bounds of a feasibly beheld transaction.

Short Time: 'I think I hear them.' 'Peace! break thee off' (I. i). 'A little month. . . . A beast would have mourned longer' (I. ii). 'I came to see your father's funeral.' 'I think it was to see my mother's wedding' (I. ii). 'I will watch to-night.' 'Would the night were come' (I. ii). 'The actors are come hither' (II. ii). 'The bark is ready and the wind at help' (IV. iii). 'I am set naked on your kingdom.' 'One woe doth tread upon another's heel' (IV. vii).

Long Time: 'Has this thing appeared again to-night?' 'So nightly toils the subject of the land' (I. i). 'He hath wrung from me my slow leave by laboursome petition' (I. ii). 'But two months dead!' 'We'll teach you to drink deep ere you depart' (I. ii). 'He hath of late made

---

[1] *The Sh. Key*, by Charles and Mary Cowden Clarke, 1879.

B

many tenders' (I. iii). 'Wherein we saw thee quietly inurned' (I. iv). 'That you vouchsafe your rest here in our court' (II. ii). 'Even those you were wont to take delight in' (II. ii). ' . . . . your tardy son to chide' (III. iv). 'They have dealt with me like thieves of mercy' (IV. vi). 'Since he went into France I have been in continual practice' (V. ii).

II

THE subject of Dramatic Time is continued by Edward Rose,[1] with the result of accumulating proof of Shakespeare's conscious and laborious art. Indeed he concludes that Shakespeare horrified Voltaire and Corneille, yet their plays appear inartistic and improbable beside his. The plays contain conflicting and irreconcilable time, especially the tragedies, because the hurry of passion is needed to sweep us along, but we need months and years for growth and change of character. The histories irrefutably prove double time; their unifying element is a rough unity of time. Eighty-three years are dramatized, and we feel a great period does pass, yet taking all the indications of Short Time, every connecting link of day and hour, these half-dozen reigns are compressed into four years and two months. Double Time is of most use in fitting for the stage an undramatic plot. *Henry IV* is a series of unsuccessful and unremarkable rebellions; and to bind these together as a drama Shakespeare has set them in a comedy—itself a succession of scenes united by closely continuing time. We follow Falstaff and Hal from morning to night, almost from hour to hour. The affairs of Hotspur demand some weeks of interval, but the two scenes are in a Falstaffian framework.

III

SWINBURNE[2] says that a poet should be studied in his verse—and that is no question of mechanical metrical tests but a study by the ear alone of Shakespeare's metrical progress, and thence, by the light of this knowledge, of the corresponding progress within, which found expression in the outward changes. From the first plays we see Shakespeare's evil angel rhyme yielding step by step to his better genius. Those scenes of vehement passion in *R. and J.* reveal the novice; the beautiful scenes deal with simple emotions of meeting and parting. As the tragedy of *Richard II* gathers speed the temptation to rhyme grows weaker. The bonds of rhyme are fairly broken in *Richard III*. In the *Errors* rhyme shows itself a good instrument for romantic comedy. Marlowe's divine tragic instrument has found its new sweet use in *L.L.L.* The blank verse and rhyme of *M.N.D.* have equal merit.

[1] *Inconsistency of Time in Sh.'s Plays*, 1880 (New Sh. Soc.'s Transactions).
[2] *A Study of Sh.*, 1880.

Shakespeare's second period is that of his perfect comic and historical style—the most limpid language, purest style, most transparent thought, matter not yet too great to be uttered perfectly. In this stage he appears serenely able to fathom the else unfathomable depths of spiritual nature. John tempts Hubert in words that touch a subtler string in man's tragic nature than any poet has struck since Dante. In the first stage of simple emotion Shakespeare had not excelled Marlowe. Romeo and Juliet were lovers only, types of a single passion. Antony and Cleopatra are first lovers—but the thought of their love and its tragedy recalls all the forces and fortunes of mankind. Indignation at her cousin's wrong transfigures Beatrice, and brings a new element of variety in unity. Brutus is the noblest figure of a typical and ideal republican in the world's literature.

Hamlet is the bridge between the middle and last period. Shakespeare revised it to satisfy himself and make it worthy of him, not for mere stage effect. Hamlet was not over-irresolute; at times he acted with unscrupulous resolution. A real doubter would not have suspected his own weakness, and he would have doubted Horatio: whereas for long he does not doubt Ophelia. *Lear* is Shakespeare's nearest work to Aeschylus—the one tragic poet on any side greater than himself. It treats the deepest thing of nature and highest of Providence—from the roots that no God waters to the stars which give no man light— over a world full of death and life without resting-place or guidance. He is a darker fatalist than Aeschylus; we see no twilight of atonement on the horizon of tragic fatalism. The most terrible work of human genius, it reveals nature as unnatural. Othello is Shakespeare's noblest man, and Iago is an inarticulate poet—almost as far above vice as beneath virtue. The text of *Macbeth* is mutilated, especially the early scenes, but not the witch scenes. Cleopatra best shows how Shakespeare not only achieved the right thing but abstained from the wrong. He set her off by no lesser means than all the glory of the world and its empires. Elsewhere in Shakespeare we see the perfect mother, wife, &c.—here the perfect and everlasting woman.

In this third period beauty and melody are transfigured into harmony and sublimity; but in one stage humour and reality are supplanted by realism and obscenity. *T. and C.* is a hybrid, hundred-faced, hydra-headed prodigy that defies comment. In *M. for M.* justice is outraged. In the *Kinsmen* we do catch the note of Shakespeare's very voice. The *W. Tale* brings us within the very circle of Shakespeare's culminant and crowning constellation. *Cymbeline* contains tragic beauty and passion, terror, love, pity, subtly sweet and bitter truth, delight and glory of life, and grace of nature—with Shakespeare's most heavenly triad of human figures. . . .

Swinburne did not suffer fools gladly, and he is at times guilty of critical incivility. Throughout his critical writings there is a

displeasing controversial note; he writes with a sore feeling for those
who have expressed contrary opinions to his own in the past, and for
the unborn 'criticasters' who will do so in the future. At the outset he
lodges a double claim for his superior worth—his ear—and the fact
that from the first years he has made the study of Shakespeare his chief
intellectual business and spiritual delight. These claims are well
founded, but we take exception to the manner in which they are
advanced. Moreover, the presence here, as in all his prose-writings,
of what we cannot but call 'bad temper' detracts from his splendid
eloquence. The two things do not mix, and the result is a divided
total expression. Aeschylus, whom at times he worshipped even above
Shakespeare, describes the confused state of Troy when the Greeks
possessed it—like oil and vinegar in the same vessel, unfriendly and
separated.[1]

Each critic creates Shakespeare in his own image, and it is only
natural that Swinburne, who had one of the finest ears in the history of
English prosody, should stress his metrical supremacy. It has been too
often overlooked—especially by the Germans—that Shakespeare was
first of all a poet—and he does well to concentrate on this. On the
other hand, his interpretation is inclined to be narrowly lyrical. The
object of the drama is to display character in action, and successful
plays have been written by men who were not poets in the pure sense.
Shakespeare combined all the qualities of the dramatist, and critics
have pointed out the mighty effect of his simple stage-direction,
'Enter Lear, with Cordelia dead in his arms'. In fine, the key to the
individual character is through his emotions suggested by the music
of the verse, but whether the whole body of the drama can be thus
disintegrated is a question that we would rather raise and abandon
than attempt to solve. However, Swinburne does much to show how
musical speech can express thought.

Myers once said that no poetry can ever appeal to the world again
like the great passages in Homer, because the language was the most
perfect in which man has ever worked. Beside it Virgil's language
sounds elaborate and Dante's crabbed and Shakespeare's barbarous.
Perhaps this explains Swinburne's reason for preferring Aeschylus
to Shakespeare. He concentrated on the verse and extracted deeper
meaning from the richer Greek harmonies. He is often at his best in
comparing the two dramatists—notably in the sphere of fate. His
remarks on *T. and C.*, that it is the play whose best things lose least by
extraction, vindicate, in the light of modern criticism, his method of
studying Shakespeare. The part played by his magnificent praise in
attuning the reader's soul to Shakespeare must not be forgotten.
When about to treat of the great tragedies he leads us to 'the entrance of
the heavenly quadrilateral, or under the rising dawn of the four fixed

[1] *Agamemnon*, 320–3.

stars which compose our Northern Cross'. 'Beyond these again we see a second group arising, the supreme starry trinity of the *W. Tale*, the *Tempest*, and *Cymbeline.*'

IV

WORTHY of mention is James Spedding's essay,[1] because it states clearly one of the leading difficulties in Shakespearian criticism—the relation between Shakespeare's life and works. Like all written by Spedding it has the stamp of a wise and impartial mind.

He writes to disprove what he calls the 'hook and eye' criticism of Furnivall, and the assumption that the plays taken in their right order contain the true history of the growth and progress of Shakespeare's soul. He maintains that the changes follow the natural law of a man's tastes as he grows older. First come farce and tragedy of the bowl and dagger kind; secondly, the richer and more delicate humours of high comedy and historical tragedy; thirdly, the great passions which disclose the heights and depths of humanity; and fourthly, the calmer and more soothing pathos of autumnal days. Furnivall mistakenly separated the broad natural divisions into subordinate groups according to the particular prominent feature. The latter would depend on many things besides the writer's state of mind—the story, the requirements of the theatre, the public taste, the actors. Every man has some power to imagine a situation he has not experienced; and this power is said to be the special gift of poets, and above all of Shakespeare. How are we to reconcile Furnivall's theory with the fact that good and bad states of mind are dilineated with equal depth and greatness in the same play, e.g. Isabella and Claudio? Shakespeare could have imagined both but not been both. If his imagination could not transcend his experience, whence came his insight into the souls of Brutus, Hamlet, Othello, Macbeth, Lear and his daughters? The mysteries of passion in them lie beyond any possible personal experiences of Shakespeare.

Spedding concludes by saying that if Shakespeare had undergone perturbations he had risen above them; and he is right to point out the error of connecting Shakespeare's life and works in the obvious way that Furnivall and some others have done. But the question remains whether he leaves too wide a gap between Shakespeare's moral nature and his imagination. Can imagination satisfy that is not based on reality—on the emotional experience of life of its possessor?

V

J. A. SYMONDS[2] points out that Shakespeare's greatness lay in bringing the type established by his predecessors to artistic ripeness; and he describes the state of England and of the drama at the beginning

[1] 'Why did Sh. write Tragedies' (*Cornhill*, August 1880).
[2] *Sh.'s Predecessors in the Eng. Drama*, 1883.

of his career. He found a spirit of civil and religious freedom, and of nationality. Loyalty to the Queen's person coincided with a sense of national independence. This powerful grasp on life's realities was compatible with romantic fancy and imaginative fervour. Feudalism and Ecclesiasticism belonged to the past, Puritanism was not yet. Men did not curb their passions and superstitions but gloried in them. They passed abruptly from good to bad, from vice to virtue. The drama requires a national public—complete sympathy between playwrights and nation. This existed in England, but not in Italy, France, or Spain. Poetry was the only art in England, and language the one means of expressing passion. At every epoch of the world man has penetrated more deeply than at others into some particular subject. Intuition into human character was the virtue of the Elizabethan age.

From the medieval Miracle the drama inherited some well-defined characters and situations, a popular type of comedy, plebeian melodrama, widely diffused dramatic customs. The Morality developed true types of character, and made the drama self-conscious. It is not necessary to follow Symonds through his account of the rise of Comedy, Tragedy, and Romance, but we pause for a moment over the Historical play. Shakespeare, he says, glorified but did not metamorphose his historical heroes. He revived real persons and raised them to poetic level without changing their characteristics. He could flatter without being a sycophant, and reveal the dark places of the soul without prejudice. Lyly made important discoveries, but it was Marlowe who perceived the capacities for noble art in the Romantic drama. He adopted the romantic and rejected the classic drama, but took blank verse from the classic. He transfigured the right dramatic metre and the right dramatic stuff. From the first Shakespeare deigned to tread in Marlowe's footsteps.

VI

WITH much that Symonds said about the Elizabethan age, J. W. Hales[1] agrees. To him the Gunpowder plotters were typical of the age. Passion, free play of life, unfettered movement of nature favoured the growth of art in Shakespeare's day. Old things had passed away, and all was becoming new. Not only were the barriers of the earth widened, but spiritual barriers had passed away: the mind wandered free in the universe of thought. The choruses of *Henry V* show how Shakespeare could rely on his audience. The Elizabethan drama was created by its circle—the whole nation; and it was the one literature of its day, the centre of English art and thought.

The porter scene in *Macbeth* gives scope to Hales for some valuable remarks on the Romantic drama. It contained frequent juxtaposition of opposites—the meeting of extremes. This is not the law of relief,

[1] *Notes and Essays on Sh.*, 1884.

but the ambition of the Teutonic drama to embrace the whole of life. The true humorist delighted in amazing contrasts and fantastic paradoxes.

Elsewhere Hales is at his best in comparative criticism. Shakespeare and Chaucer, he says, excel in character-drawing because of their reverence for Nature. Both are realistic, and prove the intense realism at the basis of the Low German mind. He contrasts the liberties which Dickens took with human nature, and the mere trick of Sterne's pathos. Could Shakespeare have saved Cordelia he would have done so. The keenest eyes see infinite nobleness in the world, but also more meanness. Shakespeare, like all the supremest writers, has no heroes in the usual sense. Also he faithfully follows his originals—especially Plutarch—and yet subtly transforms and ennobles them. By an inscrutable magic the same words breathe a new life, and the whole scene is transferred into a new air.

Hales's criticism of *Lear* deserves a glance. He dwells on the heathen atmosphere of the play due to Shakespeare's deliberate choice of dark and barbarous ages. Passion is lord of all, and man scarcely separated from brute. Lear is of Celtic race; the Teutonic mind can scarcely follow the rapid revolutions of his fiery spirit. Cordelia also has Celtic impulsiveness. Yet the play deals with natural man as opposed to artificial. The passions walk abroad—greed, lust, wrath, but also love. In the end good prevails, and evil consumes itself. . . .

Hales speaks of the 'Celtic' Lear incomprehensible to the Teutonic mind: and yet Dowden described the play as the greatest single achievement of the northern or Teutonic genius. The play no doubt is one of passion, but at the deliberately chosen barbarous ages we partially protest—having in mind Lear's outpourings against the official classes, and the scene where he wakes and recognizes Cordelia. The age of Homer was thought to be primitive till it was pointed out that primitive men do not speak of their gods like Homer. We may say of the critics as Theseus said of the actors, 'The best are shadows': or as Byron said of men in general—they mark the earth with ruin, but their control stops on the shore of the Shakespearian ocean.

VII

A. S. G. CANNING[1] cannot be called an inspiring critic of Shakespeare. He rather reverts to an earlier kind of criticism which assumes Shakespeare to be a great poet, but judges his poetry as a splendid robe cast over all characters alike whose doings are tested by obvious moral or prudential standards. He is a stranger to the imaginative world which their reactions should create in the reader's mind. Thus he says that Shakespeare does not make Octavia as interesting as he might have done, considering her amiable, virtuous, and forgiving character

[1] *Thoughts on Sh.'s Historical Plays,* 1884.

as recorded by history. Cleopatra fears to lose Antony, because through
him she rules Egypt; and her whole object was to live in voluptuous
enjoyment. None of the persons in *Macbeth*, except a few in name,
have any Scottish characteristic. Lady Macbeth's love for her husband
is little to be commended, because she will gain by his increasing power,
owing to her influence over him. Shakespeare's noble language alone
dignifies a base, shameless character. The two run no risk, because
Duncan is killed in his sleep, and Banquo and Lady Macduff by hired
assassins—yet they exhort and animate each other in grand language
worthy of a true hero and heroine. Falstaff never shows a good quality,
being a compound of self-indulgence, falsehood, licentiousness, and
shameless roguery. The Prince makes no promises, while getting full
amusement from Falstaff's wit and profligacy. The rebel leaders—
Hotspur, Worcester, Mortimer, Glendower—are none of them equal
to Henry IV in combined valour and politic wisdom. Falstaff is bored
by Shallow and Silence, but he is too shrewd to offend people if he
can help it. The final scene between the King and Prince did much
to produce the change in the latter. It was unlikely, if not impossible,
that ruffians like Dighton and Forrest, in *Richard III*, should use such
language or feel such emotions.

Perhaps Canning rises above himself in analysing Richard III's
soliloquy after the apparitions. It reveals, he says, his mental power,
vivid fancy, and deep remorse, without real penitence, and seems to
arise more from dreamy recollections of his many victims and vague
terror at their menaces than from any sense of personal responsibility
to a higher power.

VIII

WE cannot accept the theory of Jacob Feis,[1] that Shakespeare wrote
Hamlet to refute Montaigne, but it is here included because the comparison throws interesting side-lights on *Hamlet's* character. After
affirming that Shakespeare did not exclude direct teaching in his plays,
e. g. *John* reveals the soul of the age that had conquered the Armada—
the Roman plays show his dislike of divided dominion—he proceeds
to say that in *Hamlet* he made his profession of faith. The first
English translation of Montaigne's essays was published in 1603, and
all the additions to the Second Quarto of *Hamlet* refer to Montaigne's
philosophy. Montaigne preached the rights of nature and yet clung
to dogmatic tenets. He yearned for laws and religions drawn from
universal reason, and yet he was a Romanist. Shakespeare was a
humanist, whose religion was natural, not transcendental,[2] and he
wished to counteract this pernicious influence. Montaigne disturbs
the mind and does not clear it, but produces despair. Hamlet, who
represents Montaigne, likes humanistic studies—Wittenberg—but

[1] *Sh. and Montaigne*, 1884.   [2] Cf. Birch, Watkiss Lloyd, and Wordsworth.

also adheres to old dogmas—'unhousel'd. . . '. Montaigne says man has no fixed point in himself, yet he reverenced ceremonial, e.g. the sign of the cross. Hamlet's soul-struggle is from a divided mind— 'nothing either good or bad'. His incessant thoughts of death are the same as Montaigne's, and Shakespeare makes it clear that they come from superstitious Christianity, not the free use of reason. This inner discord—superstition and humanism—makes Hamlet turn to Horatio.

Montaigne was a new and strange phenomenon in Shakespeare's energetic age—a nobleman letting himself be driven about rudderless by his feelings and even boasting of this mental disposition—who would be a humanist, yet retains the reasoning of Loyola. Hamlet has been called a philosopher with energy paralysed by thinking too much. This endangers the sovereignty of human reason. We owe everything great in the world to a full and free use of reason. Thought and action go hand in hand, and action is useless without thought. Bacon was showing that the mind can only progress if it discards trans-cendental dogmas and inquires into nature. Hamlet is unconcerned by the murder of Polonius and Rosencrantz and Guildenstern, and his arguments would palliate any tyranny. His final vengeance is done in blind passion; and Montaigne says that the most beautiful actions of the soul proceed from the impulse of passion. Shakespeare wished to warn contemporaries that to try and reconcile two opposite ideas— Nature, and superstitious dogma which declares human nature sinful —will produce deeds of madness. . . .

The defect of the above is that it ignores the historical side of the play—the material which Shakespeare incorporated from his sources. It also ignores the disturbing influence on Hamlet's mind of the events before the action opens—his father's death and his mother's re-marriage. Also it is obvious that the writer is prejudicial against what he calls 'transcendental dogmas'.

IX

THE critic has many disagreeable duties to perform, and not the least is to report unfavourably on a work inspired by true enthusiasm for its subject. No one will dispute that R. G. Moulton[1] is a genuine Shakespearian lover, and yet his essay in scientific criticism is doomed by its very nature to fail. It profits little to gain the world of know-ledge and lose the soul of art. At the best his comments are like objects in a museum; they are facts and they are there because they have served a purpose, but they will never be used again. They do not make our sense breed, as Angelo's did at the words of Isabella. For instance, it is true, but in an infertile abstract fashion, that unstable moral equilibrium is at the root of the main plot of *Lear*—unnatural

[1] *Sh. as a Dramatic Artist*, 1885.

distribution of power set up by Lear, of which the whole tragedy is a rebound.

The object with which he sets out is to present dramatic criticism as a regular inductive science. Judicial criticism compares a new work with those that exist already. Criticism of investigation does the same, but it also differentiates and registers a new type. No one now tests exclusively by classical models, yet the idea of testing is still the root idea. Sympathy is the grand interpreter, and the judicial attitude is a barrier to it. Admiration for the past paralyses faith in the future. One should analyse literature as it stands, discover its laws in itself. The inductive critic asks what view best fits with the details as they stand in actual fact. Subjective impressions produce the literary effect, but the objective details are the *limit* on the variability of the subjective impressions. Truth of interpretation is tested by the degree of completeness with which it explains the details of a literary work as they stand. Inductive criticism is concerned with differences of kind, not degree; it distinguishes literary species. The laws of the Shakespearian drama are those of dramatic practice derived from analysis of his actual works.

Character, passion, plot are the grand divisions of dramatic criticism. The leading interest of character is interpretation—turning from concrete to abstract. Richard III is ideal villainy; Bassanio may appear unworthy of Portia, if we compare their parts in the drama— but note the force with which his personality sways all those who approach him. Portia and Nerissa illustrate character-contrast, and Macbeth character-development. Passion divides into unity, complexity, movement. As regards complexity, Shakespeare and his contemporaries produced stirring new passion-effects by mixing serious and comic. When light and serious passions alternate we call it tone-play; the porter scene in *Macbeth* is an example of tone-relief; the comic irony of the trial in the *Merchant* is tone-clash; and the centre of *Lear* rises to tone-storm. Plot is the intellectual side of action. When mutual relation of parts is considered by itself, as abstract interest of design, human life being only the material to which this design is applied, then we get interest of plot. This reduction to order is where science and art meet. Criticism must analyse a complex action into constituent single actions. The enveloping action links with wider interest, e.g. the Wars of the Roses in *Richard III*——the supernatural in *Macbeth* where the human workings of the play are wrapped in a deeper working out of destiny—the passions of the mob in *J.C.*—the French war in *Lear*. The latter is outside the main issues, yet loosely connects itself with every phase of the movement, and finally breaks out as the reality in which the whole action of the play merges. Economy of plot is the perfection of design which lies midway between incompleteness and waste. It brings the various bonds

between actions into a common system; the more the separateness of
different interests are reduced, the richer will be the economy of
design: Bassanio is a link between persons; Gloucester's story seems
to spring out of Lear's. Symmetry—balance of actions—is Shakespeare's
most important economic form: *Lear* is the most intricate and most
symmetrical play.

Movement is the real basis of distinction between the two main
classes of Shakespearian dramas, not tragedy and comedy. In the
Merchant the leading interest is in the complication of Antonio's
fortunes and its resolution by Portia's device. In the tragedies there
is no such return from distraction to recovery; our agitation is relieved
only by the emotion of pathos or despair. The impression, therefore,
is the sense of intellectual or emotional unity in the movement, i.e.
Action-movement or Passion-movement. For Tragedy and Comedy,
therefore, we substitute Passion-drama and Action-drama.

Such, in outline, are Moulton's most general ideas; it remains to
give some instances of the way in which he applied them to particular plays. The *Merchant* embodies the idea of Nemesis—the
artistic bond between sin and retribution. Each detail of vindictiveness in the first half is matched by a corresponding detail in the second.
Shylock appeals to the written law, and this leads to the recalling of an
old law which crushes him. Shakespeare leads up to the bond by a
discussion on interest. The contradiction is between flesh and barren
metal. To resolve the law difficulties, Shakespeare retains the traditional plea as to blood, but puts it into the mouth of an amateur
lawyer, and then before we feel the injustice, follows up this brilliant
evasion by a sound legal plea. In *Richard III* the transcendental is made
possible by method of treatment. The incident of the wooing of
Lady Anne might be impossible alone, but becomes possible through
others it is associated with. Richard passes through a career of sin
without taint of distortion of the intellect, and with the calm of
innocence; and thus he convinces us that he is irresistible. Each
minor interest is a Nemesis, and all are linked. Those who triumph
in one become victims of the next—Clarence, the King, Hastings,
Buckingham.

In *Macbeth* sin and retribution are equal. Macbeth succeeds till
the mid-point when Fleance escapes, aand then he declines. Banquo's
murder unmasks former crimes, and the action is a complete Nemesis
—a career of sin in which the last sin secures the punishment of all.
The apparent checks to destiny become the means by which destiny
chooses to fulfil itself. Macbeth is practical and natural; he reflects
current thought and goodness as they appear from the outside. He is
almost childish in his spiritual struggles: he could not say Amen!
Lady Macbeth, on the contrary, is accustomed to moral loneliness
and at home in mental struggles. To her the sleeping and the dead

are pictures, and she has conquered the superstitions of the age. *J.C.*
gives the antithesis of charity and political science. When these
clash, outer and inner life conflict; and in Rome the individual existed
for the State. In Brutus the antithesis of the outer and inner life
disappears; he is evenly developed on both sides, does not deceive himself, and preserves his moral sense. But the antithesis reappears in
action: he admits that Caesar has done no wrong, but slays him for
what he might do. This conscious sacrifice of justice and friendship
to policy is a fatal error which produces the whole tragedy. Caesar
is practical like Macbeth, and perfect to the point where his own
personality is engaged. The tasks of the soldier and statesman are
imposed from without, but at last he comes to a crisis that involves his
personality. He attempts a task imposed on him by his own ambition,
and needs self-knowledge which he lacks. From the swimming match
with Cassius we see that he lacks passive courage born of the inner
life which gives strength to submit to the inevitable. He calls for
rescue, and so when he is sick with fever. The plot is symmetrical,
the whole balanced about the turning-point in the middle. Passion
gathers round the conspirators, and rises to a great climax like an
arch. Then it declines, since it is an error to ignore justice and
humanity. Outraged human sympathy asserts itself, after Caesar's
death, in the passions of the mob. . . .

Moulton assumes that economy, &c., of plot is a means to make
Shakespeare's poetic genius more effective, but he does not convince.
Neither do we share his belief that Shakespeare consciously directed
his plots in the manner he describes. It remains to ask whether
Shakespeare intuitively practised the scientific plot-building which
Moulton attributes to him. The critic should explore his subject's
mind, and not the least interesting of his duties is to discriminate
between its conscious and unconscious working. We feel that Moulton
is outside Shakespeare's mind, and like the scientist reconstructing
from the rocks his story of the past. His terms are too empty of
emotional content by the time they reach us to stimulate our power to
understand and admire Shakespeare. Between the impression and its
utterance there exists a scientific No-man's-land where the aesthetic
sense dies; and thus the critic uses other faculties than those which
recorded his impressions to body forth his doctrine.

Yet it is fair to add that once or twice when Moulton writes in
an impressionistic manner he holds us. We may not agree with his
opinions on Macbeth and Lady Macbeth, or Brutus and Caesar, yet
the light is so directed as to make darkness visible. And in a tract
which he published the following year,[1] he makes some discoveries
which we would not willingly let die. In *Henry V* the true punishment of the conspirators is Henry's outpouring of soul which

[1] *On Character-Development in Sh. &c.*, 1886 (New Sh. Soc. Trans.).

turns the light of heroism on to the sin of treason. All Henry's heart-searching and doubt has no effect but to draw every fibre of his soul on to the task before him. Macbeth's practical nature, as the part of him most highly developed, will be, when he surrenders himself to evil, the seat of his susceptibility to crime. But this same nature will be hindered by want of the self-discipline needed for periods of in-decision. His imagination at first restrained him from sin, but later became the Nemesis which betrayed him to the supernatural visita-tions that ruined him. . . . In all these we feel that the 'economy' of which Moulton speaks is more moral and psychological and less mechanical than we have been sometimes inclined to admit.

X

RICHARD GRANT WHITE'S[1] point of view is that Shakespeare was an unconscious genius, who wrote easily, and whose object was to produce a suitable play for the Globe stage, with neither 'philosophy' nor 'central idea', nor even art-purpose after his earliest essays. He worked up old plays and stories and made them immortal by his psychological insight and magic style. He warns the reader against the critics, even Coleridge, and especially the Germans, and thinks that those who understand Shakespeare best read the plain text and do not use critical editions. We will pass in review some of his typical sayings and note how far they help us according as they are true to his theory.

The persons of *L.L.L.* show germs of character or imperfect out-lines rather than character. The thought of the *Errors* is of lighter weight than elsewhere, yet nothing like Adriana's jealousy had been written in a modern play. *M.N.D.* shows a great advance, both in poetry and human interest. *Verona* is one of the weakest plays, written under the influence of the prose-romances of Shakespeare's early day, yet the first comedy of society in our literature which repre-sents tolerably the daily intercourse of real human beings. *Richard III* is the poorest and thinnest in thought, the least free and harmonious in rhythm—the least Shakespearian. *Richard II* is rather a tragic dramatic poem, but the best passages show Shakespeare attaining free and independent action.

Shakespeare had no system of dramatic art: *John* presents the events of a whole reign. He showed things as he saw them, thoughtless as to the past, except as it gave material for dramatic treatment. *Henry IV* presents the social life of his own day, and contains his highest humour. He knew that Falstaff was morally vile, but as dramatist he was in-tellectually indifferent to the character of the person by whom he effected his dramatic purpose. In the *Merchant* there is great advance

---

[1] *Studies in Sh.*, 1885.

of character and dramatic construction. *R. and J.* is the freshest, sweetest breath of life's spring-time that a poet's lips ever uttered. Like the hack playwright of to-day he dramatized an old ballad to make a play to please his audience, but it just happened that he was William Shakespeare who had a peculiar way of doing such things.

In *T. and C.* the individual, mental, and moral traits of the persons are not distinguished, but it is Shakespeare's wisest play in the way of worldly wisdom. It utters the Ulyssean way of life, and Shakespeare is Ulysses. Lady Macbeth is cruel, remorseless, unimaginative; but, like the tigress, she has sexual and maternal instincts. That Hamlet should spare the King at prayer reveals a fiendish malignity of purpose, if any purpose at all—but it reveals only his lack of purpose.

Rosalind had not only wit but humour, which few women have. Her character revealed under her strange circumstances makes her Shakespeare's most charming woman except Imogen. Jaques's melancholy was what we now call cynicism. The sight of so much real happiness at the end was more than he could bear, and he withdrew to a hermit's cell to hide his chagrin.

Lear, M. for M., Timon contain more revolting and alarming truths than all the other plays together. It is hard to trace Shakespeare in his plays, but we cannot but conclude that something in his experience of life caused him to produce three such plays within three years. What a marvellous, untraceable touch of art is that by which he conveys to us that Lear, in casting off Cordelia, is half conscious that he is doing wrong! His insanity he brings upon himself, for he is not driven out into the storm or driven out at all. Goneril and Regan at first are not without reason, and up to the time when Lear rushes out into the storm he cannot be justified. Strangest of all is the sustained royalty of his madness, for mad or sane, he is always kingly. The wisdom of the Fool has come from long experience of the world without responsible relations to it. He justly disappears when Lear sinks from frenzy to forlorn imbecility, because his utterances would have jarred upon our ears. The situation becomes too grandly pathetic to admit the presence of a jester, who is nothing if not professional. Even Shakespeare could not make sport with the great primal elements of woe.

Iago's character, both strong and complex, is hardly inferior to any in Shakespeare. He had little spontaneous malice, and unless for a good reason would rather serve than injure those around him. Honesty and a warm heart were his external traits; he was popular with all. His inner nature, till he was tempted to reveal it, was possibly but half known to himself. He was selfish and unscrupulous, but not disposed to malice or mischief—only cruelly heartless. Until some one barred his way, he was as free from personal malice as the man who makes

a corner and ruins unknown persons. The one peculiar element
was that he had no scruples, no moral sense—his guide was self-
interest. . . .

Grant White's mind belongs to the class that believe the hardest
problems can be solved by common sense. We must protest when he
warns us against Coleridge, and we even protest in a minor key when
he warns us against Ulrici as a mad mystic and Gervinus as a literary
Dogberry who has imposed all his tediousness on the world. The
difficulty lies between first and second impressions, and the duty of the
'higher criticism', which Grant White contemns, is to discriminate
wisely the latter. If the impression is immediately returned to the
page, the verdict may be true but barren. If it is meditated, the result
depends upon the previous culture of the mind which absorbs it: and
some critical minds are far from spiritual realities, and overworked
with systems and central ideas and abstract learning. The ideal is
that literature and life should nourish and develop each other: thus
when Myers discovers that certain lines in the sixth book of the
Aeneid beat with the pulses of the heart, he reveals his own nature
softened and refined by conversing with the classics, and he elevates
the reader by his contagious enthusiasm.

Grant White's obvious, common-sense, argumentative criticism does
not satisfy us as applied to Falstaff, Jaques, or Ulysses, but it succeeds
partially with Rosalind. It does both himself and the reader good
service when he discovers that Lear was not driven out into the storm;
and it enables him to make an excellent analysis of Iago. He is at his
best in *Lear*, especially in his remarks on the Fool. There the uni-
versal-life interest so predominates that the incoming impression is
forcibly sucked down to the depths, and even if returned at once to
the surface bears the marks of its awful experience: like the Amazon
which floods for miles with fresh water the ocean itself. The value of
his book is in its reconcentrating attention on a fact often forgotten—
that Shakespeare's style is the true foundation of his greatness. The
final expression is that only half his mind is turned upon Shakespeare,
and the other and larger half preoccupied with the misdoings of super-
subtle critics.

XI

WILLIAM MINTO[1] writes useful if not great criticism. He
states clearly the nature of the drama, the difficulties the dramatist has
to contend with, and how Shakespeare used his genius and experience
to overcome them. It stops short of the inner mysteries, but it is the
kind we should do well to carry with us as introductory to more
ambitious works.

[1] *Characteristics of English Poets, 1885.*

Shakespeare united prudence with heaven-climbing genius. He opened his mind freely to the experience of the ages; but he expressed newly the accumulated wealth of literature, and improved what he borrowed. His was the wisdom of sagacious choice and happy application. But his genius was his own, and the word that best describes him is 'myriad-mooded'. He understood the mental habits of others by passing through many changes of mood. No imagination can construct states of mind apart from all experience. In imagining characters Shakespeare fell back on the temporary attitudes of his own variable mind. In London, where he had to make his way, his doubtful position exposed him to treatment ranging from insult to admiration. For dramatic insight a wonderful combination of variableness is needed, and for dramatic execution, fundamental steadiness. Dramatic truth consists in correspondence between motive and passion; dramatic subtlety appears in the fluctuations of passion. Shakespeare combines this truth and subtlety with an incomparable energy of expression. No one has approached him in imagining and expressing the tempest in the soul from supernatural apparitions. His mastery over the keys of sadness is the most memorable side of his genius. Intense passion transfigures: there is strict dramatic truth in Macbeth's fancy that the blood on his hands will incarnadine the seas. The many-sidedness of his characters makes them life-like; they are types, but also individuals. The dramatist's most essential faculty is that of representing one character in active influence on another. The effect reacts, the reaction reacts, &c., &c. To hold your shifting data unconscious, and to keep all your results within the just limits of dramatic effect, is one of the rarest human gifts. This appears in the beginning of *Macbeth*, the quarrel of Brutus and Cassius, the scene between Coriolanus and his mother. *A. and C.* is the greatest monument of dramatic subtlety. Without the massive breadth of feeling and overpowering interest of the four great tragedies, it excels even *Macbeth* and *Othello* in range of mastery over the fluctuations of profound passion. It is the greatest play in the dramatist's greatest faculty. In drama life is condensed and concentrated, and it is unconcerned with the slight and stealthy growth of passion. In all his tragedies Shakespeare suggests the influence of destiny. How would we have felt had Cordelia and Desdemona survived? . . .

This is the criticism of the teacher rather than the seer. The words are like counters that stand for a fixed value among men. The significance of the ideas which they express has been agreed upon by all, e.g. 'the massive breadth of feeling and overpowering interest of the four great tragedies'. Old terms and epithets are not used to reveal a distinctive admiration for Shakespeare; rather we are instructed in the way that Shakespeare should affect us. Nevertheless, such teaching has its use.

XII

A book like Helen Faucit's[1] depresses the opposite scale too greatly, for personal imagination rather unduly predominates. It is a charming book, the work of an artist, and bears the imprint of a charming nature. Helen Faucit acted the parts of the heroines of whom she writes; she threw her own nature into theirs, was moved by their emotions, and thought their thoughts. Our business will be to sift her pages for criticisms which throw light on Shakespeare because of her method: and then to balance these by such selections of the merely personal or fanciful of which this method has been the cause.

The character of Ophelia was delicately outlined and shaded in with fine strokes, and revealed Shakespeare's belief in the sympathetic actor to fill up the outlines. As a child she had been lonely and given to wandering by streams. With Hamlet's rare qualities there was a certain loneliness like hers, which attracted her. She was not weak, but strong in the highest sense—that is, self-forgetting. Portia as a last resource tries to bring before the mind's eye of Shylock the horror of the deed—a gash. His fiendish nature is here revealed, and one no longer desires to extenuate him. Desdemona has been called insipid and plastic, but such natures do not win the love of the noblest and the attachment of all. State affairs absorbed her father, and she was thrown back on herself and left to dream of nobler characters and lives than those around her. Long before she saw Othello she must have pictured to herself this remarkable man who was talked of by all. Brabantio was blind because he was of strange race; and this wide difference of feeling could not have existed had there been sympathy. Brabantio's blindness must have shown the lovers that it was impossible to gain his consent. Juliet also dreams of an ideal hero, having grown up amid coarse worldly surroundings, with a rich imagination full of romance, and boundless capacity for self-devotion. Imogen acts on and influences all the chief characters in the play; we must make ourselves familiar with them to know her. The opening scene shows how much Shakespeare expected from those who personated his heroines. The actress must produce the impression of a character, from which all that is afterwards seen of Imogen follows naturally. Iachimo's exquisite art fulfils Shakespeare's purpose of keeping alive our respect for the wretched husband. The charming features in Guiderius and Arviragus are developed by her influence. Posthumus dies believing in her guilt: in such scenes Shakespeare surpasses all dramatic writers. He has faith in his interpreters, and does not encumber them with words. No words could express what passes in Imogen's soul.

In Rosalind Helen Faucit could express what was best in herself and her art. She found in her that 'something never to be wholly

[1] *On Some of Sh.'s Female Characters*, by Helen Faucit (Lady Martin), 1885.

known', those suggestions of high qualities answerable to all the contingencies or trial of circumstance. Only Shakespeare's device could place her where she could probe her lover and be sure that his love equalled hers; and only he could bring her out in triumph, losing nothing of our respect. The actress must avert from Orlando's mind all suspicion of sex, yet preserve the refinement of Rosalind's station and intellect, and by occasional tender accent and persuasive look indicate how, even at the outset, she establishes a hold on Orlando's feelings, which, in their future intercourse in the forest, deepens unconsciously his love for the Rosalind of his dreams. The image of Benedict recurs unbidden to the mind of Beatrice with a frequency which suggests that he is at least more to her than any other man: the train is laid, only the spark is needed. There was no malice in her sayings, but enough of sting to pique the self-esteem of those they were aimed at. Her nature is suddenly developed rather than changed. She neither reproaches her cousin nor seeks to extenuate the defects she is charged with. The audience are thus prepared for the high qualities she will show. After the church scene the trouble that has fallen on Leonato's house has strengthened the tie that binds them, and makes their mutual regard and ultimate union only slightly depend on the plot of their friends. Hero readily forgives Claudio, but such conduct would have chilled all love in Beatrice. We need not doubt the future of Benedict and Beatrice; they will continue to find out something new and interesting in each other's character.

We will now exemplify the dangers to which this method is liable. The following show the author relating her own experience and meditations in too narrow a sense to Shakespeare's work. Perhaps Portia's father saw her bias and took her to famous trials, or she would not have been so sure of overcoming Shylock. She would not leave the despised, deserted Jew to his fate, because his money had brought Bassanio to her. It does not occur to Othello that had Desdemona been so 'cunning', she would have bribed some one—say Emilia—to hide her from his just wrath; she would not have gone to bed and slept like a child. Imogen's final happiness hid for a time injuries that were past healing: the ordeal to such a delicately nurtured creature of wanderings without food and shelter, and the sight of her husband's headless body. Happiness came too late, and the hurt was too deep for mortal leechcraft.

We must afford two instances of her more general criticism, which show how fine at times could be the point of her analysis. She dwells on the skill with which the story of Imogen's trials is interwoven with the traditionary tales of the ancient Britons and their relations to Rome, which give to it the vivid interest of a grand historical background. In M. Ado the temporary success of Don John's plot helps the permanent success of the first plot—one of many proofs of Shakespeare's transcendent skill in dramatic construction. . . .

There are times when all Helen Faucit's powers work together
to produce a unique effect. She had feminine intuition, imagination,
and she was an actress. The harmonious co-operation of these produced judgements like those on Beatrice and Rosalind, on the relations
between Desdemona and her father and lover, and Ophelia before the
opening of the play. She had not learned her parts mechanically, but
realized them in her imagination: she had seen Ophelia as a child
wandering by streams—and Desdemona in her Venetian palace dreaming of an ideal lover. When her parts were played she did not dismiss
these pictures from her mind. They remained with her, to give to her
written words on Shakespeare's characters a mellowing effect of time
and distance.

XIII

ROBERT BOYLE[1] aims to prove that Shakespeare did not write
Henry VIII. His criticism is an instance of right method in approaching Shakespeare, that of the learned and disciplined critic who winnows
his impressions by a gradual process of meditation. He finds that this
play has not the passionate power which is the undertone of all the
later dramas. Fanciful, or pictorial, images occur in Shakespeare, but
when passion is added to imagination the pictures run into each other
and we get symbolic images. The latter are seldom fit for pictorial
representation, and embrace the most striking passages in Shakespeare's
dramas. The blending of these two classes—fancy clear and plain to
eye and mind, in less elevated scenes, with the loftier images which
impress themselves on the soul with one stroke, but which the eye
alone cannot realize—is a characteristic of Shakespeare's later plays,
and is absent from *Henry VIII*. In the women of the later plays there
is a mixture of the spirit world and the world of flesh and blood. Anne
Bullen does not share this, nor does she justify the praises other
characters give her. The heart of Katharine is equally set on the
vanities of her high station. She shows nothing of the softening
influence of misfortune—a prominent trait in all the later dramas,
in harmony with Shakespeare's psychical development, and the outcome of his life-experience. Wolsey is so little noble that even the
quarrelling scene does not degrade him. The characters do not reveal
themselves as in Shakespeare at his best; we receive impressions of
them through the opinions of others: we see Wolsey through the eyes
of Katharine and the nobles, so the picture is one-sided.

XIV

STOPFORD BROOKE,[2] whom we shall often meet again, first
appears as critic of *Richard III*. His work has not only the intrinsic

---

[1] '*Henry VIII*: An Investigation into the Origin and Authorship of the Play, 1885
(New Sh. Soc. Trans.).   [2] *Richard III*, 1885 (New Sh. Soc. Trans.).

value that we expect from such a wise man and accomplished critic and writer, but also the subtler interest (to those of us who think that Marlowe did more than Shakespeare) of his fine discriminations as to what Shakespeare added in recasting the play. He finds Shakespeare in the evolution of the hero's character. Gloucester, he says, blots out all love or capability of feeling it—a unique position in Shakespeare. His remorse is more agony of failure than of sin; conscience only intrudes in dreams; awake, he cares not a pin for his crimes. This accounts for the unbroken rapidity of crime in the play; whereas guilt is not the natural element of Macbeth.

No doubt Stopford Brooke accepted the belief of the day that *Richard III* was an exercise in Marlowe's manner, but his fine instinct led him to explain or censure what was unnatural or un-Shakespearian. Having remarked that Richard had no love and was therefore unique in Shakespeare, he says that no other man would have wooed Lady Anne as he does, or asked Elizabeth for her daughter. Only his lack of love and conscience make these scenes natural. In the scene with Elizabeth dissimulation is overdone and passes tragic bounds. In the pleasure of exercising his intellect Shakespeare has been carried away and has lost hold on the main movement of the drama and lowered the note of tragedy. Intellect without conscience cannot be fine and is sure to err in dealing with men. The scene of Richard between the two bishops is ridiculous and over-sensational, and almost touches upon farce.

Most suggestive is his criticism of the murder of Clarence, when we recall Shakespeare's use of underplots or subordinate characters. The murderers debate the whole matter from their lower and coarser standpoint, and settle it as did the kingly robbers and nobles. They remember their reward and then attack conscience as the most dangerous thing in State or society. According to Stopford Brooke the play's predominant idea is the connected moral idea of the supremacy of conscience, and in the last scene it is wrought out so forcibly that for a brief hour Richard himself recognizes that there is a conscience in him, but argues against it as impossible. . . . Would not the first part, at least, of this sentence describe our impressions of Marlowe's *Faustus*?

XV

ONE fact is worth noting in Henry Sharpe's essay on the rules for the use of prose in Shakespeare's plays.[1] After pointing out such main distinctions as we should expect for the use of prose and verse, according to character or situation, he discovers that Hamlet's natural way is to speak in metre, but he speaks prose with any one that he mistrusts. When he suspects Ophelia of being in league with the others, his manner changes and he rails at her in prose. At first he speaks metre

[1] *The Prose in Sh.'s Plays, &c.*, 1885 (New Sh. Soc. Trans.).

to the King, but prose after seeing the Ghost. Only in the grave-digger scene he speaks prose to Horatio, and that is because he continues with him the conversation he began with the Clown.[1] . . . The essay shows the tendency to explore one path after another of Shakespeare's art.

XVI

WE will first take the remarks on Shakespeare's plots. The Cowden Clarkes discover in them unity of purpose and harmony of moral principle. They maintain that he made fresh laws in art for himself, and that unity of impression is the grand secret of his dominion in dramatic art. To Rose the most remarkable thing about him is his concise and complete construction. Moulton finds him as subtle a weaver of plots as deep reader of the human heart. He has elevated the conception of plot from mere unity of action, through reduction of amount of matter presented, to harmony of design uniting concurrent complex actions. Helen Faucit comments on his wondrous skill in dramatic construction. She says that he puts aside unities for higher purposes. Time, place, action are his instruments, and he made them submit to him. Grant White maintains that after his first years Shakespeare had no art-purpose, but always an inborn instinct of dramatic effect.

Swinburne says that he was a free-thinker in the best and highest and widest meaning—a spiritual democrat and socialist. According to Hales he was no religious reformer but a great moral teacher, delighting to trace the action of the great moral laws of the world and show the fearful penalty of transgression. Moulton finds him true to modern notions of Providence and moral law. Feis says that Shakespeare thought it enough to champion 'natural things'. He advocated true and simple obedience to Nature's laws and renunciation of all transcendental dogmas. He was the greatest humanist who ever strove to raise man's soul and mind by natural means.

He was, says Rose, a man of immense intellectual power and an unrivalled observer who remembered everything. Swinburne says that he knew all things better by instinct than others by experience; that he was the mightiest and wisest scholar or teacher in the school of the human spirit. He also speaks of his untraceable personality through his plays; whereas Boyle is confident that the guiding principle which led him through his dark life was continual striving to know himself, to make use of his faults and weaknesses, and by their help mould his character into a nobler form. Hales ascribes to him a wonderfully lovable nature.

On characters we have but three outstanding remarks: Rose's, that he sets before us a whole man and his whole life; Grant White's, that

[1] Cf. Delius (1878).

by nature and impulse he wrought out the characters of his persons with the knowledge of a creator of human souls; Boyle's, that in the later plays the characters develop and reveal themselves.

On one subject Hales and Minto agree. Hales says that at times he shows us the dreadful spectacle of blind, inexorable Fate; Minto, that he recognizes overruling Destiny. Swinburne considers him a darker fatalist than Aeschylus.

Of single remarks that should not be omitted we have that of the Cowden Clarkes—that he had an intensely strong and passionately fervid appreciation of friendship; Grant White's, that as a poet he was the supremest master of human utterance, rising with unconscious effort to the highest heaven of poetry ever reached by the human mind; Minto's, that he united sure and firm-set prudence with heaven-climbing genius, and possessed clear-eyed sagacity and sanity. . . .

We notice a less positive tone in these generalities—as of a deepening belief in the mystery of Shakespeare. It is admitted that he knew the rules of art but was above them, and that if he lacked official learning he had instinct which served him better. The same applies to his religion, except for Moulton's too absolute statement. A Shakespeare greater but more remote is presented to us by the critics of these years.

Chapter XXIV

GERMANY 1876–1885

I. ELZE. II. DELIUS. III. HENSE. IV. OECHELHÄUSER. V. GESSNER.
VI. THÜMMEL. VII. CONCLUSION.

I

IT is characteristic of Karl Elze[1] that after noting the influence on Shakespeare's art of his Warwickshire upbringing and the theatrical performances which as a boy he witnessed at Stratford and Coventry, he discovers Anne Hathaway to be the prototype of the heroine in *Venus*. The description, he says, is of such 'appalling truthfulness' as to suggest personal experience. He accepts the tradition that Shakespeare was a lawyer's clerk, defends the deer-stealing episode, and rejects the story that Shakespeare, a married man and father of three children, demeaned himself by holding horses at the theatre. He speaks of his rapid rise to fame and fortune, his purchase of New Place, and the coat of arms for his father, and his wish to become a gentleman. The latter he calls his Achilles' heel, and notes that as soon as his outer position was secure, a feeling of dissatisfaction with life came over him,[2] and he speaks, more bitterly than any other writer, of the vanity of all worldly possessions.

His dramas are the productions of an unconscious, instinctive faculty of the mind; they are loosely constructed, lack symmetry in the development of the plot, at times have episodical breadth,[3] and at times hurried ending. Those German aesthetic writers go too far who regard them as organic works of art of faultless perfection. *Venus*, his first published work, is somewhat of an opium dream of sensual love. *Lucrece* shows important mental and moral progress. Both are diffuse—the reverse side of the extraordinary merit of his dramas— viz. psychological depth, and rare knowledge of the human heart, every fold and fibre of which, despite his youth, he is acquainted with. Neither the slightest nor the most secret emotion escapes him, and perhaps his early marriage proved an excellent instruction. Had he never written a play he would have become immortal as the greatest English sonnet-writer.

Shakespeare's knowledge of Greek and Latin has been questioned, and his use of translations. Whether from study or intuition, he conceived the spirit and character of classic antiquity more correctly and in a truer and grander spirit than many a mere book-scholar. He is full of small anachronisms, but his characters cannot be matched in antique truth and grandeur. He thirsted for knowledge of all kinds,

---

[1] *Wm. Sh.*, 1876 (trans. Dora Schmitz, 1888).   [2] Cf. Hallam.
[3] Cf. Rümelin.

and learned with ease—and he must have known that only by acquiring
aristocratic culture could he rise from his low rank of actor. He alludes
to foreign works, of which there were no translations in his day. He
could survey the whole realm of knowledge and see every detail in its
true relation. He may have had little of the specialist's exact knowledge,
but he had extraordinary power of observation and the intuitions of
genius. He gives an endless variety of pictures and allusions from
nature and human industry without a single error: he recognizes the
nature and very essence of the matter. Unlike Ben Jonson, who boasts
of his knowledge, he seems to owe all to divine inspiration. The
allusion to the eagle in *Venus* shows he knew it was the eagle's habit to
shake its wings while eating. In the same way he had knowledge of
falconry, coursing, stag-hunting. Writing of fishing, he speaks of
superstitions known only to anglers. But thought was his chief domain,
and he was physiologist as well as psychologist, knowing that physical and
psychical life are correlated, and the latter is the result of the former. In
knowledge of insanity he was years ahead of his time, recognizing that the
only remedy for madness is physical, psychical, and moral comfort. He
knew not only every healthy state, but every phase of a diseased state of
mind, and he contemplates it from a higher and superhuman point of
view. His pictures of dying persons are artistically and scientifically
correct. He knew that medicines, like poisons, take effect by finding
thei way into the blood. This was unknown to his contemporaries,
and he derived it from observation of nature. His anachronisms are
licence rather than ignorance: every person in the theatre must have
known Bohemia was not on the coast; and art deals with ideal, not
actual, truth. His knowledge of the nature and purpose of music is
remarkable. In the *Merchant* he fathoms with deep insight the relation
in which the various characters stand to music. And his highest praise
for music is that he makes it go hand in hand with morality and human
kindliness. He appreciates painting deeply, sculpture less, and architecture not at all: the latter is the only art which he ignores. He demands
that a picture should be intelligible, explain its own meaning, and be
true to nature. Again and again he says that the artist must learn from
Nature, find out her mysterious ways, and 'surpass' them. Witness
Timon's remarks on a picture; and this agrees with Shakespeare's
conception of music as a secular art, and a relaxation after the day's
work. If art is truth to nature and sensuous fullness of life, religious
subjects are excluded. As Shakespeare knew Giulio Romano he must
have known Raphael his master in Italian religious art. That he
ignores them shows that he thought them out of place in his poetic
delineation of life. He transmuted his positive knowledge into poetry,
so that his dramas are the nearest things to life in the whole of art.
And the result of all-embracing culture and the highest form of
poetical imagination cannot fail to be sublime moral excellence.

It is impossible to know Shakespeare's moral nature from his works.
It is likely that he was proud, and conscious of his intellectual superiority; but his ambition was based on the wealth he gained, not on his
writings. He perfected the sonnets, and the sonnet's essential characteristic is praise of love and friendship. Friendship is placed above love
because it is an absolutely moral connexion. Perhaps also Shakespeare's
unhappy marriage made him seek compensation in friendship. The
Sonnets are probably a mixture of fiction and truth, and we cannot form
from them an idea of his nature. We only know that he had a fixed
purpose and attained it by caution, energy, and perseverance: and this
opposes the theory of feminine submissiveness. We also know that
he had wrestled with the deepest problems and solved them as far as
possible. He therefore had knowledge, intuition, observation, and
self-culture; and he emerged from his experience in no cheerful,
light-hearted state. The Bible and Christianity are part of our civilization, inseparable from the world he wished to represent. It was therefore an element of culture from which he could not free himself, but
it is impossible to divine how far he was individually Christian. He
frequently advocates mercy—but the clearest indication of his religious
tendency is in the garden scene with Jessica, Lancelot, and Lorenzo.
It is impossible to know his views on Redemption or immortality: only
the heathens Antony and Cleopatra, of his numerous dying persons,
allude to meeting again after death. Nowhere else is there hopeful or
comforting prospect of a future life, or any Christian form of consolation. The constant refrain is that death is our inevitable destiny, the
common fate of all. But we cannot disentangle Shakespeare's personal utterances from his dramatic: his works might be made to prove
anything. More trustworthy evidence is his objectivity, through
which he gives every form of faith its due and shows no prejudice.
This would have been impossible had he been a strictly orthodox
follower of any special religious body. His point of view was above all
Church doctrines—it was humanity. He attacks nothing that thoughtful persons revere: though he may satirize dogmatism he is no
blasphemer. Conscience and duty are his central religious points: he
insists on an active, moral life, and on charity. If best men are moulded
out of faults, he believes in moral purification through curbing passion.
True repentance and atonement mean a new lease of life—as Hamlet
tells his mother. His characters act of their own free will: he is no
fatalist. The world is a moral organism: each exists through and for
the whole, and can only thus attain the moral perfection which is the
aim of all life. This world-organism is self-contained; it can reward
good and punish evil, and is independent of life beyond the grave.
The Beyond remains a mystery, and Shakespeare knows that he
cannot fathom the supernatural. He makes man fulfil his destiny in
this world, and therefore praises not faith but knowledge as the

highest human acquisition. He is Christian only so far as Christianity
is synonymous with Humanism. Humanism was the religion of the
best in his day when the Church and religion were dragged into the
whirl of politics. There were persecutions by both parties; people
were forced by law to attend church; and the result was that inner
satisfaction was transferred to the Renaissance of literature and philosophy.

Shakespeare was no politician, but expressed the opinions of the day.
He upheld law and order, uprightness and faithfulness, justice and
mercy as the pillars of the State and the moral community. Beyond
these he accentuates only the grades of society, which should not be
overstepped either arrogantly or with criminal intention. Yet he
condemns class prejudice, and exalts virtue and nobility of soul above
rank and birth. The freedom with which he delineates many diverse
royal persons makes it impossible to believe that he admired royalty,
e.g. Lear is Caesarism gone mad. Absolute power carried to excess
leads to mental aberration; and in subordinates to absurdity, e.g.
Shallow, Dogberry. He loves England, but without prejudice or
national hatred. He is sarcastic but not unjust to France, and acknowledges the excellent horsemanship and tasteful attire of the people.
Italy is the land of refined and fashionable life, but also of cunning,
treachery, and poisonings.

Objectivity has been the basis of our inquiry into Shakespeare's
character—a safer foundation for such an estimate than an examination
of numerous quotations from his works. From all we know of his life
we infer that he strove to live up to his own ideal. He was one of the
truest and most genuine of human beings. Truthfulness is the virtue
to which he gives precedence, and nothing stirs his wrath like hypocrisy,
falsehood, crooked ways. He denounces women who paint and wear
false hair; and almost forgets his objectivity in describing false characters—Osric. To be true to oneself is the highest ideal. His life was
not faultless, but in the end he rose above the temptations of sensuality....

We concluded our former estimate of Elze with the remark that he
left us with our eyes fixed on earth rather than raised to the stars; and
the same is true here. He is at his best in describing the arena in which
Shakespeare ran his race, not in speculating whence arose his power.

He is helpful because he makes his points clearly on Shakespeare's
knowledge of sport and natural history, of the arts, from which only
architecture is omitted, &c. It is legitimate to infer that, as he mentions Giulio Romano, he was acquainted with Raphael and Italian
religious art; and yet when he attempts these higher regions of religion
and morality his pinion droops. We cannot quarrel with his method
of approaching the great questions, or with his conclusions on Shakespeare's Christianity and other-worldliness; yet they do not satisfy us
as do those of Dowden which resemble his in many ways. The reason

is that Elze uses these terms like counters which have an agreed rather than an intrinsic value among men; he does not kindle the highest themes with the fire of his own mind. Reason predominates over emotion; he seems to argue that certain causes produce certain results, alike in history, morals, or aesthetics. Thus if Shakespeare had belonged to any definite religious sect he could not have treated religion objectively. The mountain of which the guide-book tells us is a thing that we go forth to visit, and to speculate upon its height: the mountain of the poet is that of our dreams, mirrored in the lake and untrodden by human foot.

II

NICOLAUS DELIUS[1] writes first about the Sonnets, and points out that since Wyatt and Surrey transplanted to England this courtly and fashionable style of poem, its subject was as restricted as its form. The theme was delicate gallantry, and the poet identified himself with the happy or unhappy lover, and covered the whole scale of feelings of such a lover. Surrey, Sydney, Spenser, and others, happy in their domestic relations, became in their poetry languishing wooers of a strange, perhaps a married, lady. The object was to enjoy the pleasure and art of a whole kaleidoscope of love, not to mirror the heart-circumstances of the poet. The deeper pathos of the feigned passion which breaks through the subtleties of his sonnet style, so that one may imagine a real cry of anguish from a wounded heart, Shakespeare did not borrow from his models, but owed to the unparalleled psychological insight coupled with the creative power which made him such an expert reader of the hearts of his dramatic characters. Such an interpretation is in his favour as a poet, whereas an autobiographical interpretation leaves him in a dubious light. The Sonnets are dramatic; they describe not Shakespeare's personal emotions, but those of the human heart in their bare truth—love, jealousy, friendship, remorse.

Timon shows striking contrast of style, even between parts of a same scene. The corruption of text is worse as regards metre than any other play. Shakespeare's part in *Timon* belongs to a ripe period of age when creative fancy begins to be balanced, even overbalanced, by deep philosophic thought. It attracted him to treat poetically psychological questions, to conceive individual characters in their depth and special traits, and so interweave artistically and develop for his dramatic material. In riper years, therefore, he may have set his practised hand to another's drama, not to revise its whole imperfection, but to exercise his psychological mastery on a single character, the real centre. His part in the first three acts was only fragmentary and casual; but in Act IV we see his more lively interest and energetic grasp. Timon the man-hater attracted him more than Timon the hospitable friend to

[1] *Abhandlungen zu Sh.*, 1878.

all the world—as we see from the masterful flow of the blank verse. And his art appears in his differentiation of Timon the misanthrope and Apemantus the cynic—characters which at first sight may appear to have affinity. On the whole, Shakespeare left the anonymous writer's plot as he found it, and, regardless of incongruities, absorbed himself only in the scenes concerned with the psychological interest in Timon's character.

Shakespeare's share in *Pericles* was more or less the same; here he was attracted by the moving figure of Marina. He begins his work in Act III with the close of the chorus. He changes nothing of the general scene, but the impress of his hand is unmistakable in the diction and metre of his later age in all that follows. The figures, hitherto mere marionettes, become real and life-like, in whose weal and woe, hitherto indifferent to us, we can take an interest. The rhymed sentences disappear, and also all stilted, oblique, and obscure expressions. Scene II is truly Shakespearian, the profound self-characterization of Cerimon, and the wonderful intuitive manner in which the reawakening of Thaisa is described, with no word too much, yet each word adapted to its end. Dionyza (Act IV), hitherto a colourless shade, becomes alive, and a second Lady Macbeth—except that Shakespeare never brings exactly similar figures on the stage. Marina with flowers at her nurse's grave, and the brothel, are examples of Shakespeare's liveliest and most dramatic scenes, in his own happiest manner. Marina in her purity amid such surroundings may be compared with Isabella in *M. for M.* The dialogue between the weak Cleon and vicious strong Dionyza reminds us of Macbeth and Lady Macbeth before and after Duncan's murder. The recognition scenes in Act V recall those of *Cymbeline* and *W. Tale.* The effect is gradually heightened when father and daughter meet, and Shakespeare preserves the same psychological art which we admire in these other plays. The music of the earlier scene where Thaisa comes to life has the true Shakespearian touch—as where Lear revives in Cordelia's tent. Diana appears to Pericles asleep like Jupiter to Posthumus.

Verse predominates in Shakespeare, but prose is not used by chance, and is a means of making characters express themselves appropriately. The lowest prose is that used not by the clowns themselves, but by their equals in station and mind. A better kind is used in conversation by important and cultured characters—by the higher humorists to express delicate humour. As the clowns' speech echoed that of the people so did this refined conversation copy that of the best society in Shakespeare's time: only Shakespeare adds to it a veiled or apparent humour and concentrated wit that would appeal to his contemporaries more strongly than to posterity. The highest artistic, elaborated prose is the Euphuistic, with its ornamented sentences and construction, its antitheses and use of metaphor. Its object in the early plays was persiflage; but in the later it was used in earnest, where it was a matter of orientation for the audience, of relation of actual conditions, or where a specially solemn ceremonial tone was desirable. Whereas the former style of prose was distinguished by humour and gaiety, this third style is formal in the choice of words and in the unusual structure of sentences.

The prose of *Verona* is confined to the clowns, and hardly rises above the familiar manner of speech. *Errors*: Prose only episodic, for even the clowns are influenced by their surroundings and speak in blank verse. *L.L.L.*: More frequency and variety, as prose extends to the higher comic figures, with the shades required by difference between characters. *Shrew*: Unimportant and episodic, and does not advance plot. *Merchant*: Quantitatively small, but qualitatively used in three ways—speech of clowns—of Shylock when he speaks naturally—of Portia where she plays the humorous prude and contemns the rejected lovers, in a roguish manner that no other means could have expressed. The prose of *M.N.D.* is monopolized by the clowns. *All's Well*: Richer and more many-sided than in any previous play; according to speaker's position, now polished and elaborate, now plain and natural— the speech of cavaliers and ladies. *M. Ado*: Prose the basis—elegant and conversational prose of the day—neither Euphuistic nor familiar. If one of the few plays where prose predominates, it is because delicate humour and coarser comedy outweigh pathos and romance in love relations. As the *Wives* is a realistic comedy, prose is the only practical medium of expression. *Twelfth-Night*: Olivia's house-companions characteristically express their eccentricities and peculiarities in prose. In her intercourse with them Olivia necessarily uses the same idiom, and Maria follows her example. *A.Y.L.*: Only when Rosalind sheds her humour and openly expresses a deeper feeling, does she, and those about her, revert to blank verse, instead of the fine cultivated prose of this play—a model of its kind. Prose again is used to describe actual facts (I. i).

M. for M.: Apart from that of the clowns, prose only begins where the Duke and Isabella speak on absolute affairs. Mariana's pathetic tale is told with a Euphuistic colouring that lifts the conversation above ordinary tones. The Duke also speaks Euphuistic prose to Escalus and Lucio. The introductory, explanatory scene of *W. Tale* is in Euphuistic prose. With the entrance of the Shepherd and Clown (III. iii) we get a popular comic element; but at times their speech is more elaborated than that of the earlier clowns. In Act IV Florizel and Perdita even raise the Shepherd and his son into a higher atmosphere, so that they all speak blank verse: the entrance of Autolycus breaks this higher tone. The general account of all that has happened (V. ii) is in prose—an account of pathetic and moving facts put into the mouths of cultivated courtiers who could relate them in a prose of delicate style and finished Euphuism. Shakespeare has given especial care to the arrangement of antitheses and parallelisms, grouping of metaphors, and the whole harmonious structure of the sentences.

Tempest: Prose limited to Jester and men of lower class.

Henry IV: The contrast between historical and humorous is marked by respective use of verse and prose. Falstaff's wit gives his prose a more cultivated tone than is usual in Shakespeare's merry scenes; but the liveliness and naturalness of these preserve it from Euphuism. Now and then the Prince throws off his adopted role and speaks in verse like a king's son. Cultivated and coarser forms of prose intermingle in the famous scene where the Prince and Falstaff imitate the King. *Henry V*: Prose is spoken in the English and French camps, which enables Shakespeare to give shades of provincial and national peculiarities better than in levelling verse. Henry naturally speaks prose while he mixes with the soldiers in disguise; when alone, he returns to verse.

R. and J.: Servants and clowns as usual speak ordinary prose; but here begins the more cultivated prose of the familiar and teasing conversation of the noblemen. When Hamlet throws off his natural self and assumes madness, he exchanges verse for prose; and the others respond. At times, as when he begs his young friends to tell him the truth, he is Euphuistic; but when left alone he speaks verse. Still playing his assumed part, he meets Ophelia's verse with bitter replies in prose. He speaks to the players in prose, but uses verse and throws off the mask in converse with Horatio.[1] *Othello*: Iago expresses his coarse cynicism in prose; when alone, he expounds his devilish plan in verse. Cassio in his wretchedness (II. iii) speaks prose, which perhaps has more effect as the natural outcry of a wounded heart. Othello (IV. i) in the moment of highest agitation and excitement can only speak in single words and broken phrases. Ordered blank verse would not suffice; therefore Shakespeare lets him speak in prose, contrary to custom. *J.C.*: Casca speaks coarse but not exactly ordinary prose. The contrast between him and the gravely earnest Brutus and Cassius is marked by their use of blank verse. Brutus the plain Republican seeks to make his funeral speech effective with the unadorned truth of prose; while the ambitious Antony outbids and neutralizes this effect by rhetorical ornament. *Lear*: The contrast between the high-flown expressions of love of Goneril and Regan with their later cold consultation is emphasized by the exchange of verse for prose. Edmund in monologue (I. ii) discloses his real nature in verse; in the remainder of the scene, where he masks his evil machinations to his dupes, he speaks prose. Kent in his reduced condition speaks the prose that is suited to it; Lear also, to the knight on matters of fact. In converse with Kent and the Fool, Lear (I. v) suppresses his real, heart-breaking

[1] Cf. Sharpe (1885).

feelings and accommodates himself to the prosaic speech of his faithful
retainers. The explanatory scene between Cornwall and Edmund
(III. v) is in prose that conforms to speakers and subject, and to a
certain degree is euphuistically coloured. The Fool and Edgar, as a
mad beggar, speak prose. The beginning of Lear's madness is shown
by his alternations of prose and verse; but he uses verse when, amid
his madness, reasonable reflections are expressed in emphatic words.
Macbeth: The naïve prattle of Lady Macduff's little son begins in
verse and falls into prose with increasing *naïveté*. Lady Macbeth's
prose shows the sleep-walker's abnormal state of mind. As she is
changed from her former self, so is her speech.

A. and C.: (I. ii) The frivolous conversation in the palace is in
prose: only the soothsayer adds weight to his prophecies by blank
verse. (III. v) Enobarbus and Eros speak prose to inform the
audience of the course of events. They rise to verse when Enobarbus humorously addresses the world. *Coriolanus*: Menenius the
humourist speaks prose except where he faces the rioters as a man of
superior station, and to preserve his instructive authority employs
blank verse. Volumnia and Valeria discuss domestic matters in prose,
but when Volumnia, in the ecstasy of maternal feeling, describes her
son in battle she breaks into verse. Coriolanus becomes one with the
crowd when he asks for votes, but as soon as he gains the first he
reverts to his usual blank verse. The Tribunes speak in verse to the
citizens about rendering the choice of Coriolanus null—and the
political interests involved justify verse. The humorous thread that
runs through the talk of the servants in the hall of Aufidius occasionally
gives a higher style to the ordinary clown's prose. Coriolanus (v. ii)
meets the prose of Menenius with cold and distant blank verse. The
speech of Menenius even in distress (v. iv) does not belie his character;
it is his special prose, but particularly incisive. *T. and C.*: (I.i) Pandarus
replies to the passionate verse of Troilus in calculated, cold-blooded
prose. The prose between Pandarus and Cressida is suitable to their
frivolous natures. Thersites naturally speaks the coarsest prose; and in
converse with him, Ajax, Achilles, and Patroclus abstain from their
usual blank verse. In II. iii, the blockhead Ajax vents his humour in
prose, and is silenced in like prose by the other Greek commanders.
Prose is especially suitable for the frivolous, gallant conversation
between Paris, Helen, and Pandarus (III. i)—a scene without depth or
feeling. Troilus in the love scene (III. ii) begins in verse, then falls in
with the prose of uncle and niece, but when feeling is heightened and
vows of constancy exchanged, verse again sets in. Cressida, bidding
farewell to Troilus (IV. ii), in the sorrow of parting, rises to verse, even
when confronted by Pandarus who clings to his prose. The prose of
Thersites, keen and pregnant, is most brilliant when he characterizes
Menelaus and abuses Diomedes. Pandarus (v. iii) brings Troilus a

letter and speaks in prose. Troilus replies in verse to emphasize the
grief that separates them.   *Cymbeline*: (i. v) The lords and Posthumus
speak euphuistic prose, accompanied by rising feeling and concentrated
passion. (ii. iii) Cloten, speaking with Imogen, changes his usual prose
to verse, with which he also expresses his rage at her contempt.   The
gaoler (v. iv) has a certain devilish humour, and his prose in dialogue
with Posthumus, with all its coarseness and scurrility, rises above
ordinary prose and displays some keen insight.   Posthumus falls in, and
replies in prose—a form to him otherwise unknown.

We will now give an instance of Shakespeare's use of his sources, in
order to refute any charge brought against him of failure in originality,
creative power, and characterization.   The three Roman dramas were
founded on North's Plutarch, and the casual critic might call them
dramatized biographies—Plutarch's prose translated into verse.   But
although he makes full use of the original, he re-creates all to produce
a true drama.   He varies the scenes of *Coriolanus*; he makes plain to us
in the first scene the hero's pride and defiance of the plebeians, his
strength in war, and his submission to his mother.   Plutarch begins by
relating his warlike deeds: Shakespeare makes Volumnia in her
maternal pride ascribe them to her bringing up.   In the interests of
dramatic unity and clarity, Shakespeare makes two revolts into one,
and suppresses a second campaign.   According to his well-thought-out
plan the antagonism between Aufidius and Coriolanus runs through
the whole play: Plutarch speaks casually of their earlier meetings.
Shakespeare makes the Tribunes persuade the people to withdraw
their votes from Coriolanus; in Plutarch the cause is their vacillating
humour.   Shakespeare's conversation at the close of ii. i, and Coriolanus's declaration at the close of ii. ii, give a causal nexus to events.
In other ways Shakespeare connects the loose account of Plutarch.
Plutarch's Volscians accept Coriolanus less suddenly than Shakespeare's.

As to character, Plutarch emphasizes the fact that Marcius early
lost his father, and was brought up, or rather not brought up, by his
mother.   This explains his lack of self-control; while he owed to his
original nature his love of truth, steadfastness, and bravery, his disinterested patriotism.   Shakespeare does not hint at the father's early
death or the son's lack of training, but he makes the mother most
adequate to bring him up and impress on him her spirit and character.
He emphasizes her influence throughout the play; Plutarch but refers
to her in the beginning of his biography, and she only reappears with
the final catastrophe.   Shakespeare gives his own conception of the
relationship of son to mother and wife, and also as father, arousing the
pure human sympathy of the audience, and bringing Coriolanus nearer
to us as a man.   Plutarch's Marcius was churlish, uncivil, and unfit
for any man's conversation.   Shakespeare shows him as friend, comrade,
and in other relationships impossible to the Plutarchian Coriolanus.

Sicinius is also more definitely characterized in Shakespeare. A factor with which the Tribunes had to reckon was the plebeians' admiration of Coriolanus, despite his hatred of them. Shakespeare describes in detail his undignified role of supplicant, of which he was ashamed, to the harmless citizens who had no inkling of the angry irony with which he begged their votes. Such scenes were needed in a drama which represents the conflict of the one with the many. This characterization of the plebs is perhaps the greatest master-stroke of Shakespeare's masterly work. He gets no help from Plutarch except an occasional comment on the fickleness of the crowd.

On the subject of speech, it is commonly thought that Shakespeare's style was influenced by Plutarch, or that the parallel passages and occasional borrowings from the biography introduced an alien element into the play. Against this we have the unity of the play, and the fact that borrowing was limited to a single phrase, metaphor, or antithesis. More often Shakespeare took longer passages from Plutarch, and remade them in the interest of drama, impressing his spirit on them by additions, excisions, or remodelling—always aiming to adjust speech to character and situation. The first part of the speech of Menenius to the plebs (I. i) is Shakespeare's own entirely. It has his characteristic humour, and no wonder it aroused interest and drew questions. . . . Volumnia's closing speech in Act V has whole passages that are quite original.

We now turn to a necessary element in Shakespeare's plays—the epic—understanding those parts where the poet relates or describes through one of his characters. He may relate the previous history of a character at the beginning of the plot—or the history of characters loosely connected with the plot: but he is more sparing of this method than his forerunners and contemporaries. There is also the episode, and the report or narrative to spare a separate scene—an instance of the last is Portia's humorous account of her wooers. Had Shylock's wrath and despair at the loss of his daughter and ducats been dramatized, it would have shocked the more refined taste, and prejudiced the effect of his later entrance on the scene. Contrast the quiet moving account of the parting of Bassanio and Antonio. Had Petruchio (*Shrew*) been shown on the stage in the negligent apparel with which he comes to his wedding, the effect would have been less comic than in the narration. The description of Jaques (*A.Y.L.*) at the sight of the wounded deer, before he appears in person, gives the key to the character of the misanthropic humorist, and interests us in a figure not very striking in the subsequent action. Besides, it would be as hard to stage the wounded deer as the later bear and snake. Falstaff's vivid reminiscences of his misadventures in the basket reach a height of comedy beyond the best devised scene.

In Shakespeare's later work, the fullness of matter to be dramatized

obliges him to revert more frequently to the epic form. The opening
scene of the *W. Tale* gives the history from childhood of the two kings.
But other motives than lack of stage room moved the poet to give the
long 'epic' scene before the final one. To have given scenic effect to what
is narrated would have lessened the crowning effect of the statue scene.

The epic element varies in the tragedies; it is used sparingly in
Othello and *Macbeth*. The actual murder is only related; and the
effect on the doers and those whom it concerns gives a double reflection
of murder. *R. and J.* has a good share of narrative which the riper
Shakespeare would have avoided. Mercutio's description of Queen
Mab is a pleasing interlude, but has no connexion with the drama.
Non-essential is the account of the poor Apothecary's shop in Mantua.
Shakespeare's stage could have held the pitiable figure of the Apothecary, not his miserably stocked shop. *Lear's* richness of material and
quick onrush of plot favour full use of epic. It would be impossible to
dramatize the series of misunderstandings between Lear's knights and
Goneril's household that cause the break between father and daughter.
The matter condensed in the dialogue between Kent and the Gentleman at the beginning of Act III would have needed a whole act on
the stage. The epic element in the scene by Dover cliffs is not necessary
for the progress of the drama. The finely detailed picture took the
place of scenic display, not possible on the stage, and intended to give
the audience a mental vision of the situation. It corresponds with such
descriptions as Bolingbroke's solemn entry into London (*Richard II*);
with the English camp in France on the eve of battle (*Henry V*); with
the triumphant progress of Marcius through the streets of Rome
(*Coriolanus*); with the first meeting of Antony and Cleopatra. Modern
decorative art could have described these scenes in their truth and
splendour, and saved the poet his verbal details. Lastly, in *Lear*, the
deaths of Gloster and Cordelia are narrated, so that the full attention
of the audience should be concentrated on the King.

In *Hamlet* the preparatory information is not contained in a single
narrative but scattered throughout—the murder, the doings of
Fortinbras, Hamlet's love for Ophelia, &c. Another playwright would
have made an effective scene out of Hamlet's first meeting with Ophelia
after his assumed madness. But Shakespeare so prepared his audience
for the Hamlet he is about to show them in every graded degree of his
role of madman. To further his plot he emphasized not the meeting
of the lovers under changed circumstances, but the different interpretation put on Hamlet's behaviour by Polonius and the King and Queen.
At times the epic and dramatic elements do not correspond, e.g. at the
close of Act I Hamlet will not inform even Horatio of the Ghost's
revelations; but in the play scene (Act III) we hear from his own lips
that he has told all to Horatio. Also, since the departure of Laertes for
France, we see no moment when the report of his skill in fencing could

have disturbed Hamlet (Act IV). The two last epic episodes—the relation of Ophelia's death and Hamlet's own report of his sea-voyage —could not be scenically displayed on the contemporary stage.

The earlier English historical dramas naturally show a less artistic and well-considered epic element. Hitherto we have found it genuinely poetical and with a practically calculated effect or cause; but the youthful histories give no fixed norm for discriminating between scenical and verbal treatment. This appears especially in the looser connexion of the narrative, and the less dramatic colouring of the frequently dry reports: though we must remember that his public demanded not so much art as a pageant of the glorious deeds of their forefathers. What was striking was dramatized, while all else necessary for explanation was compressed and versified and inserted with no artistic addition or characteristic individuality.

The successive messengers from France (*1 Henry VI*) are colourless throughout; and such is the Pucelle's account of her previous history— material taken from Holinshed but not worked up dramatically. Talbot's account of his imprisonment is rather more lively and coloured. The epic element of Part II shows increased mastery of historic material, e.g. the reports of the serious symptoms of growing unrest, and York's monologue, with its drastic description of Jack Cade, whereby Shakespeare introduces Cade to the audience before he appears in person. Richard's outline of his own character (Part III) is an epic sketch to be developed later. The epic elements in *Richard III* are mostly retrospective, knitting together the threads that connect this play with the foregoing. But there are other epic elements, such as Clarence's dream—distinct proof of the advance of Shakespeare's art. Scenic reproduction was here out of the question; but an episode like Buckingham's account of his dealing with the citizens might well have been dramatized: it would have lessened the effect of the pre-arranged farce that follows between Gloster and Buckingham. Shakespeare may have thought that had the Princes been strangled on the stage the audience would have been less moved than by the murderers' remorseful account.

That Gloster's murder (*Richard II*) should be reported, not shown, is justified by the economy of the play: it must be emphasized as the first item in the account against the King that was to bring about his end. The psychological effect and pathos of despair of the King's self-confession of waning authority compared with the rising favour of the returning Bolingbroke, would not equally have told upon the audience as a scene. The epic element in *1 Henry IV* is poorly represented; but we note, in connexion with the development of Shakespeare's art, the descriptions and characters of the narrators, e.g. Percy's defensive speech. Part II requires more use of narrative, as a longer period of time is covered. As the play proceeds the audience have to be made

aware of many happenings under Richard II. These are not merely
recapitulations, but new lights on well-known deeds from opposing
political points of view. We watch not only the development of the
poet's art, but his wider and deeper insight into politics. *Henry V*
abounds still more in descriptions, as a greater number of events had
to be subdued to one dramatic picture. The detailed justification of
the French war has a double object: to explain to the public that it is
no war of aggression, and to contrast the peaceful, ordered condition
of England.

Epic intervals are unavoidable with *J.C.* The comedy, perhaps
prearranged, of the offer and refusal of the crown, is only known
through Casca's scurrilous account. The intention no doubt is to
impress it more on the audience, and to show more clearly its effect on
Brutus and Cassius. It is thus also with the descriptive account of the
prodigies—even had the stage allowed their reproduction. Antony's
apostrophe to Caesar's corpse foreshadows the horror of civil war: and
this could hardly be shown on the stage in the following acts. The
complex train of events in *A. and C.* requires finely detailed pictures.
Octavius's reminiscences of the former Antony (I. iv) recall events
that could not be shown in separate scenes. The recriminations
between the rival Triumvirs (II. ii), in their historical retrospect, fill
up gaps in the knowledge of the audience of former events. Antony's
impolitic and imprudent behaviour in Alexandria, the cause of his
later fall, is told in the speech of Octavius (III. vi). The fight at
Actium is so described that the audience feels indirectly a witness of
the event. In the two last acts the psychological and personal interest
of the two leading characters outweigh the historical, so that the
tragic is scenically displayed, and there is no further need of an epic
element. . . .

Delius impresses as a persevering and unpretentious critic who has
worked over a wide Shakespearian field, seeking knowledge of Shakespeare by comparing his work of different periods, and whom as a
reward for disinterested toil Shakespeare's spirit at times has visited.
His conclusion on the Sonnets, if not the whole truth, is worth more
than a passing thought, and may be compared with Hermann Tieck's
preliminary remarks on the nature of genius. At times he shows a
lacking sense of poetic values, as when he compares Dionyza to Lady
Macbeth, or the revival of Thaisa to that of Lear; but on the whole
his criticism proceeds from the belief that the final standard is the
poetical. Hence his remark that Timon as world-hater attracted
Shakespeare more than as philanthropist. But his best services are the
detailed examination of the prose in Shakespeare, and the epic element.
Most critics roughly divide Shakespeare's characters into speakers of
verse and prose according as they are emotionally charged, e.g. Hamlet
and Falstaff. Delius not only discovers three kinds of prose, but subtly

analyses each in connexion with character and situation. He remarks
that to the cultured prose of his day Shakespeare added wit and humour;
that prose in *A.Y.L.* is used to describe facts; that the clowns in the
W. Tale are attracted into verse; that Falstaff's prose is distinct from
euphuism; that in *Henry V* national characteristics are expressed in
prose because verse has a levelling effect; that Casca does not speak
ordinary prose; that humour gives a higher style to the prose of the
servants in *Coriolanus*; that Troilus replies in verse to Pandarus to
emphasize the grief that separates them; that the prose of Posthumus'
gaoler, though coarse and scurrilous, rises above ordinary prose. The
effect of all these is to convince that Shakespeare's art was infinitely
subtle and varied, and to recall Dryden's saying about 'God's plenty'.
To one of his more important statements we demur; it seems to us
that Lady Macbeth's sleep-walking prose is hardly explained by the
reason that as she is changed from her former self so is her speech.

With regard to the epic element, Delius has performed no mean
feat in grading it—from the rough insertions of the early histories to
those accomplished passages that expose character or describe events
that could not be scenically shown. Surely he is at his best in remarking
that the Duke's description interests us in Jaques, who is not greatly
striking in the subsequent action; but the final conviction remains that
the epic element can serve well the comic interest and perhaps the
historic, but not the tragic—that a distinction exists as between hearsay
and experience. Casca's 'scurrilous' account of the offer of the crown
may be a masterpiece; and also Clarence's dream, whether or not by
Shakespeare:[1] though the last is as much soliloquy as narrative. But
can we accept without prejudice Hotspur's account of the lord who
demanded of him his prisoners?—or Ophelia's of Hamlet's appearance
in her chamber?—or Goneril's of the misconduct of Lear's followers?
Even these seem one degree removed from the intenser reality of
Shakespeare's supreme dramatic scenes—the naked encounter of soul
with soul. Yet we must admit that Horatio's final summing-up of the
situation—his words on 'carnal, bloody, and unnatural acts, Of accidental judgements, carnal slaughters'—help to deepen the veil of
mystery and horror that enwraps the play, and to unify the character
of Hamlet with the play's outer events. We think that Delius gives
his casting-vote for the dramatic in his last words on *A. and C.*, where
the personal overbears the historical, and the epic element is no longer
needed. Perhaps indirectly he helps us to appreciate Carlyle's saying
that Shakespeare's plays are truer than reality.

III

C. C. HENSE[2] says that Shakespeare far outdid his contemporaries in
knowledge of mental diseases. Observation and the instinct of genius

---

[1] See J. M. Robertson.   [2] 'Mental Diseases in Sh.' (*Jahrbuch*, 1878).

enabled him to describe madness and melancholy with a truth to nature to which no other poet has attained. To copy nature faithfully is not necessarily art; and some critics question the right to introduce on the stage anything ugly or unpleasant. We think the impulse to represent mental disease is due to an imagination which delights in great effects, and loves to represent characters in an entranced state of violence and passion. Compared with the characters of Sophocles, his are gigantic; and his criminals exceed in rage and wickedness those in ancient drama. But, with Shakespeare, aberration has the higher purpose of moral truth—madness being the enhanced expression of conscience. In life madness need not be the result of guilt: whereas Shakespeare's characters become mad from the burden of guilt which they have laid upon themselves. There is nothing about madness in the old story of Lear; but with Shakespeare he is quickly roused to violent wrath; and his repeated curses help to darken his thought and close his mind. He is without moral restraint, and 'hath ever but slenderly known himself'; his unbridled self-will leads him to disinherit Cordelia. The Lear of the old story looked on the evil he suffered from his daughters as punishment for his sins; but Shakespeare's Lear feels himself more sinned against than sinning: and this furthers his madness. His madness is ugly where it unites with wrongdoing; but the ugliness is of a kind which poetry allows and indeed requires. In a drama so rich in contrasts this madness, arising from guilt, emphasizes the contrast to the beauty of guiltless souls.

We note the same in Lady Macbeth, who stands in an inverted relation of disposition and development to her husband. We expect the vacillating Macbeth, in whom excess of imagination lessens the power of right judgement, to be the one to suffer mental derangement. That with sleeplessness added to qualms of conscience and despair he is not driven mad is due to his uninterrupted criminal activity. The stronger Lady Macbeth is overpowered by the past in her sleep. Some have regretted that the course of her madness has not been traced, like that of Lear—but in this there is aesthetic psychological truth. The aesthetic lies in the mystery and silence: and we know from Hamlet how these intensify the interest. Lady Macbeth disappears at the end of III. v, and only reappears in Act V; but the picture of the lonely brooding woman doomed to silence haunts us. Her mental aberration as sleep-walker is psychic and moral, taking deep root through her loneliness. The more painfully aware she becomes of being deceived in her husband, the more in loneliness she feels the growing estrangement, and the more active grow the suppressed feelings of her better nature which drew back on seeing Duncan's likeness to her father.

Shakespeare associates guilt and judgement of others with madness, e.g. Lear and Ophelia. He is overmastered by the thought of his daughters' ingratitude, and the wrong he has done Cordelia—and also

that he is more sinned against than sinning. This joined to a sense of
kingly power turns him into a judge; and the light of truth shines from
the night of madness. The judgement scene where he rails against
hypocrisy is reason in madness. Hamlet utters similar passionate words
on the relation between his mother and uncle: and we may compare
Posthumus (*Cymbeline*) when he supposes his wife unfaithful. Lear in
his sane days was deaf to warnings of truth and loyalty, and believed
hypocritical lies; but in his madness true insight into the actual
character of humanity developed with irresistible power. We recognize the effect of the Fool's enlightening sayings in some of the King's
expressions, cf. 'All thy other titles...', and 'When we are born...'.

Ophelia's madness may also be connected with self-reproach. She
is so far guilty that she let herself be persuaded, through mistaken ideas
of obedience, into an act unworthy of her guileless soul. She is con-
taminated by the degraded atmosphere that prevails of secrecy and
hypocrisy. She assists in the eavesdropping; and Hamlet's words are
significant, 'I have heard of your paintings...'. Then she suffers the
two blows of lost love and her father's death. Here she is more sinned
against than sinning, and in her madness, like Lear, she shows her
insight and condemnation of concealed guilt by means of symbols. She
also appears fantastically dressed in wild flowers, which she distributes
—a habit of insane persons, according to mental doctors. Ophelia shows
her instinctive sense of the truth in her distribution, e.g. she gives the
Queen rue—'herb of grace o' Sundays'—and so judges her.

To judge the advance of Shakespeare's art we need only compare
the madness of Titus with that of Lear. There is no doubt that the
latter is mad; but it is disputed whether the madness of Titus is real
or feigned. Titus has no trouble of conscience, though a far greater
sinner. Young Shakespeare, under Kyd's influence, makes mental
aberration the stimulus to brutal revenge. Shakespeare full grown in
knowledge of life and art made Lear's madness a cleansing process of
the spirit. Though Lear thinks of revenge, Shakespeare's more
advanced humanity does not let his curses materialize. In the same
way Hamlet was ready for unheard-of deeds, and would not slay the
King at prayer; but Shakespeare preferred a milder and truer conception of tragedy, and allotted a juster punishment to the King.

We may also compare his treatment of real and feigned madness.
In Edgar he follows the popular idea that madness is the work of
Satan to be cured by exorcism. Lear's healing requires no exorcist;
and here the poet's knowledge is ahead of his age....

We note Hense's opinion—as with some other critics—that Shakespeare was far beyond his age in knowledge of insanity; and we commend two of his sayings—the Fool's influence on Lear—and Lady
Macbeth's period of silent brooding. These prove that deep Shakespearian unity to which no conscious art can attain. But we accept

with reserve his main theory that madness is the result of guilt. It is obviously the cause of mental disturbance with Lady Macbeth; it can be made to sound plausible with Lear; but the meaning of the word must be unduly strained to include Ophelia. To explain Lear's madness according to rewards and punishments is to belittle it; and we rather look upon it as a revelation. The stress laid by Hense on Hamlet's words to Ophelia, 'I have heard of your paintings', is one more instance of the literal Teuton habit.

VI

WILHELM OECHELHÄUSER[1] writes that the Bottle Companions and Drunkards in Shakespeare represent every possible contrary type of character and position in life. Their only bond is the common weakness; individually they differ from the occasional drunkard to the habitual one, and also from the effect produced on each according to ethical and intellectual disposition. There is something so kindly disposed and pleasant in Shakespeare's description, so much observation of stages of drunkenness, that we can hardly mistake a measure of personal sympathy. The intuition of genius does not wholly suffice.

To one who knows human nature so well, drinking scenes would offer opportunities of interesting study. No other poet has treated with such variety drink and its effects: we have Caliban, Lepidus, Cassio, Bardolph, &c. Drink becomes an epoch in Caliban's spiritual life, but the elevation of feeling only increases his natural lowness and evil of disposition. He tempts Stephano to murder Prospero in his sleep, and when Stephano approves his plan he falls into wildest delight. With Stephano it is only wanton exhilaration of drunkenness, not calculated evil, that makes him accede to Caliban's plan; and in the end he forgets the murder in his desire to steal fine garments. Trinculo loves wine like all Shakespeare's clowns, but he is a poor-spirited creature who becomes cringing when he is drunk. The stage knows no better scene of drunkenness than this trio affords.

Barnardine (*M. for M.*) is careless and untroubled, and afraid of neither past, present, nor future. It is his drunkenness that saves him, since the Duke will not condemn so unprepared a soul. This picture of a sot is original enough to make us forget that it is bestial. It is not so with Sly (*Shrew*) who is the ordinary brawler. From the words of Hamlet and others we know Shakespeare's feeling towards these common tipplers; and Cassio (*Othello*) makes use of equally harsh expressions.

The scenes in the actual beer-house, where wine inspires wit and humour, are those that Shakespeare lingers over with a certain pleasure, and where he judges human weakness more leniently, e.g. Toby,

[1] 'Bottle Companions and Drunkards in Sh.' (*Jahrbuch*, 1881).

Andrew, and the Clown in *Twelfth-Night*. What prevents Toby from sinking to the grade of the common tippler is the indestructible humour produced by wine. He is always in good humour, always ready to jest or tease. Aguecheek is the whetstone of his humour; and on this fatuous companion wine has a highly comic effect. Drink makes him even more foolish; only when suffering from the after-effects does he become more sensible, and realize that his wooing is hopeless. Toby and Andrew represent in masterly fashion the subjective and objective comic side of drunkenness. They consider the Clown a servant, but drink abolishes social position. The Clown never appears really drunk, and is always master of the situation. He knows his own position towards his more aristocratic comrades, and tactfully makes use of it to fill his money-bag.

Falstaff has much of Toby's humour and sensuality, but in a far more refined degree. The beer-house is the only place where he feels himself comfortably at home. He is too witty and clever ever to let himself be drunk enough to lose control over his mind. Wine is for him the vehicle of companionable joviality, jest, and humour. He is ambitious to hold his own as head and intellectual centre of the mixed company of Eastcheap; and drunkenness that destroys mental powers would lose him this position. He delights to make others drunk, and amuses himself with the effect of wine on the weak-headed. Self-command is a fine feature given by Shakespeare to this delightful character: a drunken Falstaff would spoil the picture. Still less does Prince Henry descend to drunkenness, though as an exuberant youth he loves wine and its exhilarating effect on mind and mood. His whole nature remains unsoiled by excess, and he and Poins are morally superior to Falstaff. Bardolph is the regular toper or chronic drunkard, even below Stephano who retained his humour. As Bardolph tempts the Page to drink, so Falstaff tempts Silence, and thoroughly enjoys the drunken rejuvenescence of the sapless old Justice of the Peace: another little cabinet picture of drunkenness.

Pompey's galley (*A. and C.*) takes us to classic times, but drunkenness is the same in all ages. This is Shakespeare's greatest collective scene of extravagance under intoxication, but it differs in being a diplomatic banquet. The world's representatives meet to drink together, and the heterogeneous personalities become as brothers in the general intoxication. Ambitious self-seeking plans are concealed, and so are traitorous intentions, and the schisms in the political world. Now and then, in the whirl of the drinking-bout, chance words that tell of lurking, unreconciled divisions lend to the scene special fascination. The dance, at which the world's great rulers assist in a state of wild intoxication, is indeed over a volcano. Octavius drinks only for political convenience and social politeness; Antony is in his element; but Lepidus succumbs and is carried out. His political extinction is foreshadowed—and with him Shakespeare has climbed to the highest social stage of drunkenness, and also illustrated its levelling quality.

Apart from drinking-bouts, there are a few outstanding individual cases. Only drunkenness can explain Mercutio's wanton provocation of Tybalt, after the Prince had threatened with death any one who should renew the brawl. Besides, Mercutio calls the placid Benvolio quarrelsome—a characteristic of quarrelsome people in their cups, which had not escaped Shakespeare's keen observation. What moves us with Cassio is his awakening—his remorse and sorrow for his lost reputation. In *M. Ado* drunkenness is not actually depicted in Borachio, but serves to make the disentanglement of the plot less improbable. Nothing for Shakespeare was too high or too low; he describes with equal brilliance every degree of human being, of virtue and vice. . . .

We take exception to the statement that through Hamlet and Cassio Shakespeare is expressing his own condemnatory views of the abuse of wine. The bitterness of the one and the self-reproaches of the other are dramatically justified; and we need not take seriously the aspersion on Mercutio. Otherwise the disinterested note of this essay, the absence of over-emphasis make it an indirect tribute to the universality of Shakespeare's genius. Drink is shown as the stimulus under which they express their infinitely varied natures. More ambitious treatises have left us further from Shakespeare the man; and we feel less inclined to demur when he speaks of the poet's 'personal sympathy': though it is characteristically German to fall back upon literal interpretation. With the doubtful exception of the instance of Caliban, we recall Sainte-Beuve's words on Le Sage—that his irony is good-natured—he has no malice or bitterness—and in this absence of bitterness lies his originality and distinction as satirist. Oechelhäuser does well to note that drink is a great leveller, e.g. Toby and the Clown; and his distinction between Toby and Falstaff, and reminder that we never see Falstaff drunk, bring us slightly nearer to Falstaff's conscious mind. Perhaps too much is made of the galley scene by Oechelhäuser and other critics. It seems to us imperfectly fused and therefore lacking profoundest significance; and, to support the charge of want of fusion, we recall that *A. and C.* is still known as a chronicle play and ranks just below the greatest.

V

TH. GESSNER[1] asks from what standpoint we shall gain the best insight into Hamlet's character. The body is the mirror of the soul; and every stroke that a dramatist gives us of the outward man should tell us something. Hamlet is aged thirty, of low stature, stout, short of breath with exertion, yet active and dexterous in sword-play, an

[1] *Jahrbuch*, 1885.

accomplished courtier. His features are mobile, his hair curled, and standing up stiff in moments of emotion. His behaviour and speech change from scene to scene; he differs from Hercules rather in stature than lack of muscular strength: he can match Laertes, and is not to be restrained from following the Ghost. At times he uses the affected courtly tone of Elizabeth's day; but he never fails in dignified courtliness. He had the actor's power to change his face and expression with every mood of soul. In one who early knew court life we naturally detect signs of sensuality and repletion; and we see his outbreaks against sensual enjoyment. His school life yielded him no true friend of heart, and alone in Horatio he recognized a worthy friend. His behaviour throughout the play must determine whether he loved Ophelia. Only his entire being explains his love, and Shakespeare leaves both under a haze. He is a lover of the theatre, and of knightly skill.

Two bitter experiences were his before the play opens—his uncle elected king, and his mother remarried. The nobles looked upon the marriage favourably, as it relieved the state of her widow's jointure. Hamlet was justified in accusing his uncle of standing between his hopes and the election, and in calling him a cutpurse of the empire. He had two tasks to accomplish, one of which, the separation of his mother and uncle, he accomplishes in his speech to her. It is not true, as Werder says, that he was powerless, from external reasons, to revenge himself on his uncle. The King had the right to imprison or banish him, but he dared do nothing openly to one whom the people loved. The guards inform Hamlet of the Ghost, not the King; and Marcellus, the royal officer, swears without hesitation to keep it a secret from every one, including the King. Claudius orders State affairs, but his seal is only a copy of the original which Hamlet has in his pocket. Mentally superior, Hamlet is exceeded by the King only in practical wit. On account of birth, personal qualities, and social position no man might become so dangerous to the King as Hamlet. They do not stand opposed as one secure by rank, and the other with his hands bound—but as two equally balanced in power and strength. That Hamlet's task was possible seems to have been tacitly conceded by himself, Horatio, and the Ghost. Had he disclosed what he had heard, Horatio, Marcellus, and many others would have helped him. He keeps silence because he feels himself man enough to fulfil the task single-handed. It is true that his confidence ebbs at times, and his moods vary; but we find no trace that he wishes to convince the Danes of his uncle's crime. He despised the stagnant court and its nobles; and this contradicts the demands of dramatic usage according to Shakespeare's views. Few of his criminals receive their just due without some proof given by the executor of justice. A single confession of crime in a monologue, or to an accomplice, suffices dramatic requirements of justice. Werder's statement is equally untrue that the Danes would have looked on Hamlet as the murderer. Hamlet, Fortinbras, Horatio were all certain that the assembly of nobles would believe Horatio's plain narrative of facts. Had Hamlet appeared, all aglow with moral indignation, and described the crime against his father, the Ghost's story, and the effect of the play scene on Claudius, he would certainly have won over his audience.

In Hamlet's temperament, which was Shakespeare's free invention, there are three points to be noted: the temperament itself—the vacillation of mood in scene after scene—and the crystallizing point (the unity) of the whole play, around which all revolves, and which throws light on the most inconspicuous scenes. It is genuinely Shakespearian to make the natural disposition the ground of the whole being and action. Education, fateful events, and strangers all work upon it, but are not the spring of existence; the natural disposition conditions and shapes the physical constitution; and the temperament is made up of disposition, humours, and passions. Hamlet's temperament is a melancholy one; he is brooding and imaginative, and affected by troubled fancies. With Hamlet, unlike Shakespeare's other melancholy heroes, melancholy is the source of all his being: his every action and feature can be traced to melancholy. The physical description of him given above is that of the man disposed to melancholy; and outer and inner are ultimately resolved into one homogeneous natural disposition. He appears to us a plain human being, of no epoch or nationality. The play covers three months, as time is needed to show different aspects; and the melancholy man varies the most. To this characteristic is due his depth of trouble, his contempt of the world, his failure to react against the King. It is Shakespeare's master-stroke that he feigns madness, since every temperament (most of all, the melancholy) inclines to some aberration; and as the phlegmatic becomes melancholy, the melancholy becomes mad. His motive is not cunning, but it helps him to appear mad when in wild trouble and rage. He can thus equally express and hide his inner feelings. It would be more true to say that he both loved and did not love Ophelia. His natural disposition was attracted by her, and she appealed to his imagination and senses; but before love had become deep-seated, other powerful influences bridled his temperament. Love is thrust aside like a stepchild, yet remains a trouble at his heart; for nothing that impresses the melancholy nature disappears.

Shakespeare frequently unifies a play artistically by stressing one passion: in *Lear* two fathers do not recognize their children; ambition possesses husband and wife in *Macbeth*; jealousy, Othello and Iago; wild living, the Prince, Falstaff, Bardolph, Pistol; mistaken identities obtain in *Errors*, *M.N.D.*, &c. *Hamlet* is the drama of dissimulation; there is hardly a scene in which it does not appear, hardly a person who does not wear a mask. The King is a master of it, and the effort to remove his mask is one of the chief affairs of the play. He holds our interest and lessens our hate by the strength with which he cleaves to it, and the power of conscience which makes him confess his foul deed in monologue. The Queen equally dissimulates, and it is second nature with Polonius. We must not condemn Ophelia who had been brought up amid dissimulation. Before she assumes the mask of madness, she had given no hint of all that her mad songs convey; therefore modesty was her previous mask. Laertes, with treachery in his heart, makes dissembling speeches of reconciliation to Hamlet. Hamlet dissembles in many ways, sometimes purposely as when he plays either the madman or courtier, or hides himself in silence. With Gertrude and Ophelia the dissembling is that of weak womanhood; with the King and Polonius it is practised dissimulation; and with Hamlet and Laertes for a definite end. But all are naturally disposed to dissimulation, having breathed the corrupt air of the court.[1]

We never see but one side of Hamlet, never the whole man—when he stabs Polonius, hesitates to kill the King, writes love-letters, meditates on suicide, jokes with Ophelia, discourses on the theatre, rates his mother, reproaches himself, philosophizes in the churchyard, presses Horatio's hand, mocks Polonius, curses his uncle. It is the shifting mask of the melancholy man, and the heart of the riddle is his natural disposition—the veil which never lets the whole man be seen. . . .

At the outset we feared we were about to be engaged in the worst kind of unimaginative criticism, e.g. Hamlet's stature— Hercules—the widow's jointure. However, this is but the lowest step of the argument; there are three others, each of which takes us into better air. The attack on Werder is temperate, well-reasoned, and allows for psychological factors—such as Hamlet's moral indignation. If the analysis of Hamlet's temperament interests but fails to satisfy, it is the fate of all abstract criticism. We become preoccupied with the idea of melancholy, and see no clearer image of a single melancholy man. But having mounted the fourth step, we do see something of the Hamlet country in a strange afternoon light. The dissimulation, which the critic underlines, helps us to realize more definitely the foul moral atmosphere of which others have spoken; and the point about Ophelia is at least worth noting. Finally, if the problem of Hamlet's character cannot at present be solved, there are few better ways of helping on thought than an orderly statement of its difficulties: and such is Gessner's method in the proofs he advances that we never see the whole man.

[1] Cf. Hense.

VI

JULIUS THÜMMEL[1] discovers three aspects in the career of
Shakespeare's heroes. Some rise from a lower stage to the heroic
sphere; there are others of ideal manliness whose energy assures their
victory; and still others who overstep ethical frontiers and bring ruin
on themselves. Edgar (*Lear*), whom we misdoubt at first for his
credulity, develops under suffering an energy which lifts him to an
astounding height of heroism. Yet more striking instances of developed heroism are Richard II and Leontes. He who repents and
gains a victory over the old Adam is a hero. Richard II, who, in face
of upbraiding, renounces the crown and takes the loss of the throne as
his punishment, has mastered the arrogance of his natural disposition.
Prince Henry, on the other hand, always had in him the making of a
hero—though hidden by inclination to licence and wanton humour.
When the time came he stepped forth as the natural peer of Hotspur
—a hero who owed his moral elevation to individual strength of
character.

The heroes in *Lear, Macbeth, John, 1 Henry VI* represent medieval
feudal loyalty—the devoted Kent, knightly Macduff, honest Falconbridge, brave Talbot—also Salisbury and Bedford. Macduff is made
of fine clay, of mingled power and gentleness. When the news comes
that his wife and children are slain, he shows the true pith of his nature.
Falconbridge is loyal to John, in whom he sees a man's soul, whereas
the girlish disposition of Arthur does not appeal to him. He remains
faithful when all fall away, a true patriot, and his humour carries him
through every grave situation. This atones for his immoderate pride,
lack of respect, discretion, and scruple. Talbot, the genuine British
national hero and terror of the French, expresses more definitely
Shakespeare's patriotism. In true noble English fashion his only
revenge on the Countess of Auvergne is to ask to taste her wine. Beside him stand worthily Salisbury and Bedford, who seal their heroism
by soldiers' deaths. Shakespeare does not bring them into the foreground, but he binds the laurels round their fallen heads in such a way
as to give them high rank among heroes.

The third group fill us with compassion or horror. Brutus wins our
sympathy because he is noble and selfless, but his means are criminal,
even considering ancient morals. Shakespeare does not shield or
justify him, but lets the crime speak for itself. Brutus and Cassius, in
their defeat, recall Caesar; and the death of Caesar, in Shakespeare's
opinion, meets with its natural retribution. Brutus, without malice
or hatred, sacrifices his friend Caesar to the Republic; but his humane
temperament is fatal in that he spares Mark Antony. With the turn
of events in such unsettled times, this kind of humanity is politically

[1] 'Sh.'s Heroes' (*Jahrbuch*, 1885).

false. The Stoic's statecraft was broken on the rock of human friendship, although his other qualities made him a fit leader of public affairs.
Cassius is the public agitator, more practical and sharp-sighted than
Brutus, full of speculative thought which he puts into action. The
way in which he wins men over to his conspiracy shows his keen knowledge of humanity—he does not approach Brutus and Casca in like
manner. He can put aside feelings of humanity, but in the end he
yields to the irresistible idealism of Brutus—and this leads him to the
same end. These two twin brothers of patriotism, through their aims,
stand high among Shakespeare's heroes.

It is otherwise with Coriolanus and Percy. Coriolanus is a hero even
to death, a complete figure moulded in brass, finely chiselled in every
detail—among Shakespeare's most perfect creations.[1] Hotspur is the
same type, in medieval dress, with equal hot-blooded temperament and
lack of circumspection. Both declined from the heroic standard in
selfish motive—in pursuit of revenge—and involved their country in
enforced war. Both alike are upright and avoid crooked ways, but are
led by excess of passion to criminal acts.

So far the hero's fall is due to a single deed, but in Macbeth we see
one who, in the grip of dark powers, involves himself in a whole net
of crimes. No deliberate criminal, but, in the beginning, an imaginative dreamer, feverishly aroused under the mystical spell of dark powers.
These somnambulistic traits are the cause of the attraction we feel for
this hero of criminal ambition. We feel quite otherwise to Richard III,
who lacks a nobler self, scoffs at loftiness, and pursues consciously his
subtly criminal way.

Hamlet is the hero of thought, the most modern of Shakespeare's
heroic figures, rising above the level of the ordinary into the intellectual
realm. He lacked the initiative that Macbeth had in excess; and what
proved fatal to the ambitious struggles was equally fatal to its non-
possessor. There is no proof, and no hint from Shakespeare, that
Hamlet was over-conscientious. He is self-accusing, and acknowledges that the duty is too heavy for his shoulders. Besides, we doubt
his conscientiousness when we recall how he forsook Ophelia, and
forged the letter that sent his friends to their doom. His Wittenberg
studies have produced scepticism and melancholy, or rather pessimism,
which excludes the passionate feeling whence great action springs. It
drives a rich mind like Hamlet's to the bizarre, so we have his feigned
madness, &c., and for permanent feelings nervous ebullitions. The
subjective plays a greater part than in any other play, as everywhere in
Shakespeare action is the result of character. Here we have a sceptical
hero who shrinks from action, which gives a corresponding negativity
to the flow of the play, and leaves something undetermined and misty
about it. In other plays every act of the hero leads to the catastrophe:

[1] Cf. Saintsbury.

here we have the destructive power of hesitation, doubt, enervation of scepticism clearly displayed. But the inner poetic truth is the cause of the lasting interest in the play and its hero. . . .

We need say little of Thümmel's first 'group' of heroes. To unite Edgar, Richard II, Leontes, Prince Henry is to succumb to external criticism—like those generalizing scientists who include man with the animal or even vegetable creation by omitting everything that is characteristic. Richard II is not a hero, nor does he truly repent, but he interests because he is a poet, and his misfortunes draw from him streams of melody. In the same way, when he deals with the Macduff-Falconbridge group, no new light appears from the fact that these several characters are brought together from various plays. This should be the object of all grouping, and the only time it is accomplished here is from the juxtaposition of Hotspur and Coriolanus—when a feeble spark is struck out. On the other hand, there are some good sentences in the *Hamlet* criticism; and it might be compared with Gessner's—that we never see the entire man.

VII

SHAKESPEARE, for Elze, has a mysterious and enigmatic personality, a Protean nature. He had rare knowledge of every fold and fibre of the human heart, and a breadth of view that surveyed the whole realm of human knowledge and experience. He had a universal mind, he surpassed all poets and philosophers in wealth of expression, and he fathomed the whole domain of human nature. Delius gives him unparalleled psychological insight, and calls him philosopher and psychologist. Hense says that he has comprehensive knowledge of the soul and its impulses and passions. To Oechelhäuser his genius was all-embracing, and his knowledge of human nature such that he described equally well highest and lowest human beings, virtues, and vices. According to Gessner, Shakespeare makes temperament centre of all.

Elze is uncertain how far he was a Christian, but emphasizes his objectivity, which extended to religion and morals. Conscience was his central point of religion: he believed in free will, and was no fatalist. Thümmel agrees that his moral outlook was impartial; and it might be of interest to compare the opinion of Hense—that he represents madness as the result of guilt.

Elze remarks that he was a close observer of nature and human life; that his every line was individual; and of all literature his comes nearest to actual life; while he had the highest form of poetical imagination. Delius credits him with surpassing and calculating art. His characters speak individually and are true to nature; besides excelling as dramatist, he has masterly narrative and descriptive power. Hense agrees that he is profoundly acquainted with the needs of true art. Gessner finds that he gives artistic unity by making one passion prominent in a play.

Though a court poet, his poetry was democratic or national. Such is the opinion of Elze, who later on discovers that he had an aristocratic turn of mind. He concludes that he was no politician; whereas Delius maintains that he had wide and deep insight into politics. Thümmel merely subscribes to his patriotism.

Elze gives him great business capacity; his sublimest world-embracing thoughts were combined with the calculating keen perception of the man of business. He had known world-sorrow: but above all he was a humanist. . . .

These opinions do not differ greatly from contemporary English writers. The critics discover contradictions in Shakespeare; and on certain points they disagree fundamentally: with the result that the mystery of Shakespeare grows.

Chapter XXV

FRANCE 1878–1885

I. RENAN. II. STAPFER. III. BROWN. IV. CONCLUSION.

I

THE object of Ernest Renan[1] is to adapt three of Shakespeare's profoundest creations—Prospero, Caliban, Ariel—to modern thought; and in such an attempt he is well served by his sensitiveness to ideas and exquisite style. We may contrast Montégut when we hear him say that Shakespeare paints no special age or country but simply human history; and that we need trouble neither about local colour nor external costumes in these battles between pure ideas. He makes Caliban say that the island belonged to him: to which Ariel replies it did, as the desert to the gazelle, or the jungle to the tiger. Prospero, he says, taught you the language of the Aryas; and, with this divine language, reason, which is inseparable from it, entered into you. Caliban contends that human nature is ungrateful; also that master-races use the weapon of superstition and hold out the fear of a hell that does not exist. The Christian God is for women and weaklings. . . . Prospero defines God as the genius of the man of genius, the virtue of the virtuous man, the goodness of the tender soul, the universal effort to be and develop. His true definition is love. . . . In a later passage Ariel laments that his art is powerless against the people. The people contain something deep and mysterious; the spirits that prevailed against Alonzo's fleet are powerless against the people. They would not even listen to his music. Alonzo and his companions succumbed because they believed. Alonzo thought the winds and waves spoke, and the thunder rebuked him in bass tones. The people admit nothing of this; magic serves no more; realism means revolution. Alas for the day when this method of reasoning will be applied to God. The people are positivists. Gonzalo concludes that Caliban represents the people, that all civilization in its origin is aristocratic, but the people, taught by the nobles, turn against them. . . .

We must resist the temptation to follow up any of these interesting trains of thoughts, and simply inquire whether they throw any light on Shakespeare. They certainly bring home to us the depth and strength of his imaginative conceptions.

II

PAUL STAPFER[2] touches the same subject when he says that great geniuses, like Shakespeare, are always new because one never gets to the bottom of their thought. He deprecates conjectures on Shake-

[1] *Caliban suite de la Tempête*, 1878.   [2] *Sh. et l'antiquité*, 1879, 1882.

speare from his plays that rob him of his chief glory, since it is of the
essence of dramatic art to be impersonal. Shakespeare soars above his
characters with the indifference of a creator, stranger to his work.
After dwelling on the vicissitudes of Shakespeare's fame, including
Voltaire's criticism, he decides Shakespeare to be the greatest poet of
England and modern Europe, but not infallible.

He was no uneducated genius; in some plays he has observed
ancient rules; he was probably not hostile, but indifferent to classic
doctrines. He was a practical Englishman who gave the public
the plays it wanted. His self-effacement and impersonality were
unparalleled; and we therefore admire, but do not love him, because
we cannot see the man. Personal qualities, even defects, are needed
before an author can become dear to ourselves. He is fundamentally
indifferent to all doctrines; his creative activity is purely practical.
Antiquity to him is but a storehouse of materials for art. His mind
absorbed to produce, not meditate—and to the end of his life his
readings remained hasty. He did not slowly accumulate material, but
threw himself on a translation of Plutarch at second-hand, by North
from Amyot. Latin in the sixteenth century was almost a living
language; and it is likely that he knew it—as did many women. He
was simply indifferent to classic learning; it was a means to an end.
The study of Greek was no better then than now; and he did not
know Greek. He was one of the most learned men that ever existed,
but in the true liberal sense: he knew his own ignorance.

The anachronisms in his plays were not individual, but common with
his contemporaries. Such things diminish as learning advanced: since
a poet must choose his subject from a remote world, because the world
around him is too prosaic. Art should appeal to all, learned and unlearned:
a poet's first duty is to interest his public. The anachronism of the
poets of the time of Louis XIV was to put Greeks and Romans on the
scene and express them through the soul of their own epoch. Voltaire
did not understand this, but thought all else bad taste and barbarous.
The romantic revolution allowed scope for the natural anachronisms
of art. Hernani and Ruy-Blas are not Spaniards, but simply young
people of 1830. The vital principle of the drama is the contemporary
soul: history is but the frame, and local colour of minor importance.
To select a subject from the past, and express a modern soul by means
of it, is art's profound and natural anachronism. The secret of genius
is to paint eternal human nature. Because Shakespeare, in *Venus*,
neglected mythology and made Venus an amorous courtesan, his
picture lives.

The explanation of *T. and C.* is in the past and belongs to the Latin
inheritance. The subject of Virgil's epic was national, and history
and poetry were nearly allied. The savage nations that overthrew
Rome came to consider themselves kinsmen of the Romans. The

English claimed descent from Brutus who descended from Aeneas; and it became in England a popular belief and patriotic faith. Homer was unread in the Middle Ages, and Virgil became the oracle. In poetic ages men cannot distinguish between poetry and reality, and they saw in the *Aeneid* a sublime allegory. Homer, as historian, was blamed for improbabilities; and all through the Middle Ages Achilles was vilified and Hector exalted. Shakespeare mocks at every one in his play except Hector, whom he respects from force of tradition. Under the creative spell he was indifferent to all doctrines: he searched Chapman's *Iliad* to find matter for a comedy. It contains more psychology and irony than his other comedies. Instead only of clever dialogue, we have comic persons; and laughter arises from situations and also from things, e.g. the character assumed by Ulysses before Agamemnon and Nestor to make them angry. Shakespeare, versed in the secrets of art, achieves great effects by small means. He removes the trappings of office and war and shows his people in their daily life. They fall from epic heights to bourgeois comedy: and the comic effect is achieved by surprise. *Timon* has no Greek local colour, and is the inverse of *T. and C.*, which hides vast riches in its strange depths. *Timon* is the only tragedy of Shakespeare's to be more noisy than solid, and it is more like one of Victor Hugo's dramas: it is picturesque, sonorous, spectacular, and has lyric eloquence. Timon's misanthropy is the rage of a spoilt child who sees his dream disappear. *Pericles* is a youthful work, more narrative than drama—like pictures from a magic lantern: yet the scene where Pericles recognizes his daughter is one of the finest in Shakespeare.

Montaigne's influence over Shakespeare is little more than a hypothesis—but it is otherwise with Plutarch: here it is no longer a question of words but the foundation of things. Shakespeare has followed Plutarch so faithfully that his Roman plays are practically the lives of Caesar, Brutus, Antony, Coriolanus dramatized. A modern dramatist would select an extract from Plutarch, not dramatize Plutarch himself. Shakespeare, of course, does select; but we feel his own imagination, memory, science to be far above the results—his ideal to be finer than his work—and his mind to contain resources a thousandfold vaster than anything in his plays. His dramatic translation of Plutarch, therefore, only *seems* all-inclusive. Careless as a rule with his authorities, he shows remarkable modesty and deference to Plutarch. The reason is that Plutarch had genius and poetic imagination, and had already half transformed history to poetry. There are times when Shakespeare changes Plutarch's whole idea, e.g. his Coriolanus is far prouder than Plutarch's who conforms to the law because he wishes to be consul. Also the old Roman citizens, who cannot have been such vile creatures, since they produced the great city of Rome, become with Shakespeare the rabble of a modern

London or Paris—blind, unpolitical, moved by the lowest instincts,
the ready prey of the demagogue, and, above all, cowardly. Plutarch's
Antony is contemptible, even odious; but Shakespeare has mingled
some happy lights and shades with his character, so that he becomes at
least interesting if not fine. Plutarch mentions the scandal, which
Shakespeare omits, that Brutus was Caesar's natural son. If history
and poetry diverge in Plutarch, Shakespeare follows the latter. He
has unconsciously followed his poetic instinct in aggrandizing Coriolanus, idealizing Antony, ennobling Brutus, and debasing the mob.
His knowledge of Rome has been overstated, and is limited to the
poetic—to the greatness of the soul of Brutus, the patriotism of
Volumnia, the noble pride of Coriolanus. In this he was helped by
the affinity between the English and Roman character and genius. His
tragedies are poetically true, since the poet's function is to seize the
soul of things out of the crowd of details. He idealizes in removing the
superfluous, in giving to the idea an emphasis that it has not in reality.[1]
A. and C. impresses on the imagination, more than any history, the
end of an era. Aristotle says that poetry is more general than history;
and Bacon, that poetry expresses what *ought* to happen.

No work of Shakespeare's is easier to read than *J.C.*; and it belongs
to his second and most perfect manner. The theme is the same as
Hamlet; but Brutus does act, makes a mistake, and yet retains our
sympathy. The three Roman plays are moral more than historical
studies. An examination of their characters would be the basis of any
aesthetic work on Shakespeare, since character-drawing was the
unique side of his art. It is the peak of dramatic art to create ideal
individuals who live for ever, and make so-called real persons appear
shadows—each of whom has a distinctive stamp—and who as a whole
represent all human passions and human nature. Caesar's character
at first excites surprise and disapproval. His majesty is that of the
Oriental despot intoxicated with absolute power. The portrait is not
entirely unhistorical; for Plutarch says he was much altered before his
end—that he had an immoderate desire to be king, or rather he aimed
at divinity and wished his words to be laws. But when he dies the
Republic has gained nothing: as if Shakespeare wished to show that
the time of liberty is over for Rome, and henceforth the cause of
servility is not submission to a master, but inward change. The Empire
was not bound up in one man's genius, but rooted in the force of things.
Brutus failed to understand this, and hence the nothingness of his
enterprise. The play is filled not with the genius of a man, but with
a new era about to dawn—the genius of Caesarism. Antony's offer
of the crown to Caesar is a trap laid by history for poetry. Voltaire fell
into it; but Shakespeare knew there was no love of liberty in the people.
Here is an admirable example of history corrected by poetry for the

[1] Cf. Professor Stoll's remarks on the function of emphasis in literature.

sake of ideal truth. There was nothing serious in the people's applause; they would have done the same if Caesar had assumed the crown. After he dies, his spirit grows till it overshadows the whole action.

Brutus is one of Shakespeare's best characters, and we must remember his moral and chronological relation to Hamlet. He is one with the historical Brutus; Shakespeare has suppressed a few traits, but added nothing. Books were his passion; and his one preoccupation was to make himself nobler. This habit of making one's personality the centre of things is a kind of moral egoism. Self-study makes him blind to facts and reality; and he lacked judgement and knowledge of men. The conspirators sought him because he was disinterested, and had the world's respect. He was also sympathetic, whereas moral perfection does not usually attract love. Shakespeare did not change history, but gave the emphasis of poetry to Plutarch's facts. If Brutus appears self-controlled, it is because a heroic will has imposed philosophy on nature. Nothing in poetry exceeds the tenderness of Brutus —the strong man's tenderness. He hates tyranny but loves Caesar; and yet his self-communion is incomprehensible—for this avenger of the Republic shows no republican feeling.[1] Instead of taking the political point of view, his doubt is for the possible effect of kingship on Caesar's nature. But once resolved he is immovable: and here he differs from Hamlet. He characteristically spares Antony, because he wars against ideas, not men. Judging as moralist, not politician, he despises Antony because he is dissolute. Cassius, who lacked Brutus's noble qualities, at least foresaw the unavoidable consequences of his action. His was the language of vanity impatient of superiority; he was discontented more than fanatical. Brutus's idealism, Cassius's indifference to life—these are the constituents of a revolutionary reign of terror. Brutus makes ingenious excuses to Antony; but Cassius, who knows men well, flatters him and appeals to his vanity. But were he only envious and jealous he would not have won our sympathy or inspired moral interest. Shakespeare adds a few delicate touches that do not destroy unity, but lightly contradict it. He does hate tyranny itself—he thinks too much—and we know from Caesar that he lived an austere life. He loves and submits to Brutus against reason—and he is absolutely sincere. The quarrel is one of Shakespeare's best scenes, and tells us most about his divine art and unique secret. Most dramatists conceive a type and raise it to the ideal. They paint the profile—because it reveals the true character. Shakespeare paints full face, he seeks truth and life—the whole truth of temperament and shades of character. He carries truth to the point of self-contradiction, for characters are not always logical. Thus he shows us Brutus for the moment unfaithful to his nature and principles—less reasonable of the two. He should not exact from his subordinates, in time of

[1] Cf. MacCallum.

stress, a moral uprightness which he did not practise himself. Cassius
did wrong to extort money—but the war was the guilty party. If
Cassius is interesting, it is that he is not only hard and egotistical, but
also a man.

It must be possible to reconcile the contradictions with the ground
tone of each character. Antony has a noble nature, but is without
moral sense. Such men can be chivalrous and heroic, but their conduct
is a brilliant lie: they obey imagination, not conscience. Besides
interest and pleasure there is a third false rule of life—the aesthetic:
and to this type Antony belongs. He was a born disciple; his nature
was to yield to a superior force. He even yielded to Octavius whom he
despised, because he felt the ascendancy of his fortune. He was
certainly devoted to Caesar; and it appealed to his imagination that
he also might be struck by the swords stained with the noblest blood in
the world, wielded by the greatest men. He praises Brutus dead, and
even weeps: within his artist's sensibility was admiration for victim
and murderer. Having no moral idea, but susceptible to beauty, he
could unite the furthest contrasts. He was no hypocrite when he
offered his hand to Caesar's murderers, he did not at first intend to
inflame the mob. He wished to do a friend's duty, and only when
launched into the current of his discourse did it occur to him that he
might push home his advantage. He was compounded of good faith
and craft, of premeditated artifice and sudden inspiration. In *A. and C.*
he preserves this aesthetic morality which can understand and love
and even will what is honourable and beautiful. The struggle between
his better and worse instincts makes him a tragic hero. Self-caused
adversity does not make him unjust as it makes most men: he forgives
Enobarbus. He has all good feelings for Octavia except love—and he
thinks poetically of her sad destiny. In the end he, who for lack of
moral support leaned on others, is left alone. Plutarch's description
of his end equals Shakespeare's; for the hero himself is poetical.

All Cleopatra's crimes and vices are transformed to grace. Things
that revolt in men do not in women; and Cleopatra is the more amiable
for her failings. Antony, under her influence, can neither weep nor
remain indifferent at Fulvia's death. With Cleopatra's love may have
mingled some political ambition; but Shakespeare suppresses it, and
shows the woman more than the queen. Plutarch insists on her
prudence and judgement; while Shakespeare neglects this, and in the
scene where she ill-treats the messenger shows that passion and feminine
unreason can go no further. But passion exalts the meanest things, and
the violence of her love changes comedy to tragedy. Actium is the
most salient instance ever recorded of a woman's power. She fled
because she was afraid; she was a woman and her nerves gave way:
but on great occasions she could be truly brave. Or rather, she usurped
this reputation by using the circumstances of her death like a splendid

cloak in which to wrap her small feminine person. She wishes to die, not because she has lost Antony and her kingdom, but because Octavius will take her to Rome—and this her nervous sensibility cannot bear.

No uglier, more disagreeable, more repulsive person exists in history than Octavius. Were he more frankly hateful he would be less antipathetic. The judgement of poetry and human nature is one, and therefore political skill does not compensate for lack of courage. He was, however, the man of destiny, and his cleverness, of the negative kind, consisted in not standing in the way of his own fortune. He only appears to be practical—because his adversary's folly passes all bounds. Lepidus is at least amusing, and the galley scene is the most humorous in Shakespeare. Humour is not sad and bitter, but a joyful and poetic feeling of the nothingness of all things. Add to this the laughter and fancy of Rabelais, and you have the complete humorist. Shakespeare has not the humour of Rabelais and Sterne; he is more serious, and the drama too impersonal to allow a subjective thing like humour—that is also opposed to great art and true beauty—to be continuously present.[1] But as a philosopher he feels that all is vanity, and he cannot but laugh at the folly of men. The impression *A. and C.* conveys is that the world is foundering in the midst of an orgy: and it is condensed in the symbolic galley scene.[2] Enobarbus has been compared to a chorus; but Shakespeare never makes the external conflict of moral ideas the essence of the action; and no one of his characters expresses the sum total of the truth; but each discovers a part that remains hidden for the others. A chorus should be perfectly wise and just; and yet Enobarbus is a partial organ of Shakespeare's thought. What makes him original is a mixture of impersonal wisdom, superior to his own nature, and decided individuality. He belongs to a time when a long succession of civil wars had sapped the feeling of loyalty to the flag, and men easily exchanged camps. In fine, the play does not present a first-rate tragic interest. The internal struggle is not a moral one, but between pleasure and interest. In yielding to Cleopatra, Antony only loses the world, not his soul. But it is profuse in poetic riches; and Shakespeare, who was no pedantic moralist, delights as much in painting a courtesan as a faithful wife like Portia. He has the serene impartiality of the Creator who makes his sun shine on just and unjust.[3] If any one wishes to imitate Antony and Cleopatra let him do so completely: they are outside and above human conditions.[4] Shakespeare does not preach—but we see the writing on the wall.

Coriolanus has courage, the first title of nobility—but he would not be able to conceive a lowly-born honourable man. The violence

---

[1] Carlyle in his earliest essay (on Richter) says that Sterne was the first of English humorists, above even Shakespeare, as Cervantes was above Sterne, the first of all.

[2] Cf. Oechelhäuser on the drinking scenes.

[3] Cf. Taine on Sh.'s 'Immorality'.   [4] Cf. Wendlandt (1888).

of his temperament was greater than the pride of his soul; and this
personal sensitiveness is a purely modern trait, strange to the ancient
world. When banished he rises to his full height; and if the sublime
exists outside moral grandeur, he touches it here, when he seems
greater in himself than the whole of Rome. But his soul declines when
he conceives his crime; his beggar's dress must have injured his pride;
and Shakespeare's one change from Plutarch is to inflict upon him this
humiliation. Menenius plays the part of mediator, and should have
avoided extremes; but Shakespeare never stages the perfectly balanced
moralist: for such persons lack dramatic and individual interest.
Menenius is an aristocrat almost as violent as Coriolanus, but he is
ironic where Coriolanus loses his temper, and is forgiven because his
manners are popular. He does not mediate for the sake of reason or
justice, but because he is old, fat, and loves peace. He is good enough,
but without true moral or intellectual worth. Volumnia's patriotism
is purer than her son's, and she loves Rome more than him. She looks
upon him as the greatest Roman, and to her the crime of treason is not
only horrible but absurd. The finest scene is where she appears in the
double majesty of Roman and mother. Of the Roman plays this has
the most unity, but there is something hard in the sentiments and
style; it is less tragic than *J.C.*, less poetic than *A. and C.* The fault
of the last scene is that Shakespeare's language and Plutarch's are laid
side by side rather than fused. The best is where Plutarch is followed
literally—for Plutarch had a poetic and dramatic imagination nearly
of the first order.

A crowd is a person; the general spirit is not the sum of the
individuals but the average. The union of beings does not produce
intelligence: a crowd means something bestial. If 1,500 superior men
assembled make 1,500 fools, what about a similar assembly of those
who are already fools? The beast will be capable of every crime, and
also of every enthusiasm—of universal excess. In the first scene of
J.C. we see the fickleness of the crowd—and yet it reacts promptly to
the Tribunes' reproaches. The people applaud Caesar's refusal of the
crown, and then shout for Brutus to be Caesar. They hated the name
of king but accepted the fact: such is the power of words over the
crowd. The worst action of the people was to murder Cinna the poet.
Plutarch calls it a mistake, but Shakespeare knew better, and feared not
to add a refinement of cruelty and folly to the crime. He knew what a
mad crowd could do at a time of revolution. We hear the fierce vacant
laugh of a mob, knowing well what it does, light-heartedly massacring
a man because he bears a displeasing name.[1] In *Coriolanus* Shakespeare
does not discriminate the plebeians of the new-born Republic from
those of Imperial degenerate Rome, but draws the universal type of
ancient Rome or modern Paris or London—foolish, inconsistent,

[1] Cf. Jusserand.

cowardly, quarrelsome, unpolitical, easily swayed, more stupid than
wicked. Their grievances seem without foundation, and we see little
use in the Tribuneship. But Shakespeare spent all his genius on his
hero and neglected the surroundings; his interest was for great
characters and personalities. And yet the play contains his best picture
of the populace pure and simple. Democracy fosters the false theory
of the natural equality of men.

If we compare the Cade scenes in *Henry VI*, and many other passages, we cannot but conclude that they expressed Shakespeare's
personal unfriendly feeling to the people. Between his treatment of
communism in the *Tempest*, and Montaigne's, there is the national
difference of English good sense and French weakness for the visionary
political systems of Plato and Rousseau. He was no prophet, and could
not foresee the future of democracy; and in Tudor and Stuart times the
people were not yet enfranchised. History justified him in excluding
the people from politics; besides, the political sentiments usually
attributed to him harmonize with the nature of his art. Poets are usually
aristocratic, and dramatists delineate the great because their positions
make them heroes. As you decline socially, the importance of the
individual is less. Poets admire grandeur and force because they are
such, e.g. some modern poets admired Napoleon. Because Shakespeare
was a poet he made Coriolanus great and the people small. He was
aristocrat and royalist: in his opinion the man with the royalist soul
had the right to be king.[1] But he was the poet of individual creations,
not general ideas. He does not teach, but makes characters live; he was
not interested in political ideas.

His attitude to classical literature was one of disregard, but the
differences between himself and the Greeks have been exaggerated.
Except *Titus* and Gloster's eyes (*Lear*), there is nothing specially cruel
in Shakespeare. Oedipus appears with blood-streaming face; Ajax kills
himself on the stage; the Eumenides of Aeschylus snore; and the plays
of Aristophanes contain bolder fantasies than anything in Shakespeare.
At least the Greek tragedies violate the unity of time and place.
Aristotle laid down no law, but pointed out the practice of the best
writers. The ancient tragic action was confined to the catastrophe,
but from the moment when tragedy broadened till it became history,
instead of simple crisis, unity of time had no right to be.

Shakespeare's art was romantic, as opposed to symbolic or classic
art—but he was the most impersonal romantic poet—as impersonal
as Homer. Besides the objectivity of the ancients he has their moral
health and serenity; he is a stranger to our modern melancholy—not
personally concerned with the mysteries of man's destiny. Virgil is
more modern, even more Christian than he; and among the ancients
we do find modern melancholy—the idea that life is a dream or shadow.

[1] Cf. Hazlitt on Coriolanus. Hazlitt himself greatly admired Napoleon.

Shakespeare's most ancient trait is the humanity of his heroes. Racine's Iphigenia is not natural enough; more than life she regrets her honours and the glory of a great alliance. Shakespeare did not study and imitate the Greeks, but like them he followed nature. Another likeness of Shakespeare to the ancients is that he represents, more than other modern poets, the great universal sentiments of human nature—conjugal love, fatherly or motherly tenderness, the affection of brothers or sisters, friendship.

Shakespeare and modern poets have accustomed us to think of tragedy as a picture of real life: but for the ancients it never lost its religious origin, and it remained a school of piety towards the gods, of heroism, of the ideal. One of Shakespeare's marvels was variety of characters—one of the charms of ancient poetry, the stability of characters. Racine, Sophocles, Shakespeare alike aim at ideal imitation of reality. Compared with Greeks and French Shakespeare may be realistic; his theatre may represent the world more as it is—but his characters do not speak the language of common life. It has been said that he dramatizes what Sophocles and Racine narrate; but he does on occasions give lively and picturesque narrative—or his plays would be simply pantomime. Between the ideal diction of Shakespeare and the Greeks the only difference is means and measure: the essential difference is in the matter of dramatic representation. Grandeur and force distinguish the characters of Aeschylus and Sophocles: truth those of Shakespeare.

The characters of Greek plays are urged to act by a moral idea, not a personal motive. The gods, or rather the moral powers of the world, are the real actors.[1] Between man and god there is discord: family affection may be at odds with patriotism. The struggle of the gods in the human world—such is the foundation of Greek tragedy. Strife breaks out because the moral essence is divided when it descends to earth, and when gods mingle with men's passions. In the characters of the old drama there was a perfect mixture of divine and human, whence sprang their energy of will and single-mindedness. Their limitations produced their strength—but Hamlet's philosophy has the reverse effect. It is untrue to say they have no characters, for the intimate union of passion and morality gives them an indomitable steadfastness. Creon (*Antigone*) represents the State, the laws of which forbid the burial of an enemy. When Euripides brought in bad or selfish persons, tragedy had lost its great religious character. Not that great criminals do not exist—but their crimes are just. The division on earth of the gods is the cause of crime. Every human agent may be justified, but he can only accomplish the divine law in violating another law equally divine. The characters are great because they accept their lot without a murmur, and do not wish to be pitied. Character is one

[1] Cf. Macneile Dixon.

with purpose, and no modern distinction exists between intention and
fact. Hence Aeschylus and Sophocles are sublime, Euripides pathetic.
But Euripides was rather the ancestor of a new art than a decadent.
He made the important reform that henceforth the human soul was
the centre of tragic interest.[1]

Hamlet himself interests us, not his terrible and sacred duty as with
Orestes. The love of Romeo and Juliet affects us, not the family feud.
But at Antigone's fate we feel the presence in the world of a great moral
trouble, more tragic than the lot of the victim. Her lover kills himself
like Romeo, but expresses impersonally the most personal passion.
The family in *R. and J.* represents no great moral idea but only
personal passions. And yet there is no contradiction between ancient
and modern: the personal passion which moves a romantic hero can
elevate his soul, fortify his character, and raise him almost above
humanity. Juliet's energy is not inborn, but supernaturally communicated to her by passion.

The grand duel, which is the essence of ancient tragedy, momentarily
interrupts the harmony of the gods. The struggle is not between good
and evil, but between two equally moral principles. Each antagonist
is right, but in a partial way, which divides justice and is tainted with
human passion. This must disappear and divine harmony be re-estab-
lished—so the denouement consists in the destruction of passions and
people that troubled the repose of God. Tragedy so conceived is the
accidental contradiction of different aspects of moral truth, e.g. *Antigone, Eumenides.* The chorus represents man's conscience, that cannot
endure the gods should be divided, and proclaims the need of their
agreement. Its sublime function is to maintain the harmony and purity
of the divine idea which the antagonism of the heroes debases. Shakespeare makes clowns and buffoons his chorus—the natural consequence
of that contempt for the official order of the world which is the basis
of humour. Friar Lawrence represents the calm of thought amidst
passion.

The Greek plays were founded on well-known legends, but Shakespeare's stories are of trifling origin. They draw their value from the
moral and psychological worth which the poet himself has added. The
story of *Lear* is childish; in *Hamlet* the action does not exist. With
five or six passions, Shakespeare, like nature, composes infinitely
varied characters. There are numerous ways of being jealous, ambitious, miserly, in love, dissolute, cruel. Shakespeare's beings, before
incarnating an abstract passion, are real individuals: their character is
distinguished from the passion of which they become the type. Before
jealousy absorbs Othello we know him as a man. This is not realism,
but superior truth. Shakespeare's characters have grandeur, beauty,
force, but of a different kind from Greek tragedy. His heroes have

[1] Cf. Macneile Dixon.

nothing external and divine on which to lean for support. Othello and Macbeth have but personal aims; their god is selfish passion; but the nothingness of the object makes it more needful to exalt the character. Against the baseness of his criminal characters Shakespeare balances their sublime energy. He approaches the ancient spirit in that his characters, infinitely more intelligent, are no less morally strong. When Brutus resolves he is immovable; and Macbeth, after silencing his conscience, advances from crime to crime. The energy of a character absorbed by one passion is easily shown; but in a complex character, vigour of soul is extraordinarily fine. Shakespeare's women are less complex than his men, and not made up of contradictions.

If Aeschylus did not proclaim moral freedom he aspired towards it, and wished to escape from the fate that obsessed him: this struggle between a great mind and the greatest problem is as tragic as his tragedies. Sophocles is calm and harmonious, because he is more purely artist. Euripides, full of happy new ideas, contradicts himself, because he is less serious than Aeschylus, less an artist than Sophocles, and because his new ideas are less thought out than echoes of the philosophy of the day. There was one most terrible form of fate—the Greek and Hebrew—the idea of sin and misfortune transmitted by contagion or heredity, e.g. Atreus. Aeschylus does his best to absolve the gods from caprice and introduce a shadow of justice at the source of all the horrors. With Sophocles external pressure is less religious than a dramatic device. The human and divine mingle in his characters according to the laws of beauty. He has also the germ of the purer belief that the man who sins unconsciously is not wicked. It is his glory to have proclaimed that the intention is all-important. The test of a fine civilization and high morality is to regard the heart as the seat of good and evil. The Egyptian civilization was superior in that it distinguished between moral intention and material fact. The legend of Oedipus is the most terrible instance of the barbarous law that condemns a man for what his hands only have done: but Oedipus in exile looks into his conscience and knows that he is not guilty. The only fate in Euripides is that of passion. With Socrates (or Plato) there was great progress; it was never just to do harm to any one, or return evil for evil. By the time of Aristotle the idea of fate had lost its influence. In Shakespeare men's characters and their free actions are the unique cause of their good or evil fortune. But fate also has a place in the Shakespearian world—the darkness and horror of the unknown. It has been vainly attempted to prove that Romeo and Juliet, Desdemona, Ophelia, Cordelia deserved their fate. Terror, or at least mystery, broods over Shakespeare's theatre.

Aeschylus had attempted to reconcile his conscience with his belief. Euripides frankly accepted a divorce. If the gods are unjust, Euripides said, they are no longer gods. There is nothing grander in the history of human thought than the heroic efforts of Aeschylus to moralize a religion he believed in but wished purer. It may be true that a person's destiny is deeply rooted in his individuality; but Desdemona, Ophelia, Cordelia, Duncan, Banquo did not deserve death. If Shakespeare departed from absolute justice it was because he was a poet. In eighteenth-century France absolute justice was preserved in the drama —but it was an age of prose. Replace Destiny with Providence—but admit that the ways of Providence are often obscure. Shakespeare prefers to state problems in a grand manner rather than solve them unworthily. Mystery is the poetic element of tragedy; contradictions are life-giving, logic kills. Shakespeare abjures systems and unites extremes, according to his observation of real life. No artist cared less to moralize the world; but great poets, in their handling of art, naturally do the work of moralists. In practice Shakespeare's catastrophes are more moral—even Christian—than the doctrine of the partisans of exact justice. The latter deprives virtue of spiritual disinterestedness, and materializes too grossly the sufferings of evil-doers. Joy should result from duty done, and suffering from the consciousness of sin. Is death the greatest of evils? Is it so hard to die? Shakespeare's indifference to doctrines extends to religion; his utterances on religion are of course dramatic: and yet the Friar in *R. and J.* consoles with philosophy, not religion—whereas religion would fit his holy character. Romeo and Juliet never speak of eternal union beyond death—while the pagan Antony and Cleopatra cherish this belief. The Duke (*M. for M.*) speaks to Claudio only of life's nothingness. Shakespeare's criminals die like heroes, without remorse—while his devout persons are often weak-hearted, e.g. Richard II, Henry VI. If he was pagan it was because he was an artist; but he was impartial and not anti-Christian, e.g. Bishop of Carlisle, Queen Katharine, Wolsey, King Claudius. Shylock's apology and the profound truth of his character are among the most astonishing proofs of Shakespeare's religious impartiality. He leaves us free to believe what we wish, but his own thought escapes amid the supreme objectivity of his art.

Oedipus is more imposing than pathetic, both more and less than man, the instrument of fate, without moral freedom. Lear represents human liberty in its weaknesses and caprices. And yet only madness can make probable his conduct in Act I; he was previously mad, and the course of events developed the germ. He did not entirely control his destiny, but, like Oedipus, was under the influence of a superior power. There does lie in wait for man a blind and sombre destiny that has survived ancient beliefs because it accords with nature and poetry. Compare also Antigone and Cordelia, and remove from Antigone the four or five virtues that compose her—piety—filial, fraternal, and towards the dead—love of truth, and regard for duty. Little of her will remain in our imagination—while Cordelia exists independent of the great moral qualities of her part. Her words never express her whole thought—but she has no need to speak. Neither what she says nor does attracts our sympathy—but her personality, her charm—over Lear, over the Fool. She is not purely ideal like Imogen, but true with a real truth: in which she differs from the proud Antigone whose moral beauty is more than human.

The most ancient thing in *Macbeth* is the visible action of a super- natural power restraining human liberty. Only Aeschylus and Shake- speare used the supernatural truly; Goethe and Byron failed for lack of accord between poetic inspiration and popular belief. Aeschylus believed in demons literally; but their tortures were more material than moral. Orestes has no remorse, but trusts in Apollo, the enemy of the Furies: the conflict, as always, is exterior and divine. Euripides used this subject, but transformed it; he did not understand the old beliefs of holy wrongdoers. He suppressed the gods, and introduced passionate and suffering humanity: he makes Orestes tortured by remorse and subjective apparitions. Shakespeare has both objective and subjective apparitions—and in the first he followed his poetic instinct. He knew that, secret or avowed, belief in the marvellous exists in man; and his age was superstitious. The Witches are objective because Banquo also sees them, and though to some extent they personify interior tempta- tion, Destiny speaks through them—so that the play not only repre- sents an ambitious man freely following a criminal path, but also a victim of evil gods struggling against destiny. Thence the tragedy has an ancient tinge, and with its religious terror mingles some religious pity. The philosophic depth of Shakespeare's conception consists in the meeting of the bad heart of a man with outward temptation. Evil is in the atmosphere; we are affected by the sins of our fathers and contemporaries. Yet subjective apparitions predominate; and it needs the art of Shakespeare or Aeschylus, the seriousness of inspiration drawn from popular beliefs to make the scene credible. The Witches personify temptation, but do not force Macbeth; he remains to the end what man always is with Shakespeare—the worker of his own destiny. His imagination is in harmony with the spirits of darkness; hell conquers because his heart is bad. The gulf between him and ancient heroes is that he seeks a personal end. Yet there is a beauty in crime pursued with a single mind; and from the moment when he determines on his first crime, he follows evil with a demon's heroism. His misery is not remorse; he has killed conscience; the thoughts that torture him are the fears of an anxious imagination, lest success should not be sure. We do not thoroughly understand Lady Macbeth; her motives are not clear. Except with Cleopatra, Shakespeare has not applied to women his great analytic power. When his heroines are good they are angels; when bad, incarnate devils. No one has rivalled Racine in knowing and representing the heart of woman. In Shakespeare, as in the Bible, we find what we seek; and so the naïve and subtle apologies for Lady Macbeth have passed as deep. She has no morality: for whereas Macbeth killed his conscience, she has none. She belongs to our physical nature and her own sex because she is delicately nervous: she must drug herself with wine at the critical moment. In the end she succumbs but does not repent, or feel that the moral law has been violated. Clytemnestra is morally as well as physically a giant, and remains calm and self-controlled. Lady Macbeth's exaggerated speech betrays her consciousness of weakness. Clytemnestra acts as she speaks, speaks as she thinks; and every word she utters is that of a person who will do what she says. She needs no stimulant, has no evil dreams, is without fear, shame, remorse. Her crime does not shake her health and nerves, but actually strengthens her.

Hamlet is an inactive hero who has something to do but does it not. Werder's theory would destroy the interest of the tragedy by shifting the point of view from subject to object. It is either the most magnificent study ever made of man's irresolution, or nothing. Shakespeare did not produce his characters suddenly, but developed them by degrees: and each of his tragedies contains the entire history of a soul. Hamlet was probably a man of great talents and virtues, who through fault of circumstances, and also fault of just balance of qualities, undergoes intellectual trouble and moral degeneration. He is neither weak nor irresolute, and has the finest inborn moral sense. In the beginning he resembles Alceste—in the end, when degeneration has set in, Werther.[1] Alceste is the noblest character in literature, because his moral indignation is impersonal: and it is thus with Hamlet at the outset. Meditation possesses him; he admits all ideas; and it is vain to seek unity in his philosophy. A few days after seeing the Ghost he speaks of the 'undiscovered country': and this contradiction is in his nature. When he spared the King at prayer he knew there was a difference between prayer and the mere external attitude: but he uncritically accepted any excuse against action—and he had no settled ideas on the greatest questions. Abundant thoughts that lead nowhere produce physical and moral impotence: narrow intellectual bounds are the conditions of heroism. Now and then the primitive basis of Hamlet's nature separated itself from the intellectual. He was mad in the sense that the balance of his nature was disturbed. An idiot revolts, but there is something sacred about a madman—and we feel the divine touch is upon Hamlet. He is punished like Prometheus, and he has long lucid intervals, but assumed madness would have no sense. His conduct to Ophelia is either cruelty or madness. His noble idealism becomes selfish and cold pessimism, hard personal pride, lazy belief in fate. He is false to his principles, and after sparing the King loses all respect for human life. His greatest crime is to torture and kill Ophelia, and then

[1] Cf. Mézières and Montégut.

forget about her. The story is the degeneration of a noble nature: only degeneration can explain such contrasts. What makes it hard to understand is the suddenness with which Shakespeare has precipitated his hero from the heights of intelligence into the abyss of evil and madness, so that we get no transition period, and the contrasts, really successive, appear simultaneous.

That Hamlet should only strike the King after he is himself mortally wounded is opposed to the religious spirit of the action of Orestes. It loses its character of sacred duty and becomes personal revenge. Aeschylus in fear, but in faith, approved it in the name of religion—while Euripides formally condemned it in the name of morality. Although the Orestes of Euripides feels conscience-stricken only after the crime, it is a great step in advance: and here he resembles Hamlet. Fifty years separate Euripides from Aeschylus, 2,000 from Shakespeare—yet he is morally nearer to Shakespeare than Aeschylus. Euripides made the greatest recorded revolution in dramatic art when, for the external conflict of gods, he substituted the internal conflict of the soul.[1] Thenceforth man is the centre of interest. . . .

The first part of Stapfer's work is concerned with the Roman plays —the second with the differences between the ancient and Elizabethan drama. In both the effect is achieved by contrast—that of the first being between modern pyschology and ancient institutions. We say 'modern psychology', for Stapfer does apply modern standards to the characters—and the result is by no means inconsistent. He at least makes them partially live again when he says that Caesar was an Oriental despot—Brutus self-centred—that Cassius lived an austere life, and was a true man—Antony belonged to the aesthetic type and lost the world, but not his soul—Enobarbus was divided between impersonal wisdom and strong individuality—Coriolanus could not conceive a lowly born honourable man, and had modern sensitiveness— while Menenius was equally arrogant, but expressed himself ironically, and at least had popular manners. All these belong to the sphere of meditation upon the character after the event rather than interpretative criticism that helps us to realize the character in action. But to the latter does belong his judgement on Octavius, that he was the man of destiny and must guard only not to obscure his own light; and also his description of the crowd that murders Cinna. We note, closely connected, a tendency to preconceived ideas of what the drama should be, and that the moral interest predominates. He says that the internal struggle of *A. and C.* is not moral, but between pleasure and interest —and that *J.C.*, if less poetic than *A. and C.*, is more tragic than *Coriolanus*.

In the second volume of his work Stapfer delimits the frontiers of ancient and modern drama, and notes the occasional communications

---

[1] Cf. Macneile Dixon.

that pass between. As result we are more interested in Aeschylus than Shakespeare; and though Antigone succumbs to Cordelia, Clytemnestra rises above Lady Macbeth. The Shakespearian clown-chorus also pales by contrast with the majestic Greek chorus. On the whole we become well-informed as to the differences between the two dramas; but the defect of the analytic method is that it brings heaven down to earth. He is compelled to say that Othello and Macbeth have only personal aims—and that *Hamlet* is the story of the degeneration of a noble nature. But the treatment of his theme accords with the spirit of his age—and herein lies the historical value of his work.[1] It represents the thought of the decade filtered through the brain of the sensitive scholar. Times will change, and there will come writers like Professor Macneile Dixon (1924) to supply the element of mystery lacking here: meanwhile it is something to possess earthly symbols of heavenly things. Another contemporary trait is the critic's over-anxiety for moral matters at the expense of aesthetic. He is living before the time when the two are fused in a higher unity.

III

WE can omit Jane Brown's[2] analysis of Richard III, only observing that she finds in him three persons—king, man, and creation of Shakespeare's: and therefore he contains Hamlet, Percy, courtier, politician, scholar. She finds Shylock interesting as Jew, but not as man. When he speaks for his race he deserves sympathy. It is the Jew when he says that he hates Antonio because he is a Christian; but when the cause of his hatred is that Antonio lends money gratis, it is the man: but Shylock is at least great through hatred. Shakespeare always cherished contrasts: he makes Portia love the worldling Bassanio—Shylock great through anger—Antonio one of the elect, a man worthy of antiquity. If Shylock were to sell his vengeance he would realize 6,000 ducats, but he has a disinterested love of vengeance. It has become an abstract passion, and he is exalted in preferring it to gain. His soul is not normally situated; it is invaded on one side by hatred, on the other by avarice; and it is better that he should choose hatred. In her dealings with Bassanio Portia effaces herself; and no one has remarked more than Shakespeare on this trait of women in love. Antonio appears neglected, but for him Bassanio represents the future. It also accords with reality, for Antonio is the foundation of all: without him the building would collapse. Foundations are made to uphold, not to strike the eye. He appeals to us by his works; he is buried under the weight of the services he renders. Also, sentiment, such as his, does not attract the same attention as passion.

Brutus looks upon death as the end of all. Conscience, brain, heart

---

[1] There was a tinge of positivism even in Herbert Spencer's 'Unknowable'.
[2] *Répertoire de Sh.*, 1885.

—three struggling forces in a modern man—are one with him. Othello does not fear death, but he reflects on the unknown: and here we see the fine shades of difference in Shakespeare's characters. If Brutus were modern, his conscience would reject the plans of his brain; and his heart would wage war with his patriotism. Shakespeare makes us conclude that intelligence differentiates consciences. Brutus wishes to kill the soul, because for him *soul* is merely a word. He is too narrow to understand that the soul of Caesar is the idea of Caesar, which will survive. Shakespeare discovers both in events and characters a kind of logic of fate. Caesar as despot should have kept Brutus at a distance: but he makes a friend of the one man who is dangerous to him because their characters were in accord. Brutus sacrifices friendship to his ideal, and, like a sublime logician, remains faithful all his life to the same feelings and beliefs.

At the beginning of *Lear* we see Shakespeare's irony in making Lear misjudge Cordelia: man fails where an animal would succeed. Shakespeare's object is to show how far an absolute monarch must be proved before he becomes a man. Only when stripped of all does Lear interest us. It is well that he dies—for the earth will lie lightly on one who has regained his soul even for an hour, and tasted those joys of the heart which turn a prison to paradise. . . .

It cannot be said that these studies throw any new light on Shakespeare, but they interest as the work of one, skilled in the methods of the psychology of her time, applying her own tests to Shakespeare. She disturbs the surface rather than plumbs, but now and then, in the shifting of lights, we catch a new expression on a familiar face—especially in the passive case of Antonio.

IV

RENAN calls Shakespeare the historian of eternity—one who belongs to no age or country, but paints human history. With Stapfer he represents most perfectly modern romantic drama. He so far approaches Renan as to say that his self-effacement was unparalleled, that he was not interested in theories or political ideas, and the greatest dramatic poet because the most impersonal and universal: his impartiality was serene like the Creator's.

He had, says Stapfer, the highest dramatic gift—he could create characters that are distinct individuals and make real characters shadowy, and represent all human passions and human nature. Akin to this remark is one by Jane Brown on his style. After dwelling on its perfect expression of the most opposed sentiments, she says that all that proceeds from him becomes detached, and attains independent life.

Stapfer decides that his impartiality was also religious, that he was indifferent to religious doctrines, but not anti-Christian: he held man to be the master of his fate. Jane Brown agrees that he makes the evil that is in man the agent of his destruction, not external evil; and she finds a kind of logic—fate in his characters and events.

It remains to add Stapfer's opinions, that he had divine art—and that he was no flatterer of the people, but an aristocrat and royalist.[1] . . .

The impersonality of Shakespeare is the one common trait expressed by these critics directly or indirectly. They would make no attempt to confine him within a formula.

[1] Cf. Victor Hugo and Swinburne.

Chapter XXVI
ENGLAND 1885–1894

I

THE first living critic to join the ranks is Mr. Arthur Symons.[1] His essay on *Titus* interests through his method of distinguishing Shakespeare from the other dramatists. He surmises subtly how far Shakespeare was concerned with the play, and he keeps in mind the history of the drama, the influence of the Renaissance, and the audience for which Shakespeare wrote. Himself a poet as well as critic, he is able to define more exactly than hitherto the effect of the Shakespearian leaven on the crude work of nameless authors.

He considers that Shakespeare revised the new work of an unskilled playwright. Elizabethan boisterousness and strength of nerve produced the Tragedy of Blood, but Shakespeare and Webster first transformed the horrible to the terrible. Kyd ignored the most terrible tragedy—that of the soul. Marlowe at least made the blood-tragedy more artistic: he idealizes the passion of greed in Barabbas. *Titus* is a tragedy of blood in construction; but Titus himself has a fine note of tragic pathos, Aaron some vigour and fullness of wickedness, Tamora a faint touch of power—but there is nothing in the others. Aaron is one of the first types suggested by the Renaissance—wickedness without moral sense or conscience—almost an aesthetic quality. Lavinia belongs to the play's general conception; it would be absurd to call her the first of the series of Shakespeare's heroines, ending with Imogen. She abuses Tamora and makes her punishment appear part retribution. Shakespeare dignified and humanized the wrongs and madness of Titus, striking a note of pathos above the Blood group. His were the slight delicate touches by which a great poet can raise the work of a small.

II

SOME pregnant remarks on Shakespeare are to be sifted out of the *Noctes Shakesperianae*.[2] E. D. A. Morshead throws light on Shakespeare's moral quality by contrasting him with Goethe. He says that

---

[1] *Titus Andronicus*, 1885 (Studies in the Elizabethan Drama. Heinemann, 1920).

[2] *Noctes Shakesperianae*, ed. C. H. Hawkins (Winchester Coll. Sh. Soc.), 1887.

Goethe could not attain Shakespeare's innate nobility of tone about virtue and vice; that he had not Shakespeare's inward shudder at the infinite character of wrongdoing—this shudder of repentance—part of the phenomena of good and evil which compose the drama of life— that makes Shakespeare's drama more powerfully natural than Goethe's.

III

H. J. HARDY'S[1] mind penetrates Shakespeare's historical method. He finds Shakespeare unscrupulous in niceties of historical detail, but tending to idealize those facts which contained abiding lessons and laws. Events subserve principles in *John*; all the persons are historical, but they also represent classes or institutions then found in England.

IV

C. H. HAWKINS[1] writes on Shakespeare's stage-craft, the method and cunning of which, he says, is of the essence of the literary value of his work. But he finds Shakespeare indifferent to incident, and absorbed in recording the fine network of nerve and motive and passion. He agrees with the theory that Shakespeare depended en- tirely on character-study, and his plots are thin. He attributes this to a racial cause: the power of breathing life into creatures of the imagination being native to England; that of creating a groundwork of incident, and machinery to set puppets in motion, rather Italian. . .
As a corrective we glance back to Moulton, and also suggest that, in Shakespeare's greatest work, incident, character, passion, &c., are fused beyond separation.

V

L. P. JOHNSON[1] works by contrast, and thus convinces us how supreme was Shakespeare's creation of the Fool. To realize the fine gold of Shakespeare's wit he refers us to that of Farquhar, Congreve, Etherege, Rochester, Dryden, Vanbrugh, Addison, Goldsmith, Field- ing, Smollett, Swift, Sterne, Lamb, Scott, Byron, Thackeray. The Fools of other writers are either funny fellows of the stage or distorted natures. Shakespeare's have passions, humours, feelings, like yet un- like those of other men. They meet life at all turns with tersely convincing answers; they laugh with love and grieve with smiles.

VI

THE criticism of O. T. Perkins,[1] on Shakespeare's Ghostland and Fairyland is of the finest inward kind. His is the nature which is rightly impressed in the beginning and only records its impressions after full meditations, so that superfluous first thoughts have been eliminated, and the result is what the most modern critic would do

---

[1] *Noctes Shakesperianae.*

well to consider. He decides that Shakespeare's art is at its highest in
the Ghost's second appearance in *Hamlet*. The Queen does not see
it, but is dismayed by Hamlet's conduct; her inmost soul is wrung with
remorse, and she shows it by her silence to the King. Shakespeare tries
to express sensibly the promptings of an almost supernatural power
within us. The irony of Banquo's ghost surpasses the terrible irony of
Aeschylus. The spectre's silence haunted Macbeth more than words.
Shakespeare makes concrete the abstract idea of the Greek 'Ate'. It
is no mere vision; the irony is lost if Macbeth only is supposed to see
the spectre; and also the contrast is lost between his previous vacillation
and later recklessness.   Thus are presented the mysterious ideas with
which the interest of tragedy is connected.

Shakespeare's fairies are the shadows dwelling in the borderland
between night and day, ruling over the dream-sleep of men. Their
speed, imagination, idealization all have their archetype in a dream,
but they are most like in their momentary character—dreams appear
long but really come and go in the instant before waking.

VII

A remark by Bertram Talbot[1] on 'Women's Influence on Men of
Mark' is worth preserving: Othello had never known Desdemona's
mind, and as there is no union of souls, he has nothing to oppose to
rumour.

VIII

APPLETON MORGAN[2] is one of the common-sense school of
critics, like Grant White, who despise the accumulated wisdom of
commentators. Such criticism has its use as a corrective, and we
should do well to keep it in mind when considering what he rather
unkindly calls the 'gush' of Furnivall, Dowden, Ward: just as the
sublime speeches of Coriolanus and Aufidius in the reconciliation
scene are reinterpreted for us by the irreverent servants.   But such
criticism is far from being the whole truth; it reflects the mind which
reads in order to contradict, that satisfies itself with the obvious meaning, and does not wait for the finer truth suggested by the echoes in
its remoter caves.

He argues that aesthetic should not become creative criticism, that
Shakespeare was a man of like passions with ourselves, and we can
read him all the better because he was a man.   Critics like Furnivall,
Dowden, Ward would write his biography out of their inner reading
of the text. There is as much evidence that he murdered his wife,
like Othello, as that he 'buried a beloved child', like Constance.
Suppose Heminge and Condell had applied to him for a comedy, and
been refused because he was in his tragic period! The Sonnets prove

---

[1] *Noctes Shakesperianae.*   [2] *Sh. in Fact and in Criticism* (New York), 1888.

that any poem or prose romance can be tortured into a set of symbolic types or allegories; they are merely bound together by the sonnet form, and no other theory exists that is not visionary and fanciful. Plays are written hastily, under different conditions from novels or poems. Even when written at leisure a play is rarely one man's entire work.[1] We no longer think that Shakespeare wrote all the plays formally assigned to him. The poems and Sonnets are one man's work and were published under his name, but Elizabethan printers selected the name that would best sell their books.

The Hamlet of the First Quarto is manly, punctilious, rational, suspicious of intuitions, deliberate, persevering. His history is rather that of purpose adhered to—and all worthy men hesitate. The Ghost is seen by others, yet he required cumulative presumptive evidence. Even after the interview he will not admit to his friends that he believes; nor, when proof is added to proof that the Ghost's statements coincide with his own intuitions, will he base action on supernatural testimony. He rejected Ophelia because he saw that the Ghost's story was true, and he had no time for love, books, &c. There was no blunted purpose in the soul of this truly English prince. A vendetta has no time-limit, and he merely waited to satisfy himself. Only a Shakespearian commentator would suggest that Horatio—clear-minded, strong-headed, acute, practical—was a keeper of lunatics.

All commentators agree that Shakespeare despised the people, but the proprietor of the Globe Theatre loved his perquisites and theatrical concessions, and would not offend those who had the right to license playhouses. The dramatists wished to be on the safe side and flattered the ruling classes. . . .

As examples of this criticism at its best and most helpful we give the two following examples. The grave-digger scene, he says, will subdue and dominate and suspend vast audiences that would never read a volume of the commentators. Shakespeare was equal to anything, since, in the *Merchant*, he could put into the mouth of Portia the most magnificent eulogy of mercy in the world, yet find none of it for a poor Jew who had offered to loan money as a friend, but had been challenged, instead, to loan it as to an enemy in order that he might exact the penalty.

IX

PATER'S third essay on Shakespeare deals with the historical plays,[2] and he considers that they possess the unity of a common motive. The side of kingship which Shakespeare makes prominent is its irony—average human nature flung into the vortex of great events. John, indeed, has a kind of greatness, but it is counteracted by madness which takes the shape of reckless impiety. Falconbridge, with his

[1] Cf. J. M. Robertson.   [2] 'Sh.'s English Kings', 1889 (*Appreciations*).

physical energy and unmistakable family likeness, asserts almost
coarsely how nature and circumstance preponderate over men's
artificial arrangements. To Henry IV also is not denied king-craft,
but his highest self is expressed in the soliloquy which represents
royalty longing vainly for the toiler's sleep. Henry V is the *greatest* of
Shakespeare's kings, and his speeches in disguise, 'I think the king is
but a man, as I am . . .', express the key-note of Shakespeare's treatment.
Richard III, like John, is touched with an effect of real heroism
spoiled by something of criminal madness. In *Henry VIII* not the
king's splendour, but the ascendant nature of the butcher's son defines
the central interest.

Shakespeare's kings are an eloquent company, especially Richard II.
He sees all things poetically and refreshes with his golden language
the tritest aspects of the ironic contrast between a king's pretensions
and the actual necessities of his destiny. His eloquence blends with
that fatal personal beauty of which he was frankly aware. His royal
utterance is the only one of his personal gifts that never fails him—
appreciation of the poetry of his own hapless lot, that infects others in
spite of themselves. The effect of little men thrust upon greatness,
as with Shakespeare's kings, is the pathetic self-pity of the weak
becoming irresistible appeal to others as the net result of the royal
prerogative—the irony of kingship, child's play in its happiness,
children's grief in its sorrows. As with children, Richard II attains
contentment by passively recognizing superior strength. The play
belongs to a small group where dramatic form almost attains the unity
of a lyric, or single strain of music. In art unity of impression is the
note of what is perfect, and therefore lyric poetry may be the highest,
and a play artistically perfect as it is nearest to lyrical effect. The
earliest classic drama arose out of the chorus, and the perfect drama
tends to return into the unity of the choric song. The true imaginative
unity of the drama is in a vivid single impression left on the mind, not
in mechanical limitation of time and place. . . .

Perhaps these last sentences help us to realize more than anything
that has been written on the subject the true meaning of the unity of
the drama—supported as the argument is on the historical basis of the
Greek chorus. Otherwise, as was said on a former occasion, and in
a yet higher degree, there is more Pater than Shakespeare in this essay—
though it must be admitted that beautiful verse like that of *Richard II*
was required to stimulate Pater's mind along such lines of meditation.
But surely he has taken a wrong turning and wandered outside the
Shakespearian realm. It was natural that one who delighted in pictures
should be fascinated by the beauty and golden speech of Richard II,
and to him may be applied 'the irony of kingship'. To apply it
primarily instead of incidentally to the others is, we think, to strain
it beyond all due. The soliloquies of Henry IV and Henry V

rather illustrate the law of compensation, and could be uttered as well by those who have great powers as great place.

X

HIRAM CORSON[1] proclaims Shakespeare to be the greatest artist that ever existed, because all his powers co-operated. His plays were written for the stage, therefore it most imports to discover the secrets of his dramatic effects. He was a great master of contrast, he brought together high and low, sad and merry, and, like the master-artist, subjected all to a dominating great idea and profound feeling. The whole organism of a play was made to serve its soul. The unity was not mechanical, but vital from the all-pervading feeling. He had great creative power without much learning, but the greatest possible knowledge and wisdom. He perceived the truth directly through his spiritual nature; he assimilated it from the response of spirit to spirit. He was the greatest and most artistic physiologist of passion. He presents passion as related to the constitution of things. As it develops, the power of self-assertion declines, and at a given point it passes into fate, after which the subject is swept helplessly along. In his plays we feel a deep sense of spiritual harmony with the constitution of things. His verse advanced through his career from recitative to spontaneous—from strictly metrical to something like rhythmical prose where metre yields to the movement of thought.

In *R. and J.* he treats passion under the condition of the moral constitution of things, but not as a moralist. That Romeo is fitted for great love is first shown through his unrequited love for Rosaline. Had it been even partially requited he should not have transferred it. When he meets Juliet his love is more spiritual than is usual with love at first sight, due to his previous subjective state from unrequited love. The cause of his forbearance to Tybalt was outside himself. Shakespeare's dramatic purpose was to exhibit the energy from all-absorbing love in conflict with adverse circumstances. The lovers' overthrow had an objective cause; their love did not fall from its own excess. Shakespeare had dramatic, not moral, purpose, and was not occupied with the abstract. In *John* he suppresses the fierce anti-Romish spirit of the old play. The Pope is defied as a foreign power rather than on religious grounds. The spirit of the play is national and patriotic; Shakespeare knew too well the function of dramatic art to make religion the informing spirit. Constance shows outraged maternal affection apart from ambition. Personal ambition for the crown would mar the artistic symmetry and moral tone of the play. Shakespeare was always true to the fatality of overmastering passion. In *M. Ado* all depends on the relations of Benedict and Beatrice to each other. She is sensitive as to the honour of her sex, and resents

[1] *An Introduction to the Study of Sh.*, 1889 (Boston).

more because she secretly admires him. Were her affections not already enlisted, the stratagem would be silly. Her true self had been kept in the background, so there was no transformation.

If Hamlet is mad the play is not fit for art. The idea of a work cannot centre round madness. That idea must be one of health, reason, harmony with the constitution of things. A play interests in proportion to the degree in which the element of moral darkness predominates—not because moral darkness interests, but for the light which struggles with and is intensified by the darkness. Without moral darkness there can be no moral light. The light which struggles with the darkness is the ultimate aim of art. If Hamlet acts as he does in a state of insanity, and is irresponsible and unconscious of crime, he is no longer an art-subject. We cannot sympathize with crime as crime. Art must express and be in sympathy with the rational and moral constitution of things. The difficulties of Hamlet's situation are objective. His soliloquies contain high and coherent reasoning and profound wisdom and philosophy. His self-rebuke is that of a man with a keen moral sense: because he cannot do the thing he would in a rational manner. The play does not make the King proclaim his crime, as he had hoped. He had to revenge a secret murder, of which his only proof was the testimony of a ghost. Reason and common sense restrained him, not moral scruples. True vengeance demanded full proof, and when fate makes him the slayer of the King he entreats Horatio to set him right before the world. How could enormous intellectual activity have such dire consequences? Where would the dramatic interest come from? This above all we must look for in Shakespeare. The real difficulty is entirely independent of his own intellectual and spiritual temperament, but especially fitted to bring that temperament into fullest play. His thoughts, meditations, feelings are doubly interesting because of their relation to the objective difficulty.

Shakespeare's characters always start as free agents. True dramatic interest demands this. As a great passion is evolved it destroys more and more the power of self-assertion. In *Macbeth* the power of the Weird Sisters depends on that which in a man's soul has affinities for that power. Nowhere else in Shakespeare does the natural world so reflect the moral. Macbeth's imaginative tenperament deceives his wife as to his true character, and has deceived many critics. At first it shakes his fell purpose, but really he shows no genuine compunction. He has selfish fears from external dangers, intensified by his morbidly active imagination: the consequences to his soul are nothing to him. Lady Macbeth has no independent ambition, and she discovers that her husband has a different nature than she thought. Her strong will yields to remorse, and her womanly nature succumbs. Had Macbeth been naturally disposed against the murder of Duncan, had the instigation been all objective, there would be no true dramatic merit.

A. and C. is among the grandest of the plays, perhaps it surpasses all. The moral interest predominates over the historical and the political. Shakespeare worked more strictly than his fellow-dramatists under the condition of moral proportion—that which is in harmony with the permanent constitution and eternal fitness of things. His great achievement was to unite moral proportion with unrestrained play of passions. Like a true artist he uses the concrete; the abstract principles to be found in his work are involved in the creative movement, and do not, in abstract form, predetermine that movement. We are nowhere made to sympathize with the moral obliquity of Antony and Cleopatra. Shakespeare's moral spirit protects us from any perversion of the moral judgement. Cleopatra is almost divorced from the moral constitution of things. Her fascination is sexual— exerted on those in her presence. Octavius gave his sister to Antony to have a pretext for breaking with him. Antony's moral struggle keeps him within the pale of our sympathy. . . .

Corson is clear-sighted, and has strong common sense, and the latter quality was specially needed as a corrective at this period of the nineteenth century. He does well to insist on Shakespeare's dramatic purpose, and also to point out the harmonious co-operation of all his powers. By so doing he suggests a higher unity than those who see in Shakespeare a moral teacher above all. But the drawback is that in continually advancing this point of view, he tends to lose sight of the Shakespearian mystery. Shakespeare becomes for us dexterous rather than philosophic; we think of him as one who explored moral and spiritual regions simply in order to make a good play. His criticism sometimes hits the mark—as with Romeo and the effect of his love for Rosaline—or the charm of Cleopatra, and the reasons of Octavius for giving his sister to Antony. It falls short with Hamlet, where he follows Werder—though his remarks on Hamlet's madness are sound— or the character of Macbeth. No doubt he himself has felt the mystery of Shakespeare, but there is a buffer state between his reading and his criticism. Anxious to prove his case, he has concentrated upon it, and let the great thoughts move to the back of his mind. He has formed his plan, it has engrossed him, and he returns no more to the original spring of inspiration. Thus we hear a great deal about the moral constitution of things, but it remains vague. The result is we are left with Shakespeare the skilled playwright—the pillar of cloud by day rather than the pillar of fire by night.

XI

THE return of Mr. Arthur Symons[1] at this point offers a welcome contrast. He agrees with Corson that *A. and C.* is Shakespeare's

---

[1] *A. and C., Macbeth, Twelfth-Night, M. for M., W. Tale, Henry VIII*, 1889–90 (*Studies in Elizabethan Drama*, 1920).

most wonderful play—and here they part company for ever. Indeed they part at once, for Corson affirms that Cleopatra's fascination is exerted on those in her presence, while Mr. Symons notes that her power most appears when she is not there, and thus the tremendous influences felt to be drawing Antony away give the measure of the force of the magic which brings him back. There are certain critics in whose presence we stand abashed—Swinburne is one, Mr. Symons is another. Both belong to that fine species—the poet-critic—in whom the soul of the poet and the brain of the critic are equally active, and each ministers to each. But the two differ in uttering the rarer knowledge which they have acquired by their happy mental constitution. Swinburne, as we remarked before, does not preserve the amenities of criticism. As he admired Aeschylus beyond Shakespeare, we will describe him as Prometheus described Zeus—sitting on his throne bravely, trusting in his loud noises, and brandishing the thunderbolt.[1] Mr. Symons is never angry, yet each time that he uses his finest gift we are silently rebuked. In the plays that follow, we think that he excels in defining that inner, imaginative unity of which Pater spoke—especially *Twelfth-Night* and the *W. Tale*, and he does it as a poet would, in concrete, not abstract, fashion, and therefore brings it home to us more vividly.

He contemns the idea that the Sonnets are not true passion, because of the curiously individual note of their complex harmonies: and this judgement gives us an insight into his method. Other critics have treated Shakespeare as moralist or dramatist; Mr. Symons remembers that he was a poet before all else, and therefore that his city is built to music; that the imaginative world has its own laws, though it can be no more separated from the real world than can the column of light, which moves through the water, from the carved and gilded barge. The impression, therefore, on which the critical part of the mind is set to work has been made complete through music and beauty.

The following may be given as instances of the poetically receptive soul working with the finely discriminating intellect. The idea of *A. and C.* is that of giving up all for love. Shakespeare develops the characters through the medium of a crowd of persons and incidents: the lovers' tragic comedy is played out in sight of the world. Enobarbus is neither for nor against virtue; he seems to confound moral judgements, and serves the part of artistic equity. Cleopatra's fits and starts are not only played for a purpose; they break out before her women. Even in the most violent shock of real emotion she never quite loses consciousness of self. She wins an extorted admiration from the very borders of contempt.

There is little comment on life in *Macbeth*, and what occurs is

[1] *Prometheus*, 916–17.

sensation more than reflection. There is little pathos, but terror against a background of mystery. Fate and spiritual agencies are present as never in Shakespeare. The conflict is between the worse and better natures of the two; the tragedy is one of conscience. In place of virtue Lady Macbeth has imagination, and this wrecks her. Time dulls remembrance with Macbeth, and guilt degrades him. Her calmness had been overstrained and unnatural, and in the end it is her body rather than her soul which gives way. The smell and sight of blood haunt her—the physical disgust of the thing.

Twelfth-Night seems as if composed when soul and body were in perfect equipoise. Every element of the play has the subtlest links with its fellow. Tenderness melts into a smile, and the smile broadens imperceptibly into laughter. The Duke is a gentle and refined egoist, and though sadly used as a lover awakens no pity.

In *M. for M.* tragedy and comedy are in mutual contradiction. Shakespeare's full power is only in the great scenes, and he has scarcely exceeded them in intensity and depth of natural truth. The deepest tragedy is caused by the innocent means of Isabella; Claudio would have died and Angelo lived on blameless. Isabella's nobility attracts Angelo, and every virtue withers into the corresponding form of vice. Shakespeare's final word is mercy which comes of the consciousness of our need of it, and is granted and accepted in humiliation. The claim which our fellow man has on our commiseration is the sad claim of mutual guilt before an absolute bar of justice.

The anachronisms of the *W. Tale* are of no more importance than a trifling error in the count of miles traversed by a witch's broomstick in a minute. Hermione is not self-conscious, nor aware that she is heroic. In Perdita the old passion of love becomes new. Leontes' jealousy throws out in brighter relief the noble qualities of those about him. The end is reconciliation and mercy extended even to the unworthy, in a spirit of more than mere justice. We feel that life is a good thing.

Henry VIII is neither by Shakespeare nor any single writer. It radically lacks dramatic and moral coherence. Our sympathies are arbitrarily demanded and countermanded. Katharine's speech lacks the vividly metaphorical way of being direct which gives distinction to Hermione's speech. Where are Wolsey's supposed commanding qualities? He is a mere transcript from history. Compare Falstaff, where Shakespeare drives in on us the impression of the man's innate power with his every word, through all his disgraces. With Wolsey the effect is trivial and spasmodic; there is no psychology underneath this big figure. Events happen but are not brought about by the subtle logic which in *Hamlet* or *Lear* constructs the action out of character. In Shakespeare picturesqueness grows out of the real nature of things.

XII

THE object of Cyril Ransome's book[1] is first to make sure of the facts and then deduce the theory. We need hardly say that criticism of an external kind fails when applied to the great plays, viz. *Hamlet* and *Macbeth*. By reducing to a minimum Hamlet's part in the catastrophe, he says, Shakespeare emphasizes the part of Providence. Denmark is rotten; the Queen's actions and Ophelia's thoughts show her morality, Polonius her statesmanship, the ceremonious uncharitableness of the priests her religion. Had Duncan named Macbeth his heir the prophecy would have been fulfilled and the audience satisfied. Macbeth had shown himself fit, and Malcolm and Donalbain were too young, and had taken no part in the fight. Macbeth was only concerned with success here; he was too much of a statesman not to know that murder breeds murder and rebellion rebellion.

Ransome is at his best in *J.C.* where he points out that the fickleness of the mob is a symptom that the basis of true republicanism had passed away. Shakespeare does not let Caesar's personality dominate, because Caesar is the accident and Caesarism the reality. Brutus fails as soldier and politician, but as a man no one can fail to recognize the beauty of character which the old Republican world of Rome had brought forth.

Between the two are his remarks on Othello and Desdemona. Othello's misfortune is that he and Desdemona have no real community of feeling. On one hand is admiration founded on sympathy with misfortune, on the other, thankfulness for such pity. Both are strong in feeling, but intellectually weak. At critical moments neither is subtle enough to pierce through the maze.

XIII

THERE are some interesting thoughts in Thomas Tyler's[2] work on the Sonnets, but the reader must bear in mind that all that is said about the connexion between Shakespeare's life and character and his works is surmise. He calls the Sonnets poetical epistles, and reminds us that a man's letters are not autobiography. They are no mere exercises in verse, because they show intense feeling and treat real incidents. The language is that of poetry, even of compliment. In Shakespeare's philosophy are three doctrines: Soul of the World, Necessity, Cycles. The first appears in Sonnet 107 and also in the forebodings, dreams, apparitions throughout his plays. Sonnet 59 clearly expresses the doctrine of the Cycles; also Henry IV's speech, 'O God, that one might read the book of fate!' Unchanging succession makes permanent progress impossible. About this time (1600) Shake-

---

[1] *Short Studies of Sh.'s Plots*, 1890.   [2] *Sh.'s Sonnets*, 1890.

speare suffered from melancholy, and scandal was afloat concerning
him. Traces of melancholy show in Hero in *M. Ado* and Jaques in
A.Y.L., and then follows the deep pessimism of *Hamlet* and *T. and C.*
In both we get the idea of man's terribly repulsive moral disease.

XIV

J. W. CUNLIFFE'S concise and well-written book[1] throws light
on an important influence on the Elizabethan drama, without which
it would have developed slowly from Miracles. Where he touches
Shakespeare it is to show him supreme over other dramatists by his
marvellous imagination, transforming to his own nature the thoughts
of others. Ben Jonson also followed Seneca in making his characters
reflect, but missed Shakespeare's perfect art in causing the reflections
to arise naturally from the situation or character of the speaker.

Seneca is the most modern of the ancients, and greatly influenced
modern drama. In him the change from outer to inner, begun by
Euripides, is plainly marked. Fatalism is his leading doctrine, of the
hopeless Stoic kind which includes the gods themselves: and this runs
through Elizabethan tragedy. Both in Seneca and the Elizabethans
the characters are indifferent to the accidents of life and despise death.
Shakespeare's villains die with desperate fortitude; even the heroines
are stoical—e.g. Hermione. In moral actions Seneca's persons show
free will. He also influenced the drama externally, being the first to
divide it into five acts. An important step was when the chorus was
excluded from the orchestra in the Roman theatre: this diminished
Seneca's hold on the unities of time and place. He introduced stock
characters—messenger, nurse, servant—above all, the ghost, greatly
enlarged from the Greek—also witchcraft and oracles. At first
classical and popular drama were slightly connected. Marlowe made
the great change and selected classical features likely to be popular—
horror of incident, exaggerated language. Peele took these from
Marlowe, and Greene was directly influenced by Seneca. Whether
Shakespeare was directly indebted we cannot say, but *Titus, 3 Henry VI*,
and *Richard III* are much like Seneca in their continuous slaughter
and stoical fatalism. We also get reflections on the cares and risks of
high place, and presentiments of evil. Even the finished *Hamlet*
slightly recalls Seneca: chance effects the catastrophe. In *Macbeth*, as
in Seneca, a horrible theme is so treated as to rouse deep reflection.
All the characters utter brief, pregnant sayings in the manner of
Seneca. Compare 'Canst thou not minister to a mind diseased?' and
'Nemo polluto queat animo mederi'. Also 'Will all great Neptune's
ocean. . . .' and 'Non ipse toto magnus oceano pater tantum expiarit
sceleris'.

[1] *The Influence of Seneca on Elizabethan Tragedy*, 1893.

XV

HENRY MORLEY[1] helps to convince us that Shakespeare was a consummate artist, but is less successful on his moral philosophy. Dealing with *2 Henry VI* he says that Shakespeare was not content just to produce a picture, but arranged all his lines in some one simple truth of life. The whole of *Richard III* was so shaped as to set one great and simple truth at the heart of the story. In *John* expediency is the motive of action. Harmony is produced by clear reference of all the parts to the point of view from which the whole picture is taken. Thus in every play of Shakespeare is some strength or weakness of common humanity, no philosophical subtlety or historical theory. John is not true to himself, but makes peace or war accord with private interest. *R. and J.*, where love and hate are contrasted, shows how Shakespeare builds the story of a play on a discord that he may turn it to harmony. In *M.N.D.* the sport is among shadows, but they are the shadows of divine realities. Friendship, in the *Merchant*, unites the two men who are the centre of the two parts of the story. In *J.C.* Shakespeare uses historical groundwork as a parable against sedition and warning of the ills of civil war; but the real point is in nothing abstract, but in human truth that strikes home to the soul of some one man through whom it passes insensibly into the souls of all who have been interested in his story. Here the centre is Brutus.

Of *Henry V* Morley says rightly that in this play of the warrior king and famous victory Shakespeare has given the most uncompro mising picture of the cruelties of war; but we cannot agree that, to harmonize the parts, Pistol's cowardice is made a foil to the King's courage.

It is on the moral side that Morley's limitations most appear. He merely sees reflected in Shakespeare his own orthodox and genial morality, and ignores the grand mysteries. He speaks of Shakespeare's spiritual rule of three: love God, love your neighbour, do your work. In defiance of the great tragedies he says that Shakespeare always shows evil overcome with good, and that he sees life as one who has found its highest lessons in the Sermon on the Mount.

We will first take some instances where these moral lessons are applied least unsuccessfully. To him *L.L.L.* illustrates that we live to do the duties of our lives, not spend all our years preparing for them. The caskets story in the *Merchant* proves that a man must exert all his powers simply to do his duty. In Antonio man stands between two principles—justice and mercy—and Portia sets forth the divine side of the lesson. The *Venus* does bring out the innocence of early manhood proof against the blandishments of woman. In *Verona* repentance restores his friend to Proteus. To Macbeth, who

[1] *English Writers*, vols. x–xi, 1893–5.

seeks right not for right's sake, but to stand well with the world, temptation may come with false assurance of security. Apemantus sees only the low things of life and thinks it philosophy to see no more. Leontes is no tyrant outside his delusion. Home-ties are stronger than death—for Coriolanus knows that in yielding he puts his life in the hands of the enemy.

We will now take instances where the moral has been over-stressed or the motive exaggerated. The latter is most frequent with the historical plays. Shylock is foiled and sentenced—not harshly—except that he must become a Christian. The episode of the rings shows that the spirit must precede the letter even in small things. Henry IV's rebuke to his son connects Richard II and his temptations with those plays where temptations are overcome. Falstaff does attract, but he is really a thief, coward, and liar. Agincourt is the poet's symbol of the way of each of us who would be a true soldier in the great battle of life. Shakespeare makes Henry V act on the counsel of the Church, and thus frees his typical warrior from all responsibility for the right or wrong of the invasion. In *Twelfth-Night* the ideal of young love has its finer life brought out by contrast with Sir Toby and his friends. Celia's heart goes out to Oliver in the hour of his repentance. *J.C.* shows that public and private morality do not differ, and that noblest motives cannot turn moral wrong into political right. From Hamlet we see Shakespeare's view that every one who reaches manhood must do his work. Cordelia, Kent, and the Fool show that sincerity is the true salt of love. In *A. and C.* animal passion drags down the spirit with the body to earth. Shakespeare meant *Henry VIII* to open with a picture of the vain pomp and glory of the world.

XVI

THOMAS SPENCER BAYNES'S essay on Shakespeare[1] is positive in the most flattering sense of the word. He has inwardly digested his knowledge, it has reached his unconscious mind, and he utters it, not to confute others, as positive writers often do, but because he is sincerely and quietly convinced. His defect is that he cannot distinguish between fact and conjecture, because his successful meditation has subdued his material to the colour of his own mind. In describing the historical, political, and literary influences that stimulated Shakespeare's genius he is correct, but to the personal influences of scenery, parents, education, early play-going, marriage, &c., we must demur. We wish to agree with what he says, and also with his opinion of Shakespeare's character, but at the most it is probable rather than certain. His picture of Shakespeare and his work inclines to be broadly ideal.

He finds the Warwickshire scenery likely to develop Shakespeare's

[1] *Sh. Studies,* 1894.

genius—uniting, as it does, the rich and cultivated with the wild and free. Mountains dwarf human interests, and a life of lonely raptures is not for the dramatist. The hills and streams, abbeys and castles of Warwickshire have historical associations, and one of Shakespeare's most distinctive features was his lifelong attachment to his native place. His father was eager and sanguine, expanding genially in prosperity, but lacking fortitude to bear adversity. His mother was truly a gentlewoman, and not only did he inherit her firmness and ethical strength, but her bearing and example during vicissitudes must have been to him a vivid revelation of the sprightly and gracious besides the profounder elements of woman's character. As a child he must have seen plays, because the best companies constantly visited Stratford. At the Grammar School he learnt Latin thoroughly. He must have joined in escapades from a feeling of good fellowship. Lucy, a Puritan, hard and gloomy, was glad to catch Shakespeare in a technical trespass. There is no evidence that his marriage was hasty, unsuitable, or unhappy. It was one of mutual affection, and a most fortunate event as it gave him a fixed centre of affection and a supreme motive. It changed his course and ripened his character.

In London he made himself useful from the first—as Greene's words prove. The sense of joyousness and power of his plays show his exultant absorption and conscious triumph in his work. The time was fortunate, the country was united in pride and patriotism, and Protestantism was patriotism. The whole conflict reacted on the genius of the race, and especially the drama was stimulated. Love of Queen and country was a romantic passion with all, and there was complete unity of national sentiment and action. The theatre became the centre of genius and art, the living organ through which experiences of the time were expressed, Feudal and Romish ties were broken, and there was a new physical and moral world, with vivid and intense curiosity about human life and affairs, and man as the centre of interest.[1]

The realistic popular drama existed side by side with the drama from an indirect classical source. The latter was the form assumed by Greek and Latin plays in contemporary Italian, French, Spanish plays. Romantic features were added to classical construction. The popular drama contributed broad sympathy, humour, contact with actual life. What prepared the way for Shakespeare was Marlowe's blank verse, and his *Edward II*—the first real historical drama, other than chronicle drama—and the blended charm of romance and reality in Greene and Peele. Shakespeare combined and perfected all these materials. In his first period he rewrote and revised—under the influence of Marlowe and the physically horrible from Roman tragedy. The second period of comedies and histories shows harmony of

[1] Cf. Ten Brink.

reflective and imaginative insight, perfection of creative art, completeness of dramatic effect. In the third there is the same mastery of art,
but enlarged vision, wider thoughts, deeper experiences, traces of
intenser moral struggles, larger, less joyous views of life, unrivalled
power of piercing the deepest mysteries and sounding the most
tremendous problems of life and destiny.

In *Timon* and *M. for M.* he shows disturbing insight into the
world's deeper evils—the darker passions of treachery and revenge.
But he also gained fuller perception into the deeper springs of goodness.
In the four great tragedies the central problem is profoundly moral
conflict of good and evil. We learn there are more precious things
than social ease or worldly success, viz. nobleness of soul, fidelity to
truth, honour, love, loyalty. . . . In the most tragic circumstances
fidelity to all that is best in life is only possible through loss of life.
In the three final dramas there is forgiveness, generosity, forbearance,
self-control.

When he retired Shakespeare was no dreamer or sentimentalist,
but a successful professional man. He had simple and natural tastes,
love of country, strong family affection. He had realized the sovereign
elixir against the ills of life was vigilant charity, love of home, kindred,
friends, all simple things. He had a passion for the unity and continuity
of family life, and the desire of his heart was to found a family. All
contemporaries and associates witness to his honourable loving nature.
He touched life at many points, and every type of character would
attract him—local Dogberries, Shallows, &c. He could seize from
the inner side, by links of vital affinity, every form of higher character
—passionate, reflective, executive. He could portray men and women
of distant ages and different races. He united worldly prudence with
the utmost generosity and affectionateness. . . .

The warning against accepting well-meditated statements as wholly
objective fact applies equally to the second part of Baynes's essay. He
does well to remark the modern qualities in Ovid and to point out his
influence on Shakespeare, but he is inclined to overstate. However,
in analysing Ovid and contrasting him with Virgil, he throws some
light on Shakespeare's genius. He finds in Ovid's picture of nature
a constant stir of life or element of human experience, also prominent
love interest and knowledge of women, and, above all, a power of
vivid conception. This was reflected in the life and colour of *Venus*,
its passion and pathos and endless variety of magical changes. Shakespeare must have written his poems before leaving Stratford; it was
unlikely that he did so after starting the drama. In his early plays he
alludes to Ovid, but probably he was not attracted by Virgil. The
feeling of the latter was absorbed in a limited range of objects and
associations compared with Shakespeare's vivid and intense interest in
all the varieties of individual character and vicissitudes of life. Poetical,

not personal, influences stimulated Shakespeare's imagination—beauty, interest, vital unity of object. . . . He was more Greek than Latin, with the objective bent of the Greek imagination. Of the Latins only Catullus and Ovid have the distinctive Greek power to conceive a vividly impressive or pathetic scene and present it pictorially in concrete fullness. Shakespeare's poems prove that he could body forth the form of things unknown. They are the most brilliant verbal pictures in the language, and he was a diligent student of Ovid. Thence his sweet verse, choice of remote subject, latent dramatic instinct working by series of vivid images, which give the highest effect of the picturesque in words, and are a substitute for the stage. Also the unifying effect of a dominant passion—in the vivid picturing of which Shakespeare follows Ovid, but in the reflective part is far above him, having a higher ethical purpose. He recognizes the force and charm of sensuous passion, but sees through and beyond. No doubt he was himself subject to passion, and on its subsiding he would meditate on its working and issues if unrestrained by the higher influences of intellectual and moral life. The contrast of the ancient and modern world is seen in the Lesbias, Delias, Corinnas, and the Mirandas, Portias, Imogens. . . .

Baynes subtly defines the dramatic quality in Ovid, but has he proved too much? As Shakespeare's poems are in many ways undramatic, the reader must decide whether Baynes's discovery helps or hinders his theory.

XVII

BARRETT WENDELL'S [1] opinion of Shakespeare is that he is a great imaginative artist who expressed in disinterested fashion the moods of his mind; but the leading idea that emerges from his work is how far what Shakespeare expressed answered to something that is objectively real in the world. We will give some of his typical judgements and then collect our impressions.

Shakespeare's originality in his poems was wholly a matter of phrase. Marlowe describes events that do not seem to happen in a real world, but Shakespeare is minutely true to nature. Words and ideas cannot easily be separated, and the Elizabethan phrase-makers managed incidentally to say something final. One cannot combine words and phrases without also combining ideas. Shakespeare infuses his stories with a permeating sense of fact; yet this is due to the distinctive trait of his mind in which words and thoughts are naturally identical.

L.L.L. expresses a state of artistic feeling which would now express itself in polite comic opera. *Verona* is concerned with characters

[1] *Wm. Sh. A Study in Elizabethan Literature,* 1894.

rather than plot, and therefore promises greater work. The characters
are hardly consistent, but Shakespeare gives them atmosphere by
adding to the bare outline of the plot subtle touches based on observation of real life. The centre of *M.N.D.* is the love story, and the
artistic purpose of the rest is to make this plausible. The characters
are singly, not individuals, but as groups there is a strong dramatic
contrast each with each. The plot of *R. and J.* coheres through the
temperaments of the characters interacting as in life. Shakespeare's
creative imagination makes his fictions real as human beings. Romeo
and Juliet are happy, because they preserve permanently the emotional
purity which could not have survived in prolonged life. You accept
the words of Richard III as actual human utterances, but his world
is unreal. None of the beauties of *Richard II* are inevitably human
utterances, but each helps to define the character who utters it.
Shakespeare makes conventions of chronicle history express, in
mastered archaic form, his growing sense of fact. In *John* creative
imagination makes real people from previous stage types. Yet Constance rants, and real human vitality is confused with old quasi-
operatic conventions.

The art of the *Merchant* makes plausible the absurd plot. After
the first talk of the caskets the bond seems quite in order of things.
But the characters are absorbingly individual and human, and we
accept all else as a matter of course. *Henry IV* gives sense of contact
with actual life, and we are conscious only of a profound impression
that we have seen real people who have done real things. The two
parts are united by the figure—not the character—of the Prince.
The incongruity troubles us no more than that of real life. We feel
the great movement of historical forces: men are in the hands of fate
that works itself out on a scale beyond any human lifetime. In
private life also there are forces beyond human control, such as heredity.
Note Prince John's treachery and the Prince's cruelty to Falstaff.
Falstaff's self-deception in the *Wives* is Shakespeare's chief later
comic motive, and later still it is a tragic one. In *Henry V* Shakespeare
laments the theatre's limitations, which proves that his purpose was
not merely dramatic. Henry is moral rather than dramatic hero,
ideal rather than man, British rather than human.

Benedict, Beatrice, Dogberry are all beguiled by intrinsic weaknesses of nature into states of mind and lines of conduct which are
dramatic because incompatible with obvious facts in possession of
omniscience and the audience. It is not theatrical but human comedy,
and, with irony added, makes a new kind of literature. *A.Y.L.* is
purely fantastic, though art conceals this. The moralizing is beautifully phrased but commonplace. Yet the spontaneous ease of
Shakespeare's creative imagination translates conventional types into
living individuals. The Sonnets must have seemed to Shakespeare

more important than his plays. His art is nowhere more elaborately fine, and actually or sympathetically an artist must know the moods he expresses. In the sense that it must have formed part of mental life, all art is autobiographical: the real doubt is the cause of the moods. The Sonnets express the suffering of a lover whose love is of this world. If the object is human, experience must shatter the ideal, and the lasting tragedy of earthly love is what the Sonnets phrase.

In *J.C.* the mood is unpassionately ironical, because we see human affairs broken loose from human control. Caesar is himself the sport of fate, and neither great nor small men can do anything. In *Hamlet* one reason why things happen as they do is that people are temperamentally just what they are. The tragedy finally expresses the mood of the artist who has no answer for the problems before him. With one part of his being he yields to divine madness, with the other he phrases it. There is a sense of tragic fate—no judicial Greek fate, but the passionate, stormy, Christianized fate of Romantic Europe. Our ills spring from the fact that men are men and women are women. *Hamlet* expresses the mystery of sexual passion, *M. for M.* the evil. Othello's jealousy is a new phase of the fact that men are men, &c. That it is groundless revives the old motive of self-deception, now become tragic. The play is one where Shakespeare, with full control of his powers, tries to express a mood or fact foreign to self. The fine artistic problem set Shakespeare in *Lear* was to gratify the taste for rant without violating propriety. Goneril and Regan are not wholly unjustified at first, yet the intention of the plot is so carefully preserved that to this day we think them monsters of ingratitude— as do Lear and the audience. Men are the sport of fate, and emotions overpowers thought. Thought cannot help us, but to yield to emotion is the way to madness. Death is no longer a mystery, but the despairing solution of the problem of human agony. Shakespeare is intellectually alert to the verge of madness; only his mastery of expression keeps him within the bounds of sanity. The monotony of *Macbeth* is that of despair; he is a study of fate-ridden, irresponsible, yet damning crime. He is forced to sin by a power beyond self, yet held to account for acts of will perverted by sin and curse of ancestral humanity. Man is the sport of evil external powers, and life a horrible mystery. The truth to life of both characters and situations pleases, and obviates the horror of the motive. The moods of *Hamlet and Lear* might have been Shakespeare's, those of *Othello* and *Macbeth* he seems to invent by sympathetic imagination: new proof of his abnormally active mind at the time. It is the ironical view of life expressed by Calvinism. *Macbeth* reveals deeper knowledge of spiritual misery than we have fathomed before. It is the knowledge of the last word of soul-sick despair.

Shakespeare created a miraculously human woman in Cleopatra, and revives the death throes of the ancient world. It is a great poem, and no veracity of detail makes it realistic. The life brought back is not spiritual, the revived world was dying, and has an aspect of fallen grandeur. To know the grandeur of moral conquest you must realize the alluring delights of moral degradation. Plutarch's narrative is presented in a grandly objective way; the facts reveal sympathetic knowledge of fleshly delight, and splendid gleams of classic antiquity. There is a great solemnity of world ruin, and the atmosphere of the historical past is revived as never in literature. The world-movement first prevails, and only later the individuals stand out. Yet there is slackening of the profound emotional impulse which surged beneath the great tragedies. Passion is presented in a coolly dramatic, dispassionate way—though this makes the play great; and Antony and Cleopatra are the most living persons in literature. The *Tempest* is deliberately removed from reality, and though a great and beautiful poem is neither great nor effective as a play. It is deliberately imaginative, and this quality typifies the fatal trouble; it is related to real life in a way which we cannot feel is unintentional. The jealousy of Leontes in the *W. Tale* is a phase of the over-wrought self-deception and unbalance of mind which pervaded the great tragedies. Autolycus is idealized from memory, if we compare him with Falstaff who was drawn from life. The pastoral scene, though unreal, does seem spontaneous and inevitable, and revives the old mood of the best time. . . .

Wendell's discovery that words and things were more closely allied in Shakespeare's mind than in any other writer's is a valuable one; but with his criticism of the *Tempest* fresh in our minds we discern his weak point. He makes the real world too prominent and neglects the city that is built to music. In *Lear* his method is helpful because it keeps us to the truth; in *A. and C.* he is at his best, because the ancient world has become imaginative; in *Macbeth* he seems to rise above himself, till the word 'Calvinism' brings us down to earth. We commend his words on the Sonnets, but for the most part he brings us little further than the ante-room of true appreciation of Shakespeare: though, with *A.Y.L.* and *A. and C.*, he so handles abstract thought as to rekindle the reader's imagination. But if he does not quite impress his vision upon the reader, at least he had eyes to see one for himself. Thus he says that the nearer a great work of art approaches the proportions of actual life rather than the details, the nearer the imagination of its maker approaches in its scheme the divine imagination which has made our infinitely mysterious world, the more endlessly suggestive that work of art must always be.

XVIII

WE will start with remarks on Shakespeare's religion. Corson says that in spirit he is a true Christian, and that Christianity is a reality to him, to be confirmed by spiritual experience. Morley tells of his spiritual rule of three to solve life's problems: love God, love your neighbour, do your work. For him, in Shakespeare's works, we have the life of man set to right music, and everywhere this music follows those laws of the best science of harmony set forth in the Sermon on the Mount. He concludes that Shakespeare is free from dogmatism and full of the true spirit of religion. Perkins says that he discovers in us the promptings of an almost supernatural power.

At the head of the moral sayings we will place Morshead's—that his tone about virtue and vice is innately noble, that he shudders inwardly at the infinite character of wrongdoing. Corson says that he is no formal moralist, but shows everywhere the profoundest moral spirit; also that he differs from his contemporaries in working more strictly under the condition of moral proportion, and united moral proportion with unrestrained play of the passions. In Shakespeare, writes Morley, evil is never overcome by evil but by good.

As contrast to the above we may cite Wendell, that he was first an artist who expressed specific moods with little care for their ultimate meaning. Corson calls him the master-artist, because he worked with harmonious co-operation of all the soul's powers. Mr. Symons says that at times he shows the gentle forbearance of the profound and indifferent literary artist. Cunliffe speaks of his perfect art. Pater affirms that the true imaginative unity of the drama is the single impression which it should leave.

Of his characters we get the following: from Hawkins, that he was the greatest human observant of humanity, and his plots depended entirely on character-study; from Wendell, that his characters are not conceived by conscious process of psychological analysis, but by spontaneously creative imagination, and that he created more and more varied living characters than any modern writer; from Baynes, that he pierces to the hidden centre of character and touches the deepest springs of impulse and passion, has absolute command over all the complexities of thought and feeling that prompt to action and bring out the dividing lines of character, sweeps with the hand of a master the whole gamut of human experience, and has unrivalled power of piercing the deepest mysteries and sounding the most tremendous and perplexing problems of human life and destiny. Pater speaks of the profound and sombre power with which he sounds the depths of mighty character. To Appleton Morgan he was the poet of humanity, not nature.

Of more general remarks we have Corson's, that he had the most

synthetic and intuitive order of mind yet known among men, that in
his plays there is little learning, but the greatest possible knowledge
and wisdom, and a direct perception of truth. Cunliffe speaks of his
wonder-working imagination that makes others' thoughts entirely
his own. Baynes finds in his work organic strength, infinite variety,
throbbing fullness, vital complexity, breathing truth of Nature herself,
and that he had a noble well-poised nature, combining harmoniously in himself the widest range of qualities. To Wendell he is not
only the supreme genius of English literature, but also a normal
human being greater than others but not different in kind, less author
than creator, inevitable vitality being the master-sign of his great
work, central and most broadly typical figure in the evolution of the
most broadly typical school of art in modern literature, among imaginative artists unique for practical prudence.

Corson says that he delights to exhibit the moral beauty of women;
while it appears to Talbot that Shakespeare does not affirm that the
influence of women will generally be for good. Wendell remarks that
idealized women predominate in the earlier plays. . . .

It is difficult to drive a straight path through this forest of praise,
but as we have a preference for the agnostic type of critic, we will
enter a warning against those positive statements on Shakespeare's
religion made by Corson and Morley, and select that of Perkins. The
same applies to criticism of his morality; and we rather single out for
praise the remarks on his art by Wendell and Mr. Symons. As the
spectrum analysis proved all worlds of one substance, so it is by
watching the colour-changes in the prism of the soul, as the light of
the plays fall upon it, that each of us can form a partial estimate of the
greatest mind that has appeared among men—not by definite judgements. The best theory of Shakespeare will be diffidently wrought,
through the progress of decades, out of the honest impressions of
agnostic-minded critics.

GERMANY 1888–1894

I

WE return to Delius [1] whose theme is now the monologue, indispensable for filling up gaps in the action or explaining feeling and development of character. It is freely used in *R. and J.*, because it was the lovers' only means to express delight and despair— but we note that it was confined to true love and passion, not vague feeling. Romeo has no monologue about Rosaline, nor Juliet about Paris. Juliet, after her secret marriage, awaiting Romeo, utters feelings that she could not have done to the Nurse and scarcely to Romeo. When Juliet holds in her hand the sleeping-draught she is assailed by many doubts and fears. It is not a monologue of reflection, feeling, self-revelation, but of dramatic action. It comprehends a whole scene; but the scene takes place within the individual. The play could be understood without its monologues, but the characters would lack many of their finer psychological features.

We could not understand *Hamlet* without monologues, as the tragedy takes place in the hero's inner being. He makes known through these how deeply he suffered from his mother's remarriage. After the ghost scene we should expect a monologue on his plan for revenge; but instead he conveys that revenge is to be deferred. His cry that the time is out of joint reveals his love of generalizing on matters connected with his conscience—of reducing the practical to the theoretical. From this condition he is roused by the players to self-condemnation; but the further scruple arises that the ghost may be an evil spirit. In the interval comes 'To be'—the purely theoretical meditations on suicide and hereafter. He seems to undertake his journey to England as a welcome excuse to defer action. The final catastrophe is the necessary result of the tragedy that has been proceeding in his innermost being. Act V requires no monologue to serve as a finger-post for the poet's intention through the previous acts.

The same reasons enforce monologue in *Othello*, where it is the knave who cannot confide his plot to another, and the poet must use a succession of monologues to help his audience. The cause of Iago's hatred of Othello remains vague, but probably it is that the wicked hate the good from a psychological necessity. In the monologue that follows further converse with Roderigo, Iago seems to be urging himself on to the deed. The former doubtful suspicion of Othello and his

[1] *Neue Folge*, 1888.

wife he now describes as gnawing his inwards like poison. The base man finds a certain satisfaction in imputing his own vileness to others. After his scheme is launched we do not need his monologues, and the tragedy is transferred to Othello's troubled soul which eases itself in monologue. The last, in Desdemona's bed-chamber, explains the whole attitude of his mind and feelings: the tenderness that will not shed her blood, and yet the cause for which she must die. In short, the monologue is used by Shakespeare to soften Othello's deed. Othello could have revealed to no single person, without restraint, his love and anguish.

Lear gives many more instances of both kinds of the monologue, viz. the natural medium to express thoughts, feelings, hopes, plans which one or other cannot or dare not betray to others, either from bad conscience, or because of isolation. Edmund has a grievance against Edgar, like Iago against Cassio. Kent's first monologue expresses his noble intentions to his master; and, in the stocks, he makes clear coming events, when he rejoices that Cordelia's letter has reached him. As Cordelia's sole representative, he could not confide all this in dialogue. Lear himself, as long as he carried on the useless struggle with his unnatural daughters, could use dialogue; but on the heath he vents his feelings in monologue, and his passionate outburst forebodes madness. From Edgar's rhymed monologue we gather that he finds some consolation in comparing his troubles with those of his betters.

Macbeth is richest in dialogue, not because the characters are isolated, but because, in accordance with the profound feeling of his later dramas, Shakespeare is interested in the psychological development and demonstration of character as fully as in the progress of the plot. Edmund and Iago were already evil, but Macbeth lapses from good to evil before our eyes. The transformation is revealed by monologue; the inner tragedy therefore runs parallel with the outer, and we can follow both. The monologue at the close of I. iv shows the growing power over him of the evil thought. When Duncan's visit is announced, and the murder is not a question of time but a matter of the hour, we hear his monologue with all its arguments against the deed and final confession that ambition alone spurs him on. The contrast to the visionary dagger-monologue is the practical one of Lady Macbeth informing the audience that she has ensured that the actual murderer should not be discovered. Banquo's short monologue at the beginning of Act III shows that he suspects Macbeth and hopes that the prophecy will be equally fulfilled for his sons. Lady Macbeth's short rhymed monologue (III. ii) refers to her husband's melancholy mood— and this could only be shown in monologue. Macbeth would be saved by further tyrannous acts (monologue IV. i); and in Act V he betrays the collapse of his whole being. The guilt shared by husband and wife has loosened rather than tightened the bond between them; and each has to fight the inner battle alone. She now experiences all that Macbeth suffered before the murder in real or visionary circumstances. Her monologue at the beginning of Act V is a counterpart to the earlier one of her husband's. We may surmise that memory haunts her waking as well as sleeping.

Turning to the subject of friendship in the plays, we gather from biographical reports that the cultivation of friendship was a necessity of life to Shakespeare. The Sonnets, whether autobiographical or not, reveal searching study into the nature of friendship. If friendship occurs in the sources of a play he gives it wider and deeper significance; and where he finds none, he adds it as his own invention. *Verona* originally was a simple love story, solely concerned with a faithless lover and the two objects of his varying affection; but Shakespeare gives it a higher significance and more psychological interest by adding to it the contrast between the faithful and faithless friend. Proteus confesses in monologue his characteristic weakness; and Shakespeare in many sonnets warns his friend of the demoralizing and enervating influence of love. Proteus submits readily to his father's will, bids a light farewell to Julia, and expresses no word of pleasure at the thought of seeing Valentine. The latter praises Proteus lavishly to the Duke. Thus in some sonnets Shakespeare ascribes all excellent qualities to his friend, and in others complains bitterly of disillusion. There is the same lack of suspicion in the Sonnets, where the introduction of the friend to the beloved one is the cause that both are unfaithful to himself. It is even worse in the play where Valentine confides in Proteus, not knowing that the latter also is in love with Silvia. In the scene where Proteus betrays the projected elopement to Silvia's father, he is the perfected hypocrite. He plays the sympathetic friend to Valentine, and offers to be go-between with letters: as the poet in the Sonnets is intermediary between his faithless friend and his beloved. Valentine's final generosity may seem to go too far; yet the Sonnets represent such self-sacrifice as an act of heroism on a friend's part.

Friendship in the *Merchant* is founded on mutal esteem, and of a less blind and easily deceived species. The friendship found by Shakespeare in his source arose from the bond between godfather and godchild. That between Antonio and Bassanio was founded on a sympathetic spirit and mental affinity: to Antonio it is an element of life, whereas Bassanio has other interests and cultivates love besides friendship. Antonio, therefore, is the giver, and Bassanio takes all for granted. It is a delicate touch that Antonio seeks out Bassanio's scattered companions and hastens their departure. The friendship in *J.C.* Shakespeare takes from Plutarch and as usual improves on it: he introduces an idealistic element into the friendship between Brutus and Cassius, unknown to Plutarch, that softens the tragedy. That Cassius does not oppose Brutus's imprudent concessions to Antony proves the moral power of friend over friend. Shakespeare shows a predilection for friendship, but subordinates it to the main action—and he does this yet more in *R. and J.* Here, too, he introduces independently two friends of diverse character. Brooke gives no Benvolio, and a Mercutio who is only occasionally Romeo's friend. Shakespeare felt the necessity of some trusted friends to whom Romeo could open his heart; but after Mercutio's death and Romeo's banishment he has no further use for him and lets him quietly disappear.

Friendship in *Hamlet* takes also a secondary place and little influences the action, yet Shakespeare gives his hero, who has to bear his burdensome task alone, the comfort and support of a true friend. At first Hamlet does not confide to Horatio the Ghost's revelation, but he does later on, and asks him to watch with him the effect of the play. His address to Horatio—superfluous to the actual drama—gives us Shakespeare's own idea of the right choice and worth of a genuine friend. For a time we lose sight of Horatio, until the friends meet in the churchyard apparently accidentally. Horatio had previously received a letter from Hamlet, who has much to tell him; yet according to Hamlet's ever-changing mood and abrupt humour—otherwise inexplicable—instead of confiding to Horatio what the latter must have been eager to know from hints in the letter, he enters into melancholy churchyard thoughts and only later relates what has happened. In response to Hamlet's last request Horatio lives to explain all, and thus Shakespeare associates him further with his friend. Of the secondary half-comic pair of friends, Rosencrantz and Guildenstern, whom Hamlet at first greets unsuspiciously, but treats unmercifully when he discovers their purpose, and sends to death without trouble of conscience, it would appear that Shakespeare shares his views, judging by characteristics and tasks assigned to these friends in the play.

Shakespeare likewise introduces a pair of friends independently into *Twelfth-Night.* Antonio's devotion to Sebastian goes so far that he follows him to the house of Orsino, his own mortal enemy. The mistakes that follow draw from Antonio a bitter lamentation over the supposed Sebastian's ingratitude, which seems to come from the very heart of Shakespeare's own feeling of friendship, and recalls the equally pathetic passages in the Sonnets where the friend's inner unworthiness is compared with his outward beauty.

Friendship is otherwise treated in *T. and C.*, though the scurrilous friendship between Achilles and Patroclus may be explained by the manner in which the medievalized Trojan story is turned into parody. Patroclus plays the undignified part of buffoon and mimic, and later performs the duties of a valet de chambre; though he takes a better position when he adds his own exhortation to that of Ulysses. At the same time he feels himself to blame, since his own little taste for war, and Achilles' love for him, are cited as the cause of the inertia of Achilles.

Menenius differs in being much older than his friend Coriolanus. Plutarch's Menenius calms the populace with his fable, and is only politically associated with Coriolanus. With Shakespeare, as the play proceeds, we begin to realize the personal relation between them. Menenius defends his friend against charges of arrogance, welcomes his triumphal home-coming, and eagerly recommends that he should be elected Consul. He becomes his mentor, exhorts him to behave reasonably, and curb his temper for political reasons. He fails as mediator, and with tears sadder than those of a younger man, takes leave of his banished friend, whom he would have followed but for his years. At the end he pleads as father with son, and although Coriolanus yields to the women, Menenius feels that the friendship which had been the pride and delight of his life is over, and Coriolanus is lost to himself and Rome.

Friendship between women is sparsely treated by Shakespeare; though the confidence between the lady and her dependants, which often grows into friendship, is at times agreeably described, and their roguishness becomes a delightful foil to the serious dignity of the mistress. It is thus in *Verona*, the *Merchant*, *L.L.L.*, but it occurs between those of like position and age, and when present, as in *M.N.D.*, it does not stand the test of rivalry in love. The only lasting girl friendship is between Rosalind and Celia, and this more than sisterly affection was not taken from Lodge, but is part of the vitality added by Shakespeare to his borrowed characters. They both take a sisterly interest in Orlando's fate at the wrestling match—and Celia is self-banished for her friend's sake: for in Lodge the Duke banishes both niece and daughter. They enjoy forest life more than court life; their good temper never fails; and their friendship is undisturbed by their other alliances till the happy solution of marriage. . . .

Many critics with greater pretensions than Delius have fared worse. He does not seek to foist his own ideas upon Shakespeare, but delves in the Shakespearian mine for its native riches. If he makes no new startling discoveries, he presents his theories in the least arbitrary manner by letting the facts speak for themselves; and there is a fine equibalance in his process of receiving and recording impressions that suggests one of the leading critics of the present day—Professor Herford. Perhaps Delius is slightly over-confident in assigning certain opinions to Shakespeare himself—e.g. Hamlet's address to Horatio on friendship—but for the most part he preserves an impersonal and agnostic note that is modern. The result of his examination of the monologue is the conviction that it is needed for the internal economy of the play, and that the last problem with Shakespeare is the psychological. Thus he says that only the monologue could show Macbeth

transformed from good to evil before our eyes, or the pair divided
instead of united by guilt. It does not occur to him that Shakespeare
used the monologue as a means to make things clearer to his audience.
As regards friendship, he tells us that the Sonnets reveal a searching
inquiry into its nature, that where it is in the sources of a play Shakespeare has added much of his own, and that he introduces an idealistic
element into that between Brutus and Cassius. These are facts that
we must accept, though we have become over-shy of autobiographical
interpretations. But the final impressions are that it is only after long
and close acquaintance with the play that a theory forms itself for
Delius, not the reverse process—and that the most satisfying Shakespearian criticism is the receptive—at times even the negative. His
method is to argue backwards from the outer events of the play to
Shakespeare's intention, and always give Shakespeare the benefit of the
doubt, e.g. Hamlet's treatment of Rosencrantz and Guildenstern.

II

APTLY in the same year we meet with Wilhelm Wendlandt [1] who,
writing about *Timon*, says that with Shakespeare it is not possible to
draw personal conclusions from occasional expressions; and it is
dangerous to look upon *T. and C.* and *Timon* as representing his actual
mood. And yet it is his peculiarity and highest ideal to embody in some
person the scattered thoughts that compose an idea, and we see its
progress from work to work as he ripens and increases his knowledge
of human nature. In his later stage worldly knowledge, and therefore,
the intellectual, predominated, and he was obsessed by psychological
problems of more than ordinary significance.[2] Prospero, Lear, Achilles,
Thersites, Antony and Cleopatra, Timon are distinct individuals and
isolated figures with a moral right of their own, disparted from moral
bonds of duty and justice and wholesome ties of human society. But
all except Achilles and Thersites, and also Prospero who reverts to the
normal, perish from their exceptional dispositions. This conformity
distinguishes Shakespeare's latest characters, and must have been
fundamentally akin to himself. He had grown into a self-existing
individualist and become a law to himself.

Prospero, absorbed in study, suffers the same fate as Timon, and
loses his kingdom. Solitude enlightens his heart, and all-embracing
love, not hate, delivers him. Antony and Cleopatra find their freedom
in contempt of the world's praise or blame. Coriolanus carries revenge
to such a pitch that his downfall is inevitable. Only Timon in the
play becomes tragically great: for Alcibiades does not suffer the final
consequences of his bold spirit. Timon is the counterpart of Prospero,
as Alcibiades of Coriolanus; and as Timon dies and Prospero lives, so

[1] *Jahrbuch*, 1888.   [2] Cf. Delius.

with the other two. Prospero is a monument of sanity and power, and Timon of disease and power. This distempered power causes his fall, and the colouring of the tragedy is the same in the three dramas of Shakespeare's latest years—*T. and C., A. and C., Coriolanus*. But in *Timon* everything is overcharged: absolute goodness becomes absolute hardness, and distempered power sinks to power full of rage. Shakespeare's heart must have felt deathly loneliness and been much distempered to have brought forth such a creation.

Timon is not an orthodox tragedy, but stands midway between objective truth to life and subjective personal symbolism, between lofty tragedy and involuntary comedy. To make it clear Shakespeare gives his own commentary—as in *T. and C.* where Achilles (iii. iii) describes the author's own position—and in the speech of Ulysses, 'Time hath . . . a wallet . . .', which is a true picture of Shakespeare's literary fate after his retirement; and the offspring of his anger at the ingratitude of contemporaries was *Timon*. A man-hater is rather a comic than tragic subject, and Shakespeare only made it tragic by making it subjective. In Timon's large-hearted blindness lies the destroying Ate of the tragedy. Shakespeare did not intend to make him a man striving after the first place, but one to whom the first place naturally fell on account of the outer and inner gifts showered on him by Fortune. Mentally and morally he was head and shoulders above his surroundings, and he fell because he was determined to persist in good deeds. Only Shakespeare could have conceived so great a heart or painted so heavy a fate: and it proves his heart even greater than his intellect.

The two halves of the play are linked by Apemantus, who first appears in railing superiority, and is finally annihilated by Timon's criticisms. The other links are Alcibiades and Flavius, who are uninfluenced by Timon's change of position. That the gulf should be bridged by a contemptible hater of his fellow men, and by the two with their liberating spirit of unchangeable fidelity, is one of Shakespeare's greatest dramatic triumphs.

The scene with the thieves is an episode, but highly symbolic. The thieves who incline to give up their profession show better heart than the Lords. The latter were already reduced to the lowest level of commoners, and the last act is uncommonly distressing with its bare disclosure of the hideous side of human egoism. . . .

We cannot accept Wendlandt as a builder of theories, but what preserves his criticism is the force with which he feels the reactions of Timon's character, and therefore both consciously and unconsciously he vindicates its Shakespearian origin. The kind of generalization which includes Prospero, Lear, Achilles, Thersites, Antony, Cleopatra, Timon can only do so by omitting everything that is characteristic of the individual. He rightly disclaims personal inferences about Shake-

speare from single speeches, but his vision of the later intellectualized
Shakespeare is over-confident.

III

HEINRICH W. VON GERSTENBERG,[1] comparing Shake-
speare with the Greeks, says that the aim of Greek tragedy was to move
the passions, and of comedy to show human conduct in such light as to
arouse laughter. Judged by this standard, Shakespeare's tragedies are
no tragedies and his comedies no comedies. However, it is not seriously
proposed to question Shakespeare's power to move the passions, but
to assert that this was subordinated to the higher aim of delineating
morals and portraying life both idealized and natural.

We will compare Young's *Revenge*—a copy of *Othello*—with
Shakespeare's play. Young is concerned only with the power of
jealousy to wring the heart with shame, terror, pity. Shakespeare
carefully develops its finest shades and discloses its most hidden workings. Young thought of the effect of his situations on the audience—
Shakespeare of the effect of jealousy on Othello. In short, Young
describes passions, Shakespeare the feelings bound up with passions.
Young's villain is a common fox—Shakespeare's Iago, perhaps not
without cause, suspects his general, and will play him a soldier's prank,
by the way. His primary motive is not revenge on Othello, but itching
desire after Cassio's post. His creed is to hold all the world for fools,
and benefit his purse and ambition at their expense. He explains his
principles too clearly to be misunderstood; we see him from the beginning in his transactions with Roderigo; and every word he utters reveals
some shade or other of his knavery. The spectator may indeed think
he has all nature before his eyes.

No author has reflected more profoundly on jealousy or portrayed
it more strikingly than Shakespeare. Othello is firm, steady, and well-
tempered; and every little deviation from his customary manner is
subtly indicated with the lightest touch. This knowledge of the nature
of passion, and power to express outwardly its every shade, distinguished
Shakespeare from other poets. Remark the skill with which
Shakespeare contrives that as soon as Iago has dropped a hint into
Othello's mind, Desdemona does all the rest. The gradual increase of
jealous passion in Othello may seem less dramatic than the hero's
ambush and sudden action in Young's play, but it is the triumph of art.
No scene can compare with that where Othello can no longer restrain
the fire that consumes him, and strikes his wife before the ambas-
sadors. The most delicate treatment of a modern artist could not equal
this involuntary characteristic action.

No doubt Young describes brilliantly the strife between love and
rage; and yet not only might any one of these tirades be torn from its

[1] *Letters on Literature*, &c., 1888.

context, but it is the kind that could have proceeded from any other man. Because these sentiments are too general for Shakespeare, and too far from the maturely strong Othello, the latter can have thrown upon him no such moving light. Yet Shakespeare gives a complete picture, and we now see that his aim is not so much to awaken horror and pity as to show forth the nature of jealousy. The scenes that follow Desdemona's death are therefore weaker than those that precede, and contribute so little to the chief aim of tragedy that their first impression is to soften rather than heighten. Shakespeare excels in depicting passion, but it is not his entire object.

He has been accused of lack of taste, and this is unavoidable if judged from our modern standpoint. His age was the golden age of word-play: King James, the most affected speaker in the world, set the tone to Court and pulpit. Pope is therefore wrong to say that passages of this kind were introduced to please the populace. Other charges against him are affectation, subtlety, exaggeration of diction: but remember that not only each class of man but each stage of life has something peculiar in its mode of expression. Shakespeare mastered these faculties of the mind—as we see from the speeches of child, youth, man, old man—and his plays abound with fine shades of difference according to the speaker's age or class. It is hard even to contemplate a greater number of finished characters, identified at once by their mode of speech, and true to their kind in the smallest feature.

Of his histories it has been said that he has no aim in view but to take one piece after another from history and present them in the mass to his audience. But it is not so: they are an ordered whole with connexion, purpose, contrasts in character, and contrasting groups. *Richard II* gives the struggle of weak kingly dignity with the strength and cunning of conspiracy. What a contrast between the King and Boling-broke, and what variety and multiplicity of gradation in the subordinate characters! Everything works towards the main goal—the destruction of the King that so soon was to rebound on the heads of the traitors themselves. We have the mirror of the human mind, and the impres-sive lesson of inevitable consequences to all actors in the drama. When Bolingbroke is King his friends turn to enemies—a formidable cabal. There are two contrasting groups—on one side Hotspur, Douglas, Glendower, heroes of indomitable courage—on the other, the dis-solute Prince and his companions. There is nothing superfluous in this bold picture, and the Prince's wild period is a foil to his later greatness. Shakespeare would have missed his final aim had he led him along a less questionable path.

If *J.C.* were only a play about the death of a usurper, Caesar him-self would be the prominent figure—whereas he is a base on which are built up the fates of the murderers. Nothing is more impressive or instructive than the misfortune which dogs the heels of the conspirators.

H 2

These remarks apply to the remaining historical plays, in all of which there is artistic unity of design, and every part is rightly related to the whole. . . .

We say of Gerstenberg what. he himself says of Iago—that he explains his principles too clearly to be misunderstood—but we think his power to feel exceeds his power to interpret. The splendour of *Othello* subdues him, but he translates his impressions into a questionable philosophic language. Shakespeare was concerned with the individual soul, not with abstract morals; and yet a critic like Gerstenberg, who is sincere and serious-minded, has his part to play. He throws his whole weight into the abstract scale, and when it declines no whit, we become aware of the adamantine pressure of the true Shakespeare on its fellow. The rest of the criticism is the natural record of one who sets out on a voyage of admiration, viz. the contrasts of character in Richard II, and the perfect plots of the histories. We have omitted an excessive eulogy of the *Errors*, but it contains the phrase that 'perhaps nothing could be found to do more honour to the human intellect'.

IV

W. WETZ[1] is interested in the subject of the sudden changes that take place in Shakespeare's characters. We must remember that they belong to the Renaissance, that their passions have a different energy from ours, and their actions may appear improbable unless we overstep our usual boundaries. When a man is overcome by his passions, one must first understand these passions, and then he can be easily persuaded to act in a certain way. Cassius inflames Brutus to murder Caesar; and Iago reduces Othello and others to the rank of marionettes. The heroes of all the tragedies have this personal peculiarity.

The difference between the earlier and later plays is that the later are based on conscience, the earlier on outward events where there is a lack of conscience. In the later also is more emphasized inner suffering, the working' of conscience, and spiritual agony which destroys character.

It has often been affirmed that Othello was not jealous by nature; but we think this is a mistake, and that he was most susceptible to the whisperings of jealousy. In character large-hearted and magnanimous, he would resist rather than encourage jealousy; and its growth is anguish to him. To understand the difference between him and a really jealous man, compare him with Leontes or Posthumus Leonatus. With Othello the struggle is not between love and jealousy, but love and honour—and Iago's efforts are calculated to make these last two collide. With Shakespeare's tragic heroes passion waits on opportunity to break forth: and Iago and others merely offer these opportunities.

[1] *Sh. from the Standpoint of Comparative Literature,* 1890.

We turn to *M. Ado* and repeat our warning that Shakespeare's lovers are not to be judged by our modern standard—but love and jealousy were more violent and glowing in life and literature. We must therefore not condemn Claudio when we consider the pain that quivers through every word of his in the church, and his intense subsequent remorse. He was no scoundrel, but noble-minded—a man, however, of vehement temperament and likely to be led away by suspicion. Besides, he and Pedro believed Hero's father to be aware of his daughter's bad character, and to be taking advantage of their ignorance. As he had betrayed their friendship, it seemed to them right to take public revenge. Again Claudio has been blamed for jesting at Benedict—but Shakespeare's impulsive characters easily turn from tragedy to mirth: cf. Prince Henry who jests with Poins at Falstaff's letter, though deeply moved by the news of his father's illness.

Claudio and Don Pedro feel that they have acted rightly, and try to laugh off their uneasiness, but they do not joke from their hearts. Leonato and Antonio are accused of unseemly behaviour—but it is to ask too much of a father that he should be cool and self-controlled at such a moment, and calmly investigate signs of guilt or innocence on his daughter's face. Lear, Capulet, Cymbeline remind us that Shakespeare's fathers are the reverse of cold-blooded. The mistake of critics is to suspect some deep moral significance in every subordinate character, and to bestow either moral praise or blame. . . .

Wetz does well to point out the historical cause of the sudden changes that take place in Shakespeare's characters. The extreme instance is Macbeth, who prayed for a blessing when about to commit murder: but the Renaissance temperament is the answer. When the old moral landmarks were swept away, man turned as he pleased from one passion to another. In reminding us of the more energetic passions of the men of Shakespeare's time Wetz does well; but in all that follows there is much lack of discrimination. He seeks to extend his theory to *M. Ado* and confuses passion with needs of the stage, and compares Leonato with Lear and Capulet.

V

HERMANN MÜLLER[1] writes on the foundation and development of Richard III's character. From his father, York, Richard inherited ambition, but he joined to it a power of will and mind which made him, in relation to other Yorks, as a masterpiece to their attempts. We see the foundation of his character in the second and third parts of *Henry VI*, where he stands with roots in a soil hollowed out with crime, and breathes an atmosphere of moral iniquity. In him is lodged the principle of an age that knows only one law, that of egoism; and he united the traits distributed among various individuals. We must

[1] *Jahrbuch*, 1891.

consider him the sanguinary reaper sent to avenge the world's crime, and this marks his figure tragically.

The monologue that opens *Richard III* is the mirror of Richard's soul: bodily ugliness stimulates him to hate the whole of mankind. Critics have warned us not to exaggerate this deformity, or assume that an intelligent man of wide outlook would attribute to this his villainy.[1] But such a thing is possible, for evil thoughts and deeds affect intellectual life—and a distorted will produces distorted judgement. Richard does not belong to those who seek for argument to justify their deeds; but he has a hideously clear conception of the iniquity of his acts, with no shadow of inner conflict between conscience and desire. He could easily have thrown a cloak of patriotism over his behaviour, considering his brother's worthlessness and incapacity—but he knows too well that his motive is lust of sovereignty served by his iron will. His hypocrisy is the result of self-mastery and lack of conscience. We ask, What is the secret of the unfailing success of this hypocrisy? He is a man of strong nature, capable of immense passion and true and deep feelings. Thus, he has a consuming hatred for the Queen and all her kin, and under this true and genuine hatred he hides his evil thoughts against his brother. He uses real feelings to hide other real feelings that he wishes to conceal. He is straightforward towards his brother in that he pours scorn and contempt upon him, and gives free rein to his biting tongue against the Queen and her family. He gives vent to these true feelings with elementary power, masking the opposite ones that possess him. Also his harsh appearance and blazing passion would oppose the idea of hypocrisy.

The scene where his mother curses him has been called the turning-point of his career, though this is not confirmed by anything in the text; but Shakespeare often leaves out direct intimation and trusts to our intuition. Here we picture Richard depressed and disturbed by his mother's curse; but he collects his titanic powers of self-control for his next move—the wooing of Elizabeth's daughter. In this he evidently believes that he has succeeded; but Elizabeth has throughout appeared one of the most spotless of women, and it would be a disgrace to her mother-love to think that she consents. Such cannot be the purpose of the scene, and we think that she only pretends to consent through fear of the danger to her child. As she quits him the news is brought of Richmond's advance; and we see the process in him of disintegration. He is restless, irresolute, even strikes a messenger. His final monologue is an awful shuddering echo of the earliest one. He differs from Macbeth in that he masters feeling and thought, forces his conscience, and sacrifices in cold blood those that stand in his way. Macbeth is weaker willed, and so conscience-stricken that he commits his crime in feverish excitement. That Richard's conscience

[1] Cf. Montégut.

is not quite dead we see from his unrest and superstitious fear. Here Shakespeare links even the deliberate evil-doer with the better side of human nature: the last monologue satisfies our moral feelings. With demoniacal power of will he becomes himself once more, and nothing daunts him at the last. It is right that he should die a hero's death—for poetic justice is satisfied by his defeat in the unequal struggle with the moral order of the world, by the overthrow of the great criminal under shattering blows of conscience, by the utter collapse of the splendid hopes which he set on the possession of the throne. . . .

Richard's character is here well analysed by a clear-sighted and unprejudiced critic. We deprecate the comparison with Macbeth; for Richard to some extent remains a stage puppet, whereas with Macbeth we hear the subterranean waters of the soul. Yet the present critic to some extent dignifies and also humanizes Richard by explaining that he was the kind of hypocrite who manipulates true feelings rather than assumes false ones, and that the abyss which received him at the end was sorrow for baffled kingship.

VI

BERNHARD TEN BRINK [1] sets out with the object of seeing the unity of Shakespeare and his works, though he admits that no genius can be explained. All we can hope to know is that the inner development, as seen in the works, harmonizes with the historical man. Shakespeare was the finest organized and healthiest of men, with the highest material, spiritual, ethical, and aesthetic susceptibilities, and the widest and deepest sympathies for man. His simple country upbringing prevented premature development, and laid the foundation of his extensive knowledge of nature. It also made him many-sided by bringing him into contact with various forms of human activity. Warwickshire held fast to the paganism and traditions of Merry England. To Shakespeare's happy boyhood succeeded the crisis in his father's affairs and his own unfortunate marriage. We may conjecture that he sought relief in the company of wild fellows, and in a short interval passed through the whole compass of moods and feelings—from the ecstasy of passion to the chilling grief of blank disappointment. From his struggle in London he emerged not unscathed, but with a matured and strengthened spirit. The era was a great one, when England, become conscious of her mission in Europe, was developing her national spirit, and also her poetry and science. Shakespeare's interest in history and politics was awakened, and he now filled the gaps in his literary education. [2]

His spiritual life shows in his works, and we see the problems that occupied him at different periods. German critics have exaggerated his objectivity: the greater the poet the more earnestly does he regard his

[1] *Five Lectures on Sh.*, 1893 (trans. Julia Franklin. London, G. Bell, 1895). Ten Brink was Dutch, but he is included among Germans, as most of his work was done at Marburg and Strassburg.   [2] Cf. Baynes.

work, the more clearly does he reveal himself in his productions, and the more perfectly does he stamp them with his individuality. Falstaff and Thersites cannot have been conceived at the same time and born under the same auspices. Objectivity is inner wealth and complete abandonment to every effort. His youthful productions are distinguished by richness and beauty rather than spiritual significance. Thence he rises to the crowning-point of his power where form and matter are perfectly balanced. Spiritual substance grows mightier and finally threatens form: Shakespeare grapples with the heart of things, and his thoughts outrun the stage.

His first epoch was 1586 or 1587 to 1593. No doubt he wrote *Titus* influenced by outer rather than inner impulse. Tragedy seems to him uncongenial, and to demand peculiar characters and abnormal conditions. The early comedies give his true spontaneous self, his hopeful view of life with serious background. *Errors* shows interest in action, while a youthful, joyous love of life forms the key-note of *L.L.L.*, upborne by lofty sentiments and a striving for the beautiful. *Verona* treats a deeper moral problem, but there is disproportion between plot and denouement. Referring to the Sonnets we see that he could be as unselfish, as passionately devoted in friendship, as Valentine. It shows his feelings when his character was unformed, and his great heart overflowed with feelings of romantic, self-sacrificing devotion. *R. and J.* is the tragedy of youth, of love that comes into a world filled with hate. It inspires and perfects two noble young beings, but also leads them to tragic doom. Even the monstrous Richard III we are made to understand on the common ground of humanity. He was not at home in the subject of his poems: *Venus* shows glowing sensuality.

The second epoch extends to the beginning of the seventeenth century. He only elaborated the *Shrew* and *John*, but they show his delight in moral worth in uncouth forms. The *Merchant* is more refined, but we discern the same contrast of worth with show; and this persists in the stupendous series of historical dramas, unrivalled for their characters and political wisdom. Henry V is the ideal of sturdy manhood on the throne—type of God-fearing, heroic, German king of the people. A man's worth, and his practical ideals? These are the questions Shakespeare asked and answered in his own way. From history he turned to the Arcadian world of his comedy, where he now did his finest work.

The third epoch (1601) shows a glaring contrast. The fate of Essex and imprisonment of Southampton made Shakespeare ponder on the affairs of State. He interrogated the ancient world and produced the intermediate Roman plays. *Hamlet* is unrivalled in truth to nature and wealth of psychological delineation. The dramatic effect of *Othello* is stronger; *Macbeth* reveals the strange workings of a human soul; but *Lear* is the summit of Shakespeare's tragic powers. *M. for M.*

had previously by its sombre tone and weighty problem trespassed from comedy into tragedy. *A. and C.* for the first time since *R. and J.* shows a woman on an equal footing with the hero. A courtesan of genius, she attains some womanly dignity through her love of Antony. Shakespeare must indeed have passed through bitter experience to create a woman who differed so widely from his preceding heroines—a woman devoid of womanly graces, yet irresistible. A yet bitterer mood appears in the stinging satire of *T. and C.*, than which no other play leaves so unpleasing an impression. The mood culminates in *Timon*, but during 1608 there was reaction. The birth of his granddaughter was an era in Shakespeare's inner life. He contributed the story of Marina to *Pericles*; and the last three plays written in retirement breathe the fresh scent of wood and meadows, and reflect the cheerful calm of country life. There is less height of passion, but psychological truth, poetical creative power, and profound thought. Substance threatens form, and verse is at its freest. The animating spirit is the wisdom which finds joy in living, and accepts all with cheerful resignation, with faith in the higher guiding powers and all-forgiving love.

Shakespeare was fortunate in having the dramatic form, through which alone he could express himself perfectly. Even the Sonnets recall the dramatic poet—and the poems, where it appears as a weakness.[1] His abundant and intense conceptions here lack his usual means to express them. On the stage the effect brings out the meaning of a cause, a man's character appears by its impression on others, the nature of a speech by its answer. In poetry the words alone must produce the effect upon the senses. Shakespeare, in his poems, tries to express all, and overwhelms with irrelevant detail that excludes comprehensive view of the whole. He also tries, in true dramatic manner, to give symbolic meaning to every part of the action: every lock that Tarquin forces cries out indignantly. To the question why Shakespeare was gifted only for drama we reply that the epic poet is an optimist whose guiding impulse is to admire great heroic figures, mighty deeds, and strange destinies. The work of the dramatist is ideal, but in a state of conflict. His heroes are dramatically effective through the qualities that make them men more than heroes. The essential thing is conflict, and it is most impressive when the hero is vanquished. We must therefore know the causes of conflict, and see that the struggle is inevitable. We must feel that the hero in a given situation, to be true to his nature, could only have acted as he did: for not otherwise shall we see ourselves pictured in him. Epic poetry is that of youth, drama of manhood. The latter flourishes among men who see life as it is—a struggle. Shakespeare's youth was passed in happy communion with nature. Perfect content needs no artistic utterance; great inner wealth is self-sufficient. When he reached manhood a tremendous conflict

[1] Cf. Hazlitt.

rent his soul. The greatest poets take the least trouble to invent new
plots. It sounds simpler that a dramatist should invent his own plot by
taking an idea and bodying it forth. But a play so constructed is
artificial, and leaves the anti-poetic impression of being forced. The
action seems to exist to prove an abstract proposition. The normal
course—which was Shakespeare's—is to respond to the stirring effect
of a story upon his creative vein. The question is what a poet makes of
the thing which he appropriates. Shakespeare treated his sources with
freedom, but he condenses dramatic action, and by accentuating cause
and effect gives to a play the stamp of necessity. We see from *A.Y.L.*
how he seizes the gist of a plot and develops the whole from that point,
so that all seems to follow inevitably like nature's laws; but this
merely proves that he excels in the dramatic conception of given
material. The important thing is the dramatic idea, viz. the poet's
point of view. It must have a unifying effect, yet we often feel resulting
unity of action without recognizing it. *R. and J.* shows how he has
created an imperishable work of art from an ephemeral poem. Besides
arousing pity for the lovers, he lifts us to a point whence we feel a
reconciling element even in this cruel fate. Obeying his dramatic
instinct, he concentrates the action into a few days, instead of the three
months of the poem which would dispel the bloom and sink the pathos.
The Fates do not will these two to be united; they may enjoy their
love but for a few short hours, when their fate is already sealed. They
have no feeling of undisturbed possession, and upon brief joy follows
eternal parting. This is poetry and tragedy, since so much depends on
concentrated action. Shakespeare's greatness lies in uniting the conception of his characters indissolubly with the conception of his dramatic action. A thousand artifices convince us the play can have no happy
ending; and above all is the family feud.

Shakespeare possessed even more than Molière the qualities of a
comic poet. He had an unrivalled conception of the ludicrous, as we
see from the wealth of his comic figures; and he excelled Molière in
wit and in deep and cheerful humour. Where Molière excels is in
firm handling of the dramatic action, and in unity of structure of the
comic drama: though Shakespeare displays this in his tragedies.
Perhaps the centre of interest of Shakespeare's comedies is not comic
action, but romantic colouring; so that if he ranks second to Molière
as comic poet it is from too great inner wealth. He gives rein to fancy,
while Molière works with his understanding. Comedy is most effective
when the evil which it brings before us is happily overcome in an easy
natural way. The greatest comedy ever wrought is Dante's *Divine
Comedy*. Dante learns to regard divine justice, which at first seems
to him as the vengeance of the Almighty, as a manifestation of the
All-wise intent to better mankind—until finally he recognizes infinite love as its real essence—the love which moves sun and stars.

This apprehension of comedy is closely related to that of Shakespeare, who saw in the world a mixture of good and evil. Thus he interweaves comic figures and motives into his tragic action, with resulting complexity of characters. They are not types as on the ancient or classic French stage, and more individual than Molière's characters. If there is realism there is also ideality and optimism. Shakespeare believes the beautiful and the good to be realized in the souls of men [1]—and in the value of this world and this life. Optimism is present in the tragedies and histories, but, above all, in the comedies. In the *Errors* beyond the mysterious play of chance we see the ruling of a higher power. At the close of his career Shakespeare returns to the fairy tale: while most poets use comedy to mirror actual life. Chance does more than in tragedy, in a world which lets us feel the workings of a benign Providence more clearly than in the real world. Poetic justice is sometimes violated in the earliest and latest dramas, e.g. the *Merchant*. Shakespeare makes us understand Shylock by revealing his inmost being—above all, by placing him in an historical light. Poetic justice requires that his bloody intentions should be frustrated, but not that he should be forcibly converted. He has come too close to us; we have learned to know too intimately the grounds of his hatred. The decision effected by a lucky accident is out of harmony with his grand passion. We crave to feel that his fate is a necessity and his ruin inevitable—and here is the discordance. The suit about the pound of flesh embraces a profound thought—*Summum jus, summa injuria*—and the decision is poetically just in the abstract. Comedy often required abstraction to produce unalloyed enjoyment: plans that have aroused our interest can only succeed at the expense of others. But Shakespeare is incapable of abstraction, because he draws characters with equal sympathy and objectivity. Thus there is often something unsatisfying in the denouement of his comedies, which only his humour makes endurable—humour which presupposes spiritual emancipation from self.

As tragedian it is impossible to compare Shakespeare with modern poets. It is essential to perceive a connexion between the hero's sorrow and his actions, and the greater moral delinquency the harder it is to produce tragic effects—as compassion yields to the feeling of just punishment. It is Shakespeare's incomparable power that he brings his hero humanly near by transforming his crime to innocence. The aim of art is neither practical nor moral, but to heighten and strengthen our sense of life. The loftiest human standpoint is to comprehend all and forgive all—to pity, not condemn, Othello or Macbeth. The tragic stage is no court of justice, and Shakespeare's motive is to hold the mirror up to nature. He conceived tragic suffering as no accident, but the effect of the sufferer's deeds. The tragic catastrophe presupposed that the preceding conflict with the powers and laws of the world

[1] Cf. Lascelles Abercrombie.

was inevitable; and there was necessary connexion between the hero's actions and his inmost nature. In tragedy Shakespeare availed himself of contemporary ideal conditions of time and space to follow his inner psychological bent that enabled him to trace a passion through all its stages and unfold an entire character. Thus he could lay chief weight on the connexion between his tragic hero's character and acts. The events and characters of *R. and J.* play an equal part. Self-denial makes Brutus adopt a fatal decision and commit a useless crime. In *Hamlet*, for unknown reasons, Shakespeare descended deeper than he had ever done before into the abysses of his own soul. Hamlet's character and Shakespeare's real intention remain a mystery. We never see Hamlet truly confront his task. Shakespeare expresses clearly enough what he considers of moment—and what he leaves unexpressed he cannot deem essential. The remaining three great tragedies may be as profound and dramatic, but have not the detailed psychological delineation which compels us to descend into the depths of our own hearts. Othello's character is the central point of the conflict. He is jealous because he is open and high-minded; and because jealousy is against his nature it destroys him. The hardest problem was to make Macbeth a tragic hero: and Shakespeare solves it by simplifying it. He suppresses all that could palliate the murder, brings out all the good in Duncan, and makes Macbeth his own accuser. We see him filled with agony and dread, as he clutches the dagger, and we realize that he is not a cold-blooded murderer, but the victim of an overpowering passion. *Lear* is Shakespeare's mightiest work, and shows his greatest power in construction and condensation. Nowhere else is the great world-mystery presented in such lofty symbols with such remorseless truth. We see the hand of Nemesis, but there is also revealed the rule of a benign Providence in the fortunes of Lear and the lot of Cordelia. Shakespeare believes in a divine government of the world, but he worships in humility the mystery in which it enshrouds itself. He paints the world as he sees it, and it appears dark to him—but it is at night that the stars shine out. Lear in his misery first experiences what love means. We feel that the Good is the most real thing, regardless of outer success. Shakespeare loves life, yet feels that it is not the highest good—that the best thing on earth is self-sacrificing love. . . .

Ten Brink has a few pregnant sayings, but he so recalls Dowden that it profits more to notice a few details than the work as a whole. He practically follows Dowden's four periods; he styles Henry V Shakespeare's ideal of sturdy manhood on the throne; finds in *Timon* the culmination of the tragic period; and sees in the birth of Shakespeare's granddaughter the beginning of a new era. His conception of Shakespeare's philosophy and religion is nearly Dowden's, although in religion his scale inclines to the positive and Dowden's to the agnostic.

But he lacks Dowden's poetic touch, and indeed his pages are true to their lecture-type. He is the professor addressing his pupils and giving them the best general facts that can be collected on the subject. Thus we feel no great force of personal conviction behind his saying that nowhere else than in *Lear* is the great world-mystery presented in such lofty symbols, &c.

We shall do better to examine certain details which bear the stamp of first-hand experience. Although modern thought balances stage needs against the 'four periods', it is well to be told that Falstaff and Thersites were born under different auspices. At his contrast of the drama and epic we remember our impressions from Delius's analysis of the narrative element: that waft of reality from the dramatic scene that made even Hamlet's visit to Ophelia seem once removed. On the subject of plots he makes the good point that Shakespeare condenses and concentrates—and this helps us to understand the gulf between' Shakespeare's treatment of *R. and J.* and that of Brooke. It is generally conceded that Molière was a greater comedian than Shakespeare, because in comedy the plot must be resolved by the individual characters of the persons concerned: and ten Brink himself admits that with Shakespeare the centre of interest is not comic action, but romantic colouring. The comparison with Dante sounds impressive, but does not satisfy. Carlyle said that Shakespeare gives the outer life of Europe, the practice or body, where Dante gives the faith or soul. This is specially true of the comedies, where earthly life suffices with its rewards of love and friends. We do not think the problem of Shylock has been better stated; and the criticism is of that fascinating kind which shows how a writer's faults grow from his virtues. Because Shakespeare was incapable of abstractions, and therefore the most concrete of all poets, Shylock is real; and because he is real he is part of the universe, and therefore a fact—and all facts are sacred, to return to Carlyle. The most striking remarks about the great tragedies are, that we never see Hamlet truly confront his task—that Othello is destroyed by the passion that is unnatural to him—that Macbeth wins our sympathy by appearing as his own accuser—that Lear would not have known true love but for his extreme misery. In all these we see a soul alone in the universe; and that of the critic is undergoing a like experience, if once removed: but he has at least felt the stirring of the poet's wing.

VII

HEINRICH BULTHAUPT [1] compares Shakespeare and Schiller, and imagines Schiller saying, 'You see my hero could hardly do otherwise'; while Shakespeare says, 'You see my heroes could well have acted otherwise'. Shakespeare is the poet of spontaneous elemen-

[1] *Dramaturgie des Schauspiels*, vol. ii, 1894.

tary nature, and the profound tragedy of his characters lies in the
fact that most of them, though inwardly compelled, are conscious of
guilt and sin—a bitter contradiction of being which no other poet so
reveals. Not fate but their own wills lead them on, and they follow
their immanent godhead. Only from this point of view can we understand the moral monsters which he leaves without judging. Nature to
him is sacred, and his tragedies are terribly grave from this unveiling of
free self-determination. Only his humour lightens the darkness—
whereas Schiller and Goethe do not need to save themselves by humour.
Shakespeare's Clowns and Fools and comic characters have every
shade of humour, and face the turmoil and inconsistencies of life with
comic resignation.

His heroes are moral warnings, and develop along necessary lines of
nature, so that in their beginning we see the foreboding of their end.
At times in their lack of reflection, even blindness, they remind one of
senseless, inanimate elements, e.g. Lear, Othello, Richard III. There
is something elementary, unalterable, even mechanical, in them,
deprived of self-determination—an irresistible subjective necessity.
Love-sick Romeo is an elementary being in the ultimate sense; and
the purest women of the plays are less moral creatures than creatures of
nature and sense. From the heroes of Goethe and Schiller we get a
higher impression of self-determination—the best means of directing
practical life. German poets deal with pliable material, Shakespeare's
heroes are of brass. Such characters as Margaret, Richard III, Lear,
Goneril, Othello are starkly set before us, and remain consistent to
their natures which lead most of them to physical or mental distraction.
Macbeth is the only instance of transition from one determination to
another, but even here the pre-existing germ overrules the thought of
real conversion.

Othello is a wonderful work built on a weak foundation. Iago would
have failed had the other characters possessed a grain of his common
sense. Othello, who lets passion possess his understanding, is equally
responsible for the crime. Shakespeare seems to wish to show how the
terrible develops from stupidity and chance (the handkerchief), and to
crown his bold, constructive carelessness by leaving the chief factor,
Iago, without a motive. In drama we are concerned with objective,
not subjective, motive. Iago is a motiveless monstrosity, and as it is
he who produces the catastrophe, it loses necessity and artistic nobility.
Iago intermittently suspects Othello, and acts as if his suspicions were
true. Such fitful jealousy ceases to be a motive, especially when the
person who feels it is in doubt. In the original, Iago is really jealous,
and anxious to win Desdemona's favour. It was natural that Othello,
after all his glorious hopes, should feel return of chaos. But for these
hopes he would have continued on his quiet way: once they had risen
he could not do without them, and his fall was certain. To this end,

which his nature makes inevitable, a sure and marvellous art leads him
through every gradation. The seething and boiling of his savage
African blood makes him deaf to the simplest prudence. According
to his character, the scene where he overhears the colloquy between
Iago and Cassio is improbable; but otherwise we can enjoy the beauty
amid the wildest ravings. Shakespeare is never coarse and naturalistic,
but, as a true artist, discovers melody and eloquence in the stammerings
of jealousy and outpourings of suffering.

Desdemona is less simple than Othello, but though she is not to be
blamed for deceiving her father (after the manner of lovers)—that she
has no comforting word for him—argues a sensuous rather than a moral
nature. She is so possessed with the elementary power of love that all
other values disappear—and she just acts naturally. We must look on
her, Romeo, and Juliet as 'beyond good and evil'. If less blinded by
passion she would have been silent about Cassio. Her conversation
with Emilia shows her to be essentially modest and humble; there is
nothing of 'tragic guilt'; and if she faulted for the sake of love, her
punishment is greater than she deserves. There is also defect of causal
nexus, since villainous knavery and combined accidents effect her ruin.
Cordelia does not shrink from conflict with life, and is closer related to
the dark powers of fate than the delicate and sensuous Desdemona,
who is made for the joy of life. It is an untenable theory that her sin
and punishment are in proportion. But she is ennobled by her undeserved suffering; her beauty, like that of a saint, is transfigured by
her tears and death; and we forget any error that she has committed.
Nothing is more beautiful than her last words which reveal her
unconquerable love—a true Shakespearian touch.

M. Ado would be the finest of all plays that take place purely on
earth, had not Benedict and Beatrice been overshadowed by the events
of the secondary action. Shakespeare never so completely spoilt the
lively impression of a comedy as he did here in blending a sad with a
cheerful plot. Supposing Claudio had listened to scandal against his
love, he would hardly slander her in public. True love becomes a prey
to grief, not revenge, and even the gentle Hero would not have forgiven
such shameless treatment. Yet she and her old father actually drag the
whole affair once more into public light. The foolish Claudio is persuaded to marry Leonato's niece—and thus beginning and end are
flippant. All else is delicate and delightful, and the play is certain of
immortality through Benedict and Beatrice. Shakespeare never so
excelled in repartee; the dialogue never halts; and the seriousness of
the glib-tongued lovers after the church scene helps to reconcile us to
this scene: although our first impressions are true, and no critic dares
to defend the outrage at the altar. That Claudio is young, impetuous,
and a spoilt favourite of fortune may explain his credulity, but not his
malicious revenge. When he jeers heartlessly at Benedict and his

challenge, he shows a character utterly degraded and morally impossible, that drags down to aesthetic ruin Hero, Leonato, Antonio, and even Benedict and Beatrice. He is an aesthetic and psychological abortion—and such would be the girl who accepts such a husband, the father who consents and connives, and those who remain his friends.

Some maintain that all is modified by the frank gaiety and easy tone of life throughout. But it is no virtue to fuddle our judgement, and Beatrice herself well defines Claudio's conduct. Benedict and Beatrice are bound to quarrel, but made for each other. Until the church scene they have only amused us, but now we take them to our hearts. It is true genius to show them never false to their natures. The moral essence of their natures is the salt that preserves them from the insipidity arising out of the honeyed life led by the others. . . .

The gist of Bulthaupt's criticism is that the reactions of Shakespeare's characters in the moral world are out of proportion to the earthly stimulus. The problem which occupies him has been solved in our time by Professor Bradley's remark that excessive vitality is the grand characteristic of Shakespeare's heroes. Granted that he is right—that the links of cause and effect are weak in *Othello*—does this make the play less to be admired? No, for we open Shakespeare's pages to see a soul in eruption, and the glow upon the sky absorbs our attention, not the domestic affairs of the villages which the lava overwhelms. The censure of Claudio is also true—if we judge Shakespeare's work as a comedy of manners instead of romantic comedy. But again we return a negative answer to the question whether the play ceases to please in consequence. The wit of Benedict and Beatrice, the speeches of the Friar, Leonato, even the wretched Claudio, in the church scene produce so bright a daylight in the reader's soul, that he will not be perturbed by details, but will accept the clumsiest makeshifts, even down to violent dislocations of character. Bulthaupt, therefore, is one of those critics who seems to regret that he is forced to admire.

VIII

WITH Ernest Traumann we return to Hamlet.[1] Unlike Faust, he has no consuming desire for knowledge, but is defrauded of his innermost earthly happiness and falls back on himself, defying fate, and willing to succumb rather than sacrifice to gods and men his most intimate self and nobility of spirit. In the fullest sense it is a tragedy of fate, and there is no question of unavoidable obligation imposed by divine or human decrees, as in ancient tragedy. Brutus, Othello, Macbeth, Lear acknowledge certain restrictions from their characters of statesman, husband, vassal, king: and they struggle—for the human in them has its unrestricted desires. But Hamlet's free humanity has

---

[1] 'Hamlet the Tragedy of the Human Soul' (*Jahrbuch*, 1894).

no such restrictions; it is fate that obtrudes upon him, and the struggle
with this importunity causes his tragic suffering.

Hamlet followed *J.C.*, and Brutus might be Hamlet's father, but
Shakespeare now wrote with developed perception. Tragic fate was
no longer in the outer world but in a man's own breast. To feudal
heroes succeeded the modern man with his cleft heart—and conscience
was the judging and avenging power of the world. It appears in
Henry IV; it is the Nemesis at the close of *Richard III*; it distracts Brutus
throughout, but is finally conciliated. In *Hamlet* it is the jealous god,
and the salient principle of the tragic plot. With Brutus the struggle
is between duty and duty; it is a question of the higher duty, to friend
or country: and he decides without a great struggle and dies nobly.
He knows little of men, and errs only in deed—while Hamlet loses
himself and is forced to become guilty. The blows fall on his whole
existence, and he rebels against nature and the eternal powers. What
was a passing crisis with Brutus becomes his permanent state. The
world and its values have no further place for him—and the question
is between the world and himself. The tragedy of public life falls into
the background of his profound emotions; the affairs of government
and social affairs serve but as a foil; and the poet with wonderful
inspiration connects his character directly with the world's hidden
forces, and compels the observer's gaze to his hero's inner nature.

The Ghost is the moving power of the whole—a figure of flesh and
blood, clad in armour, who endures purgatorial fire like a human
personality, who loves the Queen and hates his brother. He awakes
pity, not horror, in Hamlet; he is objectively real, no reflection of
Hamlet's melancholy. He calls upon Hamlet to do no more than his
duty; in short, the Ghost is his fate, and from now onward Hamlet is a
broken man. Only a word now and then from one of his loyal friends
reminds us of what he was and paints a noble picture. One of the
play's quietly effective secrets is the sense of abdication of the past.
And yet, although he had known filial and human love, these were so
soon quenched as to leave no doubt that the essential part of his nature
was mind.

It is not surprising that the supernatural should be introduced, and
Hamlet should deal with ghosts. Those who are not rightly balanced
with the active world, whose spirits have no goal, are exposed to a
terrible danger. Shakespeare surveys his character from a standpoint
beyond good and evil. His heroes are frequently undone by their
virtues—exaggerated good becomes evil, e.g. Othello's trusting nature.
He teaches that reason is given us to curb our passions: but so large and
elementary are the passions of his heroes that their guilt seems due to
unlucky stars. Hamlet, on the contrary, asks nothing of the world; he
cannot recognize the actual evil, though he unknowingly points to it
in his bitter truth: 'There's nothing good or bad but thinking makes

it so.' It originated the suffering of our race—and he stands like the
first man who has eaten of the tree of knowledge. A chasm divides him
from his age, country, and surroundings. Brutus enters a strange
world, but has strength to face it; Macbeth longs for a more primitive
age, yet he proceeds to his goal; but Hamlet is totally adrift.

He is the living conscience in a lying world—a world where murder
inevitably follows general degeneration. The King is an ordinary
criminal—bad conscience personified, flattering where he should
command, using all for his own purpose, even Ophelia's love. The
Queen is less bad than weak, the prey of the moment—unhappy link
between two opposing generations. Polonius has a commonplace mind,
and is the man of everlasting words—caricature of a dignified age.
Laertes is the slave of passion, exact opposite to Hamlet. Ophelia is a
creature of the elements, like Undine—without will. At her father's
bidding she relinquishes her lover: and this accorded with his recent
experience of women's faithlessness. He goes on his way and forgets
her, and when they meet in the corridor they stand, death at the heart
of each, like two indifferent onlookers. Only Hamlet's love for
Horatio endures to the end; yet even this does not influence his action.
He stands alone with fate and his own being—and the Ghost's exhortation seems to fall on barren ground. He draws near to madness; his
visit to Ophelia, his conduct after the play, his words to his mother
show his mind to be severed from his heart. To rouse himself he must
take out his tables; he needs the example of Fortinbras to stir him. He
stands like the disenthroned Lear, but what he seeks is his former
passion. He cannot find what he has lost, so he wraps himself in his one
remaining garment—his mind.

The two steps he takes to fulfil his task show the sad downfall of his
spirit—his 'antic disposition', and the device of the play. The way of
cunning is opposed to his upright nature; he loses sight of his goal, and
drifts rudderless down the stream of error. Comparison between his
arguments on suicide in his earlier and later monologue show the
disintegration of his mind: in place of the canon of the Almighty we
have sceptical arguments. The prayer scene is perversity itself: the
King feels that his prayers cannot reach heaven, while Hamlet refrains
through belief in the saving force of prayer. Yet lower must Hamlet
sink when he rages against his mother—contrary to his father's
bidding; and the climax is the murder of Polonius. Now he is conscious
of his fall; he has abandoned his hold on fate; and his better nature,
with his power of resistance, is no more. He passively submits himself
to the way of death, and is led on to villainy against Rosencrantz and
Guildenstern. All will is extinct in his tired soul.

His darker instincts, hitherto checked by a higher soul and brilliant
intellect, begin to stir more and more. The 'dangerous' in his temperament awakes, and his noble nature turns to its reverse. The frank-

souled, conscientious man delivers his school friends to death without a twinge of shame. His discourse in the churchyard is defiantly materialistic. There is no word of the soaring soul from him who had felt that his immortal soul could not do certain things. There is scorn of his own delayed mission in the mechanical enumeration of his uncle's sins to Horatio (v. ii). This is not the Hamlet of Ophelia's portrait, but 'the shadow of shadows'. He makes a poor exit in a laughable duel, and so ends a life of such high promise. The way to the goal was his to choose, and his better nature could have reached it; but since this was consumed, his lower instincts had to ransom the demands of fate. He lost his earthly life, but he saved his soul, which soars above his errors, above all that our senses see and apprehend. Alone of Shakespeare's heroes he fights for nothing tangible, but for his own spirit—so he suffers of life itself. Shakespeare does not therefore contrast an ideal figure with him, as Richmond to Richard III, and Malcolm to Macbeth, but the man of action Fortinbras. And yet it is Hamlet after all who delivers his country from the strangle-hold of custom. . . .

We have endured through these pages for the sake of a perverse kind of interest which they awaken. First of all we will collect a few remarks that loom through the haze: that the Ghost retained earthly passions and inspired pity, not horror; that the Queen links two opposing generations; that Hamlet's mind is his last shelter; that the prayer scene is perversity itself; that in the end Hamlet saves his soul. With the main argument, that Hamlet exchanges his better nature for his worse and so fulfils his task, it is impossible to sympathize. The interest of the play is not in external action or logical coherence, but in the hero's character and the vast realms of thought which his words open up. But the above isolated remarks serve a purpose of their own. As opposite characters attract each other to a certain point, so where these two opposite forces of logic and emotion collide, a fitful new light flickers for a moment over the familiar play. If a common emotion may be deduced from their several impressions, it is that the rotten state of Denmark comes home more forcibly.

IX

WE will begin with remarks about Shakespeare himself. Wendlandt pronounces his heart to be greater than his all-embracing intellect. Gerstenberg calls him nature's pet genius, with every single faculty of the human spirit equally balanced and developed into a gigantic whole. Ten Brink says there has rarely been so healthy a man; he had the highest material, spiritual, ethical, and aesthetic susceptibilities, and universal sympathies. We may conclude with these the saying of Delius, that he attaches great importance to friendship.

The following are on the moral and philosophical side. Delius and

Wendlandt affirm in the same words that in later years he became most occupied with psychological problems. Gerstenberg and Wetz emphasize his knowledge of the passions, though the former adds that he had the higher aim to delineate morals. Wetz, Müller, and Traumann alike speak of the leading part played by conscience in his system. Bulthaupt finds that free will, not fate, inspires his characters. Ten Brink says that no one has so profoundly fathomed the human heart, and he is the greatest of tragic writers because of his spiritual depth and thorough reality. Also that he believes in the divine government of the world, is deeply religious, that the moral sense is the root of his religion, and for him infinite love pervades the universe.

On Shakespeare's art and character we have first the verdict of Delius that he is the surest guide and master in the field of dramatic art; and that he gives the very person heart and soul. Wendlandt calls him the perfect dramatic architect, and his the master-hand. Gerstenberg speaks of the triumph of his art; and he is Bulthaupt's perfect artist. Ten Brink discovers his unique stamp to be (thanks to the stage) a combination of deep and imperishable matter with the most intense immediate effect. He was a dramatist before all; he had matchless art in dealing with dramatic action; and though his plots are often loosely constructed, he excels in dramatic conception of given material, and the conception of his characters is indissolubly united with that of the dramatic action.

Gerstenberg says that his object was to represent sensuous nature, and that he had perception of the beauty of nature; ten Brink, that he had extensive knowledge of nature; Bulthaupt, that he was the poet of elementary nature. . . .

These critics are unanimous and orthodox. It may be noted that they are immersed in their subject rather than distinct from it. Except ten Brink, they incline to study Shakespeare as moral teacher rather than poet or dramatist.

Chapter XXVIII

ENGLAND 1895–1899

I. CORBIN. II. BOAS. III. CAIRD. IV. J. M. ROBERTSON. V. SIDNEY LEE.
VI. WYNDHAM. VII. BOWDEN. VIII. DOWDEN. IX. CONCLUSION.

I

JOHN CORBIN[1] is a critic whose method we should do well to bear in mind when considering purely aesthetic treatises. He brings before us the temper of an Elizabethan audience, and as the years go on we shall become more familiar with the historical-aesthetic school. The service he does here is to track to its source the divided impression left by Hamlet. Modern commentators have carried his work further.

He points out that Shakespeare was a popular playwright in an age when the drama was not over-reputable. Insanity amused an audience, and it was unlikely that Shakespeare wholly effaced the traditional comic treatment of Hamlet's madness. The story was derived from Saxo Grammaticus in the twelfth century and Belleforest in 1570. The date of the lost English play, probably by Kyd, was 1589—a tragedy of blood with a comic underplot. Hamlet's feigned madness seemed comic in certain of those scenes which affect us as deeply tragic in the modern play. This presumes in Elizabethan audiences an attitude towards acts of cruelty and insanity incredible to any one brought up amid the sensibility of modern life. Plays were rapidly written, a new one being required about every eighteen days, and Shakespeare's custom, in working over an old play, was first to revise it thoroughly, then, if it succeeded, rewrite and improve.[2] A dramatist is most at the mercy of the traditions and caprices of contemporaries, and he was no exception. In many plays, from haste or policy, he left whole episodes that savour of the cruder aspects of the Elizabethan drama. Hamlet was not the 'sweet' or 'gentle' youth of effusive commentators—note his indifference to Rosencrantz and Guildenstern. Shakespeare added dignity to him, and made his demonstrations of insanity mental. He had to invent expedients to hinder him from killing the king. Only in the final version he becomes highly self-conscious and intellectual. Despite modern excuses, his cruel cunning in sparing the king agrees with the Hamlet of the *Hystorie*, and with Kyd's Hieronimo in the *Spanish Tragedy*. There are two contradictory phases in his character—one is a remnant of the last play, the other a foreshadowing of his character to come. In the pre-Shakespearian story there was no real insanity, but, remodelled by Shakespeare, his mind becomes acute, sensitive, morbid under the strain.

[1] *The Elizabethan Hamlet*, 1895.　　　　　　[2] Cf. J. M. Robertson.

Shakespeare's happiest additions to the old tragedy of blood contradicted the drama's vital structure. Hamlet in action refers back to the lost play; the Shakespearian element is concerned with his reflective, imaginative, humane traits. His conduct to Ophelia is the result of Elizabethan attitude to suffering and insanity. To Shakespeare's audiences these scenes possessed the element of now-archaic comedy. *Lear* at once became popular through the king's sonorous rant, and the comic element of insanity. Compare our own attitude to the temporary insanity of drunkenness.

II

THE work of Mr. Boas[1] embraces the whole of Shakespeare. He begins with the characteristics inherited by the drama from the Mysteries and Moralities, passes on to the influence on Shakespeare of the early dramatists, of the Renaissance and the national spirit, and then proceeds to consider each play.

The English sacred drama rested on the same rock-bed of Anglo-Saxon righteousness that supports the solid fabric of Shakespearian ethics. The supernatural in Shakespeare survived from it, and the Vice in the Interludes was the forerunner of the Shakespearian Fool. English literature was always sensitive to foreign influences, especially Italian, and this was most marked in tragedy. *Gorboduc* consists of sententious monologues without character or action. England became the champion of Protestantism: the Armada quickened the national spirit; and the whole country was incarnate in Elizabeth. In Marlowe's *Faust* sin works out its own Nemesis, so the catastrophe is vitally related to conduct. Tragedy was developed by Kyd, comedy by Lyly and Greene. Kyd was the pioneer of introspective tragedy, but with a crude moral basis. Lyly introduced prose into the drama and influenced Shakespeare's colloquial prose, also lyrics, and imaginative comedy with supernatural framework. Greene depicted noble and chaste woman, and first vitally connected serious and comic, and his moral outlook was akin to Shakespeare's. Shakespeare was no pure product of the Renaissance; he inherited the English medieval spirit of which Warwickshire was most eloquent—such as class-differences, and sense of power attaching to land. But he did feel Renaissance ardours of passion and emotion—as witness his 'love without end' for Southampton. . . .

From the above we see the opinion of Mr. Boas, with which no one will care to disagree, that Shakespeare extracted all that was best from inherited influences and those about him, and from the works of his predecessors. He then turns to Shakespeare's work, and wholeheartedly accepts the four periods of Dowden and many others.

In his survey of the plays, though he most emphasizes Shakespeare's

[1] *Sh. and his Predecessors*, by F. S. Boas, 1896.

moral quality, it is the moral as enhanced by its artistic setting. He is at his best in discovering hidden links between plot and character or plot and underplot, and explaining their cause in the human heart. He considers that *Titus* is by Shakespeare because it has the stamp of unity, and Aaron, like Shakespeare's criminals, has acid humour, and adroitly turns to his own purposes the vicious desires of his fellow men. Richard III, in his sleep, utters an agonized cry of homage to the might of the moral law. A stroke of consummate art makes the scenes of farcical entanglement of the *Errors* the pivot on which turns a deeply tragic issue. Shakespeare adds twin servants to twin masters, because he saw that two improbabilities buttress each other. In the *M.N.D.* he shows extraordinary skill in devising variations on a given theme. The mistakes here are of the night, not the day, and internal to the mind, not external. The fairy world reproduces in miniature the structure of human society. The life of these tiny creatures, over whom morality has no sway, is a delicious sense-life. Bottom and the rude mechanicals, in their grotesque devices and makeshifts, really face the question of the relation of shadow to substance—the immemorial question of realism in art and on the stage. Launce and his dog (*Verona*), the fidelity of the simple servant to his poor cur, silently condemn the knavery of Proteus.

The political plot is not only the background to *R. and J.*, but an integral element of the play: the rivalry of the Houses gives tragic bias. The note of tragic predestination becomes vague presentiment with Romeo and Juliet, and moralizing with the Friar. We are not left in barren sorrow, because the atmosphere of the world is purified by the elemental force of love. The brilliant portraits of the *Merchant* minimize the inherent improbabilities of the story. A merchant is most exposed to risks, and Antonio, in his self-sufficiency, challenges fortune. Flesh, on his own showing, is the only legitimate bond of interest. The caskets show, as in *R. and J.*, that Shakespeare was more affected than is thought by the influence of fortune on human affairs. Antonio defies fortune and is punished; Portia submits and is rewarded. Shylock's claim is urged in the stubborn spirit of the narrowest Jewish legalism; Portia's saving plea is grounded on the equally slavish letter-worship of Roman law.

England is the omnipresent and immortal figure of the histories. The characters gain dramatic dignity from the width of the radius within which they operate rather than from their own force. Shakespeare surveys the energies for good or evil radiating from the throne to the extreme confines of national life. His fundamental conviction is that individual character reacts with potent effect on the life of the State. In *Henry IV* the personal interest overbears the political, and the King is not the dramatic centre. Diplomacy and determination cannot make him succeed in the highest sense, as man or king, or yield him inward peace. Prince John's likeness to the King throws into relief the grander outlines of the latter. Northumberland is an even more effective foil, as with him caution and policy degenerate into selfish cowardice. In the career of Henry IV Shakespeare proves that material success, exclusively pursued, turns to bitterness even with those most fit to achieve it. The Prince does not like the King's subtle policy, and is driven to streets and taverns to see life without veneer. Falstaff's existence is based on denial of the moral law, and his corpulence is partly responsible. One so physically clogged in the struggle for the ideal may well refuse even to enter the arena. His vulnerable spot is affection for Hal, and through this he is mortally pierced.[1] In *Henry V* Shakespeare most stresses his cardinal conception of a king—duty above privilege. Besides simplicity and sincerity Henry has grandeur and glow of soul as king, warrior, judge; but these fail him as lover. Falstaff of the *Wives* has no fascination, but he just resembles his former self in the courtier's contempt for the citizen. The Pages are equally ready to victimize their daughter selfishly.

M. Ado gives the most subtle varieties on a single idea. Perhaps Don John lacks humour because in this most radiant comedy Shakespeare did not wish to make a villain fascinating and focus attention on him. It has been condemned as improbable that the lover and his patron should be convinced of a heinous crime on slender evidence; but this strictly accords with the genius of the play where momentous inferences built on overheard scraps of dialogue result in much ado. Toby (*Twelfth-Night*) has gulled others all his life, and now exposes himself to the permanent derision of a misalliance.[2] That Orlando (*A.Y.L.*) does not recognize Rosalind must be ascribed partly to the peculiar influence of the locality. He plays rather a passive part in speech with her, but gains in sunny charm of character and seems a pervasive presence in this golden Arcadia. In *All's Well* an abnormal relation is elevated to an almost tragic sphere, that it may not become repulsive. The healing of the king's body foreshadows that of Bertram's soul. The most repulsive details all have their place in the general scheme of *M. for M.*, which is indisputably noble. Angelo's nature is just kin enough to Isabella's to feel the full seductive charm of her immaculate purity. His brutal outbreak of cruelty is of that kind which, in Shakespeare's eyes, is the reverse side of lust. Both Helen and Cressida are heartless and disloyal, yet they wake devotion. In both camps sentimental gallantry is the ruling motive, with disastrous results to true national interests.

Nowhere has Shakespeare so departed from his sources as in *Hamlet*. He gives the impression of choosing the theme as a vehicle for his own thoughts. The soliloquies are often not closely related to events. The Queen's nature is unstable and volatile, whence Hamlet has inherited

---

[1] Cf. Marriot and Rötscher.   [2] Cf. Stopford Brooke (1913), also Priestley.

his vacillating will. As to Rosencrantz and Guildenstern, each seeks to compensate for entire lack of individuality by alliance with the other. In posing as a madman Hamlet catches something of the imperfect age—its preference for roundabout, disingenuous dealings. In the end he yields to fatalism, and thus becomes indifferent to the deaths of Rosencrantz and Guildenstern and Polonius. Paralysis of will produces paralysis of moral sense. In *Macbeth* Shakespeare adds to Highland mysticism a stupendous moral significance unknown to the Celt. Macbeth lives in an imaginative world, and the wild poetry of barbarism steeps even his crimes in crimson splendour. The stern Shakespearian ethics demand a double retribution on the sinner, at the bar of the world, and in his own breast. Neither Macbeth nor Lady Macbeth had conscience, and the dramatic crux was to exhibit the action of Nemesis in such characters. He becomes the victim of self-torturing imagination, she of her acutely nervous sensibilities. Thus we realize that nature has reserve forces to punish sin. *Othello* brings into collision strongly contrasted racial types. To Desdemona he is like a being dropped from another world. She accepts his exotic birth and hue as elements in the unique marvel of his whole career. Their love is based on mutual fascination rather than knowledge. It is Iago's triumph of malignity to induce Desdemona to plead for Cassio, and discover a suicidal property in virtue itself. Had Othello's love been grounded in experience it would have been proof, but it is fed from imagination, and into imagination Iago pours his poison. Desdemona has isolated herself from her family; and the African gives no heed to the laws of a community in which he is an alien. All in *Lear* seems the wildest confusion, yet a plot of labyrinthine intricacy is steadily un-ravelled, and the majesty of the moral law is the unseen arbiter. It is not Shakespeare's greatest play, but the most stupendous expression of his genius. It deals with the uncontrollable passion of the Celtic nature, which links it not with the spirit world, but with the untamed forces of purely animal or natural life. Lear is driven mad by an incident which links the two plots. In the kingdom of the spirit nothing matters but 'the good will'. Cordelia's ardour of love is justified of itself. It exists, and in its existence lies its triumph.

In *J.C.* we see a populace weary of liberty that means nothing, and in need of an idol. Caesarism survives Caesar's death; his infirmities in the flesh are a foil to his irresistible might when freed from fleshly trammels. If no one event stands out in *A. and C.* as pivot of the catastrophe, it is because Shakespeare interweaves the love interest with the political. Cleopatra's complexity, like Falstaff's, reconciles con-tradictory qualities. She has paradoxical grandeur compounded of all that is morally worthless. It is not love, because their souls have never mingled. The foundation of their bliss is unstable: he fears treachery, she desertion. In the galley scene we see in miniature Paganism

dancing with uproarious merriment to its destruction. Amorous
rivalry persists beyond death, since the Queen competes for her lover's
embrace with her own waiting woman. Thus the passion of Antony
and Cleopatra carries at its heart the secret of eternal unrest.

The *W. Tale* is made up of three dissimilar plots united by a merely
mechanical bond. Perdita belongs alike to the real and idyllic worlds.
In Prospero we see Shakespeare's conception of a divine being's attitude
to the mortals under his sway. Ferdinand has to give more solid proof
of his loyalty than amorous vows and sighs. . . .

Mr. Boas has the power to experience rightly and express impartially,
but there are degrees in his verdicts. He is at his best in *Macbeth*,
Othello, *A. and C.*, at his worst in his remarks on Sir Toby and his
comparison of the healing of the King's body and Bertram's soul in
All's Well. And the cause is the extent to which the presence of
Shakespeare abides with him during his critical meditation. In the
tragedies just mentioned he writes under the spell of the emotion which
quickens his imagination; in the comedies, the emotion has left him
and he is merely seeking intellectual reasons. Yet some of his argued
criticisms are well worth pondering, e.g. he says that Richard III's
success as a wooer deprives him of justification for evil and shows that
nature has not penalized him. He also defends Bertram well by
observing that he is made to take a woman separated by caste, robbed
by familiarity of the magical charm of the unknown, and whose claim
to his hand violates the elementary relations of man and woman. And
the nature of Cassius has rarely been better analysed: personal jealousy
mingled with sincere republican passion which gives dignity to a
character lacking in moral elevation. One of his merits is to reconcile
poetry and fact, e.g. Othello's effect on Desdemona. He also delimits
emotion exactly—in the style of Mézières or Professor Herford. Thus
he tells us that the wild poetry of barbarism steeps Macbeth's crimes in
crimson splendour—that the love of Othello and Desdemona is based
on mutual fascination rather than knowledge—that the souls of
Antony and Cleopatra have never mingled, and their passion carries
at its heart the secret of eternal unrest.

III

EDWARD CAIRD[1] states in an original way some leading problems
of Shakespeare's personality, his art, and his times. His powerful and
philosophic mind retains a true impress from the whole of Shakespeare's
work, and all that is known of his life, and he uses this as a touchstone.
Shakespeare to him is a man of universal sympathies, and he is aware
that there are inseparable weaknesses from such a state of mind. He
thinks to detect certain regions of thought and feeling closed to Shakespeare—his aristocratic political feeling—his lack of insight into the

[1] 'Some Characteristics of Sh.' (*Contemporary Review*, Dec. 1896).

secrets of religious life—but dramatic reasons may explain these. In the fifteenth and sixteenth centuries it was less that the individual was set free than that his weal was bound up with certain great general interests. Religious reformers taught the duty, not the right, of private judgement. In politics it was national State against universal Church; feudalism gave way to the rule of powerful monarchs; the king embodied the general will. Thus Shakespeare was a patriot and con-temner of democracy.

He then extracts from Shakespeare's unlimited nature reasons why he surpassed the dramatists of the world. He could rise above all special interests of individuals to a central point of view, and so realize how in the drama of life individualities react upon each other and produce a crisis. He may have lacked strong will and firm self-defen-sive individuality and perhaps had to learn self-command by sore experience, but his deep and rich nature would help him to regain peace of mind, because it sympathized with all the elements and movements of humanity, and could not be tied to any one passion or interest, but would ultimately see the relative insignificance of personal desires.

He then proceeds to trace the clear logic of Shakespeare's dramatic thought almost beyond the limits of poetry, in a manner slightly too abstract, but none the less profoundly suggestive. The characters become conscious of themselves and almost read to us the secret of their own weakness and moral of their own fate. It is the ultimate secret of great dramatic work, and the reason why the catastrophe produces not horror and dismay but reconcilement. In the tragic crisis the movement of life had brought about a full statement of its problem; and fully to state the problem of life is almost to solve it. Passions are purified because worked out to the last issues; even good-ness must complete itself in sacrifice, and so reveal what it really is.

IV

MR. J. M. ROBERTSON[1] now enters the field where he has done and is still doing great things. He has been called Cato the Censor in the rather lax republic of Shakespearian criticism,[2] and such a title does not underrate him. This is not to imply that his intellectual power overrules his aesthetic; both are strong, and each ministers to the other. We heartily disclaim the German tendency to make criticism into an exact science; but there is a reverse danger when an unchecked fancy causes softening of the intellect. The ideal is to steer a middle course, and there are few critics who can distinguish between facts and fancies as skilfully as Mr. Robertson.

He condemns the work of Feis on the same subject as extravagant, though he agrees that Montaigne influenced Shakespeare. This influence first appears in *Hamlet* and continues beyond. The note of

[1] *Montaigne and Sh.*, 1897.   [2] *Times Lit. Sup.*, 7 April 1927.

passionate friendship between Hamlet and Horatio, absent from the First Quarto, appears in the later. There are suggestions of Montaigne in the soliloquies and the thoughts on suicide; the Duke's exhortation to Claudio in *M. for M.* is a synthesis of Montaigne's favourite propositions. In Mr. Robertson's opinion the deeper problem of Shakespeare's mental history has hardly risen till our own generation. The traces that appear of Seneca are but Seneca's stock speeches,[1] and he practically only read his own language. We should revise our conception of Shakespeare in the light of the positive facts of his life. Critics do not seem to bring those facts into touch with their aesthetic estimate of his product. Emerson resigned himself to the solution that Shakespeare's mind was out of human ken.

The poems are uninspired, pitilessly prolix, external, and unimpassioned. Their merits—inexhaustible flow of words and endless observation of detail—are not those of a superior mind. The theatre, not his plays, provided his income; thus at the outset he was not conspicuous for intellectual depth or seriousness. There needed to develop him experience and intellectual stimulus. Added to the discipline of acting was the probably real central episode of faithless love in the Sonnets. In appreciation of women's charm we see his first contact with the deeper forces of life. He is still unconcerned with the deeps of male nature, except in Shylock. His early historical figures are distinguished for visible actuality. Falstaff is an incomparable comic reality, but only comic. No doubt the originals of his heroines were women who had charmed him. *R. and J.* is a picture of the luxury of woe, not fundamentally unhappy. *J.C.* touches a further depth of sadness, and shows failure dogging the steps of the wise, destiny searching out the weakness of the strong. Culture and experience have made the man Shakespeare into the dramatist: culture that came without search and could be undergone as spontaneously as the experience of life itself. Montaigne's book was the most living in Europe; he was the first of the moderns, having discovered that the most interesting form of truth is the most intimate. The secret of all great literature is that a writer may affect us more by pulse and pressure of speech than matter.[2]

The Essays were the source of the greatest expansive movement of Shakespeare's mind. From *J.C.* to *Hamlet* he shows concrete perception of the fatality of things. In the second, perception has emerged in philosophic consciousness as pure reflection. He transformed the old tragedy of blood with moral perception. Only in the finished play emerges the sense of void left by the initial crime, that no hecatombs of slain wrongdoers can fill. We see human impotence and weariness of spirit in presence of overmastering fate. Subjective treatment of old material made moral anachronism inevitable. We trace the influence

[1] Cf. Cunliffe.   [2] Cf. Stoll (1923).

through *M. for M.* to the great tragedies where we see living stimulus and germination of fresh intellectual life. He carried the serene semi-stoicism of the essayist to a deeper and sterner conception of things. Change to tragedy must have been his own choice, and the gloom of the tragedies was partly the reflex of his experience, partly the expression of the philosophy to which his reading had led him. *Othello* and *Lear* show an overwhelming energy of the element of evil far beyond Montaigne. In the tragedies after *Hamlet* unrelieved evil is presented with sombre persistence. Shakespeare owes a lasting debt to Montaigne, and between them is lasting community of thought. Shakespeare passed his later years in accordance with the essayist's ideal. Like no other fellow-dramatist, he left London when he might have enjoyed it at leisure, and this is one of our main clues to his innermost character....

In Mr. Robertson's criticism the emotions are held in check until the intellect has done its duty. He tells the truth about the poems, and is not dazzled by the light reflected back upon them by the great works yet unwritten. At first we seem to be in company of an intellectual guide only, when suddenly he formulates an aesthetic judgement, and we discover that it is the work of the intellect which has made it possible, and also more effective in itself. Where, for instance, has the problem of *Hamlet* and the struggle in the hero's soul been better stated? As regards the direct influence of Montaigne on Shakespeare's life and works, we can only say, in the absence of biographical facts, that we regard it as conjecture; but, knowing Mr. Robertson's methods, with a strong bias in favour of its truth. In any case, it is the right way of approaching the problem of Shakespeare the man; and his last words about the retirement to Stratford are among the most suggestive. There is a Thucydidean touch about Mr. Robertson's criticism: contact with life has stimulated his aesthetic sense. We shall meet him again at Philippi.

V

THE work of Sidney Lee,[1] whose name will be honoured while Shakespearian literature endures, now claims us. While sifting his biography for its critical portions, his point of view has become plain. He makes Shakespeare's merit stand out by comparing his treatment of the same themes as earlier or contemporary dramatists have treated, or remarking on the use he makes of his sources.

L.L.L. shows the influence of Lyly, but the humanity is fuller-blooded. The farcical drollery of Launce and Speed (*Verona*) improves on Lyly's verbal smartness. Only with *R. and J.* does Shakespeare reveal poetic instinct and dramatic insight of unprecedented quality. In *Henry VI* he revised and expanded the work of others: the lifeless beat of the verse and crude language prove that the Joan of Arc scenes

[1] *A life of Wm. Sh.*, 1898 (3rd, revised, edition. Murray, 1922).

were not his. *Richard III* contains a note of lyric exaltation often caught from Marlowe; but the subtle characterization is beyond Marlowe. So in *Richard II*, which is an offspring of Edward II, does Shakespeare trace far more subtly than Marlowe the development of a self-indulgent temperament under stress of misfortune. Marlowe's influence finally appears in the *Merchant*, where Shylock is a penetrating and tolerant interpretation of racial characteristics degraded by antipathetic environment. In *John* Shakespeare flung all his energy into adaptation and produced a great tragedy. He gives new life and dramatic power to the chief characters, and eliminates the narrow polemical and malignant censure of Rome and Spain. Though *M.N.D.* consists of four incidents from well-known sources, it is an example of Shakespeare's freshest invention. He gives to the fairies a dramatic interest beyond Lyly or others, and conquers a new realm for art. *All's Well* shows a tightening grip on the subtleties of romance. He endowed the incident of the *Shrew* with the vital spirit of comedy.

Henry IV is his most convincing portrayal of broad and comprehensive humour. In Part II, which abounds with Stratford memories, he touched the comic scenes with his own magic. Falstaff's wit and jollity redeem his sensuality and untruthfulness; the contrast between his old age and unreverend way of life supplies the tinge of melancholy inseparable from the highest manifestations of humour. The *Wives* reflects low-pitched sentiment couched in colloquial vein, yet Shakespeare has nowhere so vividly reflected the bluff temper of average English men and women in contemporary middle-class society. *Henry V* is constructed like a military pageant. Only he, among Shakespeare's kings, evokes at once a joyous sense of satisfaction in the high potentialities of human character, and a feeling of pride among Englishmen that one of his mettle is of English race. In *M. Ado*, *A.Y.L.*, *Twelfth-Night* Shakespeare works over more or less serious poetic romance by another hand, and with the romantic theme interweaves original episodes of genial irony or broad comedy, convincingly interpreted by characters of his own invention. There is much penetrating reflection on grave ethical issues fused with spirited portrayal of varied comic phases of humanity.

In *J.C.* Shakespeare adds to Plutarch his own gift of glow of dramatic fire. He averts the peril of dramatic anticlimax in relegating Caesar's assassination to the middle distance by the double and somewhat ironical process of belittling him in life and magnifying the spiritual influence of his name after death. The old barbarous legend of *Hamlet* is transfigured, and its coarse brutalities are sublimated in a new atmosphere of subtler thought. It is a study of the reflective temperament in excess. The central figure exerts a pathetic fascination on minds of almost every calibre. *T. and C.* combines the characteristic features of Shakespeare's early and late performances. Shakespeare differs from other poets in depriving fickleness in love of any false glamour—a dramatically effective innovation. He did not depreciate the Greeks, but accepted medieval tradition. Irony at the expense of classical hero-worship was a common note of the Middle Ages: in *J.C.* Shakespeare had already hinted at it.

The catastrophe of *Othello* is reconstructed in masterly fashion. Shakespeare lent Desdemona's fate a new and fearful intensity by making Iago's cruel treachery known to Othello at the last. The plot and characters are treated with unfaltering equilibrium. The popular tale of *M. for M.* was a sordid record of lust and cruelty. Shakespeare diverted the course of the plot at a critical point, and not only proved his artistic ingenuity, but gave dramatic dignity and moral elevation to a degraded and repellent theme. In the old versions Isabella yields her virtue; in Shakespeare the central fact is her inflexible chastity. Shakespeare's argument throughout is philosophically subtle; the poetic eloquence of the Duke's and Isabella's homage to chastity, and the expositions of corruption caused by sexual passion, alternate with coarsely comic interludes which suggest the vanity of seeking to efface natural instincts by coercion of law. There are incidents from Holinshed in *Macbeth*, but every scene which has supreme dramatic value is Shakespeare's own. It is among the noblest of the world's tragedies, yet it approaches the bounds of sensational melodrama nearer than Shakespeare's other plays. The melodramatic effect is heightened by the physical darkness which envelops the main episodes. But the poetic fertility of language, magical simplicity of speech in critical turns of action, dramatic irony accentuating the mysterious issues, the fascinating complexity of the two leading characters lift the piece to the first rank. In *Lear* Shakespeare's tragic genius moved without faltering on Titanic heights. He ignored former endings, and first converted the story into an inexorable tragedy. The verbal and metrical temper give the first signs of the valiant defiance of all conventional restraint which marks the latest stage in the development of his style. Timon and Apemantus show his penetration amid the work of others. Timon is cast in the psychological mould of Lear.

Shakespeare concentrates on Antony's infatuation, and there expands and develops Plutarch with magnificent freedom and originality. The leading events and characters are taken from Plutarch, and, despite literal borrowings of phrase and fact, are reincarnated in the crucible of the poet's imagination, so that they glow in his verse with heroic and poetic glamour of which Plutarch gives but faint conception. It is doubtful if any character of Shakespeare surpasses Cleopatra. The note of roughness and sensuality in Antony is ultimately sublimated by his vein of poetry. As with Richard II and Macbeth, native poetic sentiment is quickened by despair. Despite liberal levies on the text of Plutarch, Shakespeare imbues the theme of *Coriolanus* with new vivacity. His detached but inveterate sense of justice holds the balance between rival political interests.

There is no tangible evidence that Shakespeare's tragic period had a personal cause, such as spiritual calamity or episode of tragic gloom. The external facts of his life show unbroken progress of prosperity. But tragedy gave scope for the full exercise of his powers. To seek in mere personal experience the key to his conquest of the topmost peaks of tragedy is to underrate his creative faculty and disparage the force of its magic.

He atones for the remote incident and loose construction of *Cymbeline* by investing the characters with rare wealth of vivacious humanity. Imogen pervades and animates the whole piece as an angel of light who harmonizes discordant elements. In the *W. Tale* Shakespeare modified the spirit of the fable wherever his dramatic instinct prompted change. He sweeps away all cause for the suspicion of Leontes; his jealousy is the aberration of a weak mind and owes nothing to external pressure. The pastoral scene surpasses all Shakespeare's presentations of country life. His final labours in tragi-comedy show increased mastery of the simple as well as complex aspect of human experience. In the *Tempest* his creative power has fired his impalpable texture with living sentiment and emotion which are the finest flower of poetic romance. The bustling energy of *M.N.D.* is replaced by steadily progressive calm. Shakespeare, through Gonzalo, adopts Montaigne's vocabulary, but puts no faith in his complaisant theorizing. The greater part of *Henry VIII* is Fletcher's, but in certain scenes the imagery has the pointed, vivid, homely strength of Shakespeare's latest plays.

Shakespeare's dramatic work is impersonal, and does not show his idiosyncrasies. We can deduce from his plays a broad practical philosophy, alive with active moral sense, but no self-evident revelation of personal experience of emotion or passion, e.g. love of country and faith in its destiny, also the humour of his race. He was a child of the Renaissance in his enthusiastic recognition of the beauty of the world and humanity. The words of his great characters make the reader think that he is hearing the unpremeditated speech of living beings: and the more closely they are studied the completer the illusion grows. . . .

The result of Sidney Lee's criticism is that Shakespeare's mind becomes a more wonderful thing to us. He begins by extricating his share from the work of others, and pointing out how he transcended it; and he then detaches his writings from his life. He insists that Shakespeare's art was impersonal, that the cause of his tragic period was not private misfortune—and to suggest such a cause is to belittle the marvel of his creative power. It is only Shakespeare's mind that he treats thus, not his works; we need but look back to his remarks on Shylock, Falstaff, Cressida, and many others to see how intimately concerned he is with life. And his last words present the eternal problem of the relation between art and reality. However, while he has experienced, and makes us feel, the mighty natural phenomenon of Shakespeare's mind, the question remains whether a writer's work can be entirely divided from his personal experience. We have cast our vote so decidedly in favour of the agnostic critic that we dare not do more than whisper a doubt whether with Sidney Lee agnosticism is not overdone?

For this reason we have reserved to the last his views on the Sonnets. Their matter is exceptionally controversial, and as all criticism is conjecture, the best use of the historian is to point out the nature of the bias of each critic's mind. Sidney Lee is naturally against an autobiographical interpretation.

There was a fashion of sonnet-writing, he says—and Shakespeare's Sonnets were of unequal value. While some are on the highest poetical level, many sink almost into inanity beneath the burden of quibbles and conceits. His mastery of dramatic power makes it unlikely that any production of his pen should present an unqualified piece of autobiography. The emotion of the Sonnets may owe much to the dramatic instinct which reproduced intuitively in plays the subtlest thought and feeling of which man's mind is capable. Elizabethan sonnets were not usually autobiographical, and, allowing for the conventions of Elizabethan sonneteering, and for Shakespeare's dramatic instinct which enabled him to identify himself with every phase of human emotion, the autobiographic element can be but slender. The duty of marriage and the immortality of poetry were two definite phases of contemporary sentiment. As to the Dark Lady, every sixteenth-century sonneteer vituperated a cruel siren. The constructive process is identical with that in Shakespeare's other works: punctilious regard for the demands of public taste, and marvellous genius and skill in adopting and transmuting for his own purposes the hints of other workers in the field which for the moment engaged his attention. The personal note may have escaped him involuntarily where he gives voice to sense of melancholy and remorse—but his dramatic instinct never slept. There is no proof that he does more than produce dramatically the illusion of personal confession. . . .

Sidney Lee does not deny an autobiographical element, but he touches it so lightly and states the opposite case with such skill, that the impression on the reader is unequivocal. We suggest that so far as is possible in such a sane, well-balanced, critical mind, he has been beguiled by his own phrases. Nothing is hinted in the way of prejudice, but it seems to us that he pondered the subject till his subconscious mind gathered force and supplied the best words for one solution, so that he became self-convinced and slightly overstated what after all belongs to conjecture.

VI

GEORGE WYNDHAM'S [1] criticism of the Poems is typical of the
last years of the nineteenth century. The theory of art for art's sake
would not have been disparaged had it always been expounded as ably
as it is here. Locke was accused of analysing mind till it became a
sensible object: we may almost say that Wyndham does the same with
creative energy.

In his view lyric and elegiac poetry express man's desire for beauty.
It matters little if Shakespeare wrote sonnets to William Herbert or
another. As in all art, something of his personal experience went into
the poems, but our business is with what he superadded—the artist's
impression on his material. We know little of his life, but enough to
prove that the poems owe scarcely anything to his personal vicissitudes.
There is nothing that points clearly to any single experience. As in
every great work of art single experiences have been merged in the
passion which they rouse to a height and pitch of sensitiveness im-
measurable in contrast with its puny origins. The Sonnets may express
Shakespeare's feelings in his own person, but are not autobiography.
The movement and sound are elemental, and the chief concern is to
worship beauty in the imagery and music of verse. Few sonnets by
Shakespeare's contemporaries remind one of his, and there are no
other poems like *Venus* and *Lucrece*. Yet these three are united in
form by lyrical excellence in imagery and rhythm. They show the
influence of Chaucer, but chiefly of Ovid. [2] You discover beneath the
general interpretation of phenomenal beauty in *Venus* a gospel of ideal
beauty, a confession of faith in beauty as a principle of life. [3]

Most of the first series of sonnets handle the theme of ideal beauty
incarnate in a mortal body, yet saved from decay by the immortality
which verse confers. The selection of themes is as much based on
current philosophy and artistic tradition as any actual experience. In
Shakespeare's imagery we watch the ceaseless passing of the year; and
when the magic is verbal it springs from immediate perception: images
are taken from subtler effects of sensuous appreciation—shadows,
transparency of windows, reflections in mirrors, jewels, apparel.
Realism is the note of these imaginative perceptions. The magic

---

[1] *Introduction to Sh.'s Poems*, 1898 (Methuen).   [2] Cf. Baynes.

[3] Prof. Gilbert Murray notes 'how many great poets seem to have drawn most
of their inspiration not directly from experience, but derivatively from experience
already interpreted in other men's poetry'. He instances Burns, much of whose
'most beautiful and spontaneous work is really a working up of old traditional
material'. The mistake, he says, 'is to apply a merely external test to something
that depends on the most intimate workings of a man's imagination'. The important thing is 'simply the intensity of imagination with which the poet has realized
his subject'. *Rise of Greek Epic*, p. 264.

springs from imaginative observation rather than unexpected verbal collocutions. . . .

Such is Wyndham's main theory; into its many and exact details we will not follow him. What he does is to define one of the fundamental problems of art. Nowadays we say rather too loosely that the artist expresses himself in terms of the universal. To Wyndham, as we see, the universal imports more than the artist's experience. Perhaps our best method of reply would be to ask a series of questions and not attempt to answer them definitely. Can any vivid interest be disparted from what is human and personal? Do not many critics say that auto-biography is the most fascinating branch of literature? How far was Pater right when he said that had the ancients allowed us a glimpse of their inner selves it would have doubled the interest of their objective work? On the other hand, do we know enough of our own minds and of art itself to separate truly the artistic from the personal impression?

And in support of the latter we will quote the words of Wyndham himself: 'Works of perfect art are the tombs in which artists lay to rest the passions they would fain make immortal. The more perfect their execution the longer does the sepulchre endure, the sooner does the passion perish. Only where the hand has faltered do ghosts of love and anguish still complain.' As a parallel to this we will set the words of a modern critic[1]: 'Knowledge must supply that which the artist meant to express and did not. Because in the early poems of Shelley and Byron there remains much untransmuted poetical activity we are helped in the interpretation of these poems by knowledge of the artist's life; we do not need it for *Prometheus* or *Beppo*.' And another modern writer on style, who holds that precision of emotional sugges-tion is the essential quality of style, or crystallization, as against rhetoric, advises the learner to leave himself out of the reckoning, and achieve personality through being impersonal.[2] We will supplement these remarks with one that has been made on poets like Pindar—that the fame which they have gained is less immortality than endless lying in state.

We had intended to raise the subject and drop it, but it fascinates us to continue. Professor Saintsbury tells how a friend objected that he treated literature 'as something by itself', and he admitted this to be true, but with the reservation that nothing human can be absolutely isolated from the general conditions of humanity'.[3] Matthew Arnold quotes Joubert's criticism that many melodramas harrow the feelings far more than the *Aeneid*; that 'the true tears are those which are called forth by the *beauty* of poetry; there must be as much admiration

---

[1] A. E. Powell (Mrs. E. R. Dodds), *The Romantic Theory of Poetry* (Arnold, 1926), p. 243.

[2] *The Problem of Style*, by J. Middleton Murry, pp. 95, 131, 143.

[3] Preface to vol. iii, *Hist. of Crit.*

in them as sorrow'. We incline to think that a poem must contain
both genuine emotion and beautiful phrasing, and that each heightens
the other. The emotion becomes more intense because the words are
well chosen; the words wake echo after echo in our minds because the
emotion is true. To insist that every poem must be self-contained, like
the above-mentioned critic of *Prometheus* and *Beppo*, would be to
strike out much of the allusive beauty of *Paradise Lost*. Byron's lines

> His love was passion's essence—as a tree
> On fire by lightning . . .

raise to an ideal level certainly one episode of Rousseau's life, if not his
whole self. They are a true instance of 'crystallization', yet would
affect us less did we not know the story of Rousseau's passion for
Madame d'Houdetot. In a favourite ode of Horace [1] occur these
words,

> Ver ubi longum, tepidasque praebet
> Jupiter brumas . . .

His voice seems to us clearest in this ode, his emotion truest because of
all that we have learnt of his nature in previous and following odes. . . .
We must perforce ring down the curtain on quotations; but if they
help to prove the central contention that in art human emotion and
fine expression must be so balanced that they heighten each other, it
follows that Wyndham minimized the necessarily true emotion in
Shakespeare's sonnets.

VII

THE work of Henry Sebastian Bowden [2] has had to knock twice to be
admitted. Except the last chapter on Shakespeare's ethics, it is worth
nothing as criticism, and it assumes throughout that the words of his
characters express his own convictions. Its object is to prove that
Shakespeare was a Roman Catholic, and it is included here that we
may get some idea of what can be extracted from Shakespeare's mind
by a prejudiced writer. Also because this kind of criticism has been
accepted in certain quarters.

   To the Protestant, he says, nature is a synonym for discord; to
Shakespeare it is no accursed thing but the scene of wondrous beauty—
the storehouse whence he drew moral lessons. According to the
Catholic Church, nature is a symphony proclaiming the praises of
God. Compare Act V of the *Merchant* where in the moonlight and
starlight the music of the heavens is heard. As regards love, the
Renaissance taught that sensuality was a virtue. In the Sonnets the

---

[1] ii. 6.
[2] *The Religion of Sh.—Chiefly from the writings of the late Mr. Richard Simpson*,
1899 (Burns & Oates).

battle of life is fought between true and intellectual and false and sensual love. Isabella (*M. for M.*) is the most perfect type of true love; her natural affections are intensified because purified by her super-natural love. *R. and J.* shows the consequences of ill-regulated passion. With Shakespeare true love is only to be won by sacrifice—an idea taught by Greek tragedy and Miracles and Mysteries, but not by the Reformers.

Shakespeare treated almost exclusively feudal times, and never wrote of the Pope's overthrow, the Gunpowder Plot, the Armada. His ideal Henry V was drawn on Catholic lines. His references to the Bible are said to prove him a Protestant; but he makes people like Falstaff quote individual texts in a strained sense for their own ends. The one indisputable characteristic of his writings is his deep discontent with and contempt for the world in which he lived. In rewriting *John* he excluded anti-Catholic passages. Henry V is the complete portrait of a Catholic hero. He does not win battles by his own strength, but solely through his trust in God. He believes in Purgatory, alms-deeds, prayer, fasting, pious foundations. Richard III's defeat and death are the consequence of personal crimes not political.

The Sonnets are of special importance as to his religion because they reveal himself, though in a partial, fragmentary, disconnected, obscure manner. He treated love in the same spirit as the leaders of religious thought: its object was the good. The work of the pure soul of true love is to fashion for itself and in itself from the earthly image that spiritual ideal which is the reflection of God Himself. The first stage is physical beauty, the second imaginative, the third ideal. The whole exhibits the three great divisions of love as stimulated by the presentation of good through the senses, imagination, reason. The same philosophy is the basis of the plays: Isabella is the ideal of true love, Cleopatra or Cressida the counterparts of the Dark Lady. In *M.N.D.* we see imaginative love to be inferior to reason. The Sonnets above all show that Shakespeare was intensely antagonistic to his time. Sonnet 66 impeaches the government of his day.

In the Love Plays Shakespeare takes his doctrine of love from Plato and knowledge from Aristotle. Absolute truth and love are one: hence the affinity between religion and love. *L.L.L.* shows that it is futile to undertake penance, study, solitude, without adequate motive —the likelihood of attaining the beloved object. Constancy in love is the corner-stone of virtue in Shakespeare's eyes. Infidelity is heresy, and even the true professions of a rejected lover are heresy (*Twelfth Night*, I. v), for love is no subjective creation but consists in conformity of thought with object. In the *Wives* we see Protestant England, but the religious element begets discord, and Evans is a scurvy model of the Parson, far other than Shakespeare's Friars and Nuns. In Fenton's defence of Anne Page, Shakespeare lays down accurately the Catholic doctrine on the subject. *M.N.D.* shows love in the second degree, when the object is created by fantasy uncontrolled by reason. Thus it is short-lived, transitory, fickle, and becomes attached in turn to any object presented to the senses. *A.Y.L.* shows the freedom of pastoral life—as if the poet were comforting a class cut off from all civil functions by proving their loss to be gain, and their moral profit more than their material sacrifice. In the *W. Tale* Shakespeare goes out of his way to describe Delphi. Rome was the Delphi of medieval Europe. Goneril and Regan find that in promising all they have promised the impossible. The true theology is built on 'distinctions' whose fan winnows away the bad and leaves the good.

Allegory was universal in the Elizabethan age, and it is possible to apply some of Shakespeare's plays in a figurative sense. The *Merchant* secondarily presents a plea for toleration. The Jew's persecuting spirit is made odious and monstrous, yet appears the natural and inevitable consequence of the treatment he had undergone. Portia says to Bassanio: 'I fear you speak upon the rack. . . .' Is not this an expression of contemptuous disbelief in all the evidence upon which so many pretended Popish conspirators suffered the death of traitors in the days of Shakespeare? *M. for M.* philosophically is the trial and condemnation of the penal code. A man should be punished for what he does, not for what he is: whereas, for the Elizabethans, to be a Catholic was treason. Also the crime must be committed, not merely intended. In describing Isabella as a novice Shakespeare shows himself completely familiar with the details of life in religion. The Duke as Friar proves in his disguise to what honourable purposes the Friars applied themselves. Ulysses (*T. and C.*) gives the palm of the virtues to perseverance or constancy, and he attributes it to grace. This is the doctrine of the Council of Trent, Catholic as distinct from Protestant. . . .

It may be once more remarked that these verdicts show what a reader with a purpose can draw out of Shakespeare's mind: notably those on *L.L.L.*, Goneril and Regan, Portia's speech to Bassanio, *A.Y.L.* He is rather better on Shylock, the Sonnets, and the historical plays. He implies that Shakespeare wrote plays to express a system of philosophy—whereas he did so to please the public and make a living. And he writes as though Shakespeare invented his plots, instead of deriving them from well-known stories. This helps to explain characters like Isabella and the Duke; though it is true that in rewriting *John* Shakespeare suppressed the anti-Catholic passages. The 'grace' in *T. and C.* is a flagrant instance of strained interpretation; and the critic whose point of view is that Shakespeare was discontented with his world and despised it cannot be taken seriously. Yet in the middle of irrelevant talk about heresies, he has made one notable discovery— that love is no subjective creation (*Twelfth Night*). This anticipates

the views of modern critics that every thought of the artist has its
equivalent in the world of sense, and it is ratified by Carlyle's counter-
saying that a fact is sacred.

We will now give in outline his chapter on Shakespeare's ethics
which is far superior to the preceding. Shakespeare is no fatalist, for if
each character were determined by the moving principle within, or
by circumstances, or by both, the whole interest, power, and pathos of
the plays would be gone, and virtue and vice be meaningless. Antony
was enchained by his passions, yet knew that he could free himself. The
sense of guilt works on Macbeth and his wife apart from fear of
retribution. The murder succeeded, yet despair reigned in their
criminal souls. Modern necessitarianism is the offspring of Calvinism.
Milton's Satan is developed step by step through the inevitable force
of the evil principle within him. Shakespeare sympathizes with the
sinner but abhors the sin. His heroines represent religious sentiment,
conscience, fidelity, truth. Ophelia has no striking mental qualities
yet wins the affection of Shakespeare's most intellectual character.
Desdemona's gentleness and sympathy first captured Othello. The
goodness of Shakespeare's heroes is not based on Puritan self-complacency but on self-conflict waged and won for God's sake and through
His grace. . . .

This is superior to all that has been previously summarized because
it reverses the method. Instead of affirming that Shakespeare wrote to
prove certain doctrines, it discovers the amount of moral truth that
appears through the working of the greatest human mind, and merely
notes that the result agrees with his favourite doctrines. It has been
said that no one seeks Nature in vain—and so no mind can interrogate
Shakespeare's without some reward. We specially commend his
words on Macbeth in these days when critics have rather stopped
short at Macbeth's preliminary speeches on worldly consequences.
The actual problem—how far Shakespeare recognized free will—
is undecided. According to Swinburne he was a darker fatalist than
Aeschylus.

VIII

IT may be of interest to compare Dowden's words on *Hamlet*[1] this
year with those of a quarter of a century before. He advances no new
theory, but we see the result of long unconscious Shakespeare meditation. His vision is clear; he treats the opinions of others, and his mind
by its own momentum contributes a further distinction; and then he
recurs to the text and the original impression undulled by learning.
Also, we who have grown used to separate the Hamlet of tradition
from Shakespeare's Hamlet may at least ponder what Dowden half-

[1] *Hamlet* : Arden Sh., 1899 (Methuen).

suggests—that the deeds which result from what is 'dangerous' in him may after all belong to his own nature.[1]

It was the intellectual subtlety of the traditional Hamlet, he says, that attracted Shakespeare, and his genius led him to refine this subtlety. He rightly defines Hamlet's intellectual character when he adds that he was not a systematic philosopher. Ulysses and Prospero were more nearly philosophers, but neither was a wit, whereas Hamlet was a wit inspired by melancholy. His madness is not deliberately assumed, but an antic disposition is imposed on him by the almost hysterical excitement after his interview with the Ghost, and he ingeniously justifies it to himself by discovering that it may hereafter serve a purpose. Also he has something dangerous—sudden impulses which come almost like the decree of Providence, e.g. his idea of unmasking the King, his reproaches to Ophelia—or when he sends his schoolfellows to death, boards the pirate, grapples with Laertes, stabs the King. . . . As to Ophelia, the ruin of an ideal leaves him cruelly unjust to the creature of flesh and blood. Throughout the play there is not one simple and sincere word uttered by lover to lover. The only true meeting is the speechless interview where he reads her soul and despairs. Only at her grave his love breaks out, as the pity of it for a moment restores his lost ideal.

IX

MR. BOAS calls Shakespeare the majestic spokesman of inexorable moral law. The focus of his moral outlook is self-sacrifice, purity, and unshaken loyalty of soul. He has constant fidelity to the eternal underlying principles of morality. Caird says that even in the darkest tragedy it is a moral principle which rules the evolution of events, and brings on the tragic crisis. In the opinion of Sidney Lee, a broad practical philosophy can be deduced from his plays, alive with active moral sense. To Bowden Shakespeare's drama was a moral discourse, and no moralist was more severe on vice.

In the matter of religion we have the words of Mr. Boas, that he always promises hope for the future; and Caird's that he is neither dogmatist nor theorist, but no agnostic in the deeper sense. Bowden says that he does not exclude the actualities of life but keeps us in the presence of one infinite, personal, eternal God, the first cause and last end of all things. His characters show that the rule of man's life and his way to perfection is no shifting, vague, subjective standard of his own making, but the unchangeable law of God.

We get the following about his characters: from Caird that he could rise above all special interests of individuals to a central point of view, and so realize how in the drama of life individualities react upon

[1] Cf. Brandes.

each other and produce a crisis; from Sidney Lee that a character would reveal itself to him in most of its involutions as quickly as his eye caught sight of its external form, and that intense character-interest triumphs over any defect of plot; from Bowden that faithful portraiture of character is his primary intention, and his characters are human because they correspond to our own experience—that every human being is free.

We get some noteworthy general remarks on Shakespeare's genius. Mr. Boas says that his soul was open to all influences of nature, and swayed by every art, especially music; and that he was the supreme type of the Anglo-Saxon organizing genius in the imaginative not the material sphere. To Caird he is the world's greatest dramatist because of his sympathetic insight by which he sees the world through the eyes of others. To Mr. Robertson he is the greatest dramatic master of eloquence, mirth, charm, tenderness, passion, pathos, pessimism, and philosophic serenity that literature can show, and he has an unequalled receptive faculty. Sidney Lee writes of the dramatic interest which intuitively reproduced the subtlest thought and feeling of which man's mind is capable, that enabled him to identify himself with every phase of human emotion; and that he limned with unerring precision almost every gradation of thought and emotion that animate the living stage of the world.

Some particularly interesting things are said on the much disputed question of personality. He defies our penetration, says Caird, by endless fullness of self-revelation. Mr. Robertson calls him the most subjective, sympathetic, and self-withholding of dramatic writers. Sidney Lee describes his art as impersonal.

Two remarks follow with which we have become familiar. Mr. Boas pays tribute to his majestic common sense, his unfaltering eye for the true proportion of things. Sidney Lee finds that he united to his gifts the shrewd capacity of a man of business.

Caird says that for him man's character is his fate; Bowden, that he was no fatalist, and recognized every human being is free.[1]

Wyndham speaks of his perfect verbal execution—diction, rhythm, accent. . . .

We are struck by the whole-hearted tribute to Shakespeare's morality and religion. The statement that he was no agnostic in the deeper sense by a critic like Caird, who was a philosopher and deeply read in German metaphysics, is worth pondering.[2] Generally speaking, criticism is becoming more exact; the critics are less inclined to judge than to discover which of their impressions are the true ones, and argue

[1] Cf. Swinburne on his fatalism.
[2] Caird is said to have been the only Master of Balliol whose intellectual predominance was great enough to make a sense of humour unnecessary. (*Times Lit. Sup.*, 7 June 1928.)

back to their causes in the nature of man. Thus even when they differ, as in the eternal problem of Shakespeare's personality, we learn something from their very differences—like branching paths that will eventually return to a common meeting-place. A remark like Sidney Lee's that intense character-interest triumphs over any defect of plot is an intimation of the break-up of the ages of faith.

Chapter XXIX

GERMANY 1895–1900

I. BRANDES. II. TRAUMANN. III. TÜRCK. IV. VISCHER. V. KELLNER.
VI. CONCLUSION.

I

GEORGE BRANDES[1] travels systematically through the land of
Shakespeare. He decides that the Cade episode in *Henry VI* is certainly
Shakespeare's, and he sees here the opportunity to watch Shakespeare's
style developing and study his method of work. We see him as critical
artist, retouching, or even rearranging words. The external evidence
that Shakespeare wrote *Titus* is decisive, and in a few lines there is the
true ring of his voice. We deduce from the plays that Shakespeare's
marriage was unhappy; and in *Errors* we catch the personal note in
the contrast between Adriana and Luciana. The *Shrew* deals with
the same topic, but these were not Shakespeare's first works. He first
began to produce independently with the light joyous comedy of
L.L.L. It has two motives: love, without passion or deep personal
feeling, tricked out in word-plays; and language itself, poetic expression for its own sake. The latter was the result of the new-born
enthusiasm throughout Europe for the stately antique literatures
beside which the vernacular seemed low and vulgar. Shakespeare
satirizes Euphuism, but parody is of little use if as tedious as the mannerism it attacks; and so far he was not mature or detached enough to rise
above the follies he opposes. In Biron we hear his own accents; and
we may assume that the vivid and tender emotions of his first years in
London inspired his utterances on love. *Errors* reveals giant strides in
technique; it has the blood of the theatre in its veins, and we see the
artist and anticipate the master. Its motive of confusion is manipulated
with astounding skill. *Verona* surpasses the earlier plays in the beauty
and clearness of outline of the young women, and the careless gaiety
of the servants. It has the exuberance of one who possesses the double
youth of years and genius among a people which is itself young. The
naïve solution is the outcome of a joyous, untried, and unwounded
spirit. Besides passion and gaiety it has fresh nature—the first breath
of fragrant midland memories.

Venus has the fresh sensuousness of the Renaissance and Shakespeare's youth, and also the tasteless Italian artificiality. The descriptions of animal life are unrivalled for truth and delicacy: the horse
recalls the description in Job. Such is the compass of style in this little
poem of Shakespeare's youth—from Ovid to the Old Testament.

---

[1] *Wm. Sh.*, 1895–6 (London, Heinemann, 1898). Brandes was a Dane, but it has
been thought better to include him among the Germans.

Lucrece is almost a didactic poem, with graphic and gorgeous descriptions and microscopic psychological analysis. In describing the paintings of Troy, as elsewhere when he mentions pictorial or plastic art, he admires realism carried to the point of illusion.

M.N.D. shows his genius fully grown, though less dramatic than lyric genius. It is one of his most tender, original, and perfect poems. The frontiers of Elfland and Clownland meet and mingle; there is no pathos, but only the romantic and imaginative side of love—the magic whereby longing transmutes and idealizes its object, the element of folly, infatuation, and illusion in desire, with its consequent variability and transitoriness. Shakespeare does not regard love as the expression of reason; he knew that the domain of the unconscious life is far wider than the conscious, and that our moods and passions have their root in the unconscious. *R. and J.* is the great and typical love tragedy of the world. It has the dual action of an absorbing love in filling the soul with gladness to the point of intoxication, and with despair at the idea of parting. Love in its passionate aspect is the source of rapture and doom. The catastrophe is not deserved, and offers no scope for moralizing. The critics who have condemned Juliet's love as unmaidenly are remote from the spirit of the Renaissance. The Renaissance means a new birth of warm-blooded humanity and pagan innocence of imagination—neither riot of idealism nor ferment of the senses, but based on infallible instinct. The vibration of the whole being is so intense that neither Romeo nor Juliet can tell where body ends and soul begins. The symphony of the play is rich enough to harmonize Mercutio's Fairyland speech with all the comedy, farce, descants of passion, and grave soliloquies of the Friar.

The Englishman of Shakespeare's day had always before his eyes pictures of extreme prosperity followed by sudden ruin and violent death. Life itself was dramatic, as now it is journalistic and photographic. English drama was addressed to the best elements of the public—the noble young patrons of the theatre.[1] The young English nobleman was both man of action and artist, and it was from such as Essex and Southampton that Shakespeare acquired his aristocratic method of regarding the course of history. The historical plays were produced in the decade when England's national sentiment burst into flower, and her pride was at its highest. In Gaunt (*Rich. II*) Shakespeare first shows his national pride, and we hear the vibration of his own voice. Richard cannot touch the reader through his divine right because it has brought no correlative duties. He has the same artistic defects as Marlowe's Edward; he so repels in the first half that he cannot efface the bad impression. Shakespeare appears as a beginner in that he leaves characters and events to speak for themselves without attempt to range them in a general scheme of perspective. The play

[1] Cf. Sisson on unanimity of Elizabethan public. Also Rümelin.

has no humour, and no harmonizing sense of style. Richard III is a Marlowesque figure, and the play is his first historic tragedy with well-knit dramatic action. Richard is a fiend in human shape, and his confession is a non-realistic unfolding of secret thoughts in words. Ambitious men were less composite, and Shakespeare depicts a historical monster of a hundred years back. But he gets an effect of complexity by producing the impression of inward infinity in the character. Deformity, conscious intellectual superiority, and lust for power are the foundations of Richard's character. Shakespeare identifies himself with Richard by substituting imaginatively the poverty which he had known for the deformity which he had not. He was himself conscious of superiority—and he was ambitious if we may judge from the restless inner force which propelled him to one great intellectual achievement after another, and from the material incidents of his life. The scene of the wooing of Lady Anne is not unnatural but unprepared. Dramatic art consists in preparing for what is to follow, and then in spite of, nay, in virtue of the preparation, taking the audience by surprise. The exaltation with which the lust of power inspires him bewilders and overbears her. It is the triumph of art that we sympathize with Richard, but we do so partly because some of his victims are worthless and deserve their fate. His wit and courage shed over his fall a glory which his coldly correct opponent lacks. Strength of character is such a rare quality that it rouses sympathy even in a criminal. It is the work of youth; the characters tell us what they are, and appear transparent and self-conscious to excess.

John bears traces of Shakespeare's grief for his son's death. He did not alter, but vitalized, spiritualized, and deepened all in the old play. He suppressed the religious element and retained only the national and political attack on Catholicism. He makes all turn on John's defective right to the throne; but as the King is too unsympathetic to serve as centre-point, and the subordinate characters draw the interest, the action is frittered away. Shakespeare's aim with Falconbridge was to present a picture of the health, vigour, and full-blooded vitality which popular belief attributes to a 'love child'. With Constance Shakespeare sympathizes as he does with all those characters who refuse to compromise with worldliness and conventionality. Shakespeare ignored Magna Carta, the result of which was a powerful middle class: or perhaps Elizabeth did not care to be reminded of it.

When Shakespeare wrote the *Merchant* he was preoccupied with ideas of money-making, &c.; he longed for land and houses and corresponding advancement in rank and position. He was discontented with his position as actor, humiliated at the contempt in which the stage was held, and looked upon his calling solely as a means to make money. There is something of himself in Antonio's melancholy— a mournful undercurrent to the joy of life which still reigned in his soul. That the magnanimous Antonio should behave as he did to Shylock makes us realize the violent medieval prejudice against the Jews. The fable of the caskets gave Shakespeare a means of expressing his hatred for empty show, and he willingly ignored its improbability. No doubt Portia represented Shakespeare's youthful ideal of woman-hood—perfect surrender in tenderness of the wise and delicate woman. She is in complete harmony with her surroundings and herself. She is the outcome of a century-old ancestry of stainless and fortunate lives, of slow-gathered riches, respect, dependants, and culture of the mind. Of a fresher stock than the nervous women of to-day, she is sustained by unfailing serenity of nature. We must realize this inner, inexhaustible well-spring of joy, or we might think her jesting forced. Shylock was more ludicrous than terrible to the Elizabethan public— and doubly despised as an extortionate usurer. Shakespeare did not share these prejudices, but had to add the enforced conversion that shocks modern readers. Respect for personal conviction, when it conflicted with orthodoxy, did not exist in Shakespeare's time. It is astounding how much right in wrong and humanity in inhumanity Shakespeare has imparted to Shylock. We see him as the inevitable outcome of his treatment. In true Jewish fashion he insists on the letter of the law and restrains his hatred within legal rights. Externally and internally he is a type of his race in its degradation. The fifth act dissipates the gloom, and the moonlit landscape thrilled with music was an image of Shakespeare's soul at that point of time. He celebrates strength and wisdom in man, intellect and wit in woman; and these most brilliant years of his life are the most musical. But his ideal of music is sphere-harmony and soul-harmony, not bell-ringing or psalm-singing.

With *Henry IV* Shakespeare attains his great and overwhelming individuality, and, at the age of thirty-three, the summit of his artistic greatness. The play is unsurpassed in wealth of character, wit, genius—heroic and burlesque—thrilling and side-splitting: and these contrasted elements move and mingle with all the freedom of life. Shakespeare despised affectation and was therefore drawn to Prince Henry who concealed great qualities behind a misinterpreted exterior. Shakespeare's whole life was just a paradox, for externally he was little better than a light-minded mountebank. Falstaff is the gayest, most concrete, and most entertaining figure in European comedy. Shakespeare was acquainted with Rabelais, who was the master spirit of the early Renaissance in France, but who stands to Shakespeare as a Titan to an Olympian god. Panurge is larger than Falstaff, an abstract and brief chronicle of the French court of his day. Shake-speare only attacks Puritanism, mildly, in self-defence—and he was, what Rabelais was not, an artist. Falstaff is a rascal of genius, with no trace of mediocrity. He has no soul or honour or moral sense, but he sins, robs, lies, and boasts with such exuberance that he charms all. In Part I all that is base and unclean in his nature is dissipated in the ether of laughter; but he deteriorates in Part II, as the contrast is prolonged with the Prince's moral strength. The soliloquy on honour sums him up in contradistinction to the other characters, for all stand in relation to the idea of honour. It is dignity to the King, renown to Hotspur, the reverse of show to the Prince; while Falstaff proves how a man can live without it. Percy is above all greedy of honour; and Shakespeare overlooks nothing about him as too trivial— his restless gait, stammering speech, absence of mind. Behind these we see into the deeper and more significant characteristics from which they spring. He is the hero of the feudal ages, indifferent to culture, a rebel because independence is all in all to him—a masterpiece of manliness, the modern counterpart to Achilles, with the same personal ambition. His is the untamed and violent spirit of feudal nobility, the reckless and adventurous activity of the English race—all the vast and infinite forces which lie deep under the surface and determine the life of a whole period, a whole people and one half of humanity. Yet he is only the foil to the hero and throws into relief the Prince's unpretentious nature.

Henry V is the national hero of England—the typical English conqueror, adventurer, and politician, unscrupulous, and, on occasion, cruel, undismayed though the enemy outnumber him tenfold—the prototype of those who were to conquer India. Henry V is not unlike his father, who was affable till he attained the throne and then sparing of his presence. The son acquires a frivolous character so as after to make a deeper impression. It pleased Shakespeare to vindicate the morality of voluntary self-reform and self-control. A new-born warmth of feeling glows behind Henry's words of dismissal to Falstaff. He will dally no more with evil, and becomes the embodiment of earnestness and sense of responsibility. *2 Henry IV* is a bundle of admirable individual passages, and the King is richer in thought and wisdom, as if drawn from the depths of Shakespeare's own experience. As a work of art, *Henry V* is not to be compared with the two preceding plays. Its theme is English patriotism and it appeals to England rather than to the world. Shakespeare strives to make Henry an epitome of all the virtues which he himself most highly values. But he un- characteristically condones Henry's massacre of French prisoners. On the whole he has descended from superhuman genius to English patriot, whose enthusiasm is as beautiful as it is simple, and whose prejudices even are not unbecoming.

Shakespeare now enters his most brilliant period, when he seems for a short time to have revelled in his own genius with a sort of passive happiness. No doubt he was happily in love, the beloved one being wit incarnate in the form of a woman. The women of the

early plays were unamiable and masculine; in the serious plays they
were ambitious and bloodthirsty; and in his later years of ripe manhood the young women are all soul and tenderness, silent natures
without wit or sparkle—Ophelia, Desdemona, Cordelia. But between
these are a bevy of beautiful young women, kind-hearted, but attract-
ing chiefly by their wit. Shakespeare mixed in the society of Southampton and Pembroke, and must have been enchanted by the conversation
of the aristocratic ladies and their playful freedom of speech. *M. Ado*
for us means only Benedict and Beatrice; and we understand that
Claudio was degraded to make Beatrice shine forth. Her unbridled
whimsicality conceals the energetic virtues of a firm and noble
character. The love of Benedict and Beatrice is Shakespeare's first
instance of careful character-development; for so far he had held to
a character scheme once laid down. Richard III and Henry V are
one and the same from first to last. *A.Y.L.* is a festival of gaiety and
soulful wit that vibrates into feeling. It typifies Shakespeare's longing
to escape from unnatural city life into the country, and he dreams of
communion between fair women and brave men in ideal surroundings.
Jaques is a misanthrope from excess of tenderness, sensitiveness, and
imagination—the first sketch for Hamlet. The wit of Beatrice was
aggressive, but that of Rosalind has no sting. She differs from Portia
in being as sensitive as she is intelligent, and she is radiant with youth,
imagination, and the joy of loving and being loved. Perhaps *Twelfth
Night* is Shakespeare's most graceful and harmonious comedy. Its
various notes of seriousness, raillery, passion, tenderness, laughter,
blend in richest and fullest concord. But we feel the joy of life has
culminated, and is about to pass into melancholy. Sir Andrew has an
inward suspicion of his own stupidity. Viola's intelligence is bright,
but her soul outshines it, and she is not untouched by melancholy.

We now see clouds on Shakespeare's mental horizon that do not
lift for eight years. Experience seems to develop in him a burning
compassion for humanity, and also a horror of mankind as a breed of
noxious wild animals. From *Twelfth Night* onwards he wages unremitting war against Puritanism conceived as hypocrisy. Earthly
life appears pitiful to him, exposed as it is to disasters brought about by
mixed stupidity and malevolence. He had grown up in England's
most wonderful period. Men and women seemed to have richer
abilities, a more daring spirit, and fuller powers of enjoyment than in
former times—with more fire in their blood, more insatiable longings,
and keener appetite for adventure. England's world-wide power was
founded at the expense of Spain; London deposed Antwerp as metro-
polis of commerce. The world which had been a little place suddenly
grew vast. . . . But with the new century came a change—and the
dark side of Elizabeth's nature developed—her lust for rule and
flattery. Conscious that her death was eagerly awaited she gave the

rein to tyranny. Shakespeare must have taken to heart the disgrace of Southampton; and the execution of Essex synchronized with the revolution in Shakespeare's mind—and grief for him was the cause of his melancholy.

The Dark Lady of the Sonnets brought a breath from a higher world, an aroma of aristocratic womanhood into Shakespeare's life. He studied, enjoyed, and adored in her the well-bred ease and sportive coquetry, the security, elegance, and gaiety of the emancipated lady. If the Sonnets do not dwell upon this happiness it is because they date from the period of storm and stress when he realized that his mistress had ensnared his friend. The tenderness of Sonnet 143 expressed the poet's whole attitude of mind in this dual relation. He consented to share her favour with his friend, but he was mainly anxious to preserve the friendship. The men of the Renaissance gave themselves up to an adoration of friendship and their friend which is now unknown; and although many of the sonnets are evident imitations, others express his true feelings. We see a side of him that does not appear in the plays—an emotional nature with a passionate bent towards self-surrender in love, and with a yearning to be loved. We see him oppressed by the contempt in which his actor's profession was regarded —lately aggravated by Puritanism. We must bear in mind his sense of the unjust middle-class attitude to realize the high pressure of his feelings towards the noble youth who had approached him full of the art-loving traditions of the aristocracy, and the burning enthusiasm of the young for intellectual superiority. There are many sonnets that are inferior, uneven, rhetorical, conventional, impersonal—but there are some whose musical quality is unsurpassed by any of the songs in the plays, or even by the finest speeches in the plays.

Brutus belongs to this troubled period when Shakespeare saw how proud and noble characters might succumb to political error and stir up rebellion on the plea of independence. During his own struggle his ideal was Henry V, but now he preferred characters whom fate balks from success. In Shakespeare's scheme Brutus had to be the pivot, and Caesar belittled into a caricature and sunk to an invalid and pedant. Shakespeare did not understand that Caesar was disillusioned, finding himself misunderstood and hated by those whom he most valued. Power had lost its sweetness, life seemed to him worthless, and he went unarmed to the senate. Shakespeare's interest was now psychological, and he dealt no more with outward conflicts but with inner crises of spiritual life. Brutus is occupied not with what Caesar has done, but with what he may do. Cassius, though frankly envious, is not base—for envy and hatred are swallowed up in him by political passion. Everywhere we feel the coming of *Hamlet*: for to brood over the incalculable consequences of an action is to make action impossible.

Hamlet has given Denmark world-wide renown, and the hero is

the only Dane famous on the largest scale. It may be recalled that
Leicester was suspected of poisoning Essex to marry his widow; also
that the murder of Darnley was not long since—and James had made
no attempt to avenge his mother's death. James was irresolute,
learned, loved art, science, acting. Contemporary history may have
supplied some outward elements to Shakespeare which, in the moment
of conception, ministered to the creative energy of his genius.[1]
Shakespeare was also acquainted with Montaigne, who had much
influence in England; and therefore the resemblance of certain
passages cannot be due to chance.[2] Hamlet is like Montaigne in
asserting that life is wretched and transitory. The indirect form of
expression had always attracted Shakespeare; it was the favourite
method of his clowns and humourists. Shakespeare made Hamlet
in the guise of apparent madness speak sharp and bitter truths that
could not be forgotten. He did what no other poet has achieved—
he delineated a genius. Hamlet's outward fortunes differed from
Shakespeare's; but these details were but symbols. He had lived
through the whole of Hamlet's experience; he had seen the unworthy
usurp the places of the great—he had discovered his ideal to be unworthy. The father's murder, the mother's remarriage—these were
only individual instances from which he inferred the dire disillusions
and terrible possibilities of existence. His own experiences with his
patron, his friend who betrayed him, the woman he loved who proved
a wanton, caused him to merge himself in Hamlet. He saw brutality
and stupidity lording it in high places, and courtiers truckling to the
great. There was nothing but wordy morality, mutual espionage,
artificial wit, double-tongued falsity, lack of principle, hypocrisy. And
the Court was the image of the world at large: but whence the cause?
Here is the problem of good and evil, and God.

   The old legend did not harmonize with the rich inner life of
Shakespeare's hero: there arose a discrepancy between this central
figure and his surroundings. Yet originality springs from this very
discrepancy between the medieval character of the fable and its
Renaissance, almost modern, hero.[3] Hamlet is no model of virtue;
besides pure, noble, moral, he can be wild, bitter, harsh, coarse, and,
when wrought up to the verge of madness, callous and cruel. He is
a child of the Renaissance, with its impulsive energy, its irrepressible
fullness of life, and its undaunted habit of looking death in the eyes.[4] He
is not incapable of action, but inaction is demanded by the technique of
this particular drama. Had the King been killed at once, the play
would have ended. His is not that entirely modern product—a mind
diseased by morbid reflection, unable to act. He has gunpowder in
every nerve, the dynamite of genius in his nature. There is no

[1] Cf. Miss Winstanley.   [2] Cf. J. M. Robertson.
[3] Cf. Montégut.   [4] Cf. Dowden (1899).

'general meaning' on the surface of *Hamlet*; the attraction of the play depends on this very obscurity. It is the kind of work to set in motion more thoughts than it contains itself, and perhaps of a different character. Hamlet typifies the solitude of soul which cannot impart itself. He is the first modern complex character who feels intensely the strife between the ideal and the actual world. The show of madness enables him to find solace in expressing indirectly what it tortures him to speak of directly. The monologues satisfy his craving at times for mental concentration. His self-reproaches express the impatience of his nature; they prove (against Werder) that the fundamental difficulty is inward. Nothing is more profoundly conceived than his relation to Ophelia: if he is cruel it is because she was weak, and tried to deceive him.

All's Well is reminiscent of *Hamlet*, and contains subtle cautious sallies against Puritanism, and reveals Shakespeare's bitter contempt for demonstrative piety. It attracted him to delineate a woman wooing a man and yet possessing and retaining all the charm of her sex. He sheds a Raphael-like beauty over Helena; and she anticipates the charm, earnestness, and boundless devotion of Imogen. The fervour and glow of her speeches surpasses the early comedies. Shakespeare only gave his whole mind to certain parts: Bertram has the right to refuse, but not for reasons of birth: Parolles has Falstaff's vices without a gleam of his genius. *M. for M.* is still bitterer against Puritanism and self-righteousness. What drew Shakespeare to such a subject was his indignation at the growing Pharisaism in matters of sexual morality. As actor and theatrical manager he saw only the ugliest side of Puritanism. One feels, even in the comic episodes, that his burning wrath underlies the whole structure like a volcano. He is too great a psychologist to depict a ready-made, finished hypocrite: he shows us how weak even the strictest Pharisee will prove if only he meets the temptations that really tempt him—and if his desire is opposed it brings out in him the beast. The play is unequally elaborated, resting on its three great scenes, and on its excellent and realistic comic scenes. The others retard the dramatic wheel and are conventional. Shakespeare cared only for the main point—the blow he was striking at hypocrisy. He probably went as far as he dared, making the giant stride from Malvolio to Angelo—and to shield himself he treated it as a comedy. A deep pessimism pervades the whole; and the Duke outdoes Hamlet's blackest mood. He assembles with art and care all that can confound and abash the normal instinct that makes for life. In no other play is the general moral so persistently emphasized.

In Macbeth we see how the man, into whose veins evil has dropped like a poison, becomes bloated, gangrened, foredoomed to self-destruction or annihilation. Hamlet who shows no remorse for a murder once committed is Macbeth's counterpart. Macbeth does not deliberate, but after is attacked by hallucinations. A crown means greatness for Macbeth, a tangible prize in this life, for which he is willing to risk his welfare in the life to come. Hamlet says: Were we sure that there is no future life we should seek death. Macbeth thinks: Did we not know that judgement would come upon us here, we should care little about the life to come. In both plays there is a breath of the spirit world, although a superhuman power does not interfere in human life. These elements are transparent symbols, but not illusions; they exist outside the sphere of hallucination. From the dramatic and theatrical point of view *Macbeth* is beyond all praise, but from the human point of view it is one of Shakespeare's less interesting efforts. Of course the text is much mutilated—clipped, pruned, and compressed for acting. The style is vehement to violence and compressed to congestion. The dialogue between Malcolm and Macduff is out of proportion, like nothing else in Shakespeare. Lady Macbeth is a lean, slight, hard woman, consumed by lust of power and splendour: her allusion to the babe is coarsely callous. The Porter scene is a fantastic interlude, an effective contrast. The dialogue between Lady Macduff and her son is one of the gems of the play. The 'To-morrow' speech embodies an absolute moral lesson—more so as in other parts of the play Shakespeare is not so much disinterested as influenced by the moral impression which he desires to produce on the audience. At this time it may have been vitally important for him to prove the strictly moral character of his works.

As far as *Macbeth* is concerned, life's tragedy as a whole—wickedness as a factor in human life—is not treated firmly and in the grand style: it is treated far more grandly and firmly in *Othello*. It is conventional to call one the tragedy of ambition, and the other of jealousy. Shakespeare does not write exercises on a given subject; he explores the tragedy of life in its origins and laws—and here the problem is the might of wickedness more than jealousy. Iago himself contains more of the grand manner than all *Macbeth*—more depth and penetrating knowledge of human nature. His one aim is his own advantage, and his impenetrable mask is rough outspokenness. He does evil for the pleasure of hurting; he is eternal envy irritated by merit or success in others. In his lack of apparent motive lie his depth and greatness. Unlike Richard III he is dishonest in his monologues, and half fools himself by dwelling on half-motives. His 'Fie: there is no such man' expresses the thought that has sheltered him. Other people do not believe that such a being exists. Shakespeare believes that this highest degree of wickedness exists, and is one of the two factors in life's tragedy—the other being stupidity. Othello has a simple soldier's nature; he is good and true, believes in the goodness of others, and is without vanity. He is little impressed with his own greatness, and thinks it natural he should be scorned. Only love made him marry

Desdemona; for he has the fear of marriage that belongs to his wild, freedom-loving nature, and he does not seek after patrician connexions. It is the sweet alluring magic that mysteriously enchains man and woman. But their union rests on the attraction of opposites, and has all against it—difference of race, age, and the man's strange exotic aspect with the lack of self-confidence which it awakens in him. He is not jealous—but the torment seizes him of feeling that one human being is a sealed book to the other. Credulity, not jealousy, is the prime cause of the disaster; also pure, deep sorrow to see his idol sullied, not mean frenzy that the idol should prefer another. Desdemona is more womanly than other women, as Othello is more manly than other men: and this is the reason for attraction between them. The beautiful proportion of all the parts and articulations of the play give it an advantage over the mutilated *Macbeth*. The crescendo is executed with absolute *maestria*; the passion rises with a positively musical effect. It is Shakespeare's only family tragedy, but in the style of the grandest. Two elect natures are ruined by the simplicity which makes them an easy prey to wickedness. The subject is restricted but becomes monumental by the grandeur of its treatment.

In *Lear* Shakespeare's vision sounded the abyss of horror to its depth, and his spirit grew neither fearful, giddy, nor faint. It is the symphony of an enormous orchestra, where all earth's instruments sound, and every instrument has many stops. Ingratitude seemed to Shakespeare the most abominable and widespread vice, and he had again and again been its victim. A giver like himself must have met ingratitude—from comrades, stage-poets, actors. It impoverished his soul, making it hard for him to help again. He was not careless with money, but could be a good comrade in practical life. Here alone we know that what we now call the social problem existed already for Shakespeare. The tragedy is written round the scene on the heath. The two stories, of Lear and Gloster, are so incomparably welded that their interaction brings out more forcibly the fundamental idea and feeling of the play. Gloster's compassion for Lear ruins him; and nowhere else are evil and good so immediately opposed. Conventional triumph of good is deliberately shunned, and blind and callous fate blots out all alike. Every passion is rendered with such power that the play, despite its fantastic basis, produces an effect of absolute truth. By a master-stroke Shakespeare exalts the traditional clown into a tragic element of the first order. The loss of Cordelia is the great catastrophe—the loss of what alone makes life worth living is the tragedy of life. We ask if this is the end of the world?—and the answer is, Yes. The ruin of the moral world, the loss of the good, does seem the end of all. What avails it that the guilty slaughter and poison each other afterwards?

Caesar's spirit lived on after his death; Antony marked the real downfall of Rome. The might of Rome, stern and austere, shivered at the touch of Eastern voluptuousness. Unlike Lady Macbeth, Cleopatra poisons in wholly feminine fashion. She combines alluring sensuality with finished culture, and could uplift even the great Antony into such happiness as he had never known before, and then plunge him into perdition along with half the world it was his to rule. Shakespeare had known such an experience, and through his dark woman his inner world had nearly collapsed. Cleopatra is the courtesan by temperament, yet with the genius for a single undivided love. The world-catastrophe precludes the action being focussed round the leading characters only. Nor must the other characters be subordinated to them completely, or the impression would be lost of majestic breadth. We have the contrast in Octavia of Roman rectitude. Love is blamed, and ambition put forward as the great man's duty. After Actium all turns on the mutual relation of Antony and Cleopatra: their love was never before so rapturous—nor their mistrust so deep. In the hour of trial they suspect each other. The drama's greatness proceeds from the genius with which are entwined the private relations of the two with the course of history and fate of empires. Roman greatness and the Roman Republic seem to die with Antony, the victory of Octavius brings glory to no one and promises nothing.

We now hear an undertone of contempt in Shakespeare; and in the next years his being narrows and concentrates itself to abhor human nature—and, correspondingly, to esteem himself enormously. The germ appeared in *A. and C.* where Antony risks all for a coquette. We see the full bloom in *T. and C.* where woman loses her glamour, and man pleases himself by seeing in her merely sex. In these years he developed the sickly tendency to imbibe poison from everything. Because he was now economically safe, his mind was freer to dwell on the eternal infirmity of human nature. Boccaccio and Chaucer had represented Cressida as lovable and frail, not base. Shakespeare pursues her with passionate hatred and bitterness: he makes her a shallow, frivolous, sensual, pleasure-loving coquette; and he aggravates every circumstance till she becomes odious. Shakespeare was many-sided, but his groups of feminine characters can frequently be traced back to an original type, and probably to one model.[1] Cleopatra was a siren, but experience cooled him, and self-deception brought disillusion. Anger at the farce of wasted feelings became the germ of *T. and C.* Perhaps he ridiculed the Homeric world to contradict Chapman's enthusiasm—being also grieved that the arrogant, pedantic Chapman should have found favour with Pembroke. He makes the friendship of Achilles and Patroclus an abomination, and covers Helen and Menelaus with mockery through the mouth of Thersites, like a Satyr-chorus. The nobly imagined Mediterranean figures, unaffected

[1] Cf. Frank Harris.

by religious terrors and alcohol, are tainted by Northern bitterness, by
Christian, not intellectual, civilization, by a narrow-minded asceticism
which has vanquished the Renaissance. Christian conception of
faithlessness in love has displaced the old Hellenic innocence and
naïveté. Shakespeare has a rigorous medieval standard: indeed the
slaying of Hector reads like the invention of a medieval barbarian.
So deep is his bitterness that he feels hero-worship, like love, to be an
illusion of the senses. Achilles is a vainglorious boaster, Helen a
hussy, the others caricatures. Ulysses is as trivial of mind as the rest.
There is a note of ridicule even in the love enthusiasm of Troilus.
In *R. and J.* no abyss appears between the soul and the senses; but it
is the lower side of love's ideal nature which is parodied in *T. and C.*
Shakespeare shows without sympathy how blindly Troilus runs into
the snare and then awakes. Pandarus is a demoralized Polonius, and
we do not enjoy his wit or sympathize with him as with Falstaff.
The decisive scene, where Cressida proves false, contains words so
weighty that we feel in them Shakespeare's soul. 'Think we had
mothers' is the pith of the piece uttered forth with terrible clearness.
The profound scattered reflections from the blockhead Achilles and
the crafty and unsympathetic Ulysses, though contradicting the whole
play, make it attractive by revealing its conflicting moods. The
answer to Achilles' question, 'What, are my deeds forgot?' reveals one
of the sources of the bitterness and pessimism. Shakespeare felt himself supplanted in popular favour by younger and less worthy men.
After his death he was eclipsed by Fletcher, and he was oppressed by
man's ingratitude and the world's injustice.

Shakespeare's mother died in 1608: she represented the haughty
patrician element of the Shakespeare family; and we see the effect in
his next work, *Coriolanus*. The subject is social conditions, and his
point of view is as personal as it can be. The root of his aversion to
the mob was the physical repugnance of his artist nerves to their
plebeian atmosphere. He had no idea of free citizenship, or of the
struggle for self-government out of which grew the Roman Empire—
and indeed was now proceeding under his eyes in England. The
opposition, consisting of the middle classes, was against him and his art;
and he looked on the Tribunes as political agitators of the lowest type,
symbols of the envy of the masses and stupidity and brute force of
numbers. He insists on the cowardice of the people, while Plutarch
testifies to their bravery. He disliked their psychology, but his contempt was still more sensuous; and it must have been at the theatre
that he encountered such human vermin. The most dissimilar
characters favour the political views of Coriolanus—which proves
that they were Shakespeare's. Shakespeare had owed his chief happiness to the friendship and appreciation of one or two great noblemen.
Such persons made life worth living, and it was this belief in hero-

worship that he now wished to make concrete. *Coriolanus* is the tragedy of an inviolably truthful personality in a world of small-minded folk; it also expresses the punishment of reckless egoism. The speeches of Volumnia reveal Shakespeare's satisfaction and relief in venting himself in furious invectives through the medium of his dramatic creations. But the Patricians are cowardly and incapable also, both in Shakespeare and Plutarch. They scarcely resist the Volscians, and are so steeped in party spirit that they rejoice in the defeat of their country because the Plebeians have brought it on themselves. This is the beginning of a certain inconsequence which henceforth becomes more marked in Shakespeare.

Probably Shakespeare revised *Timon*, the best of the verse being distinctly his own. His genius and master-hand pervade the whole, despite foreign elements. The link with the last play is that the despair of Coriolanus is active, that of Timon passive. He is more bitterly relentless than Coriolanus, and his hatred of humanity is consistent. The other characters simply make salient the chief figure, or rather his great outburst of bitterness. Lear has friends, and Coriolanus his mother, and Antony and Cleopatra love each other. Timon loses our sympathy because he loves no individual passionately. Had he ever been drawn to a friend he would not have squandered his possessions on the world. But in him Shakespeare concentrates all that he had lived through in the last years.

The power of cursing could go no further, but now we feel our ignorance of Shakespeare's life-history. Mere resignation cannot explain the marvellous softening of his long exasperated mood. Marina, Imogen, Perdita, Miranda, must have had their prototypes; and perhaps some noble-souled young woman reconciled Shakespeare once more to life. These are half-real, half-imaginary; the halo of youth and romance shines round them; the foulness of life has no power to defile them. They are self-reliant without the buoyant spirit of the earlier adventurous maidens; they are gentle but not pathetically mournful like the sacrificial victims. The young girl appears as a wonderful mystery of nature, drawn with the ripened man's rapture over her youth. Only with the birth of Marina in Act III does Shakespeare really take *Pericles* in hand. He is now led to exempt one from general condemnation of the sex.

In *Cymbeline* he has put his whole soul into the heroine. Imogen embodies woman's highest characteristics—untainted health of soul, unshaken fortitude and constancy, inexhaustible forbearance, love, radiance of spirit. We find in her the deepest love ever placed by Shakespeare in a woman's breast: though the play succeeds those filled to the brim with contempt for women. Shakespeare probably wrote from experience, but not necessarily his own, and at this time he may have gained some clear and personal insight into an ideal love.

We ask what impelled him to write, how did he arrive at the theme?
His late mood had been that life in human society is unendurable,
especially in a large town or at a court. Here the best men are banished,
the best woman is foully wronged. Let us exchange the town for the
idyllic peace of the country: this is the recurring note in Shakespeare's
best works. He had never held to the letter of the law in morals, nor
believed in unconditional external commandments. Now, more than
ever, he believes the quality of an action to depend on the will—he
believes only in the ethics of intention. Pisanio lies and deceives
because he cannot help it, but his character becomes moral, not worse
but better. All the nobler persons flout accepted moral laws and touch
evil without defilement: Guiderius kills Cloten and thereby prevents
his intended violence to Imogen. The majority who speak and act
falsely are ignoble; but he only is truly moral who follows out his own
ends, by his own means, and on his own responsibility. From this
point of view the world becomes less gloomy.

The personality of Hermione unites the distinct parts of the *W. Tale*.
From the first Shakespeare sought to prevent melancholy from cloud-
ing the later charming scenes; and to make each chord of feeling
melt away in the closing gentle strain of reconciliation. The womanly
high-mindedness and blamelessness of Hermione show brighter on
the dark background of Leontes' jealousy: she has the ideal Englishwoman's nature. Though Shakespeare never loses a chance of
satirizing the lower classes, he lets appear, with a sympathetic touch,
through his clowns, their natural wit, good sense, and kind-hearted-
ness. Perdita has Shakespeare's own favourite trait—distaste for
anything artificial or unnatural. Shakespeare now looks on love with
a fatherly eye, with a tenderness for those who yearn for happiness,
as something remote from the world and himself.[1] That Polixenes,
the better of the two kings, is rough and harsh again emphasizes the
contrast of the court. Leontes is the typical sixteenth-century, Italian,
Renaissance Prince, who at once thinks of poison and then of fire.

Shakespeare painted decoratively in the *W. Tale*, and did not
concentrate his whole strength; but he does so in the *Tempest* where
all is ordered and concise, and so inspired with thought that we stand
face to face with the poet's idea. It was written for the occasion of
a royal wedding, and contains flattering allusions to the King: although
perhaps it is ironically hinted that James imagined himself to be such
as Prospero. The grief for Prince Henry's death was fresh enough to
overshadow all rejoicing, and a joyous play would therefore be ill-
suited. Yet the festive feeling must not be destroyed, and Shakespeare
therefore alluded to the Prince's death in such a manner that grief
was lost in joy. The play lacks dramatic interest, but is so marvellously
rich in poetry and inspired by imagination that it forms a whole little

[1] Cf. Dowden.

world in itself. Prospero is tried by suffering and proves its strengthening qualities. He absolves the offenders with more contempt than
charity; his forgiveness is that of the wisdom which is no longer affected
by outward circumstance. Shakespeare's own nature overflows into
Prospero—the genius imaginatively delineated, not, like Hamlet,
psychologically analysed. Prospero is the master mind, the man of the
future, as shown by his control over the forces of nature. In him
Shakespeare unconsciously anticipated the results of time. Ariel is
supernatural, Caliban bestially natural—and both have been endowed
with a human soul. In the whole record of poetry Ariel is the one
good spirit who arrests and affects us as a living being. Caliban utters
many melodious lines; he is more elemental power than human being,
and therefore rouses not indignation and contempt but amusement.
A deep sense of the vanity of all things had laid hold on Shakespeare;
he believed in no future and expected no results from the work of a
lifetime. Like Prospero he had sacrificed his position to his art.

It is likely that his retirement to Stratford did not bring him
peace and contentment. His own family looked on him as a returned
artist-Bohemian. We doubt if his daughters could appreciate him, and
his wife was still less educated. She preferred sermons to plays, and
we are reliably informed that she opened her house and heart to
wandering Puritan preachers. That he found little favour with the
leaders of Stratford, despite his wealth and kindliness, we surmise
from the fact that he was never appointed to one of the public offices
of the town. . . . He was not only a writer, but a deep-feeling, rejoicing
and suffering man. It has been too often said that we know nothing
of him. The object of this book is to refute the idea of his impersonality.
It is our own fault if we know nothing of a man who has given us
forty-five important works. . . .

Brandes had a European reputation, and he is certainly among the
critics of Shakespeare who have plucked the golden bough. Though his
book has been called a biographical romance, it is delightful to read—
if we must admit that our high hopes at the outset were not fully
justified—and that some 'region cloud' made the sunset less clear.
The reason is that Brandes is a poetic and imaginative critic, and his
best judgements are where his instant vision comes true. Where he is
less inspired we encounter him in the over-trodden paths of Dowden,
and in those where Mr. Frank Harris will afterwards walk. In the
latter we do not welcome him, though at least he is not deserted there
by the winds of imagination, whereas Mr. Harris relies on external
facts.

Between Mr. Harris and Hartley Coleridge lies much space, and at
his best Brandes has a power of defining emotion delicately that
recalls Hartley Coleridge. Thus he ascribes the naïve solution of
Verona to an unwounded spirit; in *R. and J.* the vibration of the whole

being is intense enough to extinguish the gulf between sense and soul; we can sympathize with Richard III because some of his victims are worthless; Falstaff's exuberance in Part I dissipates his baseness;[1] Jaques is a misanthrope from over-sensitiveness; Iago flourishes because the world does not believe such a being exists—and Othello is wrecked by credulity not jealousy; Timon loses our sympathy because he loves no individual passionately; Hermione's personality unites the play; Prospero absolves the offenders with more contempt than charity; Ariel and Caliban have human souls. He rightly says that in Hamlet Shakespeare has delineated a genius, like no other poet; and we ask in all humility whether a better thing than this has been said about *Hamlet*—that its attraction lies in its obscurity. Surely here is the agnostic criticism that is most fruitful with Shakespeare—the light that makes darkness visible, and the soul of man more mysterious and infinite. Brandes is a subjective critic, and the following instances are yet more typical; they relate not to character in action but character in itself: Richard III gives the effect of complexity through inward infinity; Percy has in him the reckless and adventurous activity of the English race; Henry V is the prototype of those who were to conquer India; Cleopatra, by temperament a courtesan, has the genius for a single undivided love; Hermione has the ideal Englishwoman's nature.

Brandes is at his second best where his judgements, if not due only to direct inner vision, are modified by history—especially such as the Renaissance which is concerned with revolution in the nature of man. We are accustomed to think of the story of *Hamlet* and the character of the hero as two separate things. Brandes admits the discrepancy but gives us pause when he observes that Hamlet is a child of the Renaissance and can be cruel. Similarly, he characterizes Leontes, whose jealousy has been blamed as unreasonable, as the typical Italian, sixteenth-century, Renaissance Prince.

Where we disagree with Brandes is in his over-positive generalizations about Shakespeare's self and life. We have compared him to Hartley Coleridge at his best and Mr. Frank Harris at his worst: he also has something of the 'fatal facility' of J. A. Symonds. Of this class is his opinion that *John* contains traces of Shakespeare's grief for the death of his son, and *Coriolanus* for his mother; also that when he wrote the *Merchant* he was preoccupied with money-making, and longed for land and houses and rank. It may be conjectured that he disliked Puritanism and the middle classes; but there is no warrant for the intense hatred which Brandes describes, or for the saying that he waged unremitting war against Puritanism. And this applies to the period in which, according to Brandes, he abhorred mankind and esteemed himself enormously. Nor do we think that the melancholy

[1] Cf. Middleton Murry.

view of Shakespeare's last years at Stratford has been historically
confirmed. And yet among these generalities are to be found traces of
the critic's better manner: e.g., the moonlit landscape thrilled with
music of Act V of the *Merchant* is an image of Shakespeare's soul
at the time; in *Twelfth Night* the joy of life culminates before it
passes into melancholy; Shakespeare owed his happiness to a few great
noblemen. All these, if not literally true, are imaginatively true
enough to stimulate the reader.

Opinions on Brandes's moral remarks may be similarly divided. It
is hardly possible to discern as he does 'a new-born warmth of feeling
behind Henry V's dismissal of Falstaff'. And the Prince's 'moral
strength' in Part II, which is said to contrast with Falstaff, is rather an
external thing. On the other hand we welcome his words about the
'ethics of intention'. Here he does convey that the Good and True
are one with the Beautiful. In conclusion, Brandes has some first-rate
remarks, but he is less than the greatest as a whole. He has had to
pause to ask his way of others on his journey to the shrine. He has
not reached it by a single, imaginative impulse, like Coleridge or
Professor Bradley, who merely compare notes with others, on their
return.

II

ERNST TRAUMANN[1] finds great meaning in the secrecy of the
marriage of Othello and Desdemona—in which Shakespeare differs
from the original tale. It gives to the deed the character of imprudence,
thoughtlessness, and wilfulness, and the effect on wounded authority is
the greater, since the couple place themselves in the wrong and are
guilty. This step brings state action into the play, and sets in motion
the most diverse elements against the Moor. Brabantio is a widower,
which intensifies his opposition—and a sidelight is thrown on Desdemona's upbringing—and her wilfulness, the cause of her guilt and fate,
explained. Roderigo, Shakespeare's own creation, is driven to despair:
in the source it is Iago who plays this part. Shakespeare doubles the
figures and achieves a twofold aim by increasing the hostile powers
against the Moor. Iago, freed from the mental disturbance of passion,
can make use of Roderigo and work better on Othello. The latter, in
reward for services rendered before marriage as love-emissary, makes
Cassio his lieutenant in place of Iago. Emilia, though loyal to her
mistress, is unconsciously an accomplice of her death. Othello is the
cause of all this evil which recoils on his head. His marriage destroys
him, because it is a misalliance which carries with it the seeds of death.
Shakespeare knew that jealousy is not a tragic passion, and he makes
Othello of trustful nature, with great self-control and iron discipline.

[1] 'The Artistic Work in Othello' (*Jahrbuch*, 1895).

The drama, therefore, must show the hero shaken and transfigured to the roots of his being, become an utter stranger to himself.

Brabantio unites the worst characteristics of exalted position: he is arbitrary, prejudiced, unyielding. That he has long been a widower is a master-stroke of Shakespeare's. We picture the lonely man, joyless in his great dark palace, with the child whom he cannot understand. He invites the Moor to his house as an interesting object, to wile away the tedium of the hours. When he learns the truth he falls as from the skies, and he thinks magic must have played a part. His choleric temper overcomes him more and more; he scornfully rejects comfort, and utters his violent feelings in a curse. Roderigo is a decadent, possessed by the one desire to make Desdemona his. Like Brabantio he would have been powerless in his passions but for the organizing mind and energy of Iago. To Shakespeare's contemporaries Iago was more credible than to ourselves: and yet Richard III, who is historical, only differs from Iago by birth, position, and aim. Iago is equally the product of circumstances, and, like Othello, their victim. He makes his mind the master of his will; both ambition and jealousy inflame him against Othello: the latter may be unfounded but they gnaw. He only mentions his suspicions in monologue; they are too deep to be revealed to Roderigo; but they are known to Emilia. A materialized cynic, he is raised far above his surroundings by a strong will, sleepless observation, knowledge of man. He alone knows how to make all subserve his plan. He tries repeatedly to justify himself, till he exhausts his art and must admit envy to be his motive—the 'daily beauty' in Cassio's life that makes him ugly. What might not his powers and energies have achieved in a larger sphere of action! It is indeed a tragic fate to be brought to justice by his tool, Roderigo, and betrayed by his own wife. Emilia lets her husband keep back the handkerchief, and is silent and tells lies at a critical moment. She thinks Iago capricious and covetous, not evil. Cassio is noble and upright and, therefore, wins all hearts. Because of his harmonizing qualities of body and mind the Senate choose him to replace Othello, to whom he is far inferior in military power.

Desdemona's character is more hinted at than developed: but a passing light falls on her previous life with her lonely, irascible old father —a life without care or sorrow but equally without amusement. Othello is a revelation—and, her love once won, she is true as rock. Her farewell to her father has even a ring of hardness, but she has overestimated her strength. She does not know the world, and we see deeper into her after the brawl and Cassio's disgrace, when the powers of her loving soul become active. She is also impetuous and does not know herself; her husband's pagan superstitions alarm her, and she withdraws within herself. In the wonderful scene with Emilia we are conscious of a passing regret in her soul that she has chosen this lot; but then all her bitterness subsides in Barbara's song. It would be false to say that she is the victim of the evil contrivance of a knave who arouses her husband's jealousy. Not jealousy but his own self-deception destroys Othello. One must examine the contradictions of his nature—the contrast between his descent and calling, between his past and present. The man of royal blood becomes general of a Christian Republic; the elderly, unworldly warrior marries a young Venetian. He had bridged the chasm with will, character, and discipline. War was his element, and he loved his free condition; but he relinquishes his freedom and becomes a stranger to himself in his new world. His deepest feeling becomes his master, and in an impulsive moment he places Cassio above Iago. That he is deeply stirred and transformed by his new life we see when he, the reticent man, pours forth the story of his love. He knows Desdemona no more than her father, of whom he says in almost childish simplicity, 'Her father loved me!' At Cyprus, when his wedding night is disturbed by Cassio, his sense of duty makes him unjust. He had ordered the celebration, and might have punished his friend less heavily. Here man and soldier dispart—and there is one, viz. Iago, who knows how to excite this feeling of duty to the uttermost. He knows that to nothing but honour would Othello sacrifice wife and love. Desdemona's pleading alone would disturb Othello, for he allows no one to interfere with his official duties. Iago's boldness warrants his success: for no one would make such monstrous charges without reason. Othello wavers at the first assault; he has no knowledge of himself; his boastful presumption makes his tragic guilt:'. . . once in doubt is once to be resolved. . . .' For a time he thinks he can separate his lot from hers—that he is not inwardly shattered. Then he bids happiness farewell and is utterly overcome: the handkerchief seems overwhelming proof. In this illusion he falls entirely into the power of the evil one and conceives his murderous design. With his rough handling of Desdemona we see how he is fallen and transformed. But when the violence of the storm has burst, his soul recovers. Nothing so explains him as his last anecdote of Aleppo: he discloses the core of his being—his virtue which is also his passion. The sight of his anguish softens for us the death of Desdemona. With Shakespeare only death redeems crime and error of life. Only in suffering they came to know themselves and what was lacking in their marriage. It is Iago who exposes their error, and, if he can be justified, it is that he belongs partly to the power that wills evil and brings forth good. By this ethical conception Shakespeare lifts the action into the realm of idea. . . .

We have followed Traumann through *Othello* as we did through *Hamlet* because he is a type of his country's critics, but we failed to receive much aesthetic stimulation by the way. The one bright moment was when he recalled the words, 'Her father loved me. . . .' to prove Othello's simple character. To be forced to dwell upon this thought does bring us a little nearer to the Moor. Otherwise we draw little from his pages but the commonplace moral that men are blinded by passion. To prove his theory he has to labour certain points: e.g., that Brabantio by a master-stroke is made a widower, that he is tyrannical, and Desdemona's youth was joyless—and that honour is Othello's fetish. That he can compare Iago with Richard III is proof that he argues from outer events inwards, instead of beginning with the movements of the soul as they respond to the Shakespearian rhythm.

III

HERMANN TÜRCK [1] defines genius as honesty, love of truth, and objectivity: since to have a personal interest in a matter is to admit the suspicion of self-seeking. Love is opposed to self-seeking and therefore akin to truth; while hatred limits observation to the surface of things. An artist must enjoy in order to produce; and he cannot produce unless his mind has previously received many impressions. How are we to connect sense-reception with objectivity, love of truth, and love? We must distinguish between sensation or mere admittance of sense impressions, and feeling which is a psychic state of pleasure and pain connected with the reception of sense impressions. When a wild beast seizes its prey the process is a simple psychic one, where sensation, thought, and resolution pass into one another; and when man is subjective and pursues self-seeking interests he behaves like a beast of prey. To become absorbed in the contemplation of any object needs detachment of the mind from every personal, subjective, self-seeking interest. A timber merchant who inspects the forest he wishes to buy has no thought to spare for shifting lights and rustling tree-tops. Sense-stimulations are constantly crowding upon us, but of these we make a selection. The unconscious will directs this selection: thus the egotistical man sees and fears only that which relates to his selfish interest. It is said that man desires that which causes him pleasure—but in reality he finds pleasure only in attaining his desire. The mere sight of a gazelle would not please a lion: were he unable to approach it he would be convulsed with rage. A timber merchant would not care to see a beautiful forest which a rival had forestalled him in buying. But when a man delights only in the sight of an object, with no personal interest, he is a genius: although, since few men are quite incapable of aesthetic pleasure, there just exists in all this power of knowing the Ideas in things and momentarily transcending their personality.

To be disinterestedly absorbed in contemplating an object is to love it; and the more we abandon ourselves to things themselves, the more will they reveal to us their secret nature, and we shall approach truth.

[1] *The Man of Genius*, 1896 (trans. from 6th German edit., 1914).

By truth we mean all-unity of mind—that the world expresses the
one Being we call God. Beauty expresses visibly the relation between
observer and observed; it is divine unity in sensation. Love unites
what appears to be divided, and effects the miracle that man passes
beyond his finite personality and expands his ego in ever wider circles.
Objectivity, love, is the secret of all genius and artistic intuition: the
artist loves the object that he contemplates, and makes no outward
imitation but an original creation. Things have an inner life that they
reveal only to him who is absorbed in them, whose soul goes out to
them. To represent the purely external is not to represent the thing
itself. To the self-seeker, the object continues to be a thing apart, and
only its outward subjective impression remains. An artist of this class
may purposely select its ugly aspect; and indeed certain inferior
products of modern art seem to be the work of hatred. The artistic
genius will only emphasise what is perfect, for the nature and essence
of things consists in that which is perfect not faulty. All that is faulty
arises by outward disturbance, all perfection is the outcome of the
innermost nature of the thing itself. The original form of the crystal
is perfect, and if it fails to reach perfection it is from outward causes,
such as other crystals that grow upon it. The artistic genius sees the
essential, not the accidental, form: the eye of love sees what is perfect.
Love makes perfect: to love, to desire the existence of another, is also
to desire that which belongs to such existence, that there may be no
defect in it, that it may fulfil its purpose and idea. To love a thing is to
emphasize its perfections.

If we ask what is perfection, the answer is, the state in which all the
conditions of existence are present. And the existence of an object is
based on the harmonious concord of its parts. The more perfectly
single parts harmonize, the more will the whole be capable of existence
and have reality. With the human body as with the crystal, accidental,
external causes hinder the harmonious development of the whole.
As we judge a man not only by what he has done, but by what he has
hoped to do—by his disposition—so the artist will do justice to a thing
not when he represents what circumstances have made it, but when he
penetrates into its inner nature and expresses that for which it is
destined by its inner nature. The ideal is nothing unnatural, but
nature itself in its inmost being. So-called naturalism neglects nature's
inner essence, its desire for life and impulse towards perfection.
Realism sees in things that which reduces their reality and capacity for
existence: as uncharitableness notices all defects. It is our hearts,
our wishes, that decide the impression. The happy man sees beauty
everywhere because he sees with the eyes of love; the world is ugly
to the unhappy whose eyes hatred clouds. Love reveals the deeper
nature of things; therefore genius is love.

Shakespeare has infused his deepest and most personal sensations, thoughts, and aspirations into Hamlet. It is evident that Hamlet regards the world with the eyes of love: note the admiration with which he speaks of his father, how affectionately he regards his perfections, and with what abhorrence the defects of his uncle. But the evil conduct of Claudius revolts him more than his outer shape, and Claudius's smiles and promises do not deceive him. He is more likely to be deceived by Ophelia and attribute to her beautiful form an equal soul: but she is weak and frail and accessible to all personal influences. She lets her worldly father persuade her that Hamlet only approaches her from base motives, and is too clever to marry below his station. It wounds him to discover that she is only outwardly perfect, and is a weak, subjectively biassed woman. And yet we know from the scene in the closet that her beauty had powerfully impressed him. He delights in natural beauty, as we see from his talk with Rosencrantz and Guildenstern—and in artistic beauty and dramatic art. In the latter he requires temperance even in the whirlwind of passion; and he extols modest simplicity and natural beauty.

As a thinker he aims scientifically, to find, amid manifold incidents, the uniform law to which all that happens is subject. The idea of a thing is the law of its development; to recognize an idea is to grasp relations between things and their parts: and this is the objective mode of thought of the man of genius. A single occurrence is viewed in its relation to the whole mass of kindred phenomena and effects. That a murderer can smile and look pleasant is one experience. Hamlet compares this with his mother's apparently boundless devotion to her first husband, whom she could yet so quickly forget. He deduces the general truth that outward and inner qualities do not correspond. Everywhere men wish to appear other than what they are, but a man of genius like Hamlet grasps the truth even when it touches himself. A selfish man sees and magnifies the failings of others, but the man of genius thinks logically and makes no exceptions in his own favour. Laertes, after the murder of his father, does not lament the wickedness of mankind, but sees the act in its immediate relations to himself. He sees no typically sinful mortal, but an individual who has done him a terrible injury. That Hamlet does not at once take revenge upon his uncle is due to his objectivity and disinterestedness, his conviction that all men are imperfect and sinful. He is thus absolved from the selfish impulse to seek personal satisfaction. An injured man will revenge himself to excess, unless he be a man of genius who thinks objectively, like Hamlet, and does not regard things one-sidedly.

The tragedy of Hamlet is one of idealism: he had conceived falsely of the world. He thought the courtiers served his father because they honoured his noble character, and that his mother loved him for the same reason. His father dies, and he hastens home to see a boastful, sensual hypocrite treated by the courtiers with the same officious zeal, and by his mother with the same tender devotion. Now he realizes that power and goodness are not connected in the popular mind as in his own. His sorrow exceeds the personal, because he recognizes the dreadful truth as to the real nature of the world. Completely logical and entirely altruistic, now that he has lost faith in his fellow-men, he sees no motive to employ his great talents. A life without purpose is no life, and therefore his soul is paralysed. Too much stress has been laid on the difficulties of his task: his conduct to Polonius and Rosencrantz and Guildenstern forbid the theory that he was a moralist anxious not to lay himself open to blame by his actions. A disinterested man will not weigh the results to himself of his actions, and will keep in view his purpose. Goethe's saying is true, that the man who acts is always devoid of conscience; and the nobler a man is, the less will he think of himself in all he does.

The cause of Hamlet's inaction is his temporary mental depression. That he has grim independence of nature is obvious from his conduct in the ghost scene. He is first to board the enemy's ship, and still more significant is his outburst of energy at Ophelia's grave. It is because his whole mental life is engrossed and his desires and endeavours arrested by the recognition of the fundamental error in his views of the world. This mental crisis paralyses his natural energy, but even before the ghost urges him to revenge we see him filled with the same despairing grief at the moral weakness of man. He would kill Claudius at once, could he so remove all evil out of the world: but Claudius is but a representative of this wicked world. It is the baseness of the whole world that has injured Hamlet, and whether he perform the deed or not it makes no essential difference in his inner state of mind. When in calm moments he desires to carry out his revenge, it is more as an obligation than from any deeper impulse. The act itself, the slaying or deposition of Claudius is not against Hamlet's nature. He would remove him like a noxious insect—and there is indeed something dangerous in his nature. But pessimism has arrested his creative impulses, despairing want of faith in the reality of things, grief at the contrast between fair outer semblance and hidden inner corruption. . . .

The introductory study on the nature of genius is to be preferred to the one on Hamlet: for it is inevitable that general theories should fail at least partially when applied in detail to aesthetic matter. We doubt if the line of demarcation between genius and talent has ever been better drawn—if more valid reasons have ever been given to justify the artist-company in considering themselves remote from and above the rest of mankind. The kindred themes of love and beauty, the distinction between true and false artist, the purposes of meditation, nature, the law of development—all these are treated with a far lighter touch than is usual in such works, and are left more wonderful, not more commonplace, as the result of analysis. The mystery deepens, the universe becomes more spiritual, the artist fulfils a higher function among men. We ask ourselves if the old opinion that a great poet must be a better man than his fellows is utterly false? And then we think of Sterne and Verlaine and a score of others, and shake our heads—or counter-argue that great qualities are balanced by great defects. Yet we cannot but agree with Türck that the soul which can apprehend such harmonies must be half-divine—even if our knowledge of literary history tells us that the reactions on earth of its mortal coverings are scandalous.

So far Türck's criticism has the ruby drop of emotion which transforms in its vessel the crystal liquid of the intellect, and without which aesthetic criticism cannot thrive. The memory of his inspiration sustains us at the outset of our voyage through Hamlet, but is extinct before the end. The frailty of Gertrude, the hypocrisy of Claudius— these are well touched and brought home: for other critics have remarked that Claudius is not ignoble in his outward behaviour. Similarly with the courtiers who defer to Claudius as they did to Hamlet's father. We realize the morally rotten state of Denmark more keenly from Türck's analysis; and the cause of Hamlet's pessimism is suggested rather more definitely than by previous writers. Hamlet's great objective, disinterested mind stands like a colossus, at the base of which the small, subjective, self-interested minds of the others creep about. But when this is said all is said—and we are advanced no nearer to the Hamlet robed in the clouds of glorious words whom we wish to know. The causes of his inaction—indifference to earthly values—may be plausibly defined: and with this some quite modern critics would be likely to agree: but the abstract philosophical reasoner will not guide us to the shrine. The enlightening critic is he who makes us share his emotion of wonder at Hamlet's character—an emotion kindled by Hamlet's golden speech.

IV

WE turn to Friedrich Theodor Vischer[1] who opens his treatise with an apology for any lack of decency in Shakespeare's plays. This he ascribes to the manners of the time, since Shakespeare himself was an exceedingly moral man. That the plays at times make one shudder is the result of the roughness and savagery of the Middle Ages. Euphuism was another contemporary vice, and also hyperbole, and generally extravagant language. These are the faults of his age, but he is not without faults of his own. His action is often overloaded owing to immaturity in most of the historical dramas. In *Richard III* there is confused, effervescing superabundance of power, and at times raw historical and chronological matter. He does not seem complete

[1] *Sh. Vorträge*, 1899.

master of his material, and finds it easier to give too much than too
little.

But he transforms all into life, humanity, action, fate. Drama is
the modern form of poetry, and he has made it his element. The idea
of freedom is inherent in the drama—the will as the cardinal point of
life. Everything kindles within, becomes willed, becomes motive,
deed; and every result is a willed result. Shakespeare is the father of
the drama and of modern poetry. He is, above all, a political poet who
sets before us the great powers that rule and pervade the whole
community. What is purely human gains a higher interest when
interwoven with the fate of kings, peoples, states. That he can
handle the human fundamentals of life as finely as the political we see
from the great tragedies where all takes place inwardly. We may miss
in him a longing founded on principle for a reform of the social and
political conditions of the people—but he is no conservative or reactionary. He says to his kings: your sovereignty depends on your worth—
your legitimacy will not save you. He can transplant himself into all
forms of existence, so that his self becomes the self of all; and he
enters into the temperament and characteristics of other nations. He
can represent types of character, yet his types are individuals. Falstaff
is a type of the coarse frequenter of beer-houses, yet we shall not see
his like again. Hamlet is the type of the true melancholic, yet there
can never be but one Hamlet: he is species and individual in one.

Shakespeare was exceptionally at home with passion, the dramatist's
leading theme. When a character strives against it we become aware
of its overwhelming strength. Yet over the plays stands the invisible
motto: Act not in blinding moments of passion. He is the poet of
conscience: passion carries with it a self-made judge. No one has
better described this power of self-condemnation. His highest aim
is the majesty of fate; he is the first poet to recognize that fate is
immanent, that man forges his own fate. He does not preach but
believes in the divine ordering of the world. His justice is not mathe-
matical, for blameless victims fall, and the best are not blameless—
but it is a true picture of the incomprehensible relation between
suffering and guilt. Amid the darkness of storm there emerges the
ancient law that controls the system of the world. At times we may
feel that his outlook on life is gloomy, but however many deaths his
catastrophes bring, something still remains over of the good. Though
love succumbs, it gains increase of power: the finite is annihilated, the
eternal remains. He is a realist in the true, not the photographic,
sense, yet he introduces supernatural beings. He shared the belief of
his time in spirits, and he makes us believe in his ghosts and witches.
To nature he gives a soul, making it sympathize with human fears
and passions.

The narrative poems give the whole ground-tone of the Renaissance

—its heightened mood, glowing, gorgeous eloquence, exaggerations, and conceits. They do not give the real Shakespeare—though in *Venus* we feel the developing dramatist is putting his psychological powers to the test. Nor do the Sonnets give much insight into his innermost character, though a certain truth underlies them, and they contain confessions.

Hamlet's melancholy is choleric, not sleepy, and he is especially violent when moved by moral anger. This refutes the charge that he is purely reflective; for he who is deterred from action simply from over-contemplation cannot be such a passionate man as Hamlet. But if he looks out on the whole world and sees it mirrored in the one act that so closely affects him, the thought of revenge might be accompanied with the feeling that it is hardly worth while to punish the wickedness of the world.[1] We get a hint of his outward aspect from the ironical comparison of himself to Hercules: which points more to a finely wrought than muscular constitution. His courage when he follows the ghost is that of a great idealistic soul, all of whose noblest powers are stirred to action. The tragedy in a supreme sense is one of Providence, not of Fate only. After the ghost scene the spirit world claims Hamlet; and he will break with all he loves and renounce all natural relationships. His feigned madness is a dangerous expedient, and he only makes of it a shield from behind which to shoot his arrows of mockery. But it must also be recognized that highly gifted men are inclined to madness, however slightly. Hamlet is not actually mad, but he has as much madness as is usual with the imaginative genius in contrast with the political or military. He therefore plays the madman because he is something of one by nature, and also because of the shock to his spirit and the resulting wild riot of thought.

He has before him a hard but not an insuperable task. It is hard for him, not because he thinks too much, but because an imaginative nature falters at the thought of a practical deed. He does not desire only to kill the king, but to be able to justify the deed to himself and to the world. He never explains his difficulties, and we learn nothing directly, but only surmise indirectly. The play scene is a wise device, that springs from his sense of justice and wish to obtain evidence: but his satisfaction is only theoretic. Though he has a task to perform, and it is his duty to live, he ponders over suicide; but Shakespeare has to show the self-torturing trait of this nobly planned nature—its nervous recoil. We tremble at the thought of unknown evils far more than at known; and Hamlet is right in saying that what makes life burdensome—and also sweetens it—is imagination. The monologue has less outstanding than dramatic value: it brings us into life-like touch with Hamlet. He has reverted to a former thought of suicide instead of using the time to spur himself to action. When the king

[1] Cf. Türck.

betrays himself at the play scene, instead of drawing a dagger, Hamlet sings the verse of a song. The moral and intellectual satisfaction, the mental triumph of unmasking the king, suffices him. The play should have been the means, but he makes it the end. Where words are enough, as in the scene with his mother, he is equal to the occasion; his speech is instinct with the energy of a moral consciousness of enormous power. In the churchyard, at the sight of Yorick's skull, he takes a perverse tone and indulges in unpleasant reflections: no doubt Shakespeare wishes to represent him as morbid and distraught. The speech of Laertes to the priest expresses Shakespeare himself, who had suffered much from priests and puritans.[1] Laertes is moved by great sorrow, but he also had an object in expressing it as violently as possible; and his rhetoric affects Hamlet not only as artificial, but as something directed against himself—as if Laertes knew of his presence. His conduct in leaping into the grave proves that there was something in him akin to the madness which he feigned. He sees in Laertes the indifferent world which denied his love for Ophelia. In revenging he is also punished for his own faults; he has guiltlessly made himself guilty, and his guilt is revenged on him.

Every one in the play lives for a separate object, and works to achieve it, and so gets entangled in the net. No play shows more clearly how in human life mingle many different streams. Man is the forger of his fate, though not in the way he pictures to himself. The less Hamlet acts, the more he drives others to action. As long as he does nothing the well-conceived design of the king, like a devilish engine slowly advancing towards him, gives the high dramatic note to the play. There follows a jolt—and the complete disruption of the machine.

Macbeth is a tragedy of the abuse of conscience, and we compare the hero with Richard III. But Richard is a hardened villain, off-spring of savage internecine warfare, into whom conscience enters as a judge from without. Macbeth, guiltless in the beginning, is tempted from without, and a quality is stimulated which is not pure ambition, but ambition nourished by imagination connected with the beauty of lordship. His romantic ambition becomes a demoniac pleasure in the horrible, though his better nature counter-urges, for he has a conscience. Hamlet abuses conscience by inaction, Macbeth by action: at the end he dies with courage, but inwardly he is a wreck. Lady Macbeth is physically destroyed by conscience; and she who exercised over herself such iron control finally ends with self-betrayal. The tragedy is one where the characters are enticed to evil by the way of fanciful ambition. It is frightful how, at the first words of the witches, the idea of murder rises in Macbeth. There must have been some previous unopposed bad thought of the same kind. He is ner-

[1] Cf. Brandes.

vously excitable, aglow with inward vision, and anticipates the goal of his ambition in the same moment that temptation assails him. Imagination flares, the longed-for is already present, the actual ignored; and the stormy feeling carries him beyond the limits of humanity and destroys his own.

Lady Macbeth is usually thought a female monster with a lust for murder; but though a demon she is a human one. She has in a higher degree Macbeth's dangerous poetic nature. She has to encourage herself with frightful invocations; and she also has a better self. She knows that Macbeth is undecided, and her energetic spirit cannot bear it. To see him at the promised height is more to her than all else: it is not only ambition but love of her husband. When he appears, after the prophecy, she greets him as if all were accomplished. In this leap over the interval to the accomplishment the two resemble each other. At the banquet she appears to lack tender, womanly feeling when she recalls her husband to his senses with hard words—but as queen she had to uphold the dignity of the house before her guests. She becomes a prey to the inner torments which she only hid: her punishment corresponds to her womanly nature. Macbeth sees ghosts, but it is her conscience that confronts her. She is herself a ghost, asleep and not asleep, a stranger to herself. Macbeth expresses his real feeling in his monologue before Seyton enters. Of softer nature than Richard III, he is desolate and withered when deprived of all the tenderer things of life. In killing conscience he has destroyed other feelings—can neither love, hate, hope, nor fear—but he retains enough feeling to be conscious of their loss. And at the last he is greater than his conquerors.

The secret marriage of Othello and Desdemona is condoned, according to Shakespeare, by the father's blind anger: but it also causes the father's despair.[1] It is a purely Shakespearian touch that Othello should be naturally disinclined to jealousy. The play is the history of the slow martyrizing of a brave, manly soul; but we are left with no empty shudder, for we have glimpsed the depths of nature. It is and is not a tragedy of jealousy, for though jealousy may overcome momentarily a noble nature, there is something low and mean in innate jealousy. Othello is too noble to mistrust; the poison must therefore be administered secretly. He is imprisoned in a magic circle, and the more he consciously strives to put away the evil thought, the deeper it enters in. But his sound nature is not to be destroyed; it reaches a crisis and then violently expels the poison, through murder.

In the hands of a lesser poet Desdemona's blindness would seem like weak understanding; but Shakespeare has developed her beauty of soul out of her lack of experience. If she is to be blamed for her flight from her father's house we must remember that Shakespeare

[1] Cf. Traumann.

was occupied with essentials and leaves much to us to supplement; and also in no tragedy do we find one side perfectly right and the other perfectly wrong. It is useless to assign a double motive to Iago, since non-preferment suffices. The suspicion that Othello had seduced his wife does rankle in him, though it had not disturbed his marriage. But it illumines his intrigue and humanizes his devilry: he had known qualms of jealousy and would like Othello to suffer likewise. He has the gnawing hatred of the servant for his master; also the lust of destruction; and he hates good in itself as the refutation of his own thinking.

Shakespeare judges of suicide according to circumstances: thus, in *Lear*, Edgar impresses on Gloster that he must bear his trouble to the end. But Othello, who has destroyed a jewel and brought to naught the blessing of the happiest marriage, can no longer take part in life. He acted as judge but judged wrongly, and now he makes amends by rightly judging the false judge. Iago's abyss of soul has a certain attraction, for it shows us, even in evil, the powers of the human mind and spirit. The pathos of Othello's rage, and the cause of his downfall, is his pure moral conception of marriage. To the question whether fate is unjust, we reply that Iago destroyed life and happiness, but not love and honour. Shakespeare may seem dark and terrible, but the idealistic powers remain as unmoved as the stars of heaven.

At the entrance to *Lear* we must remind ourselves that poets do not always keep within the probable. Lear is spoilt and hence morbid, and the natural desire for love begets delusion. The weak old man judges by words and rewards hypocrites. The tragedy is that a fault, which is not a serious crime of evil will, brings down such a weight of trouble. Only a deeply feeling nature would suffer such overthrow when it meets with thorough want of love: and here pity claims us. His shattered state tells us more about his nature—sympathetic, tender, finely organized—and makes us esteem him more. Cordelia is an innocent victim, though touched by wrong in the way he speaks to her father. But no tragedy is achieved without guiltless victims; and Shakespeare also required an event that should give Lear's death-stroke. Cordelia also would have played a flat role had she survived. The tragedy is one of self-destructive wickedness, of the good that exists in suffering.

In the historical plays, what is purely human receives a different colouring and weight: and, speaking generally, power is emphasized. The early English plays introduce us to a world of rough, Nordic barbarism that contrasts with the ancient world. The common passion is to rule, the weakling is lost, and even in the few brave honest men the final word is power. The women are as wild as the men, e.g. King John's mother and Queen Margaret. Shakespeare gives us an exact picture of the horrible age of the Wars of the Roses—fierce, cruel, grimly humorous, but entirely a picture of power. Yet the grandeur of the whole group equals in power the noblest Greek tragedies.

John is not unskilfully composed, but has no true unity. We are in a world of conflicting interests, an intricate wilderness of exclusive selfishness. 'Commodity' rules: it is hard to discern on which side lies appparent right. If John feels conscience it is from outer, not inner, cause: as when he is glad that his order for murder is not carried out. Pandulph is the only consistent character, but he represents the ambition of the Church, and, willing to allow any means to obtain power, has no greatness. The Bastard, besides being clear and sympathetic, has the strong and positive feeling of patriotism. Constance is beautiful in her mother-love, but wild and ugly in her passionate rage. The more the play lacks unity, the more striking is the poetic fire of separate parts. There is no organic connexion between crime and suffering: the king's punishment comes from the Church, where he had least offended—and he only suffers physically.

Richard II is an early work, and shows traits of unripeness, but has unity and connexion, many truly dramatic scenes, and also a grand simplicity and truth of leading features and situations. It is the most appealing and affecting of any known play. Richard is an example of fate: he suffers and falls through his own fault, but his character grows with his unhappiness. The buried powers of the soul break forth, and contemplation helps to alleviate suffering. Bolingbroke lacks subjectivity, and is hard, except when politically amiable. But he is not excessively important, and we think Shakespeare might have given his calculating intellect the chance of more expression. We do not know if from the beginning he aimed to dethrone Richard. He may be compared with Octavius, as Richard with the fanciful Antony. We are left in doubt how far Richard was guilty as regards Gloster's murder. If guilty it should have returned to him in his prison monologue.

The chief value of *Henry IV* is in the character-drawing. Shakespeare gives us types of certain distinct human characters that are yet living, pithy individuals. Falstaff is the very essence of comedy, and men will laugh at him as long as laughter lasts. The play has a moral background: we have to do with justice as it interpenetrates the actions of man. The king discovers that his vassals claim the same right as he formerly did to rebel. We should find Falstaff less comic did he eat more and drink less—for the drinker stands higher than the eater. It is significant that he is stout, and relates to the fact that he has no shred of malice, spite, or ill-temper. We recall that Caesar liked stout persons and mistrusted the lean Cassius. He is timorous, because fear must be overcome by character—and how can he acquire character? His *naïveté* imports still more, without which he would not be a comic character: he is naïve although dissolute. He makes witty excuses for himself, but does not wish others to believe him, only to laugh with him. The King is of dry political mind and measured behaviour: and this alienates the Prince. The latter feigns to be worse than he is—but also Shakespeare wishes to show us that ripeness is only obtained by knowledge of depths as well as heights. We always feel that he has the power when he wills to break away from his low life. He is and remains a plain, honourable, sensible, practical man. His duel with Percy is the climax of the play. That the King has acted unjustly does not excuse the rebellion of the nobles. They are simply moved by personal envy, but what ennobles them is their warlike courage and chivalrous honour. Henry V has a right balance of intelligence, character, and feeling: he is one of the sound healthy natures. He crowns his character by giving the victory to God.

Henry VI's only crime was mildness, but Shakespeare never makes him ridiculous, and only allows a measure of irony to surround him, which leaves room for compassion. Soft, sympathetic feeling is all that he can offer to the victims of the storm. Although Margaret is a 'she-wolf', Shakespeare does not leave her without some softer traits. That she had to supply her husband's lack of power, and so reverse their relations, would in itself help towards her moral perversion. It is Henry's fault that she marches at the head of the troops and fights like a man. Such perverted strength is only bearable if it is genuine strength, with courage and firmness in misfortune—and we see these displayed in her powerful address at the battle of Tewkesbury.

With Richard III we affirm that it is not of the essence of poetry to represent a man entirely dehumanized—that we must feel some compassion at his downfall. Unlike Macbeth, Richard is wicked throughout, but like him he is disturbed darkly within, and is therefore human. He combines distinct powers like no other individual; with rough terrifying power he can use finesse; he is not only cunning, but he can play the actor and orator; he enjoys not only victory, but his own overwhelming ability. We look into the abyss, and it has for us a giddy attraction. What justifies him is the powerlessness and wasted condition of the world around him, where no one has will, or, if he has, it is perverted. The two young princes are the only innocent sufferers; Elizabeth is at least to blame in her nepotism. She and the Duchess of York awake our sympathy, but they are smirched with the prevailing corruption, and anger darkens their souls. The others who fall are bad, half bad, blind, weak, wholly egotistical. Richard appears as an instrument of punishment destroying all around him, and also himself, and thus paving the way for a fresh political life. Among self-seekers he is the supremest, and he alone is consistent. In his hypocrisy he is master of every tone—glow of love, pious humility, modesty, compassion, warm friendship—the whole scale of feeling. We see his wooing of Anne, and changes of tone in the scene with Elizabeth. His collapse is effected from within and without—his suppressed conscience begins to work. Nowhere is Shakespeare more reminiscent of Aeschylus and Sophocles.

Throughout the Roman plays breathes a truly antique spirit, and Shakespeare transfers himself into the statuesque simplicity of the ancients better than any other modern poet. *J.C.* is the best of all subjects for tragedy: a man who cannot emerge from a conflict with clear conscience will be torn to pieces in soul. It is man's lot to err when he enters into a fight between two principles partially justified. The right of Rome to remain a Republic has become only a formal one; and the anti-monarchists, who would preserve an anachronism, must resort to murder and conspiracy. The people have no longer a will of their own, and Caesar, who is in touch with his age, must incorporate the people's will. No one can handle this theme rightly who cannot appreciate the beauty of this compelling idea. The conspirators are so drawn that they represent the genuine old noble lofty spirit of Republican Rome. We know Caesar better from the description of others than his own appearance. His will is based on the majesty and energy of his character; he feels a universally historic right, yet he is not justified in appealing to this. He does not care because he believes that what he wills conforms to the spirit of the age, but because it responds to his pride. In daily matters he is vain and easily flattered; in great things he is crafty and deliberate and uses bribery. Among equals he is kind, open and true-hearted. But his undeniable greatness, and all that is free, generous, poetic, large, and brilliant in him, are here fully expressed, besides the heroic assurance with which he trusts to fate. On the whole, the play is a tragedy of principles: murder is committed without personal animosity. We could wish Brutus to be more sensible to the hideousness of murder and to his personal ingratitude to Caesar: but he would have been less the self-contained, steadfast Roman. His character is magnificently developed; he shares in the murder yet holds himself apart. He makes mistakes from humane motives which prevent success and effect his downfall.

The condensed, obscure style of *A. and C.* does not suit the grand ancient material as well as the homelier speech of *J.C.* Politics stand out, and are not justly connected with the human: hence lack of dramatic unity. Who is to rule the world, and will Antony free his soul? The political appears somewhat alien beside the human. Heroism and poetic enjoyment of life and love war in the heart of a highly placed man. It becomes the tragedy of moral backsliding, yet Antony still attracts. He was Caesar's friend and avenger, and belonged not to stern old Republican Rome, but had the larger sense of a world-conquering state. He united the lordliness and pomp of Rome, but was not man enough to withstand Eastern luxury. He was sensitive, imaginative, easily yielding, reflecting something of Shakespeare's self.[1] His ensnarer is also poetic and full of genius, so that we may feel he is not untrue to himself. Only in her love can he find the full beauty of life. Shakespeare describes every mood and phase of her mind, and how she torments and caresses Antony in the same breath. But she is not truly lovable, gracious, pleasant, and never displays her arts with winning charm. Only when Antony is dead does another spirit speak in her, as she realizes his greatness. She who loved display now experiences simple and eternal feelings of humanity: she has after all loved as far as she is able.

Coriolanus is essentially a tragedy of character, for the principle of aristocracy works in Coriolanus like a force of nature, and influences his whole temperament. If he insults the people his contempt in itself need not be wrong. Shakespeare has a growing distaste for the people, due no doubt to the behaviour of the groundlings at the theatre.[2] He blames Coriolanus for outrageous expression, not fundamental principle. He makes his faults those of a noble fiery spirit, too noble for this world. Revenge alone takes Coriolanus to the enemy's camp; he even wars against his aristocratic friends; and for this reason the tragic problem of this otherwise perfect play is not solved. According to Shakespeare it is the patricians only that he betrays: and when moved to forgo his purpose, he does not yield to the idea of Fatherland and the right of the people, but simply to the love for his family. . . .

Vischer does well to call Hamlet and Falstaff to witness that Shakespeare's characters are both types and individuals; and on the whole he excels in defining emotion accurately. The traditional faults of his countrymen still cling to him: he takes seriously Hamlet's comparison of himself to Hercules; he excuses Falstaff for the reason that it is less degrading to eat too much than to drink too much. But his method of analysing emotion proves incidentally that Shakespeare is for all time, without conscious striving to reconcile Shakespeare with modern thought. Such are his remarks on Hamlet: that he was too passionate to be deterred from action only by excess of thought; that like all highly gifted men he was inclined to madness; that he was satisfied with his mental triumph over the king. It has been generally conceded that Macbeth is imaginative and poetic, but his ambition has been denounced as worldly. Vischer discovers that imagination transfigures also the object of his ambition, and lordship is touched with beauty. Also, Macbeth's defenders have concentrated on the fact that he dies with courage; but Vischer describes him concisely as an inward wreck. Lady Macbeth is admirably summarized in the end as herself a ghost, and a stranger to herself. The remarks on *Othello* incline to the logical-poetical, but still have insight, viz.

[1] Cf. Frank Harris.   [2] Cf. Brandes.

that there is something low and mean in innate jealousy—that Iago
had known jealousy and would like Othello to suffer likewise. But
in the reasons he gives for Othello's suicide he again rises to the
heights. He says truly that only a deeply feeling nature like Lear's
would be utterly overthrown from the failure of love. On a lower
level it is well judged that he surrounds Henry VI with a measure of
irony that leaves room for compassion;[1] and he enters a sound apology
for Margaret—since it is a fact that foolish men produce knavish
women. We cannot omit his point that only in Cleopatra's love can
Antony find full beauty of life—and also that Cleopatra is not truly
lovable.

But we turn to the reverse side, and, as we said before, we discover the old faults, due to the old causes. Macbeth is compared with
Richard III; Caesar is considered indisputably great; if Antony
attracts it is because he was Caesar's avenger. We conclude that
Vischer has appreciated Shakespeare as philosopher and dramatist
rather than poet. The latter shows even in his best passage—on Lady
Macbeth—where he insists above all on her self-betrayal. His judgement has not been fined by communicated ecstasy from the Shakespearian rhythm. The following lines from *Hamlet*,

> In the most high and palmy state of Rome
> A little ere the mightiest Julius fell . . .

surely convey to us the greatness of Caesar and the majesty of Rome
more than the whole of *Julius Caesar*.

V

A few characteristic points may be extracted from the work of
L. Kellner.[2] After the horrors of the earliest plays Shakespeare first
fully reveals himself in *R. and J.*—a work of purest, most feeling
truth, of humanity in its strongest and most moving impulses. If
Shakespeare had created Juliet alone, and no other woman's character,
he would remain the panegyrist of women in English literature.
Romeo's impetuosity and passion might have made us anxious for
the future of the pair, if there had been a future. Already in *Venus*
Shakespeare had brought before us in a few words a landscape that
entrances the soul. Here also we feel the spirit of the place—how
fundamentally it belongs to the action and actors—how wonderfully
the colouring of the south is imparted. In its humour, of a broad
delightful kind, the play also far outstrips Shakespeare's youthful
work. *L.L.L.* is a firework of good and bad wit at the expense of all
that was exaggerated and over-refined in the day's speech. The
final condition imposed by Biron on Rosaline is a contrast to the playful

---

[1] Cf. Mr. Percy Lubbock's account in the *Craft of Fiction* of Flaubert's ironical
method of developing the character of Madame Bovary.   [2] *Sh.*, 1900.

tone—as between the beauty-drunk and self-seeking culture of the Renaissance, and the sober, altruistic puritan outlook on life. *Henry IV* and *Henry V* captivate us more by their humour than history. The *Merchant*, composed about the same time as *M.N.D.*, is separated as by a generation from that delightful marriage comedy. In the *Merchant* we see Shakespeare past the time when the senses exclusively determine our fate, and body and soul are governed by the love and desire of women. Friendship is now to the fore, and the passions therewith associated. It represents the highest ideal of friendship, and all else is subordinate. Not Shylock but Antonio is the hero, and his hatred for the Jew is impersonal: he hates him as a usurer who causes misery to his fellow-creatures. Shylock does not understand this impersonal hate, and looks upon Antonio as a personal enemy who has injured his business. When the chance comes he acts according to the old law of an eye for an eye.[1] No doubt Shakespeare felt like Antonio, but with his seer's gift he would understand the Jew's inner soul, and he makes him speak as if he himself had to revenge the degradation of a thousand years on his hereditary enemy. In the interest of his art he could not deny a certain greatness to the usurer, and for the sake of dramatic balance he made him no unworthy antagonist to Antonio. If we laugh heartily at Falstaff and are not repelled by him, it is because he has nothing in common with us who have by inheritance and upbringing a consciousness in the blood of morality. Falstaff as a moral being belongs to another sphere; his nature places him beyond good and evil; he shocks us no more than does an animal. *Othello* gives us the chance to gauge fully Shakespeare's power of transforming a dead original into living poetry. The most terrible and perfect of his tragedies, it brings us closest to the fate of the ancients. The last three plays reveal Shakespeare once more reconciled with life, and looking with clear untroubled eyes on the world. As if to balance Cressida and Cleopatra, he creates Imogen, Hermione, Miranda, the purest and most lovable women characters in literature.

Character is the first and most important thing with Shakespeare; the Hamlet material attracted him only on account of the psychological problem: and in this way he gives a wholly new spirit to the borrowed matter. In contrast to his predecessors he developed a technique by means of which he laid bare the innermost soul of his heroes, and made clear their motives and spring of action in their deeds. Only the characters of the youthful works explain themselves by monologue. When Hamlet analyses his conduct, it is the logical consequence of plot and character. Shakespeare mostly uses four ways to describe his characters: action, slight unconscious traits, contrast with other characters, the opinions of other characters. The

[1] Cf. Brandes.

mood, slightly perceptible with Marlowe and others, is an essential dramatic point with Shakespeare. Before each important scene something, perhaps quite slight, prepares in us the true receptive condition. *M.N.D.* would be unthinkable apart from a certain frame of mind; and the witch scenes in *Macbeth* would move us comically. . . .

Kellner is unduly concerned with moral questions; he has a kind of fatherly anxiety for Romeo, in the event of his having lived—and he feels himself of a different species to Falstaff. When he says that Falstaff is beyond good and evil he approaches a great truth of art by a wrong road—as Ignorance approached the Celestial City. But where he rings true is in defining the mood of the play—the Renaissance, Puritan mood of *L.L.L.*, the marriage mood of *M.N.D.*, the friendship of the *Merchant*. We may hesitate whether Antonio is the true hero, whether his hatred is impersonal; but in the moment of hesitation the atmosphere of the play is brought home. It is well to recognize that character is Shakespeare's great transfiguring agent; and he is thus not far from understanding that poetry is the great moving force of all.

VI

BRANDES acclaims Shakespeare as an artist who seeks truth to nature as the highest quality in art, whose art is that of nature itself. His plot construction shows incomparable artistic dexterity. Traumann alludes to his technical and artistic mastery. Türck calls him the greatest dramatic poet of all times. Vischer says that his composition is deeply designed, that he is the father of the drama and modern poetry. He is a realist, but not in the photographic sense.

We will approach the moral side with a remark of Brandes—that in his artist soul there was a peculiar blending of the enthusiast and cynic. He has also two further general remarks: the first, that with Shakespeare the morality of voluntary self-reform and self-control is the determining factor in human life; the second, that in morals Shakespeare did not believe in unconditional duties and absolute prohibitions—in external actions apart from will—but only in the ethics of intention. Traumann says that his conception was ethical; Türck, that with him moral feeling was as perfectly developed as aesthetic and intellectual. Vischer finds a stern moral kernel in all his work, and has many more things to say on the moral question: that he thinks all depends on will; he is the poet of conscience, he believes in the divine ordering of the world.

As delineator of character, Brandes calls him a Prometheus in his power to create human beings. He also says Shakespeare understood that our moods and passions are rooted in the unconscious. Traumann and Vischer speak of his knowledge of the passions. Vischer also says that he can transplant himself into all forms of existence and enter into foreign temperaments; that his characters are both types and individuals. Character is the most important thing with Shakespeare, according to Kellner.

Brandes calls his conception of history aristocratic and naïvely heroic. He was not interested in constitutional or parliamentary matters; he had no systematic political conviction, but was mostly loyal and monarchical. Yet he lacked both historical and classical culture. Vischer, on the other hand, describes him as a political poet; and if he had no social sense, he was at least no conservative or reactionary. As we have no remarks on Shakespeare's religion, except Vischer's already quoted, which bordered upon the moral, we will here include those by Brandes which border upon the political: that he had no anti-Catholic prejudice; and that he did not care for ecclesiastical matters.

We can offset Kellner's judgement, that Shakespeare does not reveal himself in his works, with a number of intuitions from Brandes: that he was full of loftiness and charm, had a deep and passionate emotional nature, was socially ambitious, &c. Kellner calls him the panegyrist of women. . . .

Brandes stands out from the Germans as illustrating the decline of faith in Shakespeare's omnipotence. His admiration for Shakespeare as a poet is equal to theirs, but it does not extend to his knowledge of religion, morals, history, &c. In the war between religion and science, the religious leaders only at last realized that Christianity was independent of history and physical geography: and so the critics are realizing with time that what matters is the fine essence of Shakespeare's poetical genius.

Chapter XXX

ENGLAND 1901–1903

I. STEPHEN. II. THORNDIKE. III. YEATS. IV. LOUNSBURY. V. MAC-
MILLAN. VI. ARTHUR SYMONS. VII. COURTHOPE. VIII. SECCOMBE
AND ALLEN. IX. MOULTON. X. CONCLUSION.

I

LESLIE STEPHEN'S essay[1] was suggested to him by the study of
the works of Sidney Lee and Brandes. The first maintains that
we can know nothing of Shakespeare from his plays; the second, that
they are more or less distinctly correlated with certain passages in his
personal history. To Stephen himself one main interest in reading is
communion with the author—though self-revelation may be involuntary or incidental. Shakespearian criticism has too often meant reckless
competition in hyperboles, and the critic should curb his enthusiasm
and seek to form a sane judgement. It is true that Shakespeare, as
dramatist, was not responsible for the opinions of his characters; yet
we know Ben Jonson from his plays alone. As Shakespeare's greatest
power was to produce varied characters, he must have been capable of
an astonishing variety of moods and sympathies. He is never didactic,
he never sentences his characters to heaven or hell, but like a true
artist simple displays the facts. Hence the difficulty of translating his
implicit convictions into an abstract theory in order to discover his
moral system.

The inference is not that Shakespeare cannot be known, but that
knowledge of him must be attained through a less obvious process.
It is one thing to know, another to analyse and formulate our
knowledge. Cross-examination might draw from critics that their
knowledge is more precise than they think. They would agree in
certain commonplaces and negations: and what is accepted about the
poetry implies conclusions about the man. A dramatist cannot bestow
talents he does not possess: therefore Shakespeare has humour.
Neither Ben Jonson nor Marlowe could have written Mercutio's
Queen Mab speech or Jaques's moralizings. Humour and fancy are
functions of character as well as reason. It is agreed that Shakespeare's
mind is vivid and subtle, and his power to blend tragic and comic is
unique: here also are indications of character. It is clear, from *M.N.D.*
and *A.Y.L.*, that he enjoyed natural scenery, and was sensitive to the
beauties of flowers and spring-time; and it is surely equally clear that
he enjoyed convivial meetings at taverns. The conception of a Puritan
Shakespeare involves a contradiction in terms. His religion, apart
from the irrelevant question of external form, included a profound

[1] 'Sh. as a Man,' 1901 (*Studies of a Biographer*, vol. iv. Duckworth, 1902).

sense of the mystery of the world and the pettiness of men's lives. He despised a pedant; and in politics he was undoubtedly an intellectual aristocrat. His contempt for the mob is good-humoured but unequivocal. In *T. and C.* he may be speaking dramatically, but he fully appreciates the argument for order.

The author of *R. and J.* must have been capable of Romeo's passion. He would not find the most memorable utterance in literature of passions of which he was not himself abnormally susceptible, or give originality to the most commonplace of all themes. To read the poems of Burns and Byron, without knowledge of their lives, would justify us in inferring that they were men of strong passions. We must, however, beware of hasty conclusions, for though it is possible to infer that a man has certain propensities, we do not know how far circumstance and other propensities may hold them in check. We put all the indications together, but cannot say which are the dominant instincts and how different impulses modify each other in active life.

His plays in chronological series enable us to trace his intellectual development, and we can compare him with himself. We see how humour checks the bombastic tendency, and the broader and deeper view of life begets temperance. The Sonnets are supposed to show that he underwent a spiritual crisis—but Sidney Lee's discovery that he was falling in with a temporary fashion deprives this argument of its force. Even if the story were true it had no permanent bearing on his life. He continued to work for the theatre and make money. Thersites and Timon may have pleased the public, or suited the part of one of his company. We do not doubt that he suffered greatly: to read the catalogue of evils in *M. for M.* is to feel the presence of a real man. If we infer that he felt intensely the emotions which he expressed, it is possible to invert the argument. His life does not explain his genius, but makes it a puzzle: and we wonder, with Emerson, how the supreme poet could have lived the life of an actor-manager.

The antithesis admits of conciliation: he does not idealize in the sense of neglecting the actual. From Hamlet's expressed regard for Horatio ('Whose blood and judgement', &c.), and Henry V, the one character who, as commentators agree, represents a personal enthusiasm, we see the value, in his eyes, of self-command.[1] The Prince's speech, 'I know you all . . .', is partly undramatic; and Shakespeare expects us to approve the exile of Falstaff. He sympathizes with Coriolanus and Antony—but they fall because they do not unite the two characteristics, because blood is not 'commingled' with judgement. This suggestion is illustrated by Shakespeare's life. He had the same temptations as Greene and Marlowe, and did not escape them by coldness of temperament. He could dream, but he was also keenly awake to a living world of men. Insight into human nature is a good

[1] Cf. Brandes.

qualification for business. His ambitions and preferences were probably like Scott's: he wished to live like a country gentleman, he admired men of action above poets, and he held aloof from literary squabbles. He wrote his plays to make money—and only in the greatest the inspiration lasts throughout. He puts out his power when the situation holds him, but there are many signs of indifference—haste, flagging of interest, readiness to forgive a character, or accept an unsatisfactory catastrophe.

In sum, we have an abnormally sensitive man, who accomplished a prosperous and outwardly commonplace career. He overcame temptation, but rejected Puritanism. He could sympathize with every passion, but not with the overstrained heroic of Marlowe or Chapman. Humour keeps him from bombast, and he sees facts clearly enough to realize the vanity of human wishes. These are personal traits that practically agree with what we know of his life. . . .

Like everything that Leslie Stephen wrote, this essay has a sound logical basis. The ground conquered will not be yielded again, the characteristics which he has disengaged—humour, love of conviviality, sense of mystery, self-control—are Shakespeare's beyond dispute. If they do not explain the whole man, it is, as the critic admits, that we lack concrete instances in his life, and therefore cannot tell the proportion of his qualities. However, Stephen has built a half-way house on the great road, which no traveller can henceforth neglect: and its design and use are characteristic of the builder. We are just touched with surprise that he accepts Henry V as autobiographical, and Falstaff's exile intended to be approved—and of the examples drawn from the plays that of Romeo is the least convincing. Here he hardly allows for the 'disrealizing power of the imagination',[1] and we would quote against him Professor Gilbert Murray's warning not to apply a merely external test to something that depends on the most intimate workings of a man's imagination; and his further remark that the most important thing in a poem is the intensity of imagination with which the poet has realized his subject.[2]

II

MOST critics agree that Shakespeare was influenced by the fashions of the stage, but few who accept the four periods allow for it. Mr. Ashley H. Thorndike[3] makes this the basis of his theory which is skilfully worked out. He also indirectly contributes some sound general Shakespearian criticism by noting how inevitably Shakespeare transcended his models.

After his early experimental period Shakespeare's debt to his

[1] Saintsbury.   [2] *Rise of the Greek Epic*, p. 264.
[3] *The Influence of Beaumont and Fletcher on Sh.*, 1901 (Worcester, Massachusetts).

contemporaries has been little noticed. When he retired, Beaumont and Fletcher were the most popular playwrights of the day. Their work was a new development in the Elizabethan drama, and the theatrical tradition was mostly continuous. Elizabethan dramatists kept closely in touch with theatrical conventions. Beaumont and Fletcher created the heroic romance, and Shakespeare was most ready to make use of what was popular. The romance-traits were a sentimental love story, a rapid succession of tragic situations, and a happy ending. There must have been an objective cause for Shakespeare's change from tragedy to romance.

Before Shakespeare retired Beaumont and Fletcher were famous. Shakespeare produced his tragedies 1601–9; and between 1607 and 1611 Beaumont and Fletcher produced six romances. To find any close resemblance to the material of the romances we must go to plays before 1601. Between 1601 and 1611 satirical and realistic comedies held the stage, or thorough-going tragedies. Shakespeare's romances and those of Beaumont and Fletcher departed from the practice of contemporaries; whereas other dramatists kept to farces, satires, and tragedies. It may be as important to note that when in 1601 Shakespeare turned from romantic comedy and chronicle history to tragedy he was following a general dramatic movement as much as personal experience.

The plots of Beaumont and Fletcher are ingenious and improbable; they treat heroic persons and actions, kings and princes, conquests and usurpations. The scene is laid in far-off places to permit strange happenings. There is always a sentimental love story, contrasted with one of gross sensual passion. To ensure a varied emotional effect they never construct a play about one central passion. Shakespeare's great tragedies are constructed according to the chronological outline of an historical narrative. Beaumont and Fletcher never imitated history, but sought to give a series of situations each of which should interest of itself, and all lead up to a startling climax. They were not truly dramatic like Shakespeare's tragedies where action was in part developed from character, but theatrically effective. Each situation may not promote the main action, but tells by itself on the stage. In the *Maid's Tragedy* a number of situations, some not uncommon, are welded together in a denouement perhaps unequalled by any other in Elizabethan drama in power to hold the interest of an audience at fever heat. There is also the use of tragi-comedy, the violent contrast of comic and tragic emotion, and the peculiar handling of the happy ending. The conflict is dramatically heightened between tragic and sentimental emotions. Pure love is constantly on the rack of tragic circumstance. In *Philaster* and *A King and No King* the happy ending is an effective and surprising culmination of a series of tragic situations. To the last scene their romances are all tragi-

comedies or all tragedies: and then comes the tragic or happy denouement. Their style is the result of effort to be effective on the
stage.

Characters are necessarily little individualized among collections
of situations which give vivid momentary pictures of passions. Philaster
is presented in such varied moods that he is slightly individual. All
are either bad or good, for if there is any hesitation the situation loses.
Evil is sharply set off by good, at the expense of reality. Characters
are presented by description, so that the interest of the audience may
remain centred on the plot. At the same time sympathy is enlisted for
the proper persons. There are conventional types—love-lorn maidens
depending for their charm on the poetry that describes them—evil
women with no shame—faithful friends.

Fletcher's style abounds in feminine endings and end-stopped lines,
and the whole effect is that of unpremeditated and disconnected
discourse. Yet in the change from the period to a looser style there is
a structural difference—a gradual advance which influenced Shakespeare's later verse. Fletcher formed his style with special reference to
stage action. In some cases—e.g. in *Bonduca*—he even surpasses
Shakespeare at his best. Every line helps to give the effect of unpremeditated speech. Beaumont's verse is more like Shakespeare's middle
period; his imagination in intensity and originality is nearest Shakespeare's of all contemporaries. He, too, gives the effect of natural
speech, without Fletcher's mannerisms, and while far less revolutionary
than Fletcher, represents a general advance to thoroughly dramatic
verse. All characteristics of romances serve the same end—to make
them act capitally.

Shakespeare's plots in his romances are other than in his earlier
plays. He has not stories of gross sexual passion like Beaumont
and Fletcher; the basis is pure and sentimental love. The material is
not from history or real life, but 'romantic', giving theatrical novelty
and variety. The story of Imogen unites idyllic and tragic events in
more marked contrast than anything before in Shakespeare. The
emotion is varied, not centred, as in the tragedies and best comedies.
The romance method is in the plot, where a series of effective situations
are connected to lead up to a telling denouement: the sole aim being
theatrical effectiveness.

The transition shows in *Cymbeline* where the historical part is
little connected with the history of Imogen, &c. The method is to
link together a series of situations involving intense and varied action,
and preparing for an elaborate denouement. In *Cymbeline*, the
W. Tale, and the *Tempest* the tragic incidents are not carried to
a tragic conclusion. The happy end in *Cymbeline* is caused by violation
of poetic justice; in *W. Tale* it is substituted for the tragic end of
Greene's novel; in the *Tempest* it is expanded into the entire play.

Shakespeare may have written these plays to inculcate forgiveness; he certainly did write them to be acted on the stage.

The characters are less individuals, less consistent, subtly drawn and plausibly human, and more creatures of stage situations. As in Beaumont and Fletcher, their salient characteristics are exaggerated, and they are often heightened types of perfect virtue or utter depravity. Leontes is not a very real human being; we see, by comparing him with Othello, that his feelings are intensified to suit situations. Hermione, the Queen in *Cymbeline*, and Sebastian and Antonio in the *Tempest* are also creatures of situations. Imogen, like most perfect people, is not real but idealized, and compared with Shakespeare's other women lacks details of characterization. Shakespeare with his delicate and pure fancy and exquisitely fit verse achieved what Beaumont and Fletcher were always trying to do with their Bellarios and Aspatias. She has little trace of individual character, and what she says suits the situation. Her various acts can hardly be recognized as of the same individual, and her character is presented largely through the comments and descriptions of others. Perdita and Miranda are still less individuals. The ideas of Perdita's beauty and grace of her character come from what others say, and from her silence. She is a conventional romantic heroine beautifully described, but not a successful piece of purely dramatic characterization. Miranda says still less, and is therefore regarded as more ethereally ideal. On the stage Shakespeare's heroines hardly differed from those of Beaumont and Fletcher, and yet Shakespeare drew no sentimentalized heroine in the eight years between *Twelfth-Night* and *Cymbeline*. Beaumont and Fletcher fail to suggest the same delicate sentiment as Shakespeare. Shakespeare transformed the heroine into a beautiful idealized being characteristically his own, but on analysis as stage personage she still presents the characteristics of Beaumont and Fletcher's ideal maidens. Even Imogen is no other than Bellario plus Shakespeare's poetry. If character yields to situations the cause is the demand of the London stage.

The verse, compared with *A. and C.*, shows puzzling decadence. There are more double endings, also an effort to conceal metre, so that verse borders on prose. As with Fletcher the aim was to imitate speech. It is obscure partly because the broken sentence structure is carried to extreme, and partly due to Shakespeare's intense and rapid imagination, in which he differed fundamentally from Fletcher. In the *W. Tale* the bear, the dances, the change of clothes are all for stage effect and the craving of the audience for novelty; as also Caliban, Ariel, and the vanishing banquet—while Prospero is an imposing spectacular figure. Shakespeare was combining the construction, pageantry, and devices of the court masque as Beaumont and Fletcher did in the *Four Plays*.

The success of *Philaster* must have interested Shakespeare, and with his usual quickness to take advantage of anything the contemporary drama offered, he forsook themes with which he had been dealing for seven years and started to write a play in friendly rivalry. He saw that a happy ending was effective, and he specially laboured over a happy denouement. It is significant that he abandoned romantic comedy for tragedy at a time when other dramatists were turning from romance. He never originated a dramatic type, and *Cymbeline* differs markedly from any play he had previously written.[1] Its differences prove to be traits similar to those characteristics of the Beaumont and Fletcher romances. It was an experiment in new fields made by a consummate adapter, and in the *W. Tale* and the *Tempest* Shakespeare transforms the experimental form of *Cymbeline* into something indisputably his own. In the *W. Tale* he does not weave idyllic scenes and sentimental love story into the main plot, but adds them in an almost separate play which occupies the whole of Act IV. His original treatment of the idyllic element and reality is unapproached by Beaumont and Fletcher. Only this fourth act has the atmosphere of reality in romance; in the fifth, the two distinct plays are united with due regard for an unexpected and effective denouement. The play is a succession of situations, and in the fourth act Shakespeare originally develops the inevitable idyll largely by introducing characters from real life. Perdita's vitality is rather from the atmosphere of real life in country scenes than anything individual in herself. The whole of the *Tempest* is a surprising romantic denouement. Shakespeare was striving for stage effect—the island, Prospero's magic, Caliban, Ariel, the pageantry—all appealed to an Elizabethan audience. The characters were mostly developed conventionalized types. . . .

It would certainly be difficult to refute arguments, like these, that are moderately stated, well-balanced, and preserve a due mean between inner and outer—the requirements of the Elizabethan stage and Shakespeare's transcendent genius. The author does not force facts to suit his theory; he seems rather to have first become dispassionately convinced of it. There is a certain kind of criticism which sets out to be aggressively original and to condemn as lumber the accumulated wisdom of the past. We have specially noted this with some previous American critics—the natural result of a younger inherited civilization and culture. Mr. Thorndike is certainly not aggressive, and he is original in a quiet, unconscious manner. Facts present themselves to his mind and he records them for their own sake, whether or not they break with tradition. If we are right in our distinction about American criticism, this is the better side of it. His

[1] Dowden writes: 'It is not proved . . . that *Cym.* did not chronologically precede *Philaster*. And . . . the type of the Shn dramatic romance had been at least outlined or sketched in the Marina romance of *Pericles*.' Intro. to *Cym.*, Arden edit., 1903.

remarks on Shakespeare's characters in the romances are especially noteworthy; they explain Leontes and also the heroines. It is true that Imogen is the creation of Shakespeare's poetry, that dramatically she cannot compare with the heroines of the comedies. So is it with Miranda, but in a distinctly less degree with Perdita—and we rather doubt if Mr. Thorndike appreciates Hermione, or the *Tempest*, as a play.

III

THE essay of Mr. W. B. Yeats[1] is an instance of what one who is himself a great poet, though born in a distant age, and concerned with far different themes, but with an intensely original mind, can discover in Shakespeare. He argues against the man of action and complains that the Shakespearian critic has become a vulgar worshipper of success. You cannot know a man from his actions because you cannot watch him in every kind of circumstance—and abundance as often as emptiness makes a man useless to the State. Fortinbras, Aufidius, Henry V are not greater in the divine hierarchies than Hamlet, Coriolanus, Richard II. The latter failed partly because he lacked qualities which his scullions possessed, ánd more because he had certain qualities that are uncommon in all ages. According to Mr. Yeats, Shakespeare saw that such a man through sheer bewilderment and impatience can become as unjust or as violent as any common man, any Bolingbroke or Prince John, and yet remain 'that sweet lovely rose'. And he notes that Henry V fails in the end, as all men great and little fail in Shakespeare.

In these last two sentences Mr. Yeats's temperamental criticism is at its best: there are times when it dwindles into prejudice. He speaks of the growing conviction among Shakespearian critics that the commonplace shall inherit the earth. Henry V has a resounding rhetoric that moves man as a leading article does to-day. He has gross vices and coarse nerves, and turns his friends away when they have served his purpose. He adds that the finest thing in the play is the way Henry's old companions fall out of it broken-hearted or on their way to the gallows. This is certainly true of Falstaff, but hardly of Pistol and the others.

Lastly, he deplores the influence of Italy and the Renaissance on English history, because even Shakespeare cannot write perfectly when his web is woven of threads that have been spun in many lands. From these self-revealing words we see how he conceives of the poet's task—how, for himself, the dream-world overcomes the real. Hamlet, he says, saw too great issues everywhere to play the trivial game of life.

[1] 'At Stratford-on-Avon,' 1901 (*Ideas of Good and Evil*. Bullen, 1903).

IV

MR. THOMAS R. LOUNSBURY[1] shows why Shakespeare was depreciated as an artist until the close of the eighteenth century. He proves satisfactorily that the art which Shakespeare was accused of neglecting was merely convention, and finally gives examples from the plays where the inner truth depends on that higher art which Shakespeare consciously practised.

Scholars in Italy succeeded in making the drama conform to the rules of the ancient stage, and in the late sixteenth and early seventeenth centuries Italian influence was strong in England. The controversy about the unities is confined to time and place, because no one will dispute unity of action. Did Shakespeare lack art because he ignored unities of time and place? Aristotle was no law giver, but an observer who registered Greek practice. Italy was their real birthplace, and France their cherished home. The early English dramatists ignored them, but Ben Jonson became their champion, and he was the literary autocrat of his age. Yet only with the Restoration was there general assent, due to French taste. This increased in the eighteenth century, with Voltaire, and it was dread of the critics, not the audience, that made the English writers keep the unities. Dr. Johnson and Dennis opposed them, and there was growing dissent, and yet the playwrights observed them strictly.

However, such was the universal deference to Shakespeare that he was exempted, and granted the divine right to act wrong. Lessing was the first to see in him as great an artist as poet, and to show the unities were unfit for modern drama. The Greeks observed unities of time and place for the sake of the chorus. Is it morally possible that events should happen in one day which are supposed to do so in the drama? Not the physical but the moral unity should be considered. The fundamental distinction is that the drama which disregards unities gives the widest possible scope for display of different passions; that which observes them brings on the scene man under the storm and stress of a single dominant passion: and men are not single-minded. Dryden's *A. and C.* shows no trace of conflicting currents of thought and feeling as in Shakespeare. Shakespeare's plays were frequently acted in the eighteenth century and produced a deepening impression. They were gradually accepted as fullest examples of that art which held the mirror up to nature. Critics are divided as to whether he was a conscious artist, but it is unlikely that the greatest dramatic genius of his time should not know what every playwright must have discussed. Note the Prologues to *Henry V*; and in the *Errors* and *Tempest* he designedly kept to the unities. In modern drama prominence of love is against the unities.

[1] *Sh. as a Dramatic Artist*, 1902 (New York, Scribner).

The classicists condemned tragi-comedy, and the French censured
the grave-digger scene in *Hamlet*. Another gulf between him and the
French was that he included all sorts and conditions of men and
let Fools speak to Kings. He proved that his method conformed to
nature and highest art, and he saw possibilities in the contrast of opposed
characters. The all-licensed Fool utters what others think but fear
to say;[1] while mingled comic and tragic represents life as it is. In
most tragical events there is a humorous element, and vice versa.
Shakespeare knew that humour relieved the strain, and added by
contrast to the effect of the serious. The grave-digger scene shows
the world's indifference to private sorrow.

In the French theatre which gave the law to Europe there were
no violent scenes. Classicists excluded from the stage what would
be disagreeable or painful in life. The Teutonic nations differed, and
Shakespeare, of course, followed custom, but a great way off. His
genius enabled him to seize the good and reject the bad, but he fully
sympathized with the principles of the romantic school. The French
were right to reject horrors on the stage, because they may stir more
in narration. The murder of Duncan affects more because it is not
seen; the soul is thrilled and the susceptibilities not offended. In this
the art of *Macbeth* is above *Lear* and *Othello*. Eighteenth-century
English criticism was subservient to French, and but for Shakespeare
the English race with its love of action might have yielded to that
kind of drama where declamation and narrative take the place of
action and are considered the only true art. Fortunately the audiences
of the pit and galleries did not pretend to like what they found tedious:
and they instinctively recognized Shakespeare. Shakespeare mixed
rhyme and blank verse and prose, and introduced prose into tragedy,
and was guilty of every dramatic sin. In time it dawned on men that
conventions concerned only the mechanism of a play and had little to
do with its character as a work of art. This depended on whether or
not it produced effectively the result at which the writer aimed.

In the Restoration period Shakespeare was eclipsed and Ben Jonson
preferred, and also Beaumont and Fletcher for their licentiousness.
Yet critical literature reveals a steadily growing conviction of Shakespeare's immense superiority. At last it was inferred that what
Shakespeare did was artistically great and possessed therefore that
enduring vitality which belongs to everything so created. The
eighteenth-century alterations to his plays show that dramatically his
fine speeches can never be safely wrenched from the characters who
utter them. In the *Merchant*, through Antonio's foreboding, Shakespeare, with artist-like care, prepared us for the horrible reality.
Lansdowne discards this in his adaptation. A word altered in the trial
scene impairs the flawlessness of the perfect whole. Lest Shylock

[1] Cf. Thümmel.

should seem too hardly used it was necessary to bring out his malignity. This is done by the emphatic way in which he refuses the money offered to him thrice over. Again, Lansdowne omits this. The intense and agonizing feeling which slowly but steadily deepens and broadens on both sides is no longer felt. In Lansdowne Shylock ceases to be exalted by the wrath of his race. He does not show the sublime hate which awes by intensity and gives grandeur to malignity. He is willing to sacrifice some money to free himself for good from a man who has thwarted him in his bargains. His antipathy is that of a business investment, and he is no longer the representative of the long martyrdom of a race.

At the end of the seventeenth century professional criticism took 'inspired barbarian' views of Shakespeare—that his vast genius was independent of the rules of the highest art. The eighteenth century admired Shakespeare and admired itself for doing so—for being catholic enough to condone his faults. They admired in fact what in theory they were bound to condemn. Shakespeare took possession of the heart—though the understanding might protest; whereas those dramatists who kept all the rules were uninteresting. They fell back on the theory that Shakespeare was somehow above art; it never struck them that he neglected not art but convention. In the last quarter of the eighteenth century there was less regard for foreign opinion—which itself was beginning to feel Shakespeare's influence. The modern view was slowly forming, that Shakespeare was not ignorant of the rules, but knew them to be inapplicable. At times he goes wrong—puns, quibbles, Valentine's surrender, Helena's pursuit of Bertram, &c.—but as a rule all is vigilantly foreseen not to jar. Gloster's leap from the cliff has been censured—but he was an easy victim to superstition, and his mind and body were unsettled by terrible experiences.

Shakespeare's poetic justice has been assailed, but one cause of his fame's increase, the unchanging deference paid to the pure in literature, is a tribute to the permanent hold which high things have over the human heart. There are licentious allusions in the plays, but the Elizabethan drama was the representative national literature and appealed to all classes. When Shakespeare sins thus it is only in connexion with verbal quibbles, rarely with the business of the play—unlike Beaumont and Fletcher where it is engrained into the texture of the plot. But his greatness as a moral teacher is not confined to delicacy —and deeper insight made him reject 'poetic justice'. He succeeded as a moralist because his moral is not obtrusive, and comment rises naturally from the situation. But his real moral greatness is that he steadily unfolds before our eyes the inevitable results of sin, crime, errors of all kinds. He knew that to observe poetic justice was to please rather than instruct, and that responsibility for our deeds cannot be measured by the results which we ourselves willingly or unwillingly encounter. In *Macbeth* there is an element of poetic justice, but subsidiary. What arrests is the gradual transforming power of sin when once it has fully possessed the soul, and its different way of devastating different natures. Macbeth becomes a tyrant inaccessible to remorse and pity; his wife's finer and higher-strung nature pays full penalty in remorse. It is not Greek fatalism, but the idea that what unites all is existence of a reign of law, inexorable sequence of cause and effect. . . .

Before Mr. Lounsbury's book the discussions on Shakespeare's art were rather vague. It was said by early critics that he lacked art, and then that he was exempt from rules and followed nature. Later came treatises on the construction of his plays, and talk about Nemesis, and collisions, and underplots, &c., but all these things are preliminaries. Mr. Lounsbury has made a useful historical summary of the view of seventeenth- and eighteenth-century critics, and brings out Shakespeare's greatness by their limitations. The impression left by successful art is one of heightened life: the poet should so use words as to make this world appear more real, more beautiful, more mysterious. In what he tells us of the *Merchant* and *Macbeth*, Mr. Lounsbury proves that Shakespeare discarded conventions in order to use the drama in this extended way. This is the first impression from his book; the second is that criticism is an art which grew slowly, and with many a set-back, and that the public were wiser than the doctors. We may compare his work with Mr. Thorndike's, and recall our sayings that American criticism reflects a younger culture. This appears in some of the aesthetic points which Mr. Lounsbury makes, which are half-facts, e.g. that it was necessary to bring out Shylock's malignity lest he should seem too hardly used.

Mr. Lounsbury's second book[1] is indirectly important at this moment in the story of Shakespearian criticism. It summarizes the history of his fame in France to the end of the eighteenth century, in its fight against classicism, represented by Voltaire. It is well to keep in mind his remark that few realize how mighty was Voltaire's influence throughout Europe during the eighteenth century.

Of Shakespeare's plays Voltaire was best acquainted with *J.C.* and *Hamlet*, but he had no great knowledge of English literature. He did make Shakespeare known to Europe, but perhaps retarded true appreciation of him. He did not scruple to misrepresent, and he was responsible for the estimate of Shakespeare through much of the eighteenth century. He strengthened the conviction that the unities were of the first importance. In Shakespeare's English defenders there was an apologetic tone; yet they insisted that beauties produced by observing rules were secondary, and could be attained by lesser men,

[1] *Sh. and Voltaire*, 1902 (New York, Scribner).

that to be a great dramatic poet you must have natural qualities and power to excite passions. Shakespeare excelled in this genius of the first order, and also in character-drawing.

Voltaire had not taken Shakespeare seriously, but as time went on he became alarmed at the admiration of him. He had admitted he could produce admirable scenes, but that each of his works was deficient as a whole. As the French had been ignorant of Shakespeare there had been no one to contradict, but now things were changed. La Place—about 1750—was far in advance of his time. Voltaire had contributed little to the real understanding of Shakespeare, but had indirectly stimulated interest in him. Now his vanity was excited, and he dwelt on Shakespeare's faults. In the depth of him was a rugged intellectual honesty; he was as much attracted by Shakespeare's power as shocked by his practice. He became more hostile with years, but his change was due rather to the change in France than to his own opinion. He secretly dreaded lest the careful dramatic art in which the French excelled even the Greeks should be swept away by the rude brute strength of a savage barbarian. He explained that Shakespeare was popular because he appealed to all classes; he had deluded himself to believe it would be easy to interest if one paid no heed to rules, and never thought it was not the thing done but the manner of doing it.

His translation of *J.C.* was a travesty, but he relied on the ignorance of his readers and their faith in himself. The French were vaguely realizing that what their drama had gained in beauty it had lost in naturalness and power, that no literature can succeed permanently which does not strike its roots deep down into national character and life. Voltaire did not understand this; his disbelief in Shakespeare grew; he employed all his powers of irony, sarcasm, invective against him, also misrepresentation and calumny. Besides, he knew what he owed to Shakespeare and had never acknowledged. His misrepresentation was not wholly intentional, but partly the result of ingrained habits of mind: he could make himself believe what he wished. He imposed on many, for his admirers thought him impartial and intimately acquainted with Shakespeare's works. He never really changed, but in later years he stressed Shakespeare's faults. He was angry at undue admiration, and he was sincere in believing that he was defending good sense and taste. . . .

We think Mr. Lounsbury overdoes the charge of misrepresentation and calumny. Our opinion has not changed: that Voltaire from first to last looked upon Shakespeare as an inspired barbarian, but in early years he concentrated upon the inspiration and in later upon the barbarism.

V

MR. MICHAEL MACMILLAN[1] has some noteworthy remarks
on the characters of *J.C.* They are more fine and subtly distinguished
than what have been previously written, but they owe their being to
these earlier verdicts. Except with Antony, they seem the result of
renewed reading and meditation over the opinions of others, until
a more delicate offspring of the same stock is created rather than
a new species.

Writing of the defects in Caesar's character, he says that it is the
conspirators who insist on them, as is dramatically proper. When
Caesar reveals them it is in the privacy of his home. Nor are these very
marked, nor incompatible with true greatness. Brutus has the imprac-
ticable idea of conducting a conspiracy to murder on moral principles.
He cannot extort money, and gets Cassius to do it, and is unjust when
the latter cannot give all he wants. No other Shakespearian hero
rises to such a high pitch of moral perfection. He has the pride of
conscious virtue, and his earnest pursuit of virtue is a refined kind of
egoism. He is ambitious as Caesar, but of personal honour—the
honour to be derived from living a consistently virtuous life. The
harsh, choleric disposition of Cassius makes him unattractive, and
this gives pain to his nature which was passionate and loving and made
him secretly hunger after the love of his fellow men. He could be
unscrupulous, yet did not consciously try to seduce Brutus from the
path of honour. He was a true republican, but his passionate temper
made him feel a strong personal hatred against the tyrant. Had envy
only moved him, he would not have won the devotion of his followers
and the friendship of Brutus. Antony is susceptible to every kind of
beauty, even that of virtue to which he does not pretend. Thus he
can appreciate Brutus, while the latter never thinks him formidable.

Two more of Mr. Macmillan's remarks on the play, as it appears
to modern eyes, are worth noting. It has often been said that Shakespeare contemned the mob. Mr. Macmillan speaks of his scorn for
the appearance and habits of the mob as unpitiful, and alien to the
spirit of modern democracy, because nowadays we regard these
things as misfortune rather than fault. He also discovers that Shakespeare was not deeply interested in political questions, since there are
no political discussions. Although the play records a great struggle
between the principles of monarchy and republicanism, neither party
argues in favour of either.

VI

THE grand merit of Mr. Arthur Symons's essay on *R. and J.*[2] is that
it instructs us in the true nature of the passion of the lovers. We see,

[1] *J.C.*: Arden edit., 1902 (Methuen).
[2] '*R. and J.*,' 1903 (*Studies in the Elizabethan Drama*, Heinemann, 1920).

through him, their new outlook on life, their new relation to the world, even the new quality in their speech, born from the transfiguring force. And this force is something elemental that uses the individual to manifest itself, and therefore fills us with hope for nature and man's destiny.

Youth, he argues, for once is conscious of itself and we remember the play as if it were love itself.[1] They have but one desire, which they attain, so they succeed in life. The unrealized idea of love can suggest to Juliet neither reservation nor ending. The first garden scene is a duet of two astonishments; it becomes incredible to them that anything else could have happened. Their love is a sacred madness; it exalts and purifies their words with its own intellectual purity, as it had transfigured their souls. We see love living its own deaf and blind life in a world busied about other matters. The people round Juliet are set there for their fixed opposition to her fixed resolve: age, custom, the family, the vulgar—the world itself. The Friar represents philosophy among the passions; he sets them moving to his own pattern of abstract wisdom. The passion of Romeo and Juliet is nature itself: sex, the idea of sex, is overflowed by a divine oblivion.

VII

W. J. COURTHOPE'S work[2] does not show insight, neither does it stimulate the reader's mind. He has collected a great many appreciative general remarks on Shakespeare, but he does not seem to have experienced them. He fails in applying them to the detailed criticism of the plays; and his comparison of one play or character with another —especially characters of different periods—are often entirely external. His relatively original general remarks incline to be fixed ideas— such as the dramatic value of Machiavelli's conception of *Virtu*— the power of the free, resolute, unswerving exertion of the human will—which he says Shakespeare learned from Marlowe. Nor can we accept his statement that a profound sense of earthly vanity pervades all Shakespeare's writings.

He first notes the effect on the drama of the Miracles, &c., and then the influence of Marlowe, especially the latter's will-worship and lyrical bias. Shakespeare's life appears to him prosperous and uneventful, and hard to connect with his varied and impassioned dramas—but the Sonnets give the key. He finds Sidney Lee's interpretation of these too logical, and doubts not that in some he unlocked his heart. The allusions justify this, for, if fictions, they would be pointless. The lyric character of the profound view of life expressed in Sonnet 104 runs like a thread through all the sonnets, poems, and plays. Compare all with all and we get insight into his poetic motives. From

[1] Cf. Montégut.   [2] *Hist. of Eng. Poetry*, vol. iv, 1903 (Macmillan).

the first division of the Sonnets we see there was a dark period in Shakespeare's life, when his ideal was shattered and his friend lost. The second division shows a still more remarkable blending of universal human experience with individual feeling and veins of dramatic thought running through the plays. Compare the Dark Lady and Cleopatra—the overwhelming power of love. We recognize in the plays the lyrical intensity and depth of personal feeling of the Sonnets—Shakespeare's craving for the world's good opinion and Macbeth's 'golden opinions'.

The early comedies are remarkably varied, each being highly individualized. In the later histories, and romantic comedies, and tragi-comedies, he is at the height of his power. The action reveals the depth of his philosophy, and the philosophy illuminates the large extent of action. The later tragedies combine the Machiavellian principle of the tragic action of the early tragedies with the principle of philosophic reflection of the histories and romantic comedies. Their vein of passionate thought and emotion shows the choice of material was affected by a profound change in the whole view of life. The tragic view of life presented by Lear and Hamlet is the same as the lyric cry of the sonnet: 'Tired with all these for restful death I cry'. . . .

Courthope deals too easily with the problem of Shakespeare's self, and uses the Sonnets too readily to interpret the plays—but as already stated, we quarrel less with his general than his particular criticism. Though he may not convince us, he at least affirms that Shakespeare excelled in thinking universally and portraying the individual, and he praises him for fusing organically dissimilar things. The best of his particular judgements are as follows.

In *John* Shakespeare retained the historical framework, but altered the philosophical aspect. He shifted the interest to Arthur, and thus showed John's character in its true light and increased the human interest of the action. In the *Errors* we see how Shakespeare had learned from the art of earlier poets to produce that unreal and poetical atmosphere which is the great charm of his Comedies of Illusion. Note the state of mind produced in Antipholus S. and Dromio S.— how the latter doubts his identity. The chief action of *Verona* is not developed so as to explain the extraordinary inconsistencies of character. The dethronement of Richard II never ceases to affect Henry IV. A large variety of characters in *A.Y.L.* are all connected with the main plot by separate underplots, so as to represent different moods aroused by the idea of romantic Arcadia. Touchstone's particular observation makes him even more strongly apprehend the deepest truths of things than Jaques. Among the influences that restrain Hamlet from action is a sense of irony. The Fool in *Lear*, like Touchstone, most clearly perceives material things in themselves.

The following illustrate the critical defects already pointed out.

Margaret (*Richard III*) is a forecast of Lady Macbeth, and the argument between Clifford and Cade anticipates Menenius (*Coriolanus*). Lyly's influence shows in *R. and J.*, as regards the manner of expressing medieval feeling of the unreality of things, and paradoxical ideas connected with the passion of love. Henry V utters Shakespeare's own most intimate thoughts about life and morality. His philosophic, ironic side attracts him to Falstaff, while his manly energy and sense of reality prevent him from falling into Hamlet's irresolution. Falstaff is a genuine representative of the selfish side of human nature; he is an absolutely transparent coward, yet content with himself. He ministers to the Prince's contemplative tendencies, but when the moment for action arrives the Prince realizes the true requirements of honour. Through this double personality the drama unfolds the meaning of the Prince's apparently sudden conversion. In *Twelfth-Night* mistakes of resemblance are balanced by the exhibition of errors produced by self-love in Malvolio. Hamlet has a double nature like Henry V. The central portion of *Macbeth* is the same as in *Hamlet*, but Lady Macbeth supplies the external stimulus. In *Lear* the medieval doctrine of the vanity of the world is made to modify that of Machiavelli—that all things are permissible to absolute Power. The episode of Gloster is not essential. Nothing in Plutarch suggests Shakespeare's conception of the multitude. It was the fruit of suffering inflicted on a sensitive nature by the unjust judgements of the world. Antony (*A. and C.*) is orator, soldier, debauchee—a Henry V without his power of self-control.

VIII

MESSRS. THOMAS SECCOMBE and J. W. ALLEN[1] see in Shakespeare at his highest, that is in the great tragedies, a fusion of passion and character in unity of poetic conception. They trace his advance through the comedies and histories, noting the isolated appearance of one or other trait, afterwards to be so fused and unified.

The one distinctive Shakespearian thing in *Richard III* is the ethical import; and he is Shakespeare's first complex character-study. Between *Richard II* and *J.C.* humour is the most salient thing; there are no great heights of poetry or depths of vision, and except for Shylock no tragic import. Women are tentative and incomplete until near the end. Romanticism and euphuism are fused in Mercutio (*R. and J.*). The play is far removed from Marlowe because of its humour. *John* is declamatory and rhetorical rather than impassioned or poetic; and has no centre of interest. The main plot of the *Merchant* is a tissue of absurdities. Shylock's avarice and malice are secondary to his sense of racial wrong; he is Shakespeare's first great character, and none of the others are fully realized. Because Bassanio is a needy adventurer,

[1] *The Age of Sh.*, 1903 (G. Bell & Sons).

the interest in the love story is diminished; and his relations with
Portia and Antonio are carelessly handled. No play is a more harmonious whole than *M.N.D.* The unreality of the love story is no flaw
because passion would be out of place. Falstaff is the height of Shakespeare's creative humour, the supreme expression of his joy in life.
A.Y.L. is a pastoral poem of surpassing lyrical richness, and in Jaques
and the Duke graver notes are heard. *M. Ado* is one of the brightest
and most finely balanced comedies, but its brightness is not from its
plot which is gloomy. Nothing in comedy is more brilliant than the
interplay of Benedict and Beatrice, and it is Shakespeare's triumph of
art to convert their mutual irritation into a basis of real and lasting
affection. In *Twelfth-Night* there is a blended harmony of prose and
verse, alternation of lively, tender, and severe. The group of comic
figures is unrivalled, and the marvellous wealth of life makes us forget
the slenderness and repetition of the plot. In *All's Well* the skill with
which Shakespeare precludes any doubt as to the essential purity of
Helena's nature, despite the ugly situations she is placed in, is one of
the miracles of his art.

When Shakespeare attained to mature thought and style he abruptly
turned to tragedy. To separate this persistent selection from his own
inner life would be psychologically absurd.[1] His tragedy is always one
of weakness; his hero fails from weakness or folly, not from his own
nobility of character or purpose. Antony would have thrown himself
away and fallen before Octavius had Cleopatra never existed. Shakespeare's heroes are not heroic, but all are finely or even splendidly
endowed, with great qualities or intellect.

In *J.C.*, which is badly constructed, Caesar's disappearance makes
an anticlimax, and Brutus is heroic but a dupe. Shakespeare is in two
minds about Caesar; he could neither wholly sympathize with regicide
nor distort Caesar into a tyrant. *Hamlet* shows a far more concentrated
interest and organic unity than hitherto. Every person and incident
is related to the hero, and for the first time poetry and life are fused,
and Hamlet's soliloquies are not comments, but the drama itself. His
mind is the theme, and the incidents but modulate its reflections.
Shakespeare's supreme dramatic craft and poetic power are here
most completely balanced. To spare the brutal ending of the original
story of *M. for M.* he employs an ugly and absurd device. With
Othello he again attains complete unity of high tragedy, and concentrated
interest equal to *Hamlet*. It is his most purely realistic play, but the
fault is that Othello has no moral right to his conviction. Even
greater concentration of interest rules *Macbeth*. This and the hurry
of events makes the tragic note most dominant in Shakespeare. *Lear*
is more terrible than *Macbeth*, more piteous than *Othello*, profounder
than *Hamlet*, but less human than any of them. All is fused and made

[1] Cf. Thorndike's opposite opinion.

one—folly and wisdom, madness and sanity, pity and rage. Shakespeare ignores the suggestion of political aims in Cleopatra's passion. It is only not his greatest tragedy because the theme is smaller and the construction faulty and the unity imperfect. Antony throws away his sovereignty for love rather ignobly—for he hankers, almost in the arms of his mistress, for the political position slipping from him. He is most unstable, and there is nothing terrible or very piteous in the tragedy of this splendid but weak man. Cleopatra is in love with his power and splendour, but without any depth of feeling. The play suffers from the lack of concentration on the two chief figures.

Cymbeline and the *W. Tale* show utter disregard of plausibility, with minute and finished realism in presenting individual figures or situations. They contain some of Shakespeare's most beautiful passages and perfect characters, with profound wisdom, divine poetry, but psychological absurdities. The *Tempest* combines solemnity, irony, broad humour in shining serenity. Between Prospero and Caliban is the whole range of human character. . . .

The fault of this criticism is that the authors, having formed a certain judgement of Shakespeare at his best (no doubt a true one), treat the lesser plays as imperfect attempts rather than stepping-stones to the highest. They make a conscious attempt to be fair, and not be betrayed into accepting the whole of Shakespeare as equally great. The result is that on the whole they do not help us to appreciate. It is criticism from impressions grown cold and is therefore uncreative, and does not pass into the reader's unconscious mind and strengthen it to return to Shakespeare. Of this kind are the remarks on the *Merchant*, on the plot of *Twelfth-Night*, on Shakespeare's heroes generally, on *J.C.*, on *Lear* which they say is the least human of the great tragedies, on *A. and C.* Of a far better kind is that on *M.N.D.*, *M. Ado*, and especially *All's Well*. The tribute to Hamlet's soliloquies is noteworthy.

IX

WE have met with R. J. Moulton before, and disagreed with him, while acknowledging his learning and enthusiasm. We fear that the present treatise [1] does not vindicate its title, or tell us much about the mystery of Shakespeare. It has a literary interest of its own, but that is somewhat akin to a Sherlock Holmes story, of which, when the denouement is reached, we no longer trouble about the events that led up to it—nor do we care to re-read. Thus when Moulton utters a theory we wonder how he will work it out, and his dexterous manner of doing it keeps us surprised and busy to the end—when we discover that the relation is hardly maintained with the first cause. He has shod his critical horses backwards, and when we follow his

[1] *The Moral System of Sh.*, 1903 (New York, The Macmillan Co.).

trail and reach our journey's end we discover ourselves at the opposite point from Stratford.

The basis of Shakespeare's moral system he finds in the plot, the study of which reveals the forces behind life that determine its issues. Richard III at first does evil for the sake of ambition, till in the end evil itself becomes the attraction. Ideal villainy is projected into a universe presented as a complex providential order, of which every element is a varied phase of retribution. Not that retribution is invariable, as we see from Cordelia, where fate leaves out nothing, not even her life, to make her sacrifice complete. Accident comes between character and fate, because, if guilt always brought ruin, life would be mechanical. Accident brings Romeo into a situation which causes his banishment—a doom instituted on account of the factious violence which he tried to resist. Dramatic plot is a revelation of moral providence. Redemption, the profoundest of moral principles, is an ideal of Shakespeare's. In *Cymbeline* six separate wrongs, illustrating degrees of the moral scale, make a sixfold complication. The separate trains of evil are unified in so far as they all strike at Imogen. Her sufferings are foremost among the forces of resolution. Each case of perverted right, as if by natural law, works through suffering to its redemption.

The three Roman plays give us in evolution the pure ideal of the State and the outer life yielding before the growing prominence of the inner life and claims of individuals. *Coriolanus* represents the patrician ideal of service to the State. The plebeians put forward individuality reduced to its lowest terms—right to exist. Coriolanus embodies absolute devotion to principle; he is neither personally ambitious nor proud, and his scorn expresses righteous indignation. All the others, including Volumnia, are ready to compromise. Even patriotism is a compromise with principle; it is devotion not to the ideal of government, but to a particular government with which the individual is connected by the accident of birth. When Coriolanus is dismissed by Rome he is free to transfer his service elsewhere, and he serves the Volscians equally well. Julius Caesar is Coriolanus on a larger moral scale. He has an all-round personality with infinite resources of intellect and lofty moral power, all concentrated in governing men and founding the Roman empire. But he has no inner life, and apart from serving the State appears not wrong but weak. The result of the irresistible advance of popular claims is the Empire, and in Antony we see an individual become the State. Cleopatra emerges as a new force; she is arbitrary individuality incarnate. The rivalry of the State and the individuality is now within Antony's personality. If he chooses to give himself to public affairs he has the Empire in his grasp: but he can find his world elsewhere. Yet when his outer life is plunged in tragic ruin the inner reveals itself.

Angelo is devoted to a cause, not a principle, and hypocrisy does not explain him. Isabella is passionate for purity, but cold to love. Mariana is all passion, but within the letter of the law. In Claudio and Juliet passion is in conflict with the letter of the law. The antithesis of law and individual begets a great moral conflict, and mercy is the reconciling force. It transcends justice and holds allegiance equally to the law and the individual—giving scope for warmth of passion while it does reverence to the light of purity.

Character is one of life's forces, and a man's character is the momentum of his past. We see this in the Caskets scene of the *Merchant*, where character, not reasoning, influences the choice of the suitors. Conscious choice is merely self-deception, and only Bassanio comes as a true lover. Macbeth had first suggested the murder, before the beginning of the play. His character was that of a man of action; he vacillates as a thinker. Suspense discomposes him, where there is no outlet in deeds. The age was superstitious, and having no inner life of his own, he is defenceless against what the age accepts. His soliloquy about murdering Duncan is nothing but a practical man's weighing of practical consequences.

The real question of the supernatural is of its function in the plot. Can something outside nature influence men and events? Does foreknowledge imply predestination? A superhuman power of reading the future is implied; but the future so read is brought about by natural cause. The supernatural cannot influence men except by their own consent. As we see in Hamlet, who doubts of the apparition, the supernatural can disturb the imagination and emotions, but only the regular order of natural influences can govern action. The supernatural is rather addressed to the spectator, and Shakespeare inherits the ancient conception of Destiny. Foreknowledge is needed for dramatic effect; it gives to the course of events the colour of mystery—e.g. Birnam Wood.

Has accident a place in the moral system? The universe which manifests itself in the form of law is limited by law. If a higher will shows itself it must be by some machinery outside the course of the law. According to men's philosophy, accident reveals destiny. *Hamlet* is a blending of character, accident, Nemesis. These moral accidents are sudden openings into the unknown, giving scattered intimations of a supreme Power behind the visible course of things. Prospero is an overruling Providence who directly controls Ferdinand and Miranda. The same thing in Romeo and Juliet seemed the result of accident. . . .

The above are fair specimens of Moulton's method, and if the reader has not stumbled hopelessly over the characters of Coriolanus and Angelo and persevered to the end, he will be rewarded by some suggestion of mystery in the Shakespearian world. No one can touch

Shakespeare without gaining some virtue from him; and in explaining the supernatural and the accidental, and also the final resolution of *M. for M.*, he abandons his formulas. Otherwise the book consists of moral maxims which need not have been centred in Shakespearian characters. To prove his theory in the Roman plays, for instance, he is forced further and further back into the land of abstractions, where the individual dies for want of his native air. With his main argument—that Shakespeare's moral philosphy appears in his treatment of plot—we agree; but plot and character can hardly be separated, and in Shakespeare's characters sleeps a moral lightning, the incalculable force of which is not recognized by Moulton.

X

AMONG these late critics occur some general remarks which can hardly be classified, yet, when brought together, reveal something of the thought of their time on Shakespeare in its larger sense. According to Stephen, his plays in chronological series witness to the most remarkable intellectual development on record. Thorndike speaks of his immense creative power. To Lounsbury he is the great poet of human nature, who conformed to nature, truth, life, and penetrated into nature's profoundest mysterious. Courthope ascribes to him universality of idea and individuality of character combined, which mark off his style from others. He also calls him a great and philosophic mind always learning new lessons from experience and observation, with imagination of infinite power and grandeur, and knowledge of man's relation to the world in all its aspects, moral, religious, social, political, and power to embody in ideal form the operation of universal passions. Seccombe and Allen speak of his broad and genial sympathy with human nature; they call him an idealistic artist who lived in the centre of the actual, greatest of all poets who have dealt with human life, the poet of universal humanity, impersonal and impartial.

We get a great many tributes to the moral side of his genius. He is pre-eminently a moral poet, in Lounsbury's view, and his greatness as a moral teacher appears in questions that affect life and conduct. Instead of poetic justice he gives the sway and sweep of those moral forces which, once set moving, work out their inevitable course in human conduct. Macmillan says that he idealizes justice by introducing a specially appropriate relation between crime and punishment. Courthope just notes the moral character of his idea of life. Stephen says that he never judges, but looks on good and bad men alike as part of the order of nature, that he has the impersonality of the true artist. Seccombe and Allen call his plays about as moral as life. Like nature, they say, he preferred virtue, and his moral attitude was that of the sane, normal man, with no trace of fatalism. Moulton says that we recognize in him the moral government of the world, and that his plays are profoundly ethical.

Lounsbury calls him a conscious artist, who did his work as deliberately as audaciously, with the keenest critical sense. Courthope says that he had an extraordinary power of fusing conflicting elements into organic action—a complexity of workmanship and variety of resource which is the sign of the highest art. Seccombe and Allen remark that, as artist, he dealt with the artistic worth of humanity, not the beauty of nature. Stephen finds him unequal, inclined to let interest flag through indifference, and only preserving inspiration intact through the greatest plays.

His highest merit, to Stephen, was his extraordinary variety of vivid and original types of character. He had, says Lounsbury, an intuitive perception of the minds of persons he set out to portray, and the strength and sweep of imagination to project himself into any situation in which they might be placed. His women were of the loftiest type known to literature. To Seccombe and Allen his characters were never extravagant, but perfected types of the normal.

On the ever-alluring subject of Shakespeare's self we get the following: from Stephen, that he was infinitely complex—he united the ideal and practical—he was abnormally sensitive to every human passion, yet self-controlled—in politics an intellectual aristocrat; from Thorndike, that, unlike contemporaries, he kept his plays free from satire, and perhaps this affords a safer hint at his personality and artistic emotions; from Courthope, that his nature was very open on one side to the attractions of sense, and on the other most sensitive to judgement of conscience, and animated by deep religious feeling. . . .

It strikes us, as the years go on, how little the critics differ in the most general terms of praise which they apply to Shakespeare—such as his universality. In the moral sphere the note for him is still unanimous —and also in the artistic. A remark in the right spirit about his personality—negative rather than positive—is made by Thorndike; but on this matter the honours fall to Stephen, whose essay has already been compared to a half-way house. The technical defects noted by Stephen will be resumed by future critics.

Chapter XXXI

ENGLAND 1902–1908

I

PROFESSOR A. C. BRADLEY[1] is acknowledged to be the greatest living Shakespearian critic, and one of the very greatest in the history of Shakespearian criticism. He combines wide philosophic outlook with grasp of detail, and synthetic power with analytic. In treating a single character he never forgets its relation to the impression produced by the whole play. His mind is powerful enough to cope with the entire world which Shakespeare has hung in chains over chaos, and it is fundamentally poetic. His analysis is effective in so far as it is helped by memories and associations stirred up by the poetry of Shakespeare. He is never merely philosophic, like some of the critics we have previously considered. There are occasions when imagination partly retires and yields place to a more purely scientific method, and in these, as we shall see, he is less successful.

We will briefly summarize his general views of Shakespeare's tragic world. The reader, he says, must realize the inner movements which produced such words and deeds. The substance of Shakespearian tragedy is a tale of suffering and calamity leading to death. His heroes are highly placed, that their fall may present a contrast. Calamities do not befall but proceed from men's actions—actions expressive of the doer. The centre of tragedy is action issuing from character, or character issuing in action—not mere character or psychology. Abnormal mental conditions do not originate deeds of dramatic moment. If Lear was mad when he divided his kingdom, he would cease to be a tragic character. The supernatural has no compulsive influence, but confirms and makes distinct movements already present. Accident is a fact of human life, but, if largely used, would weaken. Shakespeare uses it sparingly, when the action is well advanced and causal sequence too firmly fixed to be impaired. There is the outer conflict ending in the hero's death, and the inner conflict of his soul. 'Spiritual force' is an inclusive term—meaning all that can drive a man's soul. Shakespeare's heroes are exceptional beings but not eccentrics; they are of the same stuff as ordinary men, but intensified. Desire, passion, will, attain in them terrible force. They are one-sided and identify their whole being with one object or passion. This for Shakespeare is *the* tragic trait, and though it is a fatal gift it has a touch of greatness when

[1] *Sh^n. Tragedy*, 1904 (Macmillan).

joined to nobility of mind. *Cymbeline* and the *W. Tale* end happily because the chief characters are not tragic, but Shylock is really tragic.[1] The tragic hero need not be 'good', but must be great enough to reveal the possibilities of human nature. Hence the mystery: man is wonderful and his greatness ruins him.

What, then, is the ultimate power since individuals are not? The Elizabethan drama is secular, not religious, and the ultimate power is neither 'moral order' nor fate. The tragic world is one of action, to which accidents and character contribute, but there is a moral order and necessity. Agents are responsible for their actions, and the catastrophe is the return of the action on the agents. There is justice, but not poetic justice, and we will therefore discard ideas of justice and merit and speak simply of good and evil. In Shakespeare evil is the main source of the convulsion—plain moral evil. Romeo and Juliet die because of the senseless hatred of their houses. Hamlet's situation is formed by adultery and murder. If it is evil that chiefly disturbs the order of the world, this order cannot be friendly to evil or indifferent between evil and good. The ultimate power must have a nature alien to evil. Evil in a man destroys others but also himself; therefore the inner being of this order must be of one nature with good. It reacts through the necessity of its own moral nature, and tragedy shows this convulsive reaction. We are not left rebellious or desperate because we see suffering and death arise from collision with a moral power. And yet evil is also within the order, and, in expelling it, the order loses part of its own substance, so that the tragedy is the waste of the good involved. The contradiction is that the order seems to have a passion for perfection, yet engenders this evil within itself, and in the effort to overcome and expel it is agonized with pain and driven to mutilate its own substance and lose not only evil but priceless good.[2] . . .

One might almost say that, by means of Shakespeare, Professor Bradley has advanced one of the most practical existing arguments in favour of the moral government of the universe. Though a learned man, he is not over-concerned with the thoughts of others: he has gone straight to the heart of the matter and brought back an answer from the oracle delivered to him personally; and there must be a specially Shakespearian quality in his mind to make such a thing possible at this late critical hour. In speculative regions he perceives the fact— that evil acts like a poison and produces the convulsion and is therefore something abnormal. Much has been written about Shakespeare's

[1] A. W. Ward also observes that Shylock grows to a tragic hero; but does not his outcry over his money, and his assertion that he would rather see his daughter dead, with the jewels in her ears, than lose them, degrade him from this level?
[2] Cf. Dowden's saying, that evil is abnormal and self-destroying; also Hales's, that in the end good prevails and evil consumes itself.

philosophy and theology and his belief or scepticism, about his personal
views, and the chances of ascertaining them by comparisons among the
plays, but so far this central fact has eluded the critics. Nor could it
have been discovered but by the combined philosophic and poetic
gifts of Professor Bradley. For these general statements could only
have proceeded from one who had experienced Shakespeare's truth
through his beauty—for whom Shakespeare was, above all, a poet. He
does not shrink from the further fact that the order engenders the
evil which it seeks to cast out, but he has done most to prove that the
world's greatest genius believed in a moral order: and consequently
he fills us with hope.

We are inclined to think that his analysis of *Hamlet* is too purely
scientific, and depends as much on his general experience of life as
his aesthetic experience of the play, and is therefore less impressive
than some that are to follow, though we except the sentence about
Hamlet's interview with his mother. It seems to him that all turns on
the peculiar character of Hamlet, and there is no question of external
difficulties. He assumes that he *can* obey the Ghost, and that he *ought*,
and says nothing of moral scruples. In the crisis of his life he shows
hardness and cynicism. The theory that it is a tragedy of reflection
does not answer to our imaginative impression. Excessive reflection
is not the *direct* cause, but melancholy—an abnormal state of mind is
the cause. Before his father's death he was more than a scholar—he
was the observed of all observers, &c. He had exquisite moral sensibility, unbounded delight and faith in all good and beautiful things,
aversion to evil, and care for human worth. Such a nature would feel
any shock intensely. It was a tragedy of moral idealism. Although no
technical philosopher, he had intellectual and speculative genius, and
he did not live the life of a dreamer. But after the shock there was no
immediate call to act, and he had time to sink into melancholy. If the
call came now endless questioning might result. Thus the speculative
habit was one indirect cause and would reappear as symptom. Moral
sensibility and imagination are now his enemies, and his condition
one of melancholia—not to be dispelled by the will. But it is not
insanity and he is not irresponsible. The immediate cause of inaction
is disgust at life. The result is otiose thinking, unconscious weaving
of pretexts for inaction, aimless tossings as on a sick-bed; and it also
explains his energy. In the interview with his mother his desire is to
save her soul, and he is at home in this higher work, unlike the rough
work of vengeance. The fatal feeling, 'It is no matter', never appears.
The play is neither Shakespeare's greatest tragedy nor his most perfect
work of art, but it most brings home to us the sense of the soul's
infinity and the sense of doom which not only circumscribes that
infinity but appears to be its offspring.

The defect, if defect it is, is remedied in *Othello*, the hero of which play Professor Bradley sees imaginatively as a whole. He finds some-thing colossal in the later heroes. Othello holds a volume of force which in repose ensures his pre-eminence without effort, and in commotion is like the elements. Jealousy like Othello's makes human nature chaos and liberates the beast in man—in relation to one of the most intense and ideal of feelings. It is like a story of private life, and the characters come close to us. The part played by accident accentu-ates the feeling of fate. If it is slightly below the other three tragedies, the reason is that the imaginative atmosphere is comparatively confined. It does not, like the others, dilate the imagination by vague suggestions of huge universal powers working in the world of individual fate and passion. In the *Tempest* and other plays we feel this power and seem near to Shakespeare; here we do not feel ourselves in contact with the whole of him. The hero, therefore, seems to have less of Shakespeare's personality than many inferior characters. Othello is not a noble barbarian who retains savage passions beneath a surface of civilization. He is the most romantic of Shakespeare's heroes; he comes as from wonderland; his nature is romantic—more poetic than Hamlet's. His life is crowned with the final glory of love, and no love, not even Romeo's, is more steeped in imagination. But he is simple, ignorant of women, and of the corruptions of civilization, and trusts absolutely where he trusts. The differences in blood increase the bewilderment with both Othello and Desdemona. The wreck of his faith and love is the deepest source of his suffering. Even pity vanishes, and only love and admiration remain in the majestic dignity and sovereign ascendancy of the close. Some critics have been horrified because Shakespeare imagined Othello as a black man. When Desdemona's soul came in sight of the noblest soul on earth she made nothing of the shrinking of the senses, but followed her soul till her senses took part with it. . . .

We need only dwell on that one superlative touch—the romance of Othello—his coming as from wonderland—whereby Professor Bradley heightens for us the glory of Shakespeare—before passing on to Iago. Here again, as with Hamlet, the analysis is colder and more informed by knowledge of life outside Shakespeare than inspired by direct com-munion with his mind: yet in the last sentences we feel the creative energy renewed.

Dismiss the idea of 'Italian' villainy, because with Shakespeare differences of period, race, nationality, locality have little bearing on inward character.[1] Iago has superficial good nature, and had lived an outwardly decent life. He was a thoroughly bad, *cold* man, who was at last tempted to let loose the forces within him. He had powers of intellect and will, and greatness of a kind. His creed was that absolute egoism is the only rational and proper attitude. He professes and

[1] Cf. Montégut on French kings, and on Macbeth.

attempts to stand outside the moral world; but he has no positive ill will. He is keenly sensitive to anything that touches his pride or self-esteem. He has a spite against goodness in men because it weakens his satisfaction with self. We do not know why he so acts, and his soliloquies do not explain it. If it was only from desire of advancement and hatred of Othello he would be no extraordinary creation. He has no vestige of passion—that is the horror of him. It was not 'motiveless malignity'; the popular view is right in making it disappointed ambition, &c. Love of evil that advances my interest and hurts my enemies differs from love of evil simply as evil. The most delightful thing to such a man would be something that satisfied his sense of power—if it also gave scope to his abilities and afforded the excitement of danger. The perilous time would be when such a man's sense of superiority had been affronted. He did not clearly understand his own motives. This seems to be the unconscious motive of many cruel acts which do not spring from ill will. To the satisfaction required by his thwarted sense of superiority add his abnormal deadness of human feeling. His strongest motive was the longing to satisfy his sense of power, and he was also an artist. We admire and even partly sympathize with him because all he has, though it goes to evil ends, has great worth in itself. He tries to make egoism and want of humanity absolute, but cannot. There are faint traces of conscience, shame, humanity. He is not indifferent to the opinion of others, as his irritation at goodness shows. What he says of Cassio proves that he dimly sees the goodness of goodness. He never seeks Desdemona's presence after the plot begins; he betrays signs of discomfort, even remorse. He is destroyed by the power he had attacked—love—because he could not understand it. He misjudges his wife, and does not know that she *loves* her mistress. This combination of unusual intellect with extreme evil is a frightful thing, and, although rare, it does exist.

Lear is the greatest work, but not the best play, as it is too huge for the stage. It appeals less to dramatic perception than poetic imagination. Its chief structural weakness, in the fourth act and beginning of the fifth, arises from the double action. There are too many characters and events, and the reader's attention is overstrained and unaffected by the battle, which is critical, and by the deaths of Edmund, Goneril, Regan, Gloster. The material is too vast to use with complete dramatic effectiveness, however essential this vastness for effects of another kind. Shakespeare was set on the dramatic effects of the great scenes, and careless of small things. Yet this vagueness and overcrowding have value for the imagination. There is a feeling of vastness, and gloom peopled with strange shapes. The secondary plot is an effective contrast, suggesting that Lear's sorrows are no accident, but due to a malignant influence abroad. There is conflict in the world of the powers of good and evil. Few of the characters are of high psycho-

logical interest but Lear himself. There are two groups: devoted love
and hard self-seeking. Love and hate are the two ultimate forces of
the universe.

By his references to the lower animals Shakespeare seems to be
asking himself whether that which he loathes in man may not be due
to some strange wrenching of the frame of things, through which the
lower animal souls have obtained a lodgement in human forms and
there found—to the horror and confusion of the thinking mind—
brains to forge, tongues to speak, and hands to act enormities which no
mere brute can conceive or execute. He shows us these terrible forms
bursting into monstrous life and preying on those who are weak and
defenceless because they are old, or human and lack the dreadful
undivided energy of the beast. The only comfort is that this horrible
world cannot endure. On the stage this mass of suggestion is lost; in
Macbeth the storm scenes do not lose their essence, but here they do.
For the imagination, the storm and Lear's passion must be one thing.
It is the powers of the tormented soul that we hear and see in the
roaring wind and rain and sheets of fire. As references to wolf and
tiger made us see man reeling back into the beast, so in the storm we
see Nature convulsed by the same horrible passions, turning on her
children. It is Shakespeare's most terrible picture, but were the final
impression one of darkness it would be a serious flaw. Not that *Lear*
contains a revelation of righteous omnipotence or heavenly harmony,
or promise of reconciliation of mystery and justice. But neither do
Shakespeare's other tragedies; nor do they suggest justice or equity
in the adjustment of merit and prosperity. Yet man is no plaything of
blind or capricious power, suffering woes unrelated to his character
and actions; nor is the world given over to darkness. The key-note
is, 'The gods are just . . .'. Pity and terror are carried to the extreme
limits of art, but blended with the sense of law and beauty, so that we
feel the consciousness of greatness in pain and solemnity in mystery
we cannot fathom.

If we forget that Lear liberated the storm his fate would not be
tragic. He is choleric, old, but not irresponsible, and he repeats his
error in his quarrel with Goneril. But we feel hate for her and sympathy
for him, so that we forget his violence. Though he has recognized his
injustice to Cordelia his disposition is unchanged. We see the world of
the play is not subject to mere arbitrary power, but so far rational and
moral that it holds the law of strict connexion between act and consequence. Nothing is nobler and more beautiful in literature than
Shakespeare's exposition of the effect of suffering in reviving the
greatness and eliciting the sweetness of Lear's nature. He owes all to
those sufferings which make us doubt whether life were not simply
evil. The business of the gods was to lead him to attain through
apparently hopeless failure the very end and aim of life. There is

excess of evil in the play, yet evil is merely destructive. It exists only
on the foundation laid by its opposite, and it is self-destructive. Thus
the world is unfriendly to evil, and its convulsion is due to evil. There
is no answer to the question why the world generates that which con-
vulses and wastes it, and it goes beyond tragedy. But there is the same
abundance of extreme good as extreme evil.

If we condemn the universe for Cordelia's death we should remember
that it gave her birth.[1] The passion of Kent's life is love for Lear, and
through his eyes we see the Lear of Lear's prime. He is old—over
sixty—and if we forget his age we cannot realize the full beauty of his
thoughtlessness of himself. Imagine the tragedy without the Fool and
you hardly know it. Cordelia speaks about one hundred lines, yet no
Shakespearian character is more individual or ineffaceable. A suggestion of infinite wealth and beauty is conveyed by her very refusal
to reveal this beauty in expansive speech; and we risk forgetting her
share in Lear's sufferings. At the moment where terrible issues join,
Fate makes on her the one demand which she cannot meet. Other
heroines could have made Lear feel that he was loved: Cordelia cannot
because she is Cordelia. Also she told less than the truth. We ask a
reason why she dies—but the destruction of good through the evil of
others is a tragic fact of life.[2] Besides, the effects of good spread
beyond the doer of good. Yet there is a touch of reconciliation. If
a heroic being fails, he is in another sense superior to the world he
appears in, is untouched by his doom, and rather set free from life
than deprived of it. This idea, if developed, would make the tragic
world no final reality. Suffering and death would count for little, and
greatness of soul for all. However, with Cordelia we simply feel that
what happens to such a being does not matter. All that matters is
what she is, and the force of the impression depends on the violence
of the contrast between her death and her soul. The more unmotived,
unmerited, senseless, monstrous her fate, the more we feel it does not
concern her. The only real thing in the world is the soul, with its
courage, patience, devotion, and nothing outward can touch that.
Pursued further this would destroy tragedy—for it is necessary to
tragedy that we feel that suffering and death matter greatly, and life
and happiness are not worthless. . . .

We break off to draw attention to the remarks on Kent's age, on
the result of omitting the Fool, and, above all, on Cordelia. These
coming after the suggestions about the lower animals and the storm,
prove our former statement that no one like Professor Bradley has so
grasped the impression of the whole and analysed the part played by
every detail in building it up. He points out that evil abounds, but is

---

[1] 'Cordelia dies, but she has existed' (Dowden).

[2] Moulton says that Fate leaves out nothing, not even her life, to make her
sacrifice complete.

self-destructive, and good abounds also—and, most of all literary critics, he gives us reason for hope—in Shakespeare and the universe. We admire his perfect balance in suggesting other-worldliness and restraining it within due bounds. This world marks a definite stage in the soul's progress, and its loves and hatreds, its suffering and horror, and its beauty are no illusion.

Macbeth is the most vehement and concentrated, perhaps the most tremendous of the tragedies. Blackness broods over the play, though the blackness of night is stained by blood, and there is hardly a thought of peace and beauty. In nature something is felt to be at work sympathetic with human guilt and supernatural malice. The obscurer regions of man's being are shown, his strange half-conscious life. He seems in the power of secret forces lurking below, and independent of his consciousness and will. Supernatural alarm is excited, and dread of the presence of evil all through and around our mysterious nature. Shakespeare used the best of current ideas about the Witches. They are ragged old women, but have secured from evil spirits certain supernatural powers. Their influence is great, but is only influence, with no question of external power. Macbeth was not innocent when he first heard them, or he would not have started with *fear*. The idea of murder was his own—he never says he is compelled. The Witches not only represent the evil in his soul, but the obscurer influences of evil around him in the world, which aid his own ambition and his wife's incitements. The idea is that inward powers of the soul answer in their essence to vaster powers without, which support them. The Witches' words are fatal because something inner corresponds, but they witness to forces which never cease to work in the world around, and on his surrender entangle him in the web of Fate.

The two great terrible figures most inspire awe of the tragic heroes, and are never detached from the surrounding atmosphere which adds to their grandeur and terror and is continued into their souls. Within them is all that we felt without—darkness of night lit with flame of tempest and hues of blood, haunted by wild shapes. They are proud, ambitious, all for station and power, but with some feeling for honour, conscience, humanity. They are tragic and grand to the end, and the action is built on the contrast between them. His passion for power and instinct of self-assertion is so vehement that no inward misery could persuade him to relinquish the fruits of crime or advance from remorse to repentance. He has the imagination of a poet which produces disturbance of mind and body. His wife ascribes his awful images—protest of his deepest self—to nervous fear, and he ascribes them to dread of vengeance. His conscious or reflective mind moves chiefly among considerations of outward success and failure, while his inner being is convulsed by conscience.[1] After murdering Duncan he

[1] Cf. Coleridge.

is nearly mad with horror, but not horror of detection. His soul speaks in the shape of imagination: when the latter sleeps he is domineering, brutal, or a cool, pitiless hypocrite. He tells himself that his sleepless torture is fear of retaliation. Even at the end he never entirely loses our sympathy. A soul to which evil was congenial would not have thought of honour, love, &c.

The first half of the play is the greater, for there Lady Macbeth predominates—Shakespeare's most commanding and awe-inspiring figure. She has an inflexible will, and there is no separation between will and deed. She leans on no one but herself, and is appalling but sublime. Were she 'fiend-like' the sleep-walking scene would be impossible. She has no remarkable intellect, and her imagination is comparatively dull. At the most terrible moment things remain to her as at the calmest—plain facts which stand in given relation to a certain deed, not visions which tremble and flicker in the light of other worlds. The knocking is no mystery to her, and even in the sleep-walking scene it is the direct appeal of facts to sense that has fastened on her memory. Her want of imagination is fatal, in that she does not foresee consequences: had she understood her husband she would not have urged him. She did not realize his strange fancies would gain such power as to ruin the scheme. Her development is the opposite to his. After the murder the discovery of its hideousness, through the effect on her guests, comes with the shock of sudden disclosure. The glory of her dream fades; she becomes a prey to disillusion and despair; and her nature gives way, not her will. Up to her light she is a perfect wife; she gives him the best that she has; she urges and appeals for a practical end, and never recriminates. Her taunts have no personal feeling; she despises his weakness, not him. Shakespeare meant awe, grandeur, and horror to predominate. The sleep-walking scene inspires pity, but awe to a greater extent. There is no contrition in her misery; she is too great to repent. What Shakespeare most felt was that evil is incalculable, and in meddling with it we do we know not what. The minor characters are lightly sketched, with little individuality. Perhaps Shakespeare felt that to individualize subordinate figures would diminish the effect, and so sacrificed the part to the whole. In the sleep-walking scene it is not disordered imagination, but intense suffering speaking in strikingly bare diction. Compared with Macbeth's excitement it expresses far more desolating misery. The impression is breathless awe: those brief toneless sentences seem the only voice of truth. . . .

To the effect of the storm in *Lear* we may compare that of the atmosphere in *Macbeth*—the blood-shot darkness which adds to the grandeur and terror of the central figures. We also note the distinction between Macbeth's conscious and imaginative life. Modern critics as against Coleridge have belittled him as one who valued only the world's good opinion. Professor Bradley has carried on the thought of Coleridge, and rightly summarized Macbeth's soliloquies as the protest of his deepest self. These two points exemplify his power—his steady poetic vision which brings him nearest of critics to Shakespeare's mind, his meditation on this vision which does not fade, and his analytic power. He also has the seriousness of one to whom the great things unveiled by the reading of Shakespeare have been no external show, but a strange and wonderful experience.

Lastly, we may touch on the relation of Shakespeare's plays to the external world. We shall meet, if we have not already met, critics who condemn the *Merchant* as unreal because Antonio with his credit and his friends could easily have raised the required sum, &c.— and make similar remarks about other plays. A work of art which has no basis of reality is not likely to endure; a work in which reality predominates cannot claim to be art. The truth remains that some reality is needed to crystallize imagination, and the last emotion we receive from Professor Bradley's book is of the external world transfigured, but not overthrown, by imagination. Thus from another side we appreciate his perfect balance, and that singularly unprejudiced mind which quickens both his vision and his analysis, and is a further link with his great subject.

We must deal briefly with his remaining writings on Shakespeare.[1] The gist of his Falstaff essay is that the conclusion of *Henry IV* pains the reader, and Shakespeare did not mean to produce a painful impression.[2] The explanation is in Falstaff himself who transcended Shakespeare's first intention. Considering Henry V's practical and politic character, and his wish to impress the world, it was natural he should dismiss his associates; and as the play was a serious historical one, such an end would be fitting. But the character of Falstaff overrides all conventions. He is the humourist of genius, more ludicrous to himself than to you. Because sack makes him witty, and because of his humorous attitude, he is freed from slavery to it. This freedom makes his enjoyment contagious: his essence is the bliss of freedom gained in humour. He makes all serious things seem absurd—truth, honour, law, patriotism, courage. . . . When he tells lies he never expects to be believed; he is no coward, but he wishes to live and be merry. The main source of our delight is his humorous superiority to everything serious and the freedom of soul enjoyed in it. In Part II Henry becomes graver and Falstaff betrays his seamy side; but all devices fail because Shakespeare has not clouded over his humour. He is the

---

[1] 'The Rejection of Falstaff', 1902; 'A. and C.', 1905; 'Sh. the Man', 1904 (*Oxford Lectures on Poetry*. Macmillan, 1909).

[2] Morgann's contention that the rejection comes at the moment when Falstaff's success in extracting £1,000 from Shallow is made known is worth more than a passing notice.

II   P

greatest comic character in literature, because he had the freedom of
soul only to be attained by a mind which had received from Shakespeare's own an inexplicable touch of infinity. Hamlet, Macbeth, and
Cleopatra had this—but not Henry V. . . . Professor Bradley
has said elsewhere that Hamlet, Iago, Falstaff, and Cleopatra are
Shakespeare's most wonderful characters.

He does not consider *A. and C.* a rival to the great four. There is
little action in the first three acts, and the first half is not tragic in
tone. Nor do we see inner struggles: Antony's return to Cleopatra is
only reported, not shown. The hollowness of the outer world—e.g.
the galley scene—blunts our feelings of the greatness of Antony's
fall from prosperity. Our deeper sympathies are focussed on his
heart, and his inward fall. The greatness of the two in their fall is
so heightened by contrast with the world they lose, and with their
conqueror, that the reconciling element strongly appears. Their love
is destructive, and clashes with the nature of things, yet it is love, and
we sympathize with it and feel in it man's infinity. Had Antony
truly loved power he would have made a sterner struggle. Her love
for him raises her; the 'fire and air' in her have transfigured her other
elements during her life—and this spirit will not be extinguished. We
are saddened by the very thought that the catastrophe saddens us so
little. It is better for the world's sake that the lovers should fail and die.

We can but give the conclusions of 'Sh. the Man'; but, with the
critic's learning, taste, and impartiality fresh in our minds, it is needless
to insist on their value, or to remark that the process of reasoning,
which we have not space to follow out, is wide, disinterested, and
sympathetic.

He finds it impossible for a man to write all that Shakespeare did
and betray nothing of himself. His readers do form some idea of him:
he was more of the type of Fielding or Scott than of Shelley, Wordsworth, Milton. From external evidence we know he was 'gentle',
'civil', 'honest', convivial: and these would seem probable from his
works. He was more gay than grave, not splendidly powerful, but
nearer to Romeo and Hamlet than Hotspur and Henry V. His
heroes were 'open and free', and the sufferings of these is his favourite
tragic subject. He is specially interested in the somewhat undramatic
theme of the unreality of the feeling of love in imaginative natures
such as Romeo and Orsino. Considering the 'dark lady' sonnets we
conclude regretfully that Cleopatra and Cressida were drawn from
his experience. He had an 'unhappy period', and we detect something
unusual in his tone regarding certain vices of the blood. In the galley
scene of *A. and C.* there is no trace of disgust, but Hamlet's intensity
of loathing for his mother's lust is unexampled in Shakespeare. An
aesthetic test proves the sonnets to the friend to be genuine. No great
poet would have invented such an obscure, unattractive story. He

does not care for men who act on principle, for the precise, or even the saint-like. One cannot imagine him enthusiastic for an 'idea'. The vices he most hated were servility, flattery, feigning in friendship, ingratitude, also unforgiveness and the tendency to prefer justice to mercy. All these are specially connected with prosperity and power. The root of bitterness to him was the divorce of goodness and power. He was not a religious man in the distinctive sense of the word, but he nowhere shows dislike or contempt of Christianity. He had a lively sense of 'conscience', and the mystery of life. *A.Y.L.* most truly expresses his nature and habitual temper, but Hamlet reveals most of his personality. Only Hamlet, of Shakespeare's characters, could have written the plays; and this may explain why Hamlet is the most fascinating and inexhaustible character in imaginative literature. . . .

The negative criticisms are especially satisfying: and we have ever been inclined to prefer negative over positive on this subject. Professor Bradley is impartial, and he makes his mystical power serve his judgement. He compares with other critics as Shakespeare himself with other poets, or Scott with other novelists. The characters drawn by Scott and Shakespeare do not reveal the personal likes and dislikes of their authors: and so, did we possess no criticism by Professor Bradley except these essays on Shakespeare, it would be hard to say what kind of literature he himself most affected. We have alluded to a true Shakespearian quality in his mind: this now shows itself in his power to convince when he speaks of Shakespeare's preference for 'open and free' heroes—for justice over mercy—of his dislike for men who act on principle. He convinces because his process of critically re-creating the scenes of the plays is something similar to Shakespeare's imaginative process of creating. Here again—as we said with Coleridge—is absolute critical truth; and those writers should take warning who oppose the requirements of the stage and need to please the audience, against any attempts to know Shakespeare.

II

J. CHURTON COLLINS[1] has immense knowledge of English and other literature, but he is a positive and determined rather than a subtle critic. He is better in the work of preparation—in clearing away unessentials and showing where criticism should begin—than in defining his direct impressions. And he is too absolutely confident and unaware that he has but limited insight.

Dealing with Shakespeare and the classics, he wishes to prove that Shakespeare was familiar with Latin authors before they were translated—Plautus, Horace, Lucretius. The Duke's speech to Claudio in *M. for M.* is the quintessence of Lucretius. That he read Greek

[1] *Studies in Sh.*, 1904 (Constable).

classics in Latin versions is proved by some remarkable parallels in idioms and peculiarities of diction and rhythm. Cf. 'unhousel'd, disappointed, unaneled' in Hamlet, and line 1071 of the Antigone of Sophocles. Shakespeare's creative energy was never self-evolved, but, his imagination and enthusiasm once kindled, all he had read or observed or meditated would come into play: and thus the classics would affect him. Both Lady Macbeth and Clytemnestra are impelled by sexual affection. Both have neither pity nor scruple, but nerves of steel and wills of iron which overawe husband and paramour. Compare Antigone and Isabella, Angelo and Creon. The first incarnate the law of the heart, the second the letter of the law. The Greeks had a superstitious reverence for custom, as we see from their drama; and this is Shakespeare's philosophy. They looked on man as a dream or apparition; and Shakespeare expressed this thought in Hamlet, Jaques, Prospero. In neither was there a flavour of cynicism, but both had a true sense of the tears in human things. Shakespeare was Christian, yet the real metaphysic of his dramas is akin to Sophocles and Euripides: as we see in the speeches of those about to die, or of the survivors. He is silent on a future life, and equally Greek in the practical resolution of formal theology into moral law. Unlike his contemporaries, and like the Greeks, he is didactic in the lessons implied in the plots and aphorisms of his plays. He followed Aristotle in making as cause of the calamity an error of judgement, flaw in the character, or inherited taint; but with him the flaw determines the course of the action, and he postulates free will. . . .

One must needs be impressed by the likeness between the lines in *Hamlet* and the *Antigone*, but otherwise the comparisons are superficial. If we look forward to his words on Montaigne we shall see that he almost supplies the arguments to refute himself. The truth is that his wide and varied reading easily affords apparent likenesses, but as soon as the inner mind begins to work upon them they fail. Thus we dismiss the comparison between Lady Macbeth and Clytemnestra, considering the utterly different impression of each which our imagination finally bears. Nor can we assent that Shakespeare was in the received sense of the word a 'didactic' poet. If we learn truths of life from his plays, it is in the same way as we learn wisdom and experience from life itself.

The essay on 'Shn. Paradoxes' illustrates to the full this blunt critical method—its over-confidence and superficiality. He maintains that Shakespeare wrote *Titus*, and that the play shows the 'timid servility' with which he followed models. There is as little reason for questioning the authenticity of the three parts of *Henry VI*. Titus foreshadows Lear, and Aaron Iago and Edmund.

Turning to 'Sophocles and Shakespeare', can we agree that irony is the most striking parallel? No doubt dramatic irony had its place in

Shakespeare, as witness Desdemona's appeal for help to Iago, and the sayings of the Witches in *Macbeth*; but does it ever predominate throughout a whole play as in *Oedipus the King?* In the course of this comparison the critic observes that Shakespeare recognized universal law controlling the physical and moral world and the greatest and smallest facts of life; and that tragedy sets in when an ill-regulated mind or ill-governed home disturbs this equilibrium;[1] and that Sophocles, too, admits that law is all-pervading. However, when he summarizes Jocasta as coarse, reckless, and impious, and Oedipus as intemperate as Lear, we decide that his limited insight into Sophocles cannot justify the personal, aesthetic, and moral likenesses which he discovers between the two dramatists.

Of a far superior order is his essay on Shakespeare's prose. He alarms us at the start by affirming that it is more remarkable than his verse— but when he gives the reason—that it is his own creation—we are reconciled. It unites, he says, the graces of rhetoric and colloquy, and Shakespeare was the first to see how the mechanism of prose and verse differed, and how far the laws which govern the rhythm and cadence of metre might operate beneficially on the rhythm and cadence of prose. He has five distinct styles: (1) Euphuistic from Lyly. (2) The realistic and colloquial only afterwards equalled by Bunyan. (3) Prose of the higher comedy, of which he was the absolute and immortal creator: it unites colloquial ease and literary eloquence, a language at once real and ideal. (4) Rhetorical: e.g. the shipwreck in the *W. Tale*. (5) Highly wrought poetical prose, the rarest of all his modes of expression. 'This goodly frame, the earth . . .' (*Hamlet* II. ii). In Shakespeare's later style his verse is often obscure, perplexed, and abrupt: his prose is uniformly smooth and lucid, and much purer in idiom and phrase. His verse is full of mannerisms, his prose always easy and natural. As regards correctness his most characteristic prose is above his verse.

The essay 'Sh. and Holinshed' alternately pleases and discourages. It is certainly helpful to be told that Henry V, who is said to be Shakespeare's ideal man, was modelled trait for trait and touch by touch on Holinshed's summary of his characteristics. But he has surely overstated the problem of *Macbeth*. He says that nothing illustrates so strikingly Shakespeare's method as what he has evolved out of a single sentence: 'Then Donwald though he abhorred the act greatly in heart, yet, at the instigation of his wife. . . .' Against accepted opinion he holds that Shakespeare wrote all *Henry VIII*, but he discovers that Wolsey, Katharine, Cranmer, Gardiner, reproduced in every trait and quality their prototypes in Holinshed.

As regards Montaigne, he thinks that Shakespeare was acquainted with him to a limited extent, and that except in the *Tempest* the

[1] Cf. Bradley on the part played by evil in the Shakespearian world.

parallels may be by chance. The same themes attracted Shakespeare
and Montaigne; there is nothing in them not to be found in Lucretius,
Cicero, Seneca, Plutarch, and filtered from them into innumerable
works popular among thoughtful people in the fifteenth and sixteenth
centuries. Montaigne's essays were almost as much a cento of philosophical commonplaces as Burton's *Anatomy* of quotations. Ben
Jonson speaks of authors stealing from them (*Volpone* III. ii). Shakespeare and Montaigne accepted ultimate problems as insoluble; both
were theistical agnostics. . . .

This last sentence perfectly illustrates the quality of Churton Collins.
Its first clause is general and suggestive; its second particular and
over-confident.

III

WE are already acquainted with Sidney Lee's views, but his book of
the present year[1] treats some of the same questions as that of Churton
Collins, and teaches by contrast. After explaining that the aim of
the Renaissance was universal knowledge, Sidney Lee suggests that
even Shakespeare trespassed unwisely on tracts of knowledge outside
his province—law, geography, scholarship. His knowledge of the law
was intuitive rather than professional; instances of 'bad law' are almost
as numerous with him as 'good law': and it was the same with his
fellow-writers. On the other hand, Churton Collins affirms that his
memory was simply saturated with reminiscences of the law, that in
and out of season he presses it into the service of expression and illustration, and at least a third of his myriad metaphors are derived from it.
Such legal knowledge, he continues, could not have been picked up
in an attorney's office, but only by attending the Courts, at a pleader's
chambers, and on circuit, or by associating intimately with members
of the Bench and Bar.

As regards the classics, while noting that the Elizabethan drama
was built largely on classical foundations, Sidney Lee remarks that
the curious verbal coincidences between the Greek plays and Shakespeare barely do more than suggest the community of sentiment that
binds all great thinkers together. He, too, deals with the Montaigne
problem, and says that Tasso, Ronsard, Cervantes, and Montaigne
were all subject to the same influences, and the results of their work
bear an amazing specific likeness. To him there is little justice in
representing the one as a borrower from the other, since both gave
voice in the same key to that demand of the humanists of the Renaissance for the freest possible employment of man's reasoning faculty.
He approaches Churton Collins in saying that the main resemblances
in sentiment concern the two men's attitude to far-reaching questions
of philosophy. . . .

[1] *Great Englishmen of the 16th Century,* 1904 (Nelson).

In Sidney Lee's pages we feel the finer mind and more disinterested thought: he aims at truth rather than victory. His subject absorbs him, and he meditates upon it impartially till his thought reaches its end. To some extent it is conjecture, and we do not feel the certainty with him that we do with Bradley; but he holds the scales exactly between his impressions of Shakespeare, and his acquired learning of the external influences on the Shakespearian drama. He is at his best in the two following instances.

Shakespeare, he says, was not a finished scholar but widely read in the literature at the disposal of cultivated men of the day. His dominant imagination at once assimilated, digested, and transmuted what he read. His mind was like a highly sensitized photographic plate needing the minutest exposure. A hurried perusal of an Italian story of a Jew in Venice conveyed to him a mental picture of Shylock, with all his racial temperament in energetic action, and all the background of Venetian scenery and society accurately defined.

Secondly, he deprecates the saying that human nature is the same throughout the world, and maintains that Shakespeare recognized that men and women, when yielding to universal emotions, take something from the bent of their education, and from the tone of the climate and scenery that environs them. Compare the love-making of Henry V, Romeo, Ferdinand. Caesar and Brutus live more with him than in Mommsen. In *Hamlet*, the one northern play, introspective melancholy infects not only the hero, but his uncle, and even his mother and Horatio. Cleopatra represents the over-ripe Egyptian civilization.

IV

THE central idea of the work of Sir Edmund K. Chambers[1] is that the drama to interest must achieve unity. He deals ingeniously with Shakespeare's method of reconciling in one effect the different planes of romance, realism, &c., and above all in showing what Shakespeare himself contributed to his ready-made material. One is inclined to say that he errs in admitting too much of the external world into the precincts of Shakespeare.

After dealing with the chronicle play, the object of which, he says, was to make the dead past live again, and dismissing *Henry VI* as artless and chaotic, he finds that *Richard III* does contain Shakespeare's personality, but at most his individual variation on a traditional manner of the English stage. The moral ideas hardly express Shakespeare's personality more than the elements of style. He has simply taken them over from Marlowe and Kyd and treats them as dramatic material. The battle of the Vices and Virtues survived from the

[1] Introductions to *Red Letter Sh.*, 1904–8 (Blackie). Reprinted as *Sh.: A Survey*, 1925 (Sidgwick & Jackson).

Miracles and Moralities: so here are the broadest issues of good and
evil. There are two motives: Retaliation or Nemesis, and the Machiavellian idea, 'Evil, be thou my good!' Shakespeare makes Richard
revel in adroitly playing on the ambitions and weaknesses of those he
would make his puppets; he makes evil his good for sheer joy in the
technique of villainy. He enjoys not the fruit but the success of his
machinations. So far Shakespeare is not primarily interested in moral
ideas, and Richard convinces only as an actor. To the *Errors* he adds
the emotional interest, the note of romance; while in the *Shrew*, if
he did not conceive the idea, he did all he could to express it laughably.
His standpoint is not ethical, but that of a dispassionate and humorous
observer. Farce differs from comedy in that it is brutal or cynical
rather than sympathetic or ironical, and it perverts the normal facts
of life. In *Verona* Shakespeare first confronts the problems of structure
and essays to be original. It is neither tragedy nor comedy but touches
the heights and depths of sentiment. Motives appear which recur in
the later plays, and the play interests in showing what preoccupied
Shakespeare. One must read the play in the light of the Sonnets:
the Sonnets are no mere literary exercise, but there is heart's blood in
them. The central theme of the play is love viewed professedly in the
abstract, but pursued with a commentary not wholly free from personal
bias. Proteus is a portrait of the false friend, and this personal note
emphasizes the romantic unreality of the end. Had he been a mere
puppet we should not have grudged him a puppet's reward. *R. and J.*
reflects something of the emotional disturbance of the Sonnets. Both
R. and J. and *M.N.D.* are the attempts of a reflective and youngish
man to state life in terms of the force by which he has been nearly
tripped up and is still obsessed. Love to Mercutio is the same as to the
author of *M.N.D.* Love is mighty but destiny more so; and the conflict
of these Titanic forces crushing the young lives between them is the
issue of the tragedy. The Friar proves that the wisdom of the ages
is no more able than the ardour of youth to withstand the courses of
the stars. At the end, besides reconciliation, there is the consciousness
that the splendour of love in life is not wholly obliterated, even when
life and love are blotted out together. Love made Romeo into a man
and Juliet into a woman, and the exaltation of this endures, so that
after all love, not destiny, seems the indomitable force.

In *M.N.D.* Shakespeare turned fairies into elemental spirits in
touch with all the dainty and delicate things of earth and air. He had
the Renaissance positive spirit for which such love had little meaning
save as material for poetic craft. He need not believe in the objective
existence of such powers. He used them either to attune the mind of
the audience to a tragic or ironical issue or as a symbol for mystery.
Here love as interpreted by the comic spirit is the undisputed theme.
It is not an integral part of life but a disturbing element in it: the

lover is at odds with established order. When Demetrius returns to Helena the dream easily becomes actual, so the supernatural effects nothing that might not have been without it. The magical love-in-idleness merely represents symbolically the familiar workings of actual love in idleness in the human heart. The mystery is the existence of a freakish irresponsible element of human nature. With the fairies this transitory disturbing element is the normal law of their being.

Richard II compared with Bolingbroke is like a comparison of deeds and dreams. Richard only feels for himself, yet his sensitiveness of soul enables him to hold the hearts of those with whom he enters into personal relations. Shocks of misfortune only stimulate him to exercise more and more subtly his incomparable imagination. In Shakespeare's psychology he is the artist type, and Bolingbroke is incarnate efficiency. The latter's courtesy is deliberate, not instinctive; and he is quite successful here, but in the next play he shows his weakness—want of sympathy, whereby he offends the nobles and misjudges his son. The total dramatic effect of *John* is the most disappointing of Shakespeare's mature plays. It is backboneless and contains little more of Shakespeare than hackwork. Shakespeare adopted the structural outline of the old play, and the historical incongruity in the presentment of the principal character destroys dramatic unity—e.g. the plot against Arthur where the king plays an unheroic part.

The total impression of the *Merchant* is emotional not critical. How, then, is comedy to be taken here? Comedy is the vehicle of ideas and reason predominates in it. However, in comedy the emotion gathers only to pass away and dissolve in triumph and laughter and clash of marriage bells. The Elizabethan drama had always the tradition of the Morality behind it, so the theme here is conflict between love and hate. Shylock embodies Hate, Antonio and Portia Love. Antonio's melancholy is out of harmony with the play's sunny atmosphere. The intrusion of the personal note from Shakespeare's private life is explained by the Sonnets. Falstaff unifies the two parts of *Henry IV*. He is the stuff for comedy because his intellect has survived the shipwreck of his morals, and his quick wits save him from humiliation. Comedy preaches sincerity by the ironic exposure of shams. *M. Ado* is a typical example of inconsistency of purpose and the clashing of dramatic planes—melodrama, pure comedy, tragi-comedy. But because Benedict and Beatrice are the most interesting their atmosphere predominates, and the incidents of melodrama are forced out of their own plane into that of comedy.

Henry V is the completest expression of Elizabethan heightened national self-consciousness. Henry's secret is that he fully represents his fellow-countrymen. Shakespeare's style reaches its zenith of objectivity and rhetoric; but the limits are that he plays on life's surface, concerned with the idols of the forum. *J.C.* has the same theme and manner and eloquence. It was the period of Shakespeare's career when his speech was most perfectly fitted to the precise ideas it wishes to express. Caesar's infirmities throw into stronger relief his powers of will and personal magnetism. He speaks of himself with awe, and this creates an atmosphere of dramatic irony. Shakespeare has passed to the despondent view of life where righteousness fails against efficiency. *A.Y.L.* is incarnate romance; the sudden changes of fortune show a beneficent disposer of events. The Falstaff of the *Wives* is the same as in *Henry IV*, but now the laugh is against him. He formerly triumphed over a careless prince and tavern riffraff, but now we see him at odds with the impenetrable chastity and practical wit of the English middle classes. *Twelth-Night* is the comedy of spiritual self-deceptions. Emotions are not really felt but regarded as modish or delightful. Shakespeare interprets Orsino and Olivia by placing beside them others like in kind but of grosser purport. Viola, with the specific of simple truth, purges this pestilence of artifice and rhetoric.

Interest of the universal, not the particular, dominates with Hamlet —not his mother's sin but the frailty of women. The key-note is the tragic ineffectiveness of speculative intellect in a world of action. In *T. and C.* a disillusioned Shakespeare turns back on his former ideals and the world's ancient ideals of heroism and romance and questions them. Do love of woman and honour of man really exist? Cressida is no professional wanton, and it is in her humanity that the bitterness of it lies. *All's Well* is drenched in irony. Helena tricks a man into marriage, and consummates it by another trick—an unsavoury adventure for no great prize. In *Hamlet* and *J.C.* we saw noble manhood disabled by intellect and idealism; here noble womanhood is disabled by womanhood's highest quality—love. Such unsmiling comedy proves how perturbed must be the once sunny spirit. Had Shakespeare any clear issue in *M. for M.*? It seems the work of a man searching somewhat vaguely for truth in unfamiliar paths. There is a corroding atmosphere of moral suspicion. Has Isabella had her ordeal and failed? Is she wholly justified in the eyes of her creator? It is hard to see anything but Shakespeare's satirical intention to theories of the moral government of the universe. So far there is ineffectiveness, not deliberate ill will, in the order of things.

There is more pity in *Othello*, more awe in *Macbeth* and *Lear*. Neither Othello nor Desdemona can oppose the forces that beset them, so they fail from destiny, not character. The play is a duel between goodness and evil. Iago is essentially inhuman; he knows his opponents' good points, and on these fastens the web of intrigue. That he should be called 'Honest Iago' shows virtue defenceless in the eternal conflict. His type fitted in with something profound in

Shakespeare's tragical apprehension of the world. Macbeth is cosmic tragedy—good and evil contemplated as much in the totality of things as in the individual. Shakespeare has three types of tragedy: external (villainy), psychological (character), cosmic (fate). About 1601 he lost his faith in the world, but the attempts to connect this phase with external events are shadowy conjecture. However, for eight or nine years he proceeded to analyse victorious evil. Macbeth is driven from sin to sin by resistless powers beyond his own control, and the enveloping atmosphere is one of moral and spiritual gloom. From the cosmic view-point the facts of sin and retribution are the springs of tragedy. Is free will illusory? If not, why is Macbeth determined by suggestions he does not initiate to ends he does not desire? It means the presence of external forces. *Lear* is analytic rather than constructive; it understands but offers no remedy. It is concerned less with man's nature than what is around and above man. In *Macbeth* sin and its retribution are represented as two closely related parts of the mysterious curse imposed on the sinner from without; and the symbolism of the witches shows its superhuman origin. The result is everdeepening pessimism, since humanity's frailties can be ameliorated, but not external forces. Lear is absorbed in his emotions and blind to the fine shades of expression and conduct in others. The cosmic side of tragedy is when the heavens are equally deaf. Wind and rain rather than unkindness beat him into submission. Shakespeare indicts forces that make sport of man's nothingness. In *A. and C.* Antony's capacity is his undoing. We see the two equally hypnotized by each other, and the intensity of this gives tragic dignity. Honour is the shattered ideal of *Coriolanus*, but beneath the mask of honour lurks the subtle sin of egoism. Egoism is at the root of Coriolanus, and he becomes tangled in the web woven more by the threads of his own nature than the intrigues of his enemies.

Shakespeare's conversion rather than transition to romance was so fundamental and sudden as to need drastic explanation. His style also changed to relaxed and structureless periods. There is nothing to show whether *Philaster* preceded or followed *Cymbeline*,[1] and certainly the late Shakespeare and early Beaumont and Fletcher have common devices of construction and types of character. *Cymbeline* is a symbolical and idealized rendering of life, where there is no clashing of dramatic planes. All are puppets, and Imogen is perfect when not compared with a Cleopatra or a Cressida. The influence of Beaumont and Fletcher does not account for a profound change of spiritual mood. The universe, lately chaos, is now an ordered and sunlit garden of God. This fundamental metamorphosis is not due to mere desire to rival others in exploiting dramatic convention. This would refuse spiritual content to tragedies and romances. The profound cleavage in Shake-

[1] See Thorndike.

speare's mental history about 1607–8 must have been due to some spiritual crisis. The plane of the *W. Tale* is not wholly kept; in Acts II and III there are scenes that touch too near the quick for romance. In the *Tempest* the dramatic spectacle of Prospero's omnipotence takes all vitality from the plots which he unravels; and the loves of Ferdinand and Miranda stir us but faintly. . . .

There is no question that Sir E. Chambers has thoroughly assimilated Shakespeare, and that the impression left in his mind is a well-considered one. Shakespeare as a human being has become clear to him; he rejects with scorn the theory that the Sonnets are a literary exercise, and he sees personal reasons for the comic, tragic, and romantic periods. He has also clear ideas as to the technique of the drama, and the question for him is how far Shakespeare was perfect in it or not. For us the question is how far the critic helps us to understand what is universal in Shakespeare; and in the present case he does it by describing to what extent Shakespeare gave unity to his plays. He is at his best with the ultimate impression left by *R. and J.* and to a lesser extent by *M.N.D.* His opinion of Proteus, though conjecture, is one of the weightiest arguments ever advanced to explain the great psychological error of the play. We can whole-heartedly accept his distinction between the planes in *M. Ado*; but his criticism of the effect of Caesar's infirmities is of the kind which fascinates and sets the imagination to work but cannot quite convince. He accurately defines the result of Henry IV's want of sympathy, but not that of Antonio's melancholy (*Merchant*). The latter instance recalls our complaint at the outset that the external world was over-present. In estimating what the dramatist should do he inclines to forget what the poet has done. Only if we forget that Shakespeare was first a poet and then a dramatist can we accept his strictures on *John*, the *W. Tale*, and the *Tempest*. Even more salient is his acceptance of Falstaff of the *Wives* as the real Falstaff, for the reasons specified. He is puzzled by *All's Well* and *M. for M.*, but, as he accepts the Folio, the suggestion that other hands are in these plays would not commend itself to him. The 'cosmic' tragedy of which he speaks, the lessening of individual responsibility with Othello and Macbeth, and the decisive action of the storm in *Lear*, does not seem to us entirely satisfactory—but for answer we must refer back to the work of Professor Bradley.

V

THE mind of Stopford Brooke[1] was of the sensitive, poetic cast, inclined to stress the moral side of Shakespeare but never separating it from the aesthetic. This perception of the interdependent good and beautiful helps us to realize the higher unity of Shakespeare's plays. It is specially marked in the tragedies, or those parts of the

[1] *On Ten Plays of Sh.*, 1905 (Constable).

comedies and histories that lie nearest tragedy. Otherwise, in the comedies, he excels in showing how the individual is related to the world of his play—whether fairy, Renaissance, or other. We will follow him through in his own order, and as we pass from his lighter to his graver touches we see by contrast the divided origins of the single impression of beauty left by a play of Shakespeare's.

The women of the *M.N.D.* still preserve their constancy in love, unlike the men. The fairies are in their own atmosphere and do not share the unreason of dreamland. This seeming real and reasonable fairy region is one of Shakespeare's creative triumphs. He keeps the elfin atmosphere quite untouched by humanity. The one human thing in this shadow world is difference of sex: this gives Oberon and Titania sympathy with mortal affairs. The life of all the characters of *R. and J.* is that of youth, even with the old men. The Nurse has neither morality nor conscience, yet her immorality is natural and primeval. When she is heartless it is more due to the society in which she has lived than to her original nature. The love of Romeo and Juliet is that of a power without, whose object is to punish and end the feud. They dimly feel a fateful presence in their love; their whole nature is heightened; they believe in the divinity of natural love. Death adds to imagination a last intensity. When life has reached the top of joy death counts for little.

All Shakespeare's historical plays are rooted in patriotism. He shows how the justice of moral evolution punished the kings and nobles who made England bleed; but his lessons are indirectly given. He aims to represent human life in action and thought within the events which history laid before him. These eight histories are united into one drama by the justice of God. They contain in their living tapestry such a great and various representation of human life as never yet was brought together and harmonized by any genius in the modern world. The shadow of fate lies dark and deep on Richard II. Even when not on the stage his solitary figure dominates the play. Sorrow changes him, and by waking his imagination exalts him above the common herd of kings into the realm of art. *Richard III* initiates a new England purged from guilt. All the avenging forces are knitted round the supernatural image of Margaret. Richard's iron will seems to make and lead events, but really he is the servant of Justice. Shakespeare does not insist on this but makes us conscious of it. Richard has no love and so no sense of right and wrong; absence of conscience is rooted in absence of love. The cause of his crime is unmodified presence of self alone, and his 'remorse' is agony of failure. He does not hesitate like Macbeth—because guilt was not Macbeth's natural element. In the end, lovelessness spoils Richard's cunning. The cursing is too long to be intense, to have the closely knitted passion which lifts the curse into the world of art.

Amid the lightness of the *Merchant* is a weighty strain of thought, and all is perfectly amalgamated. Bassanio knows he may be accused of seeking money, but he knows he desires Portia alone. Also Antonio's friendship is romantic: and yet romance is less prominent than the tragedy of life. We see nothing of the beauty of the sea-city, but we get the atmosphere of its world-wide trade. Historical reality gives weight to imaginative work. Belmont is reality yet romance; the play is as various as life itself, with its sunshine and shadow, &c. None of the characters lack the active intelligence of the New Learning. Antonio's friendship exalts Bassanio in our eyes. Shylock is the darkness to Antonio's light; and the centre of the play is the struggle of darkness and light, good and evil. Antonio's greatness is his carelessness of gain for gain's sake. Shylock's sordid care for money lost him his soul and was the cause of all his evil passions, and these at last consumed even his love of money. It was like Shakespeare to gather some vague pity round him at the last. Circumstances made him bad, even more than the degradation of the world and the love of money. His two passions—personal and national—mingle and strengthen each other. Portia knits together the two parts of the play, but her inmost self appears in her first talk with Nerissa. Shakespeare wrote *A.Y.L.* for his own delight; it has no conscious moral purpose. He believed in love at first sight; but the love of Celia and Oliver was more of the senses than the soul; and this stains Celia's pleasant image. Few plays are wiser and fuller of affectionate experience of human nature. Still greater is the beauty of character in Rosalind and Orlando. To live with them is to live with moral beauty; their life will do good to every one they meet. The mantle of her sweetness is over all; and even Jaques is not as bad as he has been. If he was ever a cynic he has now put his cynicism away, but keeps it in his pocket ready to put on and off like his cap. He is the tired man of experience who mocks the world, but would like to find the freshness of life again. He is really interested in the fate of the wounded deer, but he is over-vain of his thinking. He has imagination—a power too noble to lodge with a cynic. The one thing his great speech wants is passion.

The outward crimes and events in *Macbeth* are but shadows of the inward realities of which they are the dread result. The Witches influence only the soul that has admitted evil to dwell in it; and Shakespeare subtly delineates the effect of suggested evil on two souls. No outward terror is so deep as that in Macbeth's soul; the scene after the murder is unsurpassed in literature: the awful, silent solitude of the mind—the true supernatural. Nothing so isolates man—and Macbeth has no remorse, but the recklessness of one who has shut himself off from his fellows by a fatal act of dishonour. Imagination in him transforms the murder out of vulgar assassination into the archetype of all terrible, soul-shaking murders. He drags in the

remotest things, and mixes up his deeds and self with Nature. Ambition
is a heavy temptation to one like himself—imaginative, supernaturally
fearful, with no moral foundation for his honour, without the conscience that is honour's guard. Lady Macbeth's desire is made stronger
by love; her emotion is so intense that while it lasts it lifts her above
nature. When the storm of impulse is over she realizes the horror
and returns to herself. Her conscience awakes, and she dwells on
the irreparable past—which he, who only seeks to secure the future,
does not. When passion dominates in a woman it acts apart from
thought: Lady Macbeth's intellect did not exist for the time.[1] She
acted like a law of nature, and now all the thoughts her passion had
concealed rushed upon her. Loss of womanhood is avenged by return
of womanhood. He has faced the consequences beforehand, and now
transfers with the sympathy which belongs to a poetic nature his own
failure to all humanity. All is illusion.

In *Coriolanus* Shakespeare appears as a less absolute dramatic
master. The poetry is as lovely as ever, but the co-ordinating power
is less. He saw all sides and sympathized with the struggle of the
people, showing what was just in their demands and modest in their
conduct. To stress this he places their cries in the mouth of a shouting
demagogue. He did not love or approve Coriolanus, and nothing is
more rigid than the steady drawing of his inevitable punishment. His
pride is not that of a great or strong man, but the servant of his choler.
That he should be so fine a character among his own class makes his
conduct to those not of his class all the worse. Even love of his mother
is founded on her encouragement of the self within him. At his best
he is thrilled by natural affections. His relationship with his mother
is the inmost heart of the drama. Love glorifies them and creates
round the haughty woman and terrible warrior the gracious atmosphere
of home.

The jealousy of Leontes is partly motived by friendship having
changed into weariness and nervous disgust. Shakespeare wisely
makes Autolycus enjoy nature; it is preoccupation with ourselves,
not wrong-doing, that prevents us from enjoying her. Though he
robs everybody he makes everybody happy. Prospero is human
enough to be interesting in spite of his art. Solitude brutalizes one
who has had no sorrow or love, but makes forgiving and tolerant one
who has had both. Having forgiven he forgets: and this is the temper
of God. The main drift of the play is to teach forgiveness—indirectly
as art should do. We feel that Shakespeare himself forgives the world
and so reaches fresh life. Ariel's exquisite refinement of nature is a
kind of conscience in him. He is more elemental yet more human
than Oberon. Prospero's speech on illusion fits the temper of his
mind at this instant of the play. He and Shakespeare were too sane

[1] Cf. Guizot and Montégut.

and experienced to imagine life as illusion or ourselves as the stuff of dreams. . . .

If Stopford Brooke is at all inclined to over-stress the moral side of Shakespeare it is in the historical plays. Such a comparison as Richard III and Macbeth is hardly now in the order of things. It may be noted that, writing of *Richard II*, he finds the characters of the early histories more isolated and less dramatically interwoven than later on. Certain modern critics who detect the hand of Marlowe in the said play might compare the impression of Sir E. Chambers in the presence of *M. for M.* As was said in the beginning, the good and the beautiful are inseparably combined, and the basis of the emotion is social. Eternity surrounds us, but this earth is not to be despised, and happiness is a thing that counts. This feeling of the joy of life points his criticisms on the Nurse in *R. and J.*, on *A.Y.L.*, Autolycus, &c. Above all is it true of Macbeth, the awful solitude of whose soul he brings home to us after the murder, and thus takes us furthest into the Shakespearian mystery. Perhaps his most typical judgements are those on Bassanio, Jaques, Autolycus, Prospero, and Ariel. The momentum of the critic's life is behind his pen. In matters of pure intellect life can be disparted from letters; no one feels Hume's privately admitted religion through his sceptical treatises. But the aesthetic writer must use his experience of beauty, and we feel that Stopford Brooke's insight comes from a wisely ordered life—above all, his power to decide where the good and beautiful become one. It proves again that the critic who would interpret Shakespeare must dedicate his whole being. There are critics, especially in these later days, whose method is elimination and correction of earlier critics, and who give off something of themselves in the process. Others— such as the present—contribute to their subject a part of their inmost self: and the fine essence of Stopford Brooke is a cultivated moral beauty.

VI

SWINBURNE'S books recur like thunder-storms: we are familiar with his views on Shakespeare, and, alas! with his critical manners also. We have winnowed the present volume[1] for instances of the good, the doubtful, and the exaggerated among his impressions. The last are always expressed in the defiant tone of one who will not be contradicted. His method here is distinctly impressionistic; he is kindled more by a part of a play—a character, or selected speeches, or a certain strain—than by the whole. This is notable in *T. and C.*, and he affirms that the Sonnets cannot be read as a sequence. We will deal first with his exaggerations.

He accepts *Arden of Feversham* as Shakespeare's, and says that nothing in the early plays is more impressive or productive of terror

[1] *Sh.*, 1905 (Oxford Univ. Press, 1909).

and pity. In *Henry V* Shakespeare matches himself with one greater
than Homer or Dante, viz. Aeschylus; and he compares it with the
Persae. *All's Well* contains some 'farcically magnificent comedy'.
Anne Boleyn (*Henry VIII*) must be Shakespeare's creation, because
Shakespeare never left us as subtle and significant a study of female
character as this finely-finished and ambiguously attractive sketch.
In simplicity, sublimity, purity of pathos and harmony of impression,
Pericles is above comparison with any but the greatest of its author's
works. Imogen is the most adorable woman ever created by God or
man. Iachimo is a subtly consistent and credible figure of a heartless
and fearless villain. The socialism of the revolutionary, even subver-
sive, sympathies which imbue with thoughtful passion Lear's inspired
insanity, is Shakespeare's own. It was only possible to treat *Coriolanus*
from the patrician point of view, and to make the patricians base and
malignant. . . .

The cause of these errors, if such they are, was Swinburne's
imagination which worked on when its subject was removed, and
recreated the impression not always truly. As regards *Coriolanus* we
may look back to Stopford Brooke's words on the subject. We will
now delight ourselves with his best manner—his poetic insight and
splendid expression:

Shakespeare flavours the fun of the *Errors* with an exquisite infusion
of poetry. We infer from *Hamlet* that he did not write merely for
the stage but always with an eye on the future and studious reader.
If he has improved on the original *Shrew*, it is rather by process of
refinement in detail than principle. Shylock's plea for righteousness,
his claim for manhood, and appeal for charity, would not have been
so forcible if spoken by a good Jew. That truth should speak through
Shylock was a conception beyond the reach of any other dramatist
or poet that ever lived. The poetry and romance of *A.Y.L.* are
interwoven, rather than inlaid, with half-divine realism or naturalism
in humour. *M. for M.* is a great indefinable poem or unclassifiable
play. Shakespeare created one of the supreme glories of all poetry
out of the shameful agony of a shameless coward in face of nothing
more terrible than death. In *T. and C.*, out of most inadequate and
unattractive material, he has fashioned some of the most glorious
poetry in the world. The woodland scenes of *Cymbeline* are wonderfully made in keeping with the rest of the poem. *Macbeth* proves how
independent of the interest excited by imaginative sympathy with
virtue the inner action and passion of a great poem may be. *Lear*
grapples with the best and worst imaginable possibilities of human
character. Nature is but a background to the deeper and more dreadful
harmonies and revelations of humanity. The immense and living
variety of subordinate figures of *A. and C.* throws into fuller and more
vivid relief the two which command them all. . . .

The words on *Lear* might be compared with those of Sir E. Chambers. We now offer without comment certain of Swinburne's judgements:

The charm of the *Merchant* is greater than its interest. The *W. Tale* is as unique among poems as is Shakespeare among men. No other poet has ever made or will ever make a blameless hero (Brutus) at once credible by human belief and lovable by human infirmity. Lady Macbeth is the one wicked woman that Shakespeare has made heroic. It is too great a transmutation and downfall that the Witches—prophetic agents of a doom sublime enough to change the face of kingdoms and destroy the souls of heroes—should be found begging chestnuts and killing swine.

VII

WE promised to meet Mr. J. M. Robertson at Philippi, and the hour has arrived.[1] The gist of Mr. Robertson's criticism is that the plays collected in the Folio contain much that Shakespeare did not write. Many persons are inclined to agree with him, and in the case of plays like *Henry VI*, *Titus*, *Henry VIII*, and *Pericles* it is no new thing; but Mr. Robertson has gone far beyond these preliminary marches and entered closed territory so far thought to be inaccessibly Shakespearian. He brings to his task a wide and accurate knowledge of Elizabethan literature—he has read over and over again the works of Shakespeare's predecessors and contemporaries, so that on the slightest hint of a resemblance he can produce a line to correspond from some dramatist scarcely known by name to the general reader. He has the self-confidence that results from first-rate intellectual power, and also a fine aesthetic faculty—a delight in the beauty and music of verse. As it is thought best to play with cards on the table, we will admit ourselves converts to Mr. Robertson's theories, after an initial shock. For some years when reading the longer speeches in plays such as *Henry V* or *J.C.*, we were half-conscious of a hardness, a want of rebound in the verse, that was not Shakespearian—and Mr. Robertson's books supplied the reason. We think the problems he has raised will occupy the Shakespearian critics of the future; but we will endeavour to condense his views and present them impartially so that the reader may judge for himself.[2]

At the outset Mr. Robertson stresses the need to compare Shakespeare's plays with the signed and unsigned work of his predecessors and contemporaries. In aesthetic matters he dismisses the inductive

---

[1] *An Introduction to the Study of the Sh. Canon*, 1924 (Routledge). A revised and much enlarged edition of *Did Sh. write 'Titus'?* 1905.

[2] Hints of other hands in the plays may be found in the following critics: Pope, Malone, Seymour, Coleridge, Bowdler, Appleton Morgan; Corbin, also Herford, on *Hamlet*; S. Brooke on *M. for M.*; Brander Matthews on Laertes; Marriott on *Richard III*.

methods of Sir E. Chambers, and proposes to trace impressions to
their concrete sources. Shakespeare probably revised *Titus* metrically
and added single lines, but no entire speech. As a whole the play does
not rise above the Kyd-Peele-Greene level of dramatic imagination,
but it has been metrically levelled up so that every speech tells for its
purpose. Mr. Robertson likewise dismisses Professor Parrott's theory
that Shakespeare used the double-ending more frequently than his
predecessors—since the percentage of double-endings in Shakespeare's
undoubted early blank verse is 8·6, while that of *Titus* is 29–30.
Where Shakespeare led the way was in run-on lines with varied pause,
and the ending of speeches on a short line—the latter with the pause
variation being his most marked advance. We must abandon *a priori*
hypotheses for scientific analysis, and remember that in the ten years
after *Titus* was first published Henslowe records that plays were
produced by three or four collaborators.[1]

It is difficult to prove scientifically that a play is not Shakespeare's,
because many undisputed parts of the early plays are comparatively
inferior. *Titus* should be compared with the work of all the other
known English playwrights of Shakespeare's early years. It will help
to prove that Shakespeare did not write the play if we establish its
real author. The style, verse, workmanship, matter are un-Shakespearian. Meres does ascribe the play to him, but that is the bare
statement of a contemporary publisher. That Shakespeare had once
revised the work would justify the theatrical company to claim it.
The theatre assigns to Shakespeare the three *Henry VI* plays, which
Meres does not ascribe to him, so the authority of Meres is open to
challenge. No doubt *Titus* is a recast from an older play, *Titus and
Vespasian,* and the latter is adapted from a lost Italian original. Greene,
Peele, and Kyd read Italian, and Kyd's *Spanish Tragedy* shows equal
Italian and Senecan influence. If Shakespeare had been other than
a collaborator before he wrote *Venus,* he would not have called the
latter 'first heir' of his invention; yet this is ignored by those who stand
or fall by 'external' evidence. All chronology of Shakespeare's plays
should start from 1593—the date of the dedication of *Venus.* He
would not regard as heirs of his invention plays in which he modified
other men's drafts or shared with others the task of revision or composition; and it is generally agreed that of such a nature was the
Henry VI group. Surely then we may believe that he had collaborators or
draftsmen for *Verona, L.L.L., Errors, Richard II,* even as he refashioned
other men's work in *R. and J.* and rewrote previous plays in *John,* &c.
Collaboration was unavoidable because plays were commissioned by a
given date—so the dramatists pooled their ideas.

[1] Grant White (1885) wrote that Shakespeare worked up old plays and stories
and made them immortal by his psychological insight and magic style. Appleton
Morgan (1888) said that a play was rarely one man's work.

The plot of *Titus* is so far the most elaborate in English drama, and here it differs from Shakespeare's two earliest plays, *M.N.D.* and *L.L.L.*, but it absolutely lacks *moral* unity. Act I alienates our sympathies from Titus, Acts IV and V reclaim them, while the intervening sub-plot is preposterous. Churton Collins called Shakespeare's characters prototypes, but the figure of Richard III was handled by Marlowe and other dramatists before Shakespeare, and the evil personalities of Iago and Edmund are a world removed from the bold daub in *Titus*. By recognizing the kindred quality of the rubbish in *Titus* and in many of the plays of its school we shall reach a just conclusion. Churton Collins insisted on the legal allusions, but Sidney Lee has pointed out that these abounded in all plays and poems of the period—in Spenser, Jonson, Chapman.

The test of style is one of the most essential in such an inquiry, and Mr. Robertson now applies it, having in his mind a clear conception of Shakespeare's power over verse and situation as shown in his poems and early undoubted plays. He opposes those critics who assign Tamora's speeches to Shakespeare. He compares her speech, 'My lovely Aaron . . .' (II. iii), with that in Peele's *David and Bethsabe*, 'Now comes my lover tripping like the roe . . .'. He finds in both the same verse-movement, with the development of two run-on lines, and the same taste in imagery and saccharine diction. He considers the gross and undramatic taunts which Bassianus and Lavinia cast at Tamora to be characteristic of Peele's method as exhibited in *David*, which was to give a strong provocation or example for every deed of violence, without regard to loss of sympathy with every character in turn. Here Bassianus and Lavinia become offensive, and the situation is worsened morally and aesthetically in a manner far removed from Shakespeare's earliest work. The plot-work suggests Kyd more than Peele—e.g. Aaron's hiding of the bag of gold. But both Kyd and Peele use constant phrases, and rhetoric without fire, whereas the young Shakespeare neglects style contraptions and has plenty of rhetoric touched by passion. Professor Parrott finds a parallel between the conceits which Marcus spins before the mutilated Lavinia and the line in *Lucrece* (st. 248), 'Her blood, in poor revenge, held it in chase'. But in *Lucrece* the bad taste is merely aesthetic, consisting in the pursuit of the verbal conceit or image beyond the verge of congruity. Shakespeare has made the psychic or spiritual overlay the physical: the figure of the trickling blood occurs when Lucrece is dead, when the long moral agony is over, and the tragic vision is one of mortal peace. In *Titus* it is an intolerable expatiation on a living agony, and such a violation of dramatic decency is utterly un-Shakespearian. In *Lear* he lets the blinding of Gloucester scene speak for itself, and shrinks from verbal equivalent. Youth does not explain this, for the highest genius does not emerge from the grossest lack of artistic judgement. Classical allusions reveal the same contrast of terseness and point in Shakespeare and weak discursiveness in *Titus*, e.g. 'Cerberus at the Thracian poet's feet' in the latter, and the allusion to Pluto and Orpheus in *Lucrece*.

Titus is admitted to be the most horrible Elizabethan play, so that if Shakespeare penned it, we conclude that he who developed the most exquisite taste began with the worst, that he who most spiritualized tragedy began by brutalizing it. Parallel passages do not guide us; they abound in Elizabethan literature; and Kyd, Greene, Lodge, Peele, Marlowe all repeat themselves and copy others. Versification is the test, also frequent use of particular phrases, general or frequent notes of manner and mannerism, peculiarities of vocabulary, tics of style and forms of phrase which are not noticeably epigrammatic in character: although clues of word and phrase must be subordinated to the test of style, or we may find Shakespeare in a score of anonymous plays. There are fourteen or more classical proper names, allusively used in *Titus*, which appear in no other play of Shakespeare's, and one or two more which occur only in disputed or composite plays. If all or nearly all appear in the works of one or two contemporaries, who for other reasons also seem part authors of *Titus*, the argument is strengthened. And yet more so if the words special to *Titus* are found in the works of these same contemporaries. Thus 'palliamant' occurs in *Titus* and in no other Shakespearian play, but in Peele's poem, *The Honour of the Garter* (1593). 'Chase' meaning 'park' or 'game preserve' occurs twice in *Titus*, nowhere else in Shakespeare, and four times in Peele's *Arraignement of Paris*. It has been argued that Shakespeare imitated Peele, but as parallel passages occur in works printed after *Titus*, it would have to be argued that Peele imitated Shakespeare. The problem is lightened if we agree that Peele wrote most of *Titus*, repeating himself as freely as in his avowed works, as did Marlowe or Greene. Many of Peele's words in *Titus* recur in admittedly composite plays, such as *Henry VI* and the *Shrew*—and this is further evidence. In Peele's play *Locrine* we see the same peculiarity as in *Titus* of names varied in form for metre's sake. 'Saturnine' and 'Saturninus', 'Philomel' and 'Philomela', 'empress' and 'emperess' in *Titus* are paralleled by 'Locrine' and 'Locrinus', 'Estrild' and 'Estrilda', 'Gwendolen' and 'Gwendolena'. We pass over alliteration and reiteration, common alike to Peele, Greene, and Kyd, assuming that Greene himself supplied the diction in *Titus*. But if *Titus* is adapted from an Italian play, Kyd is the likeliest playwright, because no other pre-Shakespearian had treated so complex a plot and one of such regular progression. The test of vocabulary also yields a number of passages that savour of Marlowe. In Act I there are suggestions of Marlowe after Bassianus seizes Lavinia; the quarrel is more life-like, less wordy, and produces a tension rarely attained by Peele. Traces of Marlowe appear in IV. iv, where the verse-movement is more nervous than Peele's and is unlike Greene's. In V. i, we get the same nervous versification, though it is sad stuff for Marlowe.

The final test is the style test, and it proves that Shakespeare had no share in *Arden of Feversham*[1] or *Edward III*. The verse of the Countess scenes of the latter play does accord with that of *Verona*, for alone in *Verona* of Shakespeare's early plays is there this vivacious monotony of line-ended iambics. *Errors* and *Richard II* may have the line-ended stamp, but the iambic movement is not the same. *Edward III* combines the line-ended norm with the marked iambic proclivity of Greene; the rhythm ends with the line even when the clause runs beyond it. Did the young Shakespeare write line-ended, monotonous iambics? Yes, if he wrote *Verona*. No, if we judge from *M.N.D.*, the first scene of *Errors*, and *L.L.L.* His command of verse was infinite, and he would not write alternately as a man possessed by one monotonous verse tune, and as a born master of rhythm. No two lines of Titania's speech, 'These are the forgeries of jealousy', have the same pulsation; but we get ten succeeding different variants from the iambic norm. Not only the verse but the diction and thought of Greene prevail in *Verona* and the anonymous play: and so the case is fairly complete. The second speech of *Errors* likewise shows the endless variation of rhythm which Marlowe and Greene at their best only approach. But if the whole play is Shakespeare's it would mean that after preluding it with a scene absolutely in his own early verse manner, he had hypnotically copied Marlowe's versification. Such is the Imitation Theory which represents him as impartially and industriously imitating four different styles in *Titus*. *Arden* is a powerful and original play, but neither its psychology nor its style attains to the delicacy of Shakespeare's early work. The critics who assign it to Shakespeare disregard these vital tests; even Swinburne showed himself temporarily style-blind and rhythm-deaf while charging his antagonists with being able to 'hear only with their fingers'.

The problem of *1 Henry VI* can only be solved by metrical tests. Critics have assigned the Talbot and Roses scenes to Shakespeare, but the latter contains twenty-seven per cent. double-endings, that would place it in Shakespeare's third period, that of *Hamlet* and *Othello*. The verse, which is end-stopped, is rhythmically below his second period. The Clifford speech was rhythmically impossible for Shakespeare in 1592; it was in the manner of Northumberland (*2 Henry IV*, I. i). The total effect of the Clifford speech is one of varied pause and rhythm of which the Roses scene has no trace. So do the metrical phenomena of *Titus* forbid us to assign it to Shakespeare. Its higher percentages of double endings are characteristic of Marlowe, Greene, Kyd, but not of Shakespeare before 1596; while

[1] Cf. Swinburne (1905).

its other traits are inconceivable as his as late as 1593. We know a
poet as much from his rhythm as his diction. Most speeches in *L.L.L.*
begin with iambs; in *M.N.D.* iambs and trochees predominate over
spondees. The first act of *Titus* has 111 blank-verse speeches, of
which 37 begin with trochees, 33 with spondees, and 41 with iambs—
very much as trochees and spondees are distributed in Peele's *David.*
The opening scene of *Titus* is monotonous, feeble, and unlike Shakespeare in rhythm. Every line is end-stopped in rhythm, even when
there is no punctuation pause, and the lines are in series, not 'periods'.
Compare the opening of *Errors* with the pulsation of the verse and
vibration of the tense diction. We get a prehensile construction of
six lines, all in poised rhythm but continuously interfluent. The *Errors*
was probably written in 1591, so Shakespeare from the start wrote
his own verse and sang with his own voice. Greene, Kyd, Marlowe
were all line-steppers; the best poetry in *Tamburlaine* is free-flowing,
but linear, without involution. A specimen of Shakespeare's visibly
early work is his insertion in *Richard III* (III. vii), the speech of Buckingham, 'The supreme seat, the throne majestical . . .'. Though partly
line-marked, we have an unbroken period of ten lines followed by
one of seven, in a 'delicately pompous' diction, distinct both from
Marlowe's loud force and thrasonical stress and Peele's commonplace
mouthing. From the outset Shakespeare had a verse-movement of
his own and never imitated Marlowe. His verse is long-breathed,
and as thought reaches beyond line, there is 'periodic' control even
when clauses keep to line-measure. He eludes the line limit even in
punctuation, carrying on clause and varying pausation. (Cf. *Richard II*,
I. iii, 'Never did captive with a freer heart.') Marlowe, who is said
to have taught Shakespeare, never wrote thus; and we are asked to
believe that the 'beginner' who could write such a winged *cantabile*
as 'Within the hollow crown . . .' (III. ii) deliberately folded his
wings and coarsened his voice to frame in the same play the raucous
vituperation of the Marlowese scolding-matches and the careless and
unashamed linear imitation of a Marlowese allocution. The stumbling-
block is the assumption that Shakespeare *must* have written all in the
Folio; but the student should be faithful to the 'star-y-pointing'
testimony of the true Shakespearian work in early composite plays.
His true voice is throughout *M.N.D.*, and the fact that his manifold
verse did not need the relief of double-ending is proof that frequent
double-endings in the early plays are the work of other men. The
double-ending came to him gradually as a minor form of freedom.

The construction of *Titus* is due to Peele, Greene, and Kyd, but
not to Marlowe. They applied the Aristotelean maxim that a good
man should not suffer without cause. Revenge is the key-note of the
Spanish Tragedy, and the victim in *Arden* had himself treated others
cruelly. In *2* and *3 Henry VI* the alternate murders by Lancastrians

and Yorkists tell of the same academic formula. Titus in Act I commits the gross moral blunder of sacrificing Tamora's son, and so forfeits sympathy when he suffers in turn. Vengeance is the fundamental moral motive, derived from Seneca (cf. *Hamlet*). In both the *Spanish Tragedy* and *Titus* Revenge is personified—a reason for surmising the collaboration of Kyd. There is also progression in atrocity, and *Titus* combines the horrors of all its predecessors. The sexual element of the plot suggests Peele, the complication and artifice of the whole, Kyd. Revenge and rant were traits of the pre-Shakespearians, and the classicism is obviously non-Shakespearian. The pedantries of *Titus* are as alien to the spirit and method of Shakespeare's real work as its atrocities and moral stupidities. Youth certainly imitates, but youth of genius imitates what it admires. Shakespeare was not likely to write the most brutal tragedy of the era a few years before he wrote the *Merchant*. That *Titus* was effective on the stage makes it more likely to be the work of practised dramatists. Shakespeare's early plays—*M.N.D.* and *L.L.L.*—were not effective on the stage, and only after years of practical training and handling of other men's plays which he revised did he add stage-craft to his mastery of the higher elements of dramatic and poetic art. To the end his higher faculty was apt to function in disregard of the other —as a appears in *T. and C.*

If Shakespeare merely revised the verse of *Titus* his company would claim it as his, on the principle of theatrical property. To work vigilantly through such a play is to realize what a patchwork quilt an Elizabethan drama can be. . . .

Mr. Robertson applies to the study of Shakespeare the analytic and comparative methods of the sciences—and these are not always successfully applied to aesthetic problems. We remember Gulliver's voyage to Laputa and meeting with those commentators who were disowned by the poets they professed to elucidate. But such a fate will not be Mr. Robertson's, and as the most purely scientific discovery requires a preliminary act of faith, so at the centre of Mr. Robertson's system, and the stimulus to his researches, is his appreciation of the beauty of Shakespeare's poetry. His best remarks are on Shakespeare's verse, and he excels as a critic in convincing the reader, by comparative methods, of Shakespeare's infinitely varied power. Next comes his power to diagnose scientifically dramatic quality and weigh his impression in the golden scales of art—as when he notes that Act I of *Titus* produces tension beyond the power of Peele—or differs from Professors Saintsbury and Parrott that Aaron's self-portraiture is 'genuinely Shakespearian'. No doubt they were thinking of Richard III, Prince Henry, and Iago: and we shall find occasion to remark in a later page that some of Professor Saintsbury's Shakespearian criticisms lack subtlety. The more external criticism—tests of vocabulary, &c.—is a witness to Mr. Robertson's industry; but even in these outer circles the road is always left open to the aesthetic heart. Intellectual power, aesthetic understanding, industry, and clear thinking are Mr. Robertson's attributes; and to the last is due the balance and subordination of the rest.

VIII

THE most important general statements of these last critics deal with Shakespeare's religion and ethics. Professor Bradley says that it is uncertain if he expressed in his works his deepest and most cherished convictions on ultimate questions, or even that he had any. With him the ultimate power was neither a 'moral order' nor a fate; but it was alien to evil because it shows itself disturbed by evil and reacts against it. Good, in the widest sense, was the principle of life and health in the world, and evil a poison. He does not attempt to justify the ways of God to man, and was little concerned with differences of doctrine or church government. He was not a religious man in the distinctive sense of the word, but he had a lively and serious sense of 'conscience', and never doubted it is best to be good. All for him in the end was mystery.

Churton Collins believes that Shakespeare had inherited Christian traditions and that he treats the Christian religion uniformly with profoundest respect and reverence. The theological element scarcely exists in him, but he had an awful reverence for religion, for the mysterious relation between man and God. He accepted popular religion on the ethical, not the metaphysical, side; he contemplates man rather in relation to himself, to duty, and to society, than to the unseen.

In the opinion of Stopford Brooke he had a profound conviction of a power which worked for the whole and was apparently careless of the individual. He knew that in men's affairs long-continued evil will be tragically broken up by the suffering it causes, and be dissolved in a reconciliation which should confess the evil and establish its opposite good, and this was the work of a divine justice proclaiming all hatred to be against the universe. Swinburne says that of good and evil, in all their subtlest and sublimest forms of thought and revelation, he knew more than ever it has been given to any other man to know.

We will now deal with the characters, beginning with Professor Bradley's important remark that Shakespeare's heroes are no eccentrics, but exceptional by intensification of the life they share with others. Churton Collins observes that he scarcely ever invented a character, but required just a hint from without. According to Stopford Brooke, sex difference was vital with him, at the root of half his power over humanity. With Swinburne, his judgement and treatment of character casts all other men's into the shade.

On the subject of artistry Professor Bradley says that Shakespeare is often a conscious artist and often sins against art, that he had not the sureness of taste in words of some smaller writers. He also praises him for impartiality. Churton Collins calls him a reflective artist, and one who less creates than realizes—who never invented a plot— an industrious, vigilant and scrupulous workman, thoroughly faithful to the essentials of art. Sir E. Chambers says that he combined the devices of the popular entertainer with the interests of the freely moving thinker and artist. Like all great artists, says Stopford Brooke, he set forth things without analysis and moralizing. Mr. Robertson thinks he was the greatest and most subtle dramatist of his age, and that the higher elements of dramatic and poetic art which he mastered were right feeling, vision for character, and command of perfect utterance in admirably rhythmic verse. He was a born master of rhythm, achieving without effort the widest variety ever yet attained.

Of more general tributes we have that of Churton Collins—that his intellect and genius were amazing alike in receptivity, tenacity, and combinative power, with the plasticity and fertility of Nature herself; of Sir E. Chambers, that he saw all round life and saw it very normally; of Stopford Brooke, that his deepest root was delight, even rapture in life, and this made his judgement sane, and also his tragedy intense. He further remarks that his intuitive judgement made his work like nature, and that he is England's greatest intellect and finest imaginative soul.

Of single remarks that should not be overlooked we have Churton Collins's on his irony—that it is the essence of his most characteristic humour—subtle and profound sense of the relation of what seems to what is. Sidney Lee's, that no writer had a keener, quicker sense of atmosphere. Stopford Brooke's, that he had a strong belief in the constancy of women.[1] . . .

Again we see that much Shakespearian eulogy survives intact, and is expressed almost in the same words. But we notice a welcome change from positive to agnostic, initiated by Professor Bradley, in writing about Shakespeare's treatment of the cosmic problem. The gist of his criticism is that no formula can fit Shakespeare, and he is ably seconded by Stopford Brooke and, of course, opposed by such a critic as Churton Collins. If it is possible to include Shakespeare's tragic heroes in a generalization, Professor Bradley has succeeded. Mr. Robertson guides us towards an exacter appreciation of the beauty of Shakespeare's verse. The ultimate impression from these critics is of special knowledge employed on a subject of universal interest, and tending to the same conclusion—of wider horizons, greater problems, and deeper mysteries: and this includes Mr. Robertson's contribution in the sphere of rhythm.

[1] Cf. Heraud on *W. Tale*.

Chapter XXXII

ENGLAND 1906–1907

I. SIDNEY LEE. II. LYTTON STRACHEY. III. BRIDGES. IV. LUCE.
V. DEIGHTON. VI. CASE. VII. RALEIGH. VIII. BAKER. IX. ARTHUR
SYMONS. X. CUNINGHAM. XI. HAMILTON THOMPSON. XII. STOLL.
XIII. CONCLUSION.

I

THE following passages from Sidney Lee's essays on Shakespeare's philosophy and patriotism [1] are worth noting when we reflect on their author's criticism of the Sonnets. Coming from a learned, fastidious, and diffident writer, they encourage us to hope that the problem of Shakespeare's personality is not insoluble.

He says that Shakespeare ignored philosophy as a formal science and despised logic, but that he was a natural philosopher who excelled in the philosophy of common sense and wisdom about men. He knew that character, thought, passion, and emotion were the raw material of ethical or metaphysical systems. He miraculously adapted his philosophical speeches to the idiosyncrasies of his characters, but there are utterances as of a natural philosopher, repeated at different periods, and unlikely to be repeated if against the author's private conviction— e.g. mercy is the crowning virtue in rulers. . . . Man should be judged not by his office but his character. . . . Obedience is a duty, and there should be order and degree in a State. . . . Vice is never made amiable. . . . Man's noblest ambition is to master his own destiny. . . . An active instinct of patriotism promotes righteous conduct. . . . The kernel of sound patriotism is respect for a nation's traditional repute, for the attested worth of the race.

II

MR. LYTTON STRACHEY [2] wishes to prove that Shakespeare's final period was not that of reconciliation which has been commonly supposed. If, he says, the character of a play is the index to the writer's state of mind, then a writer of farces would be habitually merry. The general opinion is that Shakespeare, after a happy youth and gloomy middle age, reached serenity. From 1601–8 he wrote tragedy of character, and then began his last period with *Coriolanus*, where, as also in *Timon*, he ignores great situations in favour of rhetoric. After the latter play, which is a splendid storm of nastiness, did he turn suddenly to joy and forgiveness? Although we only think of the charm-

---

[1] *Sh. and the Modern Stage*, 1906 (Murray).
[2] 'Sh.'s Final Period', 1906 (*Books and Characters*. Chatto & Windus, 1922).

ing characters of the *Tempest* and *W. Tale*, these plays contain a series of portraits of peculiar infamy, and it is a fallacy in proportion to forget them. Paulina is unsurpassed for violent expression; and there is brutality of phrase and cruel coarseness. We find charm and gravity in Shakespeare's other plays—Ophelia, Brutus, Cordelia. It is argued that they end well—but so does *M. for M.*; and the world of the last plays is one of enchantment where all must end well. Conventional closes to fantastic tales, and charming heroines, do not prove the writer's serene tranquillity. What of Leontes, Iachimo, Caliban! Some characters are boring and do not live—unlike the early plays. Shakespeare must have been bored with all but poetry and poetical dreams. Thus, then, we imagine him at the end—half enchanted by visions of beauty and loveliness and half bored to death: divided between ethereal songs and bitter and violent speech. Prospero, if wise, is also self-opinionated and sour. Compare the guileless group of English mechanics in *M.N.D.*, and the hideous trio of the 'jester', the 'drunken butler', and the 'savage and deformed slave' in the *Tempest....*

Mr. Strachey as usual writes brilliantly, but the net result is that after weighing his arguments we do not revise our opinion that the final impression of Shakespeare's last plays is a happy one. The strongest believer in the four periods—such as Dowden—did not argue that Shakespeare could go through life unscathed; hence the *Tempest* has not the light-heartedness of *M.N.D.* But we do not take Leontes or Iachimo seriously as villains, and the beautiful concluding speches of both the *W. Tale* and *Cymbeline* leave us melted in joy. No doubt there was prejudice already existing in Mr. Strachey's mind, which he transferred to the Shakespearian page—and also a certain eagerness to contradict. We do not suggest for a moment that his criticism is one to be dismissed, or that it springs from anything but true sensitiveness: but it is ordained that every critic who touches the hem of Shakespeare's robe springs erect in his own shape.

III

THE essay of Dr. Robert Bridges[1] is of the conjectural kind, and further proves the innumerable angles from which Shakespeare may be observed. According to him, Shakespeare's genius was radically affected by the character of the audience.[2] The latter were iron-nerved and enjoyed realistic horror, brutality, or even foolish verbal trifling. The coarse terms in which Claudio repudiates Hero enfeebles the plot of *M. Ado*. Offences of the first rank—Proteus, Angelo—are too readily overlooked: this was perhaps due to Shakespeare's gentleness

---

[1] *On the Influence of the Audience*, 1906 (vol. x, Stratford Head Sh., 1904–7).
[2] Cf. Corbin, Jusserand (1911), Sisson.

of mind, while the audience would forgive from indifference and moral
bluntness. Perhaps he took advantage of this to help out his plot. In
the *W. Tale* he relied on their stupidity to admit inconsistencies or
impossible situations for the sake of dramatic effect. Angelo shows no
remorse till he is found out: how should the disgrace of exposure
remodel such a villain in fifteen minutes?

A man like Macbeth, with great qualities, would not have committed such actions: but Shakespeare less reveals than confuses. Was
the murder preconceived, or imposed by the witches, or his wife?
If his predisposition was only in the exact balance required for other
agencies to carry it out, it is still contradictory to the picture of nobility
impressed on us by Shakespeare and essential to the play. This
veiled confusion of motive is so well managed that it must be a device
intended to escape observation. Shakespeare's art is to create a hero
superior to his actions. When the audience is preoccupied with his
personality actions follow as unquestionable realities, and in *Macbeth*
they are even preordained and prophesied. Macbeth is shown possessed
by the shame and horror of the crime, but fascinated by the presentation
which is deluding the audience.

The delicate Imogen was unfit to be associated with the details of
the gross Italian story—but when the story was chosen and the
characters decided on, Shakespeare's imagination overrode difficulties
so as often to outrival nature. To enrich his picture he will transplant
incidents detached from the original story without their causes, as we
saw the hero's actions taken without his character. In the old story of
the *Merchant* Antonio is Bassanio's godfather. Perhaps to Shakespeare
unmotived conduct seemed more effective dramatically. It would be
easy to give a better ground for Othello's jealousy. Iago could not
mix unsuspected in the world: Desdemona would have shrunk from
him. What hurts at the present time merely pleasurably excited the
Elizabethan audience. The fact that it is uncertain if Hamlet's
madness was true or feigned, shows it was Shakespeare's design to put
his reason under suspicion. Does not the hypothesis of such a design
reconcile all? Wherefore the mystery of his earlier relations with
Ophelia? . . .

These are interesting questions, but they cannot be definitely
answered. If it was due to his uncritical audience that Shakespeare
chose to paint Sistine roofs rather than work in mosaic, then the
audience is devoutly to be thanked. No doubt a critic of faultless
taste like Dr. Bridges is pained by some of Shakespeare's verbal and
psychological lapses, as Voltaire and other eighteenth-century writers
were by his neglect of 'art'. But we rather think that Dr. Bridges
overvalues what is correct and consistent in poetry. If we remember
right, in criticizing Keats's ode, he deprecated the nightingale's 'plain-
tive' note of the last stanza, after the 'ecstasy' of those preceding.

IV

MORTON LUCE[1] takes all Shakespeare for his province, but is hardly among the greater critics. He admires Shakespeare with all his might, and has not a fault to find with him, but he is too confident, and though he can be subtle at times, he has not the power to doubt and re-question his impressions which at times serves the true critic well. Since the work of Professor Bradley we have a higher test; for he touches the centre of the problem, and all his judgements are born of the original impression. Luce at times may be directly impressed, but the impression merely sets working the thoughts native to his own mind, and the theories which he constructs are only partly developed from Shakespeare contact. He overworks the moral theme, and though he admits that Shakespeare was first a poet and then a philosopher, he does not act upon it. The effect in art of the mystic alliance of the True, the Good, and the Beautiful is that the good becomes more so because it is beautiful: but he does not convince us of this.

He says that Shakespeare's work is the greatest mental achievement of all the ages, and he was never a beginner. In his first work he may be inexpert in the externals of poetry, but he is comparatively mature as a prose artist in words, as an observer and thinker. His knowledge is as wide, if less deep, in *L.L.L.* as the *Tempest*. There are passages in the earliest plays that show some kind of maturity, while in the latest are crudities, foibles, conceits, carelessness, errors in taste. The supreme power and charm of his work is the creative presence of the artist himself. In every play we find extra-dramatic antitheta, e.g. the speech of Theseus in *M.N.D.*, 'The poet's eye . . .'. Hamlet and Prospero reflect Shakespeare's main features, and they discuss the whole business of the theatre. He is too deep a thinker and great a poet to be a mere objective dramatist—a machine for making plays. He was first poet and philosopher, then playwright. . . .

Thus confidently does Luce travel over the dangerous ground, and raise a smile in those of us who have so often returned baffled from the quest of Shakespeare's personality, and, when most hopeful, have been suddenly chilled by the thought of the needs of the theatre. Further, he rejects alien authorship, and accepts the Folio, though he admits other hands in the most obvious cases such as *Titus*, *1 Henry VI*, *Henry VIII*. It contents him that as a beginner Shakespeare had freaks of style or deferred to popular opinion. Admiration of *Titus*, and perception in it of germs of later plays (above all, the saying that Tamora is related to Cleopatra), is characteristic of such critics as Luce, who become intoxicated by the great things in Shakespeare, and thenceforth discover the same beauties in anything suspected to be by his hand.

[1] *A Handbook to the Works of Wm. Sh.*, 1906 (G. Bell).

In the following judgements he is at his best, though we are divided on the subject of the poems. He is right to say that they show artistic, not spiritual, enthusiasm, but hardly that they do not bear the impress of youth—that always in Shakespeare is there judgement, restraint, advanced philosophy, profound knowledge of human nature, wonderful faculty of drawing character. But he shows true insight in deciding that in *Venus* unrestrained passion is heightened by transference to a woman, and in *Lucrece* heroic chastity is heightened by association with wedlock. If *Henry VI* is the divided work of Marlowe, Greene, Peele, Shakespeare and others, the resulting miracle of homogeneity is greater than that of single authorship. Through the three parts a continuity bears witness to oneness of design and revision. The poet of the *Errors* already outbids the dramatist. The comedy of *Twelfth-Night* is relieved and heightened by interwoven exquisite romance, while strains of the finest poetry make perfect harmony with the comic undertone. At every point drama and poem mingle and are transfigured. Notes of wisdom and merriment, tenderness and raillery, joy and sadness, melt into the controlling harmony of love. *T. and C.* allows free scope for Shakespeare's excess of reflective tendency. The incongruities of the double theme are unmanageable. The leading features of a character in Shakespeare and the main incidents of the drama are always derived from some preceding author, or differences between these authors, or more or less vague tradition: and this accounts for inconsistencies.[1] In Cressida at least three previous sketches are combined, while Hector is that of the popular stage. Yet he never fails to give to each character a new and striking individuality. Shakespeare began with Chaucer's Cressida and ended with Henryson's. In an hour she changes from a fair, pure, and true woman to a willing and impossible wanton. *Othello* has the most absorbing interest and overpowering pathos in Shakespeare. In every detail is artistic oneness of treatment, and Othello is duped because he was a Moor. That was regarded as a frail vow between an erring barbarian and super-subtle Venetian; therefore a love like his implied trembling jealousy. Desdemona is murdered, and does not die for love; her death is almost unheroic and unredeemed. In no other play are pain and wrong left in brute reality, but there is always a glimpse of ideal justice and restitution. Othello and Desdemona lack worldly wisdom; in a perfect world they would have been perfect. Iago does not seek vengeance, but enjoys the sense of power, and in this we see some principle of his humanity. Octavia (*A. and C.*) reminds us that sooner or later our sense must undazzle. Such devotion, on the part of Enobarbus, Charmian, Iras, to such nobility suspends the moral— 'Let him that is without sin'. The final splendour of poetry is unmatched even in Shakespeare. . . .

[1] Cf. Bridges.

There is much to be disputed in these judgements, notably on Cressida, Desdemona, and the final effect of *Othello*, but they are true criticism. If not the whole truth they are at least part of it, and help us to realize the nature of the problem. From the main body of his criticism we will now give those characteristic portions which treat of Shakespeare himself, his moral progress, and the part played by women. We will repeat the warning that the stream of his original thought does not always mingle with the stream of thought aroused by his impression of Shakespeare. In *Lear* he has almost succeeded in crossing chaos by the moral bridge.

L.L.L. gives a display of almost all topics set in almost all lights, and therefore of opinions that are no more final than considerations of mere vocabulary and language. Thus early he used the drama as a mirror, and in the end he succeeded in educating the people up to the level of the highest form and spirit of the highest art, the poetic drama. *Titus* sets forth his practice of concluding a feast of horrors with Aristotle's saving grace of pity and fear, and teaching us that vengeance is wrong and love right. Gaunt (*Richard II*) is one of the sententious characters that are Shakespeare himself, and Polonius is a descendant of Gaunt and York. The love of Romeo and Juliet has the beauty of earth compared with that of Ferdinand and Miranda which has the beauty and holiness of heaven on earth. Even in Shakespeare's day the coarseness of Mercutio was a reversion in art; there is none such in Trinculo, Stephano, Caliban.[1] Portia (*Merchant*) is a type of Shakespeare's women at the ideal stage of development. The Middle Ages are behind, and the 'Understanding Age' before: they are neither the slaves nor the apes of man. Shakespeare pursued the quest of the ideal till the vision of the perfect woman was revealed to him in Miranda. There is nothing good to be said about any of Shakespeare's heroines, unless it refers to the whole process of their evolution and keeps in view the womanly perfections that culminate in the astonishing ideal of Miranda. Years after *A.Y.L.* Shakespeare set himself the artist's supreme task—to paint a woman not as a man paints, but as an artist—Marina, Imogen, Perdita, Miranda. At present he is a man who plays with his women, not an artist who reveres them. So far he has most excelled with women of lower life —the Nurse, Mrs. Quickly.

Hamlet sounds the deepest abyss of thought, and the hero almost stands for humanity. No wonder at times Shakespeare forgot the theatre and never finished the character. The process of refining on assumed madness disguised Hamlet, and Shakespeare himself did not know he was mad. His habit and love of ambiguity baffled even himself. In most of his plays are discrepancies,[2] but we are content if our main impressions are consistent. Isabella (*M. for M.*) is Shake-

[1] Cf. Strachey.   [2] See Bridges.

speare's best woman, that is the most moral, which accords with the whole scheme of the play. Her hesitancy has peculiar charm: but for Lucio she might have withdrawn from the contest. As she proceeds love dominates moral scruples, and she illustrates the enormous advance in Shakespeare's art and ethics. The lesson of *Lear* is that we can call nothing our own but love—and when this is learned the whole man is changed. Death is then the consummation of life, as love implies sacrifice. Shakespeare tells us clearly that the one thing valid in this mystery of humanity is ethical progress from selfishness to charity. Also that we are what we are not by circumstances, but in ourselves. Lear was changed from a bad man to a good man, and thereafter nothing mattered. The end of the drama is the dawn of everlasting day. Cordelia is Shakespeare's noblest creation: in a perfect world she would neither be possible nor wanted, but she is wanted in our world of warring good and evil. Giving may cause us pain, but the giving is all; and here again we come upon the ideal—progressive morality grown in the gardens of art. *Macbeth* treats of the bipartite— the ideal human entity. Even Shakespeare now recognizes that either sex alone is half itself. This adds a higher truth and deeper seriousness than Aristotle dreamt of. The tragedy is double in scope and two-fold in effect and interest. But for her the murder would not have been, but Shakespeare never forgets the essential differences of sex. Her reckless impulse is followed by reaction; and he who was deliberate becomes reckless.

In *Coriolanus* Shakespeare sets before us the mental and moral deficiencies of the mere fighting man. The atmosphere of *Cymbeline* is love—and repentance and atonement as with the other late plays. It proves that for Shakespeare the end was infinite hope and therefore joy and peace. The cumulative force of his own experience now compels into one astonishing combination all past elements of tragic passion and comic laughter. Dramatic construction suffers; the plot is weak and there are unreal incidents and anachronisms. Here and in the *W. Tale* and *Tempest* we get pure and perfect youth; and these, with the women their counterparts, are the crowning glory of Shakespeare's romances, and of all the conceptions of art, morality, beauty, goodness. Paulina is the rarest creation of the ideal—a woman whose attractiveness must be sought in moral rather than mental and physical qualities.[1] The *Tempest* has the sacredness as of Shakespeare himself speaking to us words of farewell. Through Miranda we discover the meaning of the wonderful series of women who represent every phase of the mighty and holy passion. Caliban reflects in himself the supernatural, social, and political topics of the day. He shows vice its own image beyond every other character in Shakespeare. Shakespeare draws together the various ideal threads that run through his previous dramas. We

[1] Cf. Strachey.

have also the ideal of marriage, education, character, final education of
good from evil, virtue, the supernatural, Providence. The play is an
autobiography, and the style a revelation of soul.

Shakespeare's philosophy without his verse would be a body without
a soul. What he saw he embodied in forms more beautiful and abiding
than any other poet. It is impossible that he should tell all the great truths
and not feel them. Love to him is the most important thing, and the
theme of sexual love most present to him—from *L.L.L.* through
every phase till we reach the ideal in Miranda. *Twelfth-Night*
summarizes his views, and Viola is the connecting link between
Rosaline and Imogen or Juliet and Miranda. *Twelfth-Night* also
illustrates Shakespeare's religious, political, and social doctrines. Of
Shakespeare's two decades, joyous humour prevails in the first, and
in the second humour becomes pathos. The laughter of the years
before 1600 ceases so abruptly that the effect is appalling. At first
slightly dramatized chronicle could be relied on to fill the Elizabethan
theatre, for history was story to the mass of the people. Then growing
dramatic education called for characterization—the two Richards and
John. Then Court life must be supplemented by the drama of complete human life—hence Falstaff. The presence of the ideal monarch
pervades the histories, even *Henry VI*. Tragedy shows ethical progress
to be the one thing valid in the mystery of humanity. If the Greeks
wavered between the old belief in malignant Fate and new hope or
trust in beneficent Providence, so Shakespeare, if he also wavers, will
end by throwing his higher morality—a bequest of 2,000 years—into the
scale of Providence. This he does even in *Lear* where the balance is
nearest equal. He never allows evil to triumph—and this is poetic
justice. Self-sacrifice to death—such as Cordelia's—is the ideal of ethics.

The dramatist aids us to match the law of moral progress, as it is
impossible to detach morality from art. Moral considerations are the
chief factor in the problem of Shakespearian tragedy. We cannot approach
it unattended by our fundamental notions of right and wrong. The
deaths of Cordelia and Macbeth are not to be explained by the same
tragic principle. Shakespeare must have deeply pondered and questioned
Aristotle. His tragic art is Aristotle plus twenty centuries of moral
advancement. The ἁμαρτία principle supplies the unifying element in
most of Shakespeare's tragedies and some comedies. The character in
some ways greatly fails because placed in circumstances where moral
law operates with ideal precision and makes ἁμαρτία prominent and
fatal—Hamlet, Brutus, Caesar, Coriolanus, Lear, Antony, Timon.
Aristotle's emotions of pity and fear would exclude moral considerations. He also says that poetic justice will not allow the good to be
sacrificed. The opposite is now the fact, and a lofty character is
rather degraded with worldly rewards. In Cordelia Shakespeare gives
us the most exact definition of progressive morality that has ever been

framed. The literary artist must be moral, for poetry reveals the
poet's soul. The sculptor, painter, musician, express themselves
through a medium that is no integral part of the mental and moral
being. Aristotle could not see, as we do, that all aesthetic influence is
ultimately moral. The theme of *Lear* is love of humanity as it
broadens into love of God. We cannot eliminate morality from art
unless we detach it from life. The 'tragic idea' will not disabuse us
of our all-pervading sense of right and wrong. Goodness is above
greatness, and at the close of a play Shakespeare drops the showman
and moralizes as one of ourselves. He dismisses Hamlet to heaven.

The main motive of the comedies is love of the sexes. The romances
are the most original of his works, and perhaps the most delightful.[1]
They renew the wit and wisdom, pathos and power, truth and beauty,
of all the former plays, but add fresh delight in nature, firmer trust in
God, kindlier belief in man and man's destiny. . . .

There is partial truth in Luce's summary of Shakespeare's philosophy. It helps us when he says that we cannot approach tragedy
unattended by our fundamental notions of right and wrong, and that
the poet must be moral since his art compels him to reveal his soul.
But when he asserts confidently that Shakespeare must have studied
Aristotle deeply, we at once perceive his limits. Our last impression,
therefore, is not of Shakespeare, but of the impression left by Shakespeare on a cultivated and orthodox mind. The morality which he
stresses is rather the self-protective kind devised by associated men.[2]
Hence he overpraises the romances with their enforced happy endings.
With a passing allusion to the fact that beauty is truth and truth
beauty, we will ask the reason for our sympathy with Macbeth, or—
in extra Shakespearian subjects—with the wars of Frederick or the
poems of Baudelaire. The intellect and moral sense are mysteriously
allied, and a book like Carlyle's *Heroes* teaches us that if a great man
is also good he becomes better in proportion to his greatness. We
rather think of the world shown in the lightning of Shakespeare's
genius as a progressive one, a place of striving, without fixed standards.
Thus we sympathize with Macbeth's longing for the crown—as we
do with Frederick's struggles to defend his ill-gotten gains—or
Baudelaire's to wring beauty from the corruption of old cities.

V

MR. K. DEIGHTON has some remarks on the characters of
T. and C.[3] that are worth pondering. He says that Ulysses is not

[1] Cf. Thorndike.
[2] e.g. in his introduction to the Arden edition of *Twelfth-Night* (Methuen, 1906),
he says that 'the impression we receive from the entire play is that of a dispassionate
inquirer into the principles of love and marriage'.
[3] *Arden Shakespeare* (Methuen, 1906).

degraded much below the *Iliad* and is certainly not meaner than in the *Philoctetes*; and that Thersites has the same features though painted at fuller length. Against Luce, he finds Cressida from first to last consistent in levity of character. Her grief at leaving Troy is violent, but of shortest duration. Chaucer's Pandarus is never as vile as Shakespeare's; therefore Shakespeare must have derived him from his own inner consciousness. He also denies, against Luce, that Ulysses violated Shakespeare's impersonality by speaking for Shakespeare himself.

VI

WRITING of *A. and C.*,[1] Mr. R. H. Case gives excellent reasons for not admitting it to the level of the four great tragedies. In the first place it belongs to a type of play defective in construction and absorbing centre of interest. Also the world-tragedy is too little insistently obvious, and depends too much for its effect on the constitution of a reader's mind, to surround the sufferers with a deeper gloom than their destiny can bestow. But the core of the matter is the contrast with the appalling situations of Macbeth or Othello. Antony and Cleopatra know nothing of such abysses; their utterance, though magnificent in poetry and pathos, is more conscious, and has something of the luxury of woe, on their own plane of enchantment. He also points out one of those links where plot and character are inseparable. Thus it is the holiness of Octavia, and the subjection of his genius to Caesar, that impel Antony back to Cleopatra. Finally he throws new light on the character of Enobarbus—who understood every one but himself, and knew neither the strength of the ties that bound him to Antony, nor his risk of remorse, nor inability to bear it.

VII

WALTER RALEIGH[2] has said some of the greatest things about Shakespeare. He is less central and philosophic and psychological than Professor Bradley, but his book ultimately conveys to us a special kind of mystery and vastness in Shakespeare that no critic has yet shown us. We can imagine Professor Bradley having congratulated Raleigh in the same spirit as Jowett congratulated Pater on his *Plato and Platonism*. What first strikes us is his robust temperament and 'large vitality. He is impatient of unnecessary details, and we shall see later the part this plays in determining his mannner of approaching the great problems.

At the starting-point he gives out that to read one of the great plays brings us nearer Shakespeare's heart than all the business of the antiquary and commentator. Every thrill of feeling an author communicates from his page must have been alive in his own mind, and therefore

---

[1] *Arden Shakespeare* (Methuen, 1906).   [2] *Sh.*, 1907 (Macmillan).

sincerely felt. Shakespeare utters truths, but we do not know what events and moments brought them home to him. After the end of a tragedy we feel the comfort that he is with us—that he found in splendours of courage and love a remedy for despair. He states both sides and expresses his mind by refusing the choice. He reveals all his mind, which is not small enough to be comprehended with ease. He is at home in the world, and we complain the place is too large for us. Hence critics compare him to Nature, though no two mean the same thing.

It cannot be inferred he was a deep student of the Bible: whereas *Elia* is a tissue of Biblical phrase. The deeper vein of scepticism in the mature tragedies is said to be borrowed from Montaigne. Certainly there is much of *Hamlet* in Montaigne's *Essays*, but it is the natural kinship of questioning minds. Montaigne exults in doubt: Shakespeare's eye and heart are at mortal war. The poems are works of art before everything: there is no remission from the sense of conscious art, no feeling for human situation. They are painless, due to preoccupation with art; the emotions they waken are those felt in the presence of art. The main motives are love of beauty for beauty's sake and wit for the exercise of wit. Than the Sonnets, no more wonderful or beautiful expressions of affection exist in English. The forms and conventions and restraints of art give dignity and quiet to turbulent feelings, and make passion tolerable. Had they been dramatic the situation should have been made clear. The Elizabethans wrote sonnets to express personal feeling, not dramatic fantasies. As regards the plays, it is unsafe to go behind the authority of Heminge and Condell—our only safe anchorage. Only his middle period is unchallenged; at the beginning he used the work of others, and at the end others used his work. There is ordered beauty and musical development in his plays because he subordinated stage effects to the needs and methods of poetry. His magic is greatest in reducing wild diversity of means to a single purpose. . . .

The problem which preoccupies Raleigh is Shakespeare's soul. He is concerned with the general impression of a play; he dismisses Montaigne in a breath; the poems do not interest him; he accepts the sonnets because they utter genuine emotion, of which his own heart is the witness. He is in quest of reality, and we must bear this in mind as we proceed further into his book.

Shakespeare first gives a situation and then gets to work on characters. Even Cordelia is invented for a situation, so we cannot argue from character to plot. In the great tragedies story and character are marvellously adapted to each other, but less in the early comedies and latest plays. When there is no further use for a character he sometimes disposes of him in the most unprincipled and reckless fashion—e.g. Antigonus. The characters in *All's Well* are designed for their parts, but even Shakespeare cannot teach them to do their dramatic work and keep our sympathy. His carelessness is part of his magnanimity; it is not poetic justice, but the larger scheme of things. He accepts the story as a kind of Providence and abides by its surprising awards. If Othello's suspicions grew in the normal fashion and were matured by jealousy, there would be no tragedy. Shakespeare makes him after his own heart, and raises him to the top of admiration. That Othello never loses our sympathy is the measure of Iago's greatness. Shakespeare seeks a real situation and then his characters live. It is a miracle of Nature—the true Nature, goddess of wasteful and ridiculous excess pouring forth her gift of life. Wherever the situation becomes tense surprises of reality intrude. Shakespeare dared to follow characters into dim recesses of personality where the hunted soul stands at bay and proclaims itself greater than law and opinion. Barnardine's death was arranged, but he suddenly comes alive and so endears himself to his maker that his death is felt to be impossible. The plot is managed without him, yet if omitted he would be sadly missed. Compared with the Jew of the story, who is a monster of medieval imagination, Shylock is a gaunt tragic figure whose love of his race is as deep as life. Act V is distraction, not solution, and though defeated Shylock still possesses the play. His memory gives to the beautiful closing scenes an undesigned air of heartless frivolity. Falstaff was intended as a mere tavern rogue, but Shakespeare lent him his own wit and metaphysic, and nearly spoils the play to glorify him. In every play there is a clear enough point of view—a character or group through whose eyes the play must be seen if the perspective is to be right. Miranda is Prospero's Miranda; we see the King through Hamlet's eyes; Bassanio is sketched lightly as Antonio's friend and Portia's suitor. Shakespeare gradually made his scheme more and more adequate to express his thought. In the great tragedies there is no escape from it; in the comedies much is sacrificed to story, criticism of life is incidental and plot symmetrical. In tragedy all mechanical expedients are discarded. The perfect temper of the earlier comedies gives warrant of reality to the later and darker plays. . . .

At this point we will take a backward look and collect ourselves. The words on Barnardine, on Falstaff, on Shylock and Act V of the *Merchant* make clear the critic's point of view. He compares Shakespeare with Nature, but in a different fashion from the eighteenth-century critic. Shakespeare, according to him, is perfecting the drama into an instrument to express his own thought clearly, dispensing with superfluous characters or details of story: as one, in new-modelling a cathedral, might remove arches or projections likely to set up broken echoes and impede the rolling sound-waves of the organ. We have one more reach to travel before we are in the gorge of tragedy, but already the current is swifter.

The critics of *M. for M.* are more moral than Shakespeare, but less experienced. He appeals to thought, and they respond by a display of delicate taste. What they shun in life they shun also in the drama, and so shut their minds to nature and to Shakespeare. Angelo's logic is unshaken by Isabella's most eloquent assaults—and Shakespeare is here nearest to direct treatment of the moral problem. Angelo's hypocrisy is self-deception; like many others he has a lofty, fanciful idea of himself; and his public acts belong to the imaginary person. At a crisis the real man surprises the play-actor. As Shakespeare holds virtue empty without beneficence, he touches even Isabella with his irony. There is no one character through whose eyes we can see the questions at issue as Shakespeare saw them. But his own thought is interwoven in every part, and his care is to maintain the balance. His wonderful sympathy travels back through the ages and revives the solemn heroic temper of the Roman world—and it also crosses the barrier of sex. His men have less practical genius than his women; their imagination often masters them, and self-deception is a male weakness. Lady Macbeth accepts all the details and consequences of the crime with the crime itself. Shakespeare's women act on instinct;[1] they are either good or bad, whereas the middle region belongs to men. They are often witty and daring, but never made all of wit and courage. Cleopatra is no type but her own unparalleled self. Shakespeare cares for the type, but more for the individual: neither Ophelia, Desdemona, Cordelia belong to a type. Each in a sense is born of the situation and inspired by it, and as in life character is made by opportunity. His most beautiful characters depend for their beauty on impulsive response to the needs of the moment. His women are simpler than his men: Cleopatra is at one with herself, unlike Antony. Goneril and Regan are hard and cruel and utterly self-assured. The women of the comedies are the spirit of happiness; in the tragedies they are the only warrant and token of ultimate salvation, the last refuge and sanctuary of faith. Therefore we have no reason to talk of Shakespeare's pessimism, because his sheet anchors always hold.

History at first steadied Shakespeare's imagination; then his vision of reality widened to include in one perspective comedy and history. In time his instinct for reality led him to use comedy and tragedy as a touchstone one for the other. Only the sham solemnity of grief is impaired by laughter. It is a great advance on the early histories when in *Richard II* he brings the king to the ordinary human level. Like Hamlet and Falstaff Richard juggles with thought and action. He is a creature of impulse, and when impulse fails he lightly discounts it by considering it in relation to the stars and the great scheme of things. Henry V is less inwardly conceived than Richard II; his qualities are more popular and commonplace. If Henry V falls short of intended

[1] Cf. Stopford Brooke on Lady Macbeth.

perfection it is the price he pays for having made a companion of one greater than himself who robs him of his virtues, makes him a satellite in a larger orbit, and confines him to the narrower domain of practical success. Falstaff gives the whole of himself to enjoyment, and the measure of the Prince's inferiority is that Falstaff to him seems rather ludicrous than witty. The Prince's qualities do not teach him the way to our hearts, and our chief concern is that Falstaff shall never be outwitted. He is a comic Hamlet, and his escapades give renewed occasion for the triumph of spirit over matter. He scorns opinion and follows his own ends, intellectual to the finger-tips. He is never entangled in his own deceits, and the judgements of others affect him not.

Politically Shakespeare was a friend to order. His thought was that of a poet, and he views social order as part of a wider harmony. He dislikes the crowd—and the impression is that only here he shows partiality. He is impatient of dullness and men of slow wit. He retained some prejudices of verbal education: to be a stranger to all that brilliant craftsmanship and all those subtle dialectical processes which had given him so much pleasure was to forfeit some hold on his sympathy. Chaucer understood social differences as Shakespeare never did, therefore they counted for less with him. . . .

The real Shakespeare is gradually forming in Raleigh's mind—as we first see from his criticism of Angelo and Isabella. He boldly exalts situation above character; he praises impulsiveness; he recognizes that Goneril and Regan were single-minded. One of Falstaff's qualities was that he cared not for the opinion of others. We are ready for the final plunge into the reality of Shakespeare's tragic world.

Shakespeare now faces the mystery and cruelty of human life. The world of romance had never satisfied him, and the order of his plays shows a gradual invasion of reality. The citadel of life is shaken and stormed by this onslaught of reality. Shakespeare does not trust to doctrines and philosophies, but his tragedy reveals a dazzling vision of humanity's pitiful estate. The reader takes refuge in morality because morality is in man's reach. Good conduct avails not in an earthquake, and morality is overwhelmed and turned aside by the inrush of the sea. Shakespeare's tragedies deal with greater things than man— power and passions, elemental forces . . . the central fire which breaks through the thin crust of civilization. He knew man's orderly habits to be precarious; at any moment the forces which struggled in chaos may reassert themselves. Character is not destiny: Othello is not jealous by nature; Macbeth is a man possessed. To Shakespeare what his heroes suffer is out of proportion to what they do and are. They are presented with a choice, and the essence of the tragedy is that choice is impossible. Shakespeare's tragic stress is laid on the hopelessness of the dilemma that follows, and his great pity for mortality makes crime a lesser thing. Othello, like Hamlet, suffers for his virtues.

A play is not a collection of biographies, but the grouping of certain facts and events round a single centre so that they may be seen at a glance. Hamlet's mind is the centre: not what he does appeals to us, but what he sees and feels—and his actions surprise himself. There is a sense of fate in the tragedies, there is the classical irony which plays with the ignorance of man and makes him a prophet in spite of himself. Othello has lived by faith, not sight, and Iago's game was won when he listened. Desdemona's unlikeness to himself was part of her attraction. The formalists who accuse her of untruth should be forbidden to read Shakespeare. In her distress she clutches at words which express one truth at least—that she has done him no wrong. All the cold passions of humanity are compacted in the heart of Iago. He can calculate, but takes no account of self-forgetful passions. If there is a moral it is that the greatest virtues must suffer for their greatness. Desdemona and Othello are made perfect in the act of death, so the idea of murder is lost and forgotten in the sense of sacrifice.

The last plays are pervaded by quiet and happiness, forgiveness and reunion. The new happiness is wrung from experience. Shakespeare explored the abysses of human suffering by means of imagination, and in the end fatigue loosened his grip on the hard facts of life. The marvel is that he won his way back to the world where play was possible. The worst terror is when it begins to appear that Shakespeare himself is not aloof and secure. In *Lear, Timon, Hamlet, M. for M.* there is a note of disgust towards the mere fact of sex. Passion goes beyond its occasion, and we hear Shakespeare's voice blaspheming the very foundations of life and society. Only a man of extraordinary strength and serenity of temper could have emerged from these experiences unspoilt. . . .

Raleigh's two greatest remarks are that Othello was not jealous by nature, and Macbeth was like a man possessed. He boldly says that character is not destiny, that Shakespeare was not chiefly concerned with character, that it is his own voice which we hear. Many critics have uttered their opinions on Shakespeare's self, but with Raleigh it is experience rather than opinion: his soul has just seen Shakespeare's passing by in the wonder-world of the plays. When all is past the impression that remains is of force and motion. And we feel what Wordsworth expressed in *The Recluse*, that neither Chaos nor Erebus can breed such awe as when we look into our own minds. If the message of Professor Bradley's book is hope for man, that of Raleigh's is awe at the mind of man. But the scales in which Professor Bradley has placed himself and his impressions of Shakespeare are equally balanced; with Raleigh the subjective scale is depressed.

The unique thing about Raleigh is a certain elemental force of mind which has not been subdued by the highest culture. On the contrary, he has succeeded in harnessing this Niagara, and thereby gained the right to approach Shakespeare. At times he overbalances, as when he speaks of the 'heartless frivolity' of the last act of the *Merchant*, or says that Shakespeare was impatient of dullness. But it enables him to take large views of Shakespeare's life, e.g. his remark that the perfect temper of the earlier comedies gives warrant of reality to the tragedies; and it quickens his sense of the values of such things as character, morality, practical success in their relation to the universe.

VIII

G. P. BAKER aims [1] to prove that Shakespeare gradually learnt to express the best in himself while complying with the needs of his audience. The latter required a story, and he was above all interested in character. In *L.L.L.* dialogue prevails, yet it is the first play to emphasize the love story. In *Verona* we see that Shakespeare recognized the value of a complicated plot and of creating suspense in the minds of his hearers, but he could not yet proportion his story or develop it firmly, or properly satisfy the suspense he had created. With *Titus* he has gained swift climatic exposition of a story which grips the attention from start to finish. He adds the love element to the *Errors*—to which the public heartily responded. And he threads his way through the confusion of the last scene of Act IV and the development of Act V, as he could not do in *Verona*. Between 1588 and 1598 Chronicle Plays were most popular. Shakespeare gradually saw his way to get the largest emotional returns in telling the public of the past: but only *Richard III* and *Henry V* are unified. When the relation of the audience to story-telling is considered, you see why only *Richard III* holds the public. He had not yet attained the art of developing a well-unified plot out of history. After 1598 the chronicle play declined, because the public were responding to increasing unity and technique in comedy and tragedy, and expected it in history. Shakespeare was restricted by fact, he painted the individual, not the type. The Elizabethans could not devise a fable and construct a plot round it. Shakespeare's scenes at first depended for effect on contained incident. Gradually he acquired the feeling for the emotional possibilities of incidents—e.g. York's discovery of Aumerle's conspiracy. He is best when absorbed in the emotional content of a scene rather than in portraying some figure so well known that his sense of fact restricts him. Within the scene, even in history, he became theatrically competent, but he could not bind all this crowding incident together except through some one central figure like Richard III or Henry V, nor discern behind the historical events the great laws and forces.

In *M.N.D.* he interweaves three groups, but in the chronicle plays he could not interweave material not more diverse. He can now look at his material from the outside, but as yet situation is above character.

[1] *The Development of Sh. as a Dramatist*, 1907 (New York, The Macmillan Co.).

R. and J. shows mastery in craft as regards insight into character and phrase. In the *Merchant* story is above character, as Shylock disappears after Act IV. He can now interweave perfectly strands of interest. His audience liked a crowded plot and love stories, but he uplifted them by characterization, thoughts on life, poetry. He could hold two points of view at the same time. His character-drawing is now so true that it makes the improbable acceptable. He has mastered the art of narrative in drama—the romantic story in *R. and J.* and *Merchant*. He can hold throughout the sympathetic attention of the audience and draw from it the largest emotional return. Comedy depends on point of view (selection) and emphasis. In *Twelfth-Night* the comic scenes are so emphasized that sympathy is with the tormentors. In pre-Shakespearian drama comic situation tended to farcical, and only gradually was evolved the comedy of manners and romance. The object is to awaken thoughtful laughter, and in *Twelfth-Night* one should appreciate not only the practical joke on Malvolio, but the contrast between what he thinks himself and is. High comedy needs superior characterization; it should depict the subtler moods of women under the finer feelings stirred in them by men. In his high comedies Shakespeare draws subtle and complex moods in masterly fashion, and he appeals to permanent interests. Though a character may be placed in unusual conditions, he finds the universal in the individual placed in those conditions. His beauty of expression helps to present the situation more clearly and swiftly. His superiority in phrasing comes from assured grasp on character. He studies a situation for what it can reveal of the characters involved, and he expresses their individual reaction on it. There is a broad human sympathy and cheery optimism in these plays, and they are perfect specimens of dramatic story-telling. Complex moods in a complicated story are clearly and easily set forth, and transfused with beauty of thought and phrase—unequalled union of plot, charm, dialogue, beauty.

Tragedy emphasizes with seriousness the causal relationship of incidents. Shakespeare knew the public loved a story, and for the public these tragedies were dramatic stories. This may explain his fourth act which has been said to drag. He probably had no theory, and his tragedies developed normally out of the chronicle play. Interest in prince or noble as human being came to supersede interest in him as king or ruler. Hotspur is better shown as man than historical figure. In tragedy Shakespeare uses history to make his characters clear. His object is to expound circumstance in terms of character. Character is his interest, story that of the audience. The problem is to set character in an illustrative story of strong dramatic action. *J.C.* shows the chronicle play resolving itself into tragedy by means of emphasis on the essentially human side of the characters involved. No early tragic causes account for later catastrophes. Shakespeare changed to romance because, like the perfect poet, he tries to subdue his mood to that of his guests.[1] His genius most appears when he wins popular acclaim for fulfilment of his artistic desires. . . .

Mr. Baker's criticism, if extensive rather than intensive, is above all useful. It sets forth clearly the difficulties presented by the dramatic form and the Elizabethan age. If more like a coasting voyage than a voyage of exploration into the interior, it at least takes us past rivers and estuaries where access to the interior is possible. This appears above all in his comments on the historical plays: and we remember how Dowden and others have remarked how hardly Shakespeare fused the tough material of history. Comedies such as *M.N.D.* and the *Merchant*, where mastery of a complex plot is attained, precede the 'episodic' parts of *Henry IV* where the thought is maturer. It has been said that Shakespeare was merely content to dramatize selected scenes, but the modern outcry for the rejected Falstaff justifies Mr. Baker. And his speculations on the development of history into tragedy are a perfectly legitimate sequel. He is likewise suggestive in explaining how Shakespeare preserved plot and story in his high comedies, despite complex character and expanded dialogue. The gist of his book is that Shakespeare developed his own powers as poet and thinker, while serving his public; and he argues back from the work itself, like Thorndike, rather than in the fashion of the system-makers such as Moulton and Snider.

IX

AS usual Mr. Arthur Symons has fine things to say about the two plays which he treats this year.[2] He succeeds because he is a poet; his insight is always imaginative; beauty ultimately reveals itself to his longer vision, or its absence disturbs him to utter critical truths. We commend his analyses of the characters in *Cymbeline*, with the exception of Iachimo. We cannot agree that the latter, after his repulse by Imogen, shows finesse in convincing her that his intentions were innocent—and that he is a faultless study in Italian temperament. That Posthumus doubts Imogen, he says, proves that he has never known her. The irony of the play is that he has always failed to destroy his own happiness. The Queen has criminal intentions, but all she does is to provide Imogen with a sleeping-draught. Cloten is one of Shakespeare's mockeries of the gentleman by birth who is scarcely a man by wits; and even he can transmit heroism by mistake. The two youths live courtly lives in the open air, and Shakespeare shows us what is intrinsic in noble descent. The soliloquy of Posthumus in prison is a masterpiece of that difficult kind of writing which has to

[1] Cf. Thorndike.
[2] *Cymbeline* and *T. and C.*, 1907 (*Studies in the Elizabethan Drama*. Heinemann, 1920).

wring a kind of emotion out of the absence of emotion in the speaker. The writing is closely modelled upon the thought; Shakespeare's aim is that last refinement where strength comes disguised and beauty seems a casual stranger. In apparent approach to the form of prose verse finally becomes its most authentic self.

In reviewing *T. and C.* Mr. Symons tells accurately what it achieves and where it fails: and his last remarks leave the impression that failure outweighs success. He treats rather more definitely that disgust at the mere fact of sex which other critics have attributed to Shakespeare in his dark period. He calls the play the most tragical of all comedies and the most comical of all tragedies. In his opinion it is not all by Shakespeare,[1] and the workmanship is of different periods. The deeper intention came gradually into his own work. It is a kind of *Don Quixote* where serious and burlesque are hard to dispart. Shakespeare makes the fall of Troy into a parable of the world, and he shows the two prime heroisms—love and glory—through the eyes of Thersites. We see the petty inside of war and the shallow and troubled depths of woman. Pandarus is love's broker, as Thersites is the broker of glory. Thersites is the Falstaff of a world that tastes bitter. His foulness is forgotten in his fierce and ever-armed intelligence. In the Paris-Helen scene love appears sickly, a thing of effeminate horror, which can be escaped only by turning·it into laughter. The speech of Troilus, 'I am giddy . . .', is a rendering of sensation sharpened to vanishing-point. It is the comedy of pure mind, with its detachment from life, to which it applies an abstract criticism. To the pure reason emotion is something petty, ridiculous, or useless. To write drama thus is to lose most of the material of drama. It makes the puppets cry out—See what puppets we are!

X

MR. HENRY CUNINGHAM [2] discriminates skilfully between the twin masters and attendants of the *Errors*, and reveals subtler character design than has yet been suspected. He points out that the sedate and melancholy Antipholus S. is cleverly associated with the merry and jesting Dromio S., and the impatient and passionate Antipholus E. with the precise and discreet Dromio E.: and yet had this contrast been overdone it would have destroyed the illusion. He says that Antipholus S. is of finer grain than his brother, and there is a like contrast between the two Dromios, but the needs of the piece did not require the latter to be carefully worked out. It also seems to him that the most strikingly imaginative comic effect is the state of mind produced in the wandering Antipholus and his attendant: each doubts his own identity. Mr. Cuningham points out that this 'more spiritual form of illusion' is medieval, and Shakespeare borrowed it from Lyly.

[1] Cf. J. M. Robertson.   [2] *Errors*, 1907 (Arden edition. Methuen).

He is right to point to other influences than Plautus which have hitherto preoccupied critics; and he finally remarks that though the scene is idealized for dramatic purposes, it is Shakespeare's London. He draws attention to the legal references in Act IV, and concludes that Shakespeare's mind must have been early steeped in the minutiae of practical and technical legal work. Legal references are an ingrained and ineradicable part of his vocabulary and thought and could only have been acquired by regular study. . . . However, it has been pointed out by other critics that such legal terms are used as frequently by Shakespeare's contemporaries.[1]

XI

MR. A. HAMILTON THOMPSON'S remarks on *Richard III*[2] are characteristic of a later criticism. They express clearly what the play lacks, and therefore correct a great deal of irrelevant praise in the part. He says at the outset that this conventional Marlowesque play is at least invested with a real human interest—but it leaves our deeper emotions untouched. The characters are good or bad without compensation, they win without reflection, and their punishment is purely mechanical. Richard, like all Marlowe's heroes, is absolutely consistent, and there is no room in him for any real development of character. The figure is imposing, yet the conception is mechanical, for the character is made to order, to fulfil an ideal plan. Only Hastings among the characters does not realize his own villainy and believes in Richard's good faith.

XII

THE first time we meet Professor Elmer Edgar Stoll[3] he is concerned with the Ghosts in Shakespeare. Are they real ghosts of superstition, or hallucinations and symbols of nineteenth-century philosophical criticism? The question affects the interpretation of Shakespeare's artistic method: Caesar's ghost either seeks revenge or embodies Brutus's sense of failure and the end of the Republic. The ghosts of the Elizabethan drama, like those of folk-lore, came to achieve a definite end—to wreak revenge, protect a loved one, prophesy, crave burial, or as omen of death. Shakespeare represents all but the last; and revenge especially, in *Hamlet, Richard III, J.C.,* and *Macbeth.* The idea of an embodiment of conscience did not occur to the Elizabethans: the ghosts impel the action and influence it.

In the scene of Banquo's ghost everything is objective: Macbeth changes completely and abruptly, and both parties show a spirit of merely personal antagonism—unremorseful fear and defiance in

---

[1] Cf. Churton Collins and Sidney Lee (1904).

[2] *Richard III*, 1907 (Arden edition. Methuen).

[3] 'The Ghosts', 1907 (*Sh. Studies.* New York, The Macmillan Co., 1927).

Macbeth, ironical vindictiveness in the ghost. Macbeth is not stirred
by conscience, or thinks the ghost unreal, as he did the dagger. Even
more objective and revengeful is the ghost's appearance at the Witches'
Cavern. An Elizabethan audience, seeing Banquo take his seat at the
head of the table, would infer that fate was getting even with Macbeth:
and this meaning could not be if the ghost were subjective. It accentuates the irony that Macbeth utters the wish that he were present.
Ghosts do not come unless they are called: as witness the old superstition against naming the dead.

Shakespeare, with the Elizabethans, conceived of Nemesis as personal
revenge. The victims in *Henry VI* and *Richard III* are avenged in a
blood-feud; their fate is due to Margaret's curse. Even in *J.C.* the
Nemesis is personal, and does not take the form of an outraged society.
So Macbeth does not fall merely as a usurper, but at the hands of
Macduff to appease the ghosts of the latter's wife and children.
Shakespeare's Nemesis strikes from without, and appears like a personal
or supernaturally personal vengeance: and of this Banquo's ghost is an
instance. Not that Shakespeare ignores higher aspects of justice and
retribution: the swords of Richmond, Macduff, and Hamlet also
represent fate and outraged humanity. But there is always a concrete
human agent. Nor does he forget inner and social retribution: Lady
Macbeth feels the one, Macbeth the other, as he laments honour,
love, friends.

Critics, including Professor Bradley, have argued that Macbeth was
prone to hallucinations, and instanced the dagger. But he himself
acknowledges the dagger and the voice to be the creations of his fancy.
And if with him imagination is the cause, why do others like Richard III
and Brutus see ghosts? The scene itself does not favour such an interpretation. Macbeth is not in the same spiritual state as when he saw
the dagger. He is glad to have the murder done, and disappointed
when he hears it is only half done. He is struck with horror when the
ghost appears, but recovers himself as soon as it vanishes. His speeches
show no real remorse, but a deep sense of insecurity when the ghost is
present. It has also been argued that the ghost is subjective because
Macbeth's description reproduces the murderer's words: but by the
laws of folk-lore, a ghost in outer semblance is merely the corpse
revivified. When Macbeth himself, on its disappearance, asserts its
unreality, it is because the ghost's vengeance is the horror and menace
of his presence—of which the murderer is glad to be rid. There is
more force in the argument that at the end he himself regards it as an
illusion—but it is a natural reaction. No one else has seen it; the
queen has rated him; and we remember that when the witches
vanished he asked, 'Were such things here?'[1] Shakespeare subtly used

[1] Cf. Brutus, Posthumus, Hastings, Caesar, Antigonus. Also *M.N.D.* Also
Horatio and Marcellus before the Ghost appears.

wonder and doubt to express the supernatural, and make us realize it was a being from another world. The doubts satisfy our artistic cravings, not our intellectual, and make the ghost more real. Scepticism prepares the way for the supernatural and breaks it to us gently. It is true that the ghost appears only to one person; but the crucial test of objectivity is that it appears also to the audience—and the audience was never made a prey of illusion. Shakespeare gives his audience a key to the situation which they should accept, and not put themselves on a level with the characters on the boards. Thus Ariel is invisible to Trinculo and Caliban, but not to the audience. It is a fairly absolute rule that what the Elizabethans represent on the stage is actual and objective.

Much that has been said of Banquo's ghost applies to the ghosts in *Richard III.* A thorough Machiavel has little to do with conscience or remorse. If he explains the ghosts as figments of conscience, it may be that he is trying to shake off the great dread that has seized him. But even if Shakespeare intended them to be a dream, and no more than the pangs of conscience, he has not succeeded. The lights burn blue —an immemorial token of the presence of ghosts—and the same ghosts appear and prophesy to Richmond, and are recognized by him as Richard's victims.

Although *J.C.* is a political drama, it has little politics or statemanship, but becomes an Elizabethan murder and revenge play, of which the latter half, like *Hamlet,* contains a ghost to preside over the revenge. We see this most clearly where Shakespeare deviates from Plutarch. The last words of Brutus and Cassius, in recognition of Caesar's fulfilled vengeance, and the words of Brutus about Caesar's spirit walking abroad, are Shakespeare's own. There are passages in North's Plutarch which Shakespeare might have used had he wished to interpret allegorically.

In fine, Shakespeare's ghosts are concrete representations of Nemesis according to the world-old conception of it as a blood-feud beyond the grave. His witches are those of James I, who ride on a broomstick and sail on a sieve; his portraits are literal and binding signs and tokens. The curses in *Richard III* are literal and superstitious, and hold by the letter only. Of course, the early historical plays are crude, and in his later work Shakespeare has spiritualized superstition, and made ghosts dramatically and psychologically appropriate. Banquo's ghost is real, but has also moral and philosophical significance. He does not bring marvels on the stage, but lets them be reported by superstitious persons. And by means of the scepticism and wonder of ghost-seers he gives to the supernatural a subjective colouring. A vague and brooding treatment of the supernatural accords with his later imaginings.

Unlike the modern writer, Shakespeare has only poetic disbelief to cope with, or imaginative apathy. He does not leave us in doubt of supernormal influence, like Ibsen, but works by awe and wonder. We must remember that his age was not entirely that of the Renaissance; and the minds of the boldest cannot pass beyond the pale of ignorance and superstitious prejudice in a generation or even a century. It required a century to make the Copernican theory accepted in England. When Shakespeare wrote *Macbeth* the rage of witch-hunting had begun; his style is deeply coloured with the superstitions of his time. Superstitions and supernatural elements are constantly cropping out even in the historical plays where the supernatural was not the subject in hand. Later romantics like Scott and Coleridge treated it in a decorative, literary way: Shakespeare drew it out of his native air and soil. His ghosts do not echo Seneca, but speak in the accents of Stratford and Warwickshire. We might argue that he himself believed in the supernatural because he represented it so successfully: but we must beware of confusing literal and poetic faith. The poetic depends on the imaginative—and the imaginative is not fettered to experience.

Much of the superstitious element has constructional import: omens and forebodings such as 'Beware the Ides of March'; but there is much that has no such import, and reflects Shakespeare himself and his age. Only his highly developed men see ghosts; the villains express doubts, and the foolish ignore portents. In the end doubt of the supernatural is unfounded; and the sceptics such as Iago and Edmund doubt human virtue even more than the marvellous. Glendower is mocked by Hotspur, but he is reckoned a formidable warrior. There are no frauds in Shakespeare, nor is the supernatural treated comically. When *Macbeth* was written, James I, the champion witch-hunter, and introducer of fresh and fierce legislation, had just come to the throne. We think Shakespeare would have revolted at paying the compliment of the 'king's evil' if he had not accepted the prejudice. Shakespeare always kept off debatable ground, and the fact that he dealt freely with witchcraft disproves any recognized difference of opinion.

The royal favour or that of the groundlings has often been advanced to explain a divagation of Shakespeare's in sentiment or art. But the world's greatest man could not wholly suppress himself, and a great popular artist is one with the people. We can see that he despises mobs —but he expresses the whole of Elizabethan superstitions without an ironical accent. He either believed in much of it or was hardly a man at all. As popular dramatist he reproduces prevailing forms of art, but does not discover truth or extend the boundaries of knowledge. He thinks in images, accepts belief, but has no use for unbelief. He is not superstitious, and, like Sophocles, is untouched by the spirit of zeal, cruelty, or gloom. He was no Puritan, but, like his generation, of the world, worldly. He has no brooding sense of the supernatural, but

relegates religion to a man's last moment. He entered imaginatively
into his superstitious creations, but had little in common with the
foolish notions which gave them birth. His supreme art in dealing
with the subject is compatible with detachment. . . .

We have noted before that American critics are prone to reject
tradition and acquired knowledge in favour of common sense—it
being an old error of mankind that the fastest intellectual stronghold
must yield to common sense. We do not wish to create prejudice
against Professor Stoll, who is among the first of contemporary critics,
but we note that common sense is his ultimate tribunal: though he
does not use it as an excuse for disregarding the opinions of others.
On the contrary, his strength is that it enables him to appreciate their
relative value, while he yet stands alone in presence of Shakespeare.
But the two following points, on which he will insist in his next
essay, are the pillars of his critical method: that we must think first of
the artist's intention, because a work of art referred only to the critic's
personal impressions may mean anything, everything—that is, nothing;
and that as emphasis is the artist's chief means of expression, the
interpretation of literature is mainly a study in emphasis. And yet,
as we followed his argument, two remarks of Professor Saintsbury's
were persistently present with us: the first, that 'extreme method in
criticism is something of a superstition, and . . . the greatest critical
book of the world, that of Longinus, has . . . very little of this . . .';[1]
the second, that Pater stands alone in clothing his criticism 'with an
extraordinarily sympathetic and powerful atmosphere of thought and
style'.[2] To the first we must admit that Professor Stoll is pointing to
the highway of the best criticism of the future, though we ourselves
may regret the romantic method. More and more, as the classics
recede in time, criticism will draw near to research—to a study of
conditions of the age, of the books which inspired the author, &c.
The impressionistic method will yield to the historical and comparative, and for the latter Professor Stoll is admirably equipped,
with his exact knowledge of the drama from Aristophanes to
Ibsen, and of imaginative literature from the classics to the most
discussed modern writers such as Anatole France and Henry James.
The second loss—the atmosphere of thought and style—is implied in
the first; for method implies classification and results, whereas meditation tends to go on indefinitely without beginning or end. Criticism
like everything else has changed in the present century, and the result
of its more business-like method is that the unconscious mind becomes
something like the hired servant of the conscious. We may deplore,
but we are met with the inevitable retort of 'progress'—as at the spread
of the town, or the presence of motor coaches in beloved country lanes.

In the present essay Professor Stoll succeeds in conveying to us

[1] *Hist. Crit.* iii. 221.   [2] Ibid. iii. 545.

what the ghost meant for Shakespeare's audience. The ghost of
Banquo was simply the corpse revivified, the concrete representation
of Nemesis; it had objective as well as subjective reality; for the
audience were never made the prey of illusion. The dagger and the
voice Macbeth himself admits to be the creations of fancy. It is in
such instances that we see common sense and historical knowledge
working harmoniously together.

XIII

AMONG these latest critics the most interesting general remarks are
about Shakespeare's thinking power. Sidney Lee calls him a natural
philosopher who excelled in the philosophy of common sense and
wisdom about men. He was no respecter of orthodox doctrine, but
in his world vice ruins him who practises it, and ultimate justice
governs the operations of human nature and society. Critics of all
countries agree that he is the greatest of thinking men. Luce says that
he believed in Providence, and that all things work together for good.
His doctrine was seldom based on religious dogma and he was a poet
before a philosopher, but he had the most comprehensive mental and
spiritual vision of any writer. His final conceptions and convictions of
morals or love or life are the most profound and noble in literature.
He sets before us the highest known ideal towards which progressive
morality is striving. Judging from his whole work we say he gives
free and undramatic expression to our best belief—in God and love
and immortality. To Mr. Arthur Symons, his wisdom, as appears
from his whole work, is neither optimism nor pessimism, but includes
both. Raleigh says that no labels of creed or party suit him, that he
was one of the few who rediscover Christianity for themselves, so that
the Gospel is born anew. In ultimate problems he had no help of
doctrine, theory, metaphysics, morals—and he trusted little to philosophy and reason. Mr. Baker speaks of his broad human sympathy
and readiness to believe in the good rather than the bad side of human
nature. Professor Stoll says that Nemesis to Shakespeare was personal
revenge, but he also recognized the higher aspects of justice and
retribution. His work is the spontaneous utterance of himself and his
age, and he has its philosophy, politics, and religion.

   We also get some important remarks on Shakespeare the artist.
According to Luce, he created a drama absolutely ideal in compre-
hensiveness—combining classical, medieval, popular, tragic, romantic,
farcical—and also national and inspired. His work is the greatest
achievement of all the ages, and no artist was ever so deliberate; he
was the best ideal craftsman of the world. Raleigh speaks of the craft
and experience of his plays. Mr. Baker discovers an underlying
artistic ideal that rounds and completes artistically the plays in a way

never seen in the work of others. Professor Stoll calls his art naïve and literal, although refined and subtle.

About the man we set down the following. Luce asserts that he was too deep a thinker and too great a poet to be a mere objective dramatist. To Mr. Deighton his impersonality is a cardinal doctrine in the interpretation of his mind and art. Raleigh says that he was the rarest of all things, a whole man. Mr. Symons thinks that nobility of soul was the part of his genius which grew most steadily to the last. The impression of Shakespeare to Professor Stoll is one of tolerance, geniality, common sense, imaginative power and fervour, rather than extraordinary enlightenment. The foremost man of the world could not wholly suppress himself.

As usual the remarks about women have a peculiar interest. Sidney Lee thinks that he sometimes denies free will to women. Luce says that the relation of most of the plays to the growth of his art is clearly indicated by their women: even in the early comedies Shakespeare's women were a new creation in drama.

Among single remarks worth preserving is Raleigh's, that a profound sense of fate underlies the tragedies;—Mr. Baker's, that he depends much for dramatic contrasts on the sure creation of atmosphere;[1] —and Professor Stoll's, that no writer has treated the supernatural so well—that he treats superstition finely and delicately while keeping firm hold on its material reality. . . .

That Shakespeare is unique is an old truth: the present age is helping to discover why he is unique. The weakness of agnosticism— especially such a doctrine as Herbert Spencer's 'Unknowable'—is that it definitely decides what can and cannot be known. The best of these critics help us to realize, implicitly if not explicitly, that art is the great reconciler: but only the supreme art of Shakespeare. They agree with their predecessors that Shakespeare was a moral and religious artist, but, thanks to his final creative energy, he transcended all known achievements in morality, religion, and art. Admiration is salted with common sense, thanks to Professor Stoll.

[1] Cf. Sidney Lee (1904).

Chapter XXXIII

ENGLAND 1908–1909

I. FURNIVALL AND MUNRO. II. SCHELLING. III. ST. JOHN. IV. BEECHING.
V. HARRIS. VI. SWINBURNE. VII. SIDNEY LEE. VIII. CONCLUSION.

I

TO this year belongs the *Century Sh.*,[1] edited by F. J. Furnivall
and J. J. Munro. We are already acquainted with the work of
Furnivall, and the first thing we notice is that his 'links' persist. We
cannot take all these seriously, but as we formerly attempted to
classify them, we will now merely refresh our memory with a random
selection.

Fickleness of love links *Verona* with *M.N.D.*, and in both there is
a Duke and a wood. In both *John* and *Richard III* cruel uncles plan
nephews' murder. The *Shrew*, like the *Merchant*, deals with the
self-surrender of a woman. Hotspur resembles Kate the Shrew, but
in armour and a man. *M. Ado* repeats the moral of *L.L.L.*—that wit
and the mocking spirit are worthless. The spirit of *A.Y.L.* anticipates
the fourth period—that repentance and reconciliation are better than
revenge. Macbeth repeats Jaques' philosophy—men and women are
but players. The grand resolves and speeches of Hamlet that result in
nothing are like Richard II's. The leading feature of *Othello, M. for
M.*, and *Hamlet* is lust. Supposed lust in Desdemona is the cause of
Othello's jealousy and thus the main motive for the action. Iago is
the Richard III of the third period. Othello and Macbeth are alike
great commanders, and are tempted from within and without. Iago
is passed over, and the Prince of Cumberland is advanced before
Macbeth. Emilia knocks at the door after the murder, like the
Porter in *Macbeth*. Love of husband before father shows in *Lear* as
in *Othello*. Timon and Lear think to buy love with gifts. Paulina
is a truer Emilia.

Furnivall and Munro believe in the four periods and in Shakespeare's
systematic development. For them his metre, words, grammar, syntax,
move but with the deeper changes of mind and soul of which they are
the outward signs. In four such periods the story of a man's heart
must be wrapt up. A poet must write what he learns from experience,
and the greatest work is based on emotional experience, not observation.[2]
He was fond of kings and queens—in the Tudor spirit, because they
stood for country. He was patriotic, no book reader, he loved nature
like Wordsworth. The Sonnets are intensely autobiographical and
self-revealing—at one with the spirit and inner meaning of his growth
and life. Critics forget his impulsive nature and long absence from

[1] *Century Sh.*, 1908 (Cassell).   [2] Cf. Raleigh.

home. Adultery was then treated with indifference. What was new is that which Shakespeare shows us—his deep repentance for sin committed. Those who declare the Sonnets to be conventional do not explain why the figures in them are not conventional types.

It thus appears that the authors are well decided in their view of Shakespeare, and we will now take some specimens of their method, adding a warning that their criticism inclines to the positive, and is shut in by strict poetic justice and conventional morality.

In *L.L.L.* we see the contrast of London wits with the Stratford-bred Shakespeare. He showed them he could beat them with their own weapons, and that their wit and fine talk were nothing compared with real good heart and work. The Antipholus-Luciana episode in the *Errors* marks the first uprise of serious, tender love. The love which bursts into full force in *R. and J.* is the lawful passion in woman and man. *Richard III* is embodied ambition. In a world where there is hardly a true friendship or a noble figure it is natural that the most callous, crafty, and remorseless man of all should triumph. The scenes with Anne and Elizabeth are an early testimony to Shakespeare's tremendous dramatic power. The misgovernment in *John* is not of a cruel tyrant but a selfish coward. John is a hero while he impersonates England, defies the foreigner, and opposes the Pope, but he is only bold politically, and morally a coward and sneak.

The *Merchant* belongs to Shakespeare's second period where sadness is but a cloud-shadow on an infinite sea of joy—in the positive forces of the world, beauty and tenderness of women, strength and comrade-ship of man, faith in the highest qualities of the human heart, compassion and love and mercy. One feeling does not dominate, but there is a symphony of grace and fierceness, mercy and vengeance, friendship and love and fiend-like hate, wit and humour. Shylock is a strong nature capable of good: the fallen angel makes the worst devil. Bassanio is something of an adventurer, yet he must be noble since Antonio and Portia love him. If the Prince in *1 Henry IV* utters his true motive for leading a reckless life, he is a charlatan and snob. Hotspur is passion's slave: himself and his own glory are his gods. The moral of Falstaff is the same as *L.L.L.*: what is mere wit, that men so value, really worth? The scene with the dying king throws a shadow over the whole play. The Prince's rebuff to Falstaff is generous: he allows him a competence which is above his deserts. Henry V not only proclaims the glory and gallantry of Shakespeare's hero, but his own full manhood's spirit, his rejoicing in his strength and success in life. Shakespeare could not make Falstaff really in love (*Wives*) or it would have redeemed him. Athwart the sunshine of *M. Ado* he brought the shadow of distress or death, for he represented life as it is here on earth. *A.Y.L.* is the sweetest play because sweetness is drawn from the bitters of life. When we look past the comic characters of *Twelfth-*

Night we feel the beauty of those who stand in the half-light behind.

With *All's Well* we enter the gloomy time, yet Shakespeare recognizes the same true woman's love undergoing a more repulsive trial—that of unwomanliness. The fundamental idea in his mind is that the way of nature—the beautiful office of fatherhood and motherhood—is the best and noblest way for the best and noblest of mankind. Through the strife of the fate of nations of *J.C.* comes the cry of the betrayed friend that persists through all future plays. Essex's rebellion made Shakespeare anxious to enforce the truth—that rebellion for insufficient cause will be followed by death, even if the motive is noble. Brutus is one of the noblest figures. Compare his notion of honour with that of Hotspur or Henry V to see his finer nature. Hamlet is the type of the weakness of us all: before he knows of the murder he thinks of suicide. Only Polonius and the women think him mad: not the King with a head. In his soliloquy—'To be . . .'—he degrades conscience to the level of his dread of death. He says he could 'drink hot blood', because big words bring relief to weak creatures. In the scene with his mother he is noble and strong. In his diseased view of life, shirking of duty, doubts, &c., he typifies each of us at some time. Isabella (*M. for M.*) is a contrast to the lust and weak will of woman and man. She is the highest type of woman yet drawn, and cannot have the mere charm and tenderness of an ordinary woman. She, Cordelia, and Volumnia, are the three splendid women who illumine the dark third period—and she is the highest of all. Angelo is a self-revelation to any man who has striven for purity, fancied himself safe, and failed in the hour of trial. The play would be intolerable but for Isabella. Justice, which seems to be struggling for life all through, fails at last. Behind the nobleness of Othello were yet the jealousy, the suspicion, the mean cunning of the savage: death to the adulteress was the practice of his race. Iago is self-sufficient and imitates no one in his inhuman designs. *Macbeth* shows separation from man as well as God—the miserable trustless isolation that sin brings in its train. Macbeth is a worldly man, and without the witches and his wife he would not have erred. Lady Macbeth shows the ready wit of all Shakespeare's women. Cleopatra is his most wonderful study of woman, and he makes us look on her with admiring hate. *Coriolanus* gives a contrast of heroines—the heaven of Italy beside the hell of Egypt. From mothers like Volumnia came the men who conquered the known world, laid the foundations of our laws, bequeathed us their arts, and have left their mark for ever on the nations of Europe. There was a theory that Plebeians and Patricians were distinct races—the former aboriginal Ligurians, the latter Umbrian Sabines who conquered them. Loftier ideals of life maintained the division. The Sabine matrons instilled into their sons their own deep reverence for the laws and principles of their fathers. Shakespeare sympathizes with Timon, as always with sufferers, rather than the practical Alcibiades who takes the right means to revenge. Apemantus does give a sound analysis of Timon's character.

The *Tempest* links earth to heaven with Miranda, and earth to hell with Caliban. The complex and detailed plot of *Cymbeline* should not blind our eyes to the genius which has woven its different strands into such fine poetry. Both Iachimo and Iago are types of the subtle Italian intellect called Machiavellian; they are masters of innuendo and suggestion, but Iachimo can repent.[1] Few if any of the plays leave a pleasanter picture in the memory than the *W. Tale*. We hope Leontes really repents—but he gets the benefit of Shakespeare's fourth period which restores to him the wife and daughter he does not deserve. Hermione is Shakespeare's most magnanimous and noble woman. Compare her self-defence with that of Hero, Desdemona, Imogen— and we see Shakespeare's splendid development. Art can go no further. . . .

In the above criticism we see that the moral predominates, and it remains to show where it has quickened and where blunted insight. To the latter belong Falstaff, and the general remarks about *J.C.*; to the former the characters of Hotspur and Brutus and the analysis of *All's Well*. Both Isabella and Hermione are over-praised from moral rather than aesthetic reasons—and surely the moral nature of Leontes is totally misconceived. It is needless to say that these critics are not likely to befriend Cleopatra; but with *Coriolanus* again moral and aesthetic truth interpenetrate. The remarks on *Timon* are true, and even partially so is the defence of Apemantus.

The criticisms of the great tragedies—*Hamlet, Othello, Macbeth*— are on the border-land. If they do not penetrate far, if they assume too much knowledge of Shakespeare's character, they are at least suggestive. We read them and then think of the alternative explanations, and as our minds make the passage we are conscious of the abyss. It is less that they stimulate than awaken echoes.

II

F. E. SCHELLING [2] deals with influences on the Elizabethan drama, and notes where Shakespeare, working with the same materials, surpassed his fellow-dramatists. There were the religious, national, and Italian interests of the drama, and though Shakespeare was thoroughly English, he owed to the transforming atmosphere of Italy the fact that he is alike the most realistic of dramatists and most romantic and ideal of poets. The Italian spirit seeks beauty in strange and often un-

---

[1] Cf. Arthur Symons (1907).

[2] *Elizabethan Drama*, 1908 (London, Constable; Boston and New York, Houghton Mifflin).

promising materials, and produces effects of art by untried courses. Marlowe gave the drama passion and poetry, and the chronicle play appealed to national instincts. . . .

It has long been admitted that Shakespeare's early histories owed much to Marlowe. Schelling points to more detailed resemblances, especially in *Richard III*, and explains the further influences that succeeded Marlowe—and where Shakespeare's own mind breaks through.

Richard III, he says, is less criminal than diabolical; his energy, hypocrisy, cynicism, &c., dilate into the heroic. This concentration of interest in the heroic dimensions of a unified personality characterizes the drama of Marlowe. Also it is without comedy, and there is a certain fixity of character, coarseness of stroke, violence of speech and deed, and a lyricism which converts whole scenes into the expression of a single emotion. In *Richard II* Shakespeare adds poetic delicacy and more searching insight into character. In both parts of *Henry IV* he weds the chronicle play to the realistic comedy of everyday life: he is the Dickens of his age, but true to fact. Henry V's 'fidelity to fact' translates the vulgar lust of mere conquest into a great national war. Shakespeare took the chronicle play out of itself and glorified it in two of his greatest plays. *Macbeth* and *Lear* derive in subject from the same sources, and their conduct as dramas is not unaffected by their extraction. The personality of his characters interests Shakespeare: Macbeth's imaginative egoism, Lear's senile dementia, contemptible in itself but transformed into the effect of grandeur by his years, royal dignity, and pitiful situation. . . .

In the following section Schelling will explain to us how Shakespeare developed romantic comedy to grace and lightness without flippancy or triviality. He learnt his first lessons from Lyly, and gradually used his supreme poetic gift to outdo his fellow-workers and transform his material.

The *Wives* proves that Shakespeare was pre-eminent in the domestic drama as elsewhere. Lyly provided him with a general model of intercourse between refined persons, and unity in constructing plot. *L.L.L.* followed Lyly's ideal, which seldom rose to the conception of a drama superior to momentary and local applications. *Verona* gives the first glimpse of Shakespeare's true and simple romantic art. The *Merchant* is the last play to show traces of art other than his own. Perhaps it remains a comedy rather than a tragedy because of the masterly union of the pathetic with the grotesque—a union as daring as psychologically true. *Twelfth-Night* is the perfection of light and joyous romanticism. The superficial atmosphere and adventure may be unreal, as are their romantic sources: but the characters are entirely English. The interest of the comedies is the kaleidoscopic groupings and changes of the persons of the drama. Romance prefers the marvellous and beautiful to real life, and takes us back to the golden joys and illusions of youth.

The art of *M. for M.* is realistic, but Shakespeare ingeniously adds Isabella's unassailable chastity and the pathetic figure of Mariana. *T. and C.* contains cynicism, irony, worldly philosophy, and bitter wisdom. . . .

In connexion with the tragedies Schelling just touches upon influences, but it is evident that they play a smaller part than in the preceding plays. We therefore conclude that by this road he has reached the opinion that the tragedies were Shakespeare's most original work—despite what has been said about *Macbeth* and *Lear*.

The Elizabethan tragedy was overwhelmingly romantic; its quest was for material out of the range of ordinary experience, apart from customs and wont of time, expressed in the accepted terms of the present. The influence of Seneca does not contradict this; he was the most romantic of classics and the most modern of ancients. In *Hamlet* we see Shakespeare's care for character; it was man, not his doings, that interested him. Plot, setting, staging, were nothing to him when seized by the fervour of imaginative portraiture. His persons live and change under his hand as men do in this world. Here he gives us a new artistic character-analysis and self-questioning—unlike the scientifically critical eye which views life from without. The naturalness and spontaneity of *R. and J.* make it unlike the romantic tragedies of the day. It is the supreme dramatic embodiment of the tumultuous passion of adolescence. In the last two acts of *A. and C.* Shakespeare expands his sources with regal power. As in *Macbeth* and *Lear* the play rises out of its particular into the imperishable triumph of unfettered art. Cleopatra is the veritable goddess of eternal change, the legion of whose caprices, frivolities, and blandishments the master dramatist has somehow contrived to sum up into an heroic figure, the incarnation of passionate abandonment to a love that rages like fire and consumes all! Abandon is her surpassing quality, and Shakespeare alone among dramatists dared to paint this passion with all the light and darkness that affect it. In *Othello* he has most ennobled and elevated his theme and practised the transforming alchemy of his art. To Othello it was wonder and rapture that a maiden so fair and delicately nurtured could love him. Love grounded in disparity is unstable, and Iago practised on that. . . .

Of the Roman plays we need only include Schelling's remark that *J.C.* has the atmosphere of dignity and restraint of ancient Rome; and we cannot agree that *Coriolanus* is a glorified chronicle history. But his best criticism is of the romances, and we may well contrast it with Thorndike's. He does not deny the influence of Fletcher, but he sees how Shakespeare transcends Fletcher, and above all points out the true relation between the special kinds of characters and incidents of the romantic tragi-comedy.

He denies that Shakespeare's characters may be reduced to types of Fletcher's. The persons of Shakespeare's romances are breathing realities, whereas Fletcher's tragi-comedies are consummate pictures with the limitations of their art on them. Shakespeare bowed to the fashion of the moment when he ended the *W. Tale* happily, and disturbed the ethical sensibilities of the modern reader in letting Hermione forgive Leontes. In the *Tempest* he transformed the gross superstition of the sailors into a tale of romantic beauty. The scenes of Fletcher's tragi-comedies are laid within the Court; they deal with love intrigues, ambition, revenge, contrasts of sentimental passion with tragic feeling and situation. Shakespeare's romance wanders over strange seas and lands, delights in shipwreck and adventure, touches imaginatively on the supernatural. Fletcher's tragi-comedies are well knit and the characters are types; Shakespeare's romances are loosely constructed, recalling the epic quality of the old chronicle plays, and his characters are as individually distinctive as in the older plays. Fletcher had only a general influence on Shakespeare. . . .

We may fitly leave Schelling here, with his best sentences fresh in our memory. He brings home to us something of the special quality of Shakespeare's mind by analysing the material at the disposal of himself and his fellow dramatists alike.

III

WE interrupt the stream of laudatory criticism to deal with a strange collection of essays edited by Sir Spencer St. John.[1] The twentieth century has its Rymers, and though we cannot say of the present author that he writes of Shakespeare without experiencing him, he at least experiences him in the wrong way. That a work of art should not be put to the same tests as a legal work, is one of the thoughts that rise in us as we read verdicts on the plays such as the following:

R. and J. lacks constructive art; Juliet was not bound to take the potion, whence the whole catastrophe: even the Friar says she might have lain concealed in his cell. Timon was prodigal not generous, and his self-burial is a farce. The plan of *Hamlet* is confused and inartistic. After a splendid opening it diminishes and ends miserably. Polonius becomes quite different from Shakespeare's first design. Hamlet's father would not have given power to a shallow babbler. Iago is the cornerstone of *Othello* yet has no adequate motive. Nothing in *Coriolanus* is natural except the domestic scenes. *J.C.* has faults, yet is full of exquisite poetry, delicate sentiments, and the highest kind of eloquence. Few women can compare with Portia. Historical truth cramps Shakespeare's genius without offering an equivalent in strict adherence to facts. Yet throughout there are many beautiful and wise and imaginative lines and passages, and these make reading tolerable. Shakespeare's best comedy is in history, because the strain of pure

---

[1] *Essays on Sh. and his Works,* edited by Sir Spencer St. John from the manuscripts and notes of a deceased relative, 1908 (Smith, Elder).

comedy led him to semi-tragedy for contrast and variety. Falstaff's wit sinks towards the end but reappears in full blaze in the *Wives*. Malvolio is original but inconsistent; he is no Puritan or stern enthusiast, but a piece of starched propriety. *A.Y.L.* is one of the calmest and sweetest plays, where evil only enters enough to produce a contrast. Prospero waited so many years for revenge that Miranda might grow up and engage in inspired love-making. . . .

After these selected judgements on particular plays we will turn to more general statements, remarking that they are personal in the narrow sense of the word and akin to prejudice. Herbert Spencer called Homer tedious and Plato silly—and A. C. Benson observed that these were the opinions of a fourth-form boy.

Shakespeare had a low estimate of women; he considered them as objects of man's passion, incentives to action, victims of his or their own vices. He sought to rival Juliet in Imogen, Portia, Helena, Desdemona, Ophelia, but all are far below her. In conception of love and beauty his imagination was only once prolific. Men to Shakespeare were bad rather than good; the best is Romeo as he has no gall. Othello's love is a delusion, and he is jealous because he concludes Desdemona cannot love him. Orlando is silly, and this saves him from our disgust. Only Horatio has no flaw; he is more disinterested and self-sacrificing than Hamlet. Shakespeare's treatment of love in *Venus* and the Sonnets is most derogatory to the sex; but in time the turbulent elements were co-ordinated into one beautiful whole such as Juliet. Othello only exhibits the jealousy of a middle-aged gentleman lest his female plaything should be taken from him; but the love of Brutus for his wife is as noble as any that we may imagine to exist in heaven. Rosaline loves Orlando for his strength in wrestling. . . .

The same perverse method obtains in the discussion on Shakespeare's philosophy. The writer argues back from particular speeches of characters, and attributes to Shakespeare any confusion that may result.

Claudio has committed no great crime but is in agony at the thought of death. It was the doctrine of Shakespeare's age, and linked with the belief in fate, that the guilt of one may be expiated by the sufferings of others. Shakespeare does not believe in necessity, but he is deeply perplexed and falls into a wilderness of paradoxes. Hamlet is the exponent of one class of his speculations, Iago, Edmund, Richard III, Macbeth of others, and the Duke in *M. for M.* and Friar in *R. and J.* of still others. He felt himself out of place in the social system of the time, and the aim of his philosophy is to blunt the edge of disappointment. From *Timon* one can see that his views of the English social system were most unfavourable, and in *A.Y.L.* he argues that there is greater sweetness in seclusion from the world. He loves all but Jews and Puritans, but his convictions were revolutionary and he did not approve kings. In his eyes they are usurpers, murderers, despots, knaves, and all the misery of the world comes from the worship of power and grandeur by the multitude. It is falsely believed that he thought humbly of himself: on all sides he saw no one superior.

IV

A LITTLE book by H. C. Beeching [1] is worth mention because it deals skilfully with some vexed questions. Shakespeare is said to dislike crowds: but who likes them? he replies. If we take his mechanicals singly he does not deny to them human virtues, and the Citizens in *Coriolanus* refute Menenius in argument. He treats the subject of Shakespeare's melancholy with mingled insight and common sense. Perhaps Shakespeare felt a temptation to melancholy, he says, but all that we know of his outward life gives the opposite impression. His comparisons of Shakespeare's rogues are worth recording, and the eternal problem of Falstaff's degradation. He suggests that the latter may be due to the fact that he comes into an historical play instead of a pure comedy, and adds that nobody wants Sir Toby put on the black list as a tippler, or Autolycus sent to gaol for filching linen from the hedges; but when the world of comedy touches the real world, social offences have to meet social punishment. In answering the question how we are to get behind Shakespeare's writings to the man, he recalls Raleigh. We must ask ourselves what is the impression left on our mind after a careful reading of any play, because that will be Shakespeare's mind speaking to ours, and the general impression from the great volume of his work is no vague one. We are conscious of gentleness and manliness, and a conviction that good must fight evil.

V

IN the opinion of Mr. Frank Harris [2] Shakespeare can be detected in his work, because an artist is bound to reveal himself. Shakespeare, he thinks, was weak-nerved and passionate, with feminine rather than masculine virtues. The event of his life was his passion for the 'dark lady', whom he identifies with Mary Fitton. Shakespeare could not paint a man of action, but in all his plays and poems painted one man —himself—and one woman—Mary Fitton [3]—until a collapse came and he retired to Stratford. Mr. Harris's book is well written and appeals to a wider circle than most critical treatises, and is likely to convince the unprofessional reader that it is the whole truth about Shakespeare. We will endeavour to present the gist, and to show how much truth it contains, and we will remark at the outset that the final effect of such a book is to belittle Shakespeare.

Mr. Harris argues that Romeo and Hamlet have the same pensive

[1] *Wm. Sh. Player, Playmaker, and Poet*, 1908 (Smith, Elder).
[2] *The Man Sh. and his Tragic Life Story*, 1909 (Frank Palmer).
[3] Cf. Brandes.

sadness and loving sympathy. Jaques is the same, though painted with lighter strokes: he has humorous sadness and intellectual curiosity. Macbeth is like Hamlet, with his irresolution and untimely love of meditation, and both have exquisite intellectual fairness. Macbeth at first loves thought and hates action, and like Hamlet loses his foothold on reality. After the murder his nerve is gone, and we see nothing of the ambitious, half-barbarous chieftain. A strange murderer is one who longs for 'troops of friends', and he complains of bad dreams, like Hamlet, and, like Hamlet, his philosophy ends in utter doubt and contempt for life. His speech to Macduff, 'Of all men else . . .' is a confession of pity and remorse, like the gentle kindness of Hamlet to Laertes or Romeo to Paris. The speech of Duke Vincentio to Claudio shows deeper hopelessness and pessimism than Hamlet's. It must be Shakespeare's own thought, as it is out of place to a doomed man, and the Duke is not callous. He is a pensive poet-philosopher talking to lighten his own heart.

Shakespeare is said to depict men of action, but they are sketches compared with his intimate portrait of the aesthetic-philosopher-poet. His men of action are taken from history or tradition, and the traits are supplied by the chroniclers. He adds no new quality to Falconbridge, but Arthur is all his. Having just lost his own son he has learnt pathos from weakness and suffering. In the old play Arthur faces the unknown with a man's courage; the pathos is the work of gentle Shakespeare who hated war and bloodshed. Richard II is cruel at first, because Shakespeare began with the traditional view, but when he saw it would yield no emotion, he veered round and discovered amiable qualities in him. He paints himself as led astray by bad friends. Richard's hasty blow is no sign of courage—which should be founded on stubborn resolution. Arthur reveals Shakespeare's qualities of heart, Richard of mind, and both are parts of one nature, and prove Shakespeare was affectionate in a feminine manner.

Shakespeare gives Hotspur's impatience superbly, his courage lamentably. Take away historical qualities and see how little Shakespeare added. Shakespeare's Hotspur hates poetry yet utters long poetical descriptions; but when Shakespeare does reveal Hotspur's real qualities, his magic makes him live intensely, despite false strokes. Compare the Prince to see how poorly Shakespeare conceives entirely manly qualities. At first he is a prig, then a colourless replica of Hotspur, but he never reveals his soul, and his changes are sudden and unmotived. When watching by the dying King Shakespeare openly speaks through him. When he dismisses Falstaff Shakespeare adds the bitter contempt; it was distaste for his own past that made him severe on Falstaff. *Henry V* is one of Shakespeare's worst works, and Henry is embarrassed by the need to speak as soldier-king. The puppet becomes ridiculous through infusion of the poet's sympathy and emotion. Shakespeare cannot express courage; 'Once more unto the breach' is not valour but its make-believe; and the 'tiger's rage' not brave but angry men. Richard III was drawn under the spell of Marlowe, but the first impulse was soon exhausted, and Shakespeare fell back on himself and made Richard keen of insight and hypocritically blunt of speech—a sketch of Iago. 'There is no creature loves me', shows Shakespeare's own gentle, loving nature. Shakespeare, who was no hero but a neuropath and a lover, took the feminine view of courage as love of honour.

The Duke's speech on music in *Twelfth-Night* is the most complete confession of Shakespeare's feelings. His self-contradictions are those of self-revelation. Shakespeare speaks freely without much care for coherence of characterization. In every play we see his love of music and flowers. Hamlet and Macbeth express his mind, Romeo and Orsino his heart and poetic temperament. Critics have overlooked his gentle, passionate side. Orsino is the complement to Hamlet who is entirely in the shadow, but something still lacks. It is humour that brings him into touch with reality, so that his ideality is not one-sided humour produced by love and sympathy. When a feature is accentuated by repetition it must belong to a living model. In neither Hamlet nor Richard are the principal traits accentuated so grossly as in Falstaff. He was taken from life and studied from outside, so Shakespeare could not paint him again. He had exhausted his model and only echoed him in the *Wives*. . . .

So far, says Mr. Harris, are the outlines: and we pause to remind him of two old truths—that Shakespeare had a universal mind, and that human nature differs in degree rather than kind. The first should teach us that every critic, according to his bias, can find himself reflected in Shakespeare; the second, that the meditations of Hamlet and Macbeth belong to a different school. Also, if we judge Shakespeare's characters by their actions as well as their minds we see that the effect made on the world by Hamlet is other than by Macbeth. It has been rightly said that 'To be'—the most universal speech—could only have been uttered by Hamlet. As regards courage and men of action, we would counter-suggest *R. and J.*, with its trio of Romeo, Tybalt, Mercutio: though of course we agree that the finest poetry is drawn from inner not outer experience. Where Mr. Harris convinces is in pointing to a continuing meditative-poetic-philosophic strain in the roll of characters; but he would have done better to suggest rather than assert. And he most fails where he is most definite—as in transferring Shakespeare's life-experiences to his work—the loss of his son, and his supposed riotous youth.

We will now give instances of touches in the plays whereby Shakespeare, according to Mr. Harris, is self-revealed. That Adriana (*Errors*), who is not blamed for her age, defends herself against it, proves that Shakespeare meant his wife. The Abbess condemns her in needlessly emphatic terms. The first scene of *Verona* gives Shakespeare's reasons for leaving Stratford; the needless argument proves personal confession. He desired love and honour and saw the drag of his marriage. No merchant ever made or kept money like Antonio—who does not esteem worldly goods. Shylock hates Antonio more than he loves money, and there is the same prodigality in all the plays—Brutus, Lear, Timon. Shakespeare must have been thus—and Ben Jonson calls him open and free. In the Sonnets he reveals his feminine qualities—passionate self-abandonment, facile forgivingness, self-pity. The unlikely story partly proves it true. Proxy-wooing is treated in three plays—*Verona, M. Ado, Twelfth-Night.* The story of Shakespeare's passion for Mary Fitton is that of his life. Rosaline (*R. and J.*) is minutely described, though she does not figure in the play, and Shakespeare seldom describes his women. Biron calls Rosaline (*L.L.L.*) wanton, and this lessens our sympathy with Biron, his love, and the play. When Shakespeare fails in art the cause is strong personal feeling.

Shakespeare's sensuality unites creatures of his temperament with those of his intellect—Romeo, Jaques, Orsino, Hamlet. It is the source of his kindness and wide sympathy. He added nothing to virile virtues and vices, but he did to feminine, and it was desire that most inspired him. He was a born aristocrat, who loathed the common people, and admired cultured young noblemen—Bassanio, Benedict, Mercutio. He omits to say that the English bowmen won Agincourt. The Sonnets to the youth are conventional; to the women they display a terribly true passion. Shakespeare's liking for William Herbert was heightened by snobbishness; when he lost him it left in him bitterness and contempt for ingratitude, not grief for loss of affection. Mary Fitton was the passion of his life, and appears in play after play, long after the sonnet period. . . .

Mr. Harris writes in an interesting manner and is himself convinced, but he is impressionistic rather than deep. He knows the mere facts of Shakespeare's life and instantly finds something to correspond with them in *Errors* and *Verona*. He repeats the old charge of Shakespeare's 'snobbishness' because of obvious scenes like those of Jack Cade or the mob in *J.C.* We would remind him of the dignified rebuke addressed to Coriolanus by the citizen—that the price of the consulship is to ask it kindly. In London or New York at the present day no doubt Antonio would be considered a bad merchant; but we recall Carlyle's saying that the ancestors of the great Mirabeau carried on business in the 'Venetian', and therefore 'not ignoble' manner. We now approach the final period.

After Shakespeare's disillusion all his heroes fail. Brutus is the most complete portrait of Shakespeare at his best. There is nothing in Plutarch of the different passions and war with himself of which he speaks. Shakespeare did not understand the republican ideal, and made Brutus a conspirator without a cause. The more perfect Brutus is the more cogent should be his motive to kill Caesar. When Shakespeare realized that he had been fooled and scorned he replied with *Hamlet*. He knew himself to be irresolute and half excuses, half realizes himself. Brooding on revenge is the heart of the play. Most men would not blame their mother, but Shakespeare identified her with Mary Fitton. No one ever felt such intensity of jealous rage about a mother or sister.[1] He never thinks of challenging the King to fair fight, but meditates assassination in a feminine manner. Shakespeare excels in magnifying this secondary weakness into the chief defect of the whole tragedy.

We see from *Othello* how jealousy and revenge gradually possessed Shakespeare. When Othello tells how he won Desdemona he falls out of character. Shakespeare knows he has fixed Othello's outlines, and therefore lets himself go. The lover of realities deserts facts, the man of action thinks lightly of reverses. Othello talks too much, and like a poet in images.[2] As soon as jealousy is broached the man of action disappears, and Shakespeare takes his place. Shakespeare's jealousy is compounded of sensuality, and no pages exist of more sincere and terrible self-revealing. Othello was first presented as sober, solid, slow to anger, master of himself. Like Leontes and Posthumus, he is driven mad by imagining the sensual act. As murderer, when he should be most sincere, Othello speaks as a soldier and utters no word of profound self-revealing. When he knows the truth he is passionate as a woman and magical in expression. Othello the captain is a mere sketch; his jealous, tender heart is Shakespeare's. Take that away and we have but the colour of his skin.

A. and C. is the supreme expression of passion for Mary Fitton. To win universal admiration and love, and imperishable renown in death, is to succeed in spite of failure and suicide. This is the lesson Shakespeare read into Plutarch's story, and he sympathized with Antony because he was passion's slave. The traits taken from Plutarch are what Shakespeare had not himself. He gives to Cleopatra low cunning, temper, mean greed, and so transforms her from a historical marionette to the most splendid specimen of the courtesan in literature. The praise of Enobarbus is Shakespeare's true opinion of Mary Fitton. She is faithless to Antony without cause. After his death Shakespeare is forced by history to give her heroic attributes, but ninety-nine in a hundred would have followed Plutarch and made Cleopatra's love for Antony her mainspring and cause of suicide. With Shakespeare it is imperious pride and hatred of degradation.

[1] Cf. Ernest Jones.

[2] See Bradley's description of Othello's poetic nature: one of the most beautiful pages of criticism ever written.

Cleopatra and the 'dark lady' are one beyond all doubt. In *Lear*
Shakespeare drinks the cup of disillusion to the dregs. Madness is
the keynote, and he dwells on Lear's blindness. Lear at his bitterest
shows erotic mania, the source of all Shakespeare's misery but quite
out of place here. *Timon* is a mere scream of pain, and marks the
utmost limit of Shakespeare's suffering.

At this point there is a break, due to breakdown in health. Perhaps
his daughter saved him from death and taught him that a maiden can
be pure, and he therefore deified her. Marina, Perdita, Miranda, are
the same figure. Imogen is full of sexless perfections. The joy of the
youths in getting to know her echoes his own pleasure with his
daughter. Prospero's confession of how his daughter preserved him
is impertinent to the play. Ariel was in prison for twelve years, and
Shakespeare was twelve years in torture for Mary Fitton. The age
and weakness on which Prospero insists are out of keeping with a
magician; but at last Shakespeare sees himself as he is—a monarch
without a country, but a great magician, with imagination as attendant
spirit. . . .

In his analysis of *A. and C.* Mr. Harris comes nearest to persuading
us that there is something in his theory, but otherwise we diverge
increasingly from his views as we proceed with the tragedies. The
fault he finds with Othello is an extreme instance of his method.
Poets are no race apart, but the well of poetry exists somewhere out
of sight in the depths of the commonest man. The greater the poet
the more he reveals to us of ourselves. It was Othello's distinction
that he had meditated over his past, and could use his great actions,
softened by memory, to make his daily speech beautiful. We repeat
that Mr. Harris's book is easy and pleasant reading, that he himself
is sincere and convinced; but he is positive in the bad sense, his distinctions are not fine, and the image of Shakespeare which he succeeds in
impressing on our minds is not one of a great world-poet. Imagination
may need an earthly starting-point, but after its huge circuit in space
it lights down on a far stranger land.

VI

WE have often met Swinburne before, and are not over-charmed with
his critical manners, but no collection of tributes to Shakespeare should
omit some of the splendid sayings contained in the little book that
belongs to the year of his death.[1] As usual with Swinburne it is the
single impressions that strike, rather than the plan of the whole. The
following are selected because of their imagination—which answers
like a burning-glass to the sun of Shakespeare's own imagination:

Through his wonderful intelligence Iago rises to the dignity and

[1] *Three Plays of Sh.*, 1909 (Harper).

mystery of a devil. Edmund's last wish is to undo his last and most monstrous crime: a wish that would be impossible to either Goneril or Regan. Of the Fool in *Lear* he says that the utmost humiliation imaginable of social state and daily life serves only to exalt and emphasize the nobility and manhood of the natural man. Having occasion to refer to the child of Iago mentioned in Cinthio's novel, he denies it to be possible, in Shakespeare's world, that monsters should propagate: that Iago should beget or Goneril and Regan bring forth. When Desdemona exclaims that the sun drew all such humours as jealousy from Othello, it would be a noble stroke of pathos were she wrong, but the higher, unequalled Shakespearian pathos consists in the fact that she was right. . . .

It has been previously remarked that Swinburne rated Aeschylus above Shakespeare. In this last treatise on the subject he still does so according to the letter, but we rather think that in the spirit he inclines to Shakespeare. Where reason determines a verdict he is for Aeschylus, where imagination plays the greater part he is for Shakespeare. It is to be noted how justly, despite enthusiasm, he uses his great powers of reason and imagination in these highest walks of criticism.

What, he asks, is the hereditary horror of doom once imminent over the house of Atreus to this instant imminence of no supernatural but a more awfully natural fate with Lear? On the other hand, Aeschylus excels Shakespeare in the more technical and lyrical sense of the word, no less than in height of prophetic power and depth of reconciling and atoning inspiration. The conclusion of the Oresteia impresses us with a crowning sense of spiritual calm and austere consolation in face of the mystery of suffering and sin. Shakespeare did not share this supreme gift of the imaginative reason, but no one like him set before us the tragic problem of character and event, action and passion, evil and good, natural joy and sorrow, and chance and change. As poet and thinker, he concludes, Aeschylus equalled if he did not surpass Shakespeare; as creator, revealer, interpreter, infinite in insight, truthfulness, tenderness, wisdom, justice, mercy, no man can stand beside the author of *Othello*. Lastly we set down his opinion that truth of imagination transcends accident of fact—as a foil to critics who censure Shakespeare because his plots were often improbable. That an event may have happened, he writes, means nothing; that a man such as Aeschylus or Shakespeare imagined it means this: that it endures and bears witness what man may be, at the highest of his powers and noblest of his nature, for ever. And we may correct this with Carlyle's saying that every fact is sacred.

VII

WITH a book like Mr. Harris's fresh in our minds, and considering the growing tendency to treat the plays as autobiographical, it is well to spend a few minutes with Sidney Lee.[1] We remember his former decisions, and they are summarized in the title of the present essay, but at the same time we think to detect a more yielding note about the Sonnets. Their dominant topic, he says, finds no place in the plays, and this suggests that if Shakespeare's personality lies on the surface of the Sonnets it is concealed in the plays. He still believes dramatic forces to be at work in them, which produce the illusion of a personal confession but do not offer sure evidence that Shakespeare is literally transcribing a personal experience.

Otherwise Sidney Lee wishes to prove that Shakespeare's dramatic greatness depended on his impersonality. The result is to leave in our minds not a belittled Shakespeare like Mr. Harris's—because the reader throughout leans on the staff of the critic's undoubted admiration —but a Shakespeare diminished from the inspired teacher of Swinburne.

The dramatist's art, Lee argues, made Shakespeare invest his characters with irreconcilable emotions. The sentiments which he reiterates are not distinctive. There is no external evidence of tempestuous catastrophes in Shakespeare's life, akin to those of Hamlet, Othello, Lear. His life was one of uninterrupted progress in prosperity. There are comic interludes in his tragedies; tragedy is the acme of dramatic art, and every supreme master has concentrated his mature powers on tragedy. Searing personal anxiety would have stayed Shakespeare's approach to artistic perfection, would have disturbed the unfaltering equilibrium of *Othello* or *Coriolanus*. Strong emotion dims the intellect, and no dramatic triumph awaits one who suffers from passion or agitation. The dramatic poet is spectator, not actor, a student of emotion, whose art sternly limits the active range of passion. He reproduces tragic passion not as it is, but so as to create an illusion of truth. The murder of Duncan and death of Desdemona are two of Shakespeare's most tragically intense scenes: yet who would say that he had private experience of murder? The possessor of imaginative genius can live in fancy more lives than one.

VIII

THE opinion of Furnivall and Munro is that Shakespeare was a splendid all-perceiving man impressed with the soundness, beauty, and admirability of man; that he had wonderful variety and many-sidedness and was kin to all natures. Schelling speaks of the matchless portraiture of men and women that makes him pre-eminent in English drama and the literature of the world, and calls him the quickest, subtlest, and

[1] *The Impersonal Aspect of Sh.'s Art* (English Assoc. Leaflet, No. 13, July, 1909).

deepest knower of the human heart. According to him, Shakespeare was totally absorbed in character and neglected story and plot; while St. John suggests that he addressed himself to the source of all interest in human compositions—the yearning of the soul. Mr. Harris says that he was the finest spirit ever born, but absolute abandonment to passion made him the supreme poet. To Swinburne he is the greatest of all poets in the literal sense—as creator of man and woman—above all as revealer and interpreter, infinite in insight and truthfulness, tenderness and wisdom, justice and mercy.

Furnivall and Munro think that Shakespeare was an orthodox Christian of the day. Schelling says that the essence of his tragedy is truth to fact, fidelity to right, to the actualities of human conduct and the main-springs of human feeling. Beeching maintains that he looked on the world as a moral order, and believed in free will.

He knew men but adored women; his reverence for women was the most beautiful trait in his character. This statement of Furnivall and Munro may be supplemented by Schelling's praise of the purity, ideal sweetness, and frankness of innocence of his heroines.

Two further statements may be contrasted: that of Furnivall and Munro that he was no democrat but had open-hearted humanity; and Swinburne's, that beneficent and bloodless social revolution was the key-note of his creed and watchword of his gospel.

Sidney Lee speaks of the omnipotence of his imagination; and Furnivall and Munro proclaim all his attributes to be agents of that imagination which made him the greatest poet of the world.

Schelling's tribute to his 'inexhaustible art' does not agree with his former statement, already quoted, that he neglected story and plot. According to Sidney Lee he attained the highest pitch of artistic perfection, and treated plot and character with unfaltering equilibrium. . . .

These two years show rather a marking time in criticism than any new discovery; but it is well that the first place should be given to imagination, as the poet's primal function.

ENGLAND 1910–1911

I

THE work of Mr. M. W. MacCallum[1] on the Roman plays is the most important of its kind. He shows in detail where Shakespeare followed or diverged from Plutarch, and with what result. To determine how far the picture of ancient Rome in the three plays is correct, he examines Shakespeare's methods of composition, his supposed preferences, and the condition of contemporary England.

After 1600 there were no more English historical plays, but the Roman play, developed by Marlowe and other university men, had become popular. All critics agree that in history Shakespeare treated his sources more reverently than in comedy or tragedy; but whereas in English history form yielded to contemporary historical interests, in Roman history there was need to select episodes of salient interest and catholic appeal. Shakespeare could only choose his point of view, and he does not attempt accurately to reconstruct the past. He did not detect the peculiar features of ancient Rome—the primitive republican life of *Coriolanus.* He could sympathize with the orgies of *A. and C.,* and understand the political crisis of *J.C.* from analogy, but he knew nothing of zeal for republican theory. Thus he only gives the notes that Rome possessed in common with all civilizations and his own especially. He quickens antique material with modern feeling, and the result is more truly antique because living energy and principle are reproduced. . . .

So far we gather from Mr. MacCallum that Shakespeare was no antiquarian, but that he saw certain universal passions at work in a distant age and foreign mind. Whether or not these are made salient by anything characteristically Roman, we shall see as we follow him through the plays. He also discusses the influence on Shakespeare of North's translation of Plutarch, and decides that while North supplied Shakespeare with the only Plutarch he could understand, his influence was more of suggestion than control.

Unlike Plutarch, Shakespeare establishes an inner connexion between the details in *J.C.* Plutarch admires Brutus's noble character, which all reverence, and the conspiracy of the Romans safeguarded by no vows, but he does not associate them: whereas Shakespeare traces one to the other and views them as cause and effect. Shakespeare interpolates some vital things: e.g., Brutus's soliloquy as he rids

[1] *Sh.'s Roman Plays and their Background* (Macmillan, 1910).

himself of scruples. But he does not utter the positive essence of republicanism—enthusiasm for the State where all lawful authority is derived from the whole body of fully qualified citizens.[1] Shakespeare did not grasp the antique point of view or Brutus's political theory. To harmonize his purpose with his idealist doctrines he furnishes him with new reasons instead of the old obvious ones. The genuine republican of old needed no justification for dispatching one who would be king. The craving for inward moral sanction is typical of the modern mind. Shakespeare transmutes the character of Brutus and revives the past by endowing it with his own life.

He makes clear that only the rule of a single master-mind could solve the problem of the time. The plebeians are fickle, violent, greedy, irrational; the governing classes envious, ambitious, covetous. For the populace, removal of the master means submission to the unprincipled orator. Shakespeare omits Plutarch's graver charges against Caesar and invents his physical, mental, and moral failings. Only minute analysis reveals the defects, which do not make the general impression contemptible. Also Shakespeare has invented some noble traits, viz:—'What touches us ourself shall be last served'. His more selfish aims do coincide with the good of the whole, and Shakespeare treats the plenary inspiration of his life that made him the instrument of heaven and was to bring peace and order to the world. But Caesar is carried away by his own conception, and cannot withhold homage from himself as incarnate *Imperium*. He represents the empire, and has to live up to an impossible standard, and must affect to be what he is not. The contrast is between the shortcomings of the individual and the splendour of the ideal role he undertakes. He has lost his old sure vision and power to act, and pays the penalty by falling below himself. He rushes on the fate which a little vulgar shrewdness would have avoided. But the idea of Caesarism, rid of the defects and limitations of its originator, becomes the more invincible. This Shakespeare perceives, unlike other dramatists who have treated the theme.

The faults of Brutus are suppressed, but he too is led to pose. He cultivates perfection and incurs the dangers of the specialist in virtue. He is divided between love for Caesar and hatred of the crime he contemplates; yet he must determine his conduct not by instinct or usage but impersonal, unprejudiced reason. He debates his difficulty with himself as an abstract problem of right and wrong. He must give the undertaking the form of ideal virtue and wisdom before he can proceed to it. The quarrel lays bare the story's significance in tragic pathos and irony. It is all in Plutarch, but Shakespeare adds the accumulated import, at which Plutarch only guesses remotely. He brings out the ideal aspect of Brutus's deed and shows it to be foolish

[1] Cf. Stapfer.

and disastrous in view of the facts. He has caused the overturn of society by assassinating the one man who could organize it. Superfine Brutus will not be guilty of extortion, but Cassius may—and then he will demand to share in the proceeds. He will interfere in Cassius's necessary measures with his moral rebukes; he will play the Infallible to such purpose that with his loftiness of view, &c., he gains authority over Cassius's mind that has disastrous results. He is never so great as in his doom, when stripped of all adventitious aids. The satisfaction to his private affections—his friends' refusal to kill him—is supreme with him at the end.

Cassius is an Epicurean, to whom death is a refuge, not an evil. He is free from superstitions and not deceived by shows. He sees through Casca and is not misled by Antony's frivolity. His lurking sense of unworthiness in himself and his purpose will increase his natural impatience of alleged superiority in his fellows. He would level down, yet is capable of high enthusiasm for a cause. He can reverence Brutus, and the episode of Popilius Lena shows him more swayed by personal hopes and fears than Brutus. He owes his death to this defect of endurance, and his want of inward strength explains the ascendancy of Brutus over him.

No self-interest moves Antony, only nobility of deed. This generous sympathetic strain in his nature is one of the things that make him dangerous. In his oration he turns against Brutus his superiority to personal claims and his patriotism and disinterestedness, which none can appreciate better than Antony, and he accuses him of black ingratitude. He never answers Brutus's charge, on which he rested his whole case—that Caesar was ambitious. . . .

Needless to say this is the most thorough analysis of the play and its characters that has yet been given to the world. Whether it helps us to reread with greater enthusiasm is another matter. Perhaps it rather accentuates weaknesses in the characters than discovers forces, though we except Antony and Cassius. Although with the latter it is a fault that comes to light—want of inward strength—so much action hangs upon that fault that it has something positive. With regard to the much debated character of Caesar, his failure as individual has never been better explained; but can we honestly detect the 'idea of Caesarism' in his unfortunate speeches? Is he not rather living on his former exploits than imagining himself a symbol? The 'spirit of Caesar' belongs to the latter part of the play; and—to venture for a moment on burning ground—those who recognize a Marlovian figure in Caesar and maintain that Shakespeare revised the play, might here state their case. In handling Brutus Mr. MacCallum shows the dividing line between ancient and modern worlds, and Shakespeare's historical lapses. At first we are tempted to think that the failure of Brutus to grasp the republican ideal, and the 'new reasons' supplied to him, throw light on Shakespeare's self: but there rises the old alternative of the needs of the theatre, and the public liking to see individual character in action. As usual the Shakespearian problem can be stated but not solved.

A. and C. is a gorgeous mingling of West and East, and also has something of the story of passion enshrined in the Sonnets. On one hand no play is more inspired and spontaneous from the author's heart, on the other, none more purely historical. Shakespeare reproduces the general contour of the historical landscape as visible from his point of view. He rearranges and regroups minor details and so gives them new significance. He does not alter fundamental traits of character but adds vividness and depth to the presentation. He omits the Parthian fiasco because it detracts from the glamour of absolute soldiership through which he wishes us to view Antony. He reads the soul of greatness through the sordid details, and explains them by the conception of Antony at his grandest, if not his best. The play is a chronicle history in its deference to facts, in its essence a tragedy. Shakespeare's Antony is capable of grand passion, but Plutarch has no eyes for the glory of his madness. Because it was sincere it reveals in him unsuspected nobility and depth. In the world freedom is lost, and there is no patriotism. The contagion of intemperance has spread from east to west; there is no moral cement to hold together this ruinous world, and the cult of material good prevails.

Responsiveness is the trait of Enobarbus; his tragedy is one of position—in that evil time his reason can furnish him with no motive for his loyalty but self-interest and confidence in his leader, or at least fame. His instincts pull one way, his reason another. In such a man instincts unjustified by reason lose half their strength, and even his revulsion of feeling is caused by appeal to his worldly wisdom. But when his judgement is convinced his deeper and nobler nature finds free vent in self-recrimination. Personal attachment, the one ethical motive left, is the inspiration of his soul. There is as little trace of love in Octavia as in Antony: and this is a gain, as he does not offend us by fickleness in his grand idolatry. She brings the atmosphere of another life, beside which the carnival of impulse is both glorified and condemned. Eros proves that the sole chance of escape from spiritual as well as physical servitude is personal enthusiasm for his master. Octavius is practical, sober, self-contained; and these middle-class virtues become in him almost aristocratic. They develop his self-esteem into pride and dignity. He opposes the solid mass of the west to Antony's loose congeries of Asiatic allies and underlings, whose disunited crowd typifies his own unreconciled ambitions. He is adroit in playing on the weakness of others, and, when winner, uses his advantage with more appearance than reality of nobleness. He would save Cleopatra to bring her to Rome—not for the sake of clemency and generosity but to parade these qualities. His only fault is to overact. He can recognize greatness when it redounds to his own credit by implying the conqueror to be still greater.

Our blood may prompt us to call Antony a demigod but our reason calls him a futility. All his energies are focussed in Cleopatra; his strategy is broken up to mere shifts and expedients that answer the demand of the hour. He will use his virtues in his own behoof— a vulgar attitude but redeemed by the vastness of the orbit through which his desire revolves. He sinks in but is not submerged by pleasures. His ideal is an infinity of pastimes under the presidency of his love— but any ideal dignifies those whom it inspires. In Plutarch he is recalled not because Fulvia dies but because she is alive, and she only dies as he nears home. In Shakespeare's Antony the removal of external hindrances gives new force to those in his own heart. Entreaties of friends and call of Rome have more force; yet we feel the impulse will soon be spent, and is a sign rather of weakness and indecision. The reconciliation with Octavius is hollow; and the easily-roused emotion soon subsides and yields to contrary impulsion.

Cleopatra is perhaps even Shakespeare's most marvellous creation— where nature that inspires and genius that reveals are most used in ideal truth. She is the incarnate poetry of life without duty. Shakespeare's delineation is more impressive and aesthetic, as he sacrifices the one-sided claims of the conception in which he delights to the laws of tragic necessity. If the first freshness is gone, the intoxication of fragrance, flavour, and lusciousness are enhanced. Like Plutarch, Shakespeare makes beauty the least part of her spell; therefore she is removed from the sphere of sense to that of imagination. She is so versatile and various, such a creature of moods, that we can forecast nothing of her. In Antony's absence she is flighty with herself. It is natural that she should wish to be present in the battle, and her panic is equally natural. Shakespeare's art effects more through conscientiousness and self-restraint. He detects a flaw in the resolute yearning of Cleopatra; the body of her dead past weighs her down; she cannot advance steadily in higher altitudes. She wavers in her resolve to die: as with Enobarbus, external stimulus is needed to the nobler course. How can we reconcile her new dignity and strength with her craven hankering for life and desire to retain by swindling a share of its gewgaws? It is hinted that she is in collusion with Seleucus, and the whole affair is a comedy arranged to keep open the door of death.

The passion of Antony and Cleopatra was due to the conditions of the time, when the individual was a law to himself. The master passion will supply the grand effective bond when other social bonds fail—when nothing else will enable man and woman to overleap some barriers of selfishness and merge their egoism in sympathy. Passion, enthusiasm, self-forgetfulness do command respect; and only one of

grand general outlook could so feel when he had tasted the sweets of
conquest and power. Relatively passion may be extolled, but, absolutely,
condemned. Each is untrue to the other; there is jealousy on one side
and fear on the other. She employs such wiles to retain him that we
ask if it is love? Yet if there were no real love, Antony's follies would
cast him beyond the pale of tolerance, and Cleopatra would be a mere
'courtesan of genius'. His feeling is deeper and higher than the senses;
and in catching him she has caught herself. Their love, if not sympathy
with the deepest and highest, is founded on correspondence in all
things great and small—completest *camaraderie*. Though their love
is often a divine orgy rather than a divine inspiration, Antony in death
has no thought of self. Cleopatra's love is deepened by trial, and
though her weaknesses do not disappear, they are but as fuel to the
flames of her love. Shakespeare makes her feel in death that now their
union has the highest sanction. . . .

The criticism is far more creative than that of *J.C.* Mr. Mac-
Callum's analysis of the characters of the latter tended rather to
separate them, here it is to unite them. We see the human heart
responding to the changed conditions brought about by the invading
East. The old moral landmarks are submerged; there only remains
personal devotion to link human beings with each other; and we see
its different phases in Eros, Enobarbus, Octavia, and others, till it
culminates with Antony and Cleopatra. It is the one thing that
survives, and we see its force when Antony rejects power and conquest
for its sake—and its weakness in the numerous wiles that Cleopatra
must employ to hold Antony. Carlyle said that when all other creeds
are done, hero-worship is the adamant below which man cannot fall:
and this last clinging of soul to soul, this need of worship, however
distracted by material cares, is written here. As Mr. MacCallum
proceeds, the human interest overbears the historical—and his
knowledge of the finer shades of emotion is equal to his knowledge
of history.

The story of Coriolanus comes first and absorbs the material.
Experiences are utilized in the interest of the play; the play is not
utilized in the interest of experiences. It would be falsely called a
drama of principles rather than character, because Shakespeare is
always first concerned with the fable, which explains and is explained
by human nature in action. In treating character it is not possible to
omit ethical considerations, since character is linked with conduct.
Political considerations cannot be excluded from a drama that moves
through a constitutional crisis. It has been said that Shakespeare
hated the people: but the vituperations are dramatic. He believes in
the sacred obligation of governing them for their good—and he often
makes nobles and kings cut sorry figures. Popular government must
be wrong, but royal or aristocratic government need not be right.

Shakespeare appreciates the greatness of his heroes and explains their offences so that we sympathize with them, but he makes these prominent and shows how they bring about the catastrophe. Coriolanus strikes as an example to eschew rather than imitate. Shakespeare selected the things nearest to his own experience, and certainly he effaced some of the antique colouring. The material is comparatively easy to shape dramatically, as the hero's personality dominates, and the character contains in itself seeds of offence and separation.

There is admirable balance and composition of the whole—throb and pulse, ebb and flow throughout. To achieve this Shakespeare was bound to reshape more freely than usual with history. He borrowed much from North's Plutarch, but added picturesqueness, passion, and dramatic significance. These never clash with his personal contributions which are far more important. All is subdued to the tone imposed by the dramatist's purpose, yet there is no loss to individuality of character. Plutarch's Volumnia does not pervade, and his Virgilia is a nonentity, while Shakespeare's Virgilia, though she speaks little, makes a definite impression. The Tribunes are colourless in Plutarch; their policy, not their character, concerns him. To Aufidius Shakespeare adds darker hues—his unscrupulous rancour. The danger to Rome at the outset of her career gives the legend a certain grandeur of import. The general scheme of the biography and the play is the same, but Shakespeare recasts it so as to give new significance. His is a fuller and more concrete picture, yet his innovations are not opposed to Plutarch, and may be suggested by his hints: e.g. Shakespeare makes Volumnia—as Plutarch does not—persuade Coriolanus to submit himself to the judgement of the people. Also unlike Plutarch he makes the centre the behaviour of Coriolanus as candidate: and as a result the Romans appear less unreasonable.

In Shakespeare the accusations against Coriolanus are just, and he would have been a tyrannical Consul. Shakespeare even softens down the worst traits of the proceedings of the people against their enemy, and thus emphasizes the hero's insolence. His pride is the cause of all, and when he invades Rome the people play a more intelligible and less dastardly part than in Plutarch. Shakespeare all but rejects the intuitive political capacity which Plutarch attributes to all classes of citizens in the young republic, which afterwards became the distinctive genius of the Roman State. Yet he just has enough sense of it to suggest a general impression, because he is deeply penetrated with Rome's greatness. Still he does not perceive the real issues between plebeians and patricians; he omits to say that the plebeians were reduced to distress by fighting for the State. They are worthy fellows driven desperate by misery, who, as a result, meddle in things too high for them. Yet they vote for Coriolanus, and see the two sides of the question more than he does. Shakespeare gives this right feeling and

appreciation of greatness—which Plutarch does not; but he conceives
of the people as a giant not yet in his teens, subject to spasms of fury,
panic, greed, only fit for useful service when under the right leader,
easily duped by flattery. He treats the Tribunes severely, but hardly
presents the Nobles more favourably. They retain caste pride but lose
class efficiency. Does this adequately represent the young republic that
is to become the world's mistress? To get the play's total effect we
must look at the general aspects of the story. The intolerance of
Coriolanus has threatened destruction from without, and the threat
has been averted. The intolerance of the demagogues has been discredited by results. Patriotism leads Volumnia to conquer herself
and her son. Thus we get the feeling of the majesty and omnipotence of the Eternal City: how it not only inspires and informs its units
but stands aloft and apart from its faulty representatives as a kind of
mortal deity.[1]

The passion of maternity hardens rather than melts Volumnia; her
influence on her son's choice of a military life is more stressed in Shakespeare than Plutarch. Menenius is not a good example for Coriolanus,
who adopts his headlong frankness without his tacit presupposition of
good-humoured hyperbole. Menenius represses his prejudices when
emergency requires, but not in his familiar circle, and as a lad Coriolanus would hear all this from his old friend. Coriolanus is general
and statesman as well as soldier, and it goes to his heart to see Rome
weakened by encroaching plebeians. He has political grip but not
political tact. Shakespeare adds the qualities of tenderness to his wife
and delight in his son. He changes his host of Corioli from rich to
'poor' man, and thus gives a wider range to his humanity. Is Aufidius
sincere, or does he soothe his wounded vanity by patronizing a once
successful and now unfortunate rival? Against him we feel that
Coriolanus strives for the realities of honour, and measures actions by
the standard of absolute desert. His self-respect and ideal of attainment
are abnormally developed, and every glory achieved becomes a pledge
he must redeem. He focusses the most valued traits of various social
fellowships greater than self. He represents a great family of a great
aristocracy of the great city of Rome. The domestic tie is closest, and
as son, husband, father, the depths of his nature are reached. His
mother sums up his ancestry and fills his soul with religious reverence.
Country, caste, family, cannot quite transfigure egoism, for all have
an egoistic aspect. They are the products of nature, instinct, passion,
and need not become rational principles. Their relative importance
may be mistaken; and so with Coriolanus it is feeling, not moral
conviction; passion, not reason. Lastly he misplaces the three objective
ethical principles: he loves nobility more than Rome, but he loves his
family as himself. His surrender to family ties is less noble than

[1] Cf. Franz Horn on *Coriolanus*.

Volumnia's to obligations of State. The collapse of his purpose is the victory of his strongest impulse. He neither acknowledges his offence nor renews his character, nor forgives, nor will return to Rome and endeavour to establish a lasting alliance. He is no martyr to patriotism, but victim of his own passion. . . .

Mr. MacCallum has impartially resolved the play into its elements, and distinguished between the Shakespearian and Plutarchan portions. As in *J.C.* he tells us of the distinctively Roman trait which Shakespeare misses, and we offer the same reasons for not accepting it without question as a lapse in Shakespeare's own nature. It is a most interesting suggestion that we get the feeling of the majesty of the Eternal City apart from its faulty representatives: but is this a definite impression from the play, or rather a moral to be drawn from reading it through the eyes of a learned historian? Perhaps Mr. MacCallum does not add anything new to the character of Volumnia, but he certainly does to that of Coriolanus when he contrasts him with Menenius. He takes soundings of Coriolanus's nature and finds love of family to be his deepest passion, and thus by a circuitous path reaches the conclusion of most critics, that Shakespeare was above all concerned with the elemental passions of the individual.

The tone of Mr. MacCallum's book is first of all historical, but the result of his impartial and almost scientific analysis is that the plays do not reveal themselves in order of interest according to their strict historic setting. History prevails in *J.C.*; history and human nature contend together in *Coriolanus*; history yields to human nature in *A. and C.* Against the critic's preoccupations, the latter play reasserts itself as the most Shakespearian. On the other hand, there is a certain kind of history concerned not with laws and institutions and battles won or lost, not with consuls and tribunes and patricians and plebeians, but with the essence of all these as relating to man in the past and contrasted with man in the present. And as in *A. and C.* we get the deeps of human nature, so we also get this abstracted, romantic history. It most conveys to us the feeling of Rome—and Mr. Mac-Callum's criticism deepens the impression. At times we lift our eyes from the spectacle of the gorgeous East, as if waking from a dream, to see, slightly sunk below the horizon, the walls and towers of the Eternal City. Rome has a meaning for us, to a certain extent beyond even Greece and Judea: it threatens because our conditions are more like. Cleopatra chose to die rather than be led in triumph through its streets—and to the Roman Triumph Plutarch applied the startling word 'terrible'. And the last word is that all this is merely one track in the vast Shakespearian forest.

II
THE views on Shakespeare of Professor George Saintsbury [1] naturally command attention. In the analysis that follows we will endeavour to give only what springs from the author's special qualifications for his task —his vast knowledge and his unspoilt power of direct vision; and thereafter we will consider how far these lighten the Shakespearian mystery.

Starting with Shakespeare himself, he affirms that all we know of him is that he wrote the great mass of work attributed to him and was generally liked and respected. The Sonnets are not reliable material for biography because we do not know the proportion of fiction and fact. The *Errors* lacks character; the verse is rough-hewn, and there is uncomely word-play, but it contains some beautiful poetry, and signs of future power over character. *L.L.L.* shows youth's prodigality and want of selection, but all the characters are of the true Shakespearian family. To deny *Titus* to Shakespeare is to pass the bounds of rational literary criticism; it is his one play of the Marlowe school. Thenceforth he advances dramatically from the panorama to the picture. *Verona* and *All's Well* have closer-knit plots, and the verse settles down to blank verse of the free kind. Helena may be either a wronged woman, or one who practically swindles a man into indissoluble connexion with her, and, compared with Cleopatra, is the more really vicious. Later on Shakespeare would not have left it uncertain, but if his experiments do not now succeed, the reason is that they aim higher. The farce of the *Shrew* has a general appeal.

What hitherto we have seen in touches becomes general with *R. and J.* The characters take the play into their own hands and work it out so as to give the story tenfold power and interest. All the characters are transformed; the whole of the Montagu and Capulet houses are alive. The subject of *M.N.D.* is worked up into action with a skill not yet displayed. Incident counts for more than character, and the several motives work into each other and work out each other most artfully. It contains the stuff of half a dozen poetical comedies. The actions in the *Merchant* provide a wave-like change of intensity and relief. The early casket scenes are of the Marlowe verse period; and some of the Gobbo business is like the unripe clowning of the *Errors*. But the trial is among the apices of dramatic poetry, and Shylock and Portia among the dramatis personae of eternity. Probably the parts are of different dates.

The chronicle drama offered the best field for Shakespeare's method. He imparted his poetry and character into 'formless agglomerations'. Richard II was conceived with a curious immature splendour like nothing else in Shakespeare. But he is not well supported; Gaunt makes great speeches but is not a great character. Shakespeare incomparably heightened the presentation of *John*, and made it into a piece

[1] *Cambridge Hist. of Eng. Lit.*, vol. v (Camb. Univ. Press, 1910).

of life rather than a sample of chronicling. It is almost the best example of his craftsmanship in verse and phrase. By adding, cancelling, smoothing, inspiriting, he turns the lame line or passage into a beautiful one. *Richard III* is full of life, and has nothing of Marlowe's peculiar dream quality. A large part in *Henry VI* is Shakespeare's. It gave him a chance to develop his grasp of character and to organize his unique conception of the loose many-centred drama kept together by character. In *Henry IV* the merest brute material is transformed into magnificent art: the historical part is wonderfully entwined and enforced. Every member of Falstaff's Bohemian circle has vital touches. It is the most genial if not the most poetical of cycles, where Shakespeare was prodigal of home memories, and yoked domestic minutiae with public affairs.

We now lose Meres as a guide, but we still follow the internal evidence of versification and dramatic craftsmanship. *Pericles* is probably not all his—yet no part might not be his—and the choruses are most Shakespearian. Perhaps he completed his own immature sketch. There is little character, and that still less concerned with working out the action. It is idle to lament the decadent Falstaff of the *Wives*. Shakespeare preferred artistic convenience, and Falstaff does not fall very hard. The character and dialogue are equal to any play, when allowance is made for kind and atmosphere. In the *Wives* Shakespeare gives, like no one else, in the bourgeois condition of prose, as high a standard of wifeliness as in Hermione and Imogen, but human. He lavishes a nepenthe of poetry on the unattractive theme of *M. for M.* Probably he revised an early work, and would not have chosen such a theme later. Pompey and Lucio are unfinished studies, akin to Launce and Launcelot. The Shakespeare of 1604 would have created a better Duke than one who involves his servants to rescue them as a rather shabby Providence. There is one loose stitch in *M. Ado*: Margaret is neither traitress nor fool. Otherwise it works out with perfect ease of action. Benedict and Beatrice are as good touchstones as any in Shakespeare. *A.Y.L.* may claim to be his greatest comedy. Its one fault is to end with a narrated 'revolution'. Otherwise nothing exceeds the romantic license—for so they lived in Arden. The vividness of every scene and passage is unmatched in Shakespeare. Arden is an earthly Paradise, but with nothing beyond the reach of any human being. Wit, wisdom, poetry, are the only transfigurers. The verse, lyrics, and prose are now perfected, and in no play are all so perfectly displayed. The purest comedy is *Twelfth-Night*. The Duke is one of the subtlest because most faintly nuanced critics of life. Viola, Olivia, Maria, are an extraordinary triad even for Shakespeare. Malvolio for all his defects is a gentleman, a man of honour and of his duty, with parts and merit.

Henry V is one of the greatest if not of the most attractive of Shakespeare's creations. The play is a pattern of the hard task of vitalizing chronicle by character. Here it is done by character diffuse rather than compact—by vivacity of different persons rather than interest concentrated in a hero. We rejoice in the triumph of England rather than Henry. *Henry VIII* is patchy, with hardly any marks of a 'first-draft' character. Instead of transcending the materials of *T. and C.* Shakespeare fails to bring out their possibilities. But for some of the speeches and touches of Ulysses, and the parts of Troilus and Cressida, it is the least Shakespearian play. *Timon* is chaotic, with no character that interests but Timon himself. Yet he is so good that the mature Shakespeare could not turn him over to underlings. *J.C.* is prodigal with poetry, but the interest is rather diffused. Shakespeare gives splendid poetic utterance even to insignificant characters. It lacks from the point of view of unity of character; only Brutus is continuous, though at first rather thin. It is a panoramic play, of sequence, not composition. The characters of *Coriolanus* interest in relation to the hero. The changes of Aufidius contrast with those of Coriolanus. The latter is not flawless, but one of the noblest figures in literature,[1] and his nobility is largely Shakespeare's work. Even Hamlet does not so much overshadow others. *A. and C.* is infinitely various; its characters are of the best; and the beauties of its verse unparalleled in number, diversity, intensity. The powers of the two great poetic motives, love and death, are utilized to their utmost possible extent. On the technical side it is the type and triumph of a chronicle play: a whole year of history is dramatized. Nowhere is there such a hero and heroine: Antony is at once ruined and ennobled by his passion; Cleopatra's frailty is sublimated into the same passion. Both are heroic in their weakness and royal in the way in which they throw away their royalty.

The character presentment of *Hamlet* informs and transforms the incidents. It is the richest and fullest in Shakespeare, and not confined to the central figure. Shakespeare neither liked nor disliked Claudius, but as creator he 'saw fair'. Claudius does not behave ill, and he has a real affection for the queen. He is a villain but a man, yet no one ever better deserved the final sword-thrust. Ophelia, Polonius, the Queen interest for themselves, not merely through Hamlet. *Othello* has still intenser pity and terror. Iago is less complex but almost as interesting as Hamlet. It is by no means certain that his suspicions of Othello and Emilia are pretended, and he has intellect, will, and courage. *Macbeth* was written at different times. Macbeth himself is a marvellous variant sketch of Hamlet—only *he* can never leave off, while Hamlet can never begin. He 'metaphysicalizes' on things he does, Hamlet on things he does not do. Lady Macbeth is peerless, and the handling of the supernatural illustrates Shakespeare's fertility. *Lear* has regality of tone like *A. and C.*, and like *Macbeth* is a tragedy

[1] Cf. Thümmel (1885).

of pity. It contains Shakespeare's most special ἁμαρτία: Lear's fate may seem excessive for his offence, but not as consequence for his frailty. The interest of *Cymbeline* is maintained among a tangle of interests by the charm of Imogen. Shakespeare has equalled but never surpassed her. There are faults of construction, but we should look at the body, not the skeleton. Perdita is exquisite but has no character; the jealousy of Leontes is touched with ferocious stupidity; Hermione is admirable to a point, but not quite fully shown. Above all, the whole is suffused with quintessenced poetry. The *Tempest* is most regular; the contrast of Caliban and Ariel is almost classical in conception and ultra-romantic in working out. Prospero is extraordinarily subtle, but the main charm is in the poetry, to which the prose adds not a little. There is no doubt of actual leave-taking in this perfect creation.

It is important to get the Shakespearian atmosphere, to feel the breath of his spirit. That consists in subjecting all things to the romantic process of presenting them in an atmosphere of poetical suggestion rather than sharply defined and logically stated. To this add philosophical depth and width of conception of life. He united romance, pure poetry, drama. From the first he gets freedom, from the second power to transport, while the third prevents vagueness. He never presents the narrow, unmistakable type character. His characters reveal themselves in their soliloquies, and nothing more helps his system of developing plot by development of character. They are marvellously adapted to the characters' idiosyncrasies, and it is impossible to distil the essence of Shakespeare's self out of them. In morals his severity is tempered by tolerance: he understands all and is therefore strictly impartial. His verse has no mannerism, no 'hall-mark' like Milton and Dante. The greatest utterances of different characters bear no relation to each other in mere expression. Above all merits is the easy and unforced breaking up of the line itself for the purpose of dialogue. The lines are induced to compose a continuous symphonic run, not a series of gasps. He enlarges the line's capacity by infinitely varying the cadence.

Venus early reveals his power of 'disinfecting' themes. No poet of the time could have done it so charmingly. It has vividness, presence of flesh and blood, absence of shadow and dream, that no one would claim for Spenser. As evidence of genius and source of delight it is hard to put *Lucrece* on a level with *Venus*. It is a better school exercise but more of one. Lucrece is not individualized; even Shakespeare made her less of a person than Venus or Adonis. No limit is possible to fanciful interpretations of the Sonnets, but it is rash to assume that they were literary exercises. Sidney Lee proves the majority of sonnet phrases, &c., to be conventional, but all poetry deals more or less in common form. The poet's essence is to make the common as if not common. No one questions Shakespeare's dramatic faculty; but could he create and keep up such a presentation of apparently authentic and personal passion? Intense feeling combined with the most energetic dramatic quality would induce complicated disguise and mystification in details of presentment. We see how the power, turned into other and freer channels, would set the plays a-working. The sonnets' attraction consists in subduing all—verse, thought, diction—to the requirements of absolutely perfect poetic expression. They are the absolute high-water-mark of poetry for those who believe that poetry less consists in selection of subject than fashion of handling the subject chosen. . . .

Professor Saintsbury's mind bears easily its immense weight of learning; it hinders in no way his power of seeing directly into the heart of the matter he discusses, and it frees him from any kind of nervousness in dealing once more with the most overworked critical subject in the world. To this we owe his remarks on *A. Y.L.*, on the characters of *Hamlet*, on Shakespeare's contribution to the chronicle play, on the non-Falstaff parts of the *Wives*, on *T. and C.* and *Cymbeline.* He says most subtly that *Richard III* is full of life, and has nothing of Marlowe's peculiar dream quality; but otherwise we detect in Professor Saintsbury's criticism a certain lack of subtlety—the defect of his quality of instant, direct vision. This appears in his manner of attributing *Titus* to Shakespeare, his remarks on Helena, on Falstaff of the *Wives*, on the Duke of *M. for M.*, on Henry V, on the greatness of Coriolanus, on the suspicions of Iago, his comparison of Hamlet and Macbeth, his censure of Hermione and Perdita, his conviction that Shakespeare spoke through Prospero. Indeed, the remarks on Helena and comparison with Cleopatra have a quality that we have described as 'American'. Perhaps he is most informing when he uses the test of verse to decide the period of Shakespeare's life to which a play belongs; and no doubt one of his best judgements—on *A. and C.*—was stimulated by the incomparable verse. For the same reason, the discussion of the Sonnets is the fairest and most satisfying that has yet emerged.

There are some writers, at the head of whom stands Milton, who do not meet their readers on equal terms—and among them is Professor Saintsbury. He is not rude to us like Swinburne; we do not stand abashed in his presence as with Mr. Arthur Symons; but we dispute with him with the greatest diffidence, as with our schoolmaster. As we frame our objections we imagine him blowing them into air with a Homeric laugh—a hearty, as well as ironic, laugh, for there is nothing ill-natured about Professor Saintsbury. If then he appears at times like a schoolmaster, he is the friendly schoolmaster: and a most delightful friend the schoolmaster can be.

In Professor Saintsbury's essay, *Shakespeare and the Grand Style*,[1] he is again at his best. Arnold insisted on high seriousness; but he defines it more widely as the perfection of expression in every direction

[1] English Association. Oxford University Press, 1910.

and kind, acquiring force enough to transmute the subject and transport the reader. Shakespeare can produce more constant, varied, and magnificent instances than any other poet of the kind which appears when needed. Even in his novitiate he can command it: and we are given instances from *Titus, Errors, Verona, L.L.L.* But he is perfectly ready not to use it: unlike Milton who wore his Grand Style as a continental officer wears his uniform, and at the cost of enormous *tour de force* of mannerism, Shakespeare can produce it with five repetitions of 'never' (*Lear*), or a miracle of negative expression, 'The rest is silence' (*Hamlet*). He seems to have deliberately determined that no special mould, no particular tool, no recipe, should be pointed out as his secret of attaining grandeur. He simply uses the grand style as his attendant spirit. . . .

Professor Saintsbury compares Shakespeare's style with that of Homer, Dante, and Milton, and makes us feel that behind Shakespeare's was a special reserve of power. We are frequently told that Shakespeare is the greatest world-poet: he makes this general statement a little more definite.

III

AS psycho-analysis is a subject that interests we will give a summary of Dr. Ernest Jones's pamphlet,[1] but will attempt no comment beyond pointing out the arguments for and against. The first is that at least it covers all the facts—the second, that for one fact, psycho-analysis has a hundred theories.

An artist ignores the source of what he wishes to express. Freud says that creative output is sublimated manifestation of repressed wishes. Shakespeare, without conscious tendency, described human conduct directly as he observed it. The cause of general weakening in energy is due to the functioning of abnormal unconscious complexes. Apart from his task Hamlet can act decisively. The picture is of a strong man tortured by some mysterious inhibition. It must be that at heart he does not wish to carry out the task. He does not know why he revolts from it: here we approach the core of the mystery. Psychoanalysis proves that mental trends hidden from the subject himself may be discovered by the trained observer. But the play produces effect because it finds an echo in the hearer's mind.

Hero, poet, audience are moved by unknown feelings. We can safely dismiss all Hamlet's alleged motives: at the thought of Hecuba he arraigns himself in words which dispose of the view that he doubted where his duty lay. What is his hidden motive for shirking the task? Those mental processes are most 'repressed' which the society by which a person is influenced most disapproves. The 'natural instincts' are those repressed, and chiefly the psycho-sexual trends, because on

[1] *The Oedipus-Complex as an Explanation of Hamlet's Mystery,* 1910.

these the herd lays its heaviest ban. Therefore the more intense and obscure is a given case of deep mental conflict, the more certainly will it be found to centre about a sexual problem. The positive striving for revenge to Hamlet is a moral and social one; the suppressed negative striving against revenge arose in some hidden source connected with his more personal 'natural' instincts.

His uncle had committed both murder and incest. Before he knows of the murder he is deeply depressed. His mother's second marriage must have awakened some slumbering memory which is so painful that it may not become conscious: as though he had found it hard to share his mother's affection even with his father. When his father dies the memories he had repressed would become active. In childhood jealousy is closely related to desire to remove a rival by death. A child regards encroachments on its privileges as meaningless cruelty; and as to death, it only realizes a person is no longer there. A boy resents when his father disturbs his enjoyment of his mother's affection. It is the deepest source of the world-old conflict between father and son— and Freud first showed that it rested on sexual grounds.

In Hamlet's early affection for his mother there was a dimly defined erotic element—corroborated by her sensual nature and passionate fondness for him. On his father's death he sees some one—and some one of the same family—usurping the place as he had once longed to do. Then comes the news of the murder—and his second guilty wish is realized by his uncle, to procure fulfilment of the first. In his unconscious fantasy the death of his father and remarriage of his mother had for years been closely associated. He therefore hates his uncle as one evil-doer hates his successful fellow. He cannot denounce him as he does his mother; to do so would stir up his own unconscious and repressed complexes. He disobeys the call of duty to slay his uncle because it is linked with the call of nature to slay his mother's husband. The dammed-up feeling causes irascibility, and also physical disgust. Paralysis arises from fear—common to all—to explore his inner mind.

IV

THE criticism of Mr. John Masefield[1] resembles that of Mr. Yeats in being strictly that of a poet. He contributes something to Shakespeare's method of treating the passions, evolved out of his own poetically meditative mind. He uses his own poetic experience to interpret a part of Shakespeare's genius.

In his opening remarks on Shakespeare himself he says that work so calm can only have come from a happy nature happily fated; that he was a shrewd man of affairs, and like all wise men cared for rank and an honourable state. The plot of *L. L. L.* intends to show intellect turned from high resolve by the coming of women who represent

[1] *Wm. Sh.*, 1911 (Williams & Norgate).

natural intelligence. Later it is betrayed indirectly by women, but more by the sexual emotions which idealize the most worthless women. The play seems to free Shakespeare's mind from doubts as to the right use and preparation of intellect. The conclusion is that poetry is not given to trained or untrained minds, but to the quick and noble nature earnest with passion. Shakespeare wrote about life and must therefore accept it for what it is—a largely animal thing. *Verona* shows a troubled mind and the same mood as the Sonnets. In *L.L.L.* only fantastic vows are broken; here is the first idea that treachery caused by some obsession is at the root of most tragedy, which remained the pole-star of his dramatic action. Strength of will blinded is the commonest cause of treachery. Only the *Errors* among the plays lacks a deep philosophical idea. Adriana's speech is unendurably real, and such reality is the only cure for obsession.

In *1 Henry VI* Shakespeare's hand appears in Act II, over which a big tragic purpose broods. He could not have planned a play where the moral idea is a trapping to physical action. He worked to revise Part II with a big tragic conception. It lacks the final writing that turns imagination to vision. The Simpcox and Cade scenes have more sadness and horror of heart than humour. He added little to Part III —but the idea that mercy has no place in war. The idea of *M.N.D.* is that those blinded by the obsessions of passion are made so at the whim of a power outside life, and that accidents of life, bad seasons, personal deformities, &c., are due to something unhappy in a capricious immortal world, careless of this world but easily offended and appeased by mortal action. The obsession of *R. and J.* is the blind and raging one of sudden, gratified youthful love. It ends family affection, and makes a sweet-natured girl a deceitful, scheming liar. It causes five violent deaths and a legacy of broken-heartedness. The blood of those killed in the feud cries out for the folly to stop that life might be lived. What had Tybalt and Mercutio to do with death? The Nurse is tragical—and it is most sad to see the fine soul turning to the vulgar in need. Still sadder is it to see wisdom failing to stop tragedy through hotness of blood and unhappy chance. If Shakespeare's self is in any character it must be in those whose wisdom is like the many-coloured wisdom that gives the play their unity. He is in calm, wise, gentle people, like Friar Laurence, who speaks largely from a vision detached from the world.

A number of people with obsessions illustrate the idea of treachery in *John*. Throughout the histories Shakespeare broods on the idea that our tragical kings failed because they did not conform to a type lower than themselves. Henry V conforms to type and succeeds: not Henry VI who is a Christian mystic. John does not conform to type; his intellect is bigger than his capacity for affairs. He cannot conform to the standard of his own ideas; his nature is unequal to the promptings of his intellect. To persist in any one course of treachery would make him great. *Richard II* illustrates the treachery of a king to a king's duty, and a subject to a subject's duty. He fails because he is not common: and the world calls for rough common virtue. Bolingbroke only cares for justice; and the clash is between the common and uncommon man. Life has made Richard king, and is as much to blame for the tragedy as temperament. *Richard III* deals with the coming of that justice which life renders at last—even if to the dead or mad or broken. Blood foully shed cries from the ground, and the human soul wrought to an ecstasy has power to draw God's hand on the guilty. Also self-confident intellect is terrible and tragical, and life will avenge the sin of being certain—the obsession of self-confidence. Only Richard triumphs by moving by a light other than his own. He knows the world stays as it is from something stupid in the milky human feelings. Part of the tragedy is that Richard is nobler than the sheep he destroys. A great intellect is embittered because cased in deformities—the tragedy of intellect turned on itself. Also is it partly tragical that not intellect triumphs, but the stupid though righteous something that cannot understand intellect.

Antonio is obsessed by tenderness for his friend—Shylock by lust to uphold intellect in a thoughtless world that makes intellect bitter in every age. One Gentile beguiles his daughter and teaches her to rob him; another signs a mad bond to help an extravagant friend to live in idleness. Half the evils in life come from the partial vision of people in states of obsession. Shakespeare in the *Shrew* indicates the tragedy of a manly spirit born into a woman's body. She is humbled into a state of submissive wifely falsehood by a boor, who cares only for his own will, her flesh, and her money. Henry IV has become a swollen, soured, bullying man. Hotspur is opposed to the rough stupid something that makes up the bulk of the world. The Prince is neither thinker, hero, friend. Shakespeare was too wise to count any man a hero; he saw the sun shining on just and unjust, no less golden though soul like clay triumph over soul like flame. The Prince is a common man, who cannot feel, so can change his habits as interest bids him. He is callous at first if he breaks his father's heart, and has no sincerity or good nature. The interest of Falstaff is that he is base because he is wise. The king when dying knows the bloodshed was vain, and that his successor will toss away the power. Life was never so brooded on since man learned to think, as in this cycle of tragedies. Henry IV fails in the hour of triumph from his manifold failures in life during his struggle for triumph; and Falstaff fails in the same way. The prize is to the careless, callous man, and no two scenes are more awful than Lancaster's treachery and the rejection of Falstaff. Henry V is the popular hero, as common as those who love him.[1] He

[1] Cf. Yeats.

has the knack of life that fits human affairs for all that is animal in them. Courage tempered by stupidity is what he loves in man. The *Wives* is full of external energy. Shakespeare has now worked out his natural instincts, the life known to him, his predilections, his reading. He was at the moment which separates the contemplative from the visionary, the good from the excellent, the great from the supreme.

Life does not interest Jaques (*A.Y.L.*); his interest is in his thoughts about life. Like all wise men he thinks that wisdom, being always a little beyond the world, has no worldly machinery by which it can express itself. In this world the fool is chorus and interpreter, and Jaques the wise finds his place occupied by one whose comment is platitude. *M. Ado* shows report to be stronger than any human affection or acquired quality. It belongs to the greatest creative period where every person is passionately alive about something. *Twelfth-Night* is the happiest play and one of the loveliest, where mirth is mixed with romantic beauty. Three souls suffer from the sickly vanity that feeds on day-dreams. Orsino's mood of emotion is unreal, because love is active. Olivia's mood of mourning is unreal, and Malvolio thinks ceremony the whole of life. Over-delicate life is decay, reality is the only cure. Olivia is roused through some one who despises her —Malvolio because other minds have seen his. But all three cease to be interesting, beautiful, pathetic. The obsession of *All's Well* is removed by making plain to the obsessed by pitiless judicial logic the ugliness of the treachery it causes. Bertram's rage becomes obsession that blinds his judgement. Helena, obsessed by love, is blind to the results of her actions. She practises a borrowed art for a selfish end.

J.C. is the first of the supreme plays, but Shakespeare was not particularly interested in the victim. Caesar was a touchy man of affairs whose head was turned. The subject was the working of Fate which prompts to murder, uses the murderer, and then destroys him. *Hamlet* is the tragedy of a man and an action continually baffled by wisdom. The action consists in the baffling of life's effort to get back to her course, because the instrument chosen is a little outside life— as the wise must be. The result is arrest of life and deadlock. The world in which Hamlet must act is governed by the enemies of intellect, the image of the world as intellect is made to feel it. Justice to a wise man is more a scrupulous quality in the mind than the doing of expedient acts on sinners. Hamlet's mind is nicely balanced, which gives to all that he says the double-edge of wisdom. He knows the sword will not reach the real man, since damnation comes from within. When life is wrenched from its course it must either be wrenched back or kept violently there. When he decides there is to be no wrenching back, his destroying wisdom decides that it shall not be kept in a strange channel. The two extremes in him of slowness and swiftness set up in life the counter-forces which destroy extremes, so that life the common thing may continue to be common. Hamlet's mercy leaves the King free to plot his death; his swiftness gives the King a hand and sword to work his will. *T. and C.* was hurriedly written, is undramatic, and lacks wit and beauty. The two or three finished scenes are among Shakespeare's grandest—in thought, not action. The setting is above the subject, and Shakespeare's mind wandered from Troilus and Cressida to brood on Helen's obsession that betrayed Troy. *M. for M.* is one of the greatest works of the greatest English mind. Shakespeare saw common prudential virtues sometimes due not to virtue, but starvation of nature. Chastity may proceed from meanness, coldness, cowardice. Both Angelo and Isabella have obsessions and exalt part of life above life. The play shows the difficulty of doing justice in a world of animals swayed by rumour. Like all the greatest plays it is so full of the illustration of the main idea as to give the illusion of infinity like life. The thought is more penetrating than impassioned.

The same ideas govern *Othello*: life seeking to preserve balance, and obsessions which upset it betraying life to evil. As in the *Merchant* the chief character is a man of intellect warped out of humanity by the world's injustice. Iago is as mysterious as life; he has a fine natural intellect, but it is superseded by the educated man. Shakespeare brooded on the power of warped intellect to destroy generous life, as in *Richard III* and the *Merchant*; he looked at life clearly and was baffled by what he saw. In *Lear* we see that man is only safe when his mind is perfectly just and calm. Any injustice, trouble, hunger in the mind deliver man to powers that restore calmness and justice by means violent or gentle according to the strength of the disturbing obsession. It is unnatural that Lear should give his kingship to women and curse Cordelia, that Gloucester should make much of his bastard son, that Lear and Gloucester should believe evil suddenly of the best beloved and most faithful spirits in the play. Fate's working to restore the balance is equally violent and unnatural. Had Kent at first been milder and Albany blunter, it would have spared the unnatural treacherous evil that comes to pass because for a few fatal moments they were true to their natures. On the excessive terrible soul of Lear Shakespeare pours such misery that the cracking of the great heart is a thing of joy. Macbeth interprets with his worldly mind things spiritually suggested to him. He looks on the letter of the prophecy till it becomes an obsession. At first we feel less horror than unbearable pity for his mind, but horror comes later when crime spreads. The private action of *A. and C.* is played out before a grand public setting. The man of large and generous nature is hounded down by the man of intellect. The obsession of lust results in treachery and tragedy. A cruel bungling suicide leaves him lingering in dishonour. This is Antony—this mutterer dying—whom no one loves enough to kill. *Coriolanus* shows that

Nature will check the excessive to maintain the type, and progress must be of the whole mass. In *Timon* we see how ingratitude, the commonest form of treachery, leads quickest to the putting back of the world because it destroys generosity of mind. It is called gloomy, but a great mind working with such glory of energy cannot be gloomy.

Craft working on want of faith for personal ends is defeated by the simple and instinctive in human nature (*Cymbeline*). The subject is only partly extricated and the treatment coloured with romance. Something fine is trying but failing to get free. In the *W. Tale* Shakespeare saw blindness suddenly falling on a person can alter life violently—and he believed that life must not be altered violently. We get the results of human blindness on human destiny. The greater plays are studies of treachery and self-betrayal—this of deceit and self-deception. Leontes is deceived by his obsession, Polixenes by his son, the countrymen by Autolycus, life by art. True friendship is mistaken for false love. It is the gentlest of plays, and the strange tenderness makes some scenes in Act V passionate with grief for old injustice done to the dead. Remorse is a romantic, not a tragic, passion, the mood which follows the tragic mood. The betrayed of the *Tempest* live to forgive the traitors. Shakespeare treats the power of the resolved imagination to command the brutish, base, noble, spiritual for wise human ends.

In *Venus* evil comes of obsession. *Lucrece* describes the results of a treachery inspired by an obsession. The Sonnets are personal poems written in many moods to more than one person. Men with imagination enjoy sweeter and closer friendships than the many know. The many, mulish as ever, therefore imagine evil. Until we can identify the persons we had best accept them as beautiful poems. . . .

Mr. Masefield's criticism casts a deep subjective shadow over the Shakespearian landscape. He is not subjective in the narrow sense, but rather he is the poet's critic; he writes for those who have become interested, through meditation, in finer and subtler feelings. He is not interested in the preliminaries of Shakespeare's art—the sources of the plots, the requirements of the stage, the restraints of history, but in what is left when these have lifted like so many veils—the experience of the human soul. His business is with the passions, and it remains to decide where his mind has worked true, or where we suspect his earthly presence in the intellectual scale—as Aeneas weighed down the bark of Charon and admitted the marsh. He writes like one who cannot suffer Philistinism—and when anything in a character suggests this quality his aesthetic balance is disturbed.

In the latter case we note how he condemns Henry V in over-strong language, much as did Mr. Yeats; and in his respect for 'intellect' he is inclined to palliate the faults of Richard III, Shylock, Iago. Likewise, is it fair to include the epithet 'bullying' among

those which describe Henry IV?—though we admit that note is
heard in his peremptory order to Hotspur to yield his prisoners. But
there is a middle region with Mr. Masefield, where he interprets
Shakespeare correctly but over-stresses him, so that we know not in
what proportion to derive the interest from Shakespeare himself or
his critic. Instances of this are the 'sadness and horror' which he reads
into the Simpcox and Jack Cade scenes (*Henry VI*); the tragical
Nurse (*R. and J.*); the 'excessive' and 'terrible' soul of Lear; the rejection of Falstaff 'awful' as Lancaster's treachery. The last is certainly
a ghastly thing—but otherwise we are reminded of the Greek
Plutarch's personal recoil from the 'terrible' Roman Triumph. Where
he excels is in showing the enduring effects of passion and the mysterious relations between those who have died from it with the living
occupants of the world—as with *R. and J.* His reason why Hamlet
spares the king at prayer is one of the best things written on that
vexed subject. He sees through John, he is suggestive with Iago—
'mysterious as life itself'—but is disappointing with Antony in the
moment of death. He shows the poet's longing for an earthly paradise:
the object of the powers above the world is to restore calm, though by
violent means. Perhaps he is at his best in the *W. Tale*, where the
anger of Leontes is forgotten in the last beautiful impression. But his
most original discovery is that interest departs from the Duke, Olivia,
and Malvolio after their respective crises. How would Henry James
have treated this situation?

V

THE work of Darrell Figgis[1] is subtle and inward, yet his book
stimulates more as we read it than when we look back upon it. He
rather grasps the Shakespearian mystery and then lets it go, for his conclusions are not unlike those of others. For instance, his thoughts on
Shakespeare's personality, though fetched from a greater depth,
resemble those of Mr. Frank Harris.

The Elizabethan stage, surrounded on three sides by spectators,
enabled the actor to speak poetry more naturally. Poetry is the most
intimate of all things, the confidence of soul to soul, and it therefore
creates the illusion in the actual minds of the audience. In all art there
is one unity only—effect. Before writing his play Shakespeare would
imagine its various scenes, always with his stage before his mind's eye.
The natural movements of drama are Introduction, Action, Climax.
He made it stronger by dividing and distributing crisis and climax,
leading to concluding climax through a crisis that was an antithesis to
it. An illustration of this is the fourth act of *Hamlet* where Laertes
rises up as an avenger, so that Hamlet has two enemies. The histories
teach us little of Shakespeare the playwright searching for a vital

[1] *Sh.: A Study*, 1911 (Dent).

principle of construction. Yet there are traces, and even in *M.N.D.*
the antithetical principle is asserting itself on his instinct. Act III
concludes with sleeping lovers, and in Act IV appear Theseus and
Hippolyta, rapt from us since the Introduction. The drama does
not reproduce but transfigures life, and Shakespeare's characters
attained heroic stature. The ancients sought to express ideal life by
means of unity of Time and Space. Freed from mundane limitations
the spectator's mind could move unhampered through scenes of
death, life, love, passion, fate, beauty—the great realities of existence.
Illusion is Eternity translating itself in terms of Time—and we demand
illusion in the drama. Unlike the Greeks Shakespeare banished Time
and Space by not recognizing them. Athens and Alexandria were
never in the matter, but in the spectator's mind. He was not concerned
with construction as such, but his characters moulded the plot according
to their natures: whereas Ibsen's characters, though they live, are at
war against their author's architectonic desire. Hamlet is the great
example, yet even here at times one suspects some lack of agreement
in the perfect working of the machine. To this we owe the problem
of Hamlet, for more than once, when his irresolution is particularly
difficult to understand, there comes a hint that the plot is in danger
without such irresolution.

Art and craft are to be distinguished, and the poet has to reproduce
Nature, to re-create symbols to take their place beside the appearances
of Nature, as clues to colossal powers behind. Thus Shakespeare's
sunrises suggest thoughts of eternity and wake our divine hunger. In
Hamlet, before the ghost appears, the remarks on the cold air strangely
pent with emotion help to attune us to sympathy with the action.
Drama conveys happenings to the mind, and as the medium is words
they must be charged with metaphor. As it deals with life's great
moments, with men at their greatest, noblest, terriblest moments, not
with sordid realism but with reality, speech must correspond. Shakespeare therefore wrote in verse, but he alternated with prose according
to the tension. The Nunnery scene in *Hamlet* most reveals how his
exquisite adjustment of prose and verse truly expresses the realities of
the minds at work. Falstaff of the *Wives* loses his splendour because
of the *suspicion* of a deeper interest. Diction is of prime interest because
words express the drama: and here Ibsen fails because his characters
speak prose and he can only reach poetry through symbolism. The
drama requires that the actual be directly presented—though there
is symbolism in Shakespeare, as when Hamlet is futile through his
virtues. The basis of man's life is emotion, and with this the drama is
concerned. Poetry is the obvious speech of emotion, and Shakespeare
was right to conceive of the drama poetically. His poetic characters
are always dramatic, his prose characters seldom. Falstaff is not really
dramatic, but interests like a jolly interlude. In the *Wives* he is more

dramatic and less Falstaff. Shakespeare deftly distributed undramatic matter through tense dramatic interest, and strengthened it by varying the pace. Lear, Hamlet, Macbeth, Romeo, and Juliet would not be the same persons in prose. Shakespeare conceived in poetry or prose, Ben Jonson only in prose, and then translated. Hamlet was not mad but mentally overburdened, and the cause, as always with Shakespeare's men, was overwrought emotions. His perplexity dated from the fineness of his susceptibilities. He spares the king at prayer because to kill him prematurely might frustrate his second object—to discover whether or not his mother was innocent. Thus the play is intelligible when we regard the crucial part from the standpoint of his emotion. When he recollects his actions the emotion has passed away and only the discrepancies appear. This process is repeated when Shakespeare's plays, that are compact of emotion, are intellectually criticized—e.g. that time lacks in *Othello* for Cassio to become intimate with Desdemona. The fourth act of *Othello* contains no antithetical movement lest Iago should fail to keep Othello at full heat of passion. In *All's Well* the volume of emotion mocks the intellectual artifice of the comedy and ruins the play. The destiny of comic characters lies outside themselves; they must be subdued to certain requirements, because a strong emotional concatenation—as in tragedy—would pluck destiny away from artificial conception. Comedy can just subdue Hero, but neither Helena nor Isabella. The Romances were tragedy, at the end of which Fortune graciously interposed.

Shakespeare's tragedy is a supreme paradox. *R. and J.* is calamitous, not baffling; the later plays are situations, where the tragedy lies in terrible conjunction of characters. Perplexity is supreme when virtue, not vice, causes ruin; it is honourable sensitiveness that ruins Hamlet. If we compare Hamlet and Othello in each other's position we see how the several situations would never have arisen. Through the histories one can trace Shakespeare's belief in fate, and he finds that the wave of destiny was set flowing by Richard II—one whose graces become vices. Mutation and permutation preoccupied Shakespeare; he wished to 'read the book of fate'. But he did not pretend to unravel the secrets of the Almighty, he concerned himself with the counsels when they worked themselves out in the ways of men. Now and then he thinks past men to God—as in Henry V's wooing, the result of which is the weakling who loses France. *L.L.L.* shows how Academies fail when we contend with the powers that urge the cosmic destiny. The tragedy of *R. and J.* is not inevitable, but due to accident; it is self-contained. Our minds are oppressed by the thought of sardonic spirits hovering round luckless mortals and defeating their plans: and here is the connexion with *M.N.D.* The action of *R. and J.* is constantly interfered with by Divinity, so the play is concluded within itself, and the interest not projected into the infinite Beyond, as in *Lear*.

The change had to be that Divinity and action should be separate, lest misfortune in one should seem malice in the other. Don John's villainy (*M. Ado*) is Shakespeare's first farewell to the old order, to mechanical identity of Divinity and action. The future is with human purposes and characters, and the Divinity is in the type of play. For the present it is comedy, where the place of Divinity is at the end, but he comes to hold it precariously, and must soon be thrust forward by the swelling strength of the characters and driven from his post at the end of the five acts to some position in the further Beyond. *J.C.* is a transition play that gives both, but in *Hamlet* there is no vestige of present settlement. *M. for M.* is tragedy arbitrarily turned to comedy; the characters drop their destinies and become puppets. Action is now the allegory of life, as drama should be. Desdemona is crushed, but we doubt not that Divinity rules the play. We esteem her, not Iago—as we do Hamlet, not Claudius. We do not actually see Macbeth die, for then we should see Divinity standing within the play; but his words, 'To-morrow and to-morrow . . .', with their utter world-weariness, grip our sympathy more effectually and project the interest more surely beyond. Potential nobility ruins Hamlet, Othello, Lear; but Macbeth fails through crime, Antony through viciousness, Coriolanus through haughtiness. There is something of present judgement in the end of the latter three, but it is not the whole solution: and now we see the connexion with Shakespeare's last period where the Divinity has its representative in the very action. It appears a character so richly forgiving and so perfect that only the word Divine suits the occasion.

That Shakespeare gives no sharply defined philosophy of the universe proves that he was of a nature opposed to a hard dogmatism of thought. Throughout his great tragic period he shows nausea and abhorrence towards the sex-question; but in his last period he exalts women. These are attributes that reveal a personality; they show he was extremely sensitive to the subject of sex. He makes the characters fail whom he must have loved, so there was something severe and inexorable in him. We do wrong to over-emphasize his material success; his great tragedies cannot have been bids for remuneration. Hamlet's directions to the players are Shakespeare himself, and show that his first concern was to achieve an art worthy of himself. Even if the Sonnets were conceits, the same expression from the author of *Lear* would mean more than from Drayton or Daniel. He responds sensitively to influence and environment: when he regards the suffering poor in *Lear* he is angry and bitter; when confronted with their bodily presence he is offended at their atmosphere. He put much of himself into Romeo and Hamlet—in whom with all their fine traits there is something ruthless—and, in his gentler mood, into Prospero. But when Hamlet handles Polonius we feel that so would Falstaff after his rejection have searched the secrets out of men. The answer to the question how Shakespeare developed in this singular way—from Romeo to Hamlet and Prospero—and through Falstaff to Jaques—is in the Sonnets. The story is unpleasant and so unlikely to be used as fiction. The friend seduces the mistress, and this revolts his whole being. After the treason, Romeo and Falstaff give place to Jaques, and when the reflective cycle is completed, to Hamlet. The incest of which Hamlet accuses his mother is an echo of that intimate relation between friend and mistress. The dark mistress appears in the re-written *L.L.L.*, and the sex-storm rages through the tragedies till it wears itself out, and the last plays show recovery of soul. Shakespeare was a large and wasteful worker, averse to care for detail; the concen-tration which he needed was supplied by his private tragedy. . . .

Figgis does well to remind us forcibly that emotion is the common basis of life and drama, that poetry is the most intimate of all things, and that the final issue is with the mind of the spectator. He also brings home to us the true function of the fourth act which some critics have found to drag. He is most original in his remarks on unity and contrast of Shakespeare and the ancients. Other critics have remarked that unity is no mechanical rule but a need of human nature—but he has proved it. Otherwise it is the steps of the argument rather than the argument itself that appeal to us. We accept him as guide through the labyrinth, but he excels in engrossing us as he leads us rather than reaching a new point. Such are his remarks—most original in the telling, but less so when all is told—about the place of Divinity in comedy and tragedy: yet it is true to say that when he touches Romance the thought is so perfectly expressed that it informs as well as stimu-lates. It has already been suggested that his thoughts on Shakespeare himself resemble those of Mr. Frank Harris.

VI

AND this fitly introduces Mr. Harris's second book [1] where he repeats his former arguments, but makes them turn on Shakespeare's relations to women. He says that there were four women who influenced Shakespeare—mother, wife, mistress, daughter. In his early plays he knew little of women: they were historical or traditional lay figures—Venus, Lucrece, Margaret. Suddenly appears an angry woman—Adriana—painted by shadows or faults and showing personal feeling—Shakespeare's wife eight years older than himself, whom he had been forced to marry. She is out of place in a farce of mistaken identity; no jealous woman would mention her age as she does; she excuses her 'dull discourses' and 'barren wit'—Shakespeare's charges against his wife all naïvely out of character. His vanity was wounded by his marriage; he was beaten in the sordid strife and forced to fly,

[1] *The Women of Sh.*, 1911 (Methuen).

but the scene of the wooing of Lady Anne proves that he still held man the master and harped on the thought to strengthen his belief. The *Shrew* was also a salve to wounded vanity, and her final lecture is most foolish. *John* belongs to 1596 when he revisited Stratford after eight or nine years, just after his son died. He makes Constance a termagant without cause because he had just seen his wife and cannot help it; but as soon as she thinks of her son her voice takes the true accent of regret.

In the second period he shows us girls running after men. He had succeeded brilliantly in London, and no doubt love had been offered to him on every side. Of Hermia and Helena at first we only know that they are both in love; they are not differentiated until the quarrel scene. But Julia was painted with astonishing realism and decision; she is the first sketch of Shakespeare's great love—twin sister to Juliet and reminding one of Portia. Juliet is the finest woman's portrait that poet ever painted—Antigone is an outline, Gretchen a sketch, by comparison. And the charm of Juliet is that her character is fused in the furnace of a first passion. He then only knew Mary Fitton slightly, so he painted her outside in Rosaline, and gave Juliet the spirit qualities that he believed to exist in her. It explains the extravagant sensuality of all Shakespeare's pet heroines. There are two sorts of portraits that accord with his mood—the happy and idealistic, and the proud, false, and sensual. He created half a dozen characters out of a few features; but most readers and critics are blinded by names and do not recognize the same person in Hamlet and Macbeth. Portia has no one quality that would be out of character with Julia. To be quite honest, Portia is infinitely less complex than Charles Reade's Margaret; her beauty and magic are in Shakespeare's poetry, not in his revelation of her character. She has no faults and is therefore unreal. Mary Fitton's lecherous, change-loving temperament, the natural complement of Portia's passionate sensuality and love of suggestive talk, is not only ignored, but transmuted into tender loyalty and devotion. Beatrice is created from Portia's wit and vivacity; Rosalind from her love and tenderness, with touches of archness added.

Mary Fitton changed the world for Shakespeare, and though he soon found out that she was a wanton, it intensified his passion. In Rosaline of the revised *L.L.L.* (1597) there are a hundred astonishing traits. Bodily and spiritual identification are alike complete; no other character is painted with this photographic exactitude. Shakespeare's passion must have reached the intensity of the sex duel. It was then the fashion for poets to praise red hair and fair complexion as compliments to the Queen—but Shakespeare says black surpasses red —uncharacteristically, because he was most subservient to rank and authority. In the Sonnets there is no disguise, and he speaks soul to

soul. His friendship for William Herbert, who betrayed him, has been
much exaggerated and was based more upon respect for rank. He never,
forgot his art when writing to the youth; when writing to the woman
he was not artist but lover. *All's Well* gives clear portraits of Mary
Fitton and Herbert. Helena is supposed to be a pure maiden, yet she
speaks most coarsely, and confesses her love in a most unrestrained
manner. Bertram's unnecessary rudeness makes one identify him with
Herbert; it is exaggerated beyond the needs of the play and consistent
with the history of his character and relations with Mary Fitton.
Helena's final stratagem is more revolting than her plot to make him
her husband. The whole story was unsuited to the character of a young
girl, but it satisfied some personal need of self-expression with Shakespeare. We see his opinion of Herbert, whom he forces us to detest,
contrary to his usual custom with his heroes. The needless contradictions betray personal feeling. He had no reason to change in the
end, and the mature Shakespeare does not blunder thus crudely.
His confession that he had possessed Diana-Helena was unnecessary;
it must therefore be Shakespeare telling us the actual truth about the
connexion between Herbert and Mary Fitton. Whenever Shakespeare is excited by personal feeling he spills himself into this or that
character almost indifferently.

All Shakespeare's great tragedies were phases of his insensate passion
for this one woman. At first he is realistic and idealistic, later he
becomes slanderer and caricaturist. Mary Fitton made him long for
purity and love, and he created Ophelia, Desdemona, Cordelia—
abstractions of patience and affection. No son ever felt a mother's
unfaith like Hamlet: but Shakespeare is thinking of Mary Fitton's
faithless lechery. When he compares the two kings he is thinking of
Herbert's high rank, and limits the superiority to 'natural' gifts. The
scenes with Ophelia are not half realized: yet love should be stronger
than jealousy of one's mother. He makes Ophelia talk obscenely because
he is obsessed with erotic mania. He wished to revenge himself on
Herbert, but knew that his position shielded him. Othello's jealousy
is almost inevitable, and he is the mouthpiece of Shakespeare's own
passion. Othello, Posthumus, Hamlet, Leontes, all picture the act
and excite themselves to mad rage by their own imagining. Like an
Englishman, Othello will kill Desdemona with the sword of 'justice'
Lear and *Timon* are like steps leading down into the dark places of
desire and despair. Shakespeare exaggerates Lear's foolish trust to
deepen the pathos of his disproportionate punishment. Every person
talks bawdry though it has nothing to do with the action and is out
of keeping with such a serious tragedy. Lear—Shakespeare's intense
passion springs from erotic mania, and the consciousness that he
is growing too old for love's lists. The undramatic monotony
of *Timon* is due to his exceeding bitterness of soul. Timon's men

friends betray him, but he rails at women. Herbert is painted fairly as
Alcibiades.

Next to *Timon*, *T. and C.* is Shakespeare's bitterest play. Besides
Mary Fitton's unfaith, Chapman's rivalry had embittered him.
Chapman was a pedant who had glorified the Greeks, so Shakespeare
jeers at them. Cressida again is a dark beauty with astonishing wit,
who talks lewdly. The speech, 'I am giddy . . .', is Shakespeare's
supremest utterance of passion. Sonnet 23 gives the same desire and
dread. No reason is given for Cressida's faithlessness, and Shakespeare's
lust and jealousy rages in every word of Ulysses' condemnation of her.
In *A. and C.* Shakespeare gives us the greatest woman portrait ever
painted; but action was remote from his nature, so he succeeds in
depicting Antony as a lover, but not as captain. The soldierly achievements which he attributes to him from Plutarch merely obscure his
character. But Shakespeare paints himself as the ideal lover with the
best tongue in the world. 'I found you as a morsel . . .' is the truth
at last about Mary Fitton, but all this insane jealousy is the obverse
and intense desire. Antony—Shakespeare has lost everything, including honour, yet finds treasure in the richness of his soul. His conduct
to Enobarbus shows him the gentlest, wisest soul that ever revealed
its sweetness in literature; but the Roman general's armour suits
Shakespeare ill, and so Antony's last words are true to the Roman, but
not to the poet. Cleopatra's death redeems her, and we forget the
wanton blood in the 'immortal longings'. Two groups of qualities in
Mary Fitton struck Shakespeare—her cunning pretence of restraint
gilding utter wantonness—and her dominant personality armed with
quick wit and quicker temper. He usually stresses one set.

Coriolanus again shows that Shakespeare could not depict a man of
action. He exaggerates his faults and makes a braggart of him. He
worsens Plutarch's character, and so reveals his own snobbishness—
as he did in that scene in the *Merchant* where young noblemen insult
the fallen Shylock. The interest centres in mother and son, and the
mother's greater influence than the wife's, though derived from
Plutarch, is emphasized. Shakespeare's mother died in 1608, shortly
before this play was written; and Coriolanus praises Volumnia, as
though she were dead. 'Thou hast never in thy life . . .' is Shakespeare
in sorrow who feels he has not done enough—for Coriolanus has
shown every courtesy.

In 1608 Mary Fitton married for the second time and left Shakespeare for ever. He retired to Stratford a broken man, and was restored
by the care and tenderness of his young daughter. The new figure of
an innocent young girl now figures in all his plays. He did write the
greater part of *Pericles*; the master is on almost every page; e.g. the
melancholy of Pericles is as uncaused as that of Jaques, Hamlet,
Antonio. What proves personal feeling in the *W. Tale* is that in

Leontes he merely copies the jealousy of Hamlet and Othello. Perdita, like Mariana, has the same love of flowers and innate purity. But she is not individualized, and has no faults. Only passion can teach a man what a woman is. Neither does the faultless Imogen live, but Shakespeare, as Posthumus, is stirred by memories of the old pain. He has thought over every fault a woman can possess. Miranda is all pity, love, humble courtesy—an ethereal shadow-shape. Prospero the magician confesses strangely that his daughter won him back to life and endurance.

All Shakespeare's mature work was coloured and inspired by his love; all his great tragedies were steeped in his insensate passion. He could not have written the four great tragedies without her, nor pictured Cressida nor Cleopatra. He might have been happier, but would never have reached such self-knowledge or attained such glory He was weaker and more yielding than the average man, near to the poet-priest: even his fools preach. He was more like our Lord than any other man; from the beginning he insisted on repentance and forgiveness. Despite his passion and failings he was the nearest the ideal of the singer-saint. . . .

Mr. Harris is sincere and therefore has power to convince up to a point, but when the first shock has subsided we return to our usual state of mind—that we know little of Shakespeare, and his theory does not fill the gap. We accept him in the same spirit as Thackeray's half-imaginary portraits of Addison and Steele in *Esmond* or Dr. Johnson in the *Virginians*. 'If it were true, how would our world be changed?' we ask: and this streak of light makes the darkness visible. At the best, Mr. Harris has not brought ready-made ideas to Shakespeare; it was study of the text that inspired his theory: but he is superficial. We utterly disagree that Shakespeare only drew one type of woman successfully, and that he fails with men of action. There is poetry in the depth of most men's souls, and it is the duty of penetrative imagination to reveal it: as Shakespeare does with Macbeth, Othello, Antony. Chatham had what Carlyle calls a beautiful strain of feminine, poetic delicacy, but he was a great man of action; and so was Canning, although he hesitated and blushed when he spoke in the House of Commons, and his love of fun stamped him as a trifler with solemn mediocrities. Mr. Harris forecasts ingeniously what might happen if literature were thinly veiled autobiography, and he is most convincing with *All's Well*—but he ignores that the small acorn of fact can produce the wide-branching oak of imagination. He is at his worst and crudest in *Coriolanus* where he compares Volumnia to Shakespeare's mother. He says that Desdemona, Perdita, Imogen, and other faultless heroines do not live. We deny it, and we re-read the plays a hundred times, whereas to read a few times Charles Reade, whom he contrasts, is to exhaust. Mr. Harris derides the 'Professor-Mandarins', but the 'man of the world' as such cannot solve the highest problems of literary criticism. It might be said that he belittles Shakespeare, but there are some fine sayings in his last chapter, 'Shakespeare, the Singer-Saint'.

VII

PROFESSOR STOLL opens his study of Shylock [1] by reminding us that we must think first of the artist's intention. A work of art referred only to the critic's personal impressions may mean anything, everything—that is, nothing—and it is little use to discuss it. It is possible to divine Shakespeare's intention; the study of Elizabethan ideas and technique reveals to us that he was not impartial and inscrutable. The exceptionally severe sentence on Shylock, including outrage to his faith—not to be found in any other version of the story —proves that Shakespeare did not favour him. The good characters, and indeed all who have dealings with him, speak against him, e.g. Antonio remarks that the devil can cite Scripture for his purpose. It is the same with the ordering of the scenes: reports of his villainy and absurdity are circulated—as in *Twelfth-Night,* where Maria announces to the audience how ridiculously Malvolio is acting. Thirdly, he himself avows his motives—and we can rely on what Shakespeare's villains say concerning their purposes to themselves or their confidants. Twice Shakespeare appears to sympathize with Shylock—'Hath a dog money?' 'Hath not a Jew eyes?'—but either plea ends in such a fashion as to alienate the audience; it becomes an excuse to indulge in revenge with all its rigours. Miser, money-lender, and Jew—three immemorial objects of hatred and ridicule—are united in one person. In other Elizabethan plays the Jew fares still worse. Shakespeare, most of poets, reflected the settled prejudices and passions of his race.

Some readers have resented that Shylock should be despoiled in the end, but, considering the treatment of the race lingering in men's memories, it is natural that Jessica should carry off his jewels and ducats, and the Duke should spare his life at the cost of all his goods. Coercion of unbelievers was also a recognized practice in the days when 'personal religion' was unknown. Had Shakespeare wished to make Shylock a serious and sympathetic figure, he would not have made him like those created by the prejudices in his day—avaricious, miserly, crafty, treacherous, hard-hearted, pitiless, blood-thirsty—a cur and devil, to be spurned and spat upon, despoiled and forcibly converted. In him as money-lender and Jew are embodied two of the deepest and most wildly prevalent social antipathies of 2,000 years, prevalent still, and in Shakespeare's day sanctioned by religion.

It has been attempted to represent Shylock as the product of his environment: but this does not accord with the thought of the time. Men believed in retribution, in heaven and hell, villains and heroes.

[1] 'Shylock', 1911 (*Sh. Studies,* New York, The Macmillan Co., 1927).

Shakespeare only forgives in comedy; he does not forgive Macbeth,
Othello, Richard III, Iago; he is on the side of Henry V who dismisses
his old associates. He treats the poor as they are—hard-hearted,
greasy, ignorant, ungrateful. He does not extenuate a scoundrel
because he is a bastard or low-born, but turns it to a reproach. If it
explains his depravity it does not explain it away, but sets the seal upon
it and confirms the prejudice, that noble and ignoble blood differ.
The tale of Shylock's indignities softens our heart but hardens the
Elizabethans'; it confirms the prejudice that Christian and Jew
differ. The point of view is that for everything there is some one to
blame—and no one more than he who has the worst of it.

The final problem is whether Shylock is a pathetic creation. The
interpretation of literature is mainly a study in emphasis—that is,
manipulation and arrangement, unification and subordination, repetition or contrast. Those who would make Shylock pathetic do so by
perverting the artist's chief means of expression—emphasis. They
lighten what is dark and stress what is important; and therefore make
both the author and his work irrelevant. In the second place it is said
that comedy often skirts tragedy. Yes, but such tragedy is of our
making, not the dramatist's. Under the comic spell we indulge in
laughter, not grief, not our sympathetic passions, but our social prejudices. When the change comes—as with considering Molière's
characters—we have passed from under the author's spell. The comic
dramatist, in the words of Bergson, isolates his material: a deceived
husband is an object of derision on the stage, from Aristophanes
onwards. Sympathy spoils sport, blights and kills comedy. On the
stage Shylock is a harsh father, miser, usurer, and Jew. Thirdly,
comedy assents to the customs and prejudices of the time. In Shakespeare's London there was no refined society or sensitive social
consciousness—but a vindictive social consciousness. Sir Toby and
his friends sport with Malvolio in torment; and Autolycus delights
the audience when he fleeces trusting souls. Singly as Jew, miser,
usurer, Shylock would repel the comedy; therefore in these roles
united how could he appear pathetic? Lastly, the Shylock scenes are
said to contain so much formal external comic technique that he may
be in part pathetic. To support this, critics have quoted his lament for
the jewels that belonged to his wife: but they err in viewing the text
piecemeal, and not as a whole. Now and then a phrase may seem
pathetic, but, on the whole, the daughter-ducats scene plays the familiar
dramatic trick of deceiving the audience for a moment and then clap-
ping on the pathetic sentiment one that is cynical, selfish, or incongruous.
Besides, the outcries of robbed misers have entertained 'hard-hearted'
audiences from the dawn of drama. Then there is the inversion, the
tables turned at the trial. Against those critics who discover a pathetic
meaning we think his defeat brings home to us the comic fact of

retribution. Portia and Gratiano echo his words; and every turn of the course of justice which he welcomes while it favoured him is greeted with shouts of laughter. To sympathize with Shylock we must turn against Gratiano, Portia, the Duke, and all Venice. The spirit of retaliation rules in the judgement scene; the laughter is harsh and vindictive.

In our modern sentimental fashion we think Shylock pathetic because of his picturesque aspect—his dignity and isolation. But we ignore his bad traits—that he is a trickster, a whining and fawning hypocrite. He belies his oath and horror of perjury by clutching at thrice the principal which he had refused; and he abandons his suit as soon as he hears that a drop of blood means the confiscation of his goods. He would keep them at the cost of perjuring his soul. He would have commanded our respect if he had reverenced his oath, or followed his losing suit to the bitter end; but he is no hero even in racial revenge and hatred. His dignity is external and vanishes when his fraud is revealed. The true critical spirit is the effort to read the words by the light in which the poet wrote them, to search for a meaning, not to impart one. We have tamed and domesticated Shylock and drawn his fangs: Shakespeare and the Elizabethans shuddered and laughed at him. . . .

We have already anticipated Professor Stoll's two basal thoughts that intention and emphasis most import. With these in mind we think he has proved his case that Shylock was not a pathetic figure on the stage of Shakespeare's day. It is beside the mark to ask whether the modern reader is justified in being impressed pathetically; such an inquiry is too alien to Professor Stoll's mood. He is concerned with Shakespeare's intention in view of the prejudices of his audience; and the gist of his argument is that in the Elizabethan age noble blood was thought to differ in kind from ignoble; that if Shylock is pathetic it is because the author's emphasis has been perverted; that sympathy spoils sport, and if a deceived husband is an object of derision on the stage, how much more so is a Jew, miser, and usurer! The good sense in practical affairs which Professor Stoll adds to his learning makes him positive rather than mystic. He says boldly that Shakespeare was not impartial and inscrutable, and to prove it he discovers as Shakespeare's own the exceptionally severe sentence on Shylock. This is not the time to insist that the greatest art speaks to every generation in its own language. Professor Stoll recalls us to the author's intention and discriminates between the happenings on the stage of the Globe Theatre and those countless stages that come and go in the abysses of the souls of individual readers.

VIII

MR. MacCALLUM says that Shakespeare is an inspired artist, and that his moral insight gives him an unrivalled position among the interpreters of men, but he is an artist, not a moralist, who wrote for the story, not the moral. Professor Saintsbury ascribes to him a fairly severe system of poetical justice and marvellous impartiality; he had morality in the wide sense, sanity, justice, tolerance—an impartial attitude because he understood everything. Mr. Masefield says that he neither praises nor blames, but his task is to see justly that his mind is always brooding on the working of fate. With this we compare the words of Professor Stoll that, except in comedy, Shakespeare has not the spirit of forgiveness. Mr. Harris says that his intellect always stands for morality, even conventional morality. Figgis discovers his power to make his characters search all moral depths in some weighty apophthegm that was yet strictly dramatic. And among tributes to his philosophical as well as moral power we include the latter's saying, that his thought had system and orderly evolution; and also Professor Saintsbury's, that his conception of life had philosophical depth and width. We will add this from Mr. Masefield—that his instinctive power is as large and happy as his intellectual.

Professor Saintsbury has many interesting things to say about Shakespeare's characters. He calls his power to vivify astonishing, and it was that which distinguished him from his predecessors. His two greatest gifts were sheer poetic expression and character creation, and his portraiture had curious and universal humanity. Plot with him was mainly evolution of character. It seems wonderful to Mr. Masefield that the mind which saw man clearest should see him with such exaltation. He also says that Shakespeare's characters belong to the kingdom of vision, not to the mind through which they came. In the opinion of Figgis he created the characters that should themselves achieve their destiny. His characters are of heroic stature symbolic of Life itself. They were the plot, for with construction as such he is not concerned. Against these we set Mr. Harris's strongly expressed views that he could not understand men of action.

To the later saying of Figgis we may oppose Professor Saintsbury's —that in telling a story or constructing a drama he is greater than often allowed; and Mr. Masefield's, that his masterly power of exposition makes his first acts like daybreaks.

Shakespeare was a woman-worshipper, exclaims Professor Saintsbury; and we recall how Mr. Harris describes him as passion's slave and denies life and character to his good women. Mr. Masefield decides that he had a great and happy mind. Professor Stoll thinks that study of his work and his fellows, as expressing Elizabethan ideas and technique, shows that he was not utterly impartial or inscrutable.

All in Shakespeare is a growth, rooted in present and past, in stage tradition and the life about him. . . .

Through the best of these qualities we see the truth lightening that Shakespeare's creative genius transcended the material it worked in— even when that material is religion, morality, human character. His is not the art of expressing best what others think, but of using the world's knowledge and experience in a mightier spiritual game of which he is the supreme master. Again we recommend Professor Stoll as a corrective.

Chapter XXXV

ENGLAND 1912–1913

I. HERFORD.　II. MABIE.　III. BRADLEY.　IV. STOLL.　V. IVOR JOHN.
VI. MOORMAN.　VII. STOPFORD　BROOKE.　VIII. MATTHEWS.　IX.
TRENCH. X. CONCLUSION.

I

PROFESSOR C. H. HERFORD [1] begins his study with an outline
of Shakespeare's life in which he takes a modified view of the four
periods. He says that Hamlet utters the mortal agony of disillusion
with unsurpassed poignancy, and that the typical humour of the tragic
period was that of Barnardine. But the bitterness of *Hamlet* and *Lear*
is lightened in the later Roman plays, and the Romances witness to
a serener inner world.

L.L.L. shows not only amusement of the country-bred poet for
the extravagances of Elizabethan culture, but also unconfessed admiration. Sentiment, even pathos, appear in the situations of the *Errors*:
Adriana is warm-hearted as well as sharp-tongued. *Verona* is a not
very successful experiment, but Julia moves us, and there is a vein of
humour in Launce fresher than has yet appeared in clown or jester.
In *2 Henry VI* there are hints of large conception and comprehensive
grasp of cause and issue. *Richard III* is Marlowesque but reveals
Shakespeare's larger compass. In his success is an element of paradox,
and he takes a sporting delight in it, shared by his creator.

Richard II belongs to the lyric period, and shows the weakening
influence of Marlowe. The action is a prolonged duel between
Richard and Bolingbroke, and the two figures are contrasted with a
subtlety and delicacy of imagination so far unapproached. Richard's
tragedy is one of the mind, and his end is heroic rather than pathetic.
The lyrical quality appears in Mowbray and Gaunt, and at times even
in Bolingbroke. Shakespeare has woven the delightful comedy of
M.N.D. out of the sheer caprice which seems to preside over love-
making and falling in love. The Athenian youths and maidens are
rather commonplace, but violent and exclusive in their adorations
and disdains. The fairies are mixed English, romantic, classical, and
the result is a subtly blent magic atmosphere. They are neither good
nor bad, too slight for morality or passion, but touched with the indefinable air of immortal beings. *R. and J.*, despite its tragedy, still shows
Shakespeare more inclined to mirth and wit than pathos. The rebuffs and
collisions between Romance and the unromantic world suggest Cervantes. Capulets, Benvolio, Mercutio, Friar, Nurse—might all have been
in comedy. There is no hint of mental conflict as in later tragedies. The
horrors of the vault appal Juliet's imagination, but do not move her will.

[1] *Sh.* (The People's Books, vol. li), 1912 (T. C. & E. C. Jack, Ltd.).

Its serious story and realistic air distinguishes the *Merchant*. Verona,
Athens (*M.N.D.*), were mere names, but Venice is very actual, despite
the fantastic plot. Of all Shakespeare's characters Shylock most reveals
his creative processes. Shakespeare imposed on him a more vindictive
penalty than does the original story, but the poet and artist rose unconsciously above. He entered into the situation and soul of Shylock with
such intensive imaginative understanding that the after-world has
mistaken it for sympathy. Shylock intends more harm than he suffers;
and the commanding charm of Portia forbids us to ask whether the
Venetian government needed to be reminded of its own laws. We
feel that she would have been equal to the task had Morocco chosen
right or Bassanio wrong. King John is invested with a dignity which
fits ill with his mean acts, and his miserable end provokes pity. The
play shows an advance in feeling for weakness.

The Induction is the best part of the *Shrew*, with its local realism
that Shakespeare now began to affect. His humour was turning
from word-play to the unconscious incongruities that are overheard. The Falstaff scenes of *Henry IV* belong to that highest
type of comedy which seems to be the humorous quintessence of life
itself. Falstaff is neither criminal nor coward; but honour, honesty,
good faith mean nothing to him. Yet he is not the real subject, nor
is the king: for though the latter is powerfully individualized, and
has pathos, we forget him in his absence. The centre of the play is
Hal—and Hotspur, the mere soldier, is a foil to him. Fluellen
(*Henry V*) partly compensates for Falstaff, and though his humour
is not to be compared, it is quite as original. But, unlike the Eastcheap
scenes, the by-play never competes with the main interest. Henry
expresses his quality by his self-possession, his disdain for the conventional values men set upon themselves, and his clear-eyed sense of
what is due under all conditions, and to men of all conditions. *Wives*
has an admirable plot, but little of the true Shakespearian quality.

Personality and humour had begun to dominate even in history,
and humour is the crowning glory of the three brilliant comedies.
Shakespeare can make womanly wit irresistibly charming, but he
endows Hero (*M. Ado*) with an exquisite silence. Claudio seeks her
hand but knows nothing of her heart, and so feeble strategy suffices
to break down a fragile structure. In Rosalind (*A.Y.L.*) woman and
wit are yet more finely mated than in Beatrice; they are allies rather
than competitors. No villainy can enter the forest, and it is not wholly
unreal, while romance and reality similarly cross and mingle in the in-
mates. Touchstone is a rustic who has learnt the trick of court raillery
without forgetting his native mother-wit. His comments and those of
Jaques add a critical or hostile element which puts romance on its mettle,
and gives it occasion to vindicate its own soundness, sweetness, and
truth. The crude incidents of *Twelfth-Night* are related to vividly

real characters, and share their vitality. Viola and the Duke are studies, the one of real womanhood, the other of a lover, in the stress of a fantastic situation. Sir Toby's gross body is of the man himself, not, as with Falstaff, the material and plaything of a masterful and inexhaustible wit.

Shakespeare cannot quite reconcile Helena with her actions (*All 's Well*), but he has never drawn the delicacy or the daring of virginal passion more exquisitely. Himself no ascetic, he recognizes with Isabella (*M. for M.*) that asceticism can ennoble character. The Duke is ineffectual like Hamlet; he deputes while Hamlet postpones; and Angelo is a rigid doctrinaire. The devices that save Claudio, &c., are unworthy of the mature Shakespeare. *T. and C.* is even harder to reconcile with Shakespearian art, for though the scenes are framed in a kind of epic fragment, and the heroes are magnificent persons, the latter are touched with solemn futility.

The action of *J.C.* makes clear that Brutus was the cause of the ruin; and he is the first example of Shakespeare's interest in greatness removed from outer success, and which even predisposes to practical failure. Hardly tragic himself, he undergoes but a preliminary mental conflict. Hamlet's despondency was not inborn, but the disposition to it was, and it paralyses his will. This 'overthrow' of a noble mind, though not by madness, is the tragedy. The plot in substance is superb melodrama, but it is touched to issues which provoke 'thoughts beyond the reaches of our souls'. In *Othello* only the hero is a tragical figure, and his horrible delusion is more tragical than any of the events of the play. *Lear*, in which the very elements mingle, is even greater as poem than drama. Goneril and Regan are more terribly real, because they have at the outset a certain low justice on their side. Lear's unreason is sublime, and his disturbed brain begets a new and larger wisdom. Gloster is but a commonplace foil, as his tortures are of the body, and his misery without greatness. No other tragedy is so full of pain or crime, or so radiant with heroic goodness. Shakespeare has amazingly clothed with surpassing grandeur two dastardly criminals —Macbeth and his wife. The witches stimulate Macbeth's inborn thought, and his life becomes henceforth a terrible dream. His nerve hardens as he commits crime after crime, but to the last he retains some vision. Lady Macbeth's initial terrific will-power is the nervous exaltation of a high-strung, sensitive woman. The Porter scene compels us to accept the awful preceding scene as entirely of the actual world. Here for the first time woman becomes an active tragic force. Cleopatra's sex-magnetism produces tragedy less harrowing but richer in consummate poetry. The last two acts belong to the highest level of Shakespearian achievement. Antony's heart enlarges as his judgement flags, and imminent ruin exalts Cleopatra. Her dying speech expresses her whole womanhood. Coriolanus is a primitive hero, and he, too, is influenced by woman. After his exile he gains a new dignity, and the story is only surpassed in power by the greatest tragedies. The Tribunes are drawn in Shakespeare's thinnest manner, and the People conceived with bitter political animus. In preceding plays the strain of denunciation is a single note; in *Timon* it becomes a fierce unbroken monotone. The play is only partly Shakespeare's, but Timon is made in the mould of the men to whom, in Shakespeare, tragic events happen. He has Lear's profound *naïveté* and sublime arrogance. His shallow universal benevolence becomes shallow universal hate.

The last plays neither harrow nor greatly amuse. Characters and action decline, and scenery gains dramatic value. Imogen is Shakespeare's loveliest and most lovable woman, and she is real. *W. Tale* shows extravagant things happening to people more real than those of the actual world. The *Tempest* is across the borders of fairyland; the wisdom of the Old World meets the marvels and innocence of the New. As nowhere else, the spell of personality and intellectual suggestion masters the story-interest. Of the characters, only Prospero, Miranda, Ariel, and Caliban concern us. Prospero is a wonderful study of a human intellect equipped with the attributes of a Providence. The Sonnets are a perennial encouragement of that 'marriage of true minds' over which no earthly condition can triumph. . . .

What strikes us about Professor Herford's criticism is its fine distinctions, as we see judgements that have become fixed and accepted subdivide still further at his touch, e.g. the note of unconfessed admiration in *L.L.L.*, the death of Richard II, the special kind of tragedy in *R. and J.*, the atmosphere of *M.N.D.* He says that Portia would have found a way out had Bassanio chosen wrong, &c., and this, with his remark on the Porter scene in *Macbeth* where he conflicts with De Quincey, and the 'solemn futility' which he superadds to the heroes of *T. and C.*, makes us realize that earthly values do not obtain in the world of the imagination, but two contrary opinions may be equally true. We agree that though Henry IV is powerfully drawn we forget him in his absence; but we cannot accept Hal as the centre of interest, though we do not condemn him as utterly as Mr. Yeats and Mr. Masefield. We also think his admiration for Coriolanus excessive, as we did Professor Saintsbury's; and against the remark that the people were conceived with bitter political animus, we again recall the citizen's home-thrust, at which Coriolanus might well have flushed with shame—that the price of the consulship was to ask it kindly (II. iii). He is excellent with *M. Ado*, and if it is possible to excuse Claudio he has done so. He does not deny a certain 'low justice' to Goneril and Regan, and after some hesitation we accept his verdict on Gloster. He lays his finger on the main motive of the Sonnets, and enables us to say in conclusion that within his limits he is the ideal critic. Intellect is keen and emotions fine, and the two pull well together in harness.

II

THE object of Mr. Hamilton Wright Mabie [1] is to present Shakespeare as a man, not as a series of problems associated with a name. In Shakespeare's early work he finds his imagination responding to the different masters of his art. The excessive puns and quibbles and conceits of *L.L.L.* show how he escaped the peril by discerning it, but also that he was concerned with the right relation of the individual to moral order, family, State. *Errors* sees the national genius triumph, for Shakespeare changed classical to romantic by means of complex character, involved plot, and un-Latin pathos.

In the beginning he saw rather than meditated, he was more engrossed by the marvellous spectacle of the world than its spiritual order. His poems are from classical models, and show the joy of release from medieval gloom. Personality has once more space and light to develop, but Shakespeare was not subjugated by the classical world. *Venus* is curiously cool and offends more by frankness than warmth. *Lucrece* is also treated objectively, by an imagination stimulated but not possessed by its subject. *R. and J.* is the flower of his poetic genius, but also tells us of deep and radical changes springing out of tragic resistance and defiance—the searching reaction of the assertion of individuality on the social order. The fairies of *M.N.D.* show forth, as in a parable, the magic properties of love when love touches the whole gamut of feeling. The Sonnets probably disclose Shakespeare's experience, but not his outer history.

Richard III is as clear and vital as any character in the plays, but the attempt to combine Marlowe's method and Shakespeare's spirit makes the play lack artistic coherence. With Falconbridge (*John*) he began to blend comedy with tragedy and history. Other plays show higher moods, but none discloses so completely the full range of his power as *Henry IV*. It has construction, characterization, pathos, humour, wit, dramatic energy, and the magical Shakespearian touch, in free and harmonious unity of dramatic form. No other play deals more easily with discordant elements; the heroic note of the old ideals of chivalry is sounded as distinctly as if Falstaff's rollicking humour did not exist. *Henry V* is not dramatic in the deepest sense, but is treated with such vigour that it has the dignity and interest of a drama. It expresses nobly the deepening of the national consciousness, and gives the secret of the expansion and authority of the English race. These plays mark the transition from epic to drama—from stories shaped by fate to those shaped by character. In his histories Shakespeare disclosed the race spirit, and in so doing developed the racial qualities of his own genius. He so exalted liberty and represented the English temper and institutions as to make patriotism the deepest passion in the hearts

---

[1] *Wm. Sh., Poet, Dramatist, and Man,* 1912 (New York, The Macmillan Co.).

of English men. He studied well the actual world before entering the ideal. These many-sided dramas exhibit the play of the divine law which binds the deed to the doer and so moralizes experience. We see the justice of God working itself out through historical events and persons, and there are hints at mercy and redemption. Royal trappings make John and Richard III more criminal, Richard II and Henry VI weaker, and Henry IV and Henry V more energetic.

In his comedy, which was more of life than manners, he expressed his ease of mind. He saw men's weaknesses against the background of the spiritual kinship and destiny of humanity. Unlike Marlowe's Jew, who is a monster, Shylock is stamped with Shakespeare's humanizing spirit, and appeals to us because he makes us feel our kinship with him. Hatred of Jews was at fever-heat, and Shakespeare did not intend to modify the popular conception, but he recast the material in the light of his marvellous imagination. The *Wives* is intellectually below his work of the period, and lacks his touches of humour and poetry. *M. Ado* is the highest point of his creative activity in comedy. Tragic and humorous are most perfectly blent, and contrast of character is most comprehensive. *A.Y.L.* is still in the sunlight, but there are premonitions of sadness. Jaques for the first time pierces the illusions of place and power and passion, and touches man's great desires and inadequate achievements. Freshness of spirit redeems artificiality, and Rosaline harmonizes purity, passion, and freedom. The vivacity and humour of her speech save it from extravagance. Within the serious framework of *Twelfth-Night* is a beautiful vein of poetic feeling and uproarious fun. It surpasses in inventiveness, freedom, and the grouping and harmonizing of diverse materials. Shakespeare parted with comedy at the moment when he had mastered the art of touching men's minor sins with the wisdom of great knowledge and the gentleness of one who loved his kind rather for what they had lost than gained.

The outer events of Shakespeare's life, from the beginning of the seventeenth century, and the revelations of the Sonnets, justify us in ascribing his choice of tragic themes to a prolonged spiritual crisis. *J.C.* shows a rigorous selection of incidents with reference to their dramatic value, and a masterly unfolding of their significance in the story. The new order in the Roman world, personified by Caesar, is the shaping force of the tragedy. Shakespeare's sense of reality and ability to give facts their full weight is nowhere else so apparent. The tragedy of Brutus is the conflict between a great nature, denied the sense of reality, and the world-spirit. That *Hamlet* should present a great spiritual problem in a form so concrete is the highest evidence of Shakespeare's genius. This drama of the soul never for a moment loses touch with reality, and Shakespeare's own personality pervades the play. Helena (*All's Well*) shows exquisite delicacy and skill, but suffers from the repellent atmosphere of the play. She cheapens the love she finally wins by a sacrifice greater than love could ask or afford to receive, and her victory is purely external. Shakespeare's mood was the passing one of cynical distrust, and to bring out one quality he ignored others.

In the later tragedies evil has become a burden on Shakespeare's heart; in *M. for M.* men are corrupted by the air they breathe, and human nature is mean and repulsive. Yet Isabella's impregnable purity gives the whole play a saving sweetness. The special irony of *T. and C.* is the confusion brought into private and public affairs by lawless or fatuous love. As a tragedy of disillusion it is saved by a rich and many-sided knowledge of life. Merely to cross the gulf of race between herself and Othello, as Desdemona does, is to create a tragic situation. Pathos is the chief trait of the play, from the spectacle of two noble natures defeated by pure villainy. Macbeth gives an impression of massive and inevitable tragedy, though the hero is not in the hands of fate, but deliberately sets in motion the tragic forces. A criminal, yet he makes us admire him by the massive simplicity of his character, his concentrated purpose, and direct action. *Lear* lifts the curtain on the most appalling facts of life and makes no attempt to rationalize them. The end of art is not to solve the problems of existence, but to deepen and freshen the sense of life; and, as in the Book of Job, the vastness and mystery of the problems suggest the only adequate and satisfying answer. The irony of *Timon* is in the fierce light thrown on those who had benefited by his lavish mood. Shakespeare had often shown how tragic disaster issues from unregulated passion, but nowhere is that tragedy set on so great a stage and so magnificently enriched with splendid gifts of nature, noble possession, and almost limitless opportunities of achievement as in *A. and C.* It is the drama of East and West, and the East succumbs to the superior fibre and more highly organized character of the West. Cleopatra is a superb embodiment of femininity, untouched by pity and untroubled by conscience.

Shakespeare was first poet and then philosopher; he incidentally discovered the ethical order of life. Starting with personality, the problem is to bring the individual will into harmony with the institutional life of society, organized in family, Church, State, and to harmonize these with the immutable principles of righteousness. In tragedy the individual collides with established order, and his inner subjective force sweeps into light through action. By means of action, impulse and thought become objective and concrete, and the inward nature of the human spirit is given external form in this world. Life becomes intelligible, and gains moral significance and immortal hopes. Shakespeare did not penetrate into the region of pure spiritual impulse, but dealt with the region of action, where spiritual impulses are worked

into character. Yet he had visions of a diviner reconciliation between
conflicting elements than is accomplished on the narrow stage of the
world. Otherwise events would be blind happenings—brutalities of
fate. He thus agrees with the soundest religious view of life and most
intelligent psychology, and his mediating principle gives his tragedies
their authority.

Cymbeline shows that he had recovered serenity, but could never
see life again without tragedy: though it is subordinate, and serves to
bring out gracious qualities of nature. In the last plays tragic forces
are arrested by repentance; they are set in motion to furnish a background for penitence and reconciliation. Shakespeare the man and
artist were vitally related: and in the end he came to look on men
with deep and beautiful pity. Fortitude under calamity, charity for
human weakness, faith in the power of human sweetness and purity,
pervade the Romances. Perdita is half-woman and half-creature of
fairyland; she mediates not only between conflicting persons, but
between nature and man. The *Tempest* is one of the most beautiful
existing poems—where Shakespeare bids farewell to his art. The
chief figures of the last plays are men and women who have borne
heavy sorrows, against a lovely pastoral background—and it was in
such a mood that Shakespeare retired to Stratford. . . .

Mr. Mabie's motive is to present Shakespeare the man—and his
opinions on the parts played by the histories, tragedies, and romances,
in developing Shakespeare's soul, are not unlike Dowden's. But when
we compare his work with the recently studied one of Professor
Herford's, we ask ourselves whether the latter, who merely submitted
his mind to impressions from the plays and endeavoured to interpret
them exactly, did not tell us more about the great ocean-mind. We
confess to getting more light from Professor Herford's criticism of
R. and J. than Mr. Mabie's account of Shakespeare's moral and
philosophical and mediating power. But we must not deny that there
are times when Mr. Mabie can be helpful by means of the theories
which he ascribes to Shakespeare: notably the effect of the office of
kingship, both on the king's self and his subjects. He also says well
that events would be blind happenings were there no suggestion of
reconciliation beyond this world: though we may remind him of
Swinburne's opinion that Shakespeare was a darker fatalist than
Aeschylus. *All's Well* is an instance where he says good things
despite his theory, and he also throws light on the *Merchant* and
A.Y.L. However, as a whole active criticism predominates over
passive, and at this hour of the Shakespearian day the passive is most
desired. The tendency reappears to confine Shakespeare within a
system and make him fit a theory.

III

PROFESSOR BRADLEY [1] assigns to *Coriolanus* a lower place than the four great tragedies and *A. and C.* because it has not their imaginative atmosphere. The forces that meet in these stretch beyond the group of persons and tiny tracts of space and time in which they appear. Coriolanus is not imaginative, he feels the rapture but not the poetry of war, and has no inner conflict. It has been said that Shakespeare hates the people, but his abuse is never dramatically unfitting, nor is it given to his most attractive characters. Coriolanus's provocation must be great to preserve our sympathy when he turns on his country. Yet the people are not ungrateful; they merely want to be treated humanely and acknowledged as part of the State. If the conflict is hopeless it is because Coriolanus is impossible. He is an innovator who would abolish the Tribunes and refuse all rights to the people—an Aristocrat with a high but narrow ideal, to which he is true—and never truer than in the scene where he tries to be false to it—Shakespeare's proudest man, but unaware of pride. He is really modest, and never dreams he has attained the ideal he worships, yet the sense of his own greatness is twisted round every strand of this worship. And because he is impatient of praise he lacks human sympathy. He has no introspection, and the events of his exile are due to self-ignorance. The thought grows in his mind of *burning* Rome, as it seems to him that even his fellow-patricians and his wife and mother have deserted him; and this was Shakespeare's own idea. His vision was of a hero enslaved by his passion and driven blindly forward, for—thanks to ignorance of self—he does not see that either success or failure would be a catastrophe. In the scene with Volumnia one is anxious for his soul; we know his life is lost, but he is above pity and life. It is as much a drama of reconciliation as a tragedy, for what we see is the conquest of passion by simple human feelings. It is a tragedy, but the catastrophe scarcely diminishes the influence of the great scene, and his death strikes us with awe, not pity.

Menenius is a pleasant old gentleman whose humour tells him how to keep the peace while he gains his point. Aufidius is a man of straw merely wanted for the plot, and his sneer at the hero's tears creates an emotion of disgust out of place in a tragic close. Volumnia's early exultation, and anger at her son's banishment, form a contrast with her final scene of pleading, and make it doubly impressive. Virgilia's silence, like Cordelia's, suggests a world of feeling in reserve. She and Valeria bring out the poetry and tender affection in the huge violent heart of Coriolanus. He might loathe the people, but he would never injure or insult one of their daughters. . . .

As usual Professor Bradley impresses with his simultaneous grasp

[1] Annual Sh. Lecture, 1912 (Oxford University Press, American Branch).

of the whole and every part. We surrender ourselves to him as to a guide, because we feel that with his wide outlook and unprejudiced mind, and discriminating knowledge of the passions, he is nearer to Shakespeare than at least any other living critic. He never loses his way in the intricate paths of Shakespeare's human nature. He has done good service here in separating *Coriolanus* from the other great tragedies as less imaginative; in defining the hero's character and the inevitable catastrophe which it produces, besides the catastrophe's relative psychological importance.

IV

PROFESSOR STOLL [1] wishes us to realize that Shakespeare's criminals are not depicted from our point of view, and cannot be proved real. The atmosphere Shakespeare breathed was charged with the dualism of the Middle Ages. Good and evil were poles asunder; God was in his heaven, but the Devil was in the world. Shakespeare does not represent men as overwhelmed by anything so vague and neutral as social forces, or only by their own passions, but by other men's passions and deeds. Besides, a play is a story on the stage; the very word 'plot' means conspiracy, and the drama requires external action and struggle.

In accordance with the temper of Shakespeare's time, Richard III considers that his deformity puts him beyond the verge of all that is human, and sets the seal on his depravity, instead of explaining and extenuating it. No psychology enters into the question, but, like other Machiavels, he boasts and fawns on his victims, and plays the hypocrite. But on the eve of battle he experiences something like remorse—and this is quite untrue to the criminal nature. When criminals regret it is because they have not committed more crimes, or have let themselves be caught. What prompted Shakespeare was his morality; he cleaves to the conscience of the Elizabethan age—external conscience, the voice of God rather than of the better self within.

Macbeth is commonly spoken of as a tragedy of remorse, but neither hero nor heroine have remorse. They have a horror of murder and blood, and even in horror of crime they perpetrate it: the thought first comes to Macbeth as a 'horrid image'. All that follows is Nemesis, and there is no sheer dread of detection or punishment, nor is there remorse or repentance, but bodying-forth of unearthly fears and more than mortal misery. Conscience appears in the form of fear among the simpler peoples, e.g. Orestes. In Shakespeare and the Elizabethan drama conscience concerns itself with punishment rather than sorrow for sin. Leontes looks upon his misfortunes as a judgement; and so do Gloster and his two sons look upon his blindness. Character after

---

[1] *The Criminals*, 1912 (Sh. Studies. New York, The Macmillan Co., 1927).

character in *Richard III* hears the voice of conscience only when he suffers. Claudio, Othello, Leontes, Borachio, Posthumus, Iachimo, long for punishment and feel that it relieves them: yet it is impossible that either Borachio or Iachimo could have such feelings. The Machiavels are cheerful and untroubled to the end, and therefore nearer to the true criminal nature; the less evil suffer the external spiritual pains of Nemesis. But the facts of the world are that the wicked are for the most part contented and cheerful—actors not so much in a tragedy as a comedy.

The limitations of the dramatic form must also be taken into account. The good characters—Othello, Brutus, Imogen, Miranda —are aware of their qualities—because the dramatists cannot comment on them in his own person. The dramatic form of Shakespeare's age was not completely evolved, and it was not realized that a character acts and does not tell his story. Don John and Borachio call themselves villains, and Angelo describes his passion for Isabella as lust: like the devils of the miracle plays who proclaim to the audience that they are full of wrath and envy; although plain-speaking and self-description appear in Sophocles and Seneca, in the French, German, and Spanish drama, and in the English drama until after the day of Ibsen.

Shakespeare makes his criminals conform to the moral standard even in their nonconformity. Macbeth and Lady Macbeth call it a murder, whereas the truth is people do not speak more honestly than they act or think. A thief frequently protests that he is innocent, even after the booty has been found upon him. Sin also is spontaneous and unconscious, and Shakespeare's hardened villains do not realize this. Falstaff, Autolycus, Panurge, are conscious and therefore malicious villains—and this was the method of Plautus and Molière. We do not rejoice to see Falstaff fleecing his landlady, the helpless conscripts, or even Justice Shallow. The frankness of Shakespeare's criminals exceeds technique and the needs of the audience. There is much unnecessary plain speaking, and the villain need not speak so truly and justly of the good, e.g. Iago, Oliver, Edmund. It confuses the outline of his character, makes him either demon or angel who sees more than mortal can; whereas, characteristically, he should consider them dolts and asses. Thirdly, the moral point of view is not more adjusted to characters of mingled nature than to the wicked. We see this where there is indecision before the deed whether to turn to right or left. The atrocious Tamora exclaims 'pitiful'; Cassius, who thinks himself honourable, talks about seducing Brutus; Iago calls his love for Desdemona lust, as Angelo does for Isabella. Men act from inclination, and do not headlong incline to what they hate. Parolles confesses his cowardice at the end when it can serve no dramatic need; and Cressida is such another with her soliloquy of remorse. Lastly, this self-description involves indifference to the unpleasant effect of self-consciousness: e.g. Caesar's boasting, Brutus's stoicism when he hears of Portia's death. The Queens in *Richard II* and *Richard III* hug their sorrow like the women in ancient drama. Cleopatra and Imogen remember their pale cheeks at critical moments, Miranda her innocence. All this self-consciousness exceeds the limitations of dramatic form; but one cannot separate form and content in a great popular artist, who speaks the vulgar language yet in the end expresses himself. Shakespeare of all dramatists could take a character's point of view, but he betrays himself where morals and conscience are concerned. A character, however vividly realized, suffers from a self-descriptive and self-conscious manner. But the doctrine of the point of view simply had not arrived. There was as yet no Ibsen in the drama, no Henry James in the novel, no *Ring and the Book*.[1]

In life the criminal is neither remorseful nor self-descriptive, but he has his own natural point of view: he calls a thief a 'fingersmith'. The universal instinct is to admit neither moral nor physical defects. Fielding in *Jonathan Wild* remarked that thieves speak as much of honesty, honour, and friendship as other men. Like others, criminals have their weaknesses and virtues; and their weaknesses have become crimes under the pressure of public opinion. The polygamous Mohammedans deny themselves wine; the stealing and double-dealing gipsies enforce chastity on their female children. Many blood-thirsty Jacobins were Puritans: but where are the virtues of Richard, Edmund, Iago?

Critics have explained away Iago's baseness, like that of Shylock and Falstaff, and given him an apparatus of self-deception like Hamlet. The tendency of modern criticism is to read contemporary ideas into works of art, new or old. Humanity and *bonhomie* have been discovered in Iago—and the inhuman and diabolical are neglected. He is a dualistic Machiavel who scoffs at conscience and revels in his villainy. He puts himself in the wrong by virtue of his self-consciousness; the accumulation of his motives and flimsiness of his suspicions show the hellishness of his purpose. He thinks as we do but is as we are not; and though he has motives he acts as if he had them not. But to discard them would be to discard Shakespeare and his words; we had better, therefore, let him run his course regardless of words, like Aaron, Richard III, Marlowe's Barabas, and other stage villains. The subconscious is too intangible for dramatic art, and is certainly out of keeping with the Shakespearian. When a character deceives himself it is in soliloquy, like Hamlet; and all hypocrites of the drama are conscious and deliberate. The soliloquy is the clue given to the audience, and must be the truth itself. The process of Iago's thinking is that of a human devil. But what makes a character immortal is individual tone and manner, expression, life-giving touch, not motives and

[1] Cf. Delius (1888) on the monologue; also Mézières, and Jusserand (1904).

internal mechanism. Only when we consider characters too curiously do they become riddles.

Heredity and environment play no part in Shakespeare, yet the world will have it so—with the result that the intention and purport of his writing is turned awry. Thus the wickedness of Lear's daughters is imputed to their father.

To prove further that Shakespeare's criminals are too conscious and consistent, they are atheists, enemies of God, in accordance with an old literary tradition: yet modern statistics prove the contrary. In real life the criminal acts simply and naturally, is often kind and sentimental. On the stage from the days of Aeschylus and Seneca criminals have glorified in their wickedness and defied man and fate. Horrors and portents have preceded crime, as if to prove sin beyond the bounds of nature. Not so is evil done in Ibsen or Pinero. The critics still insist that 'Shakespeare is nature', and herein lies the difficulty. Michael Angelo knew the human body as well as Shakespeare knew the human soul: yet some of the attitudes of figures on the ceiling of the Sistine Chapel are physically impossible. Lesser artists would make no such mistake to-day. Though not identified with nature they have studied her, and discovered that no word or attitude can satisfy unless it accord with this larger method of truth. . . .

What Professor Stoll first achieves in this essay is to make us realize that conscience meant something external to the Elizabethan, the voice of God, not of the better self—as in a former essay he defined the true nature of contemporary ghosts and witches. He then proceeds to show that criminals do not suffer from remorse; the facts of the world prove that the wicked as a rule are contented, that sin is spontaneous and unconscious, and that a criminal is rarely an atheist. They do not call murder by its name, like Macbeth, and commit it in horror of blood. All this helps to prove that Shakespeare is not nature; it injures him as a realist, not as a poet. Professor Stoll would be the first to admit this, as indeed he says that it is the life-giving touch which makes a character immortal, not interior motives. We continue to maintain that the tree of art grows from the root of reality, and if the root suffers from the disease of over-fancy the tree becomes barren. It is by bringing the crude real world nearer to the ideal Shakespearian that Professor Stoll achieves his effect, and the Shakespearian world is not belittled as a result. Whether this holds good of Professor Stoll's second main contention that the frankness of Shakespeare's criminals exceeds dramatic technique and the needs of the audience, we hesitate to affirm or deny. To prove it he approaches the Shakespearian world to that part of the real world which is expressed in the writings of artists less inspired but more technically perfect because of a later age, and therefore the inheritors of a longer literary tradition. This may or may not represent Shakespeare as more historical but less universal.

Professor Stoll characteristically infers that Shakespeare reveals himself where morals and conscience are concerned.

V

MR. IVOR B. JOHN has thrown some new light on the structure of *Richard II* and the character of its hero,[1] and consequently on the limitations of the play. He says that, as with the central figures of the greater Shakespearian tragedies, the possibility of tragedy inheres in Richard, and also that of salvation. When these are dangled before us throughout a play we get a crude summary of the essence of tragic drama. Dramatic art also demands an inevitable tragic climax, and we should also get this did we know the circumstances. But we do not know them till after we have read the play, so we arrive afterwards at the sense of inevitability by a process of retrospective analysis. Richard has not powerful forces to contend with, and is without either heroic strength or heroic weaknesses. Any unheroic, plain, straightforward person would have done better: and we never think this of the central figures of the later tragedies. On the whole we despise Richard because the only thing he cares for is a telling situation. When Northumberland bids him read out his past misdeeds he is more dignified because unprepared with a part to play. We must not assume that Shakespeare here conceived the character of Bolingbroke as it afterwards became. We find no hint of a deliberate plan to seize the throne. He returns to claim his own and has glory thrust upon him; but there is no trace of his controlling power behind events; for it was not his policy or strength that dispersed the Welshmen or made the nobles revolt. He had self-control, quiet strength, and the power of quickly meeting a situation and profiting from it. . . .

Mr. John does well to emphasize the opportunist character of Bolingbroke, and to warn us against accepting him and Henry IV as the same person.

VI

IT is the duty of the modern critic to avoid generalities and define more closely and subtly, and Mr. F. W. Moorman fulfils this admirably with the *W. Tale*.[2] He maintains that pastoral convention had always seemed unreal to Shakespeare, and in *A.Y.L.* he had corrected Arcadianism with a strong realistic element. He does not now succumb to the temptation, and the wit and wisdom of the old shepherd savour not of Arcadian dreamland but the farmstead and the byre. Autolycus proves that Shakespeare preserved his wit and gaiety to the end, but there are no more wit-combats between the lovers. They do not now conceal love beneath a mask of pleasantry. Reconciliation must prevail at all costs, so Hermione is kept alive despite improbability.

[1] *Richard II* (Arden edit. 1912, Methuen).   [2] Arden edit. 1912 (Methuen).

Perdita's reconciliation is related so that Hermione's may be the crowning scene. The strength of character which enabled Hermione to refute her husband's charges without bitterness has enabled her to endure the seclusion of sixteen years; and it is also an act of heroic submission to the will of the gods in accordance with the religious spirit of the play. . . .

With the last sentence only do we disagree, for we think that the interval of sixteen years belongs to the fantastic element which is certainly to be found in the play, and that Mr. Moorman should not try it by the standard of realism; and also that he discovers in the play more religion than it actually contains.

VII

STOPFORD BROOKE,[1] writing of *M. Ado*, finds the sad strain in it to be Italian, the gay Shakespearian. Yet he pronounces the wit of Benedict and Beatrice to be Italian, and he defines subtly the peculiar nature of Italian wit. There is little plot but much character, of every sort and condition, like a pageant of life. Benedict and Beatrice are the quintessence, and they reflect the stream of life brighter than they receive it, and radiate it still more. The characters are presented in doubles, so that we see the same type but a different individual— Verges is the echo of Dogberry but also something more. Only Benedict and Beatrice are far from all conventional types, their difference is one of sex. They do not see at the outset that they are antagonistic because alike; but they were not in love at the beginning of the play. Their new gravity, after they love, changes the atmosphere and prepares us for the deep shadow. The church scene is repulsive; and even with the excuse of extreme youth, Claudio disgusts us. Shakespeare's literary nerves must have been affected, and a wrongly conceived subject was wrongly executed. He fails with Claudio, Leonato, and Hero, but uplifts Benedict and Beatrice. The two passions in Beatrice stimulate each other—pity for Hero and love for Benedict: the latter is now transformed from mere requital to personal passion. . . .

The statement that the love of Benedict and Beatrice prepares for the shadow is, we think, an exaggeration, but otherwise Stopford Brooke is a sound and delicate interpreter. He has not the large grasp of Professor Bradley nor the perfect balance of Professor Herford; there is more of himself than Shakespeare, but he does much to restore the balance by a sympathy—backed by his own experience of life— with the moral-emotional side of Shakespeare. His analysis of character in modern terms brings home to us Shakespeare's universality.

Twelfth-Night is the gayest of all plays, ranging from the delicate fantasies of love to jovial humour. Its sadness is not serious sadness:

[1] *Ten More Plays of Sh.*, 1913 (Constable).

even Malvolio is happy in his self-conceit, till he is gulled. We see Love the prank-player of the world, Cupid in his freakishness. The Duke loves his own ideal of a woman and knows nothing of Olivia. Viola loves truly and imaginatively, and gains the wisdom of a deep inner experience. In her difficult position she never makes a mistake; she has the frankness of Shakespeare's women to whom love is a glory and joy, and she infects with love all about her. Olivia has always been flattered, so that when her fancied love is repelled, it becomes passion. She interests as one of her class—rich and unoccupied; and she might be vulgar were she not so reckless. She is too great a lady to trouble about disorders in her house, and when Malvolio enters cross-gartered, is scarcely aware of his existence, and later on only regrets that he has lost his senses. Sir Toby and Sir Andrew represent the ill-behaved folk such as probably were often about the houses of Elizabethan nobles. Their wit almost excuses their excesses, even Andrew is humorously silly, but Toby cannot be compared with Falstaff. The latter is never drunk, and is wittiest and wisest when he is musing alone upon the world. Toby marries Maria for her wit, and this ideal choice reconciles one to him.[1] Malvolio represents a disagreeable Puritan element—one who opposed all mirth and used his grim morality as a ladder to self-advancement. His self-love is more wicked than the drunkenness and recklessness of the others. . . .

We spoke of Stopford Brooke's sympathy and hinted that it was not unlimited, and it rather fails him here in his judgements of Olivia and Malvolio. He takes the latter too seriously, and applies predominantly moral rather than imaginative tests to the former. We might think that he compensates for this by becoming reconciled to Sir Toby; but here again it is marriage which appeals to him—as if the world of human affairs was the one reality. Yet he contrasts pleasantly with those critics who say that Toby's 'misalliance' is poetic justice—that he who mocked others is himself made ridiculous. He is excellent with the character and influence of Viola.

The political interest of *J.C.* is the natural war between Liberty and Autocracy. Righteous revolutions do not always succeed, because the men who make them are not disinterested: here only Brutus has a single aim. But he has no form of government to replace Caesar and thinks Rome will govern itself. Shakespeare takes no side in the quarrel, yet on the whole inclines to Republicanism—as we see in the heightened phrasing and intenser soul of the speeches he gives to Brutus, whereas Caesar speaks almost like a fool. The interest is political, and the conduct of the drama is not affected by the relations of Brutus to his wife or friend. Caesar's spirit dominates, though he himself belongs to the past. There is little of human passion at its height; Brutus's passion for liberty is that of the student; while envy

[1] Cf. Boas and Priestley.

is the passion of the other conspirators. Brutus doubts whether Caesar will be tyrant or not; and this scepticism is naturally unimpassioned. Antony's friendship for Caesar is mixed with his political selfishness. Brutus lives in a world beyond Cassius, and even in reconciliation he condescends. There is deep emotion in the scene between Brutus and Portia, but it hardly belongs to the drama. The true catastrophe is the fall of Republicanism in the death of Brutus—the struggle of the hero of a past world against the victorious pull of the present. He is morally right, so his fall does not lower him in our eyes, and his soul is unconquered. But we come to see that Caesar's death, which he thought would restore freedom, was the event which riveted on Rome the Imperialism which he hated: and few situations are more poetic. In the quarrel between Brutus and Cassius Caesar is an over-shadowing third; and were no atmosphere created by the besetting thought, Caesar's ghost could not have appeared. Defeat and ruin strengthen the deep loving-kindness of Brutus's nature; he gains a double soul in Shakespeare's hands. Cassius, too, wins back his soul, and is lifted by Shakespeare's divine genius into our pity and affection. The reproaches of Brutus break through his angry experience, and make him tender instead of furious. He leaves his old nature behind and becomes young again. . . .

Recalling all that has been written about the play, and comparing the foregoing, we conclude that this critic specially brings home to us the human side of wars and revolutions. He has said nothing absolutely new about Brutus, but he makes us realize the depth of his nature by his power of moral sympathy. The last sentence about Cassius is certainly 'some new thing', which will abide with us for ever and modify for good our conception of the character. His words about the share of Caesar in the quarrel and the cause of the ghost discovers an unsuspected unity in the play.

The main human lines of each character of *Hamlet* are extraordinarily simple, but Shakespeare has added to the simple outlines the most subtle and complex representation of thought and feeling. Hamlet is one of humanity's great types, but also all the variations within it. His thoughts are the ordinary ones of his type; they are not of exceptional range or excellence, and do not set him on a pinnacle above other men; but they are clothed with a splendour of poetic words and made to seem greater. The King and Queen, Polonius, Laertes, Ophelia, belong to the practical type, ignorant of its own soul, and, when forced to see it, crying out, 'What is this place? where am I?' Hamlet is not mad but eccentric, and conscious of a world beyond the senses: Horatio, in whom he had wisely confided, never thought him mad. Consider his position—transported from a student's life to the active world of terrible events. He seeks relief from the present by abstract reasoning; his imitation of madness is bad; his sanity forces him to link thought to thought. But he always glides away from the hated outer life to the inner life, where he finds doubt and hesitation. He spares the King at prayer because he dislikes killing when his blood is cold, and can only act on passionate impulse. When he sees his mother, his soul is in confusion from the dark ground-swell of his situation. It is beyond the world and its realities—hence the death of Polonius is but an incident compared to the horror which involves him. His behaviour to Rosencrantz and Guildenstern does show the cunning of a madman; it was an act of mean treachery, and then, if ever, he passed the limit between feigned and real madness. The King is neither bold nor resolute, and all his talk is of a bluffing honesty. Fear awakens his drugged conscience into idiotic speech. It relieves him to confess his crime and bluff heaven with a desire to repent: it may give him renewed power to sin again. In his final murderous treachery he is twice as bad as before his prayers. Ophelia when mad casts off her littleness and commonplace, and rises to the super-sensible world, among the spirits beyond the earth. The child within the maiden reveals all the deep fineness of her loving nature, now unladen of convention. When she slips, as common in delirium, into a certain grossness, it is primeval nature speaking, and neither her delicate sorrow nor her piteous gaiety are injured. The unconcerned grave-diggers enhance the tragedy, and also the gulf between classes which makes the tragedy of States. Death, which the prosperous fear, is a subject of rough humour to these men. . . .

The statement that Hamlet was no exceptional thinker is at least worth pondering: and on the side of it we may set the universal popularity of the play. The critic helps us to realize that Hamlet was not mad, through his relations with Horatio, including his timely confidence. He also keeps before us the continual surge of the storm in Hamlet's mind and its consequences—notably the hardly remarked death of Polonius. We should agree wholly with his stricture on the episode of Rosencrantz and Guildenstern, save for the reminder that it occurs in the original story. Sympathy fails him with the King, and the result is a critical blot. If ever a man's soul is laid bare it is when the King confesses his misdeeds. Ophelia is exquisitely touched because sympathy returns, but it rather fails with the grave-diggers. Do the rich fear death more than the poor? Does the idle man gain time for fine feeling, as he says? We should distinguish between idleness and leisure, and reflect that the intellectual man, who develops his brain, has time for fine thought and feeling, and also great sorrow, while the idle man too often becomes a hypochondriac.

The characters and poetry of *M. for M.* are great only in patches.[1] No doubt the subject repelled Shakespeare—a society eaten to its core by fornication—and drove him to create extremes of human nature—

[1] Cf. Pater.

Isabella, Angelo, Claudio. He rather forces the ugly story to represent high-souled chastity, outward virtue breaking up in sensualism, the fear of death, and also the danger and limits of authority. Probably there had been a twist in Shakespeare's life, or the change from *Twelfth-Night* to *Macbeth* and *Othello* is hardly explained. His plays expressed not his personal circumstances but the general temper of his soul. The present play is between the cynicism of *T. and C.* and *Timon*, and the pity of the great tragedies. Here we have no pity either for Mariana, Claudio, Angelo, Isabella. Justice is not done, and natural justice is lightly and therefore cynically treated—so that all—even Isabella—are lowered in our eyes. The Duke knows what is right but lacks intellect to rule rightly, so becomes a spy. The irony is almost too deep when he marries Isabella. There is bare and ugly realism unrelieved by humour. As the elements and characters were not strong enough for tragedy, they had to be made into comedy. Shakespeare therefore invented Mariana, that the characters might go home in peace and continue sinning. Did Shakespeare write with a mixed moral and artistic aim, and lose his grip on the main issues, and produce broken, unequal work? The outward morality is not interesting or attractive: we do not love Isabella, and are repelled by the Duke's morality, while that of Mariana is on her lips not in her desire. The Duke is thinker, not ruler; Angelo is chaste because cold, and has no virtue to oppose temptation when it comes. All Shakespeare's powers combine in the first meeting between Angelo and Isabella. The question of Authority, the fear of death, the nature of sin—are the three great subjects of the play. Isabella is harsh because innocent; it is the experience of one's own guilt that awakens mercy. Claudio's thoughts on death were natural to a cultivated man in a luxurious age, and contrast with Barnardine's. . . .

We think that Stopford Brooke is absorbed by the subject rather than its treatment, by the painful nature of the scenes rather than the poetry which Shakespeare has worked into them. He does not allow for the fact that the subject was ready-made, and Shakespeare lighted it up with his genius. He speaks of a 'twist' in Shakespeare's life, and is one of those critics who think Shakespeare's life and art to be closely connected. He is over-moral in condemning the Duke and Mariana: he speaks of the latter's 'excited desire to have Angelo for life as a husband'. His best criticism is about Isabella and Angelo: he excuses Isabella's outburst but not the offence of her words. His remarks on the fears of Claudio and Barnardine recall the same discussion in Hamlet—and we would remind him that Barnardine looked on death as a drunken sleep. On the whole we think that he fails to separate the real and poetic life of the characters.

Shakespeare did not write tragedies to use for art's sake his knowledge of the darker side of human life. The foundation of his soul was other than when he wrote the comedies. His belief in a divine Justice was shaken in *Hamlet* and now disappears. He cannot explain the problems of misery and evil and the sacrifice of the good. In *Othello* Chance or Unreason, blind and deaf, is at the centre of human life. We abhor a universe without law and despise ourselves and our race. Othello is noble, but Desdemona's love for him was improbable. It was strange that a young man like Iago should show such hypocrisy, hatred, and cruelty. Neither we nor himself know the reasons of wickedness—and he was thought honest and open. It was improbable that Emilia should live with him and never think ill of him. Othello, at first an experienced soldier, comes to trust absolutely this young man of twenty-eight. The handkerchief episode bristles with improbabilities, yet Shakespeare's creative and formative imagination made them all seem probable. The deepest source of all the woe and guilt is Desdemona's innocence. Iago bases his plot on it; because of it Desdemona misunderstands Othello's rage; and owing to it Othello suspects her so easily: and yet we feel its loveliness. Iago's character seems simple enough, but its variety is almost incalculable. He has a keen and subtle, not a high intellect; near Desdemona he looks blacker than hell; and it required little wit to gull Roderigo. He would have succumbed in a day to ordinarily intelligent folk. His plot is ill-constructed, as he should have stolen the handkerchief unknown to Emilia. The centre of him is self-love, which excludes all other love and therefore all goodness. Sensual as the brute, he becomes cruel, for the two are inseparably linked, and he grows to love cruelty for its own sake. Othello is stately, noble, self-contained, and the essence of the tragedy is to reverse this dignified image. He has never quite understood why Desdemona loved him, and he is all of a tremble, over-tense with the advent of love, his whole nature upturned by love. He becomes stupid with pain, and it is vain to deny that he was jealous—and the root of jealousy is selfishness. The notion of grave justice evaporates in the heat of personal rage. Shakespeare was baffled by the cruel irony of life and writes in a passion of pity for men and resentment for their pain. . . .

The subject of drama is passion, and the effect of passion is to stupefy, so it is no wonder that Othello should err. Stopford Brooke does right to dwell on the improbabilities, of which the greatest is Desdemona's love for Othello—and on Iago's second-rate intelligence; but does he allow sufficiently for the working of fate? Again he is plausible but not wholly convincing in explaining psychologically Shakespeare's tragic mood. He speaks of the tempest in Shakespeare's heart, but says nothing to explain the calm that descends on the reader at the close, as the victims—even Emilia—speak words that hint at another country and home of the soul. He examines Iago on all sides but does not appreciably lighten the mystery; but he does well to emphasize Othello's jealousy, though some critics—even Swinburne—have denied it.

All humanity and even the gods are clothed with chaotic darkness in *Lear*. The good suffer for their goodness more than the wicked for their crimes, and Nature is either blind or pitiless. Shakespeare was in hell with more personal suffering than Dante: yet he climbed out of it again. He was exploring the primeval brutalities of uncivilized man, and the slums of human nature. The characters in *Lear* are emerging from savagery but remain half brutal—e.g. Gloster's light talk before his bastard son. The filial impiety of Goneril and Regan is pure savagery developing itself with frank selfishness in the atmosphere of irresponsible power. Unlike the world of Aeschylus, that of *Lear* leaves us in darkness that can be felt. Goneril and Regan feel no remorse, and no divine Justice saves Cordelia. We get furious passions, wild land, untilled society, savage beginnings of the world. Edmund's repentance is modern, and seems out of harmony; his treachery is a civilized vice of the Machiavellian type. Kent and Edgar disguise to express their true character and shake off their conventional ones. Goneril and Regan must have undergone repressed suffering from their overbearing father, and they had his temperament. Cordelia was born good, and suffering had developed her goodness. Lear is a giant smitten to the heart and finally broken down. The inner tempest heightens his powers, and he sees not only himself but the fate and sorrow and crime of the whole world. Also the hypocrisy he has met with urges him to pierce deep into the hidden blackness of mankind—down to its shameful roots. We hear the first condemnation of the black villainy of the Social State. The Fool is angry at Cordelia's banishment and therefore speaks bitterly. Lear understands, and this is their mutual secret. The Fool mixes sense and nonsense, sanity and insanity, and this adds to the mystery of his nature and the feeling that he belongs to another world. Only out of the Eternal Love in a man come scenes like the meeting of Lear and Cordelia. Lear's soul is redeemed, for he comes to know that love solves the mystery of the world. . . .

In the above Stopford Brooke refines upon accepted views and explains rather than initiates. By stating definitely certain things he brings them home to us—such as the degree of savagery in the human nature of the play. We knew before but not in so detailed a manner that Lear's passion increased his powers. If it is possible to vindicate Goneril and Regan to some slight extent he has done so—and here his criticism gets an imaginative tinge. If he is right that the Fool was angry, this is indeed something new: but we will leave it undecided.

Shakespeare's *John* was the old play rewritten but transformed. He added the emotion of Constance, Arthur, Falconbridge—and he slew the King on a burning couch for wronging England. He paints

John as mean, greedy, crafty, selfish, a murderer—yet he must be supported for the country's sake. Pandulph is represented as despising public morality and private humanity when the interests of the Church are in danger. Of all Shakespeare's plays this most appealed to national heart and honour and wrath with Rome. John was an able soldier and politician, but morally bad; his dominant passion is to keep the crown he has unjustly taken. Policy defeats conscience, but he fears his own design to kill Arthur, and even dreads to hear it in words, for then it is irrevocably shaped. We may compare it with Macbeth's soliloquy before he murders Duncan. Now conscience speaks, now the politician, and the two motives are subtly varied. And yet Shakespeare half forgives one who stood against France and Papacy. Falconbridge slowly attains great nobility of character, as great affairs lift him to greatness. When Constance is present the others are but scenery for her wild figure. Her grief is touched with imagination, and her wildest cry is in intellectual order. Her every word is charged with the physical passion of motherhood—unmodified by civilization. . . .

Where the problem is predominantly moral the present critic is a trustworthy guide, and he skilfully values the degrees of blackness of the blots on the character of John. We do not feel the moral subject is intruded, and the moral-aesthetic limit is finely suggested in the scene with Hubert—where the King dreads to hear his design in words. His treatment of Constance recalls that of Lear; but again we think he is over-confident in affirming Shakespeare's personal patriotism.

In its greater parts *1 Henry IV* is of Shakespeare's greatest; the thoughts and passions and meditations of a wide range of observed characters are imaginatively revealed. Execution equals observation, and the personal spirit of the artist kindles the reader. Shakespeare clings to truth but departs from annalism, and creates life as it exists in country, town, camp. It is less a regular drama than a dramatic representation in tableaux of a continuous series of events. The Prince gives unity to the scenes, and Falstaff to some extent. We are not in a democratic country but one likely to become democratic: even the lowest people have got into history. To the King's former character as Bolingbroke is added a control of temper which brings victory but irritates his enemies. Yet when he bids his son imitate that part of his character which has caused the quarrels, and then advises him to be like Hotspur, we feel Shakespeare's irony. Later on we forget the crafty King in the father, and we part in peace with him because he loves. But his craft has been so great in the past that when he offers the gentlest terms to his enemies they cannot believe in him. The Prince separates himself from his father because he understood his character and was out of harmony with it. He was attracted by Falstaff's wit, but he had inherited his father's craft, and deliberately

STOPFORD BROOKE 1913   335

intends to forsake his low companions in the future. He has a pliant
mind and can turn easily from the tavern to affairs of the kingdom.
At times he is as quick and witty as Falstaff, and when war comes all
his follies vanish. At first the contrast of the downright, uncalculating
Hotspur relieves us, but when we find that he has little but animal
courage and desire for fame, and no self-control or consideration for
others, we lose something of our pleasure. It is pitiful that only in
death can he live beyond the present.

The King combined craft with strong will, but Northumberland
combined it with weak will, and so ruins the rebellion. Death softens
the King and at last father and son understand one another. They
are quite affectionate and quite worldly-minded, and personal lovingness
and political craft are mingled with delightful skill. We part from
the King forgiving all, as we part from most of Shakespeare's characters.
We could wish that Henry V had dealt otherwise with Falstaff, but it
was amazingly insolent of Falstaff to approach him at the solemn
time of the coronation, and he had lately degenerated into a mere
cheat, so that his fall is justice.[1] Falstaff has no malice—and this at
least veils his rascality and sensuality. He was no hero but had ordinary
courage: an old fat man could not face two young and vigorous high-
waymen as at Rochester. He was a man of birth, and now and then
his ancient quality and honour emerge to touch us with the pity of
their loss. We forget rather than forgive his faults because we enjoy
his good humour and intellectual power, and because he has the courage
of his situation. . . .

The characters of the King and Hotspur have rarely been better
analysed, and there are some good things said about the Prince and
Falstaff, but also some notable defects with the two last. The Prince
was not witty, and Falstaff was harshly treated—though it is true
that he chose his time ill to address the new-crowned King. But
Shakespeare had to concede something to the facts of history and the
needs of the theatre, and the result was a sudden emotional collapse.
It is too often tacitly assumed—even when formally denied—that
Shakespeare invented his plots, including the historical ones—and an
internal reason is given for what has an external cause. The day of
perfect fusion of plot and character is not yet—so we are not reconciled
to the rejection of Falstaff as we are to the death of Othello—but the
struggle with the histories (as Dowden witnesses) did much to bring it
about. Otherwise the general historical spirit of the play is well
conveyed by the critic.

Shakespeare was glad to turn from the civil war, and in *Henry V*
let himself loose on the honour and greatness of England. He gives
the events of war in tableaux and describes action rather than the
present souls of men in dialogue. Being Shakespeare he cannot help

[1] Cf. Morgann, Bradley, Marriott, Bailey.

showing us the speakers' hearts, but his main object is to inculcate
love of country. The war was aggressive, yet a people would naturally
wish to overcome its opponents, and Shakespeare shared this passion
and common excitement. Patriotism produces national contempts, but
it also commemorates great national qualities. The latter exist apart
from the folly and greed of rulers who cause war; and on these deep-set
noble qualities, as embodied in the King and others, Shakespeare most
dwells. Shakespeare was never greater in historical plays than here,
where he shows the temper in which nobles and soldiers go to death
against enormous odds. At the same time he hated war, which sacrificed
the many to a selfish ruling clique, and he depicts in masterly fashion
the ecclesiastical hypocrisy of mitred rascals. Henry does not appear
entirely noble but the crafty politician and steadfast leader of men.
He has made war with all its horrors for its own purposes; in disguise
he answers the soldiers sophistically; but the hour of revelation comes
when he sees what he is and the difference between him and his
peasant soldier. It is Shakespeare's finer vision of the man within the
King's trappings. The end is self-deceit, and the wonder is that
Shakespeare, who saw clearly the poor stuff of men and heroes, had
yet great reverence for human nature. The balance is perfect between
an unjust and selfish war of aggression, and magnificent and magnanimous courage at death's door. The noble soul of England conquered
at Agincourt. . . .

   There is no doubt that the object of the play is to celebrate the glory
of England, but we do not know in what proportion Shakespeare was
yielding to the demand for patriotic teaching or obeying an internal
impulse. Otherwise Stopford Brooke has used his moral genius to
make some fine aesthetic discoveries—notably as to the King's character and the general structure and balance of the play. It is the kind
of play, with its many moral problems, that such a critic would be
likely to overrate.

VIII

BRANDER MATTHEWS[1] thinks that study of Shakespeare as
a dramatic craftsman has been neglected, and that attention should
be focussed on the plays as plays. They were calculated for the stage
and only there disclose their essential dramatic quality. They were
also written to be performed by a special company of actors, in a
special theatre, before a special audience. The true ancestor of the
Elizabethan play, when Shakespeare began to write, was the dramatized
gospel story of the fourteenth century—a haphazard sequence of casual
episodes performed for the benefit of spectators who could not read.
Shakespeare took the drama as he found it, and never strained to be
original. It is likely that he only revised *Henry VI* and *Titus*, adding

   [1] *Sh. as a Playwright*, 1913 (Longmans).

but rhetoric, not construction or characterization. Remember he was an Elizabethan, with the stout nerves[1] and insensibility to pain of those spacious days. Later on, like all great poets, he used his strength to interpret rather than invent.

The early comedies were lyric and tentative, the result of juvenile cleverness. The story of *L.L.L.* is little related to real life, and its action is external rather than internal—since the author directly intervenes and restricts the free will of his puppets. The King, Princess, courtiers, ladies are less true characters than pleasant parts for the actors; the humorous characters are traditional stage-types. The wit is verbal and the jests of the various persons transferable. *Errors* is one of Shakespeare's most conscientiously worked plays as regards plot; it has an adroit crescendo of comic perplexity, and to farce is added a human quality. *Verona* is more romantic but less well constructed. The situations are reached by improbable means and are ineffective because Shakespeare calls our attention to his unveracious psychology. The play shows how slowly his power to handle character developed. *M.N.D.* has his first truly comic character—Bottom, who is not deliberately witty, and so far above traditional comic figures. In him and his mates we see imagination working on observation. It is the most exquisite of his comedies, if not one of his absolute masterpieces. It has as many comic situations as *Errors*, and mechanical dexterity far more concealed. If *L.L.L.* and *Verona* are comparative failures they are equal to any comedy so far composed. Shakespeare was groping for a formula of comedy, and if he only perfected the romantic comedy, and never achieved the true comedy of manners—which Molière afterwards accomplished—it was because he has no frame to adopt acceptable to his public.

The earliest chronicle plays do not attempt to be harmonious wholes; at most they have the arbitrary unity due to a coercive central character. *Richard III* convinces more in the theatre than the study, and its methods are still primitive: Richard's opening soliloquy is not psychologically true. *Richard II* lacks theatrical effect, but—also unlike *Richard III*—has truthful character-delineation. Events merely happen and are not brought about by deliberate intent. Bolingbroke becomes king rather through Richard's weakness than his own strength. *John* is a medley of scarcely related scenes, where only contrasted characters and abundant eloquence stand out. Falconbridge is outside the story, and the railings of Elinor and Constance are unseemly. Yet the characters, though external, have now become living men and women, not merely parts. As playwright Shakespeare has not improved in these three plays.

R. and J. is the first to withstand the double test of stage and study. The tale is fiery with passion yet chilly with the sense of impending

---

[1] Cf. Stoll and contrast Frank Harris.

doom. Shakespeare exerted his powers when his subject attracted him; otherwise he followed the line of least resistance. In only six or ten of his plays do all his powers work at their full height. Plays were then for the stage, and if the Elizabethan playwright attempted to reach the highest plane of purely artistic excellence, it was from internal stimulus. Shakespeare here works for his own delight and gives to his subject a unity which no other playwright had striven for. Poetry and character are made effective by the framing of the incidents into a plot which rivets the spectators' attention. All the characters obey the law of their own being, and by their implacable purpose sustain the action throughout. The flaw in the plot is the non-delivery of the letter—and to urge that accident plays a part in life is to confound the realities of nature and art.

The two parts of *Henry IV* are less well constructed but more character-creative. The medieval drama allowed lofty and base characters to be mixed, and the Teutonic race does not demand close unity of construction. Shakespeare's power over character is so developed that he can call to life at will as many varied and true human beings as he may need. In these two plays and *Henry V* his power of inexhaustible creation becomes a fact. The key to Falstaff's character is that he is human, and Shakespeare was never more detached.

The structure of the four romantic comedies is curiously alike. They cannot be defined as the highest type of pure comedy like Molière's, where the action is the inevitable result of the clash of character on character. The sub-plots in Shakespeare are romanticist, often archaic in unreality of motives, and only tolerable because we are willing to make believe. These plays are frankly medieval in their devices, though the characters are Renaissance. The truth of the latter makes us believe the story: the pound of flesh and the caskets are inconceivable in any world; but Portia and Shylock are true to life. Portia was the central figure of the *Merchant* to Shakespeare, since Shylock appears only in five scenes. The play is a comedy in its blithesome tone, and a tale of true lovers. Madness and rage were comic to the Elizabethans, and Shakespeare means his spectators to hate Shylock and laugh at him. But he builded better than he knew, so that now we see in Shylock much that is human and pathetic.[1] In defence of the plot of *M. Ado* it may be said that the Elizabethans preferred illogical unexpectedness to credibility. A forward step is that Benedict and Beatrice are not the same at the end of the play as at the beginning, but develop before our eyes—a foretaste of Shakespeare's supreme gift. No one grieves deeply in *A.Y.L.*; it is the most fanciful and lyric of Shakespeare's plays. Rosalind's part is played by a youth, and she attires herself as a lad and then pretends to Orlando that she is a girl—a trick of surpassing theatrical effectiveness. Jaques

[1] Cf. Herford and Stoll.

supplies the element of sub-acid humour which contrasts so pleasantly with the happiness of all the rest. Shakespeare's mastery of stage-craft is proved in *Twelfth-Night* by his skill in connecting the two plots—pensive melancholy and sentiment and riotous humour. The comic characters are no longer traditional, for Shakespeare can now individualize every character, however unimportant. Jokes are no longer extraneous, but are either evoked by situation or express character.

Shakespeare's characters are also parts prepared for particular actors —according to his intimate knowledge of the histrionic abilities of his fellow-players.

Philosophy, psychology, poetry, belong to the subject of *Hamlet* as Shakespeare sees it, and are not externally applied. But even were the characters puppets, the sequence of ingenious situations would hold an audience; but as it is the characters produce the episode by force of their individualities. The play becomes what it is because Hamlet is what he is. Hamlet is not obscure on the stage, and he knows what he wants to do. He is not weak of will, or spectators would lose interest in one who does not know his own mind. Even yet Shakespeare is not fully grown, and there are some irrelevant things. That Laertes who is manly should agree to treason is like Kyd's summary psychology before Shakespeare,[1] and Beaumont and Fletcher's after him: but Elizabethan playgoers liked transformations of character. There is little originality in Hamlet's musings,[2] for Shakespeare was not an original thinker in the narrow sense; but he was in the broad sense: old thoughts born anew from the travail of his mind became fresh and young to him.

Shakespeare had made himself a playwright by hard work, yet he wrote three plays comparatively empty of dramatic power. He wilfully violated the dominating principles of drama that by now were second nature to him. The theory of personal experience is not trustworthy; but he always responded keenly to contemporary influence, and sex-problem plays by Middleton and Marston were then in fashion. The story of *All's Well* leaves a straggling sequence of episodes of mere narrative badly presented in dialogue. The heroine degrades herself by pursuing such an unworthy man. Comic characters are extraneous, and there is a return to the 'clown'. The subject did not attract Shakespeare and his effort was slight. The theme of *M. for M.* is repugnant though not uninteresting, but haphazard as a whole. The play depends on Isabella, and she does not rise to the possible heights of the situation. The Duke has not wooed her, so that she sells herself for rank, though she would not do so for her brother. *T. and C.* is unworthy of Shakespeare as playwright, but may heighten our opinion of him as poet and philosopher, and even more as psycho-

[1] Cf. J. M. Robertson.   [2] Cf. Stopford Brooke.

logist. These three plays prove that he had not found a formula for comedy.

With *Othello* we first get the full richness of true tragedy, without the lyric note of *R. and J.* or that of the revenge-play of *Hamlet*. In form and structure it is Shakespeare's best, though the story is too swift to let the plot be flawless; but the plot is wrought with the care that Shakespeare only bestowed on what attracted him. He shows a mastery of all the tricks of the trade common to the most different playwrights. It is a true tragedy in which the characters exist for themselves, and the action is what it is only because the characters are what they are. Othello is romantic in himself, by birth and career; Romeo's romance is from the circumstances of the story. We may doubt that a human fiend like Iago can exist; but when we see him before us we accept him. He need not justify himself, he acts so because he is Iago. Shakespeare only wishes us to know that he believes he has a reason to detest Othello. In the eyes of men a perfect woman was characterless—and this explains Desdemona, though she is colourless rather than characterless with Shakespeare.

The dramaturgic method of the Roman plays is that of chronicle plays, but the spirit that of the greater tragedies. *J.C.* is an effective stage-play, with vast theme and world-wide background, with strongwilled characters who know their own minds, with abundant oratory, and a succession of striking episodes all integral to the story. *A. and C.* has the lofty elevation and imaginative energy of the mature Shakespeare's tragedies, but the lax form of the chronicle plays of his youth. Things happen rather than are caused by the persons, and the play lacks a controlling purpose. The poet and psychologist were unsupported by the playwright. Antony is infirm of purpose and therefore less dramatic on the stage. But their appeal to each other is intellectual as well as sensual; it is the whole woman and the whole man, soul as well as body, which draw them together. Selfish and callous except to each other, they feel no need for self-respect. There is more willpower in *Coriolanus*, but it does not make the play theatrically attractive: perhaps because it is narrative in dialogue rather than drama. It presents a single character dominated by a single unlovely characteristic.

Shakespeare gets so absorbed in his work that he transcends the needs of the theatre. A play gains in epic grandeur but suffers in being charged with a message too mighty for it. *Lear* is not plausible on the stage; the action is unreal and the theme medieval and remote.[1] The opening test scene is fundamentally absurd. The characters are truly dramatic because they are well endowed with will—even Cordelia knows her own mind. The scene on the heath is supreme, and the play in its higher aspects is a masterpiece of the master poet

---

[1] Cf. Bradley's saying that the material of *Lear* is too vast to use with complete dramatic effectiveness.

of the stage, and in its lower moments it is adjusted to the baser likings of the Elizabethan rabble. The characters took possession of Shakespeare's imagination and compelled him to let them utter their inmost thoughts—and so the poet ousts the playwright and the drama becomes epic. Perhaps he was weary of the dramatic form, for all the plays after *Lear* are more loosely constructed. He comes to rely more and more on his power to vitalize characters, and on poetry and wisdom.

He never again put forth his full power to make a play as perfect as he could in construction and cumulative effect. The plotting of *Macbeth* is careful and conscientious and the action breathlessly rapid. We see deeds disintegrating a once noble character, so that the drama is not external but internal, in Macbeth's soul. The last third of the action is not sustained by equal constructive skill. Yet the story as a whole is firmly put together, and serves as a frame for the portraits of Macbeth and Lady Macbeth. The higher truth appears that character is destiny, and the supernatural becomes an integral element of the story and contributes to the atmosphere of the play. Richard III was a typical stage-villain, but Macbeth was potentially good. Macbeth's power of vision redoubles his sufferings, and he knows that his better nature is being destroyed. Lady Macbeth has no imagination, and is cruel, insensible, and unrepentant. We abhor them, yet they fascinate us by their stern persistence in evil. Shakespeare uses his characters to illustrate the laws of life, and makes us understand and therefore pity them. He points no moral, but the ultimate morality is clear enough. Macbeth is unconscious of the fateful web about him, but Shakespeare sees it and uses magical means to make us see it. The poetry cannot be detached from the drama, and here Shakespeare most proves himself to possess the double qualification of the dramatic poet.

Shakespeare had never sought for an original form, so he readily adopted the dramatic romance. *Cymbeline* lacks reality, is artificial, and ingeniously clever. There is no decline of poet and philosopher, but there is of psychologist and playwright. The characters are slaves of the situation, with no independent life. The final discoveries and recognitions astonish only the characters in the story, for they reveal nothing new to the spectators. The *W. Tale* is even more broken-backed, but the recognitions are more effective because the audience did not know that Hermione had survived. Some characters live independently—Paulina plays her part urged by her own individuality. Perdita is more than the story requires. In the *Tempest* Shakespeare uses the framework of dramatic romance to achieve a beauty all his own. The fantastic misadventures are logical because due to the magician. . . .

Matthews plays the useful part of reclaiming land on which the sea of Shakespeare-worship has unduly encroached. He reminds us that the plays were written for the stage, and he supports his point of view with two strong arguments: that Hamlet is not obscure on the stage, and knows what he wants to do; and that though we doubt such a human fiend as Iago, we accept him when we see him. The worst side of such criticism is his remark that the Duke (*M. for M.*) has not wooed Isabella, so that she sells herself for rank, though she would not do so for her brother. But on the whole it is the best kind of common-sense criticism, not unlike but far surpassing those who would reject all previous opinions and reread the plays with nothing between their minds and Shakespeare's. It tells how the Shakespearian drama rose out of chaos into the perfect form of *Othello*; it explains the shortcomings of the chronicle play, and also of the romantic comedy compared with Molière's true character comedy. It does well to raise the question of technique and to point out that only in six or ten plays did Shakespeare achieve full dramatic expression: we are reminded how Carlyle insisted on the power of intellect needed to construct a play of Shakespeare's. And yet the problem of Shakespeare's genius as ever escapes the formula. *Lear* is intrinsically greater though technically less than *Othello*; and the disadvantages of the chronicle method do not detract from the poetry of *A. and C.*

IX

EXPRESSION is the end of art; and character, with its outcome destiny, is Shakespeare's great concern: these two points are made clear by Mr. W. F. Trench[1] at the outset of his study. In no play does character interest so completely submerge that of incident as in *Hamlet*. Liberty is not no-restraint: a tiger appears free but is governed by inexorable law. Man needs a truer freedom based upon will; to live in liberty and progress he needs to be controlled by a higher law than the tiger. He stands alone in that he is not compelled to obey his own law, which is moral law—and he feels within himself passion warring against this law. In morals these may be reconciled by transforming passion into love; in art by transforming it into love of beauty—passion become passion for beauty, the source of perfect order.

The core of the situation is that an idealist is brought face to face with actuality, and must play a man's part in a simple and primitive form of life's conflict. Responsibility deteriorates Hamlet; the formerly religious man curses his birth. If it falls out that the hero, once greatly refined, becomes obscene; that he who was charged to avenge the death of one innocent person occasions the death of several innocent persons; and that he who was once scrupulously moral becomes indifferent to homicide: then indeed was there never greater irony in the world of art—especially as the cause is man's chief glory—intellec-

[1] *Sh.'s Hamlet: A New Commentary*, 1913 (Smith, Elder).

tuality. But he fails through a definite defect in his will; he had contemplated suicide, which means that the will renounces control. He
decides on a course of inaction, and incurs the inevitable penalties
from weakening of will.

Pressed down by his new burden he needs the support of love and
friendship. Ophelia fails him, and so do Rosencrantz and Guildenstern
—though he is unjustifiably severe in sending them to death. It is
hard to understand him, as even Shakespeare found—and he cannot
understand himself. The truth is that his whole life is changed beyond
his recognition: the philosopher must be a politician, the moralist a
manslayer, the theorist and idealist must give out energy and practical
efficiency. The Ghost's words stimulated him to 'remember' and note
down in his tablets—the player's to speak passionately and then to
write a play. It would be an excuse to postpone, did he doubt the
Ghost's identity (which he had never doubted before), so he writes
a play.

He has now missed his chances, and the slaying of Polonius involves
his doom. Speaking, reading, writing, were congenial to him, and the
form of action he had turned to was suicide. When thought became
intolerable he sought relief in insulting Ophelia. She reveals herself
in her lament, not the real Hamlet: for the conventional and proper
heir-apparent existed only in her imagination. There is much matter
in Shakespeare that impressionism cannot discover. He was often
careless of stage-effect, and wished solely to present character perfectly,
to satisfy himself, not the theatre. Hamlet lectures the actors to express
his own character, not Shakespeare's own views of the drama. After the
play scene he discovers the madman's impulse to kill: suicidal tendency
becomes homicidal, though he does not think of killing Claudius. The
Queen is in instinctive terror for her life, but not after he has killed
Polonius. Shakespeare ignores stage-effect and declines to make things
easy for us to follow; but it is absurd to say that the play is full of inconsistencies. Hamlet knows that he kills Polonius undeliberately, and does
not repent, but feels he acted as a scourge in the hands of God, than
which nothing is more dangerous. Is there any hope for such a Hamlet?

Impressionism does not suffice for the criticism of the greatest
plays because it may miss a whole series of details the cumulative
effect of which should be to modify the character estimates of first
impressions. Ophelia's description of Hamlet does not arrest us because
we are affected by the situation, and do not expect detail just here to
reveal character. We enjoy the passage but miss its character value,
which in drama is the most important thing, and when this has occurred
in passage after passage we reach character estimates due more to our
sensibility than reason and imagination. We must criticize rationally
and imaginatively, and also carefully examine Shakespeare's methodical
plot structure. The latter will make clearer his attitude towards and

treatment of character and destiny. There is a definite break between each act, though not necessarily one of time; and thus the fourth act of *Hamlet* should begin with scene 3—when Hamlet leaves Denmark. The fourth act belongs to Claudius, and the moral question is not what the agent shall do but what he shall be. Claudius will not regain peace by renouncing the kingship, and as one cannot be the same after a self-conscious decision, he falls lower and decides on a second murder. Hamlet in his soliloquy accuses himself of failing to exercise his reasoning powers, of not looking beyond the present moment: can the mistakes of self-analysis go further? If Gertrude's speech be regarded as the account of Ophelia's actual death, it is absurd and undramatic; but she had been terror-struck when Laertes demanded his father, and now there was another death. To lessen its bitterness she therefore urges that it was purely accidental and painless. She lacked refined sensibility and was awkwardly imaginative; she expected Laertes to be as dangerously angry at Ophelia's death as at his father's. Shakespeare does not strain after stage-effect and distinguishes between dramatic and theatrical value.

The philosophy of the grave-diggers goes deep enough to search the very foundations of society, and in the presence of death Hamlet and the clowns meet upon a level. A most inadequate psychology would ascribe his outburst at the grave to feigned madness. It is want of self-control, and as with Polonius he claims irresponsibility. Now at the end he is confident in the overruling hand of God, and repudiates voluntary action. He is wrong to deny chance, and here we see the dramatist making us face mysteries of destiny. In Act 1 he decided to let himself go, and so proclaimed his madness. He left his duty undone, and trusted to God to bring things right, and so denied freedom, responsibility, manhood. The 'divinity's' plans are worked out by means of free men; Hamlet was given a chance of doing his share, but he failed and brought about disaster. When Ophelia deplores the loss of his reason Shakespeare is poking fun at her; and when you deplore his death he is poking fun at you. Fortinbras praises him, but the truth is that, under the rule of a philosopher, things in Denmark would have become still rottener; an idealist should have no kingdom but his own mind. . . .

Mr. Trench's point of view has become clear during the above analysis: he stresses character value and denounces impressionism. But there may be another cause for the failure of impressionism—the disharmony between the character of Hamlet and the primitive incidents of the play. He does well to distinguish between dramatic and theatrical effect, and his arguments in favour of Hamlet's madness at least stimulate thought. Nowadays we say that if Hamlet were mad he would be irresponsible, and the play would lose moral interest; but he gives a moral reason for Hamlet's irresponsibility. However, he shares the fate of all critics who insist on keeping in their depth while studying Shakespeare. This most appears in his verdicts on the eulogies of Hamlet by Ophelia and Fortinbras, and the speech of Gertrude on the death of Ophelia. We may compare the latter to Cleopatra's words as she feels her spirit loosing:

I am fire and air . . .

. . . .

As sweet as balm, as soft as air, as gentle . . .

When death is in the air, men and women say and do strange things.

X

PROFESSOR HERFORD says that Shakespeare's tragedy always centres in personality. In his supreme dramas the mystery of personality and the human fates rooted in it is more deeply explored than anywhere else in literature. Profound and intimate fellowship with the souls of men went to the making of the great tragedies. Mr. Mabie, that personality is the basis of his conception of authority and significance of human nature. Stopford Brooke, that his tolerant, almost divine way of seeing humanity gives him at least a fourth of his power over mankind. Matthews, that he had a vibrating sympathy with the characters of his great tragedies. Mr. Trench, that he had unequalled imaginative sympathy and power of identifying himself with his characters; that the aspects of human character and phases of human experience which he set forth were innumerable and infinitely complex; that he does not discuss or analyse a character but impersonates it with complete dramatic objectivity and unlimited imaginative sympathy. Against these Professor Stoll affirms that, in accordance with the Renaissance, he was indifferent to psychology.

On the subject of morals and philosophy we have Mr. Mabie's tribute to his moral sanity and ethical soundness. He is among the greatest ethical teachers, not by intention but by deep and clear vision: being the closest observer and most daring idealist of his age. Professor Stoll gives him a moral bias: when morals are concerned he breaks the character's point of view to let himself appear. But he conceived of remorse in a rather external, spiritual way, and did not realize that sin is spontaneous and unconscious; nor do heredity and environment play any part in him. In the opinion of Stopford Brooke, the universe to Shakespeare, where evil destroys itself, was naturally moral; but he also says that during the progress of his tragedies belief in divine Justice came to be replaced by belief in Chance. Matthews finds in him the universal toleration of universal understanding. Morality to him is not something that can be put into a play but something that cannot be left out—implicit, not explicit, ethics. Mr. Trench notes that he constructs his plots about a moral centre. Also that in his philosophy Providence asserts itself through accident. In his great heart is some kindliness or benignity, some tinge of a charity like God's, intermingled with sarcasm or grim irony, and some sort of pitilessness like Nature's.

The supreme expression of his art, in the words of Professor Herford, was tragedy. His, says Mr. Mabie, was the marvellous harmony of the expert craftsman united to the poet's superb imagination: he had extraordinary genius for seeing concrete fact and unrivalled power of irradiating that fact with the insight and vision of the imagination. Against the judgement of Stopford Brooke that he had intense persistency in finish and careful art, we set that of Matthews, that he was not incessant and conscientious in striving to attain perfection, and attained it only now and again.[1] Matthews also says that he had the gift of inexhaustible creation, that he was a poet by the gift of God, psychologist by observation and intuition, philosopher as the result of insight and meditation, playwright by hard work; and that he is richer in the life-giving faculty than any other dramatist.

The following are more purely general remarks: Mr. Mabie's, that he was always sane and large-minded; Stopford Brooke's, that he had a nature of indelible sweetness, and extraordinary balance of judgement.

Two other remarks to be set side by side are Stopford Brooke's, that his personal sympathy was on the side of Republicanism, and though he may not actually have been a republican, he was opposed to despotism; and Matthews's, that he had intense human sympathy —the noblest quality of our modern democratic movement.[2] Both these writers describe him as an ardent patriot.

Matthews says that he has noble portraits of women but no line in praise of the sex itself. . . .

From the most significant of these remarks we gain the impression that Shakespeare revealed to man something new and mysterious in his own soul. He reduces us all to the type eloquently described by Stopford Brooke, ignorant of its own soul, and when forced to see it, crying out, 'What is this place? Where am I?' No less than before he is considered a great moral teacher, but his morality also is less definite and more mysterious, like nature's. Only a few positive statements about his politics or religion persist.

[1] Cf. Bradley.   [2] Cf. Swinburne (1909).

Chapter XXXVI

ENGLAND 1914–1917

I. GILBERT MURRAY. II. STOLL. III. HOLME. IV. SIDNEY LEE. V. DE
SÉLINCOURT. VI. MATHEW. VII. MACKAIL. VIII. J. M. ROBERTSON.
IX. BEECHING. X. CONCLUSION.

I

PROFESSOR GILBERT MURRAY[1] explains that Hamlet and
Orestes were traditional types, and *Hamlet* was gradually built up
like most of the great Elizabethan plays. In all versions it is essential
to the whole dramatic character that both heroes should be under the
shadow of madness. Something in Hamlet makes us wonder if his
madness is assumed; and something in Orestes makes it easy for him
to go mad. Orestes soliloquizes and doubts and hesitates like Hamlet.
He also suspects that God, who commands vengeance, may be an evil
spirit in disguise. Both express violently cynical opinions about women.
There are also slighter coincidences; in both traditions the hero is
away from home when the drama begins; both go on a ship, are
captured by enemies but escape. . . . When the sagas were worked
up into tragedies, the old similarities remain and new ones are developed:
Aeschylus, Euripides, Shakespeare, resemble each other in points that
do not occur in Saxo or Ambales or the Greek epic. The hero's
madness is the same in Shakespeare and Euripides, but differs from
that in Saxo or Ambales; yet Shakespeare did not study the Greek
tragedies directly. Where is the connexion?

A group of legends produced the Orestes-saga: Kronos cast out
Ouranos, and Zeus cast out Kronos. A Summer-king or Vegetation-
spirit is slain by Winter and rises from the dead in the Spring. Or
each Year-king comes first as a wintry slayer, weds the queen, grows
proud and royal, and then is slain by the Avenger of his predecessor.
The Hamlet of Saga resembles Orestes when we find that he is a
bitter fool and king-slayer. Hamlet's mother plays the strange part
of wedding her husband's slayer. The King's wife in the saga, under
the shadow of adultery, incest, murder, remains motherly and sympathetic: so Gertrude—who is the right character for our Mother Earth
—loved to be happy and see others so. Thus the origin of the Hamlet
and the Orestes sagas is in the prehistoric and world-wide ritual
battle of Summer and Winter, Life and Death. As happens in religion,
the fundamental identity still shows itself. The subjects appeal to
deep-rooted human instincts and move us in profound and poetical
ways, as though we had known them always. Tradition effects

---

[1] *Hamlet & Orestes*: Annual Sh. Lecture, 1914 (N.Y. Oxford Univ. Press,
American Branch).

that myth is corrected by life. That is where realism comes in, and literary skill and imagination. The writers in the greatest ages of literature preserve a due proportion between the expression of boundless primitive emotion and the subtle and delicate representation of life. In *Hamlet* or *Agamemnon* or *Electra*, besides their perfect art, we have an under-current of desires and fears and passions, long slumbering yet eternally familiar. The power to stir this stream or move with it is one of the last secrets of genius. . . .

Such criticism is the work of a learned man who is also a poet. As spectrum analysis proved that all worlds were made of one material, so Professor Murray helps us to realize that the human mind is one in all ages. And the result is to make us take more seriously even art itself, and the artist who knows something of these subterranean streams. If ever we had thought art depended on artifice and was a matter for the individual, we should do so no longer. The origin of life, the mystery of creation: these are the ultimate problems of the world. As they touch the world of art, Professor Murray has done something to make them less impossible to solve. It has been well said that we are bound by strange ties to our common mother, Earth.

II

PROFESSOR STOLL opens his essay on Falstaff[1] by disagreeing with Morgann and the romantics. A great dramatist does not dupe us deliberately, but on the contrary accentuates what is in the foreground. The cowardly flight from Gadshill stands first, and therefore dominates the whole. The principle that what is most prominent is most important is the beginning and end of art. Gadshill is an example of the practical joke, according to Elizabethan usage, played on a braggart or coward. There is no instance of a character making a fool of himself on purpose; and if a character feigns, like Prince Hal, we are informed of it. To Falstaff's cowardice we have the testimony of the Prince, Poins, and Falstaff himself who proves it when he roars and runs away. Shakespeare's cowards, like his villains, bear their names written in their foreheads—and such refinements as Morgann suggests were foreign to his stage. After the robbery Falstaff swaggers and calls the Prince and Poins cowards; and this charge of cowardice against the brave by the coward is a perennial stage situation. The same applies to the practice of hacking swords with daggers. If Falstaff had lied and escaped in fun, there would be no fun in confuting him. He jokes and quibbles to cover up his cowardice and confusion.

Shakespeare will have him a coward if Morgann will not. On the

---

[1] *Falstaff*, 1914 (Sh. Studies. N.Y., The Macmillan Co., 1927).

eve of the battle he whimpers, 'I would 'twere bed-time, Hal, and all well', and then says his catechism of dishonour. He feigns death, like all clowns and cowards; like them he wreaks himself on a dead body, and then plots to take the honour of killing Hotspur. Men of principle who scorn glory do not snatch at other men's. His pretence and appearances of valour, like his boasting and philosophy of discretion, merely heighten the comic—the cowardly—effect. It is true that the Chief-Justice pays tribute to his service at Shrewsbury, but the explanation is that Shakespeare knew his audience would not now go astray, and having sufficiently exhibited Falstaff's character and established his reputation, he secures a comic effect by reminding us of his martial exploits and letting him profit by the acceptance of the rumour.

We must remember that the original of Falstaff was Sir John Oldcastle, and Shakespeare was dealing with a coward of popular tradition. As with his English kings or Roman heroes he always stands by popular tradition. Falstaff belongs to the type of the braggart captain; he has all the qualities of this ancient stage-figure—cowardice, bragging, gluttony, lechery, sycophancy, and pride. He appears a sycophant when he wheedles the Prince, and proud when he insists on his title. All these traits are inherited from the Italian popular *Miles Gloriosus*, Capitano Spavento. But Falstaff is not silly and affected, only boasts when there is need, is not beaten and knocked about the stage, but keeps a sort of dignity, and is a humourist and wit. No doubt these have impressed critics, but all his other traits are those of famous clowns—Panurge, Sosie, Scarron's Jodelet. Had Falstaff not added cowardice to his other failings he would have disappointed the audience, for cowardice is the most comic. He is not a figure drawn from real life; cowards do not go to war and become captains. But on the stage a coward who does not rob on the highway or follow the wars is no coward. We might as well call Parolles brave, who yearns for the wars in Italy and persuades his master to take him there. Falstaff goes to war to furnish matter for comedy.

We now turn to the 'incomprehensible lies' of the buckram story. It sounds unplausible that he should exaggerate to his own cost and discredit, for the malicious pleasure of Poins and the Prince; but the unplausibility is to be paralleled elsewhere. Benedict is equally clever, but exposes his disgrace after he stumbles and falls, instead of endeavouring to conceal it: he at once betrays that he is lovesick, after all his railings against love and marriage. He is jeered at and laughed at like Falstaff, and he and Beatrice are the last people to expose themselves. The idea is that the dramatist should secure a telling and immediate comic effect—that of the scorner scorned, the boaster and liar as a coward laid bare. Shakespeare aims to be dramatically effective not psychologically consistent. When Falstaff is not a wit he is naïve, and the pith of the humour is when his appetite for purses or mirth bursts in an instant the bonds of his penitence. He is as unconscious as inconsistency ever has been on the comic stage. Naïve as well as witty, he does not wish to make himself ridiculous for the sake of a joke, to step into traps for the fun of wriggling out of them. From Aristophanes and Plautus through the Renaissance to the present day there are comic characters whose dearest desire, after saving themselves, is to save their faces.[1]

If Falstaff steps into the trap on purpose, little would depend on his evasions: but here lies the centre of interest. The Prince and Poins press him hard and embarrass him, so that he turns from bluster to coaxing and wheedling. It is fine to speak well, but finer still when need arises. Dryden, Johnson, and Addison recognized Falstaff's need, but Morgann and the Romantics did not. To be caught in a trap and try to explain his way out of it was the typical plight of the coward in medieval and Renaissance comedy. How could the audience, without a hint, discover that this seeming coward was not really a coward, and these seeming excuses mere make-believe?

It is in his wit and somewhat in his purpose that Falstaff's excuses differ from those of Bessus, Bobadill, or Jodelet. Compared with their subterfuges his are gay, aggressive, triumphant, and laughter-provoking. He has an impudent dignity, and though he does not expect to be believed in his evasions, he does in his bragging lies. He makes up for all that he has lost for reputation for valour by what he gains in reputation for ingenuity and gaiety. The main thread we are seeking to trace, which explains much in Falstaff, is the principle of a looser unity-identity in dramatic function and tone rather than in mental quality and processes. He must be entertaining rather than plausible, and this explains his jokes amid carnage, regardless of ultimate pyscho-logical propriety, but in the manner of Elizabethan clowns. Shake-speare may be careless in detail, and he seldom conceived his characters apart from the plot—and this explains why Falstaff fights with Pistol and captures Coleville.

It is part of Shakespeare's greatness that he does not keep strictly to a scheme: he conceives Shylock in prejudice, but now and then touches him with incompatible tenderness. If Falstaff is unabashed before the King at Shrewsbury, it is characteristic of Elizabethan drama that any comic character jokes with a king, and a king jokes with anybody. It matters little whether he and Panurge are gentlemen. Criticism is wrong to insist upon details and draw fine-spun deductions —upon his knighthood, seal-ring, bonds, pension.

The fatal objection to the theory that Falstaff is feigning is that he keeps his joke to himself. There are no such jokes on the stage;

[1] Cf. Fauconbridge in *Look About You* (1600), Middleton's *Family of Love*, Passarino in Cicognini's *Don Juan*, Beaumont's Bessus, Chapman's *Widow's Tears*.

and with Shakespeare the battle is to the strong, and success never
looks like failure.   Comic effect consists in swift transition from
unreality to reality, or the reverse—and there must be no uncertainty.
If the joke is not on Falstaff, and his courage is real, then the joke is
on ourselves.   The play is for the stage, not a closet drama to be explained
by solitary and anxious perusal.   Morgann himself admits that the
audience took Falstaff for a coward.   Uncertainty in the individual,
disunion in the audience, is the death of laughter.

Falstaff has been given a philosophy, has been called a military
free-thinker and moral nihilist, not void of principle but inspired by
an anarchistic sort of principle.   But his soliloquy on honour comes
from his wits, to cover his shame, not from the heart.   His
'philosophy' is but a shift and evasion; he is not dead to morality,
but takes refuge in sophistry.   Half a dozen cowards in contemporary plays talk in Falstaff's vein.   In Panurge above all the
ironical method is obvious.   Falstaff's philosophy is a bundle of evasions,
to escape from himself, not Poins and the Prince.   It resembles the
ironical method of Anatole France shifted to the first person—the
method of Fielding, Sterne, Molière, and others.   Falstaff calls sack
the cause of valour, which is a confession of cowardice; and Benedict
declares that the world must be peopled.   The result is to dissolve
away the speaker's pretences; he does not express but exposes his
inmost self.   Perhaps this method of ironical self-betrayal is a thing
outworn; psychology—born of sympathy—rejects it as external and
double-tongued.   It seems to confuse for us the lines of the character,
to make the author peer through and wink at the audience—to the
harm of our sympathy and craving for reality.   But, when we come
upon it, our mistake is to adjust it to the modern spirit instead of
adjusting ourselves to the Elizabethan.

Critics who have not learned to think historically have lifted
Falstaff out of Shakespeare's reach.   Morgann protests that he is
without evil motive: but he lies and jests for profit, cheats and swindles
his unsophisticated admirers, is gluttonous and lecherous, robs on the
highway, and is a coward.   In contradiction to some of his apologists
he does cheat the weak and prey on the poor, e.g. Quickly and the
conscripts.   All this was once funny, but is now base and pitiful: as
much that was funny to the Elizabethans or Louis XIV is now pathetic,
like Shylock and Harpagon, Alceste and George Dandin—and 'dis-
gusting' and 'terrible' like Falstaff or Tartuffe.   Even now it is
impossible to see Falstaff on the stage without a shudder.

If Englishmen like Falstaff it is because their pleasure in the
picaresque still lingers.   Also Falstaff appeals more by his speech than
his conduct; he is supremely poetic, and though he talks prose it is
the most marvellous prose ever penned.   Besides its vitality and spirit,
friendliness and good humour, fancy and wit, it is more heavily

charged with the magnetism of a personality, and has caught more the perfect intonation of an individual human voice than any other prose or verse. Englishmen cannot escape the strong infection, though foreigners may prefer Sancho. In this lies the contradiction—for all of us, like Prince Hal and Mrs. Quickly, take to a man for his charm, not his virtue. We must also reckon with Shakespeare's comic art— the isolation and comic emphasis that we saw with Shylock. Shakespeare does not insist on Falstaff's sins and vices but subordinates them to his comic effects. His boasting and lying are not needless, but the revival of enthusiasm after ignominious lapses, the glow of reaction after escape. His roguery is not professional but human and incidental. He is only scared for moments; he can assume a virtue, though he has it not the next moment. His promptings of conscience are real, but not too real: a call for a bawdy song ends them when he is in health. Yet they prick him a little on the battle-field, and are just present at his death-bed. Were he perfectly happy he would not be so human, and his distinction is to override obstacles to happiness. He rises superior to all immaterial things, but not to circumstances. He does not laugh when he is cast off: as he would do if the critics were right. He is planted on this earth and cannot dispense with her favours. He does not regret the Prince, nor does he crave love—but he requires good fellowship. He is by nature a guest, not a host, and has found it more blessed to receive than give. He has been able to dodge duty, but he cannot dodge discomfort and cold fact. The King is harsh and priggish, but character and situation are true, and the game of evasion cannot last for ever. . . .

Much of our comments on Professor Stoll's previous essays would apply to the present one; it is therefore not necessary to repeat them, and we will discuss a few of his remarks that apply in the narrower sense. We naturally ask whether he has confuted Morgann and the romantics? From the historical point of view the answer is Yes— for if emphasis is the artist's chief means of expression, it is by perverting (dramatically) this emphasis that Morgann and others have achieved their effects. In the ultimate court of appeal, the individual soul, impressionistic criticism may rank higher than historical—but we cannot neglect the historical, especially at the present day. For reasons already given the reader will recognize as typical of Professor Stoll's learning and psychology, the description of the stage-coward who always goes to war—the saying that cowards do not go to war and become captains—the remarks on ironical self-betrayal, and the conclusion that men attract by charm, not virtue, and Falstaff does not regret the Prince but requires good fellowship. His remarks on Falstaff's prose are noteworthy, and refer back to the last essay where he says that the life-giving touch creates character, not interior motives—and look forward to the essay on Shakespeare himself.

They may also be compared with Mr. Middleton Murry's theory why Falstaff declines in Part II.

III

MR. J. W. HOLME'S criticism of *A.Y.L.*[1] is a fine piece of work He reminds us of Professor Herford by his insight and power to express his thoughts with perfect balance and absence of prejudice. He calls Touchstone Shakespeare's most complex, purely comic character, and he says that Shakespeare transforms him from the family-fool to the keen dissector of insincerity; though it is often hard to say where buffoonery merges into courtly cynicism: his grotesque courtship is itself a piece of broad parody of pastoral love-making. Despite his marriage he stands outside the symmetrical arrangement of characters; he has a roving commission of parody, of reducing to strict common sense the affectations of the others. He states grotesquely the opposite point of view and strips off inessentials; his comments are the true touchstone of the false position into which his companions have argued themselves. Jaques is the Italianate Englishman, and his function is like Touchstone's on a higher plane. But his cynicism is often a pose, and at times one is inclined to think he does not himself believe in it. He anticipates certain tragic possibilities undeveloped as yet in Shakespeare. Like Brutus he is an intermediate stage in Shakespeare's process of evolving Hamlet. The melancholy, now but a potentially tragic excrescence, was to become dramatic and produce the climax. Rosalind, like Beatrice, is a perfect portrait of the high-born, cultured, witty court-lady, who yet loses nothing of womanly charm and tenderness. The wit of Beatrice, Portia, and Rosalind never lapses from their constant level of high-bred, cultured, fine ladyhood. Shakespeare transforms the atmosphere by introducing realistic peasants, as in the *W. Tale*; in both plays he refuses the artificialities of his model. The secondary incidents do not interfere with the larger plot; and when the minor persons hold the stage the larger interests are not neglected. Thought, language, verse, are perfectly wedded; the flexibility and restrained speed of the prose fit it to represent closely the easy flow of contemporary high-bred conversation, and the pithy colloquial talk of shepherd or country-wench. It is the consummation of Shakespeare's work before he turned to tragedy. . . .

We note the fine tribute to Shakespeare's art, and to his imaginative insight in portraying Rosalind—and the critic's sense of the beauty of the play and also its relative importance in the Shakespearian scheme It is well to note the significance of Touchstone's name.

[1] Arden edit. 1914 (Methuen).

IV

SIDNEY LEE [1] affirms the immense debt to Italy of modern literature, philosophy, science, law, art. When the Turks overthrew the
Byzantine Empire in the fifteenth century the literary art of Athens
was driven westward in full flood. Feeling for form, delight in life,
free use of reason, dawned on the modern world. Cardinal Bembo
summed up the new gospel by declaring that only when one said of
the world that it is beautiful did one serve the cause of truth. The creed
of the Renaissance frankly acknowledged the earthly elements in man's
being, yet insisted on the power of reason to raise him ultimately to the
angels. Reason and beauty had one purpose when man's mind discovered and revealed the ultimate beauty and order underlying matter.

The Renaissance came late to England and was only literary. Shakespeare was the greatest of humanists because of his catholic sensitiveness
to external impressions and power to transmute them into something
richer and rarer. In the garden scene of the *Merchant* we hear the
dominant notes of the Italian Renaissance. Italian fable is the basis
of his dramatic structure, but the changes he made best reveal the
greatness of his faculty and the breadth of his intuitive grasp of human
passion and sentiment. He transforms Iago from a conventional
Italian criminal to the profoundest of all portraits of hypocrisy and
intellectual villainy. The Sonnets prove how deeply he had drunk of
the spring of Italian philosophy. From Petrarch downwards, sonneteers
preached that beauty was ideal, and isolated it from its physical embodiment. Shakespeare says his friend's beauty is a 'shadow' of the true
'substance' of perfect beauty. He identifies beauty with truth—an
entity independent of matter and time. It was by way of Italy that
such doctrine reached Shakespeare in England. His humour and his
power over the drama were his own. . . .

We here get clearly and comprehensively stated the different
elements in the Renaissance—their influence on Shakespeare, and
his power to transcend them.

V

PROFESSOR E. DE SÉLINCOURT [2] discovers that Shakespeare
was profoundly impressed, as the modern artist is not, with the individual's relation to the nation. He treated neither tragic nor tragi-
comic theme without giving it an historical or quasi-historical background. The hero's relation with his State intensifies or complicates
the situation. His root-principle is that of *noblesse oblige*; he believes
that the great are surrounded by great temptations, and they are only

---

[1] *Sh. and the Italian Renaissance*: Annual Sh. Lecture 1915 (Pub. for Brit. Acad.
by H. Milford).
[2] *English Poets and the National Ideal*, 1915 (Oxford University Press).

great when they surmount them. *M. for M.* shows how those in authority and under it may endanger a State. Baseless attack on those in authority is the worst and most dangerous crime. This is not aristocratic bias but profound criticism of a State's greatest peril— which grows in proportion to the power of the people over their country's policy. In our days the people have become the autocrat, but the problem is the same. Richard II's love for England was based on what England could do for him; he ignored that duty which the very existence of a community demands from all its sons. The nobles who surrounded him were patriots, but they warred with each other, so we conclude that 'patriotism when there is no moral order means civil strife'. Except in *Henry V*, England is the hero of the historical plays; the reigning monarch typifies some vice in the nation —with Richard II love of pleasure, with Richard III unscrupulous ambition, with John treachery and opportunism, with Henry IV personal selfishness in diplomacy. Shakespeare maintains that policy will only succeed if it is just, and observes the same laws of conduct as do private individuals. A ruler must no more break moral laws in the interests of a community than in his own interests. Richard was unfit to rule, but Bolingbroke had no right to usurp. Shakespeare admired his efficiency, but censures his ambition: he can do no permanent good. For Henry V as a ruler—though not as a man—Shakespeare has nothing but praise: he is simple, sincere, selflessly devoted to his country, and, above all, religious. He was no hypocrite, and Shakespeare did not doubt his claim to France. His teaching was the counterblast to the prevailing Machiavellianism. He saw that Nemesis worked in States as well as individuals; the sins of the fathers were visited upon the children, and there was a redeeming power in virtue and the consciousness of right. . . .

The value of this work is that it establishes on a secure foundation a test for Shakespeare's historical characters. As they bear themselves to their country their natures appear—and the contrast with each other follows inevitably. Professor de Sélincourt believes that Shakespeare's root-principle was *noblesse oblige*, and he argues back from the facts in such a way that Shakespeare compares with himself. This is the best method for proving that Shakespeare had any particular belief or principle—because comparisons of Shakespeare with other writers are apt to be unprofitable. We may say that in these pages Shakespeare becomes self-convicted of a high political morality, and that the criticism is a fine balance between positive and agnostic. After a preliminary act of faith the facts are left to speak for themselves. . . . There are certain questions that we prefer to raise without attempting to answer: thus we ask, Did Shakespeare believe that Henry V had a true claim to France?

VI

THE motive of Mr. Frank Mathew's[1] book is to make us understand Shakespeare by teaching us the right order of his works. He
rewrote or retouched nearly all his plays, so that mature and immature
work are blended. Probably he began to write short plays of the nature
or length of Interludes—because the separate parts visible in most of
his plays seem to have been of an appropriate length. *Titus* may have
been written first as a poem, and it remains lyrical: its terrible doings
are absolutely innocent. *T. and C.* belongs to different periods, but
the Troilus part to this one. Also the first version of *Coriolanus*,
which is external and rhetorical and Marlowesque, and differs from
the other mature tragedies which ache with sympathy. Had he written
it when mature he would have transfigured Plutarch as he did with
A. and C. At this time the influence of Kyd predominated with
Shakespeare; *Lear* in its first form seems based on the *Spanish Tragedy*.
The blinding of Gloster proves that Shakespeare could have written
the horrors of *Titus*. The faults and merits of *Cymbeline* are those of
good work; and the fact that *Cymbeline* and *Lear* are the two plays
most akin to *Titus* prove that they were first written in youth. Autolycus was too wise for Shakespeare's earliest mood and too merry for
his latest. Such contrasts prove that he wrote these plays when young
and revised them when mature.

Shakespeare's supposed mood of reconciliation is not peculiar to
the *W. Tale* and *Cymbeline*, but belongs also to *Verona*, *M. for M.*,
A.Y.L., and the *Merchant*. The *Tempest* is partly based on *M.N.D.*,
and an innocent fantastic Romance, with the sweetness of *Pericles*,
seems to survive in the satire and weariness of a final revision. The
alacrity of *L.L.L.* seems combined with the mellow mood of *Twelfth-
Night*: the Fortunate Island is as sequestered as the Forest of Arden,
and Jaques sees the folly of youth as soberly as Prospero. Shakespeare
is not moved by any grief for Antigonus or Lavinia or Imogen.

There were three seasons in Shakespeare's life as writer—spring,
summer, autumn. *R. and J.* and *M.N.D.* are companion plays: the
latter is a humorous comment on the illusions of love. It has another
companion—the woodland tragedy of *Titus*, and is linked with the
Tempest as a fairy-tale. It also has links with *A.Y.L.*, *Errors*, the
Shrew, and *Verona*. Thus we see that no play can be studied apart,
for each is illuminated by others. The ironical setting of *M.N.D.*
turns the fairies to ridicule as well as the rustics. There are two
separate Interludes—the fairy-tale and the farcical one. The doings of
Bottom and his friends were a comment on Fairyland as those of
Falstaff and his on Chivalry. These Interludes brought Shakespeare's
country in touch with the real life of his day—the true things in his

[1] *An Image of Sh.*, 1915–20 (Jonathan Cape, 1922).

work before he could attain the darker truth of his tragedies. The *Merchant* reconciles a savage tale like *Titus* with the gaiety of the amorous youths in *L.L.L.* and *Verona*. Perhaps *Shylock's Revenge* and the *Choice of the Caskets* were separate plays, and Shakespeare revised and blended them in a comedy in 1594. The *Merchant* can only be expounded by recognizing that it was rewritten in a different mood. Shylock's collapse and the scornful pardon it earns are appropriate to a comical villain, like Parolles. *A.Y.L.*, *Twelfth-Night*, and Act IV of *W. Tale* are the work of a man old enough to see life as it is and young enough to take delight in it still. Parolles (*All's Well*) is impossible because he is drawn in contradictory moods; the Parolles of the first act could never have been fooled in the fourth. Bertram survives from the days when Shakespeare could admire such a boy. *Twelfth-Night* must have been an early work, and is linked with *Errors*, because the story of the deception is heartless. Shakespeare could not have chosen a noble gentleman's heart-break as the theme of a jest after he had drawn Jaques. Malvolio underwent a change like Shylock; he began as a laughing-stock, fool, and hypocrite. The metrical tests suffice to prove that these plays were all revised later.

The historical plays may have been written as separate scenes and united later according to the different reigns. Nearly every scene is founded on the older plays: the second part of *Richard II* openly imitates Marlowe's *Edward II*, and thence he derived his sorrowful kings. But his chief aim was to please the Pit, so he introduced fighting and din and passages of deliberate fustian. Yet he found his own tragical voice while writing this Pageant, and thus his tragedies have a national root. *Henry VI* contains little of Shakespeare and is mainly the work of Marlowe, Greene, and Peele. The scenes of *Richard III* where the hideous King fascinates Lady Anne and Queen Elizabeth probably survived from old plays, because neither Shakespeare nor any man of his time could have been primitive enough to imagine them. A few passages, like Clarence's dream, ennobled a play as crude as *1 Henry VI* and foretold the great tragedies. *Richard II* is like two separate scenes of the Pageant, and in the vigorous first part there is little of Shakespeare. The Richard and Bolingbroke of the first part are transformed in the second. The scenes of a rhetorical pageant in blank verse of *Henry IV* conflict with others of vulgar humour in prose: they are both too admirable and too distinct to have been written together. *John* shows false pathos (Arthur and Hubert) and conventional ranting blended with the dawning supremacy of the tragical mood.

Excessive strength is the theme of Shakespeare's tragedies, even *J.C.* Hamlet is too great for his time, Lear too great to be a King, Othello too great to live among the Venetians. Antony is strong enough to conquer the world and then cast it away. Each, including Coriolanus and Timon, has no weakness, but excessive strength that weakened his heart. All are on the brink of insanity, and this insanity is the dotage of strength. In Seneca's tragedies madness was inspired by the gods, or by ghosts in search of revenge; it resembled possession by evil spirits; and Shakespeare copied this— in Brutus, Macbeth, Hamlet. These three should therefore be dated first, for when Shakespeare turned to tragedy he followed Seneca. The latter's tragedies were frames for rhetorical recitations, not meant for the stage. Their influence checked the action of *Hamlet*, but it fades as if Shakespeare outgrew his master and saw that philosophical arguments impede a story of passion, and victims dominated by ghosts must be subordinate.

J.C. is old work rewritten, probably made up of two plays, one dealing with Caesar's fall, another with the revenge of his ghost. Brutus is not the hero, and no Hamlet, but on one side, a vain dupe, sham Stoic, and mouther of platitudes—meant to excite the hatred of the audience and leave their sympathy with Caesar unchecked. The play was written after Essex had failed: Essex who had struck because he trusted the Londoners. We must know historical facts to understand Shakespeare. After the Queen beheaded Essex she lost the love of the Londoners. The two pictures of Brutus and different manners suggest an earlier version. Most of the characters are drawn without sympathy, and there is a tepidity and weakness as if Shakespeare wrote the play when he was too young to do justice to its theme, and rewrote it when he was writing still with dexterous stage-craft, instead of emotion, and feeling his way to his own tragical method. We can imagine that Shakespeare had Essex in mind when he drew Brutus and Hamlet, and this explains the connexion between these two characters.[1]

There are two Macbeths, as there are two Othellos, two Shylocks, and several Hamlets. The first is he who says, 'The Prince of Cumberland! that is a step . . .'; the second as described by Lady Macbeth, 'Yet do I fear thy nature'. The first is juvenile and akin to Aaron, the second is mature and akin to Hamlet. One Lady Macbeth is like Tamora, the other of the sleep-walking scene. Macbeth as he is now drawn could not have murdered his benefactor asleep. Also the beauty of the play is stained by shambling blank verses and passages of juvenile fustian surviving from an earlier form. Belief in witchcraft was on the increase, and the Weird Sisters were changed to Witches. This change dominates the mood of the play, for instead of merely prophetic beings from Shakespeare's country they became bearded old women. They are openly in league with the Devil, and one effect of the change is that Macbeth is overcome by the Devil. The play is thus made popular and fit to attract the roughest audience, but its atmosphere is changed from poetry to prose.

Shakespeare's last Hamlet has more in common with Essex. All

[1] Cf. Winstanley.

the meditations are as old as the hills, and this is one of the reasons why the play is immortal. Mediocrity ensures them a fame denied to difficult greatness.[1] If Hamlet's madness were assumed he would not begin by longing to kill himself: there is no doubt about Edgar's pretended madness. When Dr. Johnson wrote that Hamlet causes much mirth, he was repeating the verdict of the people who saw Burbage as Hamlet. The tragi-comical idea of Hamlet would explain why he mocked the Ghost and Polonius and jested with the Players and Grave-diggers. The things that are faults in a tragedy are justified in a pantomime, which is a picture of life contrasting sorrow and laughter. The chief picture of Hamlet shows him holding a skull and making the most obvious reflections on it. Because he is a spectator he is in touch with the audience—a fault in a tragedy. He interprets the tragedy, which is part of the Pantomime, instead of controlling it, and he is the victim of his own meditations. He has a vague character, since Coleridge, Goethe, and Schlegel identified themselves with him —and they had little in common with the Elizabethan English.

There are two separate tragedies in *Lear* and different manners. Prentice work, such as rhyming lines, is combined with the most beautiful prose and perfect blank verse. Some incidents also prove that he wrote a form of the play in youth—the first scene and the blinding of Gloster. *Lear* is a tragedy of the dotage of strength, but as with Hamlet and Macbeth, his dotage preceded the things which crazed him. Goneril and Regan speak of Lear, and Edmund of his father, as Essex might speak of Elizabeth. Lear raged against Cordelia because he loved her too much, and this links his doom with Hamlet's and Othello's. Even Lear's madness is open to doubt, because Shakespeare cannot have meant pitiless insight to be a sign of madness when he gave it to Hamlet and Lear and Timon. These men were set apart from the world by their greatness and misery, and saw it better because they were apart. The two other supreme tragedies, *Othello* and *A. and C.*, and also *Coriolanus* and *Timon*, are apart from any creed and influenced by no ghost. Lear is so great that he surrenders this world's greatness without a thought: he only values his kingdom because he can divide it among the children he loves. He towers over his only rivals in greatness, Othello and Antony, because they are dominated by women, while his love is a father's and only asks to give all.

In *Othello* chance dominates even more, and controls the story throughout. Perhaps Shakespeare first wrote it as a tragedy in the days of *Titus*, and rewrote it after the *Merchant* and gave it a fortunate ending. This would explain why Desdemona speaks after she is thought to be dead, and why so much of the tragedy has a comical mood. The first act is a prelude and extenuates Othello's behaviour in a way contradicted in the rest of the tragedy. It shows that he did

[1] Cf. Stopford Brooke and Brander Matthews.

not woo Desdemona till her love was made plain, but in the third act
he says that Cassio had acted as a go-between. Iago's only motive is
that he is not made Lieutenant, and this feeble beginning is in the
tragi-comical method of the *Merchant*. The other tragedies open
tragically, but here there is nothing to indicate Othello's mood. There
are two Iagos—one tragi-comical, the other whose deliberate wickedness was tempered by Hamlet's introspection and doubts. He contradicts himself when he first says that Othello was constant, loving,
and noble—and then that he had seduced Emilia. Desdemona's love
is not unnatural, because Othello is great and noble; but in the first
form of the tragedy it was meant to be horrible, and therefore it ended
in horrors. Iago was first like Aaron, then more like Edmund, while
Othello resembles the Prince of Morocco in the *Merchant*. Othello
is left childishly credulous and suddenly savage, every inch a negro,
in spite of the stateliness borrowed from the Prince of Morocco. He
became a true negro instead of an impossible one like Aaron, as
Shylock became a real Jew instead of the bugbear of the traditional
stage. The miracle is that all our sympathy is with him.

All these were Revenge plays of the kind popular when Shakespeare
was young. *A. and C.* is the only play written slowly with deliberate
labour. Its story of passion is told with dignity and calm. Lepidus is
the only comic relief, but, like the Porter in *Macbeth*, he is dominated
by the mood of the tragedy—unlike *Hamlet*, *Lear*, *Othello*, where
comedy breaks the tension with laughter. Shakespeare differed from
Plutarch in making Antony's surrender to Cleopatra exalt him to a
greater nobility. It is the world's greatest Poem of Love, and Shakespeare never toiled with the same passionate emotion again.

He wrote or rewrote his later tragi-comedies with a flagging hand
and under the shadow of his tragical mood. *M. for M.* and *T. and C.*
comment on the faults of the great—as Shakespeare naturally might
do in days when he saw the English Monarchy falling. About 1601
he may have combined two juvenile plays—the stories of Hector and
Troilus, adding that of Thersites and Ajax. On this form he founded
a dark tragi-comedy, and used these stories as episodes in a picture
worthy of *Timon*. The play proves that he did not know Greek, for
had he read the *Iliad* in Greek he could not have degraded its heroes.
Many of the speeches appear as if they came from a note-book and were
assigned to characters at random—one of the proofs that the play
in its last form is a sketch. The first Achilles clashes with the last;
the first Cressida, the humorous girl of the early plays, with the last,
a false and evil woman; and the first Troilus, a lover like Romeo,
with the last, who is elderly and noble like Antony. Shakespeare left
the play a sketch because a more splendid vision soared from its ashes.
Cressida became Cleopatra, whose falsity was part of her charm, and
the boy Troilus inspired the dream of an Emperor Antony.

M. for M. is a noble tragi-comedy blended with a juvenile comedy already revised. The solemnity of the tragical mood connects it with Shakespeare's final tragical work. The Duke's speech is a man's last meditation, and an answer to Hamlet's puerile statement that but for fear of other ills after death a man would rather die than endure such things as 'the pangs of despised love . . .'. That the man should tell of the fear of life, and the boy the fear of death, is a sign that the play is later than *Hamlet*. And the Catholic Duke's Roman mood is a sign that the revision belongs to the Roman group. *M. for M.* is confused by the blending of incompatible plays: the first form had the gaiety and juvenile heartlessness of *L.L.L.* and *M. Ado*. Lucio was first an entertaining Italianate gentleman, but he became detestable. There are two Angelos—one the mere hypocrite of a juvenile comedy—while the second loved holiness and justice and fell tempted by holiness. Shakespeare worked half-heartedly on *All's Well*, because he had to deal with the intractable stuff of boyish invention. The story would only be pardonable if fantastic, but if meant to be true it would be repulsive. As it is, the bleak light of *T. and C.* conquers the glow of an Italianate comedy. Perhaps Shakespeare saw this and conserved some of his younger work in his latest plays—such as the fourth act of the *W. Tale* or Imogen's adventure in *Cymbeline*. The first three acts of the *W. Tale* were probably a juvenile tragedy; the fourth a separate comedy of the time of *A.Y.L.*; and the fifth was added to unite them with the rest and ennoble the play by the passion and dignity of the second Leontes. The light of the *Tempest* is an afternoon glow, yet it has links which unite it with early plays, e.g. Ariel is transformed from a spirit belonging to a story of magic to a humorous fairy. It is Prospero's tragedy, for he is robbed of his child and has forsaken his magic and his beautiful island and has abandoned his dreams of reforming Caliban and has only to wait for death. Prospero's long tale to Miranda may survive from a form written before Shakespeare had learnt that drama should be written in dialogue. In Act II Sebastian and Antonio indulge in the tedious jocosity of *L.L.L.* Iniquity ends in virtue as suddenly as with *A.Y.L.*; and all the wickedness is forgiven because everything in life is illusion. . . .

Mr. Mathew says that it was Shakespeare's lot to earn his bread as a jester, spending his wit to win the laughter of fools, and he did this as naturally and lightly as Touchstone. He concludes with some remarks on Shakespeare himself that might be compared with those of Mr. Frank Harris. He thinks that Shakespeare began as a fragile and effeminate youth, excited and over-confident, superfluously friendly to all, and pleased with himself; and that he grew quiet and subdued with years, and ended wan and emaciated and quieter still, exhausted by his passionate dreams, and in the silence of a man who remembers that he has spoken too much.

Criticism is more or less of an adventure, and one can but exchange impressions with a critic, and either return a 'Yes' to his 'No', or the reverse. There is little that can be proved; the last court of appeal is the heart of the individual; and we will therefore say that Mr. Mathew diverts rather than satisfies. He interests, but we know quite well as we read that we do not intend to accept his theory that Shakespeare's plays were built of separate pieces. We would remind him that no work of art can endure that does not leave a single impression; and also that Shakespeare was a child of the Renaissance when the passions were liberated as by another Aeolus, and the ships of morality were all but wrecked on the high seas. Men turned from one passion to another, like Macbeth when he asked for a blessing as he left Duncan's bedside; and this accounts for the 'two Macbeths', the 'two Othellos', &c., on which he insists. On the other hand, a book like this helps to prove that the modern mind does not accept the entire Folio; but instead of detecting other hands in the plays, like Mr. J. M. Robertson, Mr. Mathew explains inequalities as due to the work of different periods.

Mr. Mathew also inclines to judge by the letter rather than the spirit: thus he says that Shakespeare's mood of reconciliation belongs to *Verona* as much as to the *W. Tale*. But there is a difference of degree as well as of kind—that will appear if we compare *R. and J.* and *Hamlet*. When Capulet says, 'O brother Montagu, give me your hand', we hear the voice of the individual Capulet; but when Laertes says, 'Exchange forgiveness with me, noble Hamlet', it is a voice as from the centre of the universe. There is also some lack of humour in his remarks on *Twelfth-Night* and *T. and C.* Malvolio is hardly a noble gentleman,[1] and Shakespeare might have read the *Iliad* and yet belittled its heroes. His criticism of Shakespeare's tragic heroes is personal and impressionistic rather than universal, and we might do well to turn from it to Professor Bradley's. Can we endorse his opinion of Lear's greatness? On the other hand, his view of Hamlet is subtle and stimulating, and we do not quite know whether to refuse the epithet 'vague' which he applies to Hamlet's character and substitute 'universal'.

VII

MR. J. W. MACKAIL, in his Annual Shakespeare Lecture,[2] notes how the enthusiasm of the eighteenth century became fixed idolatry, to be followed by the new idolatry of the romantic revival. Then came Coleridge and Hazlitt who opened out new regions, and soon nothing less than universal knowledge was claimed for Shakespeare,

---

[1] Professor Saintsbury also calls Malvolio a gentleman. This is truer than *noble* gentleman.

[2] *Sh. after 300 Years*, 1916 (pub. for Brit. Acad. by H. Milford).

nothing short of a doctrine and message on all the matters that concern life. Reaction began in the form of scientific criticism misapplied to the Shakespearian environment. However, modern idolatry breaks out at intervals—notably in thinking of the characters as existing outside the plays. To read a philosophy into Shakespeare is hurtful, because it stands between us and him and vitiates our view.

The Elizabethan age was one of material expansion and intellectual activity, but also of contraction, low morality, and debased art. Humanism had not struck deep in England, and the Renaissance died in the year when Shakespeare came to London. Shakespeare floated with the stream; this was the secret of his unique greatness—that he fitted into his environment. A conformist by instinct, he conformed to the ways of Stratford and London. He did not impress his contemporaries greatly, but immediately took the impress of every word, humour, quality. His fairness to his characters is the index of an indulgent temper, but more largely of a sensitiveness which is in touch with the whole of life. He neither seems to hate his villains nor love his heroines. The Queen in *Cymbeline*, in a way, was a perfect mother; and Edmund was beloved. Perhaps he shows antipathy to Iago—but Iago is not quite a real person. Nor is he the accomplished scholar, the trained lawyer, the expounder in dramatic allegories of the Platonic philosophy, the profound political thinker. He does not write about music like a musician, and his legal phraseology was the habit of his age. He is called an anti-democrat, but he merely reflected the spirit of his audience at Whitehall or the Bankside. The note of passionate pity for the poor in *Lear* was in swift response to the ground-swell of the new democracy. The body of work passing under his name is not all his, but in its massed total it has a subtler kind of unity—that of the Shakespearian touch and inspiration which vivified all the work he laid his finger upon. A few touches of the master-hand worked wonders in the coarse and repulsive tragedy of *Titus*.

Shakespeare was neither inventor nor innovator; he followed all inventions and put his own masterly technique and vitality into them. But in the management of metre, in his handling and development of the flexible dramatic blank verse, he explored as well as perfected. Otherwise, what was about him in art as in life sufficed him. Words were with him like persons and things; every word in the swarm is alive and stings. When he puts the brake on he can concentrate his power and charge a few simple words with all his accumulated reserve-force. Words like, 'Even so: cover their faces' (*Lear* v. iii), carry in them an unequalled sense of vastness. In time he became too impatient to deploy his forces; language poured on him faster than he could put it down; one thought or image would drive so hard on the heels of another that they became merged and fused. As regards verse, the metrical pattern is always there, but as the loom flies it is crushed into vast deviations. Yet the pattern is never lost, only submerged. His apprehension is simultaneous, not consecutive; the content of a speech or a scene seems to rise in his mind together, and he gets down on paper as much as he can. The action of the plays present gaps, inconsistencies, even impossibilities. This massed, incoherent treatment saves his plays from mechanism and makes them so startling a likeness of life.

He is no formal moral teacher, but sets life before us and does not judge. His lesson is like that of Sophocles, that we should not draw lessons, but see and feel and understand. Good is better than evil; but that there is a power which works for righteousness is only one fact of life. His tragedies leave us with a sense of exaltation because, through him, we have seen life as it is, neither good nor bad but wonderful. He does not teach patriotism; the love and praise of his great Englishmen are theirs, not his; only the expression is his. . . .

Mr. Mackail's criticism, that Shakespeare floated with the stream, is suggestive as a point of view, but we think that he over-stresses the passive nature of Shakespeare. It is tempting to find a master-key, such as sensitiveness, to open the secret of Shakespeare's knowledge of all sorts and conditions of men; but we doubt if creative genius can be explained negatively. However, one of the uses of such a point of view is that it forces us to dwell on the opposite—the active power needed to grasp character and present it dramatically; though no doubt Shakespeare had a passive element, and Mr. Mackail's criticism is a corrective to those writers who persist in ascribing to Shakespeare himself the thoughts of his heroes, and also acquaintance with definite arts and sciences and philosophies. As an instance of Shakespeare's passiveness he notes his transition to romance in the wake of Beaumont and Fletcher: and we are familiar with Thorndike's treatise on the subject. His opinions on Shakespeare's command of metre resemble those of Mr. J. M. Robertson—especially the effect of his vivifying touch on such a play as *Titus*. The remarks on Shakespeare's method of apprehending scenes are an instance of the best kind of impressionism— that in which contact kindles the spark of life, and from the critic is born a thought glowing with his own experience and the genius of his subject.

VIII

IN a former volume Mr. J. M. Robertson dissected *Titus*, and concluded that a play jointly written by Peele, Greene, Kyd, and Marlowe had been revised by Shakespeare; in the present [1] he discovers the hand of Chapman in several plays so far thought to be purely Shakespearian.

He begins by noticing marks of Chapman in the *Lover's Complaint*. *Crooked* in the sense of 'curved' is constant in Chapman, but Shakespeare never applies it to a curl. The line of Chapman's *Iliad* (v. 618),

[1] *Sh. and Chapman*, 1917 (Fisher Unwin).

'Whole *storms* of lances, large and sharp, of which a number *stuck* . . .',
contains two of the tic-words of the *Complaint*. 'Stuck' and 'storm'
occur repeatedly in the thirteenth and fourteenth books, and 'stuck' is
found all through Chapman. Ellipsis or asyndeton is among the main
structural marks of Chapman's style, e.g. 'That statue 'tis (that) still
weeps for former thought'. In his earlier rhymed work, including
Hero and Leander, the syllables are often wrong, so that we must
make a line lame to read a rhyme—a fault common to himself, Peele,
and even Spenser. Shakespeare set the example of reform in *Venus*,
to which *Ovid's Banquet* was the rival poem—as the *Complaint* was
to *Lucrece*. If, then, archaistic rhymes do not occur in the *Complaint*,
the Chapman hypothesis is strengthened rather than weakened. The
test of vocabulary yields sixteen words in other than Shakespearian
use. Among them are *Fickle* for delicate, *Storming* for raising a storm
over, *Occasion* for impact, *Parcels* for locks of hair, *Phoenix* for newly
sprouting (adj.). Chapman excelled in the common Elizabethan habit
of word-making. He has adjectives in *y*, *less*, *ful*; he overworks words
ad nauseam; he frequently frames or revives new or old terms 'for the
nonce' only. *Authorised* occurs but twice in Shakespeare apart from
Complaint: in *Macbeth* and Sonnet 35. The latter with its jolting line,
'Excusing thy sins . . .', might have been Chapman's. *Dialect* is
used literally in *Lear*, metaphorically in *M. for M.*, in Chapman
both. *Deified* is used once, metaphorically, in *A.Y.L.*—literally or
primarily in the *Complaint*, according to Chapman's constant practice.
In no other of Shakespeare's contemporaries do we find this preciosity
and odd contortion of thought and language. Tautology, inversion,
and the split infinitive are also marks of his style. Thus the *Complaint* is as like him as it is unlike Shakespeare; it has his eccentric
diction, his involved and forced construction, with an occasional
vigorous and elevated line.

The Sonnets show that the connexion between Shakespeare and
Chapman was partly hostile. Shakespeare succeeded with *Venus*, on
which Chapman composed the *Banquet of Sense* and thought to prevail
by superior learning and scholarship, but failed to catch the popular
imagination. His hostility to Shakespeare was more splenetic than
Shakespeare's to him. If the lines in *L.L.L.*, 'War against your own
affections, And the huge army of the world's desires', belong to the
revision of 1597, they may be a retort to Chapman's *Shadow of Night*.
Holofernes probably represents Chapman, who had been a schoolmaster, and we find in the pedant's verdict close parodies of his opinions
in the dedication of the *Banquet*, where he disparages poetry that is
merely limpid and popular.

The non-Shakespearian hand in *Timon* must be Chapman's. Chapman is full of Timonism, and in all his tragedies, poems, prefaces,
dedications, and postscript to the Homeridian Hymns there is world-

accusing rhetoric. We find his strained metaphors and verbal touches in *Timon*, and his ellipses in syntax. Cupid's address to *Timon* in I. ii, before the banquet, recalls *Ovid's Banquet of Sense* with its enumeration of 'the five best senses'. The transitions from verse to prose in single speeches are common in Chapman but are non-Shakespearian. Most remarkable is the duplication of motive in *Timon* III. v, and *Bussy D'Ambois* II. i: the theme of both is the offence of killing in a duel. The vocabulary of the opening scene is peculiarly Chapman's; such words as *particular, particularly, conjured, continuate, rapt, confluence, austere, drift, ivory* are much used by him. It may be that Shakespeare recast a faulty play of Chapman's; this would account for the heedless construction. The Senate scene is not Shakespeare's; the thesis debated, the style, the verse, and the vocabulary are all Chapman's; and the banquet scene is pure Chapman. The weakness of the play was that the plot could not properly make a play at all. This would not deter Chapman, and the slow evolution of his tragedies contrasts curiously with the rapid action of his comedies. He sets himself to invent episodes of action to eke out *Timon*, which is rather a grave comedy ending with a natural death than an Elizabethan tragedy proper; and the incoherences arise from that effort. He characteristically first makes Alcibiades rebel in his own quarrel, and then affect to be Timon's avenger. The soliloquy of Flavius in IV. i, is like Chapman's familiar exclamatory method. Pathos eludes Chapman, as it did Marlowe and all the Elizabethans but Shakespeare; and only Shakespeare could have put the touch of tears in the last speech, 'Yet rich conceit . . .'. To Chapman we assign the third scene of Act V; but great verse like, 'Timon hath made his everlasting mansion . . .', reveals to us what is beyond Chapman.

Many words in the Shakespeare Concordance occur only in *Timon*, and a large number of these are more or less often in Chapman. Seventy words peculiar to one play in the Concordance and thirty to one scene are proof of an alien presence. However, a writer like Chapman uses many words once or twice only, so that we must finally rely on tests of style, versification, imagery, purport, and syntax. Yet the once-used words occur in speeches which are not of his versification. In his recast Shakespeare turned some of Chapman's drafts into his own rhythm. Timon's speech (IV. iii. 176–96), 'Common mother . . .', is certainly Shakespeare; and here we have the verb-form *marbled*, which occurs in Chapman but nowhere else in Shakespeare; and also *unmeasurable, liquorish,* and *unctuous*. The speech is Chapman rewritten by Shakespeare.

The play contains a number of Chapman's tic-words: *jeweller, continuate, presentment, confluence*. The peculiar use of *propagate* found in Timon is frequent in Chapman. Such words as *untirable, glass-faced, steepy, unpeaceable, caked, respectively, repugnancy, dividant, fang, wappened, trenchant, turncoats, enscar, conceptious, carper, to hinge, composture, exceptless, opulency, patchery, whittle, fragile, decimation, insculpture* are all likely enough to have been used by Chapman. To the words *presentment, propagate, scope, cease, ingeniously, grave* (verb) he gave a force which Shakespeare did not. Also a number of words common to him and Shakespeare are used in a way characteristic of Chapman: *hug, englutted, conjured, rapt, austere, satiety, precédent, pomp, gratulate, importune,* &c. The line (v. i. 177), 'Contumelious, beastly, mad-brained war', contains three adjectives traceable to Chapman, one of them not found outside *Timon* in Shakespeare's plays.

No doubt Shakespeare worked over the fourth and fifth acts and may have revised and retrenched the first. It is considered a late play, but in the two long Shakespearian speeches (iv. i, and iv. iii) the percentage of double-endings is low; whereas Chapman reached a high proportion of double-endings long before Shakespeare. The manner is Chapman's, except in those speeches where Shakespeare's verse lifts all to a higher harmony. The play is ill-motived, ill-plotted, ill-constructed, and only made memorable by Shakespeare's occasional transfiguring intervention.

Chapman may have planned or recast *Pericles* and written the Gower Prologues. The first two acts contain mixed rhyme and blank verse, and there are many of his habitual words, phrases, ideas.

T. and C. has long been considered a composite work. Probably it was composed in successive strata; the Ulyssean matter, where we find traces of Chapman, having no natural structural connexion with the central theme. But the large rhythm and perfect cadence of the great dialogues are not Chapman's. There is, however, strong reason to believe that his was the intervening hand which drafted the political discussions. Like most of the dramatists he was given to pseudo-dramatic scene-writing in which theses are argued where action should be developed, and a number of persons may equally well utter any of the thoughts. A parallel to the stratagem of Ulysses to sting Achilles into action by playing on his vanity, exists in the first two speeches of the fourth act of *Byron's Tragedy*. But the final degradation of Achilles serves no purpose except to belittle Homer, and we cannot attribute this to Chapman. The Ulyssean scenes contain so much of his vocabulary and non-dramatic didactic method that we count him the draftsman.

Certain interludes in Shakespeare's plays contain traces of Chapman. In the sixty-eight rhymed lines of the interlude in the *Tempest* there are eighteen which occur nowhere else in the plays. There are a few, used once or twice elsewhere, which happen to connect with Chapman. The vocabulary of the Pyrrhus speech in *Hamlet* suggests Chapman. The two rhymed speeches in *Othello* (i. iii. 199–219) are non-Shakespearian interpolations and in the manner of the play scene in

Hamlet. The interlude of *Cymbeline* has the 'marble mansion' of Timon, and the whole of the quaint rhymed verse is more like Chapman than Shakespeare.

It has been surmised that *J.C.* as we have it is condensed from a double play, and it is assumed that this double play was Shakespeare's. May it not have been pre-Shakespearian, and may not Chapman have supplied some of the classical substratum? There are traces of another mind: such a passage as, 'How many ages hence . . .', is dramatically false. The lines are those of a scholarly person aware that the theme had already been repeatedly dramatized. The sentiment of the conspiracy and assassination is Chapman's, and may be compared with his *Tragedy of Caesar and Pompey*. But if he drafted *J.C.*, or recast a previous play, it was certainly rewritten. Wholly inadequate to its titular theme, as we have it, it cannot have been planned by Shakespeare. The first speech of Marullus carries on the key of Chapman's play, but the present anomalous drama is the result of severe compression. But the style is not Chapman's, and the low proportion of double-endings is impossible for him after 1598. The metre suggests that Shakespeare did most of his recast before 1599, and Ben Jonson further revised it and increased the proportion of double-endings.

The *Shrew* is one of the most deeply doubted plays, and the bulk of the work is not Shakespeare's. From word-clues in *Timon* it is possible that Chapman had a hand in it, e.g. transitive use of *cease* is common in Chapman—and only in *Timon*, *Cymbeline*, *Shrew*. So with *plash*, *deck*, *satiety*, &c. Of real range of vocabulary the indiscriminate statistical method gives no notion; here we have merely dealt with significant uses of words. It is precarious to take for granted what is Shakespeare's original work in any disputed play. Between the old play and Shakespeare a third, probably a fourth, hand has intervened. Otherwise the style of the non-Shakespearian parts of the *Shrew* is like that of Chapman's comedies, which is as simple as his later tragic style is turgid and involved.

In *1 Henry VI* there are signs of Chapman, though Marlowe must have begun it. There are several of his characteristic words, among them the epithet 'mad-brained', already traced to him. The first twelve lines of Scene v (Act I) have six double-endings, and we suspect either Chapman or Heywood, who were the first to practise that indulgence. The higher percentage of double-endings in the Roses scene make it impossible for Shakespeare as early as 1594. A distinct clue to Chapman in *Richard III* is the word *punched* in the dream-parade of ghosts. Only he has used it elsewhere—in *Iliad*, vi. 126.

Most of the Prologues of *Henry V* and many speeches, including the Harfleur rants, are probably not Shakespeare's. The play must be the recast of a pre-Shakespearian drama by Marlowe and Greene, a companion play to *Edward III*. Many admit Shakespeare did not write the prologue to *T. and C.*, and these prologues are about the same date and have the same general aspect. Certain words suggest Chapman, such as *threaden*, also *streamers* (*Iliad*, ix. 237), *sternage* (Chapman's translation of Hesiod's *Georgics*, ii). In the fifth prologue we note *ostent*, and *whiffler*, which occurs nowhere else in Shakespeare, but four times in Chapman. The play's proportion of double-endings is higher than that of *J.C.* which is dated later. The visibly Shakespearian verse, such as the speech of Canterbury on the honey-bees, and the soliloquy of Henry, has few double-endings. The Harfleur rants must be third-rate Marlowe, and there is much non-Shakespearian work throughout, so that the problem is to trace the early and late hands. Chapman is most suggested in v. ii, by the verbal clues. With 27 per cent. double-endings we have these once-used words—*congreeted, fumitory, coulter, savagery, keeksies, burnet*. Also *deracinate*, which occurs only in *T. and C.*, and *leas* which occurs in Chapman and the dubious masque in the *Tempest*. The scenes between Henry and Katharine and Katharine and Alice are unworthy of Shakespeare and akin to Chapman's weaker comedy; and we know that he read French. Some word-clues suggest that Chapman had a hand in the comic scenes, particularly those with Pistol. The versification of Henry's Crispian speech differs utterly from that of his soliloquy in iv. i. Its idea is that of the scene in *J.C.* where the conspirators predict that their deed will be renowned among posterity. The high proportion of double-endings (23 per cent.) indicates later work, and it may be a speech by Peele (whose style it suggests) recast by Shakespeare.

Some of the early comedies are recasts by Greene—notably *Verona* and *All's Well*. The matter and vocabulary of *Errors* suggest Chapman—such one-play words as *inquisitive* (twice), *defeature* (twice), *apparently, carcanet*. The style is like that of the *Shrew*, and a word in common is *housed*, which occurs four times here, frequently in Chapman, and never again in Shakespeare. Much of *Verona* is non-Shakespearian; in ii. iv, the proportion of double-endings is 25 per cent., in scene vi, and iii. ii, 20 per cent., and this was impossible for the immature Shakespeare. It is so much in the spirit and manner of Greene that only the double-endings cause the difficulty, but there is no doubt of his prior presence. Lines 50 to 57 in ii. vii, are likely to be by Chapman, though he did not do much for the play. Neither did Shakespeare, though he developed Launce, and may be traced in such a speech as, 'How use doth breed a habit in a man!' which has a touch of feeling beyond Peele or Greene or Chapman, though here too is probably an old substratum.

All's Well contains much prose and rhyme and nearly 29 per cent. double-endings. As *M. for M.* has less than 26 per cent. and *Hamlet*

22 per cent., to put this play later would imply that Shakespeare's art had declined. The rhyme is compressed and obscure, and not in Shakespeare's early manner. The riddle of rhyme with much double-ended blank verse is solved if we admit the presence of Chapman. The play originally may have been a *Love's Labour Won* slightly adapted by Shakespeare from a draft of Greene's. The Parolles of the opening scene is non-Shakespearian, and his dialogue with Helena is needlessly offensive. The prose beginning may be Shakespeare's revision of Chapman—e.g. Lafeu's words, 'Your commendations . . .'. The vocabulary of Helena's first speech, but not the versification, points to Chapman. Her second verse speech suggests nothing of Shakespeare, but thereafter word-clues to Chapman abound: *prejudicates, discipled, enwombed, captious, intenible,* &c. Much of the verse suggests Shakespeare's rewriting after 1602, but such a line as 'You know my father left me some prescriptions . . .' is pure Chapman. The scene in Act II between the King and Helena is non-Shakespearian, and is either Chapman or a mixture of him and older material. 'Fiery torcher' recalls 'torchy evening' (*Hero and Leander*, v. 426), and Chapman often speaks of the torch of the sun or day, and much of the rhyme is akin to the couplets in Chapman's tragedies, and differs from all in Shakespeare but the spurious rhymes in *Othello* and the play scene in *Hamlet*. The quality of a passage like, 'Ere twice the horses . . .', raises the question whether the play scene in *Hamlet* may not be a survival from Kyd's old play, and whether Greene wrote it. It has the same simple mythological machinery and rhymed verse as *All's Well*, with a like enumeration—'Full thirty times . . .'. Probably Chapman adapted Greene in *All's Well* and then imitated the effect in the play scene. A basis laid by Greene and worked over by Chapman accounts for the *Hamlet* play scene and the rhymed parts of *All's Well*, though it is not easy to disentangle their respective shares. The early dialogue between Lafeu and Parolles is unlike anything else in Shakespeare. When the King speaks eight lines of blank verse, twenty of rhyme, and more blank verse, it is utterly un-Shakespearian; whereas Chapman in tragedy interlards his blank verse with sententious rhyme. Forty-six per cent. double-endings was impossible to Shakespeare's middle period, and the blank verse is largely end-stopped and not in his later manner. Shakespeare would not have planned so evil a foil as Bertram to such a spirit as Helena, but he never got away from Greene—the inveterate inventor of villainous heroes.

The work of elimination has only touched Shakespeare's inferior work. No one impugns one of the great plays as a whole or any great speech. His superiority discriminates him, the beauty and power and charm that others lack. It is conceded that his plots were borrowed, and that he retained large parts of other men's plays. He wrote to please his audience, reserving his power to create character and beautiful speech. If a faulty plot came his way he had to handle it, but all dramatic creation is but re-creation. Thus he spent some of his highest faculty on *T. and C.*, turning Chapman's didactics into magnificent verse, and limning pictures of Cressida and Diomed and Troilus which survive the incongruities of their framework. He would not have planned the non-dramatic Ulyssean discussion of Chapman, but he transfigured them by witchcraft of style. . . .

Mr. Robertson's criticism is disposed in circles, of which the innermost is his appreciation of Shakespeare's power over character and verse, thence widening into matters of plot and structure, and finally into the more external theme of vocabulary. But the circles are interdependent, and though the criticism appears to be scientific, it springs from an aesthetic root. The critic is entirely disinterested; he does not set out deliberately to prove that Chapman wrote certain passages of the plays, but because these passages leave on his aesthetic sense an unsatisfactory impression, he recalls his experience of previous or contemporary dramatists and assigns them to one or the other. If he can fortify this inner impression with arguments from vocabulary, dates, needs of the theatre, &c., he becomes convinced and states his conclusion. Mr. Robertson is scientific in that he is disinterested, and does not wish to prove a theory or obtrude a particular dramatist: thus he will argue subtly that here is a passage originally penned by Greene and worked over by Chapman. The result is that Shakespeare is exalted, not belittled: though Mr. Robertson is not one of those who maintain that all the good is Shakespeare's and all the bad by alien hands. But he is convinced that a certain unique quality exists, which is Shakespeare, and he brings this home to us. We admire his judgement and the perfect balance and interdependence of his aesthetic and scientific powers, and his power of industry.

IX

H. C. BEECHING tries again the theme of Shakespeare's character,[1] and differs from Mr. Mackail's utterance of the previous year. That he worked hard enough to produce thirty-seven plays shows that he did not always take the line of least resistance. Spenser chose his epithets carefully in *Colin Clout*, and he called Shakespeare 'gentle'—a word which included honour, valour, generosity, good manners. To create a dramatic character it must be vitalized as well as sketched from life, and the power to vitalize springs from sympathy between what is in the dramatist's own mind and that of another. A vulgar-minded, mean-spirited man could not draw a noble character. Othello's nobility is Shakespeare's, not Cinthio's. Also there is a change of tone between the plays of different periods, between the sunny happiness of the romantic comedies and the serious benevolence of the later romances.

[1] *The Character of Sh.* Brit. Acad., 1917 (Oxford University Press).

The women's parts most show this—since Beatrice, Rosalind, and Viola are the salt of their society, while Gertrude, Goneril and Regan, Lady Macbeth, and Cleopatra are corrupters and destroyers. The Sonnets corroborate a great, if temporary, disturbance in Shakespeare's view of women. Recent critics affirm that he represented life but did not interpret it; yet the virtuous characters clearly disapprove of the wicked. He wrote for persons with ordinary moral training, and his characters impress us as he intended. His bad characters are not monsters, but men and women who act from intelligible human motives. If Shylock is compared with his original in the Italian novel, and Marlowe's Barabas, we see that Shakespeare has humanized the stage Jew. He has the dignity of ancient lineage, and passionate sense of injustice from centuries of contempt and persecution. Yet his resulting vindictiveness makes him a danger to the State. Shakespeare's tolerance arose from complete knowledge, and he instructs as well as pleases. Had Falstaff been a character in a comedy he might not have been dismissed, but he is in English history and is unpatriotic, and must therefore go—at the expense of the audience's sympathies. Cordelia dies because Lear's selfish rage had aroused forces of anarchy and brought her within their reach.

Rosaline (*L.L.L.*) tells Biron that to be a complete man he must learn earnestness through contact with sorrow; and the degrees of guilt in Alonso, Antonio, Sebastian (*Tempest*) are carefully distinguished. Thus both the plots which Shakespeare invented emphasize noble character. His praise of forgiveness shows the value which he attached to it. Tragedy with Marlowe represents Nemesis falling on exorbitant desire. Shakespeare's tragic heroes are men, not Titans, beset by temptations common to us all. With Fletcher tragedy only has victims of tyranny. It would be uncritical to attribute to chance a change of method made by a consummate artist and consistently adhered to. Shakespeare chose the Aristotelean type—a noble nature with some error or weakness.

Shakespeare valued law and order in the State (*T. and C.*), and also long tradition, sound government, security. He was imaginatively jealous of tampering with any single element in the precarious and intricate construction—with household, marriage, children, servants (*J.C., Coriolanus, R. and J.*). In *Lear* the prerogative of age is impugned, and disregard of social ties causes the catastrophe of *Macbeth*. Even in *A.Y.L.* Jaques advises Touchstone and Audrey to be married by a good priest.[1] Shakespeare is said to despise the masses, but though he shows crowds at the mercy of demagogues they respond equally to good. There would be little dramatic interest in the lives of honest humble folk; but when the time comes (*All's Well*) he shows himself the champion of the humble and meek. He is said to have neglected

[1] Cf Mézières.

the poor till interest in them, at the date of *Lear*, was popular; but the remarks of the destitute Lear were dramatically fitting, and such references do not persist in later plays. Finally, his dramas uplift because they inspire love in us for all the best things in life. . . .

This lecture is a useful antithesis to Mr. Mackail's; it is sound rather than brilliant, pedestrian rather than winged. It treats the moral question somewhat in the manner of Stopford Brooke. Its general statements excel its particular; we agree that Shakespeare did not take the line of least resistance, and that his industry and the different tone of his plays, his tragic method, and the final impression of his plays testify to this; but when he applies his theories to particular instances and discusses Shakespeare's preferences, we feel a set-back towards the criticism of the 'four periods' type. However, he is right to insist that no vulgar-minded man could write nobly, and signs are not wanting that this opinion is once more finding favour.[1] The aesthetic man, like the economic man, is passing away, and some of the angry outbursts against Ruskin, who insisted that art is a matter of the whole being, are recoiling upon their authors.

X

WITH this thought fresh in our minds we will set down Mr. Mathew's corroborating words—that Shakespeare was great-hearted, for no one can write nobly if his life is ignoble. Professor de Sélincourt calls his reading of history aristocratic, adding that he had no subtle political theory, but was a patriot who emphasized the need for national unity. Beeching whole-heartedly agrees—that Shakespeare pleaded for unity and law and order alike in state and family morals—also that he was a patriot who dismissed Falstaff because he was most unpatriotic. To Mr. Mackail he is no direct teacher of patriotism. Neither, says Mr. Mackail, is he a direct moral teacher: that good is different from evil and better than evil, is only one fact of life as he sees it. According to Professor de Sélincourt, he thinks honesty to be the only policy that can succeed in the long run. Beeching sees in his attitude one of stern judgement, and describes his tolerance as arising from his power to analyse every action and passion into its motive, so that we pity while we judge. Mr. Mathew's impression from the Droeshout engraving is that he looked on the world pallidly without consolation. Professor Stoll says strangely but suggestively that he was little of a humanist. To Sidney Lee he is the greatest of humanists.

Mr. Mathew also says that in unfolding a tale he did it with deliberate falsity, making his characters tell their secret thoughts and explain all their emotions; that he aimed to write a Book of the Living,

[1] 'He (Sterne) is the most conspicuous example that could be quoted in favour of the dangerous thesis that literary and moral excellence belong to different spheres. . . .' *Eng. Thought in the 18th Cent.*, by Leslie Stephen (1876), ii. 441.

yet does not draw his times as they were, but as he saw them in the Kingdom of Dreams, and this made his work universal. In Mr. Robertson's opinion he transfigures fable into lasting literature, and has a strange power to create living figures speaking a living yet beautifully idealized speech. Beeching affirms that he did not merely show natural man his face in the glass, but admitted a bias 'on the side of the angels'.

On the subject of art we have Professor Stoll, who says that Shakespeare aims to be dramatically effective, not psychologically consistent, and that he seldom conceives his characters apart from plot.

Sidney Lee affirms that he reformed the methods of the drama in masterly fashion, and triumphantly broadened its basis; while Mr. Robertson pays tribute to his verse, praising its flawless flow and mighty rhythm, and also his transfiguring witchcraft of style, while he considers judgement and charm to be the two poles of his comedy. . . .

Of the criticisms on Shakespeare's philosophy and politics we prefer Mr. Mackail's, because it is not too definite. To confine Shakespeare within a theory is to miss the suggestion of the infinite which is the ultimate impression of the plays. Mr. Robertson does convey his sense of infinity through his appreciation of Shakespeare's verse.

Chapter XXXVII

ENGLAND 1918–1921

I. QUILLER-COUCH. II. MARRIOTT. III. RALEIGH. IV. J. M. ROBERTSON.
V. CROCE. VI. T. S. ELIOT. VII. HERFORD. VIII. CONCLUSION.

I

SIR ARTHUR QUILLER-COUCH[1] strikes the key-note of *Macbeth* by remarking that if the supernatural is eliminated nothing is left. The sordid story of a disloyal general murdering his king and usurping the throne would not interest. The problem is to make Macbeth sympathetic, to make the audience believe he is a man like one of them. And the only method is that he should commit his crime as if under some fatal hallucination. The play more than any other is wrapped in darkness, for only in darkness can one mistake and purchase evil for good. Shakespeare had to leave the witches vague and the extent of their influence indeterminate; the very soul of horror lies in the vague and impalpable. Thus he forces us into terrified sympathy and actual fellow-feeling with the murderer, and he deliberately flattens down the virtuous characters to throw up Macbeth and Lady Macbeth into high relief. We care little for Macduff or Lennox, and neither Duncan, Malcolm, nor even Banquo are imagined intensely. When Macbeth is overthrown by men of straw we are made to feel that Heaven has conducted the work of retribution. Macbeth and his wife command us by the isolation of their grandeur in guilt. Banquo is the Point of Rest, the ordinary man beside Macbeth—as Horatio stands to Hamlet or Cassio to Othello—the sense of norm needed in great literature. After Macbeth yields, Banquo becomes a living reproach to him—a touchstone of right and wrong. The play is likest in Shakespeare to Greek tragedy—especially in its peculiar retrospective irony. The spectator is reminded as by an echo of what has been coming all the while. Compare 'Neptune's ocean' and 'A little water . . .'. After Birnam Wood we recall 'Stones have been known to move . . .'. The play resounds with such echoes, and teems with peculiar whispers of reminiscent irony.

Like all dramatists Shakespeare had to learn stage-mechanics and then unlearn them. The secret of his art is in playing human being against human being, not in devising situations. In *M.N.D.* he strove to make mistaken identity poetical but not farcical. To understand Shakespeare we had better ask ourselves how the thing was done than search among sources and origins. Poetry suffuses *M.N.D.* as

[1] *Sh.'s Workmanship*, 1918 (Fisher Unwin).

with potable moonlight, and for the first time his two greatest natural gifts, poetry and humour, find scope. Trust in an imaginative world dissolves four-fifths of the difficulties that have beset his plots. By assuming that we take the fairy-world for granted he at last achieves easy probability. The fairies and the clowns are more really imagined than the serious characters, so they take charge of the play.

The *Merchant* is heartless and leaves a chilling, disappointing effect. Antonio is merely static, and Shylock is meant to be cruel; but the rest are cold-hearted wasters. Antonio's parasites discuss his affairs sympathetically, but they always assume that it is his affair, not theirs. Bassanio counts on more love to extract more money, and such a predatory young gentleman would not have chosen the leaden casket. All this is bad workmanship, and so is his changed method of speaking as if he were addressing a Y.M.C.A. This flaw in characterization goes right down through the workmanship of the play. To the peculiar Jewish cruelty the Christians should have opposed Christian charity; but they are as heartless without Shylock's passionate excuse. Shylock gets little of the 'mercy' that Portia speaks of, and her victory is won by fantastic legal quibbles. Better believe that Shakespeare made his Venice a picture of the hard shallow side of the Renaissance —and opposed to it Belmont with its humanities and adoration of beauty. All who arrive at Belmont are at once the better for it. Shakespeare wrote greater than he knew, for he started out to make Shylock such a cruel, crafty, villainous Hebrew as would appeal to Elizabethan Christians; but he could not help sympathizing with his point of view, as with Caliban and Falstaff.[1] Shylock takes charge of his creator, fenced in by intricacies of plot and finding outlets for his genius where he can. Shakespeare's hands were tied by the monstrous absurdities of the plot, so it seemed to him best to begin with absolute realism. He first impresses us with the reality of the people, and when the pound of flesh is first mentioned in scene iii, as a jest, the characters are so real that we are at Shakespeare's mercy and accept the incredibilities to come.

In *A.Y.L.* all who flee to the forest find the values of life changed for them. The persiflage between Rosalind and Celia in the first act has a false sparkle, and the whole language of the act is curiously monotonous. Shakespeare is impatient for Arden, and the remaining four acts are not drama but fantasy. Shakespeare invented Jaques and Touchstone who are both piquantly out of place while most picturesquely in place. The Duke moralizes on the artificiality left at home; the courtiers ape his humours; and this, being less than sincere, needs the salutary mockery of Jaques and Touchstone. The characters are not in earnest, but play at life and are afterwards restored to their proper element. The play derives through *L.L.L.* from Lyly,

[1] Cf. Herford (1912).

and is Lyly carried to the nth power. Hymen is botchwork not to be explained as interpolation—like the vision of Posthumus.

To make Falstaff the hero of *Henry IV* is an innovation—a permanent artistic principle is set up in the treatment of history by fiction. *Richard II*, *1* and *2 Henry IV*, and *Henry V* carry the house of Lancaster from usurpation to the highest point—but there is an accompanying sense of fate and apprehension—of tedium in success and absence of joy. Bolingbroke wishes to make it all right with God in other ways than restitution, and he dies unhappy, having never known joy. Prince Henry has known joy, but he renounces it when he ascends the throne, and becomes an ingrate to those who brought him joy. Into this atmosphere of doom Shakespeare thrusts the jollity of common folk. To him they were types of the old Interlude—Falstaff was Gluttony, Bardolph Drunkenness, Quickly was the conventional hostess, Shallow the conventional Country Justice, and Slender—or Silence—the conventional awkward country Booby. Shakespeare's mind is working, but the whole Elizabethan drama is in ferment too—yeasting up from type to individual—to Iago from Richard III—to Shylock from Judas. The Prince is between Hotspur's challenge to honour and Falstaff's temptation to sensuality. The speeches of Hotspur and Falstaff on honour are cross-lights that illumine the whole play. Shakespeare uses the call to arms for Shrewsbury and the crown scene to convert the Prince: the whole is built on the old Morality structure imported through the Interlude. The rejection of Falstaff is the most damnable piece of workmanship in Shakespeare; and if we accept the first speech, 'I know you all', it poisons the madcap Prince in our imagination for good. Shakespeare killed Falstaff because he dared not introduce him into *Henry V*. Henry had wronged Falstaff, and Falstaff could kill him with a look. Falstaff had never hurt Henry, and Henry had hurt Falstaff to death but for continuing to be, in fault and foible, the same man in whose faults and foibles he had delighted as a friend. In the Eastcheap scenes Shakespeare wonderfully gives the old Interlude life and recaptures the spirit of Chaucer.

Nine-tenths of all that has been written on *Hamlet* is rubbish. Shakespeare wrote it as a play for an audience of ordinary men and women. If a work of art is shapeless and nebulous it is to that extent suspect as a work of art. *Hamlet* could not be a popular play were it a psychological enigma. It is the last triumph of a masterpiece that all can understand and enjoy it, and Shakespeare did not write the longest of his plays to hide what he meant. The opening scene is magnificent, and the superb diction already closes us in its grip. Laertes and Polonius are perhaps deliberately made tedious, for in this court of Denmark an abyss of horror has been half-opened to us, and on the stage—like a thin crust over damnation—the two courtiers prate meaningless saws and worldly wisdom. We ask if Hamlet was mad—but madness is a relative term, like drunkenness. Few of us are without some little kink of the brain, and Shakespeare, fulfilling the dramatist's first function, invites each of us to put himself in Hamlet's place. His mind oscillates—as the mind of each one of us would do after a shock—but is not thrown off its pivot. The Queen never thinks him mad, and she thoroughly understands throughout. No doubt that Shakespeare at the time was maddened by some revelation of the lust possible in woman—as a hundred filthy comparisons in *T. and C.*, *Othello*, *Lear* bear witness. It explains Hamlet's behaviour to Ophelia; in recoil from a mother's lust he rends the veil from that other altar of love. He enjoys acting the madman to complacent fools, but he never does so to Horatio. Critics call him pusillanimous, but he is a man of gentle scrupulous nature and active intellect. He only had the word of a ghost; the responsibility rests with his own conscience. He would naturally shrink from such a charge that had been imposed upon him. A dramatist must make his hero sympathetic, so that we feel what happens to him is happening to us. The key to *Hamlet* is what each of us will find in his own breast.

A mellowly romantic atmosphere pervades Shakespeare's last work. The theme that engages him is that of a woman wrongfully used. Imogen is Desdemona rejudged and tenderly vindicated. Unity of time is set aside, because the process of repentance and forgiveness is naturally slow. There may be some relaxation of grip, but no loss of mental power. It is as if Shakespeare, who had triumphed over the possible, was starting out to conquer the impossible. We feel that human forgiveness for the wrongs men do us is nobler even than God's revenge for murder. How can any God of our conception vie for our pity against Imogen? It cost Imogen all she had in the world, whereas God has so many things to fall back upon. Shakespeare in his later plays, treating forgiveness, atonement, reconciliation, attempted a harder thing than to justify the ways of God to man: and that was the reconciliation by slow process, under God, of man with man. Great artists tire of repeating successes, but not experiment. If Shakespeare failed in altering *Othello* to the *W. Tale* and *Lear* to *Cymbeline*, he failed by no intellectual decline, but in the attempt to achieve something better and more difficult. Forgiveness is gradual, and to be durable depends upon conquering a real resistance. The working dramatist is limited to three hours; therefore Shakespeare's last aim brought him up against the limitations of his art. He honourably turned his back on past success, and risked a made reputation to follow Nature.

There is truth of imagination, emotion, fact. The imaginative truth once granted (as childhood grants it without effort), the rest of the story at once becomes real. So let the reader of *Cymbeline* surrender his sympathies a little more, with wise passiveness, to the story of Imogen. She has Desdemona's fond trust, with the steel and wit which Desdemona lacks. If we allow Imogen to be Shakespeare's supreme woman, then the miracle is worked. He has done the thing he attempted, and it is idle and presumptuous to lecture him on this or that flaw in the machinery he used to accomplish it. Perhaps the play is constructed out of fragments, each like something Shakespeare has used before, and inferior if you will. But the worth of a detail consists in as much as it contributes to the total effect. If we keep our eyes loyally on Imogen, the incongruities of fact blend into an imaginative congruity.

Shakespeare deliberately worked into the one drama of the *W. Tale* two different stories in two separate categories of art. The mixing up of things that differ is in the end a matter of tact. Critics are fond of dwelling upon the play's faulty structure, but the object of these pages is to suggest ways of reading Shakespeare by which we can increase for ourselves our profit and delight in him. Our first business in the world is to judge for ourselves, but, as critics, we must discover what the author is trying to do. We will thus understand his difficulties, and it will determine our attitude to his faults. Here the gap between Acts III and IV comes of failure to do a difficult thing—afterwards accomplished in the *Tempest*. Leontes' jealousy is a caprice of self-deception, but we should have been warned of it. Hermione's resurrection is more startling, at the expense of dramatic irony. Autolycus has his place in the picture, but does nothing to further the plot. The great fault of all is the scamping of the recognition scene. The interest and emotion that we have invested in the story is cheated by the merely reported tale. Finally, the play is not compact and leaves no single impression.

The storm and the shipwreck of the *Tempest* are ten times as well managed as in the *W. Tale*. One of its loveliest inventions is the manner in which love takes charge of two young hearts and carries them ahead of its contriver, leaving him with his magic at a standstill. The log scene is the most beautiful love scene in Shakespeare, who, since *R. and J.*, had been chary of love scenes unless he could handle them with raillery. The light here is autumnal, yet the atmosphere breathes of the dawn. There may or may not be another world where wrongs are redressed, but there is a continuance of this world in newer generations: Marina, Perdita, Miranda renew the promise of the world. But the restoration of good will is a slow process, and again and again the difficulty beat Shakespeare—till he conquered it in the *Tempest*. He is more a king in this play than any other. One can imagine Beatrice or Rosalind enacted with just a touch of vulgarity, yet without offence: but not so Perdita or Miranda. Shakespeare's secret is past fathoming, and we must not test him too narrowly by the

conditions of his craft, or think of him as limited by them. The play,
like *M.N.D.*, most constantly invokes and relies on music. Is Prospero
Destiny itself? or the invisible master-spirit of all the tragedies? or
Shakespeare himself? or James I? Poetry does not work on photo-
graphs but hints, and never on persons or individuals. By its universality the *Tempest* is what each of us makes of it. More than the great
tragedies it forces diviner tears for sheer beauty, with a royal sense of
the world and how it passes away. It is the majesty of art: we feel that
we are greater than we know. . . .

Sir Arthur Quiller-Couch is greater in his likes than his dislikes:
and this is no mean praise for a critic—especially when we add that
his likes are of the dynamic kind that inspire the reader to think.
Thus he tells us of the retrospective irony in *Macbeth*, of the effect of
the fairy-world of *M.N.D.*, and of Belmont in the *Merchant*, of the
atmosphere of doom in *Henry IV*, of the thinly veiled hell beneath the
stage of *Hamlet*. He defends Imogen in language that Swinburne
would have approved: in art it is the result that counts, not the process.
All these verdicts are born of meditation continuing the work of
impressions, of intuition and imagination—and at their best they
communicate awe to the reader as he approaches the great Shakespearian mystery. But the faults he finds, as with the *Merchant*, are
more with the letter than the spirit of the play, or are overstated, as with
the dismissal of Falstaff. On the other hand, they witness to a mind not
overwhelmed by the study of Shakespeare; essentially a modern mind,
which the Victorians would have called irreverent, but we prefer to
call anti-hypocritical. He shows us that the world is changing, that
new ideas are evolving, and not everything in Shakespeare is time-
proof. His best words are on the romances, and it is at least an interesting suggestion that Shakespeare had a harder task in them than the
tragedies, whether we agree with it or not—and the same applies to
his statement that it is harder to justify the ways of man to man than
those of God to man. We agree that Shakespeare's power did not
decline—as instanced by the construction of the *Tempest*, and his
poetry never failed of its intensity. The latter point is more universally
admitted, since the faults of construction of the *W. Tale* are obvious,
Sir A. Quiller-Couch himself allowing that it makes a divided impression; and yet the poetry of the idyllic fourth act is universally acclaimed,
and to read the last scene of the play, with its living characters and
flawless rhythm, is to experience one of the finest aesthetic pleasures
in the world. But where the present critic excels is in interpreting
more definitely than his predecessors the spirit of reconciliation in the
romances. Apart from the question of another world, he says, this
world is continued in future generations. If indeed it is possible to
discover Shakespeare's self in his works, such a thought will help. Of
great importance are his remarks on the supernatural in *Macbeth*, and

the transformation of type to individual in *Henry IV*. We see what Shakespeare himself added to the play, we guess at the Spirit who brooded with mighty wings over the abyss. Lastly, if the book is decidedly impressionistic, its author's mind has been strengthened by the acquired knowledge which he has put aside in order to yield himself to his impressions.

II

SIR J. A. R. MARRIOTT[1] sees in Shakespeare's historical plays a meaning that the present generation would do well to lay to heart. They are, he says, the quintessence of the Elizabethan temper, national unity being to Shakespeare the one supreme condition of national greatness. Only national unity could deny dynastic strife, and this was the supreme need of the hour. History to Shakespeare was the play of personal forces—not, as to the modern historian, a stage in evolution. The heart of the Shakespearian drama is the Lancastrian revolution of 1399. *Henry IV* represented social order, ecclesiastical orthodoxy, parliamentary government. Parliament was to become the direct instrument of government; but the attempt failed because it was premature. Shakespeare did not make plays out of social and economic changes, but seized on the personal aspects of disorders, and the chaos that ensued from lack of government. His history is sound in the main, and even to secure dramatic effect he never falsified history. England is the hero of each of his plays.

The philosophical inspiration of *John* was supplied by Shakespeare himself, while he merely reproduced the framework of the earlier play. He shows how expediency became the motive force of the characters, and so converts a Protestant polemic into a study of human nature. But there is a disharmony between personal and political interest. John is despicable in the main, but not in the opening scene. 'Right' to Shakespeare depended on personal qualities; John had still to be tried; and not till he again and again proved his unfitness to rule does Shakespeare allow him to lose the sympathies of the audience. He is guilty of murder and treason—but does this justify the barons in revolting? As he degenerates, so does the Bastard develop under the stress of responsibility. But the real hero is England, whose life and honour are jeopardized less by external enemies than internal divisions. The warning was opportune, for though the peril of the Armada was past, Ireland was in rebellion, and the ecclesiastical situation was difficult, as the Government was persecuting Catholics and separatists.

Before the opening of *Richard II* there had been a struggle between King and Parliament, in which the King prevailed. The play is unintelligible unless one knows preceding events. Shakespeare deals with the last eighteen months of the reign—September 1398 to

[1] *English History in Sh.*, 1918 (Chapman & Hall).

February 1400. It was the climax of the prolonged struggle between
the Crown and the aristocratic oligarchy, between the new proletariat
and the propertied classes, between the Lollards and the Orthodox
Churchmen—in short, between the forces of revolution and conservatism. The struggle was not wholly between Crown and Parliament,
but more between the King and those oligarchical nobles who wished
to supersede the royal authority. Richard II is the most eloquent of
Shakespeare's kings, and a peculiar interest—part political, part psychological—makes the play one of Shakespeare's greatest tragedies. It
proves that a ruler needs high character and adequate apprenticeship,
and that these are essential to sound government. Richard's failure as
king is due to his orphan's upbringing and lack of real home influence.
Though born to command he has never studied the difficult art of
ruling. He is his own worst enemy, and the essence of Shakespearian
tragedy is that the citadel should be betrayed from within.

1 Henry IV is Shakespeare's most perfect work. The king was a
usurper and conservative, and he owed his ever-deepening unpopularity
to the peculiarities of his situation. Conservative reaction brought
him into power, for in the latter half of the fourteenth century
revolution threatened. The Black Death (1394) had dislocated a
social system that rested on manorial organization. There were three
movements: the peasant rising of 1381, the social and ecclesiastical
revolution threatened by Wyclif's followers, and the attempt to arrest
the evolution of parliamentary government. However, Henry IV
came to the throne not only as conservative, defender of orthodoxy,
and constitutionalist, but as the nominee of the baronial oligarchy who
for two hundred years had opposed the Crown; and they could not
forget the apparent ingratitude of their former colleague. Shakespeare
omits Henry's persecution of the Lollards, and concentrates attention
on the 'usurping' king and those who had aided him. His task was to
satisfy the conservative instincts of the men who had abetted usurpation—to concede the claims of the orthodox ecclesiastics without
outraging the Lollard sympathies of the House of Commons—to
accept the principle of parliamentary control without weakening the
executive power—to repress aristocratic disorder while retaining the
friendship of the baronial oligarchy. The play combines history of
a high order and some of the finest English comedy—a remarkable
stage in the evolution of the chronicle play. Falstaff is one of the
greatest creations in literature—the despair of commentators. He
was no coward, but the measure of his valour was limited by his
rationalistic discretion. He was a profligate and liar, yet retained something of the instinct of a gentleman. His lies are palpable, but are not
meant seriously to deceive. His associates feel the subtle power of
breeding, and respect him even more than the Prince. There is no
malice in him, and he maintains his ascendancy by sheer intellectual

superiority. We like him not for his rascality, but his rare wit, his superb self-possession and intellectual agility. He is always sure of himself and never taken at a disadvantage.

Henry IV's position on the throne is a contradiction in terms. He is oligarch and constitutionalist, usurper and conservative, successful rebel and repressor of rebellion. His ambition was limited to the practicable; he was not lovable and could win respect, not affection. He was too calculating to snatch at an opportunity, but he never missed one. He was no devoted churchman like his son, but he knew the political value of a good moral character. In his reign it was attempted to give to Parliament control over the executive and make it the direct instrument of government. It failed because the country was not ripe; and Shakespeare does convey political lessons, though he was above all interested in the play of personal forces, and he embodies the difficulties of Henry IV in the personal rivalries of individuals.

In all other kings but Henry V something or much was lacking to complete success, but in *Henry V* Shakespeare depicted an ideal Christian Knight, a ruler both popular and successful, a man to love and admire. And he observed the most important canon of patriotic poetry—the law of indirectness. His political moral is more effective because it is oblique. It is a great national epic in dramatic form, and the king is no impossible hero, but human, and above all a soldier-king. His early speech, 'I know you all', shows something of his father's shrewd calculation of political and ethical profit and loss.[1] He plunges into a politic but unjust war,[2] though Shakespeare makes the clergy responsible. The other blot on Henry—the persecution of the Lollards—is omitted by Shakespeare. The scene where he repudiates Falstaff is wisely got over in the last act of *Henry IV*. Nothing could more disconcert a devout churchman, still under the spell of the splendid coronation ceremony, than to be suddenly confronted with the boon companions of his riotous youth.[3] He could not have done otherwise, yet his words strike a chill. He broke Falstaff's heart, who loved Hal for himself, not for what he could get out of him.[4] There is a vein of hardness and policy in a character as near perfect as Henry V's. If, as it has been suggested, his conscience was his accomplice, not his guide, Shakespeare's hint of this in Act I is too subtle to impair the general impression of high-souled and pure-minded patriotism. There is nothing finer in English literature than the scenes before Agincourt. If the English chronicle plays are a continuous national epic, *Henry V* is the climax. The king's personal popularity hushed the sound of dynastic strife, and concealed the weakness of the constitutional

[1] Cf. Quiller-Couch.   [2] Cf. de Sélincourt.
[3] Cf. Stopford Brooke and Bailey.
[4] Boas also says that Falstaff was mortally pierced through his one vulnerable spot—affection for Hal.

experiment of the Lancastrians. The play is a model of patriotic poetry, and glows with passionate love of country and kind.

It is generally agreed that *1 Henry VI* is not in substance the work of Shakespeare, and Parts II and III represent his revision of earlier plays. One cause of the civil war was the break-down of the constitutional experiment. The barons had grown rich and powerful, and there was a revival of 'bastard feudalism' which infected justice— while the ambitious foreign policy of the Lancastrians had failed. The quarrels at home of Gloucester and Beaufort, and the victories of Joan of Arc abroad, contributed to the Lancastrians' downfall. All the play does is to prepare us for the outbreak of the civil wars. There is no skill of versification nor subtle character-drawing in Part II; York's ambition is obvious, and also the coming catastrophe—in accordance with Shakespeare's earliest manner. He connects the Yorkist and Lancastrian feuds with the personal rivalry of two ambitious women. It is historically true that Margaret was the evil genius of the Lancastrian House, and it was characteristic of Shakespeare to concentrate attention upon her. The horrible account of Beaufort's death is unhistorical. He had read the signs of the times better than Gloucester—that the constitutional experiment was precarious—only he failed to see that it was premature. Cade is an impressionist portrait of the crafty demagogue and self-seeking communist, from the hand of a master. The Cade of history is relatively unimportant, but Shakespeare's is a priceless creation. Shakespeare, like his countrymen, accepted the firm rule of the Tudors as a corrective to previous anarchy. Edward IV might have been secure had he not quarrelled with Warwick. His marriage with Elizabeth Woodville upset Warwick's diplomacy, including the independence of the Low Countries—as one of the few fixed points of British foreign policy. Trial and failure of a great constitutional experiment marked the Lancastrian period. To ensure parliamentary government, a highly developed sense of social solidarity is needed, and the will for social order, besides general agreement in the 'fundamentals' of the Constitution. None of these were present in the fifteenth century, and the experiment failed because it was premature.

Richard III shows the influence of Marlowe, and the king is not subtly characterized. In Henry V the impulses of headstrong youth subtly conflict with the promptings of policy and ambition. Richard II is torn between brave words and abject deeds, but Richard III is clean-cut and definite. Only Margaret divides the honours with Richard, and her appearance in the play is dramatically rather than historically justified. Richard III had superb intellectual endowments, and he exerts his powers to the full in wooing Anne and persuading Elizabeth. It is possible that his physical defects strengthened his intellectual appeal. Two issues were involved at Bosworth—dynastic and moral

—right and wrong. From Richmond's sublime meditations Shakespeare passes to the melodramatic ghost scene. We have work of the highest and lowest quality side by side throughout the play. We must not summarily dismiss the bad work as non-Shakespearian, but remember that he often wrote under great pressure, and that his taste in early plays was far from flawless. National unity was the text of the chronicle plays, since the prevailing dread of Elizabethan statesmen was a disputed succession and renewal of civil war. The Queen was childless, and her death might be the signal for quarrels between Parliament and the Administration, repressed under her tactful rule, to break out. That the nation might hold together, Romans, Anglicans, and Puritans must compose their differences, the new agrarian classes must deal gently with tenants and labourers, Parliament must use moderately its new powers, and the Crown must yield gracefully. All this is not explicit in Shakespeare's plays, but his leading motive is social solidarity. The Tudors were liked with all their faults because they secured it. Lack of it caused the collapse of Henry VI and overthrow of Richard III. Richmond's prowess in the field gave earnest of his strength as a ruler.

In the sixteenth century Parliament developed, and local government —the training-ground of the middle classes—was reconstructed. In a broad way the Tudors carried out the will of the people. The period between Bosworth and the Armada was an emergency period, marked by struggles to establish a new dynasty and avert civil war. Henry VIII's marriages were not unconnected with fear of a disputed succession. He might have chosen the easy path of dalliance rather than ally himself legally with unattractive women. The agrarian revolution broke up feudalism and the manorial system. The new men who possessed the land wished to make fortunes out of it, and this enriched the middle classes. In the sphere of European politics the national system emerged. England's threat to Spain quickened her zeal for maritime adventure and overseas trade: whereas Englishmen of the Middle Ages were neither conspicuous sailors nor merchants. After the Armada an independent spirit appeared in Parliament that made the future Stuart quarrels inevitable.

Shakespeare was an intense patriot, absolutely the product of his age, and the child of Renaissance England—but never more so than in the English historical plays to which *Henry VIII* is a fit epilogue. Doubt whether Princess Mary was legitimate made the King tremble for the succession. There are few finer things in these plays than Wolsey's fall. Shakespeare was too near him to be just, and reveals little of his psychology or his place in English history. He was the first English diplomatist to grasp the idea of the balance of power in Europe to protect the smaller States and curb the greater. Yet he lives in history

386 MARRIOTT 1918

as a personality, and if transmitted personality is the true test of greatness, he responds to it through Shakespeare. The moral of *Henry VIII*
is political, not ethical, for Shakespeare believed with Machiavelli that
politics are divorced from ethics. The play has political, not ethical,
unity, beginning with the arrest of Buckingham, because mention
of him as possible candidate to the throne involves the succession. It
closes with the baptism of Elizabeth, which assures the dynasty.

Patriotism is the keynote of Shakespeare's chronicle plays. At no
period of English history has the realization of national unity been
keener. National unity and social solidarity are the two dominating
ideas of the historical drama. . . .

If this is not the highest kind of criticism it is at least among the
most interesting. It states clearly the causes of the civil war and the
legacy of anxiety inherited by the England of Elizabeth. Sir J. Marriott
admits that Shakespeare was concerned with personal rather than
political aspects; but he himself is most interested in history, and he
justifies himself by keeping before us Shakespeare's passion for national
unity. It must also be remembered that one of Sir J. Marriott's objects
is to impress upon the modern reader that the problems of Shakespeare's
day were akin to our own. There is indeed a singularly modern
sound in the words which he uses to depict the struggle between the forces
of conservatism and revolution, the new land policy, the differences
between Parliament and Executive, &c. Our own day has seen the
land changing hands—and, in the sphere of foreign policy, it is well
to recall England's views on the independence of Belgium. That all
this can be read into Shakespeare is at least an indirect tribute to the
universal quality of his mind. But it is well to insist that Shakespeare
was above all a poet—and we think Sir J. Marriott is overborne by his
interest in history—though we hasten to add that he has found all this
in Shakespeare because, in the first place, he is poetically impressible.
The moral of his book is that national unity is the cure for civil
disorders, alike in past and present: and he calls as a witness the
world's greatest mind. But the danger is that he overpraises those
things which crystallize his message, apart from their aesthetic value.
Thus he sees in the characters of Henry V and Richmond, in the
scenes before Agincourt, and the whole of *Henry VIII*, a glory that has
largely departed for modern critics. Yet he is only partly wrong with
the rejection of Falstaff. The religious fervour which he attributes to
Henry is excessive; but he allows that Falstaff chose his time badly;
and this is a point that other critics have raised. If we look back on
the historical plays as a whole, we find that, apart from the Falstaff
scenes, those things which stand out are John's qualms of conscience,
Richard II's vacillations, Henry IV's soliloquies and protests to his
son—in short, those occasions when the soul labours with itself, once
removed from the practical world. And yet the fact that such jewels

of modern political wisdom can be extracted is a further marvel of the inexhaustible treasure-house.

III

SIDE by side with Sir J. Marriott, it is interesting to read Walter Raleigh's lecture.[1] To Raleigh also he was the completely representative national poet, who embodied and exemplified the virtues and faults of England. The wit of the trenches in the Great War was pure Shakespeare. He and his contemporaries gave to England a new self-consciousness and self-confidence. Through Falstaff he expressed the immense English tolerance, while in the scene between Trinculo, Stephano, and Caliban we see how the Germans failed to impress the incurably humorous British private. He was tolerant of villains; his worst villains are theorists who cheat and murder by the book of arithmetic. We find in him no elaborate hypocrite; his hypocrites enjoy themselves too much, and are artists to the finger-tips. Hypocrisy is superficial, and Shakespeare entered too deeply into the minds of his creatures. It is not easy to harmonize perfectly the outward and inward relations of the soul; and a hypocrite is one who too readily separates them.

He valued freedom but disliked anarchy; his idea being that the heart should be free to follow its impulses. His ideals were not political, but he required the impulse as well as the deed: a man, in his opinion, who does what he has no will to do does it badly. The ultimate law between man and man is that of pity. Portia's speech rises above the strife of nations and belongs to humanity. He is the poet of humanity, not of a nation or any institution. He abjures all formulas and abstractions and phrases, and reduces things to their elements. The scene between Lear and the madman, where Lear is still every inch a king, shows his test whether man, when stripped of his pretences, is noble. . . .

These words speak for themselves in relation to Mr. Marriott's. Beginning on the same theme of Shakespeare and England, he shows how Shakespeare overleaped all national bounds and became the poet of humanity. And the cause is the quality of his own soul, unrelated to anything in society or State.

IV

MR. J. M. ROBERTSON [2] warns us that all theories of Hamlet are inconclusive because they ignore that Shakespeare adapted an older play, which laid down the main action embodying a counter-sense which the adaptation could not transmute. He denies that any charge of delay can be brought against Hamlet except between Acts I and II. To stab a man in the back would hardly produce a high moral

[1] *Sh. and England*, Brit. Acad. Annual Sh. Lecture, 1918 (Oxford Univ. Press).
[2] *The Problem of Hamlet*, 1919 (Allen and Unwin).

or aesthetic effect; but Shakespeare has given critics their warrant by Hamlet's self-impeaching soliloquies. Werder and others dwelt on external difficulties and ignored his self-accusations; but they took for granted the thoroughly plannned character of the play. Werder's theory of external difficulties and need for judicial punishment is never once indicated in the play; and, like the subjective theory, it makes Hamlet recoil from the possible course and fasten on an impossible one. Hamlet is neither weak of spirit nor outmatched by circumstance. It may be true that vengeance was no solace to his soul poisoned by his mother's guilt; but this induction, though comparatively just, is incomplete. Shakespeare should have explained Hamlet's delay, but he does not because his transmutation of the play was but a process of making more and more mysterious a delay which in the earlier story was not mysterious at all.[1] The objective reasons for delay in the early story have been progressively eliminated. To understand the play we must know its history. The author of a novel, which admits of commentary, may use the device of pretended doubt as to the motives of his characters, but a play does not admit of commentary, and a dramatist should not leave a character unintelligible. The cause here must be the conditions imposed by the material.

Kyd[2] was the author of the pre-Shakespearian *Hamlet*, and some of his phrasing survives in *Hamlet*, especially the 1st Quarto. The old German play helped to remove much of the superfluous detail. The episodes of the embassies, the mission of Reynaldo, and the campaign of Fortinbras, are excrescences on the plot. The 'To be' soliloquy clashes with the appearance of the ghost, and Kyd would hardly have made Hamlet contemplate suicide immediately after vowing to revenge his father. Only in the 2nd Quarto and the Folio is it removed from its earlier place and relegated to Act III. This rearrangement tells of a protracted process of reconstruction. But the question is, how did Shakespeare turn a Hamlet who was very little of a mystery into a Hamlet who is very much one? Kyd first combined the Ghost's revelation with the mock-madness of the old story. No ghost was needed in the latter, as the murder was known to all, and Hamlet assumed madness to save his life. Kyd's Hamlet shammed madness after supernaturally learning of a secret murder, and endangered his life. The play within the play was also unnecessary, but Kyd loved to complicate motives. The Hamlet who needlessly shams madness develops into the Hamlet who unintelligibly swerves from revenge. Far better for Shakespeare's credit to admit that his Hamlet pretends

[1] Kenny (1864) calls *Hamlet* a curious psychological study grafted on the story of a half-barbarous age. Cf. also Corbin on *Hamlet* and its sources.

[2] Brander Matthews mentions the name of Kyd. He says that Laertes is manly yet agrees to treason: like Kyd's summary psychology. Prof. Herford says that the plot of *Hamlet* in substance is superb melodrama.

madness because Kyd's does so. At times he did make himself answerable for other men's artistic sins; and here he retained all the archaic machinery while transfiguring all the characters. The construction remains incoherent, and the hero an enigma. At the outset he should have told Horatio and Marcellus: since the audience believed in the Ghost the characters would do so. The King's confusion after the play is clear proof of his guilt. Kyd's tragic method is one of long-baffled action, and these devices are his machinery in adapting a barbaric story where the barbarian *must* delay because he is only one against a powerful chief. Possibly it all goes back to a sun myth.[1]

Hamlet is commonly condemned on the strength of a single recoil from assassination—and most high-minded men would have done the same. But the audience, who were under the dramatic spell, and believed in the Ghost, disregarded all questions of real time. Shakespeare makes a masterly effort to hint a psychological solution of the acted mystery, while heightening it by the self-accusing soliloquies. It is he who makes Hamlet keep the Ghost's tale secret, and he stresses the Queen's guilt. The latter—an almost intolerable motive for drama—is the new ground-note of Shakespeare's *Hamlet*. The pessimism that proceeds from utter sickness of heart makes us feel that revenge is no remedy. This implicit pessimism is Shakespeare's personal contribution, but matter remains which conflicts with pessimism, viz. displays of vigour like the killing of Polonius. A psychologically consistent play cannot be made out of a plot with barbaric action and a hero transformed to a supersubtle Elizabethan.[2]

He performs a miracle of dramatic imagination, and projects a personality which holds our minds and hearts in spite of his cruelties. He does it by sheer intensity of presentment, absolute life-likeness of utterance, phrase, feeling. Shakespeare himself is not revealed until we see how often he was compelled to handle or retain intractable material. Here he was adapting an old play for his company, and the public expected the Ghost and mock-madness. Critics in the past have tried to explain the problem apart from its genesis. Shakespeare, by immensely heightening the character, put it in still further irrelation to the action. His real triumph was to turn a crude play into a masterpiece—a magnificent *tour de force* which may ultimately miscarry aesthetically because a silk purse cannot be made from a sow's ear. But the pragmatic test is final: the miraculous puppetry of the actor-manager has kept millions at gaze for centuries.[3] . . .

The gist of previous remarks made upon Mr. Robertson may be

---

[1] Cf. Gilbert Murray.

[2] A. W. Ward says that Hamlet is conceived on a broader basis than the action of the play furnishes. The play is forgotten in the hero.

[3] Sir A. Quiller-Couch says *Hamlet* could not be a popular play were it a psychological enigma.

repeated: he keeps a perfect balance between inner and outer. He knows the history of the play and he has experienced its charm. His scientific knowledge waits upon his aesthetic; he does good work in the historical field because he has a keen sense of Hamlet's marvellous personality. From his examination of the material appears the greatness of the mind that transformed it. Because he appreciates the self-accusing soliloquies he sees clearer that the delay is imposed from without. It is well-known that volumes have been written upon *Hamlet*: but the outstanding facts are the unaccountable delay, and the gulf between Hamlet's nature and his actions—his treatment of Ophelia, slaying of Polonius, and dismissal to death of his two former friends. Mr. Robertson makes it clear to us that Shakespeare did not draft the play but adapted it—and that only in its history can we find a clue to these enigmas.

V

PROFESSOR BENEDETTO CROCE [1] separates the poetical personality from the practical, and insists that the former is the true object of study. Erroneous conviction that the two are identical is the source of vast useless labours in Shakespearian philosophy. Conjectures about Shakespeare are of no use, as it is impossible to deduce life from poetry. When a sentiment that has really been experienced is raised to the sphere of poetry, it is plucked from its practical soil and made the motive of composition for a world of dreams. Thus it may be true or not that the tragic period is connected with Shakespeare's life. Other disturbing errors are to connect Shakespeare with the history of his time, like Taine—or to trace different forms of his poetry to his reading, like Chasles.

Shakespeare was a universal poet, no particular poet of ideals, morals, politics, yet he is not irreligious, immoral, &c. He nowhere refers directly to God, but within him is an ever-present obscure consciousness of an unknown divinity. Yet the positive and negative are not reconciled in superior harmony. After a storm, though good men fill the thrones of the wicked, the desolation of faith betrayed, of goodness trampled upon, of innocent creatures destroyed remains. Shakespeare is not beyond these passions, but he is beyond being on one side or other. He receives them all in himself simply to make of them his unique world. He surpasses individual emotions but strengthens our interest in good and evil, sorrow and joy, destiny and necessity. The object of criticism is to point out exactly where lies the poetical motive. The sense of strife in vital unity prevents the vision from becoming simplified and superficial in the antithesis of

---

[1] *Ariosto, Sh. and Corneille*, trans. Douglas Ainslie (Allen and Unwin, 1920). Rather than omit so important and cosmopolitan a critic as Professor Croce, it has been decided to include him among English writers.

good and evil. Shakespeare is not a philosopher who reconciles all under theory. We must confront his objectivity with his poetic subjectivity, his impersonality with his personality. His cosmic and philosophic thoughts simply fulfil the function of poetical expression, and lose when taken from their context. In the depth of his consciousness Shakespeare appears outside all definite creeds, and only knows the vigorous passionate life upon earth, with the surrounding shadow of a mystery. Yet his moral discernment bears a strong imprint of Christian ethics. Tragic conflict arises from the union of this exquisite ethical judgement to a vision of the world moving by its own or some mysterious power. He has not Dante's historical conception of life, and lacks true political faith and passion. One must relate his mental presuppositions with the life of the time. The Renaissance had made earthly life real, and he truly belonged to it—to the side of it associated with new wants, with the spirit of new philosophical research, full of doubts, permeated with flashes from the future.

His treatment of love in the comedies is characteristic of the Renaissance. He regards it with affectionate sympathy but also curiosity, with the superiority of an expert mind, and thus with delicate irony. Love claims to be founded on judgement, but is guided by fancies, and is therefore self-deceiving, as in *M.N.D. R. and J.* might be called the tragedy of a comedy. The Poems and Sonnets are from Italian models, but he is always a poet, as he can never get away from himself. He infuses his own thoughts and modes of feeling, and harmonies and movements of the soul, so that the Sonnets have the aspect of a biographical mystery, of a poem containing some hidden moral and philosophical sense. The poetry of the romantic and idyllic plays is also rather superficial and tenuous, as the decorative background takes the first place. They have a sense of unreality, as we see in the crises of the action, where evil-doers are easily pardoned, and the wicked turn out to be harmless (*A.Y.L.*).

Critics have spoken of the 'educative' effect of the historical plays on Shakespeare, in the way that recalls the conception of art as 'imitation of nature'. The artist must give form to his own sentiment, not reproduce external nature or history turned into external reality. The question, then, is of the sentiment which inspired the historical plays. They have not the epic quality, because Shakespeare is no partisan marching under one or other political or religious banner. He goes beyond, to the universal man and the cosmic problem. Like the Renaissance, he lacked historical reflection and homesickness for the past. The cause of the internal stimulus, the constructive idea, the lyrical motive, of the historical and Roman plays, is interest in and affection for practical achievement. Henry V is more a king when he tears off the kingly mask and sees himself as a man. Hotspur is a 'formal' hero, but all his wit, satire, love, are hastened by impetuosity. Coriolanus is also a 'formal' hero, and his bravery is not founded on love of country, or on a faith or ideal, but has no other object than itself. Falstaff has a kind of innocence, the result of the complete liberty of his relation toward all restraint and ethical law. Shylock lives and speaks, and himself explains what he means; the pathetic and biassed nineteenth-century interpretations are foreign to such a character. He lacks a background, and his rapid fall is unconvincing. The characters of the strictly historical plays do not find their ideal complement. Because there lacks a definite ideal, but there is sympathy for the varying lots of striving humanity, interest is concentrated upon character-drawing—and historical material is somewhat passively accepted. On one side we get force and impetus, on the other lack of idealization and condensation. We cannot find Shakespeare's own thoughts in *Coriolanus*, because the hero, the Tribunes, &c., are looked upon solely as characters, not parts and expressions of a sentiment that should justify one or other or both groups. Henry V failed to understand Falstaff, and is not to be admired for repelling him.

In *Macbeth* the vision is wider, almost philosophical, yet includes the former practical vision. In the historical plays there are powerful but limited individuals; in the great plays there are more than individuals, representing eternal positions of the human spirit. The former treat gain or loss of the throne; the latter also, but they add to it the gain or loss of the soul itself, the strife of good and evil at the heart of things. Macbeth and Lady Macbeth tremble in their experience, at that creative moment of daring which demands the resolute dedication of the whole man. The obstacle is not material, but it is loyalty, duty, justice, piety, &c. The struggle is between savage desire and the reverence which the other idea inspires into his deeper being. Lady Macbeth, whose power of desire is absolute, discovers the cause of his weakness and applies the remedy. She strengthens his will for action—the will pure and simple—but after the crime the same atrocious discord continues. His tragedy is that he cannot hold himself right or wrong— the tragedy of reality contemplated at the moment of conflict and before the solution has been obtained.

Lear is inspired by an infinite hatred for deceitful wickedness. Lear himself is a creation of pity and sarcasm; he was mad before he became mad; but Shakespeare's creative impulse goes so deep that he assumes gigantic proportions. Goneril and Regan express boundless egoism; but love is equal to hate, and Cordelia is goodness itself. Why does not goodness triumph in this material world? Why does she, though conquered, increase in beauty till she is adored as something sacred? The whole tragedy is penetrated with this anguished interrogation.

Iago represents evil for art's sake, done through artistic need to realize his own being and feel it strong. He gains nothing, and what results from his acts is evil as an end in itself, arising from desire to prove himself superior. Othello is pierced by sensual jealousy, but is also injured in what he holds sacred—so his slaying of Desdemona is expiation. This was Shakespeare's answer to that mysterious form of evil—perversity.

A. and C. gives the tragedy of the will dominated by passions, of voluptuousness that means internal and moral death. It is composed of the violent sense of pleasure coupled with a shudder at its effects. To Antony the rest of the world seems heavy and prosaic, but it is voluptuousness not love: he sees clearly what Cleopatra is. The tragedy of the will is poetically lofty but in a low form morally.

The atmosphere of *Hamlet*, where the obstacle is internal, is far more subtle. It is the will itself in the dialectic of its becoming, in its passage from meditation to purpose and from purpose to action, in its becoming true concrete will. Brutus differs by taking a decision, though he does not hate Caesar. Strictly speaking, Shakespeare has not put more of himself and his poetry into *Hamlet* than the other plays, and perhaps there is less philosophy because it is more perplexed and vague. Even 'To be', though supremely poetical, cannot be reduced to a philosophic problem. The play is not the key to the others, but the expression of a distinctive state of the soul. It expresses distaste for life, but life is thought and will, each of which creates the other, but when certain painful events injure us this process is interrupted. A void succeeds, a losing of the way, which is a sort of death. Hamlet would have carried out the vengeance had he not begun to die internally. Everything contrary to the ideal and the joy of life, including death and the fearful unknown, crystallize round the murder of his father and adultery of his mother. He cannot love, for love is love of life;[1] his display of moral indignation to his mother is but a paroxysm. He does not know the nature of his malady, so instead of combating he encourages it—at most uttering vain self-rebukes. Finally he effects vengeance, but as if by chance. Yet the song of desolate anguish that the poet sings is so lofty that it would seem that a newer and more lofty conception of reality and human action must be born of it.

Not reconciliation but justice pervades Shakespeare. He knows neither perfect saints nor perfect sinners, for he feels the struggle at the heart of reality as necessity, not accident. The good and brave have weaknesses, and the criminal's energy of will may be a kind of spiritual greatness. Prospero, refined by meditation, experience, and science, and penetrated with the thought of the instability of life, forgives. Shakespeare is indulgent to men but neither rises to cheerful hope and faith nor sinks to gloomy pessimism, because the struggle between good and evil remains undecided for him. His characters greatly love life, yet they renounce it serenely, like a liberation. Claudio is almost resigned, then clutches at a glimmer of hope. Barnardine is indifferent

[1] Cf. Franz Horn.

to life and death yet lives and gets drunk. It is only conjecture that Shakespeare's last period was one of 'serenity', and that Prospero represented himself.

Excellence in his art was long denied or contested to Shakespeare. It was said that he was strong in character, weak in construction; but such distinctions, between characters, actions, style, dialogue are arbitrary, scholastic, and rhetorical. The precision, the delicacy, the gradations, the shading of his representations, besides the passages where he theorizes on art, prove that he had profoundly meditated the art he practised.

Much criticism of Shakespeare is worthless, but the German critics of the speculative period at least tried to discover the soul of Shakespeare's poetry: though unfortunately they imagined that it resided in a sort of philosophical, moral, political, and historical teaching. The objectivist criticism, now in full vigour, is absurd. Art only succeeds when irradiated with a sentiment which determines and controls it in all its parts; whereas historians and psychologists attempt to detach characters from the creative centre of the play and transfer them to a pretended objective field, as if they were made of flesh and blood. What Shakespeare was intent upon was the creation of his own spiritual reality. No doubt his historical origin is to be found in the Renaissance. From Italy he received his form and material, and also many thoughts that went to form his vision of reality. In addition he obtained from Italy his literary education: but the origin of his poetry was in himself alone. . . .

Professor Croce's point of view is that of the philosopher, concerned with reality and the nature of knowledge, not its diluted reactions in the physical world. At the heart of the universe there is movement and struggle; man is a self-contained world, and his actions are preceded by struggle. Shakespeare made the actions of his characters spring from the primary struggle in varying degrees of purity. The outer robe of Professor Croce's interpretation does not differ notably from that of other critics. That the early plays are partly unreal because the decorative background takes the first place; that the idea of the historical plays is interest in practical achievement; that the tragedies add the gain or loss of the soul, the strife of good and evil at the heart of things: all this recalls Dowden. It is no novel teaching that one must discard history and biography and judge the poet only by his poetry. However, this is but the approach to Professor Croce's central idea—the pangs that precede the birth of the work of art. With this purpose he withdraws from Shakespeare a definite system of morals or philosophy, formal religion, the historical sense—in order to restore them to him on the further side. Art may proceed directly out of the beautiful—but the good, the true, and the beautiful are one. Just as excitement lends nervous force to the body, and the strength of a madman is a proverb, so the mind of the inspired poet, struggling to produce, almost despite itself discovers secrets of nature and unguessed-at relations of things. Thus Professor Croce extracts from *A. and C.* a shudder at the effects of the violent sense of pleasure, and tells us that Cordelia, though conquered, increases in beauty till she is adored as something sacred. But his finest work is his analysis of Hamlet's mind —the causes that produce internal death. And when he says in the end that a greater conception of reality is born out of the agony, we feel that he has taken us within earshot of the throbbing sound of the creative impulse. Beauty born out of sorrow, hope out of earthly wrack, is the artist's goal—ranging from the merely personal writer whose mind revolves within its own shadow to the world-wide circles of Shakespeare.

VI

MR. T. S. ELIOT [1] accepts Mr. Robertson's criticism of the play of *Hamlet* historically as a stratification, and he also agrees that the essential emotion added by Shakespeare is the feeling of a son towards a guilty mother.[2] But the emotion is too hard to localize and manipulate into art. The only way to express an emotion in art is to find external facts that evoke it; e.g., Lady Macbeth's sleep-walking state of mind is communicated to us by a skilful accumulation of imagined sensory impressions. Artistic 'inevitability' is when the external is adequate to the emotion. But Hamlet is dominated by an emotion inexpressible because in excess of the facts as they appear. His disgust envelops and exceeds his mother, and as he cannot understand and objectify it, it poisons his life and obstructs action. Had Shakespeare made Gertrude more criminal, there would have been a totally different emotion in Hamlet; but because she is so negative, she wakes in him the feeling she is incapable of representing. Hamlet seeks an outlet in buffoonery because he cannot find it in action. The problem is one of intense feeling without an object or exceeding its object, and Shakespeare attempted to express the inexpressible. To understand it we should have to know the unknowable, for we assume the experience was one which exceeded the facts. . . .[3]

It is an old saying that thought without action is demoralizing, and that the anger of an irritable person exists already in his own mind. This, on a gigantic scale, applies to Hamlet, according to Mr. Eliot. We remember that Mr. Robertson declared that the pragmatic test was the

[1] *The Sacred Wood*, 1920 (Methuen).   [2] Cf. Richardson (1784), and Hudson.
[3] Cf. W. F. Trench (211–12 note): 'All thoughts and feelings seek to materialise, to externalise themselves. That is the most fundamental fact of the universe, the reason for all action, the basis of all art. Any externalising of feeling tends to "ease".' Mr. J. Middleton Murry also writes that 'sensuous perceptions are necessary for the complete expression of contemplative experience'. *Problem of Style*, p. 9.

final one, and that for centuries the play had never failed to enthral countless audiences; but on behalf of Mr. Eliot it may be suggested that the minds of dramatic audiences are filled to their full by the display on the stage of mighty passion, and the power to analyse their causes is deferred. Mr. Eliot's essay, therefore, is an interesting hypothesis, and one likely to stimulate the minds of others.

VII

PROFESSOR HERFORD[1] discovers that Shakespeare has certain preferences and exclusions which he shares with the respectable citizen rather than the finer and rarer spirits—in other words a bias for normality, which specially appears in his treatment of love and marriage.[2] Love to him is a transfiguring and joyous passion, and its effects are happy. He is interested neither in violation of marriage nor in the coquette or the prude. He touched only the fringes of the comedy of love because normal love is not ridiculous and could yield material for the comic spirit only through some fact or situation external to it. He deals with confused identities, or the rarer kind of confusion in cases like Rosalind and Beatrice where his humour is richer and finer because it derives from a hidden ground of passion or tears. Nor is much tragedy to be found in normal love, and so Shakespeare uses the kind of delusion which perplexes and rends apart. But where he excelled was in imagining such fine women's souls that slander from the man they loved wrought upon them to the most piteous extreme. Always the tragic quality springs from the wonderful presentment of the love which is wrecked.

In the beginning he was slight and superficial, inclined to paradox and symmetry—e.g., the Shrew, Lady Anne's courtship (*Richard III*), Helena's wooing (*All's Well*). Such paradoxical feats were foreign to the profound normality of his mature art. To his taste for symmetry we must add a conception of love as extravagant magnanimity (*Verona*). Viola (*Twelfth-Night*) typifies his retreat from the extreme romantic position, for in the original story she follows a faithless lover. Later on he discards even the fun of sex-confusion: Imogen's adventures are purely pathetic. At first he delighted in opportunities of pathos from situation, but his riper technique was fortified by acquaintance with the spirited and high-bred Portias and Rosalinds of his time, and he acquired the experience, the genial worldliness, the poetized normality of his riper art.

The subject of *All's Well* was not congenial to his prime, and so the reason why he revised the play must have been something in the fundamental theme which attracted him. This, no doubt, was Helena's clear-sighted resolution, in which she is a true sister of Portia

---

[1] *Sh.'s Treatment of Love and Marriage*, 1921 (F. Unwin).
[2] Cf. Mézières and Beeching.

and Rosalind. She herself must be less the active agent to conquer Bertram than the sport of circumstances. Yet Shakespeare does not solve the problem; for if she means to avoid him why does she pilgrim to St. Jaques? She fluctuates between resolute pursuit and dignified renunciation—the first of which represents Shakespeare's earlier mind, the second his riper. He tried to fit a character based upon a nobler type of love into a plot based upon a grosser.

The norm of love obscured at the outset gradually grew clear, and became the background of the most delightful comedy and most poignant tragedy. His comedy of love is outside the norm, like burlesque (*M.N.D.*). And, though more rarely, in tragedy, when obsessed by evil, he accentuated the disastrous aspects of the relations between men and women. In some of his greatest work he shows love as unstable, lawless, grounded on illusion, the cause of tragic ruin within. The union of Desdemona and Othello is precarious because they are ignorant of each other. Love in Hamlet's Denmark is naturally touched with insidious disease. Only Ophelia among Shakespeare's women renounces love at a father's bidding, and there is nothing heroic in her sacrifice. It breaks her own heart and mind, and removes one of the last supports of Hamlet's trust in goodness. Love is the spiritual undoing of Angelo (*M. for M.*), and Isabella's purity is a negative abstinence, not whole-hearted devotion to a man she loves, like the rest of Shakespeare's heroines. Troilus and Cressida are without the grandeur which makes ruin sublime. The tragedy is depressing because it strikes less deep; the harms do not rend and shatter but undermine and frustrate. Cressida's love may kindle valour for a moment, but in the end it saps heroism and romance. But passion invests the fall of Antony and Cleopatra with a splendour beside which the triumph of their conqueror appears cold and mean. Shakespeare takes no sides and does not theorize about morals, but simply shows that Antony's passion ruins him as a statesman and saps his mental and moral strength—and yet it enlarges and enriches his emotional life. As a rule, when Shakespeare is at his greatest, love has a subordinate place, yet no other poet has so united appreciation of love as it is with apprehension of its ideal possibilities. . . .

The qualities of perfect balance and fine taste which we noted before in Professor Herford are not lacking in the present treatise. It remains to ask whether any new land is brought within the sweep of his compass that has found a new centre. In the first place he helps us to conceive how infinitely delicate a woman's soul may be, according to Shakespeare: the soul which cannot bear the beloved one to think evil of it. Secondly, we may compare his criticism of *All's Well* to Mr. Robertson's of *Hamlet*, and of *A. and C.* to Professor Croce's of *Hamlet*. The Phoenix rebirth that Croce discovered in Hamlet's despair, he discovers in Antony's mad passion. This is the critic's last

triumph—to induct the reader into a larger world of beauty that
rises suddenly like a vision when the foundations of the world of sense
have given way. Finally, Professor Herford is right to insist that
Shakespeare had a strong bias towards the normal, and that even
enraptured lovers like Romeo and Juliet design honourable marriage.

VIII

WE will first deal with remarks on Shakespeare's religion and ethics.
Raleigh says that he gave up the Church and took to religion.
Professor Croce, that he was no poet of 'ideals', yet not irreligious,
immoral, fatalist, pessimist; that he nowhere refers directly to God,
but within him was an ever-present obscure consciousness of unknown
divinity; that he strengthens our interest in good and evil, sorrow and
joy, destiny and necessity; that his moral discernment bears a strong
imprint of Christian ethics; that he believes neither in Fate nor in
determination of character; that justice is everywhere in him; that
he discerns acutely good and evil, but leaves the contest between them
undecided. Professor Croce concludes that he is not a philosopher who
reconciles all under theory; and Professor Herford likewise affirms
that he takes no sides, is no ethical theorist trying exactly to measure
right or wrong, but a great poet whose comprehensive soul had room
for many kinds of excellence incompatible in the experience of ordinary
men. His was a glorious humanity.

   The last word fitly introduces the subject of Shakespeare's politics,
beginning with Raleigh's phrase (the counterpart of his former) that
Shakespeare gave up the State and took to humanity, and that he was
the completely representative national poet who expressed the immense
tolerance of the English national temper. Sir J. Marriott likewise uses
link-phrases, that to Shakespeare the moralist right depended on
personal qualities, that he clung in politics and ethics to the golden
mean, and also subscribed to the doctrine of Machiavelli—that politics
were divorced from ethics. He says that no one was ever inspired by
more ardent love of his own country, but he was no partisan, he had
Olympian impartiality, and England to him was an inspiration.
Professor Croce, on the other hand, denies that he has any true
political faith and passion.

   Sir A. Quiller-Couch calls him a magnificently indolent man
breathing life into old plots, and a mighty craftsman. Professor Croce
says that he was intent on the study of his art.

   Of purely general remarks we will give the following: Sir A.
Quiller-Couch's, that his two greatest natural gifts were poetry and
humour; Sir J. Marriott's, that he had unfailing dramatic instinct,
and no man had a nicer sense of the congruities; Professor Croce's,
that he was a universal, objective, impersonal poet, and one of the
clearest and most evident; Professor Herford's that there is little

of myth and dream in his poetry—its staple is the humanity we know.

Sir A. Quiller-Couch says that he has a sublimated conception of maidenhood. . . .

We welcome the absence of dogmatic statements in all these critics. Surely this method is the true one: to reason imaginatively from one's own experience to the Shakespearian sum. As mysticism is self-proved, because it operates identically on the furthest-removed minds in time or race, so those whose minds faithfully receive Shakespeare may ultimately lighten the vision by comparing their experience.

Chapter XXXVIII

ENGLAND 1921–1922

I. WINSTANLEY.   II. J. M. ROBERTSON.   III. CLUTTON-BROCK.

IV. DYBOSKI.   V. CONCLUSION.

I

MISS LILIAN WINSTANLEY [1] strikes a new note in Shakespearian criticism, or rather accentuates one only partially struck. She deals with the historical origins of the plays, and startles us with some contemporary parallels.

Her object is to regard a play as an Elizabethan audience would regard it, since the mentality of his audience provides the dramatic poet with at least half his material. Hamlet's Denmark would appear to an Elizabethan audience like contemporary Scotland. There was feudal anarchy, usurpation, assassination recognized as the method to remove a rival. Yet in Shakespeare's Denmark and in contemporary Scotland there was love of education, philosophical depth, power of thought and meditation. In both the Catholic and Protestant faiths exist side by side. The Ghost is a Catholic, Hamlet a Protestant, since Wittenberg was a famous Protestant University. So in Scotland the Queen and her party were Catholic, her opponents the Protestant lords. In Shakespeare's Denmark the king was murdered and his wife marries the murderer: so Darnley. Polonius is murdered like Rizzio, and his body disposed of by the staircase. Also the king has no regular army, and Laertes heads an armed band—as in sixteenth-century Scotland. In both countries there was love of strong drink, and both courts have Italian and Danish names. Shakespeare's audience would be intensely interested in Scotland because it was the country about to provide them with a king.

Are the critics right who represent Shakespeare as a modern psychologist? Even if he were three hundred years ahead, his audience would not be. He cannot have been completely indifferent to his own era, and the Elizabethan stage was closely associated with politics. [2] Lear could be more easily compared with Oedipus and Priam than with Goriot. Oedipus and Priam are not people of common life, but the modern psychologist aims at realistic portraits of *individuals*. Homer spoke of 'divine Priam', and Shakespeare's greatest figures are almost superhuman—not even extraordinary *individuals*. There are no historical records of men pathetic as Lear, interesting as Hamlet, wise as Prospero. Shakespeare hints at his characters being partly

---

[1] *Hamlet and the Scottish Succession*, 1921 (Cambridge University Press).

[2] Hints of this theory appear in Steevens, Plumptre, Hunter, Massey, Elze (1868), Montégut, Friesen, Brandes, Mathew, Jusserand, Chevrillon.

mythologic and symbolic. He places Prospero on a magic island, withdraws Macbeth and Lear into the legendary past, makes Othello symbolic by his blackness. The mythologist is fundamentally historical, the psychologist is an egoist and individualist who chooses a subject that interests himself, and makes it interesting by his method of treatment—like Flaubert with Madame Bovary. The mythologist deals with traditional matter, already interesting to his audience—like the Greek dramatists. Had Shakespeare been a psychological realist he would have invented his own plots, for his method of reconstructing and altering beyond recognition saves him no labour. He makes more improbable the already improbable plots of *Lear* and *Hamlet*. Hamlet becomes a different character; only the names are alike and the country Denmark.

Richard II and *Hamlet* are linked together because they show how intimately Shakespeare and his company were connected with politics. The partisans of Essex were suspected of using the fortunes of Richard II as a symbol. In the last years of Elizabeth the great problem was succession. Although there was prejudice against Scotland, James had the best title, and it would be an immense advantage to unite the whole island under one rule. James was learned, merciful, unrevengeful, serious, reflective, melancholy, retiring. His father had been murdered and his mother imprisoned for life. He defended himself with subtlety, verbal fence, and so great a passion for keeping his own counsel that he was at times suspected of insanity. He escaped assassination, which had befallen all his Stuart predecessors, by reticence, subtlety, and genius for evasion. He prided himself on knowledge of human nature, but the most fatal of his defects was vacillation and weakness of will, whereas the Tudors had will-power and determination. He let the younger Bothwell usurp his power in Scotland, and he admits the vacillation with which Elizabeth in her correspondence reproaches him. Yet in emergencies—such as the Gowry conspiracy—he acted with decision.

In the saga source of *Hamlet* there was no parallel to the murder, but there was in the Darnley murder in the Scottish ballads. Before the explosion an attempt had been made to poison Darnley, and he escaped the explosion to be strangled in the garden. The correspondences are the effect of poison on the body, the secret character of the murder, the body found in the 'orchard'. As Mary had been accused of poisoning her first husband through the *ear*, it looks as if Shakespeare combined the three attempts. The Ghost's attitude to the Queen is tender and indulgent, and Darnley to the last sought Mary's love. In the play the Queen is fickle—and this was Buchanan's chief indictment: that Mary vehemently loved her first husband, then soon forgot, and married a second who was inferior. Hamlet and the Ghost stress the indecent haste and contrast between the two men—and all contemporary records stress the difference of Darnley and Bothwell. Darnley was skilled in martial exercises and had a fancy for appearing in full armour. Much is said of the Ghost's armour that makes him more dignified and warlike. Buchanan and others describe Bothwell as a needy adventurer, vicious and drunken: and Hamlet alludes to the King's heavy drinking. Hamlet is Protestant, whereas the Ghost is Catholic, and admits 'foul crimes', and is grieved by nothing so much as the want of absolution. Darnley was a Catholic who had sinned and was cut off without extreme unction. His son, James I, was Protestant, and an eager student of Protestant theology. In the saga there was no ghost because no doubt of guilt; in history there was doubt: Bothwell was suspected but not openly accused. There were rumours of apparitions on the night of the murder; and Shakespeare unites these into his magnificent conception. Gertrude remained true to Claudius—like Mary to Bothwell. Among those who received the captured Bothwell was one Eric Rosencrantz—and at the court of Scotland there was a Guildenstern.

The crucial problem of the drama is the hero's character, his melancholy and irresolution. But if Hamlet does not act it was because Shakespeare was stating an historical and political problem which neither he nor any one else could solve. In the prose sources the task before the hero is quite simple. Both Hamlet and James were philosophic and meditative, and interested in the darker side of human nature. In both was the baffling trait of hesitancy combined with sudden vigour in emergencies. Elizabeth warns James that his nephew, the younger Bothwell, had repeatedly plotted against his life, and complains that he talks but does nothing. This reproach or hesitation is not in Shakespeare's source, where the hero is delayed by external circumstances. The most open practices on the part of the younger Bothwell, and most manifest insults, cannot sting James to action. At last Bothwell enters the palace in disguise and asks pardon of James on his knees. James forgives, but later on excommunicates him—as Hamlet spares Claudius at prayer till he can achieve his religious ruin. This explains how the play appealed to great popular audiences. In Kyd's original *Hamlet*, as in the sources, the motive of revenge was mainly stressed. It was a startling innovation to make incapacity for action the centre of a tragedy; but if it concerned England's future king it would fascinate. Shakespeare combined the two Bothwells: the crimes of Claudius are those of the elder, more striking and dramatic Bothwell; but the relation of Hamlet to Claudius is that of James to the younger Bothwell. James was careless of dress, and Hamlet was indifferent to dress and scornful of courtiers. James always carried tablets to take notes, and it is Hamlet's first action after the Ghost-interview. This can have had no other object than to show a personal trait. Hamlet's policy delivers him from many perils, and

James was the only one of his race to escape violent death and live out his natural days. Shakespeare's method is not portraiture, but he takes the central situation, the Orestes-like motive of the play—the murderer of the father has married the mother—the man who should avenge but cannot. The Duke of *M. for M.* is inferior to Hamlet, but more like the historic James—because, when Shakespeare wrote *Hamlet*, he had not seen James, when he wrote *M. for M.* he had. *Hamlet* must have been a pamphlet in favour of the Scottish succession.

Neither the play scene nor the motive of the voyage to England was in the saga. After the Darnley murder pictures were circulated of it among the excited people, and, above all, a banner which had a dreadful effect on Mary. Hamlet knows the king's designs, yet lets himself be sent on a dangerous voyage, and leaves his country in the power of a villain. Such a mingling of hesitancy and rashness can only have been represented because there was a real historic parallel. James set out on a stormy voyage to bring home his bride—Anne of Denmark —and left the younger Bothwell to his own devices. Shakespeare retained the incident because it shows a power of vigorous action in emergency coexisting with a certain rashness and weakness in the very circumstances which enable the vigour to be shown. When Hamlet returns he again forgives and attempts to be friendly with Claudius: as James again forgives the Catholic earls and Bothwell.

The murder of Polonius resembles the historical murder of Rizzio by Darnley, but not the saga. In the play we get the Queen's bitter lament for the 'good old man', and Hamlet's disposal of the body 'by a staircase'—the staircase that played a principal part in the murder of Rizzio. Perhaps Hamlet's gruesome remark that Polonius was at supper is a macabre reference to the Rizzio murder where the victim was found 'at supper'. The politic worms may be a parallel reference to the wearisome and futile sittings of the 'Lords Politic' in considering the murder. These things would be accidental if alone, but in combination they convince. Polonius resembles Burleigh, and Shakespeare might make him Hamlet's enemy, as Burleigh was of Essex and Southampton. Polonius stands out as the one person who enjoys the royal confidences, like Burleigh who had outlived Walsingham and all his generation. Burleigh was a learned man who had played a prominent part in Cambridge—and Polonius obviously desires to be thought learned, and alludes to his university life. To his son Thomas Cecil, who lived an irregular life in Paris, Burleigh wrote anxious letters, and instructed friends to watch him—like Polonius and Laertes. He also wrote a number of maxims for his son, like the advice of Polonius. And he would state all the reasons for or against a particular action, with meticulous care for detail. He would employ spying— as Polonius intercepted Hamlet's letters to Ophelia. He estranged his daughter from her husband, through using her as a decoy—as Polonius estranged Ophelia from Hamlet. He was a new man who resented attacks on his ancestry—and so Hamlet's 'fishmonger' strikes home to Polonius. The humiliation of Burleigh by his scornful rival Essex was a standing jest of the court: each is made a public butt by a brilliant young man. As nothing dramatic happened to Burleigh, Shakespeare combined him and Rizzio, as he did the two Bothwells. The parallel is that both held a position of supreme trust and wielded power by underhand methods. To unite them unites the two parts of the play —James I and Essex.

The story of Ophelia resembles that of Elizabeth Vernon, wife of Southampton, and Lady Essex. Southampton's love for Elizabeth Vernon cost him the Queen's favour, and he married her secretly. Both Essex and Southampton repeatedly offended the Queen by their connexion with plays and players: and this would not have been had Shakespeare treated imaginary events. Among resemblances are the wooing with *too much familiarity*. Both Polonius and Laertes reproach Ophelia; and Elizabeth Vernon and Ophelia declare that their lover had pledged his word. They are both separated from their lovers, and in both cases the love affairs are made court affairs and publicly discussed. Marriage becomes impossible, and seduction is suspected. Elizabeth Vernon's lover went away, and she became deeply distressed and in danger of insanity. Hamlet's language to Ophelia is most coarse, and her songs are equally suggestive. Was Shakespeare carrying his friend's story a step further, and making it more pathetic? Southampton was in the Tower, in danger through this love-story. Probably Shakespeare wished to awaken sympathy for him, and the required unity was already in the minds of the audience. Shakespeare depicted sympathetically the relations between Hamlet and Ophelia, but it is an open question whether they were literally innocent—and Victorian prudery may mislead us. The conclusion implied by Hamlet's suggestions in the play scene and Ophelia's in her songs is other than innocence. His love for her only appears in certain scenes, and the reason may be that Shakespeare drew Hamlet from more than one original. He forgets about her through most of the play.

Much in Hamlet's experiences suggests Essex, and he was by nature student and soldier more than courtier. He preferred retirement to court life, and, like Hamlet, was without ambition: while the Hamlet of the saga wished to gain the crown. Hamlet's curious lack of ambition is thus explained—that Shakespeare took hints from Essex, against whom, at his trial, ambition was preferred as a criminal charge. In the last year of his life Essex was irresolute to the point of insanity, and at times longed for death and showed himself world-weary and life-weary. Like Hamlet his last anxiety was not to leave 'a wounded name'. He was closely associated with actors—to the Queen's displeasure—and the Stage then influenced opinion like the modern Press. It told against Essex that he was connected with Shakespeare's company, which had repeatedly performed *Richard II* with its deposition scene of the King and his death. Hamlet is courteous to the players and calls them 'the abstract and brief chronicles of the time'. He would not have done so had their plays dealt with Bronze-Age Britain and ancient Denmark. Nor would the Star Chamber have concerned itself with dramatists and actors that had no political influence. As Essex and *Richard II*, so it was the Gonzago play which brought Hamlet's fate on him. There is no parallel in the saga to the story of Laertes, but there is in the last years of Essex. As Claudius pits Laertes against Hamlet, so Robert Cecil pits Raleigh against Essex. Essex was haunted by the dread of ignominy to his body if he died a traitor's death—and this suggests the grave-digging scene— the insulted dead, the shamed and humiliated dust, &c. Essex had a passionate desire for reconciliation with Cobham and Raleigh—and Laertes exclaimed, 'Exchange forgiveness . . .'. Also, 'I am justly killed with mine own treachery'—and so Raleigh was destroyed by the same methods of slander he had used against Essex. As Spenser's great poem is one mass of symbolism, as symbolism is a chief method in the religious drama before Shakespeare, and also in Lyly, so an element of symbolism is probable in Shakespeare. The casket of letters was stolen from Lady Essex, as Hamlet's love-letters to Ophelia were intercepted. Ophelia's description of her lover differs from the Hamlet who resembles James I. Essex was courtier and soldier, but Hamlet expressly disliked bloodshed and despised the tricks of courtiers. These facts cannot be interpreted as psychology, but they can as history. Nothing in Shakespeare's *Hamlet* justifies Fortinbras succeeding to the throne, but it is symbolic of James I—the heir from another and more northern kingdom entering to make good his right at the head of his army.[1]

These resemblances are too close to belong to the atmosphere of the time, and they are all events of immediate interest. Shakespeare selected the *Amleth* saga as Hamlet selected Gonzago. He loved reality and wished to describe life as it is lived, and his audience would be interested in the personalities and politics of the time. His method was to shape contemporary events into good dramatic material. His plays might be defined as mythology on its way towards psychology. Great mythological figures may have been thus created—neither copied from individuals nor pure fiction, but accretions round a historic centre. The *Faerie Queene* is avowedly contemporary history, yet it looks less like it than Shakespeare. Had Hamlet's character

[1] H. S. Bowden (*Religion of Sh.*, pp. 318–24) compares Polonius to Burleigh, Hamlet to Essex, Claudius to Leicester. Mr. Mathew says that Shakespeare had Essex in mind when he drew Brutus and Hamlet.

been a psychological unity, so many critics would not have differed about it, but they would naturally differ if Shakespeare were drawing from more than one character at the same time. . . .

No one can read the above without being at least partially convinced. Such a trait as the note-taking of Hamlet and James I cannot be accidental. The greater individual likeness of James I to the Duke in *M. for M.* and the likeness of Polonius to Burleigh are specially convincing. One is constantly asking, 'But is this true?'—like the bewildered Tribune at the news that Coriolanus was marching on Rome. There is also the question of method, and the example of the *Faerie Queene* is a powerful weapon in Miss Winstanley's hands. We have been told before that the Elizabethan drama filled the part of the modern newspaper, and other writers have connected the deposition scene in *Richard II* with the fate of Essex. Miss Winstanley, therefore, does right to hold the lamp higher and show the ever-widening circles of historical interest. But she strikes us as wrong in eliminating the psychological interest, for we think that even if Shakespeare started along the broad slope of history, his final wrestle took place on the higher ground with the single human soul. We also ask ourselves whether Miss Winstanley's method of reasoning subtracts grandeur from or adds it to Shakespeare's characters? Her saying that his greatest figures are almost superhuman, and not even extraordinary individuals, might be compared with Professor Bradley's criticism. And she adds that no historical men have been pathetic as Lear, wise as Hamlet, &c. Is not our awe at the splendour and terror of a great man increased by the knowledge that he is a human being like ourselves? Lastly, we venture to say that Miss Winstanley is more absorbed by history than Shakespeare—and she effects a similar transference in the reader's mind. She disposes us to pursue historical studies rather than return to Shakespeare; she centres the interest in James I, Darnley, Bothwell, Mary, Burleigh, Essex, Elizabeth Vernon, and others rather than in Hamlet and Polonius and Ophelia.

In the Introduction to her second book [1] Miss Winstanley stresses the importance and relevance of time. She denies that one can dissociate a poet from time and space and consider him simply in the abstract—and she remarks that Professor Bradley scarcely refers to the events of the day. According to her the question is, What is the relation of the plays to England and the seventeenth century? Symbolism is to be expected in Shakespeare, and historic events appear differently to contemporaries and moderns. Schlegel and Coleridge supplanted the historical method with the psychological; but psychology also had its historical development, and that of the sixteenth century differs from the nineteenth. The method of constructing characters differs radically, and Spenser uses an individual to represent

[1] *Macbeth, King Lear, and Contemporary History,* 1922 (Cambridge Univ. Press).

the genius of a whole country, and also characters that stand both for individuals in history and the genius of a whole nation, e.g. Orgoglio and Mammon represent both Philip II of Spain and Spain itself. So with the Huguenots, Coligny is himself and the whole genius of France; and Queen Joan of Navarre is herself and also the daughter of France. If this were Shakespeare's psychology it might throw light on *Lear*—a play great enough to be the tragedy of a nation. We can imagine it as the scream of horror of England's greatest genius at the anguish of the civil war in France, which he feared might happen in his own country. Spenser's characters are superhuman, neither portraits nor fiction. It is useless to interpret Shakespeare's psychology as if it were Browning's. Hamlet, Macbeth, Lear, Prospero are greater than any individual man. The Elizabethans took a great interest in history, and the stage dealt with contemporary history: it was charged against Essex and Southampton that they had made political use of the stage. The Government, menaced by secret enemies, would not allow the most innocent allusion to current politics. In *Macbeth* and *Lear* Shakespeare uses a large element of contemporary history closely connected with immediate events. In the bare subjects there was nothing to suggest such dreadful and painful emotion. The passion of *Lear*, like nothing else conceived by the human mind, is about the domestic affairs of a remote king of the Bronze Age, whose story in the original was not a tragedy. The true theme of *Macbeth* was the Gunpowder Plot which was aimed against the Protestant Ruler of Britain and the Union of Crowns of England and Scotland. Macbeth fulfilled the Merlin prophecies by trying to avert them; and James I was greatly interested in prophecy. James compared the Gunpowder Plot to that against his father; he dreaded a repetition of it, and the populace dreaded it for him. They feared a massacre of Protestants in England similar to St. Batholomew. Both *Macbeth* and *Lear* appealed to the same complex—the Darnley murder and St. Bartholomew. Only the fate of nations and the fate of the world are great enough subjects for *Macbeth* and *Lear*.

Merlin had prophesied that the Arthurian Empire should be restored and the unity of Britain achieved when the true British line succeeded to the English throne. Macbeth knew Banquo's line was destined to succeed, and, like Oedipus, he caused the prophecies to be fulfilled by the means he took to avoid them. Britain was the great protagonist of the Protestant faith, and the union of crowns was dreaded by Spain. Those who disliked the union supported the Gunpowder Plot, and James truly believed in a league against himself directly fomented by Satan. In his reign there were repeated trials for witchcraft and sorcery, and Catholics were supposed to be guilty of such practices. He thought himself and his life were objects of dispute between the forces of good and evil. He believed in the divine

right of kings, and thought the theory would be strengthened if it
could be proved that secular prophecy had also foretold his advent to
the throne. Now we see how intensely the subject appealed to Shakespeare's audience. The people believe in divine right because through
it they assert their own right to national development as against the
Pope's claims. Macbeth would avert the Merlin prophecies—and
evil spirits try to destroy Banquo, but these very powers of evil are
forced to testify to the permanence of his line. Advanced nationalism,
and freedom of thought, and political freedom, are contrasted with
reactionary Papalism. A great Protestant Empire will set the world
free: and the subject of *Macbeth* is the furious opposition of the powers
of evil.

The Gunpowder Plot reminded James of the murder of his father,
and the English nation compared it to St. Bartholomew. The audience
would believe in Macbeth's attempt to extirpate the race of Banquo;
hence Shakespeare works to a pre-existent unity in their minds. The
murder of Duff by Donwald in Holinshed was the nearest parallel to
the Darnley murder in Scottish annals, and Shakespeare modifies it to
make the resemblance closer. The conference of Macbeth and his
wife, the bell, the drink, the silence of night, Macbeth's disrobing,
his pretence of being awakened, the knocking: none of these are in
Holinshed, but all have parallels in the Darnley murder. So in the
Banquo murder Shakespeare drew on St. Bartholomew, and its central
incident, the murder of Coligny. The latter, the Darnley murder,
and the Gunpowder Plot were all imputed to the Catholic League.
The English dreaded the Catholic League, knowing their country to
be the object of its animosity.

We remember the irony of Duncan's praise of Macbeth's castle;
and Melville in his *Memoirs* says that Darnley was lodged in Kirk o'
Field as a place of good air. There is nothing of this in Holinshed, nor
of the intense depth of night which the Scottish proclamations dwell
upon—nor of the conversation between Mary and Bothwell in her
chamber before the murder, which Buchanan reports. Shakespeare
also discards the blood feuds prominent in Holinshed, and makes Lady
Macbeth's motive ambition for her husband. So Bothwell's ambition
was insatiable, and Mary wished to gratify it. The terrible incident
of knocking at the door occurs twice in the Darnley murder—when
Bothwell knocked with a clamour on the gate of the Kirk o' Field
—and when his servant roused him. Two servants were killed with
Darnley, and two who lodged apart survived to give evidence:
thus the parallel is curiously exact. Further parallels are Macbeth's
statement that none will dare impugn the deed because the doers have
all the power—and Bothwell's impudence and audacity at the Darnley
trial. The heavy sense that no one dared speak for justice was the
burden that weighed on men's minds. The Court was crowded with

Bothwell's adherents; the Earl of Lennox (absent from Holinshed) was chief accuser; and he, and Shakespeare's Lennox, ardently desire help from England. In the contemporary plan of the murder the bodies of Darnley and his servant appear, and a dagger floating in the air above them. Also a child's picture is seen, with the inscription, 'Judge and avenge my cause, O Lord!' and a broken branch lies by the dead bodies. These resemble the figures shown to Macbeth by the witches, and all prove that the mentality of the time turned history into symbolism. Shakespeare describes the night as intensely still and then tempestuous beyond human memory. The symbolism of the Darnley explosion that made the ground shake explains this contradiction.

Further blanks in Holinshed and likenesses between Macbeth and Bothwell are that both are accused of lechery and tyranny, both have no interval of contentment or good reputation, and both are accused of witchcraft. The Queen falls into melancholy, and her epileptic fits may have suggested the sleep-walking scene. In Holinshed the blood feuds give a sort of wild justice to the crimes of Donwald and Lady Macbeth. Shakespeare substitutes ambition and personal affection which correspond with history. It is Hamlet's method in the Gonzago play.

James I believed that the younger Bothwell was associated with witches, and such belief was general. The Privy Council had ascribed the Gunpowder Plot to the evil spirits of Scotland. We hear of a witch raising storms to stay the Queen's home-coming to Scotland—the very practices of the witches in *Macbeth*. It was proved that Bothwell was connected with several witches, and Roman Catholicism was his impelling motive. He was said to be the great centre of Catholic plots and conspiracies. The essential idea of *Macbeth* is that the hero plans with the witches the murder of a king, and knows their inspiration is from the Powers of Darkness.

Shakespeare took little but prophecy from the witches in Holinshed, but he adds all the wonderful and terrible details from the Scottish witch-trials. His witches, like those of history, have familiar spirits; they have the gift of prophecy; they raise storms and pursue ships; they term themselves 'sisters'; they can pass the sea; they are associated with cats; they meet in waste places; they gain influence by telling men half-truths. . . . The aim of the Bothwell witches, and of the Gunpowder Plot, was to prevent the union of England and Scotland—and both were set on by the Roman Catholics.

People feared the Gunpowder Plot might be followed by a St. Bartholomew. Compare the wavering of Charles IX, and the taunt of the Queen, his mother, in his chamber at midnight. The commentators have only assumed that there was such an interview and previous promise in *Macbeth*. Holinshed only says that Lady Macbeth urged him on, but nothing of cowardice, of previous promise, of the excellent opportunity. The Queen, fearing he would relent, ordered the bell of

St. Germain L'Auxerrois to be sounded—and a bell is the signal to the
hesitating Macbeth—and it was terribly effective on the stage. Duncan's attendants pray, and Coligny and his people were at prayer when
the assassins reached the door. Holinshed makes a supper the occasion
for the murder of Banquo, and Shakespeare adds details to intensify the
parallel with the occasion for the massacre of St. Bartholomew—the
marriage feast of Henry of Navarre with Marguerite of Valois. There
is the same hideous treachery of making an invitation to a festival the
occasion of massacre. As Banquo was to have been the principal guest,
so Coligny. The latter urged his people to escape, as Banquo did
Fleance, and both victims were slain by torch-light. Shakespeare here
appealed to the nerves of his audience, as he did with the bell. Both
were murdered with repeated blows on the head and a terrible amount
of blood: of which there is nothing in Holinshed. Like Macbeth,
Charles IX was haunted ever after and suffered terrible remorse. In
sleep he cried out his horror of blood, as Macbeth was shaken by
terrible dreams. The Huguenot poet tells how the gutters were filled
with blood, which flowed into the rivers, staining them crimson, and
thence reached the ocean; and this recalls, 'Will all great Neptune's
ocean . . .'. Like Macbeth, Charles IX suffered from hallucinations
and sleeplessness, and he died largely through want of sleep. Shakespeare drew on this because his audience had inherited the traditions
of the religious drama and believed in God's moral judgements. France
is said to have been sunk in vice and crime in the reign of Charles IX;
the land was rife with lewdness, luxury, irreligion, impiety, magic,
abominations, disorders, treason, poisoning, assassinations: to which we
may compare, 'Alas, poor country . . .' (*Macbeth* IV. iii). St. Bartholomew and the Darnley murder were looked upon as one tragedy—the
terrible crimes by which the Catholics sought to prevent the Protestant
succession in England.

The Porter in *Macbeth* is a satire on Guy Fawkes—Guy Fawkes
who served as the watchman who mounted guard over the cellar.
What we call intrusions of comedy may be tragic-grotesque. The
Grave-digger and Porter may appear comic like Satan and Judas
Iscariot in the mystery-plays. Macbeth may be a composite character,
like Hamlet, and he is more interesting than any real murderer. His
courage, recklessness, and audacity recall the elder Bothwell, his association with witches the younger Bothwell, his hallucinations and remorse
Charles IX. He thus becomes 'the ideal murderer', a figure of superhuman horror and fascination. He would have been uninteresting as
the older Bothwell only, hard and callous, without the glamour of the
supernatural and the trait of remorse. It is not easy to unite all these
qualities in an individual; so Macbeth is more than man—a figure in
which all the elements are human, but so combined that the result is
superhuman.

The story of *Lear* was familiar to the public as authentic history, but not as tragedy. A remote king in the Bronze Age, whose original story is a conspicuous example of undeserved good luck, hardly seems a subject for one of the most terrific tragedies in the world. Shakespeare eliminates the real motive of Goneril and Regan in the story, and so makes the main motive of his drama a marble-hearted, inexplicable, inexpressible ingratitude. In a book of Pierre Mathieu we find what looks like a French interpretation of the story of Gloster. The blind father is France, and the blindness is symbolic of the blind and rash acts of that country. The illegitimate, treacherous son is Henry of Guise; the legitimate, devoted son Henry of Navarre. *Lear* is a political play in which the nations are protagonists, and ungrateful children the factions of a civil war, tearing their fatherland to pieces.

It is hard to realize now to what an extent the Gunpowder Plot had terrified the nation. The King compared it with his father's murder, and the people to St. Bartholomew, and it was supposed to be the work of the Catholic League which had produced civil war in France. The parallels with the Darnley murder were—that Darnley had been led to his doom by false professions of affection and his own credulity—that he rashly left his friends and placed himself in the power of traitors—that Mary would exclude him from the title of 'king'—that he was proud and haughty and prone to furious rages—that Mary took away his servants, forbade hers to obey him, denied him necessities, made him beggar and outlaw, thrust him naked out of doors into deserts and heaths, compelled him to shelter in a ruinous house with beggars—that he attempted to escape to France. . . . Few of these are in the old tale of Lear. The murder was repeatedly called parricide and said to violate two of the sacredest things—matrimony and royal majesty. The *Chronicle* does not give this sense of the greatest of all human duties violated and all human sacraments broken. Rizzio is insolent to Darnley, like Oswald to Lear, and both aggravate the mischief. Darnley never had more than the shadow of power, and this shadow of power and tutelage of his daughters was bitter to Lear. Darnley suspected Mary of the basest sensuality, and this was one of Lear's terrible charges against Goneril—'Down from the waist they are Centaurs'—whereas Goneril of the old story is not so accused. Rage and impotence were the leading traits of Darnley and Lear. Even Darnley's friends admitted his capricious folly. The 'fool', sometimes called a 'boy', seems like a symbol or detached personality of that second self which had ruined Lear.

Darnley was thrust out naked, barred from nobility, denied his servants—even as Goneril and Regan beat down the number of Lear's knights. In both we have causeless change from the warmest professions of affections to the bitterest hate and open and obvious insolence.

Darnley followed Mary from one castle to another, to be disdainfully excluded—as Lear rode after Regan. Darnley's heart was obstinately fixed in loving Mary—and Lear is terribly hard to disenchant with Goneril, and more so with Regan. As Goneril practises with Regan to shut Lear out of doors, so does Mary with the Earl of Murray's wife. The sources tell nothing of this refusal of fire, lodging, shelter. The 'division between the dukes' represents the factious Scottish nobles. The hovel is paralleled by the ruinous house near alms-houses for poor beggars provided by Bothwell. Contrary to the *Chronicle* Shakespeare makes intense, violent, and unprovoked hatred a main motive of his play. Only the taking away of the servants resembles the *Chronicle*.

Mary was tied to Darnley (who was actually Duke of Albany) and jealous of Bothwell's wife—as Goneril was jealous of Regan with Edmund. The Casket Letters containing Mary's impassioned letters and sonnets to Bothwell ruined Mary, as Goneril was ruined by her love-letters. Goneril arranged to marry Edmund and planned her husband's death—and we read in Buchanan of Mary's marriage contract made before Bothwell's divorce. The love story is in history, but in neither of Shakespeare's sources.

In Huguenot Memoirs St. Bartholomew and the Darnley murder were treated as parallel crimes inspired by the Catholic League, planned and executed by the House of Lorraine and Catherine de Médici, and there was direct contact with the powers of hell. The murders of Darnley and Coligny were termed 'parricide'—and the French royal family were used to call Coligny 'father'. The Huguenots called him the 'father' of his country, and compared France to an ungrateful child destroying its father. He had almost regal power, and was descended from a house one of the privileges of which was a personal retinue of 100 knights. He was known as the second king of France, and Catherine was jealous of him. The Parisian populace crowned his effigy with straw—as Lear and the wild flowers. He had been warned against Charles and Catherine, but he believed in their professions of affection. Shakespeare blended the two stories in one, and he was working to a pre-existent unity in the minds of the audience. From the story of Darnley come the supreme pathos of Lear, his helplessness and futile rages; from Coligny, as representing France, the Titanic power and passion, the heroic courage and dignity. The storm in *Lear* is an appalling conception, and the French civil war was often compared to a terrific tempest. Coligny was old and appealed to the murderers to respect his white hairs, like Lear—and like Lear he still had tremendous physical force. Lear had terrific passions, and Coligny was known to rate furiously the whole French royal family. Lear was stripped naked in the tempest and deserted by all—and with Coligny all France is exposed naked to the tempest of St. Bartholomew.

After his death Coligny's very furniture was judged and condemned to be destroyed; in *Lear* we have the bitter irony of the trial of the joint-stools. To the tragedy of one of the greatest nations reduced almost to the level of the brutes, we add Shakespeare's fear of a like fate for England, and this explains his terrific grief. The historians tell how France was like a father who preferred the illegitimate son Guise to the legitimate Navarre. Like Edgar Navarre ultimately won his kingdom by arms. Joan of Navarre was against Catherine and Margaret, as Cordelia was against Goneril and Regan; she sees through their impudent lies, but cannot fight. Coligny had been advised by his friends not to come to Paris; but he ignored their warnings and believed in the Queen Mother's enthusiastic professions of affection. His trust appeared almost senseless to his friends. It was part of the St. Bartholomew plot to withdraw Mary Queen of Scots from prison and make her Queen of England; therefore the Huguenots treat St. Bartholomew and the Darnley murder as one series of events aimed at the Protestant succession in England and France. The two crimes were connected in the popular mind and linked by Shakespeare in drama. The Queen of Navarre was murdered by Catherine, as Cordelia by her sisters. Like Cordelia the Queen of Navarre never flattered or dissimulated, and gave up all, even life, for the truth.

Catherine persuaded Charles that his nobles were a danger to the royal family, and in 1569 he was insulted by the diminution of his retinue. Lear's curse on Goneril would apply to Catherine. She was sterile for long after marriage, and then her children quarrelled with her and among themselves, and were a bane to France. A Huguenot tract of 1573 curses them in Lear's manner. Joan of Navarre stood by Coligny in his darkest hour, and on his defeat at Moncontour in 1569 she goes to him and is received as an angel. She brought with her a doctor named Ambrose Paré who made many improvements in the treatment of the insane. He replaced the old brutality with gentler treatment, including music. Coligny is the father of his country, betrayed and murdered by ungrateful children; his naked body is exposed to the elements that are less cruel than his children. He is the genius of France, and in his person all France is naked and outraged: yet she will revive and live again. Like Albany, Charles IX at first gave way from weakness, but he afterwards repented his share of the tragedy. His younger brother, the Duke of Anjou, was a willing accomplice, and his fate was like Cornwall's: he was stabbed by a servant who revolted against him. Henry of Navarre suffered misfortunes like Edgar, but finally he came to the rescue of blind and mutilated France. Mathieu says that France would have fallen to pieces had not the great Prince received and cherished her: and this is a close parallel to the central episode in the Gloster story, where Edgar receives and cherishes Gloster. Edgar speaks as a peasant; and Navarre in early life was brought up among peasants and spoke in a strong southern dialect.

Shakespeare writes symbolic mythology, and it has been so long ignored because we have assumed the same psychology in the sixteenth century as the nineteenth. It was the method of his age, and we see it in the *Faerie Queene*, Lyly's plays, Sidney's *Arcadia*, Ben Jonson's Masques, Drayton; and also in the historians such as Buchanan, and the French poets and historians—D'Aubigné, Ronsard, Malherbe, De Thou, Mathieu. In Memoirs we get historical prose on one page and the same material turned into mythological poetry on the next. . . .

On the whole we think Miss Winstanley's second book more convincing and fuller of more striking parallels than her first. The floating dagger above Darnley, Coligny and his retinue, the fate of Anjou, the character of Joan of Navarre—these and many others cannot be accidents. Now and then a parallel is overstrained, e.g. that Lear was hard to disenchant with Goneril and Regan; or the comparison of the Casket Letters to those of Goneril. However, we feel no doubt that Shakespeare was acquainted with these things, and that they worked in his mind and he derived ideas from them; but that they were equally present to the minds of the audience, and that Shakespeare wrote his plays in the Hamlet-Gonzago spirit, we do not think is proven. Of the first book we said that Miss Winstanley transferred the interest from Shakespeare to history. This is true of the second, though we do not for a moment deny that Miss Winstanley herself is impressed to the full by Shakespeare's genius. However, we must admit that for the moment we are more interested in Darnley, Bothwell, Mary, Coligny, Catherine the Queen Mother, Charles IX, Henry and Joan of Navarre than Banquo, Lady Macbeth, Lear, Albany, Gloster, Edgar, and others. It may have been observed that we did not include Macbeth in the list, and here we think that Miss Winstanley surpasses herself, and we are rapt from history into contemplating the terror and splendour of Macbeth's character. She tells how 'he has penetrated below and beyond the world itself, into dark reservoirs of unknown and unfathomable evil which the soul of man dare hardly dream of exploring, and, most tragic of all, he *knows* that he is ruined and can measure all that his soul might have been and all that his soul has lost'. She adds that 'Shakespeare cannot have found the whole of such terrible sublime in any one human heart', and that Macbeth is something more than 'a figure in which all the elements are human, but in which they are so combined that the result is superhuman'.

Here Miss Winstanley gives generously, but in the last clause the rich giver proves unkind, as Ophelia would say. Having shown us Macbeth like a pillar of cloud and fire, she tends to dehumanize him. We still think that the great soul in the great body let loose on earth is the most awe-inspiring sight beneath the sun. When Othello speaks words like these,

> Here is my journey's end, here is my butt
> And very sea-mark of my utmost sail,

we feel something that diminishes the sack of cities, and we rather sympathize with the brigand who had been in Napoleon's retreat from Moscow and confessed to George Borrow that there was 'nothing remarkable' in his life. But the obvious answer to Miss Winstanley is that we need know nothing of the Darnley murder or St. Bartholomew to appreciate *Macbeth* and *Lear*. She has written criticism of an extraordinarily interesting kind, and, in exceptional cases, such as Macbeth, of the finest, but she has also lit up historical events with stolen Promethean fire.

II

MR. J. M. ROBERTSON continues his labours with *Henry V*,[1] and, applying the test of manner, sees much in it to doubt. The limner of Hotspur and Kate, Falstaff and Harry, would hardly present war mainly as a declamatory matter of reciprocal rant and taunt. The verse is often pre-Shakespearian, and has vigour without sweetness, power without grace, and the comic relief is often dragged in by the heels rather than lightly interwoven. The Prologues hint at pre-Shakespearian drama, and the action at times heavily relies on them. After Agincourt we see undoubted traces of recomposition.

Act I has the same primitive dramatic expedient as the first scene of *Edward III*: the King must be convinced of the rightness of his cause. The Harfleur rants contain 25 per cent. of double-endings, compared with 5 to 9 per cent. in other verse of the play, and their lines are turgid and end-stopped. The first is full of bombast and boasting, the second of calculated savagery—hardly fitted to the leader of Shakespeare's manhood. Would Shakespeare have produced such work a year, or even a few years, after *1 Henry IV*? No doubt he worked over the play and wrote the scene between the King and the soldiers and some of the Fluellen scenes, but the original play belongs to the time of *Henry VI*, and the rant style to Marlowe's first crude period. Probably about 1590 a play on Henry V, embodying some of the popular matter of the old *Famous Victories* had been put together by Marlowe, Peele, and Greene. Shakespeare never vitally rehandled the play, though he inserted the best ethical and poetical matter. In the preceding play he had clearly given the King's reason for invading France. It was probably Chapman who vindicated the order to slay the prisoners— the one non-Catholic Englishman who justified the Massacre of St. Bartholomew (*Revenge of Bussy d'Ambois*). The three versions in

[1] *The Sh. Canon*, Part I, 1922 (Routledge).

Henry V of the massacre of the prisoners at Agincourt are intelligible as the result of two interpolations, but not as the spontaneous composition of any one author. Through inattention to style such anomalies have long passed muster. Shakespeare would not have copied Marlowe's diction after he had written *1 Henry IV* and Henry's V's soliloquy in Act IV.

The verse of *J.C.* is more archaic and less flexible than that of *1 Henry IV* and *John*, and the proportion of double-endings (19·5) is the same as *Richard III*, compared with 21·8 in *1 Henry IV* and *John*. Some of the verse belongs to Shakespeare's middle style, but much does not. For two hundred years it has been admitted that the character of Caesar is unsatisfactorily presented, and Fleay suggested the hand of Ben Jonson. Jonson's method is didactic, hortatory, and declamatory, and we may also compare Casca's speeches with Chapman's *Sejanus*, and his prose narrative with the prose in the latter's *Tragedy of Caesar and Pompey*. Chapman often used the standing tag about the 'many-headed beast', and like Ben Jonson he was for Pompey and against Caesar. Drayton also derides the multitude, and so does Marlowe. It was a universal pre-Shakespearian note.

The quality of the play and the lack of any unifying conception are alien from Shakespeare. It has not the flaming power of *Coriolanus* nor the wealth of portraiture of *A. and C.*, nor is it a rounded dramatic whole as are these plays. The management of the time is not un-Shakespearian, but it suggests condensation. The unfit brevity of the presentment of Caesar suggests both condensation and alien intervention. It is the work of a hostile artist—as were Jonson and Chapman: the stories told against him by Cassius in scene ii are not historical, and are invented to disparage him. The later Shakespeare, who grasped Antony and Coriolanus with such amazing power, would not fail with him whom he called elsewhere 'the mightiest Julius'. We are probably reading either alien work rewritten by Shakespeare or Shakespeare curtailed and interpolated by another. With Brutus, Cassius, Portia the play follows Plutarch, but Plutarch is not made to cohere as in the great Roman plays: the quarrel between Brutus and Cassius has no dramatic meaning. They become suddenly transformed to old friends, after Brutus had been scolding like a servitor. Except for the reconciliation the scene is undignified and unworthy. If the retelling of Portia's death by Messala was purposely left standing, it exhibits Brutus as a fraudulent *poseur*. We seem to have an *interrupted* revision of the quarrel scene, and the original handling is surely not Shakespearian. Shakespeare may have twice revised it, once retouching it, and, secondly, strengthening it by making Brutus already know of Portia's death, which in the original play he learns only afterwards. Portia is merely a hysterical nuisance and a danger to her friends; and she kills herself in the midst of her husband's supreme trial, though she had begged to be his helper. She is no integral part of the play, and her speeches do not advance the action. But if the object was to disparage her, it suggests Ben Jonson, who in *Volpone, Sejanus, Catiline* shows contempt for women-politicians. After Caesar's death the play became the chronicle history type, in which only Marlowe excelled, because he unified it by sacrificing chronology and historic detail. The wrangling scenes of the opposing leaders belong to the primitive method of chronicle plays, including *Tamburlaine*. The first hundred lines of Act V are like the debris of a pre-Shakespearian play, and also the rants of Brutus and Cassius after the assassination. We must realize the extent to which Shakespeare's dramaturgy is a recasting of previously current stage material. But if transmutation was his supreme function, why is it so inadequately exercised here?

Fleay's later hypothesis was that the play is Ben Jonson's abridgement of a *double* play. We are in the thick of a plot in the second scene before any conspiracy has been evolved—in an historical play which was supposed to teach the audience. That Caesar, Antony, Calpurnia, and six other notable personages should appear to play such brief parts is bad stage economy, and bad business. Then the triumvirate are introduced without explanation or preparation completing their list of victims for the proscription. No previous hint of dissidence preceded the sudden dispute between Antony and Octavius as to which of their commands shall make the right wing. Only the theory of a double play condensed into one can explain these phenomena. Not that the play is at all points compressed, e.g. the Portia action is extraneous; and at times the dialogue is inappropriately expanded, e.g. the preposterous discussion where the east lies. The fourth and fifth acts show the same marks of alternate expansion and curtailment of both primary and secondary work, resulting in duplication at one point, and at another truncation of episode.

The two primary plays were probably early, and the central problem is to find the date and first author of Antony's oration. As late as 1599 Shakespeare would not have written monotonous end-stopped verse, nor twice repeated Antony's intolerable metaphor of the 'dumb mouths'. Marlowe was the only pre-Shakespearian with the force to write the oration, but the style is not peculiarly his. There was a play on Caesar about 1588, and the problem is whether Marlowe's hand was in a play where Antony's oration was a main feature, and a sequel which included the scolding scene of Act V. The following are signs of Marlowe: *Gliding* ghosts only appears in *J.C.*, and in *Edward III* and the *Jew of Malta*. Cassius's speech on the omens has a pre-Shakespearian quality: compare, 'A flight of ugly ravens' (*Edward III*). The same idea is in *Henry V* (IV. ii. 51), and on that view Shakespeare uses twice in one year an archaic figment, in archaic style, from an old play of the Marlowe school. Instead of such a lapse it is easier to assume that the device belongs to the old school, and all three plays were produced in the days of Shakespeare's nonage. Antony's address to the corpse of Caesar is in the style of Henry V before Harfleur, and may also be compared with *1 Henry VI* (iv. ii. 11). Shakespeare would not have written in 1599 speeches in Marlowe's manner of 1589, in the same early verse manner and dealing in the same order of ideas. The line-ended verse of the oration is Marlovian, and long before 1599 Shakespeare had evolved a different manner. *Am-bi-ti-ous* is never in Shakespeare, often in Marlowe. In the *Jew of Malta* there are two iterative lines ending in *policy*, and three in *authority*—the kind of rhetorical effect as in the oration. The verse quality and diction of the oration are un-Shakespearian, but it has distinctive dramatic originality. It is the product of an imagination which excelled not in subtlety or truth of portraiture but in vigorous and original grasp of simple situations. If Marlowe wrote the Roses scene (*Henry VI*), he could have written the oration. The Roses scene contains a high percentage of double endings, characteristic of Marlowe, and far beyond Shakespeare before his first period. It stands out in vigour of declamation rather than psychological depth, and its author could have achieved the effect of Antony's speech. The verse of both is fundamentally like many of the speeches in *Edward II* (e.g. those of young Spencer, ii. i. 31, iii. ii. 10).

Much of the play is post-Marlovian, but it was Marlowe's fate, as a playwright, to miss to a large extent permanent appeal as against his later competitors. But his ideas survived, and here there is a Marlowe basis. He originated the play, and it was subsequently revised by other hands. The 'thrasonical' conception of Caesar has been traced to Muret, Grévin, and Garnier. It is improbable that Shakespeare knew any of these plays, but Marlowe must have known Muret's play. It is unlikely that he invented the speech of Cassius that disparages Caesar.

Granted that a double play existed in 1602, it is conceivable that it was condensed into a single one in 1607. It is impossible that Shakespeare himself abridged it, but it is just possible that Jonson did so. There are verbal reminders of Jonson, and also the stultification of Portia in ii. iv. The new attitude of Brutus to Caesar in the speech in which he describes the dead hero's sin as one of 'supporting robbers' tells of a process of revision in which Shakespeare did not largely share. The abridgement lowers Caesar's character and gives scope to the hostile case: and Jonson in *Sejanus* is strongly anti-Caesarean.

If the play proceeds upon a Marlowe play dealing only with Caesar and his assassination, there are reasons for believing that it had been recast by other hands, both before and after coming under Shakespeare's. There are clues to Drayton and Chapman. The latter wrote the *Tragedy of Caesar and Pompey* and he was pro-Pompeian. The action at the outset is in the key and spirit of Chapman's play. Verbal traces of Chapman are *replication, concave, retentive, thunderstone*. *Cautelous,* only here and in *Coriolanus,* is used by Chapman and also by Drayton. Chapman may at least have expanded the anti-Caesarian narration of Cassius in the second scene. In his *Caesar and Pompey* he embroidered history in a way that Shakespeare never did. The first presentment of Portia, the framing of a scene for its own sake, out of due proportion to the main action, is in Chapman's way, not Shakespeare's. The verse and diction of the scenes, though probably worked over by Shakespeare, are below the higher levels of his early middle period. In Chapman the lyric and didactic impulse often outstrips the business of the scene, e.g. Portia is introduced to proclaim an ideal role which she cannot sustain. In II. i. 187 we get a split infinitive—'Is to himself take thought and die for Caesar'—a specialty of Chapman who uses it nine times and is the first notable writer to do so.

The first three acts show signs of a general revision by Shakespeare, to which the verse owes some firmness and freedom. Marlowe probably originated the play before 1590, and he was then associated with Kyd, who was acquainted with the Cornélie of Garnier. The latter preserved the tradition of the boastful and self-worshipping Caesar. The play *Caesar's Fall* (1602) has disappeared, and the old sequel play *Caesar's Revenge* was perhaps revised by Shakespeare. Probably Ben Jonson compressed the two plays into one at a later date. In the case of *Hamlet* Shakespeare entirely transmuted his material, but here the theme was intractable. To uphold Caesar would antagonize the literary tradition, to applaud the conspirators might offend the Government.[1] There is no doubt of Shakespeare's hand in Caesar's speeches—the stately diction and massive cadence of the speeches in which Caesar half-deifies himself—and we surmise that in the original first part of the play he presented Julius quite adequately. Unfortunately for commercial reasons much of his work was suppressed, but it was not he who set out to portray Caesar and failed.

The primitive psychology of *Richard III* should make one doubt Shakespeare's authorship—also the primitive end-stopped verse, and the high percentage of double endings. It contains some distinctly early Shakespearian matter; it exhibits the 'restrained' and freer styles of Marlowe; and it abounds in double-endings. Briefly, it is the style of the early historical plays. Marlowe predominates, and he opens with one of his usual soliloquies that present character. The verse is utterly un-Shakespearian, vigorous and *athletic,* but never winged. It is late Marlowe, and, with its scale of double-endings, impossible to Shakespeare before *Troilus.* Its *timbre* differs as does a brass instrument from a violin. We infer that Marlowe revised the old work for Shakespeare's Company in 1592, and then recast his former sketches of Gloster in *Richard III.* Shakespeare enters in III. vii—and throughout

[1] Cf. Miss Winstanley.

Act II, after scene i, and especially in scene iv, there are traces of Kyd. Clarence's dream is Marlowe's, because the verse is not Shakespeare's, and no one else could dispute it with Shakespeare. We find a parallel to 'Wedges of Gold' in the *Jew, Hero,* and *Tamburlaine.* Compare also Richard's opening soliloquy '. . . to quaver on a lute . . .' with *2 Tamburlaine* I. iii. Richard's confessions are not in Shakespeare's way of writing or psychologizing, but they are in Marlowe's. In the later part of the play there are traces of revision and expansion by Heywood on a Marlovian basis.

Is the dialogue between Richard and Elizabeth Marlowe's, or a reviser's, or a mixture? The duplication of episode is a constructive weakness that delays the real action, and it is wildly improbable. The scene is an interpolation, and has words specially used by Heywood. Surely no one will assign to Shakespeare the parade of ghosts with their sententious uninspired speeches. The whole scene, including Richard's terror-stricken speech on waking, is but a continuation of the primary presentment of the character in the old *True Tragedie of Richard III* adapted by Marlowe. The psychology—the crude vaunt of villainy and terror-stricken avowal of guilt—is that of Marlowe's unsubtle monster. The note of Richard is that of Machiavel in the prologue to the *Jew*, of Guise in the *Massacre*, of Barabas in general. The pseudo-Machiavellian attitude towards 'conscience' is flaunted in Greene's *Selimus.*

Marlowe predominates; Kyd enters markedly in certain scenes; Heywood did some later expanding. Shakespeare no doubt revised, but he contributed only some six or seven speeches. The play is full of swarming crudities and inferiorities of style, and inferior psychology, and is melodrama, not Shakespearian tragedy. The central figure and one or two others have the Marlovian strong outline and driving energy. The play is theatrically alive from end to end and is a prodigy of historical mystification. By sheer force of dramatic percussion on the national mind Marlowe has established for centuries a notion of a man and a period as essentially fabulous as the Song of Roland. His vigorous craftsmanship has hypnotized posterity and swayed historians. Richard is not a human being but a compound of Marlowe's Tamburlaine and Barabas and Guise; he is Marlowe's traditionary cast-iron scoundrel, with his incongruous collapses of despair. Shakespeare wisely did little to the play, because its drawing power depends on its magnificent crudity. Unlike *Hamlet*, it could only be transmuted by entire rewriting. Of Shakespeare it contains but a handful of speeches and interpolations. . . .

Mr. Robertson's criticism passes before our eyes like the revolutions of a wheel, the hub of which is his fine power of aesthetic appreciation. But the prevailing note of his remarks on *Henry V* is strong common sense. He is now confident of his method, and it preserves him like

an antiseptic in the laden atmosphere of other critics' praise. He looks
at the play and reports its obvious blemishes, and then proceeds to
draw upon his knowledge of contemporary and pre-Shakespearian plays.
He rightly points out that the King's true reason for invading France
was stated in *2 Henry IV*, and in this clear light of common sense much
of the conventional admiration for *Henry V* looks faded.

In his examination of *J.C.* he uses finer weapons. He dissects the
play, and, finding its total impression un-Shakespearian, subdivides
the particular impressions of certain scenes and characters, and uses
his knowledge of other dramatists to place them. Thence he builds
his conclusion, and makes it stable with historical research—the old
French plays that were known to Marlowe and Kyd. But although
the problem is hard to solve, and Mr. Robertson takes us by tortuous
ways, at times he can discard his learning and light up his subject by a
direct flash of common sense, e.g. his remarks on Portia, on the quarrel
scene, and on the oration with its monotonous and end-stopped verse.
His reasons for assigning the scene with Portia to Chapman remind us
that the final test is aesthetic, and that he never loses sight of this. As
we read we seem to hear cracks in the foundations of the temples of
praise which less independent-minded critics have reared, stone upon
stone. In Mr. Robertson's criticism of Caesar himself we find insight
and common sense well mingled, and we do not think anything better
has been written on the subject. No critic has found Caesar's character
satisfactorily presented, and all have striven to explain it. Certainly
the lines in *Hamlet* which tell of 'the mightiest Julius' are among the
most haunting in Shakespeare.

Richard III contains some excellent criticism on Marlowe, yet so
handled as to bring the glory of Shakespeare home to us. The contrast
between the music of their verse—the brass instrument and the violin
—is specially excellent; and also the tribute to Shakespeare's discretion
in doing little to the play.

III

A. CLUTTON-BROCK [1] is occupied with the problem of Hamlet's
delay in killing the King. He says that Mr. J. M. Robertson's attempt
is not concerned with the delay but with other matters, and is therefore
irrelevant. He also differs from Mr. T. S. Eliot, saying that it is
wrong to find motives as if the play were a history of real persons.
He maintains that Shakespeare's problem was to make Hamlet behave
as he would behave in those circumstances, and out of his behaviour
to make a play. In this he has succeeded, so the problem is not aesthetic
but intellectual, and arises because Hamlet is entirely convincing. As
he acts, we feel so he would act, and no play gives a stronger feeling of
certainty. The tragedy is that he does many things which trouble us,

[1] *Sh.'s 'Hamlet'*, 1922 (Methuen).

and which seem contrary to his real character, yet we never doubt
that he would do them. The business of drama is character and action,
not psychology, which is science and not art. The notions that works
of art are to be understood only through their history, and that they
should answer questions which belong to science, obstruct the experience
of art. During the experience we hardly notice the delay but are
absorbed by Hamlet.

   The characters of a play have no existence except in their parts;
but in a play there is more than the words. To explain the delay we
must rediscover that part of Shakespeare's aesthetic purpose which has
been lost with the original business of the play. Our aim should be to
discover how Hamlet's words should be supplemented with action, and
in what mood he should speak them. When dying he insists that he
has wrongly expressed himself. What is the compulsion that has forced
him to do so in action and words? The causes of compulsion are in
the text; up to the ghost interview he is quite normal. Then appears
the first sign of mental disorder—the obstacle within himself that
prevents him from telling the others, and the actor should stress this
violent nervous shock, as of much future importance. He had consciously resolved to obey his father, but the shock had made a wound in
his mind, and the pain was so sharp that unconsciously he flinched
from it, and seized every pretext to forget it. The 'law of reversed
action' worked within him, and the more he tried to force himself to
act, the more he unconsciously invented pretexts why he should delay to
act. The essence of the tragedy is that Hamlet's irrelevance, the result
of nervous shock, causes many deaths instead of one, and causes Hamlet
to express himself wrongly. We except the soliloquies which keep the
real Hamlet before us, as contrasted with the wrongly expressed. Remove
the soliloquies and you will see that the inner Hamlet is as much a
part of the drama as the outer. He can put his conscious self before
himself with Shakespeare's own power, but the fact that he cannot
put his unconscious self before himself is the tragedy. The contrast
between the will and its disordered machinery makes the interest and
pity of the play. His behaviour to Ophelia is the result of the shock
of his mother's adultery. Men get an idea of woman from their
mothers and fall in love with women in whom they recognize the same
idea. They are truly in love with an incarnation of the divine and
universal woman. The scene with Ophelia is unintelligible if the
actor does not show that Hamlet is wrongly expressing himself under a
compulsion he does not understand. Out of extreme hatred he spares
the King at prayer. He wishes to enjoy the pleasure of killing him,
and must be in a rage to do it. It is more natural to him to speak to
his mother against the King than to kill him. To prefer words to acts
of violence is a mark of civilization, not weak will. He cannot satisfy
his hatred with any act of revenge, because what he hates is less the

King than a certain beastliness in life which the King represents. Action cannot satisfy a mind shocked by life itself. The play is bitter tragedy, but not gloomy because of the brilliance and diversity of Hamlet's mind.

Hamlet would not be worth understanding if it could only be understood in terms of an earlier play. One of the critic's main functions is to remove obstructions to experience of works of art. The play is a unity because a single character predominates—a particular, morbid state of that character. Contrary to Aristotle, Hamlet's misfortune comes from crimes in which he is not implicated, and through the nervous shock from hearing of those crimes. Perhaps a tragedy should not be made from undeserved sufferings: yet Shakespeare has done it. Art expresses values by communicating them through beauty. The artist need not make a statement of his values even to himself, but he must express them in some object which makes us value what he values. When we feel beauty the communication is made. Shakespeare in Hamlet seems to embody all that he himself most values in humanity. He is not preaching a sermon and saying, 'Here is my ideal man', but the fact that he values a certain kind of human being intensely causes him to express that value. Hamlet expresses values more completely through the presentment of a living man than any known play. It proves nothing about human nature; it *is* human nature. Tragedy justifies itself by revealing more than comedy, e.g. we most value Mercutio when he jests dying. Hamlet throughout is like a man who jests dying; his courteous welcome to the players is more moving in a doomed man than in a comedy.

That Shakespeare so fully expressed his values in *Hamlet* proves that, if he used the old play, he was not tied to his material. Before *Hamlet* no one of Shakespeare's characters compelled the play to be what it is. Hamlet came to life as no previous character; in him is a peculiarity of values never before attempted—a certain way of feeling, thinking, and acting, unknown to the world but since valued by the world. Hamlet represents the extreme of experiencing power, and because he experiences everything so fully he is more hurt by calamity than a common hero. His tragedy is that his virtues prevent him from acting effectively; but his capacity for suffering is more to be valued than the common hero's effectiveness. He is like a larger intellectual conscience contemplating himself and all things: more like Julius Caesar and Disraeli than Cromwell, Napoleon, or Gladstone. It prophesies a higher state of being, and of this fusion of the aesthetic and intellectual with the practical, Christ is the greatest example in history, and Hamlet in literature. The very discord of the double consciousness reveals its underlying harmony. The tragedy is in the conflict between the permanent attitude and the practical task. Macbeth's crime evokes what he has of double consciousness, and causes

the discord of his nature; but Hamlet's is always thus. The play gives
the sense of values apart from consequences, and so fulfils the function
of all art. . . .

Clutton-Brock does well to remind us, as Mr. Robertson had
previously done, that the play leaves no divided impression on the
audience. It is equally true that mystical experience is the basis of all
religion; and yet both truths are frequently forgotten. Yet we must
guard against mere impressionism, and remember that all good Shake-
spearians have read *Hamlet* not once but a hundred times, and hope to
do so a hundred times more; and that deposits of historical knowledge
in the unconscious mind may react helpfully upon the conscious mind
with which we read. By a different path Clutton-Brock has reached
the same conclusion—that there are two Hamlets—but he explains it
on aesthetic grounds. The interest of his analysis, expressed in terms
of modern psychology, is that it reveals something of Shakespeare's
depth and universality: and we say this with a side-glance at Miss
Winstanley. The concluding portion of the essay is the best—the
impression of Hamlet absorbing the interest of the play and thence
concentrating in himself the interest of the human race; and finally
the comparisons with great historical persons tell us something. We
are inclined to think *Hamlet* is obscure because the soul of man is a
mystery, and Shakespeare by expressing in concrete art more of this
mystery than any other writer, has made darkness visible. We cannot
say that Clutton-Brock has altered our opinion of Hamlet, but he has
fixed certain lines strongly in our understanding, and so made us realize
something of the mystery.

IV

PROFESSOR R. DYBOSKI,[1] against the four periods of Dowden
and others, prefers to think of the total of Shakespeare's work not as
one wave but several waves rising and falling—alternations of success
and failure, effort and exhaustion. Such an interpretation has a solid
basis in the law of nature. He sees flickerings of future tragedy in
Aaron and Tamora, and of future refined comedy in the women's
speeches of the *Errors*. The *Shrew* followed for relief, and then came
the early historical work, of which the second part of *Henry VI* showed
a great advance on the first. *Verona* was another early victory in
comedy, and it contains all the elements of good Shakespearian comedy
side by side, though perhaps in a crude state.

If a decline now sets in it was partly because *3 Henry VI* deals with
intractable dramatic material, and also a temporary collapse was unavoidable preparation for *Richard III*. Shakespeare had now learned
that Marlowe's method of limiting artistic ambitions to a circumscribed
theme is a surer way to success than Peele's crowded stage of chronicle

[1] *Rise and Fall in Sh.'s Dramatic Art*, 1922 (Sh. Assoc. Paper—Milford).

histories. It becomes a favourite device with him to use conscious limitation to concentrate scattered strength. The play reveals his youthful drunkenness with the Renaissance ideal of Titanic delight in unbounded power over man. *L.L.L.* radiates a triumphant sense of attained security, and is a fitting sequel to the solid achievement of *Richard III.*

A relapse followed to unproductiveness and uncertainty of touch, perhaps caused by the closing of the theatres during the plague. Shakespeare turned to epic and lyric forms; and transition from the sensuous buoyancy of *Venus* to the tedium of description and reflection in *Lucrece,* again proves the necessity of decline after a rise. So in the Sonnets we see the breadth of inspiration coming and going: gems of imagination and feeling dwell side by side with unbearable conceits. We next see Shakespeare at his lowest depth of workmanship. *John* shows that he had lost experience in grouping figures and arranging events. If Falconbridge is a prelude to the patriotism of *Henry V* he is an inarticulate one, and the Arthur scenes, though pathetic, are episodical. From this nadir he soars up to *M.N.D.*—the highest height of his poetic prime. *R. and J.* equally glorifies 'the kingly state of youth', and returns to the device of limitation of theme, compared with the rich, manifold, and frail texture of *M.N.D.*—a concentration which stamps it with more conscious effort and less divine spontaneity.

It is hard to trace the alternation of rise and fall in the next period. If *Richard II* shows decline it is in lapses into affected diction in monotonous elegiacs; while in the *Merchant* Shylock outgrows his proper place and function, though he does become the grandest type of Jew in modern literature. It is the same with Falstaff, since Part II, which largely repeats the whole frame of Part I, was written for him. With *Henry V* Shakespeare ascends—again using limitations of aims as a narrow path to victory over exhaustion. With *Twelfth-Night* we are basking in the noonday sun of Shakespeare's comic art. The likeness of Sir Toby to Falstaff and Sir Andrew to Slender show how excellent a thing happy repetition may sometimes be. The curious ambiguity of Jaques (*A.Y.L.*) spells exhaustion, and also decline of artistic resolution. Great repetition is found in *M. Ado,* and also the conventional stage villain; and so we sink to *All's Well,* where Parolles gives the last and faintest echo of Falstaff's wit.

We can only conjecture the reasons for the decline of Shakespeare's comedy and stupendous rush towards tragic excellence in the midst of his comic period. *J.C.*, though disjointed, gives a profusion of eternal truths on the weakness of heroes and fickleness of crowds, on the tragic illusion of democratic leadership, and the sacredness and vanity of revolution. Enough of this survives to tinge the dynastic drama of *Hamlet* with large-eyed criticism of rottenness in States. This social interest gives universality of bearing to Macbeth's personal ambitions, and makes loyalty to Venice the one permanent thing in Othello. It shows the abuse of official power in *M. for M.*, and deposits crystals of ripe statesman's wisdom in *T. and C.* Finally it yields in grapple with the innermost moral meaning of this human world in *Lear*. But *J.C.* remains the supreme effort of his social thought. With *Hamlet* preoccupation with the human interest began to weaken artistic control and objective grasp. *M. for M.* has sayings on life and death as profound as *Hamlet*, but strangely unequal. In *T. and C.* the wreckage of majesty, and floating fungus of poisonous growths, jostle each other on a sea of dejection. There is loss of artistic balance, and temporary disability of the artist to see sexual relations in the light of beauty. This strain exists more thinly in Iago, and appears in Lear as a disease of the mind. Aware of his gradual loss of self-control, Shakespeare once more applied the remedy of confinement to a subject of narrow range; and he produced in *Othello* one of the most clear-cut jewels of his art. From *Othello* to *Macbeth* we seem to see a rise in artistic ambition. Othello and Desdemona are conceived in a vein of noble but almost child-like simplicity, and in an oppressively fatalistic manner; but the character-drawing of Macbeth and his lady is more complex, and accompanied by more daring meditation on the fundamental problem of free will. *Macbeth* is Shakespeare's most effective *dramatic* work, but *Lear* surpasses in grandeur, as the solar system surpasses the earth. It is Shakespeare's mightiest effort towards metaphysical synthesis in poetry.

Timon was a failure, and after *Lear* no broader outlook on life and more sublime abstraction was possible. Again he returned to his favourite device of seeking renewed vigour by limiting his subject to one great concern. *A. and C.* concentrates the full light of all a manhood's experience of great men and great women and a great epoch, on a vision of love between two lordly human beings, filling a stormy age of history with its splendour. But *Coriolanus*, where the towering isolation of the hero is over-stressed, shows that conscious limitation is a two-edged weapon. Yet it marks a distinct reawakening of the social interest. Its moral is the necessary homage of a superior man to the great fact of Society, and it is Shakespeare's own supreme moral triumph over the pride of genius.

The dramatic romances are the manner of his declining years, where dramatic consistency is sacrificed to romantic incident. The *Tempest*, cosmic in its greatness, was the crowning summit of dramatic romance. In supreme earthly melody we hear suggestions of harmonies not fully conceivable by mortal ears. No further step was possible, and he returned to history—to the whole gorgeous pageant of England, with its long array of grand figures. The working out of his artistic vocation was his principal business in the world. . . .

We have included this essay because its point of view—the alternation of rise and fall—is at least original; but we have also included it as a warning—that such criticism is no longer possible, though it would have been welcome in the age of Dowden. Professor Dyboski's 'links' between the plays are rather more inward than Furnivall's, but they are equally over-subjective. He is aware that the plays contain much non-Shakespearian matter, yet he seeks to apply a system to the whole of Shakespeare. The marks of strain specially appear in the 'social interest' which he discovers in *J.C.* and endeavours to track through the tragedies that follow. But disagreeing with his criticism as a whole, we will admit some good incidental remarks—notably the strength gained by limitation of interest. When he applies this test and compares *M.N.D.* and *R. and J.*, we learn something more of each play. He also discovers that the second part of *Henry IV* repeats the incidents of the first, including the 'grand scene' between father and son in the middle of the play—that the revolt is an aftermath—and the repetition extends even to the music. Nor should we forget to commend his remarks on *T. and C.*

<h1 style="text-align:center">V</h1>

AT this point we have few generalities to chronicle, so we will start with Mr. Robertson's tribute to Shakespeare's 'all-shadowing fame', and set beside it Miss Winstanley's remark that he was a popular dramatist of intense appeal, and also her tribute to the terror and beauty and splendour of his work. Her opinion on his greatest figures, that there was something exceptional and almost superhuman in them, that they were not ordinary or even extraordinary *individuals*, should be compared with Professor Bradley's. To her Shakespeare was of all men most interested in human nature, and she allows his patriotism.

In artistic matters we have first Professor Dyboski's saying that Shakespeare was not distinguished by inventiveness. Mr. Robertson calls him the mightiest of dramatists but no faultless artist; and says that his artistic method was primarily presentative of persons, characters, and actions; and that he transfigured whatever he laid creative hands upon. He also speaks of the lithe grace of the Master's movement in verse. . . .

These general remarks justify the conclusion that the ablest critics advance the cause of Shakespeare by examining his material more and more definitely and showing how far he transcended it.

Chapter XXXIX

ENGLAND 1922–1923

I. ALDEN.   II. MIDDLETON MURRY.   III. J. M. ROBERTSON.   IV. WELLS.
V. BAILEY.   VI. NOBLE.   VII. COWL.   VIII. STOLL.   IX. CONCLUSION.

I

THE object of Mr. Raymond Macdonald Alden [1] is to distinguish in Shakespeare's work those elements of an age from those of all time. He pays a tribute to the Grammar Schools in which Shakespeare was educated, where obtained the Renaissance system of cultivating the imagination. He also notes that England had both Renaissance and Reformation—unlike Italy and Germany which had one without the other. Both Spenser and Shakespeare attempted to fuse beauty with moral seriousness. After touching on the religion, politics, sport, manners, and customs of the Elizabethan age, he decides that the most characteristic contribution of the Elizabethans to literature and the drama was not technique or a system of thought, but poetry—poetry added to the ever-present human love of story.

In Mr. Alden's opinion only *Henry VI*, *Titus*, *Shrew*, *T. and C.*, *Timon*, *Pericles*, *Cymbeline*, *Henry VIII* are not Shakespeare's independent work; and he considers Shakespeare's development as an artist remarkably regular and normal, but not necessarily related to external conditions.

Shakespeare's poems show him entirely a child of the Renaissance, and they are in the manner of Ovid. The emotion of *Venus* satisfies the taste for sentiment, but is not poignant. What most interests him in *Lucrece* is the theme of remorse and revenge as lust's followers. The soul of Lucrece is undefiled, yet she is profoundly troubled by the ruin of the body. Both poems are more Elizabethan than Shakespearian. They show him beginning to practise the art, which he afterwards perfected, of remaking familiar materials by passing them through his visual and spiritual imagination. But the chief characteristic is the sense of the magic power of words—the newly discovered art of phrasing which fascinated the Elizabethans. Sonnets were the fashion, and there is no reason to suppose Shakespeare's were written at one time or addressed to one person. He adapted the 'English' sonnet form from Surrey and Daniel. This expresses movement—thought and feeling in evolution rather than recollected in tranquillity. Some deal with the typical Renaissance themes of beauty and love. The word 'love', among Elizabethans, was as naturally used between men as between man and woman. But Shakespeare has so saturated the conventional sonnet-imagery with lyric beauty and feeling that he creates reality, e.g. the

[1] *Sh.*, 1922 (Allen & Unwin).

idea of Sonnet 31 that a great love gathers into itself all previous
affections in the lover's experience. The deepest, where we hear
Shakespeare's authentic lyric voice, are Sonnets 29, 30, 116, 123, 124,
which represent love and friendship as an inner experience triumphant
over circumstance.

When Shakespeare started, chronicle history was the most popular
type; it was less dramatic and more epic than other types, and its object
was to teach. Its structure was crude because based on succession of
events rather than causal relations, and its characters were crude
because they were types, and either good or bad. Marlowe first saw
the chance of making Edward II's fall due to his character. In
Henry VI Shakespeare took the characters much as he found them,
but to the King he added something of a new richness and reflective
dignity. In *Richard III* he converted chronicle history to tragedy by
compressing historical events.[1] He retained some of the conventions—
such as the hero's self-admitted, deliberate villainy, but he added
Richard's mind—agile, intense, and almost beautiful in malignant
perfection, so that it appeals to the aesthetic sense. Richard II is realized
like the future great Shakespearian characters, and the enormous
advance in art strikes by contrast with older conventional elements that
appear side by side—e.g. formal and typical characters such as the
Queen. Shakespeare's power of writing verse that is both poetry and
speech at once also conflicts with the traditional style. The old-
fashioned style finally prevails, where the King dies like a traditional
hero in a stage catastrophe. By altering Hotspur's age in *Henry IV*,
Shakespeare connected the two elements in a splendidly constructed
dramatic whole. For clownish interludes he substituted a richly
comic yet realistic group of persons and interwove them closely with
the serious scenes. The Prince and Hotspur are intensely interesting,
but built up on a few simple concepts, not subtly wrought. Falstaff
enters the story by the aforesaid half-legitimate process, and becomes
one of Shakespeare's few greatest creations. Part II is inferior, and
the cause of the puzzle of the coronation scene may be that Falstaff is
too attractive. In these two plays the conventional elements of the
chronicle drama are reduced to a minimum, and most characters are
realized independently of traditional types. *Henry V* reverts to older
methods and is pageantry more than drama. The King's words and
deeds are a great achievement, but not his character. Perhaps the
character was too fully ready-made, or perhaps Shakespeare's interest
was greater in those who fail. He does not realize the personality
as a vital whole, and one is forced to believe that Henry acted as he did
because the tradition of his change of conduct was so popularly
interesting. He had every claim to greatness and displayed it with
brilliant formal success, yet failed of it as a spiritual creation.

[1] Cf. Dyboski.

No clearly defined type of comedy was ready for Shakespeare. Several types existed, and the Elizabethans, who liked multiple plotting, frequently mingled them. That which lastingly attracted Shakespeare was the kind which united thoughtful characterization with romantic sympathy. The deeper irony of *L.L.L.* is the theme of aspirations and professions incompatible with the facts of life. Biron incarnates experience of the folly and satiric perception of it, and this doubling up of comic significance in a single person was characteristic of Shakespeare. Except Biron the characters are conventional, with little realism or individuality, and there is little throughout the play that depends on character other than the typical sort. The *Errors* is Shakespeare's only work to depend wholly on interest of plot. *Verona* really begins Shakespearian comedy, because love is entwined with adventure. Shakespeare followed Greene, who learnt from the Italians, and revealed the possibilities of romantic comedy—the vital union of narrative technique with poetic seriousness. No character of *Verona* interests us for himself, apart from his adventures. *M.N.D.* is a wondrous hodge-podge, that satisfied and glorified the vaudeville spirit of English drama. It was a notable achievement in technique to unite such materials, and the complication was unparalleled in comic art. *Errors* and *Verona* showed Shakespeare's tendency to individualize the minor characters above the major; and here Theseus and Hippolyta and the four lovers are faint, while the fairies and clowns are vivid and lifelike.

The *Merchant* confers perfect dramatic utterance upon all the characters. The pound of flesh and the caskets are linked by the theme of manly friendship, most dear to Shakespeare. We get a tissue of incredible absurdities—we see Bassanio change from fortune-hunter to true lover, and also reflective moralist—while Antonio becomes suddenly helpless after a vigorous practical career. But Shakespeare's technique was now such that he disguises an irrational plot by skilful evolution. The natural style and vivid characters persuade us that the characters logically produce the action. Some parts of the characters belong to familiar types, but as the play proceeds they grow upon us as newly created persons. Modern ethical sense exceeds historical, so Shylock is misinterpreted. Shakespeare was concerned with the utter and irreconcilable animosity of Jew and Christian, and he placed the facts before his audience. He was not analysing racial or religious prejudice, but probably he could not now draw a character without making it vital enough to awaken sympathy. The two seemingly-independent plots of *M. Ado* are cleverly linked. The Hero plot is conventional, the Benedict-Beatrice plot unconventional, with much of realism and satire to set off the romantic spirit. We have pure romance and high character comedy side by side. The threatened tragedy does not disturb us, because its figures are slightly characterized, and the mere action keeps us in the not too thoughtful region of romance which promises ultimate happiness. Claudio is barely a character, and Don John is an effective stage figure. The vivid characterization of Benedict and Beatrice marks the height of Shakespeare's comic period. The concealment scene is much more than farce, because three-fourths of the fun is due to our knowledge of Benedict's character, not to situation. He is transformed and does not merely find he is in love—and it is made possible and significant as comedy by the personality of Beatrice. Rosalind (*A.Y.L.*) combines the moods of comedy and romance in a single person and plot. Shakespeare was little interested in the more formal side of pastoralism, but he extracts from it the realistic charm of outdoor atmosphere. As in Portia, romance and comedy meet in Rosalind: she can be in love and make fun of being in love at the same moment.[1] *Twelfth-Night* is one great résumé of the matter of romantic comedy. Only Sebastian is known not for himself but for what he appears and does for the sake of the plot. Beyond this, nearly all done in the earlier comedies is done here a little better. If the Malvolio story, like those of Hero and Shylock, is too serious, the cause is divided between Time which has increased humane sensitiveness, and the modern actor who over-emphasizes Malvolio.

The Elizabethans loved vivid sensation and eloquent verse, and were interested in personality. The Renaissance discovered that the evil in human nature is a fascinating feature of mankind. In tragedy as in comedy there is the fundamental distinction between outer action and action which takes its meaning from within. Tragic drama begins with crude interest in catastrophe and rises to that which is spiritual. The tragic quality of *Titus* remains on the low level of sensational interest in the crash and fury of the action, yet there is some pity for the wretched father. The madness of Titus is comic at times, for here the Elizabethans were more realistic than ourselves. Shakespeare took the story of *R. and J.* as he found it, but elevated and purified the emotional values. He did not remake the story by creating personalities: all save Mercutio are less individuals than types. If the tragedy of Romeo and Juliet arises from their personalities, it is only in the sense that it depends on those universal characteristics of love in youth—passionate loyalty and headlong rashness. The tragedy is not of character but fate. Love is triumphant, and our suffering is mitigated by the comparatively low degree of individual characterization. We mourn not too poignantly for youth and beauty seen as lovely types. It is not thus with the death of Desdemona or Cordelia, or with the real friend who died yesterday. Just so far as we conceive Romeo and Juliet to be typical rather than personal, the beauty of their end is greater than its pain. The chief source of *J.C.* was

[1] Cf. Clutton-Brock on Hamlet's character.

Plutarch, and in dramatizing Plutarch Shakespeare had to determine
the series of actions which should bring out the elements of personality
most effectively. He diminished Caesar and ennobled Brutus, yet his
attitude is impartial, because he perceived the irony of the conspiracy
and the triumvirate. Caesarism and idealism fall because both are
centred in personalities that have lost their grasp on facts.

Hamlet intensifies this tenfold. We feel the delay is due to Hamlet's
mind and heart, yet Shakespeare has not linked the inner source of the
action with the outer details, as in other plays. The soliloquies which
reveal to us the hero's soul are not closely connected with the dramatic
action. Acts IV and V are a fairly normal intrigue. *Othello* is not
concerned with racial problems. Shakespeare used his sources just far
enough not to suggest anything beyond the personal experience. He
produced three dramatic creations unsurpassed in vitality and tragic
power by anything in the world's literature. Character is more than
technique, for only Othello and Desdemona, of all persons on the earth,
could undergo precisely this experience. Iago is the mystery, and
Shakespeare was now deeply interested in the place of evil in human
nature. We would give much to know why he transformed the happy
ending of the original story of *Lear* to a tragic catastrophe. He does
not attempt to attach the play closely to common life or to make it
plausible. To the conventions of Elizabethan tragedy he owed the
strange, terrifying means to dramatic power of the heath scene—
Lear's madness, the Fool's partial madness, Edgar's pretended madness, amid night and tempest. *Macbeth* with Shakespeare became a
personal tragedy, not a chronicle drama, though there are one or two
survivals of the latter, such as the long dialogue of Macduff and
Malcolm. In Richard III, and in Goneril, Regan, Edmund, Iago,
Shakespeare represented evil objectively and unsympathetically, but
here we are strangely identified with Macbeth and cannot view him as
a monster. His struggle makes for sympathy hitherto hardly known in
the tragedy of villainy. The Elizabethans believed in powers of evil,
and the play suggests the horror of that region of darkness with
which humanity may interact. It satisfies the sympathies and moral
judgement, and presents both the mystery of destiny and responsibility
of the individual will.

A. and C. is chronicle history and personal tragedy. Shakespeare
was interested in men who failed, and opposed to them the successful
whom we love less. Antony's tragedy was not chiefly political, but
that of a destructive passion. Shakespeare's supreme achievement was
to present Cleopatra's beauty and charm in action and dialogue. At
the end she becomes a tragic heroine of towering nobility, though she
has never done a fine deed in her life. *Coriolanus* rather returns to the
ironic sternness of Plutarch and *J.C.*, yet there is an inner personal
tragedy: the hero's nature is at odds with itself. At times Shakespeare

worsens his hero, according to Plutarch, and treats the Roman
populace with a severity for which there was no warrant in his source.
Thus no one is to blame, but the tragic fall is due to coalition between
the evil forces in personality and environment. A great soul out of
place destroys itself the more surely the more fully it expresses its own
nature.

The tragi-comedies were unromantic, intensely true, and acutely
critical, socially, but they did not interest the Elizabethans. The whole
effect of *T. and C.* is dramatically futile, but the mood is more baffling
than the abortive plotting. The plots are interpreted so as to alienate
the sympathies, and the effect is of a moral and emotional hodge-
podge. As to irreverent treatment of Homeric tradition, Shakespeare
only carries on traditions which the Troy story had accumulated in
preceding generations. It is not a drama but a series of scenes, whose
relation to one another is unexplained. Shakespeare changed the moral
quality of *M. for M.*, but either the material or his attitude impaired
his powers of characterization. The Duke's speech on death is a rare
survival of the undramatic interlude or monologue. *All's Well* is an
experiment on our sympathies, and Shakespeare solved the problem by
creating a heroine of precisely the character to make such conduct
plausible, dignified, and consistent with true womanliness. Parolles
is a familiar Elizabethan type who ministers to the conviction that
the world is made up chiefly of rascals. Ben Jonson's comedy is based
on this, but the mood clashes with Shakespeare's romantic plots. The
result is decline in dramatic characterization, for plots that do not
logically depend on the motives involved in them do not demand the
same vital realization of personality. The brothel scenes of *Pericles*
were a decadently popular feature of the Elizabethans of London, and
Shakespeare caters for their low tastes. In Marina he presents a purity
that cannot be smirched, and thus gives another example of the indispensable connexion of characterization with truly dramatic structure.

The characters of *Cymbeline* are slightly individualized, but they
act and react with reality. The *W. Tale*, more than *Cymbeline*, makes
the elements of human character and motive essential to the action.
Paulina is more individualized than any other serious person in the
romances. The *Tempest* gives a life-story concentrated into a single
day, and combines the riches and variety of the new romantic drama
with the technique of the classical school. The fairies of *M.N.D.*
were conventional, but Ariel and the others are new creations. They
are not toys of the fancy, but significant of deeper experiences. This
gravely mature use of the supernatural hints at a new experiment in
which Shakespeare touches the mystery of human fortune with a
vague symbolism, half personifying the forces of good and evil which
wait upon men's motives, and the ultimate order or cosmos which
brings peace and unity out of their strife. The play's peculiar conditions

justify the romantic practice—otherwise decadent—of putting action above character. When Prospero and his wand control events, they cannot arise chiefly from the personalities of those concerned. If we knew the ways of fate drama would disappear; and it is in such a position that this play puts us, and it is therefore above ordinary dramatic art. Shakespeare's later work was partly determined by theatrical fashion and the influence of Beaumont and Fletcher; but the spirit of tragi-comedy was increasingly congenial to him. Having sounded the depths of human evil, he must either relapse into sombre silence or become conscious of the forces of reconciliation. The latter did not promote dramatic effectiveness, because drama is conflict. Yet it is not weakness, but implies insight into the region where tragedy disappears because the whole course of the passions is run, and the human spirit comes into its inheritance.

In comedy Shakespeare sacrificed criticism to poetry and social anatomy to beauty, and therefore fell short of the real masters—Aristophanes, Cervantes, Molière. Yet he mingled harmoniously the comic and romantic, and only Ariosto and Scott have approached him. He accepted prevailing modes in tragedy, but transformed them by making them more intense. He was chiefly interested in character, and in him Renaissance individualism found its highest expression. Thus critics discuss his characters like persons who had lived before the play was written. Unlike Ben Jonson he was an inductive moralist, and Henry V is his only deductive character. His ideas are the outcome of dramatic thinking; his bad characters impress us as so ill-born that they could not but sin. But the tone and significance of his whole work is morally sound: evil is evil and good is good. Yet our impression remains a general one; he seems to admire courage, fidelity in friendship, serenity in hardship, readiness in action—and to incarnate these in the persons of his lovable men. Kindness with him is a cardinal virtue, and unkindness the unpardonable sin—and here he was beyond his age, for the Renaissance was humanistic, not humanitarian.

He had no obvious social or political theories. If he disliked the populace he also disliked an arrogant aristocrat. He was truly English in basing kingship not on divine order or force, but the corporate will of lords and commons, hedged in by obligations. He mostly accepts the Renaissance ideas of love. He presents marriage with purity and idealism, admitting a sensuous element which he makes the basis of something finer and more essential. This is typical of the whole process which civilization has worked out through slow centuries of toil of sense and spirit. He believes that love is permanent—that no lover by himself can destroy the product of the two. Forgiveness is a corollary from this.

It is doubtful if he had a system of thought. He gives the normal thinking of the time close to its highest level, and emphasizes things that rise from an interest in individuals rather than classes or theories. The question is of the total impression from the plays, above all, the tragedies. The latter emphasize more defect of will than trait of blood or destiny. He considers evil abnormal, and the universe to be on the side of good.[1] In the great tragedies goodness is defeated, yet they would lose their meaning were goodness not the norm from which the whole measure of life is taken.

Religion is a hazardous subject, and Shakespeare was true to the Renaissance in eliminating religious motives and ideas from most of his plays. Yet there is the great sonnet on the soul; and Hamlet—closest to himself—is the most religious of his creations. As regards his personality, he watched all dispassionately, yet must have lived within himself the life of the passions. It is the essence of dramatic composition to combine the external and internal points of view. His works are more lastingly vital than any other in human speech outside the Holy Scriptures, because he dealt in the common stuff of the passions—and passions remain unchanged. He had the art of trans-figuring the natural: his is the truth of absolute poetic humanism. . . .

Mr. Alden's point of view is clear: to discriminate Shakespeare's own contribution from the representative elements in his works. The salient merit of his book is that it is comprehensive, and does not, like much point-of-view criticism, isolate certain facts in order to prove a theory. He states clearly the facts as known to him—the conditions under which Shakespeare wrote, the needs of his public, how far his genius was thereby limited, to what extent it transcended these condi-tions; and it is on the latter subject that we get his best criticism. He yields to no one in admiring Shakespeare, but he is not dazzled like the romantics, and the result is much wise discrimination. We follow him with interest and approval through the poems and sonnets and histories, but when we come to the comedies our interest deepens. The faults which he finds with the plot of the *Merchant* heighten the effect of his subsequent praise, and bring home to us Shakespeare's unique power. His faculty to retain clear separate impressions and then mingle them in such a way that one impression subdues the rest likewise appears with *M. Ado*—as later on it does with the character of Cleopatra. But the bridge between his method of judging comedy and tragedy is *R. and J.*. It is noteworthy that by another road he reaches the same obstacle in *Hamlet* as the 'disintegrators' of Shakespeare. His explana-tion of Iago is one of the most satisfactory. The men and women of the Renaissance were interested in evil, and as madness appeared comic, so we can imagine that evil gained a strange kind of beauty: and this fascination became sympathy when transferred to Macbeth. We pass over the tragi-comedies with the remark that their lack of

[1] Cf. Bradley.

romance—bearing in mind the fullness of romance in the earlier
comedies—is a light that might not fail (we speak with all diffidence)
into the nature of Shakespeare. He rightly says that the best way to
judge Shakespeare is according to the total impression of a play, and he
follows Professor Bradley's great argument that evil is alien to the
Shakespearian world; yet we rather think that he has over-stressed the
wisdom of the final romances, at the expense of the tragedies, though
he does give an excellent reason for their decline in dramatic power.
The shortcoming of such a book, on the whole, is that critical observation predominates over critical experience.

II

PERHAPS no critic has approached Shakespeare in a more reverent
and awe-struck mood than Mr. J. Middleton Murry.[1] He seeks to
apprehend the deeper rhythm of a poet's work, the rise and fall of the
great moods which determined what he was. Such an apprehension
is most mysterious when most direct. A mysterious change takes
place in the nature of thought, that it may make a closer contact with
the nature of reality. It is a simple and strange relation like love, and
our knowledge of a work of literature, when most perfect, is a simple
apprehension. Criticism is a personal affair, the confession of a soul's
adventures among masterpieces.

Poetry longs for the things that are not—for permanence, security,
eternity. Shakespeare submits the shadow of things to the desires of
the mind more than Shelley, and is more objective and substantial.
In the 'Phoenix', which is nearest Shelley, he is secure and serene. It is
mysterious but crystal-clear and attains what Shelley longed for. The
most astonishing description of the highest attainable by human love,
it is above the plane of intellectual apprehension.

This is the harmony of which echoes accompany his heroes'
destinies. Macbeth's 'To-morrow . . .' voices the despair of mortality,
not of crime.[2] The world's noblest spirit might have uttered these lines
more truly, and they overcharge the play. They belong to Shakespeare,
not Macbeth, as do Prospero's lines in the *Tempest* on the unsubstan-
tiality of the world.

Shakespeare's reaction to death is peculiar to himself and beyond
his conscious control. He longs for finality in death, and passes from
doubt to assurance of finality. That death is triumph over life is
a sentiment that surges up through the smallest chink of opportunity,
and therefore has a personal rather than dramatic reason. We should
expect passages that express life's insignificance to be sombre and sad—
yet they are mysteriously beautiful. Macbeth rejects this life because
he knows of something better and truer. Shakespeare has a secret

[1] *The Nature of Poetry*, 1922; *Coriolanus*, 1922; *Falstaff*, 1923 (*Discoveries.*
W. Collins, Sons & Co., Ltd., 1924).   [2] Cf. Figgis.

knowledge, and memory of an experience compared to which that
of life is trivial. After the symbolic vision of perfect and celestial love
he was bewildered in the world. There is less 'serenity' in his last
plays than acceptance of his own rejection of life. His tragedies are
terrible and moving because they attempt to express his knowledge
in terms of this world. The human soul is overstrung, and madness
and hallucination count for much. They contain the double tragedy
—of the characters, and Shakespeare himself who invented them in
vain for his intentions.

After Shakespeare's early period we must trace not so much the
attitude of rejection as the varying emotion with which it is held.
Bewilderment predominates in *Hamlet*; the crimes of this world tear
to pieces a soul whose affinity is with the other. The emotion of
Macbeth is blank and deadly despair. The despair lightens in *Lear*,
where Shakespeare, through Cordelia, miraculously sounds a purely
superhuman note, and assures us of that which can be only by virtue of
the forces which seem to deny it. Lear and Cordelia are exalted to
the 'Phoenix' state. Loyalty became Shakespeare's earthly symbol of
his highest experience, and marks off *Lear* and *A. and C.* as the pinnacle of his *expression* in literature. *A. and C.* is Shakespeare's triumph
as the artist, because waste after waste is redeemed by loyalty—and
death, as nowhere else, is presented as longed-for sleep. As with the
death of Christ, the purest reality, beauty, love can only become
manifest on earth by disaster. And the effect of surpassing genius is
that the lips of the characters at last merely utter the cadence of their
deeds.

Shakespeare's intuition into reality was deepest, so his consciousness
also was deepest that reality cannot be fully manifested through 'the
imitation of emotions and actions'. The 'Phoenix' is absolute poetry—
immediate intuition into the hidden nature of things. Relative
poetry is born of the soul's adjustment to the knowledge and memory
of such an experience. To understand Shakespeare is to understand all
poetry. . . .

To lay critical hands on this beautiful essay would seem like desecra-
tion, and if we cannot quite agree with Mr. Murry's estimate of the
'Phoenix' or his conviction of Shakespeare's 'experience', we will hide
behind his own bulwark—that criticism is a personal affair, the confession of a soul's adventures among masterpieces. Great criticism is
a kind of partnership between author and critic; we do not think that
Myers could have written anything equal to his essay on Virgil had
he never read Virgil; but we do not think that Mr. Murry could have
been equally eloquent on another subject than Shakespeare—that it
is his own mind which contributes the largest portion: though this
is not to deny that his mind has been enriched by the study of Shakespeare. He has the flexible mind of both poet and critic, that can turn

easily from the critical east to the creative west. But we will add on the positive side that Mr. Murry is the first critic to convey to us the sense of a mysterious harmony between the words and deeds of Shakespeare's characters.

He finds the conduct of Coriolanus life-like rather than inevitable. He does not *deserve* to die, as a tragic hero should, and his death is rather an accident—physical more than spiritual consummation. Had there been an Iago-strain in Aufidius he might have made the death of Coriolanus inevitable, but he, too, acts in rage. Coriolanus knows nothing of himself, and is bewildered away from battle. He notices neither things nor people, and barely recognizes the wife he loves. He remembers only what he feels, and not till he sees his wife and mother is he convinced that it is shameful to threaten Rome. Shakespeare excels Plutarch in putting before us the living man whose thoughts and words were the servants only of his impulses. But Aufidius is the weak point of the play. Shakespeare at first drew him as a man of hate and conspiracy, then followed Plutarch and made him a chivalrous enemy. The two cannot be reconciled, and the poisoned plotter has to carry on the action of the play to its tragic end.[1] What Shakespeare does convey miraculously is that Coriolanus and Volumnia are one being—she the mind and purpose, he the body and strength. . . .

Mr. Murry explains excellently why all the emotion put forth in *Coriolanus* does not rise to true tragic level. We would except the scene where the mother pleads with her son to spare Rome—and here again Mr. Murry's late words solve the problem. The two natures are one, and the struggle is more internal than external. His discovery of the divided nature of Aufidius is an instance of ever-increasing modern critical sublety.

Writing on Falstaff, Mr. Murry contends that the more we know of where a great poet has taken *us*, the more we know where *he* himself has been. He lives by his power of reawakening deep experience in us. Something happened to Shakespeare to darken his world, and the greater a man is the more completely is an event merged in his inward relation to it. It is possible to know more of Shakespeare than of our dearest friends.

Falstaff was the greatest creation of Shakespeare's yet undivided being. He is greatest in *1 Henry IV*, among his equals. Hotspur was animated by a like fundamental irresponsibility. One carelessly pursued honour, the other sack. We feel they were necessary projections of the same moment in the same mood of the same genius. This radiant naturalness is only intermittent in Part II where Falstaff is as often mechanical as inspired. His wit with the Judge is thin, verbal, and boring. In the scenes where he is at his best he himself says little or nothing. He profits by the afterglow which persists from the first part

[1] Cf. Schücking on Cleopatra.

and appears at the mention of his name.   He is kept alive by transfusion of blood.   It wearied Shakespeare to go on creating Falstaff because he had in his mind an inexhaustible store of comic characters waiting to be born.   Part I had been a great popular success, and the town demanded more Falstaff: but Shakespeare, being a creative genius, could not repeat himself.   The Queen's command to show Falstaff in love was the last straw, and instead of keeping his promise for *Henry V*, Shakespeare's first mention of him is that he is dying.

Traditional Shakespeare criticism has spoken of Falstaff's moral decline and justified his rejection.   Part II is a comparatively poor play, with unrelated comic scenes, and we would naturally perceive Falstaff's dubious morality more clearly if here and in the *Wives* Shakespeare's creative power were weakening and he could no longer maintain his comic hero in the imaginative world.   His acts and sentiments are no whit less moral in the second than in the first part.   A truly comic character can only decline creatively, not morally.   When Shakespeare's creative light fails we recognize Falstaff as a rather disreputable adventurer.   He had to bring Falstaff back into the world of fact and history, and in such an enterprise the facts become adamant.   The Falstaff whom the King of England had to repudiate was not the Falstaff whom Shakespeare had created.   Shakespeare must pretend they are the same person and drag his hero down to earth and disgrace him. . . .

This essay, though less brilliant than the first, is more business-like and keeps closer to Shakespeare's mind.   In Mr. Murry's distinction between creative and moral decline we see the spirit of modern criticism at its best.   He notes that the facts are adamant, and here he is at one with Dowden's estimate of Shakespeare's difficulty in controlling history dramatically; and his last sentences might be compared with Professor Bradley's lecture on Falstaff.   We suggested that in the first essay Mr. Murry's own mind contributed the larger part: in the present this mood is chastened, but thereby the essay gains.   While keeping close to his experience of Shakespeare, Mr. Murry is equally self-revealing, and the result is that the great burden of tradition slips from our shoulders, and we feel ourselves for the moment alone with Mr. Murry and with Shakespeare, as though no other critic had ever penned a line.   It is this power to rethink his subject from the beginning that makes Mr. Murry one of the most delightful writers of criticism at the present day.   That the Falstaff of Part I appears a lesser knave because he is buoyed up on the sea of Shakespeare's creative imagination is a critical and psychological fact of the first importance.   When beauty fails the want of goodness stands out.

III

MR. J. M. ROBERTSON [1] is with us again, and his object is to establish ever more clearly Shakespeare's supremacy over his 'fellows'. He deals with *Verona*, and he finds an un-Shakespearian quality in the bulk of the versification. He suggests that it was largely the work of Greene, and that Peele supplied the comic relief. Shakespeare may have rewritten the opening scene-section, but the rest of the piece, while abounding in double-endings, is markedly primitive in respect of end-stopped lines. 'But say, Lucetta, now we are alone. . . .' Compare such woodenly uniform iambic verse with passages in *M.N.D.* and *L.L.L.* where we get trochaic openings and alternations, varying pausation, interfluence of lines, inweaving of spondee and anapaest and dactyl, elusion of caesura, elimination of 'feet'. The plays of Shakespeare dated before 1593 are but partial recasts. If they are dated later their mechanical end-stopped verse is incompatible with *M.N.D.* and *L.L.L.* Also, would Shakespeare hypnotically imitate Marlowe in *Richard II* and *Errors*, and Greene in *Verona*, yet insert in all three plays certain passages in his only early manner—that of *M.N.D.* and *L.L.L.*, and of *John* and *1 Henry IV*? On the authority of *Venus* we deny original work to Shakespeare before 1593; but we may fairly call *M.N.D.* and *L.L.L.* typical of his original dramatic manner. If he wrote such blank verse about 1594 or 1595, when did he pen the breathless tic-tac of *Verona*? To ascribe it to 1590 is to ignore his declaration about *Venus*, and to become hopelessly entangled in the double-endings problem. It varies from 18 per cent. of the latter to 20 and 25: after which, in 1595, he reverts to the low rates of *John* and *1 Henry IV*, and increases again in later plays. If the beginning of *L.L.L.* is Shakespeare's first writing, we have simple influence without imitation: but the traditionists hold that he copied Marlowe in *Richard III*, and therefore relapsed into the most slavish imitation ever exhibited in literature. The imitation theory is against all common sense: that Shakespeare, capable from the first of finer verse, greater style, subtler diction, would mistrust their attractive power, and for years try everybody else's style, down to their clichés. After starting *Verona* in his own early manner, would he imitate Greene's mechanical iambics to the last tick? The double-ending was the only device by which a writer like Marlowe could relieve his monotonous verse-form. Shakespeare least needed it because he had the greatest faculty of spontaneous variation of blank-verse rhythm. His later acceptance of it was but an item in the progressive liberation of his style. Greene would be likely to take the double-ending from Marlowe, and the comic relief in *Verona* is in Greene's manner. The fundamental moral perversity of the play is akin to Greene's *James IV*:

[1] *Sh. Canon,* Part II, 1923 (Routledge).

we are called on to forgive the unforgivable. We have like soliloquies of James and Proteus on their changes of choice, and like prattle of serving-men. Proteus passes in two minutes from the grossest black-guardism to accepted repentance. This is characteristic of all Greene's prose fiction; and yet he was the first pre-Shakespearian to create lovable and life-like women. His iambic movement is in nine-tenths of the blank verse. The numerous verbal and phrasal clues would prove nothing of themselves, because Shakespeare had to acquire his vocabulary from his predecessors, but they have cumulative force when added to similar manner and matter, verse and diction. Such wholesale imitation would have been a kind of literary prostration on the part of the master dramatist.

The style and ideation of *Richard II* is Marlovian. Peele often echoes Marlowe, and when a great passage occurs like Gaunt's praise of England, the question is whether Shakespeare's revising hand has worked on original matter by Peele or on something of Marlowe's echoed by Peele. The leading themes in Gaunt's speech are all item-ized by Peele, and as many other once-used words in the play are traceable to Peele, the primary ground for asserting his presence—the prevailing Marlowe style—is reinforced. It is hard to find Shake-speare in Act IV, and he is certainly not in the final scene of Act V: we need only contrast Bolingbroke's words to Exton with King John's to Hubert of the same period. The reader is presented with a set of styles in which Shakespeare's only emerges here and there. The duplicated quarrel scenes are railing matches on the common 'chronicle' plane, with many traits of Marlowe. The unsatisfying exposition scene is unlike Shakespeare; whereas in *John* he easily improves at each step on the old play. *John*, with *M.N.D.*, is the true starting-point for the study of Shakespeare's serious style. It has throughout the *cantabile* quality in which from the outset he shows himself unique. He could not have written *John* and *Richard II* and *Richard III* within two years, declining to 6·3 per cent. of double-endings in *John* and 5·1 in *Henry IV*, after 16·6 in *Errors*, 18·20 in *Richard II*, and 19·5 and even 20 in *Richard III*.

All proves that Shakespeare adapted an older play. Weak construc-tion, inappropriate rhyming, forcible-feeble diction, poor couplets at the end of scenes and speeches, tell of a primitive original imperfectly revised. The many double-endings point to Marlowe, for there are few in Shakespeare's rewriting. All that Shakespeare has done, includ-ing the King's speeches, belongs to his earlier manner. He probably handled but did not originate the King scenes. The play makes no advance on *Edward II* and is as loosely constructed. There is much monotonously stressed couplet verse, like Greene's, e.g. Mowbray's speech, 'Myself I throw . . .'. It has regular pausation, clause form, curt sententiousness, rhetorical key. Its manner and movement suggest Peele's *Edward I.* Faults of turgidity and bombast falling into bathos are not those of the young Shakespeare.

Marlowe must have done the Roses scene in *1 Henry VI* and probably the Talbot scenes. The couplet verse of his Ovid translation is of the semi-rigid cast of the Talbot scenes and similar verse in *Richard II. Hero and Leander* was more flexible, but Shakespeare's verse in *Venus* is not stiff. The verse of *John* has not the primary formalism of Marlowe's line, nor the prevailing laxity of style of the chronicle plays, and already the proportion of run-on lines exceeds Marlowe. Shakespeare's immaturity is his own; he learned his business like others, but he did not tread blindly and helplessly in the tracks of others.

If the verse is un-Shakespearian and like that of a contemporary, and also yields a number of words used once by that contemporary, the presumption is strengthened. If we add way of thinking, mode of metaphor, emotional key, habit of diction, duplications of non-proverbial phrase and trope, no alternative is left except deliberate purpose of systematic imitation. We must assume that Shakespeare wrote, 'Chop off his head', 'Off with his head', because Marlowe had often written it before; or that shortly before *M.N.D.* he penned hundreds of verses like, 'Never did captive with a freer heart . . .', with Marlowe's swing, heedlessness, one-line rhythm, and blare. We are asked to believe this because the theatre company ascribed to Shakespeare all the plays which it purchased and he retouched. Marlowe, Greene, and Peele echoed themselves *ad nauseam*, because they were hack-writers living from hand to mouth. Shakespeare's echoes of others are either open quotations or simple adaptations of current phrase made in the easy Elizabethan way, with his own voice and versification. He would have planned *Richard II* as a mere variant of *Edward II*, and it is to be noted that where he rewrites he does not imitate Marlowe's manner, but introduces his own. He would not write the other style when he had already compassed a finer of his own.

The bulk of the blank verse of the *Errors* is a survival from a pre-Shakespearian recast penned by one or more of the 'academic' group on the basis of the older verse. The first scene has 2 per cent. of double-endings, the second 24 per cent.—a proportion not reached in any undisputed play till *A.Y.L.* The rate in IV. i, is 19·6, and in v, 19 per cent. Probably all that Shakespeare did after the opening scene was a small amount of rewriting. The verse of the opening scene is conceivably Shakespeare's earliest, having a fairly high percentage of run-on lines; while the second scene, which is typical of the bulk of the play, has few run-on lines and many double-endings. It is of another fabric from *M.N.D.* and *L.L.L.* Less monotonous and more forceful than *Verona*, it is as often end-stopped—the rhythm being end-stopped even when the clause runs on. It resembles Marlowe, who wrote

comedy in *Faustus* and *Edward II*, and comedy and farce in the *Jew*.
If, as probable, Marlowe wrote the old *Shrew* play, he may have
written *Errors*. After the latter's opening scene the bulk of the blank
verse is the easy, forcible, and end-stopped kind characteristic of
Marlowe. Shakespeare in his early period abstains from double-
endings, while Marlowe inserts clusters in *Edward II* and 26 per
cent. in his translation of Lucan. Clues of phrase and vocabulary and
once-used words point to Marlowe, and also the bounding energy of
movement of Act V. It is a desperate compromise to imagine Shakespeare composing a series of plays in the exact verse-manner of some-
body else, after having forged and used his own great instrument.

M. for M. is one of the most perplexing problems in the Canon.
Present with some of Shakespeare's finest poetry and most moving
thought is verse of lower quality and prose evidently by another hand.
He must have trimmed or edited the blank verse throughout, but the
play remains morally incoherent as an action. The literary quality,
including the verse, is unequal, and the farcical matter irrelevant to
the serious. The total effect is so sombre as to exclude comedy—and
the total effect is created by anomalous procedure on the part of the
good characters. The Duke absents himself to secure general punishment of those whom he has encouraged to sin. Angelo's self-commun-
ings are partly Shakespearian, but the portrait is not true to life. It
was drawn rather by an anti-Puritan moralist and polemist than a
character-artist. Such a law in a city where brothels abound is fantastic,
and in Cinthio the offence is rape; but it is just intelligible as a disguised attack on Puritanism.

Angelo is a plot-puppet who leaps from asceticism to lust and
murderous fraud. As Cinthio says nothing of a man 'fundamentally
cold', this trait must have been added to present a type of repellent
Puritan. There is next to no cause for his villainous breach of faith,
and he is so intolerably wicked that when he proclaims himself ready
for death we cannot regard him as humanly contrite. And he is
assigned as a welcome mate to Mariana—who has to show a less
tolerable indelicacy than the lapse of the lovers. Except in the poetry,
where is Shakespeare's spirit? He has added much poetry and detail,
but has not reconstructed the character to its changed action: and
yet the play is dated at the period when he was at the height of his
power. The ribald matter is not like him; the scene between Escalus
and Elbow and Pompey is the merest comic padding. In serious
scenes prose and verse are mixed in un-Shakespearian fashion—not to
relieve tension, but from caprice or fatigue of the writer. It is an old
practice that derives from the Italians and pre-Shakespearians. The
bifrontal structure ruins the piece as a moral whole: Claudio is
treated by his sister and the Duke as guilty of a grave sin; and yet they
plan that Angelo and Mariana should commit the same act. Neither

in the play's better poetry nor in Shakespeare's undoubted work of the period is there sign of mental collapse—so this central flaw is more likely to be due to a draftsman of bad judgement. Isabella shows false feeling in lending herself to a plot which by her own code is unpardon-able—and this is a negation of the qualities in which Shakespeare transcends all other dramatists.

A mass of evidence in character, conception, method, vocabulary, style, phrase suggests Chapman's hand. He was known among contemporaries to lack judgement—although Greene also asks us to pardon the unpardonable. The quality of the verse in Act V resembles Chapman's, and the anomalous ethic is characteristic of him. In his signed plays he attacks the Puritans, and he has some fantastic pseudo-delicacies, but no real or healthy delicacy of moral feeling. He makes a priest a go-between in *Bussy d'Ambois*. In his signed work Chapman has never attained to such noble harmony as Claudio's speech on death or the Duke's. But the diction and rhythm of Isabella's final speech is quite un-Shakespearian. The word 'beast' that she hurls at her brother, and her final scream, are violence without poetry, and quite in Chapman's way. Perhaps Shakespeare thought it might remain, since the plot was perverse beyond remedy. If we compare the furious Charlotte of Chapman's *Revenge of Bussy*, we see that she and Isabella are alike projections of extremes by the poet of extremes. Charlotte cries to her brother who kills Montsurry and commits suicide (v. v. 199), 'Well done, my brother; I did love thee ever, But now adore thee . . .', and duly retires to a convent. It is the very art that presents to us the virago-virgin Isabella of the prison scene. When she inconsistently changes into a warm pleader for mercy we have the great versification of Shakespeare possibly rewriting Chapman with zest. The scene where the Duke propounds the Mariana plot is in a euphuistic style of prose. Compare *Eastward Ho*, '. . . let me now entreat you . . .', '. . . my kind desire to see you . . .'. Also *Tears* (iii. i). Lysander: '. . . question no more the reason of my journey. . . .' It was Chapman's habit to use verse alternately with prose, and sprinkle prose with verse. The bad verse lines, 'If my instructions may be your guide, Let the Barnardine be this morning executed', are like a Chapman medley. The octosyllabics at the end of Act III are like Chapman, and such occur in the *Gentleman Usher*, near the end of Act II. In these are two Chapman words, *morality* and *nicety*, which occur only in *M. for M.* throughout Shakespeare.

The signs of curtailment are compatible with the inference of Shakespeare revising a Chapman draft. The latter's plays are usually long, and his serious verse is obscured by verbiage. Shakespeare would aim to make the contorted and diffuse diction lucid and brief, and this would explain the aspect of every scene—the verse of three acts rewritten, the prose retained, Claudio's terror-struck appeal transfigured into pure Shakespearian verse, and Isabella's fierce tirade untouched. The last two acts, save for Mariana's song, are merely abbreviated and revised. The ribald scenes are like Chapman, in whose plays bawds, &c., continually figure. Two terms used in this connexion, *sheep-biter* and *flesh-monger*, occurring nowhere else in Shakespeare, and used by Chapman in one signed play, go to prove that his was the ribald matter. The super-elaborated plot recalls the *Widow's Tears*.

But the style most reveals Chapman. There is much of his verse and prose that survives all but a kind of planing down by Shakespeare. 'Now, gentle daughter, fear you not at all: He is your husband on a pre-contract'; 'Here in this prison, father, There died this morning. . . .' This is not Chapman's good verse, but it is his by test of comparison with his hand-to-mouth work in his signed comedies. The general manner is his—such finger-print words as 'under-globe', 'under-dwellings', 'regions', 'continents', 'earth'. It is hardly Shakespearian that the maiden of the furious invective of the prison scene should receive the news of her brother's death by hideous treachery in such wooden fashion. It is hardly Chapman, who had rhetoric enough— and it may be the intermediate play. Several words that only occur here are used by Chapman. 'Death lives in thy tongue' is a Chapman, not a Shakespeare, locution. We may compare 'Heaven doth with us as we with torches do . . .' to *Byron's Conspiracy* (iii. iii), 'The heavenly powers envy what they enjoin: We are commanded t' imitate their natures'. Compare also 'Spirits are not finely touched . . .' with Chapman's dedicatory epistle of the first twelve books of the *Iliad*, 'O 'tis wondrous much . . .'. Thus even in a scene which Shakespeare has inlaid with some of his most perfect lines he is working over a Chapman draft. Compare 'delighted spirit' with Chapman's 'delighted darts'. The word here means 'loosed off'—the spirit loosed from the body. The Duke's speech to Claudio is Shakespeare's, and above Chapman in rhythm and diction; yet there are signs of reconstruction. Here, and in Claudio's speech, Chapman may have been the intermediary of ideas suggested by Montaigne Compare 'thick-ribbed ice' with '. . . chain up thy blood In manacles of ice'; and 'snow-broth' with 'For snow and fire can hardly generate'.

Markedly in Chapman's manner are such once-used words as 'adoptedly', 'advisings', 'attorneyed', 'austereness', 'thick-ribbed', 'vastidity'. Shakespeare has revised out of the play much of the declamation usual to Chapman—but it is not his versification as a whole. The freely varying pausation of the opening scene is his. The rhythm of the scenes where Isabella pleads is one with the emotion, but the verbal clues still tell of a primary text rewritten. In the speeches of the Duke and Claudio on death, where there is a rewriting of matter well lost, we have a tragic music that Shakespeare does not often surpass. The verse of Act V is quite other—monotonous movement, rhythm normally line-ended, increased double-endings. The rhythm stresses the latter and aggravates their monotonous effect. About this time, in *Twelfth-Night* (IV. iii. 1–21), Shakespeare gives us seven double-endings in twenty-one lines, without monotony. 'Ay but to die . . .' has one double-ending, and the thrill of the verse doubles the thrill of the imagery. Chapman in his plays often gives strings of lines in one tune, aggravated by double-endings, as here in Act V; while the style of the prose of Act III is Chapman's. Shakespeare has but transfigured Act III in its great passages. Act IV, after the song, is not Shakespeare. The transitions from blank verse to couplets and couplets to prose are in Chapman's manner. 'He hath a garden circum-mur'd with brick' is in the monotonous tune, and also 'Nor, gentle daughter . . . '. The Duke-Friar, persuading Isabella and Mariana alike, is of Shakespeare's conception; and his is the rapid prose keeping up a speed of action that holds the stage interest. The repulsive and contradictory ethic is like Chapman. If Shakespeare spared the prose it was because it did not need rewriting for stage purposes, which the verse did. He lifted into poetry much of the serious verse dialogue, but did not trouble, in his maturity, to eke out an incurable unsatisfactory plot with inferior 'realistic' matter. . . .

We are now familiar with Mr. Robertson's method and need not repeat our formal general criticism. We think his examination of these last plays as satisfactory as of former ones, and he is even closer to his subject. The lever of his argument is the distinctive quality of Shakespeare's verse, and we may cite as an instance of his growing insight the remark that the second scene of the *Errors* is not Shakespeare's, because the rhythm is often end-stopped even when the clause runs on. Such a remark helps us to believe that he is not merely a critic with a theory who has shot his bolt once and for all, but that his ideas tend to divide and beget other and finer ideas. The verse-argument against *Verona* is strong and convincing.

His most important criticism here is of *M. for M.* Reviewing a former treatise on *Richard III* we said that he criticized Marlowe in such a way as to light up Shakespeare. Substituting Chapman for Marlowe the same may be said here. The high moral tone of Shakespeare's plays on which many critics have insisted appears more strongly by contrast with Chapman's 'repulsive and contradictory ethic'; it is indeed Chapman's dome of many-coloured glass that stains the white radiance of Shakespeare's eternity. The farcical matter irrelevant to the serious helps us to realize how supremely Shakespeare alone conquered his form; as also do such moral-dramatic faults as Isabella's false feeling, her outcry, 'Beast', Mariana's action, &c. All these convince us that art is not a partial thing, but an earthly symbol of the

Beautiful and therefore of the Good and the True. Browning once commented on the ease with which Shakespeare ascended the peak of poetry, and the infinite distance between him and others; and Carlyle has remarked that the power of intellect needed to construct a single one of his plays might have realized a fortune in practical affairs. Of this distance and this power we become more fully aware, not without a touch of awe, when he is contrasted with a fellow-worker in the same field. Mr. Robertson's thrust staggers *M. for M.* to its foundations: the fact that it still stands, to be re-read with undiminished pleasure, is a tribute direct and indirect to Shakespeare's transmuting power. That his critical sense never sleeps, that he never lets his theory advance mechanically by its own momentum, we see by his remark that Isabella's wooden reception of the news of her brother's supposed death is neither Shakespeare nor Chapman.

Yet it is in the realm of verse that Mr. Robertson produces his finest critical effects. We note, as complement to what was said above, his remark on the line-ended rhythm of the verse in Act V, where the rhythm stresses the double-endings and aggravates their monotony. And perhaps nothing brings home more the glory of Shakespeare's verse than the discovery that even in the greatest passages he is re-working Chapman. The core of Mr. Robertson's argument is that Shakespeare, who early developed an exquisite style—as appears in *L.L.L.* and *M.N.D.*—would not have written whole plays in the style of others, with an occasional interpolation in his true manner—and the proof is closer and more explicit in the present volume. We close it with the conviction that when all the moral and aesthetic philosophers, and psychologists, and theorists on the drama have had their say, the fact remains that Shakespeare was first and last a poet, and the duty of a poet is to convey emotion by rhythmic words.

We must continue with a further treatise on *Hamlet* by Mr. Robertson,[1] called forth by the new outbreak of impressionist criticism that followed his attempt of four years ago to explain Hamlet as a marvellous composite—the result of imposing a new psychological treatment on an old drama of delayed barbaric revenge. Clutton-Brock's process he calls one of sheer feeling in which reasoning does not enter. He contends that there can be no standard of aesthetic judgement without 'analytic processes of logic'. Even Clutton-Brock must offer reasons why his sheer impressionism shall be conclusive. If one character in a play so hallucinates us that we never ask ourselves, in the face of perplexities, whether the play as a whole hangs together, we are not experiencing it as a work of art. The statement of an impression, if more than interjection, is a collection of sensations into a reflection and a judgement. We cannot discriminate aesthetically without

[1] *'Hamlet' Once More*, 1923 (R. Cobden-Sanderson).

reflecting upon categories. An aesthetic impression must prove itself 'rational' if it is to have any status above blank self-assertion.

Clutton-Brock's book abounds in verbal entanglements, and confuses 'conviction' with 'impression', and the result is that he fails to advance the discussion. He concludes that the real Hamlet neither acts nor speaks—save in the soliloquies—but is to be inferred through the wrong expression which fills the rest of the play. The incongruity was that Hamlet acted as the barbaric Hamlet before him—because Shakespeare was transmuting an old play without reconstructing it. Clutton-Brock argues that Hamlet is continually switched from his purpose and his 'thought' by an 'unconscious self' created by the shock. Coleridge's 'overplus of reflection' becomes eviction of the conscious self by the unconscious, which makes Hamlet express himself wrongly in action and talk. No psychological law will explain how a 'conscious' can 'unconsciously seize a pretext to forget' which is 'invented' by his 'unconscious'.

Clutton-Brock says that he is 'aesthetically convinced', meaning 'aesthetically impressed'. He asserts that no one who sees the play questions Hamlet's conduct. But surely no thinking man would miss the perplexity while he is listening to Hamlet's self-accusing soliloquies. The Hamlet that Clutton-Brock presents is pathological, not psychological; and a mentally disordered hero is no subject for high tragedy unless it makes him psychologically greater for the time, as Lear. The tragedy of Hamlet is that killing the King will not still the Ghost's revelation that the murderer seduced the Queen. Clutton-Brock asserts that the reason is sovereign through all its disorder: but how can it be when the Unconscious is forcing its puppet to express himself wrongly? He speaks of Hamlet's 'double consciousness': but the opening soliloquy shows us Hamlet wholly possessed with his nausea at his mother's marriage. He cannot see his mother's case as that of an independent person.

Shakespeare has put more of his mental power and poetic magic into Hamlet than into any of the score of other men's plays which he more or less transmuted. Though there might be 'miscarriage' in transforming a barbaric into an intellectual Hamlet, with the action unchanged, Shakespeare intended to present a hero. Till 1600 he had found little scope for the higher poetic powers of his mind. How he would kindle at the chance of *Hamlet* we see from *1 Henry IV*, where all the figures talk in excess of dramatic requirement. We get reality of poetry side by side with unreal action. He had to keep to the beaten track for economic reasons, and he had the faculty of compliance; but his genius found compensation in the power to flood with his own thought and feeling whatsoever of his given material he felt he could transmute. After more or less transmuting other plays, his genius found in *Hamlet* a field for its utmost power of intensive transmutation.   In that age free utterance on great themes came only from heroes, princes, nobles—whereas priests and friars must talk in character.   In the ideal Hamlet Shakespeare saw a princely spirit vibrating under his torture, and through his own pain doubly alive to all the beauty and tragedy of the world.   The events of the play were there and he had to accept them, and in this acceptance he reveals his great idiosyncrasy.

The play was not thus planned, but evolved from an early play by Kyd.   Shakespeare transfigured the central character and transmuted the diction, but retained the action; and the result is incongruity between Hamlet's words and actions.   In the old story his mock-madness has helped him to escape death, but now it puts him in danger.   The 'To be . . .' soliloquy is incongruous after the experience of the Ghost.   Certain unnecessary scenes are retained, such as Reynaldo's mission to Paris.   The inference is that Shakespeare did not wish to reconstruct the play, but to transfigure it in literary or spiritual fashion. He cared little for plot, but was a master of stage effect, and therefore retained the 'To be . . .' soliloquy, though inappropriately placed, because he knew it would tell with his audience.

He conceived Hamlet as a sensitive, cultured, and princely Elizabethan.   The planned and delayed revenge was a familiar motive in the old drama, and it may be that Shakespeare proceeded to touch it up without inquiring the cause of the delay.   He retained the main features as he found them because he knew they would appeal to audiences. The play came to him stamped with the character of unexplained delay, and he did subtly indicate a possible explanation—that Hamlet was too deeply wounded by his mother's action to be satisfied by mere revenge on his uncle.   But this solution is inadequate to the retained action of the old play.   The play scene was an excellent device when the audience saw the King always surrounded by guards—and Shakespeare retained it as a fixed and effective feature of the play.   Clutton-Brock insists that Shakespeare spontaneously conceived the play scene as a device of the nerve-shocked Hamlet to pretend to one stratum of himself to be taking action when he was really obeying another stratum which recoiled from action.   He kills Polonius like the original barbarian, with the same cry, and the same barbaric unconcern.   Shakespeare progressively rewrote without reconstructing, and in the end it could not but strike him that man and things were incongruous. Revenge did not inspire him, and in the atmosphere he sheds we see it as inadequate to rectify the balance of a life shattered by evil.

Shakespeare had not the architectonic schemes in his head that the theorists have assigned to him.   He did his marvels by way of business, fretted neither by ambition nor thirst for fame.   To recognize his real procedure—alchemy of transfiguration—is to appreciate his mastery more intensely than to see in him a deliberate schemer of theoretic masterpieces. He is a dramatist above as well as for the stage. The one abiding mystery in him is the mystery of genius—and his genius was not subdued to what it worked in. . . .

Clutton-Brock cannot stand such horseplay—as Carlyle said of the Sections, when Napoleon opened fire with his big guns and put an end to the French Revolution. Mr. Robertson's knowledge has widened and deepened since he last wrote on *Hamlet*, and he has developed his power to appreciate Shakespeare aesthetically. His antiquarian knowledge—if the term may be allowed—has helped him to draw finer critical distinctions, and he convinces us, more than many a rhapsodist, that Shakespeare was inspired. Re-reading Clutton-Brock, however, and rejecting much that is false and merely impressionistic, we will adhere to our former opinion—that he uses the character of Hamlet successfully to focus the mystery of the human lot. We will also support his assertion of Hamlet's 'double consciousness', which Mr. Robertson denies on the evidence of the first soliloquy. For does not Mr. Robertson himself support it when he says most admirably that Hamlet, through his own pain, was doubly alive to all the beauty and tragedy of the world?

IV

IT is fitting that Mr. William Wells[1] should follow Mr. Robertson. He writes to prove that *J.C.* is an old play by Marlowe—with the possible assistance of Peele—and the present revision was begun by Shakespeare and finished by Beaumont. The language is both archaic and simple, and no dramatist had a simpler style than Beaumont. Its ratio of double-endings—1 in 6—and the end-stopped test point to a much earlier period than 1602. Such a caricature as Caesar belongs naturally to Marlowe, if we compare Tamburlaine, Faustus, Guise, Gaveston, Barabas. There are touches of Beaumont in Portia, for he was acquainted from boyhood with well-bred women; whereas Hotspur's Kate was a middle-class wife, because only late in his career did Shakespeare learn to draw distinctions of breeding. Shakespeare begins a play at the beginning, and tries to get all he can into a limited space, while Beaumont begins near the middle, relates what has gone before—as here in the second scene—and then proceeds to develop his plot. The result is much padding—as when Caesar is killed in Act III, and two Acts remain to write—so that the quarrel scene is a beautiful interlude. Too much significance has been given to links with *Hamlet*. Compare the relations of Hamlet to Ophelia and Brutus to Portia. Hamlet was afraid of suicide, Brutus committed it. Brutus was slow to decide, quick to act; Hamlet was quick in thought but slow in deed.

Arrogance and contempt of fear distinguish Marlowe's heroes. He

[1] *The Authorship of 'Julius Caesar'*, 1923 (Routledge).

also has an idea of a more than human look of majesty in the faces of strong, highly placed characters, striking fear into common mortals. Compare Tamburlaine, and also Guise: 'And princes with their looks engender fear'. Brutus's words after the murder, 'Show the reason of *our* Caesar's death', recall those of the King in the *Massacre*: 'As all the world shall know *our* Guise is dead'. The date of Part II *Tamburlaine* was 1582, and the links between it and *J.C.* show a vocabulary common to the two plays; Cassius (v. iii): 'This day I breathèd first'; and *2 Tamburlaine* (iv. i): 'O Samarcanda where I breathèd first.' The conspirators watch Caesar's facial by-play as he listens to Popilius Lena; and in *Edward II* the watchers of the Queen pleading for Gaveston exclaim, 'She smiles: now, for my life, his mind is changed'. This would date the play 1589, the time when Guise was assassinated, and yet Marlowe does not treat openly of him till 1592. Dramatists had to take care not to ruffle the feelings of the French Court;[1] but Marlowe might easily write a play on Guise and call it *J.C.* Both Guise and Caesar were warned of their coming doom and ignored it from contempt of fear. Both walked to and fro avoiding stabs, and each pulled his robe over his head. *J.C.* departs from Plutarch in stating that the time was eight o'clock, and Guise was murdered at this hour.

The probable date of *J.C.* was 1609, when Shakespeare left London and resigned his work to Beaumont. Lines 1–57 of Act I, scene i, are his, and we may infer that he intended the play to be of wider scope. Flavius and Marullus are introduced never to appear again, and Shakespeare never introduces superfluous characters. A change of style accompanies this change of plan, and there are many parallels to Marlowe and Beaumont, while the humorous scenes do not suggest Shakespeare. The members of the mob do not jest in Shakespeare's easy manner, but are heavy and slow. Yet the verse is swift and alive, and this is against its being early work. After 'Run to your houses . . .' there are traces of Beaumont, besides failure of inspiration. Thus Beaumont always dismisses a seditious assembly. Compare *Noble Gentleman*, iii. iii, 'Every man to his house in peace and quiet'; *Cupid's Revenge*, iv. v, 'Good friends, go home again', and 'For my sake to your houses'; *Love's Pilgrimage*, iv. i, 'Get you all home and work'. Shakespeare evidently meant much to be acted between the triumph and the Lupercal, and some serious business for the Tribunes. Beaumont leaned towards Aristotle, and disliked some of Shakespeare's methods. He could neither destroy Shakespeare's fragment nor proceed on the same lines, so he made a new beginning and tacked it on to the old one, afterwards relating in the second scene the intervening events between the two. When Cassius tempted Brutus he should have recalled the episode of Flavius and Marullus.

[1] Cf. Miss Winstanley.

Of the eight-line speech that concludes the first scene, the first four lines are characteristic of Beaumont, the last of Marlowe. The latter are monotonously sing-songy, and there are many such in *2 Tamburlaine*. In fine, the first and duller draft was Marlowe's, and then came Shakespeare's uncompleted revision—to be followed by Beaumont's excision and constriction of Marlowe's written and Shakespeare's purposed work.

Even when the thought is Marlowe's we find Beaumont's diction. Beaumont used the verb 'to do' far more than Marlowe or Fletcher, and here it occurs 101 times. Beaumont alone of the tragic writers took a clear view of the whole course of his play, and had the fifth act before him when writing the first. Shakespeare's methods in *Hamlet* and *A.Y.L.* are slipshod compared with *Philaster* written about the same time. The passage, 'The fault, dear Brutus...', suggests Marlowe, who, unlike the more conventional Shakespeare, had a furious itch to challenge all kinds of right, divine and otherwise. Caesar's outburst of humour is followed by complete reversion to type. If Marlowe had imagined him to be serious he would have remained serious to the end; therefore Beaumont is responsible for his conversion, and he is like the bluff wooden-headed warriors in Beaumont and Fletcher, such as Mardonius in *A King and No King*.

The tenderness and delicacy of Brutus's character belongs to a more refined age than Marlowe's; but Beaumont had great sensibility, and the Brutus-Lucius companionship is practically reproduced in Philaster and Bellario. In the *Maid's Tragedy* Beaumont repeats much of *J.C.*, and as the latter was not published in his life, and many other of Shakespeare's plays were more likely to attract him, one cannot otherwise explain why he should have gorged so liberally on this one play. The translation of the first book of Lucan's *Pharsalia* goes to prove that Marlowe wrote the earlier play. Calpurnia's speech derives from the *Pharsalia*, and the colouring of the lines is Marlovian. He frequently uses 'drizzled',—and armies in the air is a common theme with him. Marlowe had translated the first book, and drawn material from it for some of his plays, and was therefore more likely to use Lucan than Shakespeare. Portia's inconsistency owes something to Beaumont's uncertain touch, all of whose heroes and heroines are a shade too weak for their tasks.

Beaumont's verse has a grave and stately deliberateness of its own, with neither Shakespeare's fervid flow nor Fletcher's indecent hurry. Compare 'Over thy wounds now do I prophesy...' with *Richard II*, iv. i, 'And if you crown him let me prophesy'. The two passages are of the same time and piece, open in the same manner, announce similar events, sound with the same twang to which like words are sung, and are both tautological. *Richard II* is dated 1593-4, and if *J.C.* is 1600 Shakespeare cannot be judged by a progressive style-test. Again, if *J.C.* is 1600 you assume a double improbability—that Shakespeare wrote *Richard II* under Marlowe's tuition when he was writing *John* in the true Shakespearian manner, and that he returned to Marlowe in 1600, having discarded his manner from 1594 onwards. Marlowe specialized in weak kings, and *Richard II* and *Edward II* are alike, and both contain identical prophecies—imaginative, not historical. The latter device abounds in Lucan, whom Marlowe studied and used. Compare *J.C.*: 'That this foul deed shall smell above the earth With carrion men, groaning for burial', with *Richard II*: 'The blood of England shall manure the ground, And future ages groan for this foul act'; and *Pharsalia*, Book vii, where the poet reproaches Caesar for his refusal to allow the rotting carcases of Pompey's defeated army to be decently consumed.

The second scene of Act II is less great than is supposed, and might have been written by Marlowe and Beaumont in combination. When Shakespeare's characters harangue a crowd, as in *Coriolanus*, they do not shed metaphor or revert to plain syntax and simple speech; nor does Shakespeare elsewhere vary his style to suit the matter or requirements of the work. As regards characters, the Antony here is not connected with that of *A. and C.*, as Bolingbroke the subject is with Bolingbroke the King. Beaumont was subtle, and as his aim was to be explicit and appeal to the unlearned, he avoided foreign or classical words. As simplicity distinguished his manner, so irony did his matter— in which he followed the Greeks. There is irony in *Lear*, but little in *Othello* or *Macbeth*. We turn to Beaumont for Greek irony, e.g. *Cupid's Revenge* and the *Maid's Tragedy*, and we see that this quality of irony was not the gift of the authors that supplied the framework. In diction and plot he aimed at clarity, and so often imparted information that other playwrights retained to achieve surprise in the fifth act. He would anticipate a surprise by making it the legitimate effect of facts previously told to his audience. Antony's oration is Marlowe's previous work reconstructed with additions. 'Lend me your ears' is not elsewhere in Shakespeare, but is in Beaumont's *Love's Pilgrimage*, iv. iii: 'I pray you, lend your ears, And keep your voices'. 'Mischief, thou art afoot!' suggest Beaumont, who frequently personifies abstract qualities, e.g. Arithmetic, Atheism, Constancy, Grief, Sadness, Sorrow, Patience, Tumult, Wisdom.

Beaumont wrote his best in scenes where friendship prevailed, but was not likely to enter into the designs of the three rogues who plotted to gain from Caesar's death in Act IV. The following words in the quarrel scene are typical Beaumont and Fletcher bluster, 'When Caesar lived, he durst not thus have moved me'. Beaumont's characters frequently invite sudden death. Compare Cassius's words to Brutus, and the quarrel scene (iii. ii) of the *Maid's Tragedy*, 'If thou wilt strike, here is a faithful heart'. The last words of line 105, 'for I know', are repeated in the same order and place in three of Beaumont's plays, *Maid's Tragedy*, *Philaster*, v. v, *Cupid's Revenge*, IV. v. Brutus questions the Ghost in the invariable manner of Beaumont's characters when they meet with a being they do not know. The sentimental Brutus-Lucius episode recalls Philaster and Bellario, and is not vital to the story of the play. The language is at its simplest; in no other work of Shakespeare's middle period are the words of such a plain and everyday kind, while the metre remains deliberate, e.g. 'The strings, my lord, are false. . . .'

Unlike Shakespeare, Marlowe was anti-monarchist, and would write the play with a strong bias against the dictator. Cassius would have claimed his sympathy, and Brutus would appear something of a fool to a man of this world. Brutus's excessive morality is a later growth; the original author had no room for morality in his concept of life, and his characters are all rogues. Compare 'I shall find time, Cassius . . .' with the great who have no time to mourn in the *Maid's Tragedy*, v. iv. Surely Brutus had time to mourn for Cassius in a fitting manner. If all this is plagiarism it must have come from an intensive study of Shakespeare—and there was no reason for Beaumont to be obsessed by *J.C.*

The author of this treatise states that he has read the plays of Beaumont and Fletcher at least a hundred times, and he argues that such a course of reading, even if careless, must leave an impression, conscious or unconscious, on the reader's mind. The result of this intimate knowledge was that one day when passing from the first to the second scene of *J.C.*, he exclaimed, 'This is the voice of Francis Beaumont'. . . .

We naturally turn back to our analysis of Mr. Robertson's chapters on *J.C.*, and find that the two writers agree on the following points: that the verse is archaic; that Caesar is presented in a hostile manner; that the quarrel scene has no dramatic value; that the play is the abridgement of a double play; that Antony's oration is largely the work of Marlowe. They are nearly agreed about the date—1607 according to Mr. Robertson and 1609 according to Mr. Wells. They differ about Portia, and we rather side with Mr. Robertson. The point that Mr. Wells makes has been used against Dickens, but is hardly fit for Shakespeare. We need only turn to the contrast of Theseus and Hippolita with the Athenian 'mechanicals' to see that even in his earliest work Shakespeare could discriminate shades of breeding: though it may be true, as Furnivall said, that in Hermia we see the 'temper' of one of the Stratford girls among whom he grew up. Mr. Robertson's range is far greater than that of Mr. Wells, and he does not mention Beaumont's hand among those which he discovers in the play. He speaks of the old French plays whence arose the 'thrasonical' conception of Caesar; and, on the other hand, Mr. Wells makes some interesting discoveries in Lucan. For the rest, Mr. Wells is absorbed by Beaumont rather than Shakespeare, and he earns a place in the history of Shakespearian criticism as a negative rather than a positive critic. He helps to prove that Shakespeare did not write all the plays in the Folio, but of Shakespeare himself he has little to say.

V

MR. JOHN BAILEY[1] considers that Shakespeare has his place among the builders of the British Empire. In war the ultimate victory is to the spirit, and the poet moves the minds that move the nation. Shakespeare treated history in the fashion of his time, though he infinitely ennobled that fashion. History in his time meant the doings of kings, and as artist he took the personal view. You can no more make a hero out of a Parliament or a people than you can paint a people's portrait. Constance and Arthur inspire more interest than Magna Carta. Yet Shakespeare's histories are less pageants of king-ship than faithlessness. We see the usurping and conscience-stricken John, the idle and empty Richard, the crafty founder of the House of Lancaster and its hardly human destroyer and ultimate victim. The history of England becomes almost a chronicle of royal and noble crimes.

The Jack Cade scenes in *Henry VI* first show the true Shakespeare —merciless clear-sightedness mingled with sympathy for the common people. He turned stage puppets into human beings, and servants and clowns often live more than their masters. *Richard III* advances, but not into Shakespeare's own dramatic kingdom, and it does not, like most of Shakespeare, improve with reading. Richard's villainies do not proceed from character and circumstance combined, but are born before their time, unnaturally, out of the head of the monster. Richard II, on the other hand, does not act but merely suffers. Action requires will, and he has only desire. For such a man sensation is all, and love of passiveness such that he will make a luxury of pain and shame and even death. Shakespeare pities Richard, but does not accept the statement of such characters or see them as they see them-selves. Thus he did not mean Shylock to be a sympathetic figure. Because he penetrates the mystery it does not mean that he does not judge. His poetic powers attain their full and final energy in *Richard II*; we get the note, never to be absent again, where all life, joy and sadness, weakness and strength, hears itself as a harmony, sees itself as a picture. *John* brings before us the typical Englishman, and the ideal heroic England of Shakespeare's own day.

Henry IV is one of the very greatest of all Shakespeare's works. He elicits the answer of life from the coarsest and dullest human clay. The great personages are rather like stage-figures, for less successfully

[1] 'Sh.'s Histories' (*The Continuity of Letters*. Clarendon Press, 1923).

than in the pure dramas does Shakespeare bring home that great men have feelings like others behind their grandeur. There are some flaws, such as the occasional praises of Falstaff as soldier. If Shakespeare had not meant him to be a coward and liar he would not have allowed us to take him for both. Probably recollections of the real Sir John Falstaff at times displaced the imaginative Falstaff in favour of the historical. Falstaff expresses the senses absolutely—with the intellect used solely to serve them. To know all is to do more than pardon, it is nearly always to love. Were he silent he would be disreputable, but he is so divinely gifted with ingenious thoughts and witty words that he disarms our judgement and we delight in one who reveals all mankind in revealing himself. His humour is of the most lovable kind, like that of Horace, Cervantes, Scott—and he can see his own true picture and laugh at it. No man was ever closer to reality in enjoying life and thinking and talking about it, but the conduct of life requires will and conscience as well as intellect, and here—unlike Henry V—he was out of touch with reality. By means of him Shakespeare turned history into a picture of human life—that of ordinary men and women which goes on side by side with great events. The realism of genius has entered the Shakespearian drama and will kill the old semi-official chronicle-history.

Henry V is less great because less broadly human, but in it culminates the glory of the historical plays as history. It contains all the pride and all the valour of England. Agincourt was unjustifiable, and ultimately had ill-results, but Shakespeare was concerned not with the philosophy of history, but to show men acting intensely. He makes Henry V the hero King of all the line, and studies him the most subtly, as a human being as well as a hero. He can both enjoy and act, feel and think, use conscience and intellect, and has passions as well as will. He was never Falstaff's boon companion and one with his company. His eyes have been opened, but he again goes blind, like the reader—for fine and open natures, conscious of greatness and indifferent to opinion, are liable to misunderstandings. Falstaff is the only character to run away with his creator,[1] and at times defeat the intention shown in all three plays that we should love and honour the Prince. The latter may have a touch of self-righteousness, but self-confidence is a virtue, and in his soliloquies he expresses the nature of a strong man who means to shape his own life. Always in Falstaff's company, he marks his separation from it. It is Shakespeare's most monarchical play, and Henry is a masterful king, though never was king so plain a man and more at home with plain men. The man is more than either king, madcap, or soldier. He is compounded of plain man, honest man, and hero, with little of curious thought or imagination. Typical Englishman, yet he kills prisoners and casts off his old friend. The horrible speech

[1] Cf. Bradley.

before Harfleur is only a threat, yet among the ugliest in Shakespeare —due either to changed times or mere inconsistency. Shakespeare has prepared us for Falstaff's dismissal, by progressively degrading him and expanding Henry's heroic nature. If the rejection is made with insult it was provoked by Falstaff's abominable behaviour in the most solemn moment of a king's life—his coronation. Suppose a judge hailed with old mess or club jokes as he first takes his seat on the bench![1] . . .

A fine modern critical mind never fails to reveal something of its subject at the moment of contact—however worked upon by other minds that subject may be. It is at such moments that Mr. Bailey, who can describe his impressions exactly, teaches us by example what our own should be. He states at the outset that Shakespeare was before all an artist who took a personal view of history. He analyses excellently the characters of the two Richards, and Falstaff above all. Nowadays the conscience of a person who is over-scrupulous about trifles is said to be a psychological rather than a moral thing; and it is by drawing these subtle modern distinctions between moral, intellectual, social, physical, that Mr. Bailey has left upon our minds an idea of Falstaff that we do not think any other critic has surpassed. Where it seems to us that he has gone astray is with Henry V: due to the fact that he accepts the Folio as entirely Shakespeare's. The old-time critics who had once experienced Shakespeare's charm took the whole of his work equally seriously, and something of this weakness has descended to Mr. Bailey. It must also be recalled that Mr. Bailey's point of view is that Shakespeare has his place among the builders of the British Empire—and it seems to us that any extra-poetical motive in judging Shakespeare handicaps the critic. He finds Henry V a subtly conceived character, and treats his early soliloquies in the preceding plays as if they had the inner self-revealing quality of the true Shakespearian soliloquy. It were as well to compare the jangling of brass instruments with the sound of invisible flutes and harps. Mr. Bailey's analysis of the Prince-Falstaff connexion is instructive, but there is no doubt that the Prince expressed his soul in the scenes of Falstaffian revelry, and any 'separation' was an afterthought. We except from contradiction the dismissal of Falstaff—the stress laid on the solemn nature of the coronation, and the admirable comparison of the judge.

VI

MR. RICHMOND NOBLE, writing of Shakespeare's songs,[2] says that delusive simplicity conceals painstaking labour, and that Shakespeare alone saw the possibilities afforded by song for forwarding the

[1] Cf. Stopford Brooke (1913).
[2] *Sh.'s Use of Song* (Oxford University Press, 1923).

action. 'Silvia' (*Verona*) connects the two parts of the play. 'Tell me where is fancy bred' rationalizes Bassanio's choice of the leaden casket. 'O mistress mine' (*Twelfth-Night*) opens and develops the revelry that leads to Malvolio's interference and the consequent conspiracy against him. The mock pastorals in *L.L.L.* finally restore and maintain the laughing character of the comedy.[1] In the earliest comedies the singers are vocalists introduced to render the song. *M.N.D.* and *Wives* contain Shakespeare's first action songs. But Balthazar's song (*M.N.D.*), aimed at Benedict, helps to evolve the plot. The songs of *A.Y.L.* convey atmosphere and reflect the personality of Amiens. In the tragedies we find only ballads or popular songs to give colour or emotional effect. Shakespeare's songs steadily became more relevant to their context and dramatically important, and his use of song culminates in the *Tempest*. No dramatist of his time or since has been able to interweave song with action and dialogue with such natural effect.

One must not apply a literary standard to Shakespeare, but remember that his art was of the theatre. The modern picture frame stage obscures the significance of the songs. 'Under the greenwood tree' localizes the action; and 'When daffodils begin to peer' depicts scenery and objects and marks the season of the year. To present the scene is to make the song superfluous. It is also a fault of modern composers to treat the songs as detached lyrics instead of dramatically. To understand the songs one should read the plays not as literature but as spoken dialogue involving action, and picture the speaker or singer on a bare platform stage.

The comic intent of the *Cuckoo Song* (*L.L.L.*) is in keeping with the play. It dissipates the idealism of the learned men by reminding them of a certain danger which threatens married men in the spring.[2] 'Tell me where is fancy bred' (*Merchant*) performs the function of dialogue, and is vitally related to the situation. It was not luck that induced Bassanio to choose aright, and, being a gambler, he was most open to suggestion. *M.N.D.* shows a great advance in management of song. The lullaby (II. ii) relieves from awkwardness and makes interesting Titania's retirement, imparts to the whole a fairylike atmosphere, and facilitates Oberon's plot. Compare 'Pinch him . . .' (*Wives*) with its model—the song round Corsites in Lyly's *Endimion*. The latter does not forward the action, whereas Shakespeare's song not only completes Falstaff's discomfiture, but concludes the little farce of Anne Page and her suitors. *M. Ado* is the bridge between old and new, for here Balthazar, the singer, participates in the action. *A.Y.L.* is the comedy of romantic unreality, and therefore song is indispensable. The secret of the charm of the comedy is that all men dream of such a life, and song heightens the effect. The songs do not

[1] Cf. Kreyssig on the concluding song of *L.L.L.*   [2] Cf. Kreyssig.

develop the action, but the scenes appear to be created so that the songs should be sung. Their dramatic function is to convey the colour of a scene and sense of atmosphere to supply the lack of a scene painter. The two songs of Amiens are the first to reflect in the lyric the singer's temperament. 'O mistress mine . . .' (*Twelfth-Night*) outlines the very spirit of the comedy. It produces a riot which causes Malvolio to intervene, and this in turn produces the conspiracy.[1]

'Take, oh take those lips away' (*M. for M.*) partly reverts to earlier practice because it is sung by a boy whose sole function is to sing the stanza, but it is also relevant to the dramatic matter, and it provides the Duke with a suitable opening remark. No man has been limned more tersely and vividly than Autolycus (*W. Tale*) in his two opening songs. The songs deprive the theft of half its villainy, and it is the singing that has made him and stamped him on men's minds. But for these character-songs the audience would hate Autolycus. They put his would-be judges in good humour, and are in Shakespeare's final form of dramatic song. Music is the very life of the *Tempest*, and the singing is always in character—from Ariel to Caliban. Ariel gives the impression that he translates into song Ferdinand's imaginings and fears. The emphasis and repetition of 'Ban Ban . . .' is characteristic of the triumphal chorus of aborigines, and shows the minute care bestowed by Shakespeare on his characters at crucial dramatic moments.

Between 1600 and 1609 song lost its vogue. The public taste was fickle; the Children of Chapel Royal, brought to Blackfriars Theatre about 1600, had almost ruined adult actors, and their success was largely due to song. Therefore Shakespeare put song on one side and attempted to lure the public by absorbing stories. But though song is more restricted, it is of all sorts, and the experience gained in the comedies is turned to account. It heightens the tragedy of Ophelia's madness, while the sexton's perversion of his text makes the ballad bear more directly on his task. He uses 'pit' for 'house' because 'pit' is in his mind, and repeats 'spade' because of his labours and fading memory. Such instances of realism prove how perfectly Shakespeare visualized every detail of the action. The Clown could sing because custom had made his task easy, and thereby the tragedy was increased. When Iago aims to subvert military order by luring Cassio to drink, he uses song to make abandoned gaiety most inviting. Omit song and the proceedings are no longer convivial. The Willow Song makes Desdemona's misery almost unbearable. Compare the ballad in *Percy's Reliques* to see how Shakespeare both improved the form and assimilated the matter to Desdemona's sex and condition. Compare also the song of Pandarus (*T. and C.*) to 'O mistress mine' (*Twelfth-Night*). The latter is from one who would eagerly participate, the former is from a promoter of intrigue. The song of Pandarus is one of the very

[1] Cf. Kreyssig.

greatest dramatic song masterpieces in the languages. 'Hark, hark, the lark' (*Cymbeline*) is characteristically morning music to transform night into dawn and disperse the stifling atmosphere of the trunk scene. The bare platform stage taxed the ingenuity of dramatists, and song helped them to attain their object.

The later songs occur more easily, are more dramatically relevant, and are not so obscure as to purpose, as are the earliest. In no department of stage-craft did Shakespeare make greater progress than in song. . . .

The scepticism with which we opened Mr. Noble's volume declined as we proceeded. The subject was one to lend itself to preconceived ideas and strained interpretations, and it is true that Mr. Noble makes a few facile points, such as Iago's use of song to seduce Cassio, or the comparison between the song in *Twelfth-Night* and that of Pandarus. But on the whole he has proved his theory, and when he treats *A.Y.L.* and the songs of Autolycus his criticism is of a fine order. Phaethon's chariot wheels must tarry till Aurora passes through the opened gates and lightens the sky; and Mr. Noble leaves the impression that Shakespeare devised the use of song somewhat in this manner—the forerunner of his dramatic glory—a more exquisite if less resplendent beauty. He has selected one of the finest gold threads in Shakespeare's tapestry-work and shown that it has not been added as a later ornament, but that its effect was calculated with the original design, to be wrought into the fabric. He has proved his main points—that the songs are dramatically relevant, and that Shakespeare's power over this dramatic use of song developed with the rest of his art. And yet the songs yield their highest beauty no less when detached from their context.

VII

MR. R. P. COWL in his introduction to *2 Henry IV*[1] detects the influence of Ben Jonson—the use of significant names for the minor characters, and of comedy as a medium of general social satire and realistic description and portraiture. The comic spirit has become less irresponsible and joyous, not exercised on creations of an exuberant fancy, but on objects of understanding and judgement, in a world of inexorable fact. The tavern life of Part I was radiant with good humour and good nature; that of Part II is tainted with emanations of physical and moral corruption. The degradation of Falstaff—a stern dramatic necessity—is effected by stressing the vulgarity of his surroundings.[2] No doubt Shakespeare was influenced by the cynical and mordant humour of Ben Jonson, and we see it in Shallow and Silence. These, while faithful to an accepted stage type, are extraordinarily individual and living. Their characters, alike built on incapacity and folly, are discriminated with amazing invention and skill. Falstaff, besides deteriorating morally, has a keener edge to his wit, and his

[1] Arden edition, 1923 (Metheun).   [2] Cf. Middleton Murry.

humour is harsh and acrid. The Prince gives an impression of rapidly ripening manhood; he shows detachment and gravity in talk with Poins. The King is dignified by the sense of approaching death, and though conscious that he had been self-seeking and unscrupulous, is upheld by the conviction that he had been an instrument in the hands of a higher power. . . .

The suggestion of Ben Jonson's influence is interesting and probable, but surely Mr. Cowl has exceeded the mark in calling Falstaff's humour harsh and acrid, and expelling all the sunlight from the play. However, his point of view is worth including as a corrective to those who see an undimmed Falstaff in Part II. Also having in mind the Prince's many enemies, we note as something of a psychological discovery the quality of 'detachment'. But Mr. Cowl's final sentence on the King is his wisest.

VIII

PROFESSOR STOLL[1] writing about Shakespeare himself, finds his unobtrusive character in life reflected in his writings. He neither abuses nor sympathizes with the Puritans, and betrays no bias in affairs of Church or State. He says nothing of the Spanish or the Catholics, of Ireland or America, of scientific discoveries, of any theories and questions, creeds, problems, parties. He was interested in the old familiar ideas that served his dramatic purpose—pagan, or royalist. He was no seer, prophet, or philosopher; his aversions are traditional, not personal—for Jews, mobs, the French. He is the supreme spectator who stands aloof, though not afar from everything. He did not unlock his heart in the Sonnets, which are not love-letters but sonnets written in conventional and traditional language. Only he among poets left Elizabeth unsung, and he wrote nothing of his fellow dramatists, whether friends or enemies. He was conventional, reticent, impersonal, because a dramatist by nature as well as profession. In the Sonnets he avails himself of every convention to hide private joy or woe. The man who most prized character seems to have been hardly a character at all. We find an all-embracing personality in his work, but not a person. If the same personality is in the Sonnets, it is also gentle, sweet, and affectionate, but abject and timorous before his high-born faithless friend and his low social status as actor. It is not an imposing nature, but accords with that of a flexible and impressionable dramatist—and with Shakespeare's conventional and obscure private life.

Even in his two dedications to Southampton and in his will he wears a mask. His bequests are formal; he refers in no way to the individuality

[1] *On the Anniversary of the Folio*, 1923 (Sh. Studies. New York, The Macmillan Co., 1927).

of the legatees. It is difficult to reconcile this farewell to the world with any conscious greatness. It was mere business, and as he was dryer and more impersonal than most men, it is unlikely that in his actor's art which he laments, and his dramatist's which he forgets, that he should go far in the opposite direction. It is therefore improbable that in the *Tempest* he should refer to himself and no one else. His plays contain no literary men, yet most of his finer characters die mindful of fame and glory. He never treats the subject of fame ironically, in modern style, and he is not disappointed or cynical. He was not too lofty or indifferent, but the fame he craved was to found a family and leave an estate in strict entail. He was a successful man of affairs in whom instinct chimed with his country's custom.

He wrote accordingly—as actor, manager, and maker of stage-plays, to which, as they were not literature, he remained indifferent. He sought to please pit and gallery and wrote for immediate effect, expecting neither readers nor critics. Hence his work was free from self-consciousness and the confining requirements of art. He ignored not only the canons of Aristotle and the Renaissance critics, but minor matters of consistency and plausibility. Lady Macbeth seems to have had a child; the Fool in *Lear* is never mentioned after he vanishes with the tempest. Do Timon, Lady Macbeth, and Ophelia kill themselves? Is Mowbray guilty? Why does Cleopatra flee from Actium? Why do Banquo and Desdemona's Emilia hold their tongues? These are a few among the oversights due to rapid and careless workmanship. Shakespeare was concerned only for the immediate effect and the momentary; and for this reason there are no perfections like his spontaneous perfections—as the purest poetry is a song, a flight, with no self-conscious or professional taint.[1] He wrote to earn his living, and that, like the moral purpose in Dante, Milton, Dickens, is a safeguard as well as an incentive. He did not strain his voice to live up to his reputation and continue to make phrases and jests when his mind was exhausted.

He was no child of nature who ignored art, but was conscious of his aims, though unconscious of his eminence. He learned his art on the stage and in the audience; it became his element—as a foreign language is learned in the country itself. As he did not pose for posterity, he concentrated upon his characters on the stage and the audience before it. If he observed the unities, as in the *Tempest*, it was to secure greater and finer effects. Such are the ideal conditions under which art is produced: it is the difference between Homer and Milton, Aeschylus and Seneca. Rules and principles are retrospective, and out of date as soon as formulated. We may find fault with his logic,

---

[1] The following critics remark that Shakespeare concentrated on single scenes at the expense of the whole: Blair, Voltaire, Le Blanc, La Place, Chateaubriand, Villemain, Kenny, Taine, Benedix, Rümelin, Stephen, Creizenach, Schücking.

psychology, motivation—but his is the supreme life-giving power [1]—
he lends each person a particular and individual voice. We hear the
true and troubled accents of the human voice. The greatest modern
novelists are trying to conjure forth again this right accent and native
idiom of the heart.[2] If Shakespeare wanted art it was because he was
intent, engaged, and inexhaustible. His work is a vast development,
but no measurable approach to perfection. He changed in style and
metre as an organism responds to its environment, not as a result of
criticism. His virtues are positive and redundant, not negative and
corrective. His art grew and branched untrained, like a work of
nature: *Lear* or *A. and C.* are less balanced and harmonious than the
Merchant. There is not Racine's fine logical unity, but the more
precious unity of all-pervading life: humour blends with sentiment
and fancy, with pathos, even with the tragic in the same moment. It
is less the art which rejects than that which embraces.

He was too preoccupied with life to study perfection in art. He
wrote easily, impetuously, for money, but also because he liked
writing. But art and life were not one and the same to him: life, not
art, was his refuge and shrine. He might have written more plays at
Stratford, but he preferred to dream and idle. His facility in writing
was his only trait truly appreciated in his day; yet the world has not
echoed Jonson's wish that he had blotted a thousand lines. . . .

If we learn anything new about Shakespeare from this essay it is
because old facts are emphasized rather than new ones discovered.
Rightly or wrongly we have attributed certain characteristics to
Professor Stoll—something practical or positive which helps him to
use his historical knowledge boldly. This positivism, perhaps, is racial:
he is not cumbered by long traditions, but walks easily where others
walk warily. He is not necessarily wrong, but it is the cause of the
emphasis which he lays on certain facts such as the following. He says
that Shakespeare deliberately hid his feelings in the Sonnets, that he
was hardly a character at all, that he was abject and timorous before
his high-born friend, that his reticence extends to his will. . . . But
the latter part of the essay conveys to us an idea of Shakespeare's
greatness and the permanent element in him as do few other modern
criticisms. If we ever doubted Professor Stoll's power to appreciate aesthetically our doubts are silenced once and for all. Having
spent many previous pages in deciding against the romantics what
Shakespeare had not, he concentrated with a freer mind on what he
had—his absence of self-consciousness—his spontaneous perfections
—his art learned like a foreign language in the country itself, which
embraces rather than rejects—his positive virtues—his life-giving
power. . . . But though we end on a triumphant note we must return
to the beginning and survey the field as a whole, and conclude that as

[1] Cf. Jusserand (1904).　　　　　　　　　[2] Cf. J. M. Robertson (1897).

a result of historical criticism the scope of the unconscious mind is reduced—it seems to exist by permission of the conscious.

IX

MR. ALDEN considers Shakespeare a world genius whose values
are absolute and timeless—the most poetic interpreter of human
experience since Sophocles. To Mr. Middleton Murry he is the most
human of our poets but also the strangest. Mr. Robertson says that he
had a grasp of the great themes of life in a poetry with a power rising
to the height of every call. Mr. Bailey calls him in one sense a man
of his own age, in another of no single age, but of all and above
them all. Professor Stoll refuses him the titles of seer, prophet,
philosopher.

Mr. Alden credits him with supreme poetic craftsmanship, but
denies that he was greatly interested in the theory of his art or very
conscientious in its practice, and finds him lacking in taste or conscience
for perfection of form. To Mr. Robertson he is the supreme master
of blank verse and supreme master over his vocabulary. He has
unmatched opulence of rhythmic and electric speech, supreme genius
for poetry in general and blank verse form in particular. He could ride
the whirlwind of measureless passion in the most exquisitely rhythm'd
verse, raising his chosen instrument to a perfection that baffles rivalry.
His was the minimum rather than maximum concern for plot-
reconstruction, though he was an unrivalled master of stage-effects.
But his drama outgoes the critical plane for which structural form is
an end rather than means. Mr. Wells speaks of the fervid flow of
Shakespeare's verse and his full and striking vocabulary, but his go-as-
you-please methods with plot. In the opinion of Mr. Bailey he was
never the most careful of writers. Mr. Noble says that his art was of
the theatre, that his craft was superlative, and his superiority in
dramatic craftsmanship overwhelming. Professor Stoll finds him little
troubled by literary conscience;[1] but his life-giving power lends to each
character an individual voice. His art is positive not negative, that
which embraces rather than rejects.

Of general remarks on Shakespeare's philosophy, religion, and politics
we get the following. From Mr. Alden—that he was Protestant on
the political side, neutral on that of personal religion—an inductive
moralist whose ideas were the natural product of experience; that
the clearest thinkers in his plays reject Destiny, and where he excelled
was in adapting exquisitely the moral judgement to a sympathetic realism;
that his ethical thought is generally and justly viewed as essentially
Christian, and he represented accurately the normal political thought
of his generation; that it is doubtful if he had a system of thought, yet
evil to him is abnormal and the universe on the side of good;[2] that he

---

[1] Cf. Bradley and Brander Matthews.   [2] Cf. Bradley.

lacked a deeply philosophic or spiritually interpretive mind, and was no abstract thinker, yet has thought most inclusively and effectively in terms of concrete human feeling and conduct. From Mr. Middleton Murry, that his intuition into reality was the deepest of all poets. From Mr. Bailey, that no one better understood either man's equality or the equally real inequality of men; that like St. Paul he is content to accept the established framework, and indirectly to support order.

He had, according to Mr. Alden, a supreme power of individualizing character, was chiefly interested in personality, and worked miracles of imaginative sympathy—and his ideal women are clearer than his men. Mr. Robertson says that his prodigious achievement consisted mainly in laying the hands of genius upon other men's work and re-creating their inferior creations of character; that his abnormal faculty of compliance with the conditions of his age may be the coefficient of the strange power to be every one in drama; and that he had far subtler perception of character of all kinds, and far more delicate endowment of feeling than his corivals. To Mr. Bailey his lifelike truth of characters is greater than his skill in linking them into a single dramatic action; and he paints with most affection the moral and emotional beauty of women, and the honesty, justice, and good sense of men.

Mr. Robertson discovers that the one emerging speciality of his character, as distinct from his philosophy and his art, was his gift of compliance with his economic and social conditions. Mr. Noble calls him an actor and practical man of affairs—an actor dramatist writing plays for the entertainment of a theatre audience. To Professor Stoll he was dramatist by nature as well as by profession, and this made him reticent and impersonal. He was less impartial than has been thought.

A remark of Mr. Middleton Murry's stands alone: the nature of Shakespeare's poetry is the nature of poetry. . . . . .

Religion is above earthly life and yet intimately connected with it: and this is the impression of Shakespeare left by the abstracted general praises of these critics. Protestantism, artistry, politics: all these he may have used or neglected, but he expressed his true self through none of them. The point of view of those critics who think that he was careless of plot-building is quite other than their forerunners of the eighteenth century. It is his verse and his characters that outstand, as the means he used to haunt the world with a vision of absolute beauty.

Chapter XL

FRANCE 1904–1924

I. JUSSERAND.   II. JUSSERAND.   III. CHEVRILLON.   IV. SISSON.
V. LOOTEN.   VI. CONCLUSION.

I

J. J. JUSSERAND[1] says that Shakespeare's profession was to write, his business to please the great public. With the glorious, the sentimental, the tragic, the spiritual he had to mix rough popular jokes. He was practical and always treated favourite subjects. His plays reflect his time and public more than himself. He had no concern for literary immortality; he wrote swiftly and easily, in obedience to the inspiration of his incomparable genius, the plays which were to delight the world. Indifference could go no further.

We follow his progress to *John*, where he adds a few marvellous touches, such as John's insinuations to Hubert—but he usually kept close to his model. Then it seemed to him that the same public that rejoiced in horrors might be interested in love matters; so he began his splendid series of romantic dramas. *Verona* was a great advance on *L.L.L.*; it revealed his supreme life-giving power, though as yet incomplete. Thurio, Panthino, Speed are marionettes such as he never ceased to make use of—and they might figure as well in other plays. Launce, however, is a Rabelaisian character of finished vitality and individuality. *M.N.D.* is first of the universally famous plays, and nothing more proves Shakespeare's great and varied genius than that he should have written it at the same time as *Richard III*. Its musical verse alone places him beyond any rival. *R. and J.* first displays his full dramatic genius—the art of linking scene to scene, of creating atmosphere, of preparing effects and surprises by anterior indications, thanks to which we are surprised but not shocked, and moved because we believe. There is a great variety of characters, all alive: but these are only the frame of the picture. Romeo and Juliet form the centre, and they are all love. Shakespeare's other heroines are beautiful and loving and have other virtues: but from Juliet we expect nothing but love—neither intelligence nor wisdom, nor affection for her parents.

The romantic dramas bear signs of hasty composition; they are disconnected, badly put together, improbable, and take up themes that have already served. *M. Ado* has the device of assumed death as in *R. and J.*; and *Twelfth-Night* repeats *Errors*. The comic part of *Twelfth-Night* is coarse and facile, alien from continental taste but evidently suited to English taste. The hero is punished at the outset

[1] *Histoire littéraire du peuple anglais,* 1904.

when he is in the right, and rewarded at the end when he has shown himself libertine and slanderer. In the romantic dramas the woman takes the lead: Rosalind (*A.Y.L.*) makes laws for all. The *Merchant* is the best of these plays, with its mixture of tragic reality and impossible but delicious fantasy. Shylock's first words make him memorable; Antonio is thoughtful and good, with the noble and slightly pale face of an old portrait; the sparkling young lords are always ready for love. The shadowy population is brought back to life; the gentlemen come down from the frescoes where Veronese fixed them. Portia dominates all: suppress Belmont and you make the play impossible. Admit that Belmont is fairyland, and then you can abandon yourself without anxiety. The magic of Belmont saves Antonio from the Jew. As soon as Lorenzo and Jessica arrive in Belmont one forgets to despise them as thieves.

It must be noted, about the Sonnets, that no allusion is made to the friend's high Court functions or military glories. His hopes of immortality are based on his personal beauty: and this weighs against the Pembroke-Southampton theory. Also the publication of the Sonnets roused little curiosity; no collection was more coldly received. Like all Shakespeare's work they are a mixture of marvels and ugliness—pearls and mud—triumphant or despairing love-songs, ideal or bestial—accents of passion so piercing that they seem to come from the heart—details that would have no interest unless they were real; and with all this, conceits, effects of virtuosity, and imitations of others—in fine, a mixture of truth and imagination as with all poets. He is transported by his friend's beauty, and therefore uses no other moral or philosophic argument except Horace's—that time flies. When love can no longer console him he feels the melancholy pessimism of the tired Epicurean. He makes no allusion to Christianity, or chances of future reunion; he has even less hope than a pagan. If his spirit survives it is in his friend's memory; if the friend survives it is in his children and the poet's verse. The idea produces a reaction—that he also can dispose of the supreme good, beauty. It consoles him that he can confer the most splendid and lasting aureole. Neither priests nor philosophers have been able to calm his anxiety; but now the muse intervenes and dictates his finest verse.

For the first eight or ten years of the new century, when his genius was at its height, he wrote tragedy, in the mood of one who is out of love with life. He describes liberty lost—virtue overwhelmed—the good incapable of doing good in a badly organized world. The world is ill made; its glory, beauty, justice are illusions. Hamlet, created to diffuse joy, hurls the innocent into the abyss. Macbeth, though man of action, is a dreamer, highly strung, imaginative, weak-willed. The perverse genius which conducts human affairs in Shakespeare's world at this period gives Macbeth for purposes of crime what he refused to

Hamlet for justice—a will outside himself. Desdemona, model of
feminine grace and virtue, even among Shakespeare's women, perishes
in an inevitable catastrophe. Of what use is life? Whence come we,
and whither are we bound? What signify the great actions of the
illustrious, or the noble virtues of saints? What purpose serve the
feelings of the highest and purest among us ? The heroes of this period
meditate on these problems in verse of imperishable beauty, but all
reach the same desperate conclusion. Shakespeare's contrasts are too
violent, his catastrophes too terrible, and his effort to pile up evil is
apparent. *Lear* is overdone, despite its lyric grandeur, and the storm
of passion mingling with that of the elements. The monstrous contrasts of *Timon* injure truth: in the beginning a machine to produce
presents, in the end a machine to produce insults. We regret that such
a person as Apemantus should be right, because he disgusts us with
reason. The romantic dramas of the time also leave a painful impression. The Greeks of *T. and C.* are a band of stupid monsters. The
bitter humour of *M. for M.*, the horror and lowness of the scenes, the
number of distorted characters petrify rather than amuse. We care
for no one, not even Isabella.

The Roman plays are masterpieces, for although without exact
local colour, they have intense human truth, and by presenting living
human beings they come nearer to antiquity than the works of many
learned historians. Brutus (*J.C.*) has the meditative habit of Shakespeare's heroes of the period. Cassius, who sees only one side, and who
is therefore positive, throws him into relief. Like Macbeth he has an
external will to supplement his own. Shakespeare's genius has rarely
served him better; he distributes life in floods; his people are distinct,
outstanding, with clear profile, playing their parts in the full light.
As in *Coriolanus*, one of the most carefully drawn characters is the
crowd.[1] Shakespeare belonged to his own times, not to ours, and he did
not feel tenderly towards the people. He took pleasure in depicting its
ignorance and credulity, sudden fleeting bursts of rage, its contradictions
and exaggerations. His intuition discovers traits then unknown that
recent research has brought to light. Only Coriolanus and the people
import: he has never taken greater pains to describe the multitude or
leave his opinion of it on record. He follows Plutarch closely, but
darkens the picture. With psychological divination he makes the mob
commit crimes and inconsequencies, weep over them and react from
them in a manner of which he had no experience, because they only
occurred two hundred years later. All the elements are here whence
emerged the future Terrors. Coriolanus is too proud even to endure
praise. No single light touch relieves this dark picture of vanity and
popular fury. This unrelenting severity shows partisan feeling. *A. and
C.* resumes the study of diseased wills dear to Shakespeare. Antony

[1] Cf. Stapfer.

completes the series of Hamlet, Macbeth, Lear, Brutus. He is marvellously endowed by nature, but is sensual, and cannot resist pleasure's attraction. A slow and continual degradation of body, nerves, and will takes place in him; but his intellect remains clear, like Hamlet's. Cleopatra is the courtesan who knows her trade and no other; the language she speaks has neither heart, soul, intelligence, nor poetry, but simply flesh. It is also a sombre play, where the base instincts win, and the catastrophe celebrates the downfall of Roman courage.

In the romances the poet's bitterness and pessimism have disappeared. The violent agonies and terrors of the coming night are softened, and the sun sets radiant in a calm autumn evening. They end with injuries forgotten and general forgiveness. Miranda's optimism spreads its calm light even to the traitors. The problem of hereafter remains obscure, but is not contemplated with terror. In the *W. Tale* he recalls far-off childhood, and enjoys the thought of the happiness of those whose turn it is to be young.

Shakespeare's abundance and complexity were opposed to classic restraint and simplicity. His characters are as varied as in real life, even more so, as they include fairies. The audience visited the theatre after eating and drinking, and it would have been hard to fix their attention on fine shades. Strong stimulants were needed to rouse them from their torpor [1]—comic interludes, processions to please the eye. Scenes among the great are duplicated by scenes with servants: the latter explain their masters. Above all he uses contrast: he places Imogen and Miranda beside Cloten and Caliban—and beside Helena, a Bertram that Boccaccio would not recognize. The blow that fells Imogen has no object but to make her lot more pathetic. Between these extremes a space is reserved for true nature and ordinary life, for exact observation and finer shades. When he exaggerates, he does violence to his own true vision to please contemporaries. One cannot understand him apart from his century: the universal love of violent contrasts was a pre-Renaissance characteristic come down from the Mysteries, and was to appear again in England in novels of the type of the *Old Curiosity Shop*. This was against classical tradition, where the speech of secondary characters is exalted to the dignity of their masters.

Shakespeare made no attempt to reform the public, but rather confirmed the public in its taste. His ideal was simply to live at Stratford as a rich bourgeois. His natural leanings were those of the many; when they diverged he sacrificed them. A trifle betrays the sacrifice—an ironic touch lost in the dialogue—that lets an attentive reader see the depth of his thought, and discovers an ideal of art that differs from his practice. Like the spectators he was indifferent to dates or geography; and his rapid composition led him into incoherences,

---

[1] Cf. La Place, Voltaire, Chasles, Lamartine.

e.g. Autolycus changes dress with Florizel, and is clothed as a courtier —but Florizel was dressed as a shepherd. A single scene of *John* contains events of 1201, 1204, and 1212. He was indifferent to local colour: his Romans, Greeks, Trojans play cards, &c. In his day great public events took place so suddenly and strangely that the theatre might well take risks. Oxfords and Knyvets fought like Montagues and Capulets; Macbeth, like Bothwell, cried out on treachery before the body of his own victim; and also, as Bothwell, Claudius married the widow of the first Hamlet, by him slain.[1] Hermione suddenly accused would not startle Londoners who had seen Anne Boleyn's execution. Like many of Shakespeare's heroines, Mary Stuart had disguised herself as a page. After the rebellion of Essex Elizabeth was nervous, and kept a sword which she passed through the tapestry. The only rule was to please.

He could condense his knowledge of human agonies and tendernesses into a form so perfect as to pierce the crowd's thick cloak of vulgarity and touch its heart, as lightning parts the clouds; but his magnificent passages are not always well placed. The Queen in *Cymbeline* praises admirably her country, yet she is a traitress. When Hotspur describes the Severn it is the poet of *Venus* who speaks. The public delighted in word play; and Shakespeare puts puns even into the mouths of the dying. It was a fault of the age; even Elizabeth used conceits in her messages to Parliament. The crowd was his only master; to the people he addressed his explanations, warnings, recapitulations, interpretations. His complex characters have their quality written on them; they point themselves out as traitors, e.g. Richard III, Iago, Edmund, Lady Macbeth.[2] His public was not stupid but ignorant, and would take no trouble. One of the qualities which he received from nature dominates all the others, and explains why, in spite of all changes of time and fashions of art, and in spite of great faults—for he did nothing by halves —his fame continues to increase throughout the world: and that is his life-giving power.[3] The character springs from his hands—lives, moves, and speaks. In the plays we see every specimen of the human race, equally alive: Hotspur is all action, Hamlet all dream. A nurse, a porter, a boatman may cross the stage, with all their separate interests apart from the hero, and entertain us with their affairs which are remote from the drama. We risk becoming absorbed in the individual and losing the thread of the play. Shylock, intensely Jewish, and eloquent defender of his faith, reverts to a Christian marionette. We hesitate whether to side with Richard II or Henry IV. It is hard to write a play clearly about characters of mixed good and evil, troubled by contrary passions: here classic art which chooses and simplifies had the advantage.

Special pleaders have credited Shakespeare with ideas, forgetting

[1] Cf. Winstanley, Chevrillon.   [2] Cf. Stoll (1912).   [3] Cf. Stoll (1923).

opposite instances. His personal ideas do appear on the rarest occasions:
as when a person stands outside his subject and part and gives forth
opinions which have nothing to do with the play—or where an opinion
is repeated in many works so frequently that it shows a mind made up
or a fixed idea. Among these are Hamlet's complaint of the boy actors
—praise of England—praise of music—satire of the crowd. Usually
he is a true creator, and with life gives independence to his people.
In the masterpieces his dramatic power is incomparable.

He took everything from his models, including impossibilities—
showing extraordinary respect for facts and following his model
literally. He retains the coarse patriotism of *John*, and even the hero's
sudden change of character in the middle of the play. His habit is to
darken bad characters, make good ones perfect, and great ones colossal.
Coriolanus, rude in Plutarch, becomes brutal in Shakespeare; Lear is
exaggerated from the old play. If his material is good, the result is a
masterpiece; if it presents improbabilities and contradictions it appears
defective in Shakespeare. But his other qualities eclipse it—his lyric
glow and life-giving power.

Hamlet is worked in light and shade; intense realism is allied to
intangible dream; and the result most strange and moving. The key
to Hamlet's character is his inability to do consciously a violent act.
Disturbed by the tempest, the mud that lies at the bottom of every
human soul rises to the surface. *Othello* is the most perfect play as a
whole; in the others the author's genius comes and goes. Incoherences
and anachronisms are reduced to a minimum, and there are no contradictions in the characters or improbable events. The first scene explains
all; we are given the elements of the drama, and we know the characters.
Othello's gentleness makes his subsequent fury more striking. The
passion of a beautiful young Venetian for an African may seem strange,
but when she opens her lips we understand her love. The souls of
both are absolutely open and simple. There is no suspicion of the
gathering storm, but every scene contains in the germ the future
development, so that the end is inevitable. Every time the Moor cries
out the bonds are tightened; his fury dims his clear sight; the dose of
poison can be doubled, and the more reckless proofs advanced. The
plot intensifies because the chief actors are warned of their danger, and
yet rush in, propelled by invincible fate.

In life and in Shakespeare comic and tragic are never far apart,
Shakespeare hates definite classifications, and if slightly abstract characters intrude into his works they are exceptions. The first scene of the
Tempest is both comedy and tragedy, and each is as true as the other.
As the tempest rises the characters stand out more clearly: so near is
danger that the equality of after-death begins. The great ones remain
ceremonious to the end, so deeply has their profession eaten into their
nature. Shakespeare gives us individuals with their large and small

qualities, their contradictions, their families and servants and neighbours
—all the agitation of the human ant-heap. No one is a type of wisdom;
but rays of wisdom remain on every bush for us to gather. Even the
plays belong to no species; many may be either tragedies or comedies.
The gayest or most grotesque may be involved in the fearfulest catastrophe. Wit combats were popular; and he began early in *L.L.L.*
Beatrice discharges witticisms and cares little who receives them; in
the first scene she confides to a messenger her feelings for Benedict.
Mingled with these are numberless fine observations—sudden flashes
that reveal by a word the depths of human nature—its vices or greatness:
the unexpected word that either a hero might speak or a footman as
he rearranges the chairs.

The same liberty obtains in Shakespeare's style—the greatest height
and lowest deep. Each character uses that which fits his rank, emphasized rather than weakened by contrast. Mixture and contrast is one
of Shakespeare's poetic rules. To Juliet's soft words succeeds the
Nurse's coarse gossip; to Prospero's weighty sentences, Caliban's oaths.
At every moment the poet helps the dramatist; the incomparable
artist seizes the intangible. He arrests and fixes those intoxicating
moments of joy or agony, as a painter fixes on his canvas a ray of light
that has shone and disappeared. We know not if he excels most in
high or low style; he is everywhere at his ease. Is Falstaff best drawn,
or Queen Mab? His skill lies in placing words, not in making use of
curious expressions; he finds the simplest words for the most striking
ideas. The commonest object suggests infinite likenesses: he sees
naturally in pictures. Exaggeration at times leads to bad taste: he
speaks of sighs and tears under the figure of storms and oceans. . . .
In verse he practised enjambment and avoided the tic-tac of French
tragedy. The cadence does result from the accents, but never distracts
the attention from the thought. His vast fame is a unique literary
phenomenon. . . .

This criticism may be described as intense admiration buttressed by
common sense; the author appreciates to the full but is not overwhelmed
by Shakespeare's genius. In such hands we feel that Shakespeare's
true fame has not suffered from the decline of the ages of faith; but he
is admired for his good things only, and his faults are not explained
away. The common sense is distinctively Latin, the result of clear
vision maintained through long culture; it has not the conscious air of
sudden awakening to facts that we detect in some modern English, and
still more, American, treatises. He does not obtrude the classics, but
we feel his classical knowledge in the background—like a curb that
hangs loose but may be tightened at any moment. He tells us, as do
others, that Shakespeare wrote to please an ignorant public, and therefore indulged in puns and quibbles, and wit combats, and violent
contrasts, and made his villains proclaim their own villainy. He admits

the *Merchant* to be impossible—and yet it is delicious; the Sonnets are mixed truth and imagination; Macbeth is both man of action and dreamer; Timon is a machine to produce first presents and then insults; the living human beings of the Roman plays serve a better purpose than antiquarian knowledge; Cleopatra knows her courtesan's trade and nothing else; the plays belong to no species, but many might be either tragedy or comedy. A critic whose judgements are so firmly based is more likely to persuade us to take seriously his explanations of higher moral, psychological, aesthetic, or intellectual problems. Among these is his opinion that the Sonnets contain no moral or philosophic argument except that of Horace that time flies. Or he explains Cassius simply as one-sided; and finds *A. and C.* sombre because the baser instincts win; while Shylock in the end reverts to a Christian marionette. It belongs to Shakespeare's habit of violent contrasts that he darkens bad characters and makes the good perfect. The last sentence is a splendid eulogy; and we feel that here is a critic who knows history and life and many literatures, and who admires Shakespeare with discrimination for the greatest thing in him—his inspired poetry. The atmosphere is quite modern, the thin veil of time that still existed between such critics as Montégut and Stapfer and ourselves has lifted. We feel that these critics often use Shakespeare to discourse on their favourite themes; but Jusserand, like a true contemporary, sees his subject only, attempts to pierce to its heart, and has no time for side issues. In his insistence, above all, on Shakespeare's life-giving power he reminds us of so different a critic as Professor Stoll. And yet, when we re-read his criticism on the Sonnets, and on *Lear*, and his remark that the plays belong to no species, we are forced to remember that he is a countryman of Voltaire.

II

IN delivering the first Annual Shakespeare Lecture,[1] Jusserand again emphasizes Shakespeare's anxiety to please the public. The crowd—boisterous, warm-hearted, full-blooded, patriotic, loving extremes, ignorant—made or marred the fortune of a play—and therefore its part, as contributor, cannot be over-estimated.[2] But he also delighted to exercise a certain function of his brain, and this saved him in spite of himself. Hence the strange nature of his work that touches all extremes—flashes of divine light, and concessions to popular taste. Hence his anachronisms and indifference to real facts. He offers the groundlings a reign of King John without Magna Carta, and a Duke of Austria who died before the play begins. The plays had two authors —Shakespeare and the motley crew at the Globe.

---

[1] *What to expect of Sh.*, 1911. (Pub. for Brit. Acad. by Henry Frowde).
[2] Cf. Sisson.

It is wrong to call him omniscient, for he does not answer several of the gravest questions. But he places the problem before us with such force that we consider it seriously. He takes no sides in religion, but is tolerant; and though he frequently states the problem of death and hereafter, he has no answer. In their calmest moods his characters hope for sleep. As patriot he was justly proud of his country's history; but he conceded to an unreasoning crowd that their enemies were cowards and scoundrels. He wrote forcibly and pregnantly of social problems, but only as a man of his age. Towards the masses—their credulity, fickleness, cruelty, sudden changes—he appears as a clear-eyed, unfriendly observer. Few writers, who deal directly with human passions, have more suppressed their personality. In an age of disputes his disposition was to keep aloof. We gather from repetitions that he adored music, loved his country, mistrusted the mob, knew something of a classical play, objected to child-actors. The change in the tone of his plays follows the general curve of human life. His characters are alive and independent, never his own spokesmen, like Hugo's. Only the Sonnets reveal his personality; and it sufficed him to express his sentiments; he never sought to publish them.

He was unhampered by traditions, rules, religious systems: he neglected dramatic rules because they were 'caviare to the general', and yet he is nearer to Aristotle than many of the latter's learned followers. Aristotle summed up the teachings of good sense and adapted them to Greek manners. Shakespeare followed the teachings of his own sound nature and adapted them to English wants. Aristotle recognized that the rational end of dramatic poetry is to give pleasure, not to moralize. Shakespeare did not seek to instruct, but the events of his plays, as in real life, are so full of meaning that the moral is obvious, e.g. Macbeth, Coriolanus, Antony, Falstaff, Othello, Desdemona, Hamlet deserve pity as much as Oedipus. Fate has allotted them tasks beyond them, or offered temptations to which less generous natures would not have yielded. Shakespeare expands our hearts and makes us feel for others. His supreme power is to bestow life and draw characters, whose fate touches us, because we seem to know them.

The uses of art have been questioned; and, taking into account various definitions of art, and Goethe's saying that all that is great contributes to our education, we conclude that one of Shakespeare's practical uses is to set free the dormant springs of disinterested emotion. He appeals to artists by taking his stand on realities and looking straight at things. In Claude Lorraine's pictures we have nature plus Claude Lorraine: in Shakespeare's plays we have nature plus Shakespeare plus his public. Discard the share of the public, and we find that he adds to nature not his own personality, but an artistic selection from real life of what nature makes his characters distinct. In realizing the share of the public we shall understand better the contribution of his higher nature. He withdraws us from our small selves and absorbs us not superficially but intensely in the lives of others. . . .

Seven years have brought little change to Jusserand's views, except perhaps clearer sight of the dualistic nature of Shakespeare. The nineteenth-century monistic conception of Shakespeare as omniscient philosopher teaching by examples has definitely yielded to Shakespeare on one side popular entertainer, on the other divine poet. His poetry is viewed rather as a sudden escape or safety-valve than a professional activity. The remarks on dramatic rules, on the uses of art, on Shakespeare's indirect moral power to create impersonal sympathy, are well worth pondering. They advance that reconciliation of all beautiful things which it is the glory of the modern disinterested critic to seek, against all followers of the classic, neo-classic, or *a priori* method.

III

M. ANDRÉ CHEVRILLON [1] says that we know hardly anything of Shakespeare, for his person has disappeared in his work; and this accounts for much of the national worship. A hero is better deified when nothing remains of his human personality; and England sees in him the ancient spirit of the English soil. Severed from its background and atmosphere his work might not be national.

At first he may appear remote from modern England and the national type. The fundamental trait of this type, as Taine said, is force of soul resting on habits and beliefs that resist external influence, and find joy in effort—effort turned inwards to shape oneself according to an ideal, and directed to subdue the outer world. The aim of English education is to fortify the will—to achieve masculine virtues. Kipling's Indian officers and Civil Servants are untouched by the influences of the Far East. This distinct type has built up the moral vigour and greatness of the Empire. Founded on the Decalogue and the moral law, its Puritan discipline taught that the soul stood alone—alone responsible for its actions. It was hostile to the artistic nature—never betraying passion and emotion, and despising sensibility, brooding, and melancholy. It also contrasts with the Renaissance type when souls were free.

There is poetry of a practical kind—will and conscience. Tennyson sang the idea of order, and Milton preserved the secret enthusiasm of a soul self-contained, upheld by a single sublime emotion, strong by its limitations. Shakespeare is the opposite, not will but imagination, a multiple and multiform genius. He is spontaneous, intuitive, his verse is easy-flowing. We see nature without law, and characters moved by primitive passions, of a Renaissance, pre-Puritan type. We also see the secondary Italian influences—the outcome of education and fashion:

[1] *Sh. and the English Soul*, 1916. (*Three Studies in Eng. Lit.*, trans. Florence Simmonds. Heinemann, 1923.)

the characters express their emotions as if delighting in them. Hamlet has the hauteur, irony, and courtesy of a prince of the period. Behind these masks we guess at an Essex, a Southampton, a Pembroke, a Rutland.[1] Shakespeare belonged to that high, light, and unstable portion of English society, touched by the Renaissance, not to the denser layer in which the ferment of the Reformation worked. The idea of free beauty governed one world, duty and law the other. Shakespeare and Milton were the resulting types.

The Celtic race is said to have given England most of its artists and poets. The Celts are peoples living apart, driven to extreme points of islands and peninsulas—in Ireland, Cornwall, Brittany—remote from the rest of the world and subjected to the influences of nature. Moist winds from the Atlantic, pale mists where the world disappears like a ghost, the onslaught of storms: all these and more act upon the soul, reduce its vital energy, and cause alternate states of passion and dream, enthusiasm and depression. Man becomes unstable, and tends even to enjoy his melancholy. He lives in a dream tinged with a certain madness, divorced from earth's realities. Contrast Malory, Spenser, *M.N.D.*, *A.Y.L.*, *Eve of St. Agnes*, *Alastor*, *Ancient Mariner*, *Lady of Shalott*, *Richard Feverel*, *Tess*, *Peter Pan* with the Dutch character of the works of Defoe, Hogarth, Fielding. Or note those writers in whom imagination is supreme but violent, charged with stormy energy, such as Byron, Carlyle, the Brontës. English literature abounds in tender dream-stories, e.g. *Alice in Wonderland*. The poet chooses the improbable, and defies common sense, experience, and reason; and here Shakespearian fantasy differs from Germanic fables, where mystery is profound but undisturbed by sudden flights, and wonder passive and almost religious.

Shakespeare is, above all, Celtic, and probably not strong-willed; his flexible sensibility would be inconsistent with firm moral structure. Love seemed to him a malady, or intoxication impossible to resist. Under the spells of Mary Fitton he was Antony in the hands of Cleopatra. Antony, Romeo, Jaques, Posthumus, Macbeth, Hamlet are not drawn from real life, but from his own self; they embody the same soul in its changing moods at different stages in its disorder: a soul powerless for action, lacking will and vigour, possessed by dreams.[2]

Yet he is intensely English, with the passionate imagination that informs all English poetry. The contrast between Renaissance England and that of to-day is that between liberty and law: but the structure of the mind does not change. Its thought is made up of direct images with their appeal to emotion, or abstract representations. In English literature concrete imagination predominates, also sentiment over logical thought, spiritual over sensual. To the lyric element is due the supremacy of English poetry at all periods—the soaring flights

[1] Cf. Winstanley, Jusserand.   [2] Cf. Frank Harris.

and emotional power as well of the nineteenth-century novel as the sixteenth-century drama. French literature, formerly a logical expression of general ideas, has become a colourful interpretation of sensation, in both cases treating psychological events that do not permanently belong to our deeper self. In English literature the outer world imports less than the invisible life of the characters. Shakespeare's greatest dramas reveal that character is fate, and all destiny turns on the discord or harmony between two principles—the soul's innate tendency, and the pressure it endures from without. The explanation is the intense spiritual activity of England—where, thanks to the disguises of education and opinion, the visible social man differs from the real inner man. Manners may suppress the latter because it is felt to be a danger. Capacities for dream, sentiment, passion may bring about disorder. Thus the Englishman oscillates between creature of a flock and eccentric individualist. The sects which began to multiply in the sixteenth century have continued to produce mystic and religious individualists. Lady Macbeth's 'Consider it not so deeply!' shows the element of disease. Emotion works within and begets dreams and ideas, rather than spends itself outwardly in sudden gestures, as with the man of the south. The social and educational defences fall away, and the soul is banished to a world of solitude and terror. Only the Slavs, beside the English, have this visionary imagination. Most spiritualistic and telepathic phenomena come from England, and many English manors and woodlands are still haunted by the ghosts of the Shakespearian stage. Mystery and presentiment of the supernatural persistently recurs in English literature. The essence of Shakespeare is the lyric gift, haunting sense of moral realities, of a mysterious other world, concrete imagination, visionary dream, psychological insight, deep and dramatic intuitions of the dangerous energies latent in the human soul under the calm surface of reason and civilization.

Tragedy has greater power to stir our terror and pity the more deeply we see it working in the soul. Suffering and emotion make for disorder and disease, and attack reason and will. To reach its climax tragedy should overthrow the soul. Mark the birth of madness in Lear, the strange and almost solemn terror of the man who dimly feels it rising within him. After frenzy is the calm of exhaustion and ruin of the will, while the soul has become a passive, sentient thing. Hamlet is still more purely psychological—a drama of inaction, of excess of thought and imagination. The ghost had shaken to its foundation the noble meditative spirit, lonely from the first. In Lear and Hamlet the situation of the secondary characters (Gloster and Laertes) is the same, but their drama is different because the soul structure is different. Macbeth, still more a prey to his fancies, is at once swept away by the suggestions of the witches. Subjected to a stronger will he is urged to a deed beyond the power of his nerves and imagination.

But we feel that an unspeakable and solemn reality is ever present —the fateful Power that governs all tragedy. Shakespeare's dream is religious because connected with yearning for the infinite—for justice after the injustice of earth—and preoccupied with the meaning of life and death. It is to the honour of the English people that they are most concerned with the mystery of things. . . .

This is the kind of criticism that tempts us to ask whether or not it is true—and the reason is that it has a scientific touch. The writer is considering phenomena from the outside rather than identifying himself with their spirit and uttering his own emotion—as Matthew Arnold did when he spoke of Celtic natural magic, and its piercing note of regret and passion. At its worst this half-scientific criticism gives us such a contrast as Macbeth's inward brooding with the external gestures of a southerner—or comparisons with or illustrations from not only Hardy or Meredith—which would be passable—but Barrie, Kipling, and Arnold Bennett. Misery acquaints a man with strange bedfellows, but not tragedy. He also creates an independent geographical and psychological interest in the Celts that he does not entirely fuse with the Shakespearian interest. On the other hand, by consistently working out his theory, M. Chevrillon attains a cumulative force that impresses: though we dare not say that the impression will be lasting, or that he will permanently transfigure Shakespeare in our eyes. But he succeeds in making Shakespeare's imagination a shade more characteristic: and his best example is the contrast between the leading and secondary characters of *Hamlet* and *Lear*. Carlyle taught us the strangeness of man alone in the universe: and to this echo M. Chevrillon has added another, if fainter. Secondly, he brings home to us the poetry existing in the depth of the English soul—the race that has produced the most imaginative poetry in the world—and we recall a confirming passage by Dean Inge: 'The quintessential Englishman is not the hero of Smiles's *Self-help*; he is Raleigh, Drake, Shakespeare, Milton, Johnson, or Wordsworth, with a pleasant spice of Dickens'.[1]

IV

DR. CHARLES J. SISSON[2] notes the continuity of theatrical history. The style of the theatre at the beginning of Shakespeare's era had survived from the Miracles and Moralities. The Renaissance was no sudden deluge; it modified rather than replaced. Feudal organization became national unity, social solidarity, and limited monarchy. Those who direct the popular soul can create nothing, for the more their soul approaches the people's, the more widespread

[1] *Outspoken Essays* (1919), p. 104.
[2] *Le goût public et le Théâtre Élisabéthain jusqu'à la mort de Sh.*, 1922. Dijon: Imprimerie Darantière).

are their ideas; and the more the universal spirit accords with that of
the highest, the greater and more beautiful does literature become.
Curiosity and patriotism were the two chief sentiments to which
literature then responded. The first was something new: the Renaissance impatiently waited for events, while the Middle Ages always
feared that something might happen. The second had developed
beyond anything that the Middle Ages could imagine. The Renaissance freed men, and restored to them the world as an arena for
experience. Instead of patience and obedience, the new virtue is to
be a man.

The classic theatre predominated at the universities, and was a
contrast to the popular; but Elizabeth and her Court cared not only
for classic pieces, but for realistic farce, tragedy, history, and romance.
Curiosity exceeded classicism; the masses and the cultivated world
acquired the same point of view; the Elizabethan theatre became
great enough to reflect the whole national spirit.[1]

To the Globe audience for which Shakespeare wrote, dramatic
illusion was absolute: what passed before them seemed real. Their
imagination was naïve and powerful like a child's; they doubted
nothing and were untouched by abstract irony and satire.[2] They did not
distinguish between real and pretended life—as some persons mingle
history and legend. This confusion of values explains why the people
discovered relations between plays and contemporary life, and why
the most improbable romance did not exclude realism.

From the beginning classic influences set in motion currents
opposed to native currents. Only with pain the latter assimilated
what was best from ancient literatures. Classical ideas made themselves
felt throughout the world of culture. Translations supplied models;
contemporary works were judged by classic standards; and writers
imitated the classics. But the immense national vigour triumphed;
for, in the heightened life of England, the foreign Renaissance influences, like rushing torrents, were lost in the ancient rivers—in the
grand tradition of song, drama, thought, story. The indigenous spirit
triumphed, but Elizabethan literature owes enormously to classic and
foreign literatures. She owes to them the stimulus from new elements
—but she absorbed these, continued on her own way, and fulfilled her
national destiny. Chapman's *Homer* has many merits, but it is not
Greek—and so with Florio's *Montaigne*. Spenser chants classic strains,
but the Thames flows to his music. It is remarkable that the first
playwrights were university men, who adopted the popular drama as
they found it—Lodge, Marlowe, Greene, Nash. Only Ben Jonson
and Chapman opposed public taste by their classicism and critical
spirit. The critical and satiric spirit implies detachment from life and
sense of superiority; and it is no accident that nothing in Elizabethan

[1] Cf. Rümelin and Brandes. [2] Cf. Corbin, Bridges, Jusserand (1911).

literature is more unreal and artificial than the moral satires. Except *Every Man in his Humour*, which has dramatic merits, the comedy of humours failed because theory predominated. Ben Jonson was against the spirit of the age, and wished to give drama a new direction. He rejected the romantic, and opposed to it not popular classicism, but classic methods of construction such as unities. Shakespeare gave the people what they wanted and accepted popular conditions, while reserving his power to stamp the spectacle with literary grandeur.

The staging of a play affects its style and construction: the less ornament the grander poetry. Yet there is no doubt that Shakespeare, his predecessors, and contemporaries were indifferent to external ornament. The Elizabethan public was equally indifferent, and cared only for the spectacle. Scenery was symbolic and could represent several places at the same time. This favoured lack of sequence, and episodic construction, because there was no difficulty in frequent changes of place. An uncritical audience wishes its enormous curiosity satisfied by a story or spectacle—as with the modern cinema. The object of both is to draw the crowd, and their means is to tell a story by action and dialogue. The object of the Elizabethan theatre is therefore epic; and like an epic poem it consists of episodes, and it narrates history, as did the Miracles. For this reason it neglected the unities, and because its predominating object was to amuse. The power and *naïveté* of the spectators' imagination, and the elementary setting, hindered the development of a true dramatic art. The popularity of the ancient madmen, clowns, Vices made a comic interest essential, even in tragedy. Ben Jonson himself, with his delicate literary conscience, yields to this demand in his classical tragedies. The noise of an open-air theatre necessitated a loud enunciation to make verse and rhythm easier heard: thus Marlowe favoured a noisy declamation. To favour dramatic illusion, poetry must be descriptive, e.g. Elsinore. *Faust* and *Hamlet* were the two most popular and characteristic plays of the time: and they contain the highest thought and poetry. The truth is that the public taste and theatrical limitations encouraged the finest poetical genius of certain dramatic authors. Anachronisms affected not the Elizabethans: the psychological truth of Shakespeare's characters has nothing about it ethnographical or geographical. We see revealed the universal soul of man; and it is greatly owing to popular demand that Shakespeare is the mirror of a whole civilization, of the soul, of the history and manners of his nation. The Elizabethan theatre was truly national because the people were patriotic, and all classes united. But the popular poetical taste lacked discernment; the people would applaud emphasis as if it were true poetry. By degrees true poetry was to prevail; and then fine language was not enough, but the dialogue must express character, and poetry become dramatic. On these two points we must note the failure of the public taste, and distinguish what the art of the theatre owes to Shakespeare's genius. There is great difference between his earlier and later works. The Launce and Speed scenes in *Verona* are hardly connected with the chief theme. In the *Merchant* the connexion is still imperfect; in *M. Ado* the stories are the effectual complement of each other. Later, while dealing with varied and complex interests, he brings all back to a fundamental unity of action. He also simplifies and concentrates the action of a play by reducing the changes of scene. In *Othello*, which shows above all his high artistic conscience, he has most completely triumphed over the tendencies of his age, while exhausting the resources of the Elizabethan theatre.

The comic element was important and of great antiquity. The devils supplied this element in the Miracles, and they were succeeded by the Vice of the Interludes. The Vice became the professional amuser, but the chief part in the Interludes was played by the madman; and his function was purely comic. The wave of symbolism in time moralized the theatre, and even its representations of madness. The madman came to represent a moral defect, a *vice* which he must correct. The Vice then became once more the chief amuser, that is the madman—on one side he is linked with realistic humour—on the other, he is impersonal and abstract. The Elizabethan clown is detached from life and emotions—that is from reality; and pretended madness is a symbol of this detachment. Shakespeare, in later works, fixed and separated the realistic and abstract tendencies: we see Toby and Malvolio beside Feste. He delighted in humour and humorous characters; but here as elsewhere he showed the artist's concern for unity. In *Hamlet* he blames extraneous jokes; and he requires comic episodes to be linked to the main theme. Usually he grasps the subject boldly by making the clown help the main action through marvellous interpretations of character: the grave-digger scene is indispensable. If the audience wishes to see madness of a grotesque kind, he shows them Hamlet, Ophelia, Lear. At the most tragic moment of *M. Ado* we remember that Dogberry holds the criminals. The clown becomes the *deus ex machina*, the master-key of the denouement: a truly ironic commentary on the uncertainties of fortune. Touchstone is a musical, if disillusioned, critic of life; but he is man also, whom Rosalind calls faithful and affectionate—and by virtue of this he is part of the action. Shakespeare did not succeed in reforming the theatre, or suppressing entirely in his own pieces what was simply grotesque; but we see his object. As he progressed he linked the comic more straitly to the main subject, and caused it to strengthen, not hinder, the romantic or tragic. It is the fundamental tendency of his genius—from the Nurse (*R. and J.*) to the Porter and Witches (*Macbeth*) or the Fool (*Lear*); from Sly to Malvolio, and Falstaff to the culmination in Autolycus and Caliban. His works afford us examples of defects caused by popular influence on this special subject, and help us to study his artistic evolution. Ben Jonson, instead of developing comedy out of drama, adopted the contrary method of developing drama out of comedy. The basis of his play would be the characteristic humour; but logic carried him too far from the public taste and the theatre's true functions. Yet sometimes Shakespeare's comic interest overshadows the other: *Henry IV, M. Ado, Twelfth-Night*. We see characters sacrificed to intrigue in *M. Ado*: Claudio is detestable, yet he is the hero. On the other hand, he develops Benedict and Beatrice with love; or rather, like Falstaff, they gain independent life from his Promethean genius. It is thus with the tragic heroes, where we see fate and character united and lost in each other. Add this to *M. Ado* and it becomes *Othello*; but only in tragedy Shakespeare solves the dilemma. In comedy and even history the taste of the audience for romantic chances has affected the plays in their unities.

Elizabethan tragedy originated in cultivated, not popular, influences; but in comedy the popular taste prevailed. Marlowe united literary and public taste, and developed tragedy on popular lines. Shakespeare followed him, and yielded to none in the sensational and horrible; but his tragedies are the best examples of care for dramatic architecture. He assimilated the comic element to the play's general character and tragic nature. The Nurse in *R. and J.*, the people in *J.C.*, have a dramatic function; the soldiers in *Henry V* reflect the loyal impulse and English courage that inspire the play: and yet these scenes are intermediary. But in *Hamlet* and *Lear* we see tragedy united with comedy that has some importance. In *A. and C.* the clown becomes the instrument of destiny or messenger of death. Though his words are ridiculous, he is serious, and when he departs there is ominous silence. The Fool in *Lear* is part of the tempest which reflects the psychological tempest. If these examples suffice not to show the union of tragic and grotesque, we can point out the grotesque in heroic characters —Hamlet, Timon, Ophelia, Lear. Shakespeare's tragedies were no longer romantic and based on chances; he followed Marlowe, who in *Faustus* used a popular tale about sorcery to express the intellectual problems of the age. But Shakespeare transformed this philosophic lyricism into dramatic philosophy. Not only do his characters utter great thoughts that are dramatically appropriate—but the basis of the play is a dominating thought. *Hamlet* is concerned with moral problems, *Macbeth* with remorse and inevitable punishment, *Othello* with love and jealousy. All reflect the philosophy of Sonnet 116: love unshaken in tempests, courage whereby man triumphs over fate. Shakespeare in tragedy works towards unity of action and tone, and substitutes an intellectual for an epic basis. *R. and J.* is in epic style, *Hamlet* in tragic. Popular taste demanded realism, yet the people applauded *Hamlet* which united its favourite spectacle with splendid artistry. They condemned Ben Jonson who deprived tragedy of romance and realism and gave it abstractions. They demanded that art and philosophy should find expression in life. Shakespeare's tragedies were not less popular and sensational: *Hamlet* abounds in murder and revenge, Othello stifles Desdemona, Gloster's eyes are torn out. At least these are naïve horrors; and we cannot remove them from Shakespeare's plays without destroying their fundamental character and dramatic truth. Here lies the distinction between Shakespeare, Marlowe, Webster, Middleton, and those who cannot make such events spring from the character and soul of their persons.

The theatre was used for political and religious controversies, and kings saw its possible disadvantages. It therefore had to become epic, patriotic, and monarchical; in 1580 it added its voice to the national choir against Catholicism and Spain. It sounded the clarion of England's glories by presenting its past and making it live. History appealed to the curiosity of the people and their naïve imagination, as well as to their patriotism and love of realism. There were no abstract politics; the interest was epic, and confined to things, persons, events. The theatre was orthodox and loyalist, and allowed nothing seditious or critical of the foundation of the State.[1] Its conception of English society shows the importance of the middle classes and worth of the individual. Although kings are sacred they reign by the consent of their 'loving subjects'. In truth the people are king in old England; love of liberty and monarchy combine in practical understanding. In *Henry V* the soldiers from all parts of Great Britain speak to the King frankly of his duties; and it is they who win the battle by their bravery. All this is opposed to hereditary or intellectual aristocracy; but the government of the Cecils was tyrannic. Shakespeare was aristocratic in his political and social ideas, and insists on national unity, strong monarchy, and an obedient people. Henry V's soldiers are brave, but they spring as much from humour and realism as social philosophy. We admire but laugh at them; and Shakespeare never takes heroes from inferior classes. The quality of the people in his histories is comic; but, otherwise, in dramatic art, he conforms to popular procedure. He neglects unity of subject, frequently changes scenes, and scarcely reshapes historical matter. If his artistic conscience is most active in tragedy, it is half-asleep in history: the most popular form of art, showing clearest the defects of public taste. And yet the public love of realism and comedy produced Falstaff and the scenes of London life. Unity of subject—there lies the basal imperfection of public taste which Shakespeare's great genius attempted to reform. Only the three parts of *Henry VI* are real chronicle plays: and here he joins the comic element to the main theme. The Falconbridge of the early plays was detached: but Shakespeare works him into the framework of *John*,

[1] Cf. Winstanley.

and makes him represent the typical, loyal, independent patriot. The pictures of social life complete the national picture, by reflecting the development of the character of the national hero, and presenting the soul of the people. People frequented the theatre to be moved or amused—to the neglect of art. This carelessness allowed Shakespeare to develop his 'kind'—to select a dominant interest that would unify his play more strictly than a succession of events. He makes biographical history, where the King's life or character dominates the events of his reign: *Henry IV* and *Henry V*. In *Richard II* and *Richard III* he turns history into tragedy: and so we draw near to the great tragedies. He need only develop his conception of history to reach *Macbeth*, *Hamlet*, and *Lear*.

Realism and romanticism were not separate things with the great Elizabethan public; and so we can hardly classify the majority of the plays as one or the other. The romantic is firmly based on the real, e.g. *M.N.D.* The popular theatre and the popular authors revealed a higher and more serious conception of the importance of the lives and destinies of ordinary people. The social ideas of the domestic drama are evidently related to a romantic conception of ordinary life, which gives it moral and imaginative beauty. The love of Anne Page and Fenton shines through the farce of the *Wives*; and in some comedies conjugal love triumphs over the distractions of the artificial world. The union of realism and romanticism was indissoluble in the public taste to which the theatre responded. It was partly due to a profound sense of beauty which transcended narrow aesthetic limits and saw life whole—and partly to a naïve and uncritical imagination. At the theatre romantic themes were clothed in the garb of reality, e.g. the witches in *Macbeth*; and the most realistic subjects are so represented as to recall the invisible, imaginative world which gives facts their meaning. Ben Jonson was condemned by the public for treating a realistic subject realistically. After leaving its master, the public, the theatre developed each to extreme—romance without realistic good sense, and realism without idealism, e.g. the Restoration. The Elizabethan public was realistic in its morality and held to the Ten Commandments: Falstaff was finally disgraced. Only in a theatre less dominated by public opinion did romantic morality develop. Shakespeare in his tragedies perfectly reconciles these two sides of life, and interprets the character and instincts of his audience. The great public likes simple morality, and prefers the *Wives* to the *Dame aux Camélias*. No doubt Shakespeare's own morality surpasses that of his public: as witness Falstaff, Iago, Shylock, Sir Toby, Caliban. Profound touches of virtue and humanity make us sympathize with these persons; and in the striking example of Caliban, savage and brutal monster by birth, his vices do not eclipse the childlike innocence and poetic beauty which light up the strange soul of this creature of a different moral world. We note that all these characters underwent poetic justice, according to popular ideas, no matter what the poet's conceptions were: and the history of art and the theatre convinces us that the people were right. The supreme works of the creative art of the whole world are inspired by a normal conception of morality; and the English theatre owed its greatness to creative representation of life before an audience in which imagination overpowered criticism.

We differ from those who divide the Elizabethan public into classes, each with its taste. During the theatre's great period all classes were fundamentally united in taste. The theatre developed by co-operating between the taste of the public and the genius and artistic conscience of the dramatists.[1] The public taste derived as much from the dramatic traditions of the past as the psychology of its own time. This taste made prominent an epic and realistic conception of theatrical material, which saw imaginative beauty in the light of truth, and tested fiction by the laws of truth. The popular art of the theatre was finally influenced and inspired by the True, the Beautiful, and the Good. . . .

Dr. Sisson is concerned to show the historical and social influences that produced Shakespeare, and the reasons why his was the supreme art. Without these influences we might not have had the Shakespeare that we know; but he used them to attain a unique perfection. Books like Dr. Sisson's frequently explain away their subject; but his has the reverse effect: it flashes upon us the true nature of art, and Shakespeare as its greatest master. Art is earthly-heavenly, because man consists of body as well as soul; and if the highest life is spiritual progress, it must be achieved partly through the beauty of earthly things. Facts are sacred; God made the earth; and the soul is as much stimulated by the charm of women, by the bravery and independence of men, as by the prayer repeated in solitude. Pater described Newman's *Idea of a University* as the perfect handling of a theory—and we almost echo his words in connexion with Dr. Sisson's work. It is impersonal yet distinctive; its object is to establish a theory, yet its confirming examples are supplied by the writer's aesthetic experience, e.g. he says that Henry V's soldiers originate in humour and realism as much as social philosophy, that we admire but laugh at them. The balance is not wholly in favour of Shakespeare, for he reminds us shrewdly that the popular love of realism produced Falstaff and the London scenes: and when we think of oft-rewritten *Hamlet*, it is possible that the germ might have lain undeveloped in Shakespeare's mind. If we can describe one of his examples as unconvincing, it is that of Anne Page irradiating the surrounding farce. But our final emotion is that all things contributed to Shakespeare, and Shakespeare perfected all things; that in the great ages of the world realism and romanticism are one; and if they are disparted as in the France of Louis XIV or the England

[1] Cf. Lamartine, Rümelin, Brandes.

of George IV, or unite to produce the hybrid sentimentalism of the Victorian age—these ages fail morally and socially. Dr. Sisson proves to us historically, psychologically, and aesthetically that Shakespeare's greatness was founded in the deep places of the human nature of one of the world's elect ages.

V

PROFESSOR CAMILLE LOOTEN[1] affirms that no literary criticism which omits religion can achieve final truth. Critics have confounded the religion in Shakespeare's plays with Shakespeare's religion. In his thirty-seven plays Catholic Christianity preponderates. It is harder to obtain his opinion on the religious problems of his day, but it seems as if his conviction varied—as if he did not remain true to the faith of his youth, but, through a period of doubt and anguish, reached a noble kind of mysticism accompanied by benevolent neutrality to all Christian beliefs.

The first step to religion is to realize our nothingness before the mystery of the universe. Every one of Shakespeare's characters possesses this elementary form of religion. The history of religion in all ages shows how man tries to give bodily form to this unknown thing which haunts him (see *M.N.D.*, Mercutio's Queen Mab speech in *R. and J.*, Ariel). In the Roman plays we hear much of dreams and omens. Belief in dreams also appears in *Richard III*, and witchcraft in *Macbeth*. Shakespeare's characters do not doubt that there are persons who act as intermediaries with infernal powers. In *Henry IV* and *Lear* there are allusions to astrology; and, lastly, prophecy figures in *John*, *Richard II* (Bishop of Carlisle), and *Richard III* (Margaret).

All these represent the elementary forms of the religious sense. There is besides a preponderating religion to which all the characters belong—that is, Christianity and the Church. The first principle is God, a personal Being, in no way aloof from the world, a Providence, a Judge impartial but inclined to mercy, one who hates ingratitude, lying, and all evil, whose vengeance takes a thousand forms. He strikes the father through his children, and common blood brings common punishment. In short, He is the God of the Old Testament (cf. the good and evil angels in Marlowe's *Faust*).

Man must choose between good and evil, and sin varies in nature and gravity. The commonest is irregular love, but there are others less serious which may be condoned by prayer. Man has the help of conscience in regulating his moral life, but it varies from an infallible guide to a pretext for self-deception (*Henry VIII*). The Ten Commandments are the law of human action, and to these the Church has added certain laws—such as observance of Sunday, fasting, &c. Virtues

[1] *Sh. et la Religion*, 1924 (Perrin et Cie).

such as justice, truth, temperance, generosity, courage, humility, piety, and others, are the attributes of kings. Other virtues are still more ideal—fear of God, forgiveness, patience in adversity, self-sacrifice—and the crown of all is love (*L.L.L.* IV. iii). The virtue of chastity well becomes women, as we read in *M. Ado* and *M. for M.*; and in the ranks of chaste women we count Desdemona, Portia, Lady Percy, Hermione, Imogen.

Christianity completes this moral order by certain long-established ceremonies—baptism, confession, the sacrament. Even Falstaff asks for extreme unction, and Hamlet's father laments that he was cut off without the viaticum. The ceremony of betrothal is almost a sacrament (*M. for M.*), and Shakespeare surrounds marriage with a halo of dignity.[1] As bond of eternal love it is sacred, and should never be lightly undertaken (*Tempest, Errors*). The power of prayer has no limits, but there are wicked men who cannot pray: contrast Claudius, Angelo, Richmond before the battle of Bosworth. Saints' days, pilgrimages, funeral rites, are also among the outer forms of Christianity in Shakespeare.

Beliefs, laws, sacraments, rites, are vital Christian manifestations, so that we see before us the organization and hierarchy of the powers of the Catholic Church. An effect of the feudal system is that the great among the clergy own land, and these spiritual lords, equally with temporal lords, serve as counsellors to the King and fulfil political functions. The lower ranks of clergy little attracted Shakespeare's notice; the Benedictines are lightly treated; but to the Franciscans, notably Friar Lawrence (*R. and J.*), full justice is done. And he offers the most delicate homage to such a nun as Isabella (*M. for M.*). From the time of Chaucer and Langland the convent has been made the object of facile jokes—but in these Shakespeare never indulges. With his great good sense he remembers that religious vows and austerity are only for the few (*L.L.L.*), and that there is an unbecoming mysticism. Henry VI refers all to the will of God, but takes no means to bring it to pass.

If, then, religion is outer as well as inner, do Shakespeare's heroes act according to their faith? The answer is that his world is the image of reality—where many are enslaved by passion, others live in mediocrity, and a few practise noble virtues and approach the ideal.

The great majority of Shakespeare's characters live in a Christian atmosphere. In the Middle Ages Church and State were closely allied, and Christianity strongly possessed men's souls, so that Shakespeare could not have ignored this double phenomenon. Religion is as much present in comedy as tragedy, and this disproves the charge that he was an agnostic—for in comedy, if anywhere, he could exclude the supernatural. Of the two churches, Protestant and Catholic, we think

[1] Cf. Herford, Mézières. Contrast Taine.

that he favoured the Catholic: when one compares the transformed
and deformed church with the noble church found in his plays.

It is a mistake to think that Catholicism was immediately extinguished
in England. Until the Gunpowder Plot it had a vigorous secret life.
Meanwhile Elizabeth's policy was to fine Catholics heavily, and torture
and execute priests. Shakespeare and his contemporaries must have
seen many a tragedy in actual life, for the age was one of fire and steel.
At the same time, the Protestant church began to split into sects, such
as Puritanism. These religious dissensions were not confined to the
capital, but spread to the provinces and divided the people. Shakespeare,
on his mother's side, was descended from a family that had suffered
for its loyalty to Catholicism. We know from his plays that he was
acquainted with the catechism, and a passage in the *Merchant* places
beyond doubt that it was the Catholic. It is where Antonio says that
the Devil can quote Scripture for his purpose. This occurs in Jerome's
dialogue with the 'Lucifériens', and though Shakespeare did not take
it from the original, he would only need to recall a passage in the
Catholic catechism which rejects free interpretation of the Scriptures
and invokes the authority of the same Father of the Church. To
write as Shakespeare does about dogma, morality, sacraments, &c.
requires familiarity from early childhood. Of all the books which he
studied none impressed him like the Bible. It is impossible to say which
translation he used, but it took possession of his heart, mind, and
memory, as we see from his style. Among other religious influences
were the representations of Mysteries and Miracles.

We cannot doubt that a revolution took place in his soul when he
arrived in London from Stratford. Catholic writers had been hard at
work in the last twenty years of the sixteenth century. In all towns,
and London especially, religious discussions were raging, and Catholics
were on the defensive. The Marprelate controversy worked like
contagion, involving even such men of letters as Sidney and Spenser.
The dramatists, except Shakespeare, were unanimous; and the atheist
Marlowe's hatred for Catholics overflowed in torrents in his plays.
Works by Dekker, Chettle, and others in the same manner, now
forgotten, won them contemporary fame. They show the force of
the anti-Catholic prejudice, and the kind of legend that had been
created to defame Catholicism. We cannot say that Shakespeare
reached the stage of one who disregards public opinion when he has
all to lose—but he approached it. He was infinitely above his rivals
in respect for truth.

He did not wish to suffer for religion, and in London it was easy
to escape the Anglican inquisition—but he was no turncoat. In his
first published work, *Venus*, and *Lucrece*, he seems indifferent to the
great problems of the day. It is rather the aesthetic ideal that he has in
view, the cause of disinterested art. We think of Titian, Corregio,

Rubens, of Renaissance art. But such a tireless observer of men could not be indifferent. In the house of Southampton he would see ardent Catholic priests and laymen, and he would need to be blind and deaf not to be aware of the red exploits that followed the Armada. He alludes to the Armada in *Errors* (III. ii), *L.L.L.* (IV. i); and in the account of the prison in *Errors*, IV. ii, he seems to have in mind the 'pursuivants' whose business it was to track Catholics and Puritans. We know from *Lear* that he had read Harsnet's book—and from the Porter in *Macbeth* we conclude that he knew all about the struggle between Anglican and Catholic from 1590 to 1610. He knew the people and the facts, and followed the events with interest.

Shakespeare's comedies are thought to be ideal and fantastic, yet they are dipped in reality. Renaissance manners were not subdued enough to conceal original vigour. Shakespeare imbibed the present, and let it tinge past ages and characters and situations. We are therefore not surprised that he places churchmen and religious questions in romantic surroundings where they seem strange. We first meet a clergyman in *L.L.L.*—Nathaniel who is a pedant, and has a good opinion of himself. Martext (*A.Y.L.*) is the type of irresponsible clergyman appointed in a hurry to fill one of many vacant curacies. He marries people as if they were pieces of furniture. Evans (*Wives*) is only a verbal mystic; he prefers worldly occupations. He has the moral taint of cowardice, compared with the intellectual taints of pedantry and ignorance in Nathaniel and Martext. Satire proceeds crescendo, and in 1600 Shakespeare openly attacks the Puritans. Their influence was growing, and they threatened the existence of the theatre. The clown in *All's Well* opens the fire, but Malvolio is the grand instance. Between *Twelfth-Night* and *M. for M.* is the abyss that separates comedy and tragedy. Behind the devotional Puritan's mask Angelo hides a perverse soul. Evil reigns in his heart while his lips pronounce pious words. Shakespeare's language leaves no doubt that he personified in Angelo the kind of Puritan he hated. Even in *Pericles* and *W. Tale* he pursues Puritans. In fine, neither Anglican priests nor Puritans could please Shakespeare.

We will now glance at the histories that run parallel with the comedies. Shakespeare impartially reconstructed the picture of medieval England, omitting no moral or civilizing force that made its greatness. The kings are the chief workers, but the Church provided many able ministers, the bishops were the firmest support of the throne, and the Catholic English people were infinitely loyal and patriotic. From oldest times the Church, with its dogmas, morality, sacraments, liturgy, education, has controlled the generations that reared the great structure. Shakespeare is no blind panegyrist: he distinguishes between God's institution and the government of man. The centre of the group is Henry V, drawn with some predilection—Shakespeare's ideal king.

To the courage and popularity of the great leader he unites wisdom, moderation, coolness, finesse, and the power to win hearts. The change from his reckless past can only be explained by the religious sense of responsibility. At every chance and change in the great drama the idea of God is present to his mind: religion and patriotism are fused into one.

It must be admitted that the Protestant spirit reigns throughout the three plays of *Henry VI*, but the explanation is that they contain little of Shakespeare's work. The episodes of Joan of Arc, Cardinal Beaufort, and the miracle of St. Albans, are certainly by other hands. As Shakespeare progresses he becomes less controversial. He soars above petty spites and will not attack individuals or institutions. We can study his most characteristic manner when he refashions the old play of *John*. He displaces the puppets for persons with soul, will, intellect, conscience. He accentuates less the political side of the action than the motives which urge the characters, e.g. Constance, Arthur, Hubert. According to the old writer, the Church was corrupt through and through: Shakespeare omits the impious scene of buffoonery where Falconbridge plunders the Monastery, and all the tirades against beliefs and dogmas. In the same year (1591) he was writing *R. and J.*, the action of which develops in a definitely Catholic atmosphere. One cannot imagine the lovers apart from Verona and the Franciscans. To Friar Lawrence Shakespeare gives, with the utmost care and sympathy, the part of conciliator between the rival families. He shows him ready to atone with his life for his involuntary fault. The unjust charges of his enemies do not trouble his serene conviction. A last difficulty is connected with *John*. To the threat of excommunication the King replies that he, not the Pope, rules England. It is the old conflict between divine and human majesty. We conclude that Shakespeare agreed with those who denied the right of Rome to interfere with his country's political affairs. Allusions to the Armada suggest that, with many of his countrymen, no matter what their religious opinions, he shuddered at the remembrance of recent dangers. Religion is another thing from temporal power, and indeed, during the peril of the Armada, the 30,000 London Catholics, one-quarter of its population, remained loyal to the Queen. The chief English Admiral, Lord Howard, was a Catholic.

The episode of 'Oldcastle' throws further light on Shakespeare's religion. Although Oldcastle was changed to Falstaff, Shakespeare was accused of disparaging the man in whom the Protestant virtues were incarnate: and this shows on which side he was ranged. We see no sign in Shakespeare of any anti-religious philosophy or of atheism. The secular nature of the theatre forbade him to be definitely Catholic like Lope de Vega or Calderon. The union of Renaissance and Reformation was soon to demoralize utterly the theatre. Shakespeare steers a middle course between Spanish and English: his theatre is not a confessional, but it is Christian. Above the domain of human passions, where his work lies, he lives in the zone of high principles where men's motives are weighed and estimated. From these he derives his view of life, history, man's destiny, and morality. He conceives of immanent and immediate justice, conscience, hope in God, forgiveness of enemies—and the torrent of passion and prejudice and violence all round: but truth is victorious at the last. This high and firm serenity comes from the religion of his youth.

We must now examine the second part of Shakespeare's dramatic character and the last period of his life (1600–16). His material fortune and fame were assured, and all seems as if he should be happy. And yet in this period he composed his most sombre work. We see characters whose misery or wickedness is without limits—as if human perversity fascinated him, e.g. Thersites, Timon, Iago, Othello, Macbeth, Lear, Edmund, Claudius—also Cressida, Cleopatra, Goneril and Regan, Lady Macbeth. Worse still, we see virtue and innocence crushed in unequal fight: Ophelia, Desdemona, Cordelia. Such is the mystery of evil; and that in this long series of tragedies Shakespeare should always lead us back to the same point, however varied the journey, proves that he was preoccupied with the terrible enigma. His intellect and imagination could not have been engaged without his heart. Had he not suffered personally from the woes of others he would not have represented them so poignantly. Also a new spirit appears, for which nothing in the preceding works prepared us. He inaugurates the theatre of ideas, he traces facts to their causes, and so comes into contact with moral problems. Contrast Jacques' 'seven ages' and the thoughts on the meaning of life uttered by Lear, Hamlet, Macbeth, Kent, Edmund. Does Shakespeare agree with Edmund's liberty or Kent's fatalism? Hamlet's soliloquy on life beyond the grave is indecisive. Is Cordelia's death (the defeat of virtue) to be explained by Gloster's opinion that, as boys kill flies, so the gods kill us for their sport? Or does Shakespeare hold with Edgar that the gods are just? The first denies what the second affirms: and so the Christian solution remains suspended. Even when man is safe he can find no happiness on earth—if we believe the Duke in *M. for M.* And, according to Claudio, death means extinction of human personality. Shakespeare returns to negative doctrines, and adopts a hesitating attitude to the fundamental problems of morals and religion. When we consider his former disposition we are aware of a gulf. In his early period (1590–1600) he created vicious characters, but he condemned them implicitly if not explicitly. He used to think that evil would not break the bounds set by Providence, and would provoke reaction to good. Justice would overtake the guilty, and death was not the end of all. Now doubt is everywhere, and to doubt is to suffer, for our minds require certainty, as our bodies nourishment. Is, then, the sadness of Hamlet, Othello, Kent, objective? All suggests that it was personal to Shakespeare: or he would not have systematically adopted a sorrowful tone when his heroes are face to face with these cruel riddles, or persisted in expounding them in play after play through these years. He who has not suffered from this malady could hardly speak of it in so piercing a strain. The danger of these moral tempests is seen in others, such as Jouffroy whom grief killed, and Amiel. How live in peace when we know not whence we come, whither we are going, nor what we should do on earth?

We must now seek the cause, and we first note how Elizabethan authors insist on the dangers of atheism. This rarely means denial of God, but rather of supernatural religion—Christianity and its moral laws. Atheism was an Italian product, whose grand master was Machiavelli, and it had touched the politics of such men as Leicester and Burleigh. Italy not only exported the poison, but she sent emissaries, such as Giordano Bruno, who became friendly with Sidney at Oxford, and influenced Marlowe, the first atheist-dramatist. Marlowe died tragically and prematurely, but not before he had become head of a group like himself. Shakespeare was acquainted with the doctrines of Machiavelli, and he had imitated Marlowe's style (*Richard III*), but otherwise there is no trace in his plays of Bruno's pantheism, or of unitarianism. However, one of the inevitable effects of the ceaseless controversies among Protestants, Catholics, and Puritans, was to promote scepticism. Universally received ideas were questioned, and sacred things were ridiculed. The Sonnets show that Shakespeare was then at a depressed period, and at this psychological moment he met with Montaigne's essays. Montaigne doubts all things: every reason in favour of certainty can be matched by one equally plausible on the other side. The reason is that the sources of our knowledge are suspect, and our senses fail to agree among themselves. Shakespeare cannot have been unaffected by this display of our intellectual misery. Blow after blow struck at hitherto invulnerable truths must have re-echoed in his mind. This is one key to the secret of the doubts and sorrows of his tragic period. Hamlet is the supreme type of doubt-tormented man.[1] His duty is to avenge his father—but what matters duty if all dies with the body? If duty and immortality are true, then all his vigour returns to him. If he listened to himself he would revolve for ever these two contradictory thoughts: and therefore his activity is suspended—exactly in the manner of Montaigne. Like Montaigne he has dilated without end on self-destroying hypotheses. But the bitter sadness of Hamlet returns upon himself—his analysis of the rottenness of Denmark—is the expression of the poet's own agony. Timon is

---

[1] Cf. Sievers (1866) on Hamlet and the great Protestant idea—man's need of faith.

another instance: and what a gulf between Timon and the forgiving
Duke of *A.T.L.*! Then the world was vivified by Christianity: now
it is abandoned to its natural instincts. We must conclude that from
this time he no longer entirely believed in the Catholicism of his
youth.

No crisis lasts for ever, and Shakespeare solved his problem by
accepting the established order, respecting venerable institutions con-
secrated by national tradition, silencing the spirit of inquiry, conform-
ing to custom. We know from the facts of his private life that for
years he lodged in London with a Calvinist family, with which he was
on friendly terms—and this proves that he had separated from Catholicism. At Stratford he was friendly with a Puritan minister, and his
son-in-law drifted towards Puritanism. He lived in a state of religious
neutrality.

Of his latest plays the most moving things in *Henry VIII* are the
misfortunes of Katharine and the fall of Wolsey: but the sentiments
are more purely simple and human than Christian. A sweet and
penetrating autumnal beauty is shed over the characters of *Cymbeline*
and the *W. Tale*, with now and then a hint of bitterness. Prospero
is the prevailing force of the *Tempest*, and the critics are right to
identify him with Shakespeare. The play also represents Shakespeare's
symbolic conception of the world from which he is about to retire.
He sees the struggle of good and evil, but he disregards reality enough
to make good get its reward and evil its punishment here and now.
He believes in no Utopia, but he suggests the kind of remedy he would
wish for a sick humanity. It must be admitted there is little place for
religion, except as theatrical ornament. The gods only intervene
formally, and Prospero, the genial superman, does as he wills. There
is a certain spiritual atmosphere, but no dogma or definite beliefs.
Shakespeare's last work is not an act of faith in God, but in man's
creative genius, and an aspiration towards a better state. . . .

Professor Looten's book seems written to prove a theory, but it
contains no special pleading. It seems to him that Shakespeare was
born and reared in the Catholic faith, that he clung to it in early
manhood, and expressed it in his plays. In proof, he points to the sorry
figures which his Anglican ministers and Puritans cut—Nathaniel,
Martext, Malvolio, Angelo—and the halo of romance that surrounds
the Franciscans. There followed the tragic or dark period in his life;
and Professor Looten agrees with other critics that it had a personal
cause and Shakespeare suffered personally, but he adds a deeper shade
of meaning. Hitherto it has been ascribed to disappointment in love,
betrayal by one friend, the tragic fate of another, disgust with the
world in general: but Professor Looten directs our thoughts to the
waterless desert of scepticism, and in so doing makes Shakespeare
represent modern thought. The modern man is not concerned with

heaven or hell, but survival or annihilation: between these are divided his spiritual hopes and alarms. Professor Looten does not make of Shakespeare a means to express his own ideas, but, in the best spirit of modern criticism, he has let the theory form itself in his mind, till it has become detached and assumed independent life: in brief, his is a twice-born theory. Nor does he seek to prove it by isolated speeches or characters, but by the whole impression of a play. It is true that he notes Falstaff's request for extreme unction, and the regret of Hamlet's father that he is cut off without the viaticum; but his best points are that we cannot imagine Romeo and Juliet apart from Verona —or the superfluous allusions to religion in the comedies—or the gulf between Timon and the forgiving Duke of *A.Y.L.* whose world was vivified by Christianity—or the formal religion of the *Tempest*. As the central problem of the book is scepticism, the denominational issue might seem negligible, but Professor Looten has used Catholicism to shed a glow of happiness over Shakespeare's earlier career that deepens the contrast with his subsequent loneliness of soul. He describes Shakespeare's doctrines as negative and insists that to doubt is to suffer because our minds require certainty, e.g. Jouffroy, Amiel. Machiavelli was the grand master of atheism, and Montaigne of scepticism—and Shakespeare was probably under the influence of both. Professor Looten studies Shakespeare with an interest self-inspired by his own theory become objective. When he makes Hamlet question the importance of duty if all dies with the body, we ask whether the true solution of the play, its open secret, is not simply scepticism—the mind divided between hope of survival and fear of annihilation.

VI

JUSSERAND calls Shakespeare's genius prodigious and heaven-bestowed, his gifts the most marvellous ever possessed by a poet, and his vast fame a unique literary phenomenon. What made him pre-eminent above all was his life-giving power. Dr. Sisson calls him the mirror of the soul, of a whole civilization, and of the history and manners of his country. The elementary force of his genius was Promethean, he had divine amplitude of soul—and his was the supreme work of the world's creative art. To M. Chevrillon he appears spontaneous, passionate, free, of the Renaissance, beauty-loving, and, above all, Celtic. Professor Looten says that he only differed from contemporaries by his transcendent genius, that he was impartial, just, serene, with vibrating sensitiveness of nature.

Jusserand calls him tolerant in religion, an agnostic. M. Chevrillon says that he had the religious craving for the infinite, that he was occupied with the mystery of life and death. He and Professor Looten agree that he was anti-Puritan; but Professor Looten finds that he was no agnostic in early years, but a true Catholic, with the high serenity that springs from religion—but from the tragic period onwards he became an agnostic in morals and religion—and his final period was one of religious neutrality.

Of his characters, Jusserand says they were individuals, not types—characters as in real life with all its accessories. Dr. Sisson alludes to his psychological truth; and Professor Looten considers that his object was the disinterested portrayal of character.

M. Chevrillon says that with him character was fate, but declares him to be moral. Dr. Sisson says that his morality surpassed that of his time. In Professor Looten's opinion he was preoccupied with moral problems.

The few generalities on Shakespeare's style can hardly be closely compared. Jusserand alludes to his concrete art and calls him an incomparable artist. He speaks of his varied style, between highest and lowest—and comments on its simplicity in great passages. M. Chevrillon describes his imagination as visionary. Dr. Sisson gives him a high artistic conscience—and notes that to effect unity of action he made the comic help, not hinder, the romantic and tragic. He was a dramatic philosopher who made thought the basis of his play. Professor Looten observes that his theatre was a perfect image of reality.

On more wordly matters we get Jusserand's opinion that he wrote for a living, to please a rude public—in which he and Dr. Sisson are agreed. Jusserand calls him practical, no democrat, one who hated the crowd. Dr. Sisson also agrees that he was aristocratic in his political and social ideas. According to Professor Looten he had robust good sense, and was impartial, just, serene, and averse to controversy. . . .

Shakespeare is compelled to use earthly means to express heavenly visions; at a certain moment heaven and earth draw near each other, and then a vision is flashed upon us of the man Shakespeare. Such is the final French collective impression; and it may be said of the French critics, far more than the German, that they do not so much go to Shakespeare as bring Shakespeare to themselves. They stand out, they inscribe themselves upon their subject, without doing that subject wrong.

Chapter XLI

GERMANY 1903–1925

I. WOLFF.   II. KOHLER.   III. MAUERHOF.   IV. WOLFF.   V. CREIZENACH.
VI. LESCHTSCH.   VII. SCHÜCKING.   VIII. GUNDOLF.   IX. RICHTER.   X. BAB.
XI. CONCLUSION.

I

MAX J. WOLFF[1] denies that it is possible to understand Shake-speare himself from quotations from his works, or to say confi-dently that he thought thus of love, hate, religion. Shakespeare so iden-tifies himself with his characters that he speaks as they speak; but one of his few exceptions is Hamlet's allusion to 'the insolence of office': for the Prince could hardly have such cause to complain. We can, however, follow the development of Shakespeare's genius by comparing his own works: thus after *Hamlet* he never wrote another comedy. The Middle Ages—represented by Dante and Thomas Aquinas—saw a breach between heaven and earth: this world was to be renounced, and only the heavenly desired. Shakespeare belongs body and soul to the earth; the world was to him the great reality, the arena of man's whole life, and as such neither good nor bad, but a palpable fact. He sees it to be pleasing and does not probe deeper after its meanings. He greets the spring, is ravished by the nightingale, looks upon the tiniest plant or meanest insect as part of the beautiful creation: whereas Goethe concentrated solely on the divine idea. Shakespeare welcomes art that makes life more beautiful, and is inspired by music and painting.

Yet he is no thoughtless, childish optimist who overlooks the misery of the world; rather he overcomes pessimism by a higher and riper understanding. Like most highly developed men he was inclined to pessimism. The Sonnets suggest a soul tossed between love and hatred for mankind. Such craving for friendship and sympathy, if unsatisfied, might lead to pessimism, and even suicide. Such mighty feelings cannot escape disillusion: as witness Timon's hatred and flight from the world. We can trace Shakespeare's inclination to solitude and world-abnegation in his most youthful work. In *Henry VI* it is the fundamental trait of the weak being's character. The great success of the next years repressed this longing, but even in the gayest comedy, *A.Y.L.*, it receives an ironic, self-deceiving, but melancholy expression. Hamlet would gladly have escaped from the world, and lived as a hermit: but sense of duty keeps him in the battle of life. This feeling of duty in Shakespeare prevents him from succumbing to pessimism. In three of the later plays, *Timon*, *Cymbeline*, *Tempest*, Shakespeare balances the two life-principles. Timon seeks peace in the wilderness,

[1] *Studies and Addresses*: *Sh. the Poet*; *Brutus and Hamlet*, 1903.

Belarius reluctantly turns back to the world, Prospero leaves his solitude and says 'Yes' to life.

Brandes is incorrect to represent Shakespeare returning home in his last years, a broken man, to end his life in bitter solitude. If he ceased writing it was because the *Tempest* was his final message, and he retired as a conqueror. Had he been so disgusted with life he would not have continued to take such an interest in the small Stratford world and the well-being of his fellow-townsmen.

He found room for truth and beauty in this world and had no need to look for it beyond the clouds. He may have had his dark hours, at the thought of the insoluble riddle of life; but the poet—and herein he was wholly poet—did not interest himself in obscure questionings. Human pleasure, sorrow, and struggle suffice for poetic handling. He takes man from the cradle to the grave, never beyond, and knows nothing of hell for the criminal or heavenly rapture for the righteous.[1] Good and bad, virtue and vice, are rewarded and punished here; his work is a moral organism ruled by certain eternal laws. Evil cannot last, and good must conquer—and both carry on earth their own fate, apart from instant outward success. Cordelia must fall because over-powering filial love had fulfilled its mission and released the world from the curse of impiety. In fulfilling her task she had gained her reward; and Shakespeare needs no external explanation. As he is a genuine artist within the bounds of earth, so are his creations. They cling to earthly blessings, unwillingly part from life, grasp eagerly at crown and sceptre, women and gold. Not one shows desire for martyrdom. Only Hamlet has a philosophic ideal and is called upon to set the world right; and this solitary example shows how overstrained desires drain away the energies and the joy of action. Shakespeare knew that vanity or self-seeking may lurk behind the ideal, but he does not despair of the world. Human suffering and strife are great and powerful even when undergone for personal gratification. At the end there is no looking forward, but looking back to what life has been. No comfort is to be sought in glory beyond, but in freedom from the world's evils: as the Duke explains to Claudio. Imogen's dying lament has nothing about resurrection; Romeo and Juliet do not speak about meeting hereafter.

Shakespeare's women are purely women; he has created the most ideal figures and the worst criminals. Beside Miranda and Cordelia stand Regan and Goneril: but they are just women, neither angels nor demons. If they fall through love they are not pitilessly condemned, as Paolo and Francesca by Dante. Repentance and patience will restore them—as in *M. for M.*

There are no oracles to be fulfilled, as with Oedipus—and if prophecies come true it is because the prophet sees clearer into the

[1] Cf. Dowden.

future, e.g. Gaunt (*Richard II*). The witches simply materialize the ambition in Macbeth's heart; the ghosts are born of fancy or conscience.

Honour is no part of a conventional system as in the Spanish drama, but personal honour. Othello does all for honour; his need is to keep his name intact. Shakespeare's kings are like other men, with human faults and failings. A crime is a crime no matter who commits it: a crown is not lent for eternity. Calderon has types of men and women; Shakespeare knows only individuals who love and are jealous. We call him a popular poet, but not in the sense that he appealed to the masses who hungered after sensation. He stood in the midst of his nation and wrote for the people as well as the Queen and the nobles. In sharp contrast to Racine and the French dramatists he appealed to learned and unlearned, rich and poor, old and young. Calderon's love is no living power, but conventional understanding of gallantry ordered by minute rules. Love with Shakespeare is so powerful that all other feelings and considerations are flung to the winds. Nothing is too strange or fanciful for Shakespeare's stage: Racine's audiences possessed only aesthetic understanding. Shakespeare's characters are free from heroics; they are not lofty and dignified, but pure products of passion unfettered by civilization or moral training. They act from inborn necessity, indifferent to good and evil. They hate intensely and are not restrained by any questioning as to whether the feeling is unworthy of them. Racine's lovers dwell in a small highly-cultured circle; Shakespeare's among all classes, and in ancient or modern times.

His kings are less royal than Racine's; his heroes may be unheroic but are human. Hamlet amidst the tragedy exchanges words with a grave-digger; Desdemona, anxious about Othello, laughs at Iago's broad jokes; Caesar, before going to the Capitol, has a domestic scene with his wife.

Because Shakespeare is unconsciously universal he produces unerringly: in his manuscript hardly a word is erased or altered. Action or plot with him is the chief thing, according to Aristotle: whereas Goethe neglects it compared with the associated ideas. Shakespeare treats his material objectively, and is far from preaching any general truth.[1] His plays reflect nothing personal; he describes events as they are, not as they appear in the mirror of his own opinions. The personal 'I' is lost in the creative artist; and with Homer he is the most unphilosophical of poets. Since Hamlet's inactivity is negligence opposed to duty, it has the significance of an act. Goethe's heroes personify an idea, and the tragedy both of Faust and Hamlet lies in their inner being. In the German it is confined to expression of feeling; in the English progressive expression is in external events. Here Shakespeare's art is most wonderful; the slightest wavering of his highly-strung hero is reflected in objective changes. The action speaks for itself, and the

[1] Cf. Ulrici and Gervinus.

poet has no need to add or explain. Some critics maintain that Henry V represents personal traits of Shakespeare's; but the same might be said of Falstaff, or even Horatio. His reality, freedom, popularity, objectivity are all embraced in his unsurpassed art of representing humanity. The artistic personality of Racine or Schiller may be grasped, not that of Shakespeare or Homer. What Homer was to epic Shakespeare is to drama—the unattainable and unattained poet of all time.

Brutus and Hamlet have like characters and tasks, but they differ in accomplishing their task. Both have watched fearfully the progress of events before they are called on to revenge. Duty calls both, but in a dull uncertain manner; and they have not found the direction in which to act. Cassius and the ghost alike summon Brutus and Hamlet to remove the criminal who is so lifted above the law by position that only force can reach him. There is no question of law, but the demand proceeds from purely personal grounds. In either case the conflict is between 'ought' and 'non-willing', not between willing and incapacity. They feel that they should obey the call, but between decision and deed is a crippling period of consideration.

Brutus loves the republican ideal and hates the tyrant as much as Cassius; and Hamlet's anger at his uncle's crime rises to the highest pitch: but both, reflective by nature, lack strength of passion to use the dagger instantly. Neither feel the interior urge to revenge, only the naked command of duty; but as they are morally serious beings they dare not evade this, though they have no wish to obey. As they cannot assimilate the idea of murder, they first procrastinate, and ask for time to reflect—and shrink more and more from the idea of blood. Brutus thinks Caesar a great man, although he has seized autocratic power; Hamlet decides that men are knaves, and the king no worse than others: so the task seems other than that urged by Cassius and the Ghost. They would commit the act, but it is impossible, in that it will not produce the desired better result. Caesar's murder will not win freedom; the fall of Claudius will not aid mankind. Yet opposed to these speculations rises the inexorable *ought*—and this stirs up the soul of Brutus, and brings a tragic fate to Hamlet.

The Dane is far more intellectually gifted than the Roman; but to every earthly action must be added some blind belief in oneself and in the success of one's individual effort. Brutus is far from the standpoint of Hamlet, who is wholly wise with sharp insight into men and things, and waits and watches. Brutus has the narrowness of a politician, and eyes dimmed by party-glasses. Hamlet holds back because he is not sure of success; Brutus has found the point of view of the reconstitution of Roman freedom from which he subjectively can perform the ordained act of blood, although objectively worthless. He falls into the politician's usual error of confusing men and circumstances: he sees the autocrat but not the frogs that need the stork as

master. He identifies Caesar's death with freedom and so determines
to kill him. Unlike Cassius he has no personal wish to punish him
for criminal arrogance, but to undertake the impossible task of restoring
freedom. Hamlet will perform no act of personal revenge; with
deeper insight he recognizes that his ultimate aim of setting the world
right will not be won by the king's death. For him the death of
Claudius is an unserviceable means, whereas the murder of Caesar
appears serviceable to the narrower, political Brutus.

The two differ in intellect, are alike in character. To the freedom-
loving Brutus, his hopes and ideals do not come true. Hamlet fulfils
his mission, with his uncle dead and Fortinbras to begin a new era.
The cause is not his own act, but the presence and power of his moral
personality. Brutus, the representative of eternal lost causes, is overcome on the battle-field. . . .

The first of these essays, on Shakespeare as poet, presents a definite
conception of Shakespeare, without straining of facts to suit the
theory. We may not agree with some statements—that action or plot
is the chief thing—that virtue and vice are always rewarded and punished
here—but on the whole there is little to be gainsaid. The method is
the sound one of selecting without preconceived ideas—e.g. Shakespeare's inclination to solitude rising in *Henry VI* and traced through
A.Y.L. to the latest plays—the craving for sympathy and friendship
in the Sonnets and the *Merchant*—the clinging of the characters to
earthly blessings—the tendency to look back, not forward, in the hour
of death. If Wolff convinces, it is because he finds common qualities
in unlike plays and characters—but the kind of qualities that lie at the
base of Shakespeare's thought rather than its finished utterance. We
therefore accept his contribution as something to be reckoned with in
future estimates of Shakespeare the man rather than as a completed
portrait for all time.

The wisdom of the second essay, on Brutus and Hamlet, lies in its
concluding sentences. Wolff excels when his thought paces side by
side with the events of the play: when he so handles the play's outer
events that they seem to reflect Shakespeare's idea and his own, for
the moment happily married. Otherwise he shows more insight with
Brutus than Hamlet—for a semi-political theory, even to the extent
of righting the world, hardly suffices with Hamlet.

II

JOSEF KOHLER[1] divides Shakespeare's criminals into three types:
(1) those driven by passion, egotistical with Macbeth or Richard III,
altruistic with Brutus and Cassius; (2) those driven by circumstances,
like Othello; (3) those without conscience, like Edmund, Iago, Cade.

Macbeth might have refrained but for the chance that brought

[1] *Criminal Types in Sh.'s Dramas*, 1903.

Duncan under his roof. Lady Macbeth was easily excited and fired, and her conscience was of the kind that awakes after the deed. She can easily put it aside, although the suppression exacts that it bursts forth in its own time with fresh and hideous power. She makes two appeals that never fail with such a man as her husband: she affirms that he has gone too far to draw back, and she questions his courage. When she demolishes his last bulwark that the deed may miscarry, he makes up his mind. A pause follows when the unconscious soul works, and, like all imaginative natures, he is led on as if in a dream, through the dagger scene, to the hideous deed. He becomes king and the energy needed to fill his new post might have kept conscience in abeyance but for the social law that a deed cannot be isolated from its connexions, and one crime is easily followed by another. He gradually comes to feel himself exalted above all social powers, and at last impregnable and superhuman, as we see from his second interview with the witches. He succumbs not to conscience, but to the actual world which rises against him.

Brutus and Cassius offer up life for an idea, and will gladly seal their efforts with blood, to die as heroes. But for Cassius, Brutus would have remained darkly uncertain. Political fanaticism was the inner spring with Cassius, mingled with some personal antagonism. He disdained to be overtopped by Caesar who was of weaker body. Brutus only sees the surface of things, and even after Caesar's death believes in Antony's friendship. When the storm breaks Cassius knows that such a war can only be carried on with strong contributions, but Brutus stands out as the noble Philistine. Brutus again prevails about the place of battle, and now we see where Cassius is weak. He has initiative but no persistence; he yields to Brutus in everything, and kills himself at an unfavourable moment when the battle might still have been saved. His suicide was the worst injury for his army; but it is characteristic of such natures that have become used at heart to summon fate and hold life cheap. Brutus based his political fanaticism on the thought of his ancestor. His republican strivings are not pure, for he has one eye on his life-work the other on the opinion of the citizens. Cassius knew this when he threw the papers into his room. Brutus was slow to resolve, and, like all weaklings, fears the interval between decision and action more than the deed itself. He expresses himself like one who has undertaken a deed beyond his strength, yet remains determined when once decided—and also like one who is accustomed to have his will performed. He is a good citizen, bad politician, moderate soldier—he adheres to what he has finally willed. He was fatal to the conspirators, fortunate for Caesar's friends—and yet after his death Antony calls him the noblest Roman. Few understand the art of politics, and most crimes of political fanaticism spring from political ignorance and youthful dilettantism, also narrow sense of citizenship and Philistine mediocrity. Suicide at the moment of disaster in battle was just expiation.

Richard III is not a conscienceless criminal; he is haunted by dreams before Bosworth, and this is the kernel and turning-point of the play. The feeling of security so needed in the coming critical battle forsakes him. That he says, 'I shall despair. There is no creature loves me', proves that he is not outside the social order like Iago and Edmund. He must sustain himself by help of the sophism, that conscience is only a word for cowards. He is a criminal governed by an overmastering motive—a political or constitutional criminal who sins against regal decrees. He can only reach the crown through streams of blood, and the passion that makes him deaf to all moral persuasion is desire for power. It is neither money, nor possessions, nor earthly enjoyment that he wills, but the divine enjoyment of power. In many ways he is a gifted man, and also brave, and his responsibility is partially lessened by the influence of a barbarous age. His deformity further separates him from his kind. The possessor of self-knowledge above most reflecting statesmen, he consciously pursued his designs and stirred up one against another. Unequalled in hypocrisy, he can approach women tenderly and bewitch their senses. It may be added, though it is hardly an excuse, that many of his victims deserved their fate. The atmosphere must be cleared and heads fall on either side before the house of Tudor could bring peace to England. Richard's powerful hand fulfilled the historic task of curtailing the civil war.

Othello's crime is entirely due to circumstance, and only in the slightest degree to any criminal tendency. He is wound in a hellish net of deceit and suspicion, and his excited African nature overflows its bounds. The drama therefore has a national psychological character. That a refined high-born woman should love a Moor has been called impossible, but the human heart is mysterious, and women at times act perversely. He was no nigger, but a Numidian—highly placed, brave, and famous. Yet Desdemona's conduct carried with it the seeds of conflict. The Moor must have felt himself a partial outcast of society, and was easily roused to jealousy. It is right that he should die to atone for his sin—but how can we justify Desdemona's death? The struggle is between human circumstance and supernatural fate; we are lifted to heroic altitudes through the might of that fate that none can defy. Othello bears the power of Venice, and because of his stately position and the way in which he upholds it he is a prey to destruction. He becomes a criminal by circumstance, for he is not in the least cruel, his life is spotless, he is straightforward in speech, amiable, good-hearted, adoring his wife. He remained calm at the violent insults of Brabantio, and in the scene of Cassio's quarrel was a pattern of self-conscious mastery. Destructive circumstances, there-

fore, combine against his nature. In a weak moment he yields to
external circumstances, and is borne away, without startling inner
development. When a man is maddened hidden qualities come to the
fore that would otherwise have lain undisturbèd: there is an upheaval
from the abyss. Circumstance was the nurse of Macbeth's natural
ambition, and his deed corresponded with his inner being. With
Othello circumstance brings forth wholly alien things from his inner
being, and make him unrecognizable.

Edmund is under a bastard's disadvantage and calls on nature to
help. He fights with all his natural powers and keen intellectual
gifts. He has no scruples of conscience, and values men as little as
animals. But when he has done his utmost, fate supervenes, and the
social powers which he has scorned turn upon him with fury. The
anti-social man can never bring all into his power unconditionally,
and so avert fate. Something always is omitted, and here we see the
significance of chance. Chance is not anti-dramatic, but a necessary
dramatic development. In chance, society revenges itself against the
individual's tyrannous lust of power, and shows him, as in a mirror,
the whole conditional state of his being.

Cade is not interesting enough to be the hero of a play, but serves
well for an episode. The Cade scenes are among Shakespeare's best
and most effective. . . .

This criticism gives us Shakespeare in the common light of day, not
seen through the veils of imagination—but of its kind it is helpful.
It is like the lull in a storm, when the high winds have been and will
come again, and are therefore not removed from experience. Or it
discusses Shakespeare as cool-headed men discuss their passionate
fellows: they themselves are not shaken, but they know passion is to .
be reckoned with in life. These thoughts give momentum to some of
Kohler's sayings, viz. that Macbeth's criminal deed cannot be isolated
—that Cassius lacks persistence—that Brutus is accustomed to
have his will performed—that security forsakes Richard, that he is
yet within the social order, and desired only power, not wealth—that
chance vindicates itself with Edmund. Above all, he excels in defining Othello's act as an upheaval from the abyss. Otherwise we do not
think the comparative method makes the separate criminals illumi-
nate each other's psychology. The lack of imaginative interpretation
appears where he praises to excess the Cade scenes, or is surprised that
Antony still hails Brutus as the noblest Roman.

III

EMIL MAUERHOF [1] finds that no one like Shakespeare so
represents man's struggle between natural desire and deterring conscience. Ambition rages in Macbeth, but the human and rational

[1] *Sh. Problems*, 1905.

being in him has no desire to murder. He wavers, and only acts when circumstances are strong enough to overcome reason.[1] The born murderer is a monster, the chance murderer merely an unfortunate man. Lady Macbeth's description, after reading his letter, suggests an ideal nature; therefore his fall makes him both terrible and worthy of compassion.

She only partially knows him: for to know a man thoroughly you must prove him; and she only truly knows him when it is too late. Had she surmised the effect on him of the deed, pity and love would have overcome her ambition. When she speaks brutally in the preliminary dialogues we must not take her literally. She is passionate, and must satisfy her longing for the crown. She cannot do the deed herself, and his opposition excites her desire. Alone he would not have acted, and now, against his better self, he commits an irreparable deed. Thenceforth he wills to live, but knows he cannot do so in harmony with his most individual nature; he therefore descends more into the depths and suffers more intensely. The judgement of his inmost self kills him, not external enemies.

Lady Macbeth is wholly woman, and she carefully conceals her intrinsic nature. She is reticent even to her husband concerning her inner feelings; but she has a rich nature, powerful imagination, and ardent feelings. She is wholly woman in her absorbing love for her husband, and her life's aim, and also in her knowledge and conscience. She measures her husband by herself, twice she misreads herself, and finally succumbs under the double deception. On receiving his letter she sees only one man between herself and her ambition, and she decides at once that he must die, without any qualm of conscience.

He is a man of ambition, and also conscience, for which reason he forebodes coming trouble. She is all ambition and imagination—as we see her—and she lives and acts in dreams, without appreciating the actual. Her whole life-element is illusion—and this has deceived her judges. Yet natural goodness surpasses her passion, and she cannot actually do the deed. Her gruesome monologue reflects dramatically this inner struggle, but it was not conscience that held her hand—rather an involuntary, unknown feeling of horror. But she desires the crown no less, and she urges her husband to do the deed—with success because her desire is greater than her love. Otherwise she would have taken the crime upon herself. Certainly she loves her husband, even when she goads him on—and in the end she loves only him in the world, after her first look at the murderer's woe-distorted face. Passion has vanished, imagination is slain, she is deceived. 'Nought's had, all's spent', is the beginning of the night-wandering state of mind, the sign of her spiritual decline. She is tender and good, not rough and cruel, but a demonic nature without the bridle of conscience from the

[1] Cf. Kohler.

hard school of life. Her tragic fate was that the demon in her was called forth, and her passion answered exclusively to the call of her nature's behest. So finely spun are the threads of her soul that the first rough breath of wind tears them to pieces: and her shattered senses fly to the shelter of illusion.

She becomes aware of conscience as a feeling, not as a principle; and the delicate structure of her feelings which had uplifted her to those heights where neither plaintiff nor judge exists, in like manner collapsed. She is to be pitied, as a woman of the first order, excelling in feeling and imagination, who nevertheless perishes because a turn of fate made her fantastic instincts overstep her moral; and a sudden temptation assailed her which only a clear conscience could have vanquished.

The task of *Hamlet* is not to set forth divine justice, but to represent suffering. Sin is our inheritance and sorrow its fruit. Hamlet is a young man of pure feeling, and fundamentally good, who meets with circumstances that passionately arouse his moral nature. To keep himself pure he is forced to look on passively at the triumph of crime, and suffers unspeakably. At last, driven by circumstances, he decides only to suffer passively, and as this crisis is reached a strange mingling of events forces him to do the deed that contradicts his nature, against which he has so long struggled, and suffered in consequence. This is his tragedy, and this alone is the mysterious problem.

Othello is not a tragedy of jealousy. Desdemona's faithlessness would widen the breach, so far hidden, between him and society. His marriage had finally assured his position, and he had risen above the disadvantages of his race. Now chaos had returned, and hence the soul-shattering blow of his suspicion. He must punish if he is not to despise himself; though he himself cannot outlive her death. It is the proud victory of inextinguishable nature. . . .

There are few readers whom Mauerhof's analysis of Lady Macbeth would convince; the interest therefore lies in discovering where he has taken the wrong turn. That he has meditated his subject we see from his remarks on Macbeth: that he suffers and also dies because he can no longer live in harmony with his true nature. But as regards Lady Macbeth, he might have profited from Kohler's suggestion about Othello—that in the upheaval from the abyss strange things came to light. In the drama, unlike the novel, we are concerned with what characters do, not with what they might have done, or appear to themselves. Those tragic characters that deserve the name are urged by a cosmic as well as an individual force. It is not Lady Macbeth's original psychology that interests us, but the sudden expansion of her nature under temptation—the demonic weapon, like Jove's thunder, that is placed for a moment within grasp of her mortal hand. . . . The superficial remarks on *Hamlet* and *Othello* need no comment.

IV

WOLFF,[1] to whom we return, finds that Shakespeare first mastered the form of the drama with *Richard III*. Its unity of plot enables one to understand fully the rise and fall of the hero. The idea of crime and retribution dominates the play; the nature of evil is such that it destroys itself. Richard is one with himself, indifferent to curses and threats, without moral law except what is imposed on him from without, against his will. When forced to confess that the way of crime is uncertain his strength fails. In the description of his downfall Shakespeare first appears as the great reader of man's soul. He succeeds not by handling historically his powerful material, but by freeing himself from all historical condition and giving timeless character to universal humanity.

Although the groundwork of *R. and J.* is pessimistic, it does not end in comfortless despair. The sacrificial death of love overcomes the hate of the outer world. Unlike Marlowe Shakespeare understands greatness not as outer power, but the dignity of the soul, and thereby reaches the deep inward conception of the tragic. Shakespeare carries his tragic heroes to the point where they willingly die, while Marlowe's resist to the end. Romeo had to struggle with outer power, but does not belong to the great sufferers—Hamlet, Lear, Othello, Macbeth —who are stretched on the rack of their own individualities. But if this youthful drama fails to realize the highest form of the tragic, it is nearer to it than the external conception of *Tamburlaine*.

Richard II is a work of art, carefully ordered The psychological conception of the two leading figures is deeper and riper, and the tragic is of a profounder kind, than in *Richard III*. In the latter, evil continues till Henry appears and conquers; in *Richard II* the antagonists are bound together from the beginning, and affect each other adversely. Richard's character develops gradually as the result of moral guilt. He commits no capital offence, but his whole personality drives him to his end. Bolingbroke is no distinct instrument of direct judgement, like Henry Tudor, but an independent character concerned with his own interests. If the play is hardly effective as the corner-stone of the York tetralogy, it is through its weak hero, who, despite delicate psychology, fails to impress like his demonic namesake. Part of the fault may also lie in the introduction of lyric speech, alien to political drama.

The tragedy of *Othello* arises because jealousy takes hold not of a suspicious but of an otherwise free and noble spirit. Only in such large characters does it act as a poison to the whole organization. No other play reaches such psychological depth. The growth of passion in the three dialogues between Iago and Othello is conveyed with unequalled art: every word is loaded with meaning. The action

[1] *Sh. the Poet and his Work*, 1907–8.

develops with irresistible necessity from the three leading characters. Even *Lear* does not move us like the spiritual disintegration of Othello. A man who murders his blameless and beloved wife, and destroys his own highest good, is the most terrible thing to be represented.

The frightful isolation of the great is an undertone in all the plays, and it sounds most fully in *Coriolanus*. Contradictions hidden under the action of *Hamlet, Lear,* and *J.C.* are here brought to light. On one side we have all that is noble and great in man—on the other, all the weak, low, mean, and common that inspire the masses, who know of no other way to handle the great than by trampling them in the dust. Undoubtedly Shakespeare saw himself in Coriolanus.

T. and C. is a masterpiece of its kind, but *Timon* fails. The idea is undramatic, and pessimism bursts every artistic boundary. It was written at the same time as *Coriolanus,* but has no one of its excellences. Growing spiritual bitterness choked the spring of creative art. . . .

Considering Wolff's excellent first essay on Shakespeare the poet, and his reputation as Shakespearian critic, we must own to be disappointed at his more detailed treatment of the plays. He makes one good remark, on the effect of the poison of jealousy on such a nature as Othello's; but otherwise he draws his moral from the outer events of a play rather than its inner spirit. This holds good even when he appears to be judging from character rather than events, as in *R. and J.* and *Richard II*; and it is most unquestionable in *Coriolanus*.

V

PROFESSOR WILHELM CREIZENACH'S opinions on Shakespeare, scattered throughout his voluminous work on the drama,[1] may be summarized as follows:

Shakespeare followed tradition and expressed all his poetry and art and wisdom by means of traditional forms. Joint authorship was the fashion among dramatists, to satisfy the needs of the theatre; and Shakespeare collaborated with others, and remodelled the works of his predecessors.[2] It is probable that he was a slow worker, with long intervening silent periods, and that several of his plays have perished. He wrote to achieve a momentary effect on the stage, not for critical readers;[3] and therefore dismissed his plays without artistic pruning or care for balance of parts, or exact reconciliation of psychology and plot. Yet he had the double character of playwright and Renaissance poet; and even as playwright he expressed contempt for the groundlings. The Sonnets disclose his most intimate feelings, and they do not seem the work of one used to stir the masses by strong effects.

He was probably a patriotic anti-Catholic, yet there is no doubt

---

[1] *Geschichte des neueren Dramas,* 1909 (*The English Drama in the Age of Sh.,* trans. Cécile Hugon. Sidgwick & Jackson, 1916).

[2] Cf. J. M. Robertson.   [3] Cf. Schücking, Stoll, and others.

that he appreciates delicately the poetic element in Catholic institutions.[1] He contrasts the turmoil of life with the peace of the cloister; the monk in *M. Ado* and the hermit in *A.Y.L.* play distinguished parts; and though he found the Friar in the original story of *R. and J.*, he lingers over him with affection. Malvolio specially proves that he shared the dislike of his fellow-dramatists for the Puritans. Against Giordano Bruno he adheres to the old theory of the universe; and except in the *Tempest* his resemblances to Montaigne are vague. Ghosts were conventional figures, but he first used popular superstition to make them terrible. His treatment of Glendower shows him in a more sceptical mood; and we prefer to think that he did not share the coarse and crude popular ideas on witchcraft: yet surely he need not have flattered the hallucinations of the vain pedant James I, even if he did secure a fine stage effect. He avoided ecclesiastical modes of thought, and also religious dogma—as we see from Friar Lawrence, the Duke in *M. for M.*, and Prospero. If he observes poetic justice, and the punishment of the guilty, it must be remembered that so do most dramatists of the period, even Beaumont and Fletcher. He does not impute to sin the tragic end of his heroes, but rather to their own character, or to circumstances. He followed real life, where appropriate rewards and punishments are unknown. Critics have failed miserably to lay some tragic crime at the door of Romeo, Juliet, Desdemona, Cordelia. In *Othello* he discards the trivial moral that persons of alien race should not intermarry; and *Hamlet* and *Lear* are specially characteristic of his method. In the legends Hamlet won his father's kingdom and punished his enemies; Lear regained his power by his youngest daughter's help. Shakespeare alters the denouement so as to intensify the characters. The tragic conclusion accords with the tone of his work at the time. In politics the dramatists were loyal and royalist; and Shakespeare reflects this in *M.N.D.* and *Macbeth*, but he abstained from the grotesque flatteries of Ben Jonson's masques. It is strange that he never speaks a friendly word for the inhabitants of London; and the reason may be the attitude of the city authorities towards actors. His aristocratic sympathies are beyond doubt; and he takes the faithful servant more seriously than his contemporaries. It is hard to reconstruct his own opinion from the sayings of his characters, yet it does appear as if he were more sensitive to differences of rank than to the feeling of the common tie of humanity. If a plain man, humbly born, excels a nobleman, Shakespeare seems to regard him in the spirit that we rate a faithful dog above a treacherous human being. He was not interested in the social question, and no poet was more explicit on the unsavoury nature of the mob than Shakespeare.[2] He was instinctively repugnant, in a high degree, to the presence of large masses of people. He shows what a fearful

[1] Cf. Looten.   [2] Cf. Brandes, Stapfer, Jusserand.

thing a credulous and excited mob can become (*Henry VI, J.C., Coriolanus*)—and he evidently did not believe it possible to improve the intelligence or habits of the masses (e.g. Lord Say's speech in the Cade rebellion). His private feelings must have resembled those of Coriolanus.

Shakespeare used traditional material for his plays, and there is no reason to think that he chose what coincided with his own experience. His anachronisms appear to have been due to the indifference of genius rather than to intention. Local colour was little studied by dramatists; and there is nothing in Shakespeare's Italian plays to justify the assumption that he had visited Italy. There is the same freedom with Illyrian, Sicilian, French, or Viennese colouring; and in the late romances all history and geography seem to be abolished to enhance the romantic impression. He adhered most closely to his sources in the Roman plays. The classical dignity of *J.C.* is unequalled by his other tragedies, and it is due to his admiration for the majestic greatness of a vanished world. But in patriotic historical drama he revealed a fertility unrivalled by other dramatists. He drew his material from Holinshed, but we must try to imagine how he was able to discover the poetry hidden beneath the chaotic mass. He has been reproached for ignoring social development and dwelling too much on dynastic conflicts; but the history of the dynasty provided the most effective dramatic motives. When depicting national upheavals he does at times emphasize economic conditions, and he handles the crowd in masterly fashion.[1] He may have omitted Magna Carta for artistic reasons: yet it is a fact that in these plays Parliament plays a small part.

The company of enterprising dramatists at work in Shakespeare's day soon turned to account the device of mingling comic and tragic scenes, and produced new and astonishing effects. Shakespeare first conceived the masterly idea of giving expression to the many voices of the common throng, e.g. *2 Henry VI* and the Roman plays. But in some of the tragedies even he has introduced a clown merely for the sake of tradition, e.g. *Titus, Othello, A. and C.* In *Macbeth* he solved the problem brilliantly with the porter scene; and, generally speaking, he had mastered the art of mingling realistic and comic. Aaron (*Titus*) is the first instance, but Mercutio really heads the procession of 'humorous men', followed by Falconbridge, Enobarbus, Menenius Agrippa. Even Iago at first has some of the features; and, with all, the humour vanishes as the tragic end nears. As jesting appears in tragedy, so does the serious element in comedy—and Shakespeare always worked on this principle. Another breach between modern dramatists and the past was unity of place and time. It must be admitted that independence of any locality often produces the same result as classic observance; and as regards time, when the dramatists unfold an unbroken

[1] Cf. Mézières.

sequence of events, we follow in fancy and do not think of asking how
long these events would take to occur in real life. This apparent
continuousness of time is attained in the *Merchant*,' where the bond
is drawn for three months. It is more easy to distinguish the independent and characteristic features of the romantic drama: one being the
greater wealth and diversity of episodes presented. It was the dramatists's supreme task to dovetail artistically heterogeneous elements
and weld many tales into one. Here as elsewhere Shakespeare was
a master, and in *Lear* he strangely produces a tremendous effect by
welding together two similar stories. He is on guard against the
overloading tendencies of Beaumont and Fletcher and Middleton,
who obscure the general effect by elaborating detail. He artistically
balances one parallel action against another: Edgar's banishment
(*Lear*) is briefly told; and much of Octavia's sufferings (*A. and C.*)
is suppressed. His task in the English histories was concentration
more than expansion—he had to sift out from an enormous mass and
co-ordinate the dramatically valuable matter. To make a play lively and
attractive the dramatists aimed to produce a series of separate effective
situations, awaking suspense and surprise, rather than an organic whole.[1]
Shakespeare as usual excels; he combines dramatic suspense with the
inevitable trend of the action. Even at the close of *Lear* he rouses
a feverish hope in us for Cordelia. This antithesis between hope and
inexorable fate is present in the final catastrophes of *Antigone* and
Wallenstein. But with one exception Shakespeare never sacrificed the
whole impression to isolated dramatic effects: in *M. for M.* he put
his whole genius only into the scenes between Angelo and Isabella.
The comedies, in the Italian manner, die away slowly at the close.
Intriguers and miscreants are summarily punished, morality is vindicated. The rewarding of noble characters is sometimes overdone, e.g.
the betrothal of Paulina and Camillo (*W. Tale*). Wrongdoers are
often pardoned with extraordinary ease: Proteus, Angelo. A spirit of
atonement and forgiveness marks the close of the tragedies: even
Titus concludes with the prospect of a better time; and the only
exception is *Othello*. The device of the soliloquy, which now seems
to us cumbrous, was largely practised. Characters naïvely communicate their projects, or villains acknowledge their own baseness.[2]
Richard III is an instance of the latter—and, of the former, Henry VI
who reveals his identity to the listening rangers. Suffolk (*Henry VI*)
provides an instance of the speaker who bares his agonies of mind
as if no one were present. But Shakespeare followed these traditional
expository soliloquies with a series where we gain insight into the
workings of the mind which produced the plot.

One result of a freer dramatic form was that characters could
develop in an unconstrained and natural manner. Kyd in the *Spanish*

[1] Cf. Stoll and others.   [2] Cf. Stoll.

Tragedy and Shakespeare in *Titus* show how misfortunes cloud their hero's mind. The *Shrew* presents a psychological transformation: on the other hand, in *Richard III* and the *Merchant* Shakespeare follows Marlowe in drawing his chief characters with immovable features; although not till the tragic period was his full power unfolded. Each one of his various figures is individual and typical; and all attempts to analyse his methods have failed. The creative might of his all-compelling intuition silences criticism; we know his characters as intimately as if they were living beings. No other dramatist has approached his skill in grouping and contrasting comic figures. The clowns of *Verona* and the *Shrew* set each other off by contrasting qualities; while Launce and Speed represent varieties of simplicity. Other instances of varied figures of the same species are Shallow and Silence, Dogberry and Verges, and the grave-diggers. Shakespeare paid the highest tribute to the fool in giving him a part in such plays as *Twelfth-Night* and *A.Y.L.*; and in Lear's fool comedy and tragedy are blended in the most original manner.

In his early works Shakespeare rather exceeded his contemporaries in the use of rhyme and alliteration. He quickened and inspired the prose which he took from Lyly; but we cannot lay down a rule for his use either of rhyme or prose; and we must remember that imperfect texts have often confused prose and verse. The prose spoken by Iago and Hamlet often reaches the highest level of his creative genius. When Iago's insinuations cause Othello to swoon, Shakespeare's greatest effect of horror through transition from verse to prose is achieved. He shared to the full the Elizabethan love of simile, and would even work out a comparison beyond its dramatic purpose. But it was in terse comparisons, suddenly lighting up the dialogue in magnificent imagery, that all must give way before him, e.g. 'a rich jewel in an Ethiope's ear' (*R. and J.*). The comparisons of 'Jealousy', 'Commodity', &c., witness to his power of personifying abstractions: a national poetic trait handed down from the Moralities. The maxim was considered a 'pillar of Tragedy' by Renaissance poets; and Shakespeare used this form to give to the world wisdom and knowledge of life. Already in Marlowe and Kyd we find aphorisms, and afterwards in Chapman, Tourneur, and Webster. If the early drama shows the influence of the traditional classic manner, on one point the English dramatists broke away from the first. They never recognized the law of tragic gravity—the need to maintain a high level of dignity in language.[1] Between the speech of kings and clowns lies a whole range of gradations of expression imperceptibly merging into one another and producing the same impression of vitality as the mingling of comic and tragic. A supreme instance is Lady Macbeth's comparison of her husband to 'the poor cat i' the adage'. . . .

[1] Cf. Voltaire.

The dominant note of this criticism is the historical; and it is the summing up of a judge rather than the pleading of an advocate. Professor Creizenach reckons with the modifying influence on Shakespeare's genius of the age, the theatre, the audience, the conventions of dramatic art, such as the soliloquy, &c.; and he helps us to understand Shakespeare by the degree in which he outstripped other dramatists, and also through the opinions of critics: thus he tells us that local colour was little studied by dramatists, and there is nothing to justify the assumption that Shakespeare had visited Italy, since he uses the same freedom with Illyrian, Sicilian, French, or Viennese colouring. There is some risk, as in science, that generalizations can only be effected through excluding all that is individual and characteristic: thus in his roll of Shakespeare's 'humorous men' we find Mercutio, Falconbridge, Enobarbus, Menenius, Iago. And he uses *Titus* as one of the proofs that the tragedies conclude with the prospect of better times. We do not doubt that Professor Creizenach himself appreciates Shakespeare's poetic, artistic, and philosophic power—but the sentences in which he records his appreciation are parenthetical rather than integral. His criticism suggests that of the publisher's reader—though we hasten to add that some persons consider this kind of criticism to contain the greatest amount of truth. The wide experience, of which it is the fruit, at least ensures that errors should be avoided—and a foundation is prepared on which the critics of the future may safely build.

VI

DR. A. LESCHTSCH [1] believes that Prince Henry was genuinely attracted by Falstaff, and does not join his company to deceive expectations. He has not his father's diplomatic hypocrisy, but is open and honourable, and thus gained a better knowledge of men than at court. Even as king he could joke with the soldiers. He combined the humour of Falstaff and heroism of Percy. Honour has no objective value for Percy, but is a morbid, over-excited, subjective desire. A man may remain a sensualist even when he strives for non-sensual pleasures. Shakespeare sentences both severely: Falstaff is banished, and Percy rushes senselessly on death. These two qualities were more exalted in Henry.

Falstaff has an unmistakable religious trait, that proves Shakespeare to be well read in the Bible. He quotes Biblical names and incidents, and refers to hell, reward, grace. No other Shakespearian character has so many religious references. It is difficult to decide how this affects his whole character. Critics like Schlegel relegate it to the background; but to see in him only a merry good-for-nothing is to ignore the depth of his character. He is not a hypocrite, for even religious

[1] *Falstaff*, 1912.

people may joke about serious things; and his death left a good impression on the hostess. His religion was touched by his humour: he saw God as absolute and man as nothing. Hence he is resigned, and fears no man—and when the King banishes him his resignation attains a tragic height. He adapts himself to new conditions without complaint. Such a degree of submission is only found in one who lives entirely in the present moment, and can at once cut himself off from past and future. It appears in the scene when the Sheriff enters after the Gadshill robbery. He knows his danger, yet falls asleep behind the arras.

With such an outlook he is neither a coward nor yet a brave man. The man who denies worth to life will see no object worthy of risk. Lack of energy may appear cowardice; and when a man feels there is no cause to be brave he may leave the impression of cowardice. Several instances prove that he did not fear death; and one who can joke on his situation immediately after danger has no actual fear. He can be brave or cowardly according as the object is or is not worth while. Such indifference to danger is possible to one who lives solely for the moment. Neither disposition nor principle decide things for Falstaff, but circumstances only. He feigns death to escape Douglas, because he willed to live, and this was his only means. . . .

This criticism is at least thought-compelling, though it treats an old theme. Our remarks on Mauerhof's treatment of Lady Macbeth do not hold good here; for the question is what Falstaff is as much as what he does. And yet the critic's best point, that Falstaff exists for the moment, brings the argument round in a circle. If he exists for the moment, it is at such moments that we see him. We are stimulated by Shakespeare's creative impulse and rise above ordinary moral and social obligations. We blame neither the robbery at Gadshill nor the defeatism at Shrewsbury. . . . The point was none the less worth making, though we do not think Falstaff's behaviour at the moment of rejection is thereby explained.

VII

PROFESSOR LEVIN L. SCHÜCKING[1] finds irreconcilable differences as to the true interpretation of Shakespeare's characters. Since the subjective has triumphed, the impression varies with the character of the reader. The romantics read modern thought and feeling into him; but the question is how he appeared to his contemporaries, and what is the cause of the obscurity? His individuality had little free play, and plots were not then drawn from the artist's inner experience. Collaboration was frequent, and Shakespeare's art was one mighty wave of a great river. Public opinion restrained even

[1] *Character Problems in Sh.'s Plays*, 1919 (London, G. G. Harrap & Co., Ltd., 1922).

Marlowe's daring thought: his Faust cowers at approaching death. Shakespeare kept the general public before his eyes, and retained many popular elements that Ben Jonson and others were rejecting. Hence the ceaseless changes of scene in *A. and C.*, Gloster's eyes, the various anachronisms. In the Clown scenes there is a blending of comic and tragic which destroys the illusion. Things unrelated to the action are introduced which therefore fail to heighten the tragic effect by force of contrast, and produce not relaxation but disturbance. Shakespeare wished to preserve intimate contact with the masses, and thus external evidence proves the popular character of his art. His art-form combines highly developed with primitive elements—on one side inexpressible delicacy and subtlety in portraying the soul, on the other, antiquated aids and props to the understanding, and alien plot-elements.

The Shakespearian theatre was primitive, and the actor closer than in modern times to his audience, to whom he almost spoke in his monologues. Self-explanation is natural to an introspective and a sincere character like Hamlet; but the trait has so much become second nature to Shakespeare that he bestows it upon characters, such as Falstaff, who are not devoted to the truth or given to self-analysis. The clown's business is to be witty, and to stimulate laughter and wit in others. Falstaff is less swaggerer and blusterer than grand master of all dramatic clowns, and in accordance with the dramatic tradition which makes the clown the centre of the comic underplot in the serious drama.

In ordinary life if a person praised or blamed himself, we would infer his real character indirectly. In Shakespeare when criminal persons openly described their deeds as wicked, the audience accepted it as direct, not indirect, truth. Lady Macbeth speaks of her cruelty, Iago of his villainy, Cloten of his villainous orders. Shakespeare does not attempt realism, but considers the limited mental capacity of the public, and wishes to avoid misapprehension of the main outlines of action and characters. On the other side, characters such as Hamlet's father, Prospero, Cordelia, Brutus, refer to their own good traits without vanity or self-complacency. Shakespeare merely overdoes the emphasis lest he should be misunderstood, and hence we receive a false impression.[1] *J.C.* above all is misunderstood by an anachronistic critical school. It was not necessary to belittle Caesar, for since the conflict is based on a political contrast, the drama could only have been rendered more tragic by the purely human greatness of the victim. His greatness shows less in himself than in his enormous influence on his surroundings. He is the centre of all, as we see from his 'chidden train'; he reads character, i.e. Cassius; he puts off petitions relating to self. His behaviour in the assassination does not betray the 'invalid' of Brandes. Shakespeare individualized him by means of

[1] Cf. Stoll and others on the monologue.

small human traits, knowing that to make him human would not destroy the impression of greatness on which the play rests. He has been called a boaster, but his enemies do not bring this charge—and again we must ascribe it to primitive dramatic self-explanation. It is the same unrealistic dramatic tradition which lets the villain confess himself. To understand Shakespeare's characters we must take seriously what they say of themselves, unlike those of modern dramatists.

We also see characters reflected in the minds of other persons. Troilus at first appears youthful and lacking in experience, but his real nature only evolves after the great disillusion. His self-estimate, 'plain and true' (IV. iv. 101), is completed by Ulysses (IV. v. 96). We get misleading descriptions of heroes by villains, at the expense of truth to character—another primitive feature of Shakespeare's art. Thus, Oliver praises Orlando, Iago Othello, Edmund Edgar. Such things belong to the exposition, and are needed to give a clear statement to the audience. The result is a slight distortion of the villain's mental physiognomy. Iago could not believe Othello had deceived him, and yet describe him as loving, upright, true, and noble. Lady Macbeth describes her husband—but the voice of conscience is very small in his bosom. It is fear of consequences that occupies the foreground of his thoughts. What preoccupied Shakespeare at this time was a sharp contrast producing cross-currents in a complex mind. Hamlet is weak by nature and desires to act, Othello loves tenderly and desires to kill, Antony unites a world-conqueror's strength with doting feebleness. Macbeth is a weak man, and his visions of terror are produced by fear: it is weakness that sees spectres, not strength. He starts at the first sight of the witches, and his state of excitement at the prophecies shows an irritable nervous system. He is the victim of nerves, and cannot control his facial expression, but in the end his mind is hardened and blunted. His ambitious impulses are not co-ordinated into one great and continued effort of will. He regrets the murder directly it is effected, though his horror is not genuine pity but the immense agitation of a man punished by his constitution for exceeding the physical limits set by his will. Lady Macbeth incites him with taunts of cowardice and weakness, and fears no opposition from goodness of heart: therefore her characterization is not true. Throughout the rest of the play she judges him clearly: the conclusion is that it was an error of characterization, and Shakespeare momentarily misjudged his own creation. Another principle is that positive statements about outside happenings are to be regarded as correct: there is no doubt about Lady Macbeth's suicide. With Shakespeare, suicide is the consummation of spiritual self-destruction wrought by evil.

The dramatic practice of the time was anti-individual, and there may be lack of realism in the manner in which Shakespeare's characters express themselves: although this is often one of Shakespeare's strong points—e.g. Shylock and Hotspur whose moods and individualities are characterized by stylistic means in the minutest details. But in episodes the author's interest may take a different direction, and the character lose its unity. Bottom becomes witty among the fairies; the matter-of-fact Mercutio, in his Queen Mab speech, contemplates lovingly the magical microcosm of animate nature. Polonius is loquacious, diffuse, inquisitive, superficial—but his speech of advice to his son is clear, precise, and strongly marked. The inevitable conclusion is that Shakespeare breaks unity of character and expresses his own personality. He satisfied the demand of the time that tragedy should be sententious.

How far did he preserve harmony of character and action? His creative processes contain elements that resist the establishment of perfect harmony. One is the tendency to split up the action into many independent scenes. We must bear in mind the medieval view of art where similar elements were placed side by side. After the classical revival it was required that parts should be subordinated to a comprehensive idea. Hamlet refers to the distresses of London actors; the 'King's evil' is mentioned in *Macbeth*; the action is interrupted by comic scenes whence no higher unity by contrast results. Shakespeare was supremely interested in the single scene: *Richard III* impresses by combined effect of single scenes.[1] Prospero speaks of tombs on the lonely island—Horatio, Hamlet's equal in age, narrates events of the day he was born—Antony was not present when Caesar overcame the Nervii—Hamlet's task is imposed by a being from the 'undiscovered country'. We must therefore dismiss the subtle speculations of critics who have tried to harmonize the conflicting elements.

This may also influence the drawing of characters, and although there is usually no change of physiognomy between the appearance of a character in one scene and another, there are contradictions. Cleopatra in the first acts is a courtesan whose only aim is love, not a queen giving audience. She is familiar with her maids and then turns on them, she beats the messenger like a mere shrew, boasts of her distinguished lovers. She puts Antony in the wrong by her cleverness, and loves him in a selfish, superficial way. The portrait is done with consummate skill, but she is by no means a 'nobly planned' woman. We see that Shakespeare regarded the sensual attraction which she possessed for Antony as the cause of her power over him, from the reflection of her character in the mind of Enobarbus. The last two acts witness an astonishing change. She exceeds Plutarch's figure, and becomes a thoughtful and motherly woman who almost forgets her own fate in Antony's. Juliet could not show more passion-

[1] Cf. Stoll and others.

ate grief or unselfish love. Cleopatra of the first acts is a creature of
sense, trained and refined above the animal level, checked from utter
sensuality only by calculation. That she fulfils her grievous resolutions
without complaint reveals sterling moral quality. The explanation is
the single-scene method: Shakespeare has cut up Plutarch's narrative
into a succession of co-ordinated scenes. Cleopatra resembles the 'dark
lady', and may be drawn from life.[1] The sensual attraction described
by Enobarbus is clearly founded on individual impression: 'I saw her
once hop forty paces . . .'. A masterly portrait results from such
combined single realistic touches, different from the second Cleopatra
who is an ideal figure like Imogen or Desdemona. By raising her
character to a higher level Shakespeare creates difficulties from which
he cannot free himself. He took from his source a course of action
that contradicted his idealized character, i.e. the Seleucus episode.
Since she intends to die it is useless to conceal jewels. Shakespearian
critics do not understand that in drama action is above character.
Shakespeare is always working upon a given plot, along pre-arranged
lines—and at times his psychology suffers. Cleopatra proves that he
fears to depart from history in important details.[2]

Hamlet is an instance of the melancholy hero fashionable at the
time—the state we now call neurasthenia. With the Elizabethans
it was strangely accompanied by active imagination (cf. Jaques).
Hamlet is the most fascinating representative of the type. Weakness
and irritability are the basis of his character: and we find exact parallels
in other melancholy characters—Hieronimo (*Spanish Tragedy*) and
Marston's Antonio. That his mother's marriage should ruin his
constitution does not prove a particularly noble disposition. The
melancholy type is incapable of concentrated systematic activity, and
subsides into reverie. Hieronimo is devoured by the passion of revenge.
Yet Hamlet does not fear bloodshed or shrink from murder: and
the critics err who consider him over-delicate. Shakespeare refined
his feelings while leaving intact his fundamental character: he shows
piteous tenderness for his father, is shaken in his soul's depths by this
purely spiritual and unselfish disappointment. But he discovers no
beautiful traits to Ophelia and Polonius: and we should never forget
his neurotic condition. The interest in procreation, that appears
in his speech to his mother, is a regular trait of the melancholy character. It is a dramatic principle that no character should possess a
salient quality which does not affect the action: and also the action
must not depend on qualities which do not appear in the drama.
Shakespeare strictly observes the first rule—excepting Antonio's
melancholy in the *Merchant*. Ophelia's madness serves no dramatic
purpose—but it did in the older play. The danger is that qualities

[1] Cf. Frank Harris.
[2] Cf. Middleton Murry on Aufidius, and Brander Matthews on Laertes.

which do not effect action excite interest and call forth expectations that are not fulfilled. Ophelia, however, cannot excite these expectations; she is a beautiful dramatic luxury who sets at defiance the above principle. The second part of the rule applies to the crime of Claudius, which only an outcast of humanity could have committed. Dramatic appearance and reality conflict: he shows princely deportment in the first scene; his speech from the throne has great thoughts, and is manly and majestic. Hypocrisy should betray itself in the drama: Shakespeare should express the malignant villain and degenerate assassin; while the actor might emphasize his amiability. He is a true altruist in sympathy for Ophelia, and an intrepid hero when Laertes raises mutiny. Only an unstable or broken character would plunge into prayer; but Shakespeare has uncritically taken over the primitive psychology of the model, and works at what is demanded by the plan already in the story. The action required a prayer scene to convince the audience; and also Shakespeare's purpose was to make his villains recognize their sin. We conclude that the parts of this figure are not all of one cast, but are formed in accordance with the part each one has to take in the action. Each part showed a tendency to independence of scene and heightening of scenic effect.

In a few cases Shakespeare departs from the given action. He based Lear's character on his irascibility, and the acute question arose of relating character and action. Critics have misjudged the opening scene. Cordelia's conduct would naturally put her father out of humour, but not change love to hate. The Fool, Kent, Gloster, help to prove that Lear had not always been flattered. Shakespeare attempts to make his actions agree with the rest of his conduct, e.g. the sisters' conversation, Kent's banishment, undiminished impatience after abdication. He threatens the Fool, strikes Oswald, speaks to Kent in disguise like a policeman to a burglar. To be unspeakably offended by ingratitude is not the sign of a noble character. Only he who has acted from calculation and failed will be embittered by ingratitude. Yet no one reproaches him for this, and all adopt his view-point: as Shakespeare wishes the spectator to do. The dominant impression is that three of the most venerable human qualities, united in one person, fatherhood, old age, kingship, are here treated irreverently. Also an unspeakable insult is offered to a king, who yet retains his dignity among beggars and in his madness. Critics have called his career one of purification, but the passage where he pities the beggars is a solitary one; and Shakespeare was little interested in social questions. Lear merely follows the beaten track of the melancholy type, whose 'humour' delights in unmasking shams. He rails against women in accordance with a mood resulting from mental derangement. He should confirm it after his return to sanity if it is to count as a stage of development. Nothing touches more than the fact that he is no longer the old Lear—not purified but extinguished. The drama is the story of a breakdown rather than a development. Hence the weakness which creates in the masterful old man, so far self-centred, a sympathetic interest in the distress of others. He is not greater at the close, but a different person.

At times Shakespeare followed action too closely, at the expense of psychology. The sub-plot of *Lear* is untrue to human nature, and disregards all that must have occurred before the play. Gloster and Edgar should have known each other better; and the bastard would not suddenly become a villain. Shakespeare condensed at the expense of psychology, and at times was artistically careless, e.g. the clumsy intrigue of *M. Ado*—the superficial view of the problem of winning a husband's love in *All's Well*, contrasted with Boccaccio, and the disharmony between the action and the heroine's character: a woman with enough energy to win a man twice should possess more will-power and less sentimentality than appears in her conversation with the Countess. That Isabella (*M. for M.*) should make such a request to Mariana is revolting; yet Mariana readily consents. The creator of sensitive women, such as Desdemona, takes the line of least resistance. The criminal Angelo is forgiven to effect a happy ending, and it is alleged that his designs were only bad intentions. Shakespeare is unequal; he will make an enormous stride, and then revert to a primitive form, such as monologue or epical drama. Now he makes a character subtly individual, and, again, all his characters talk in the same key.

In assigning motives for action we see great irregularity. Some critics read between the lines—but Shylock's actions agree entirely with his words. Iago's expressed reasons do seem overshadowed by his love of intrigue and delight in his own malignity: and yet his reasons were not subjective imaginations. Shakespeare would not have impeded the spectator's understanding with a monologue containing subjective truths that were falsehoods. It is a feature of Shakespeare's monologues that the speaker tells the truth about his actions, that the action may be clear to the public. At times the action disproves the stated reason, i.e. Claudius does not *appear* such a wretched creature—because Shakespeare's creative process conflicts with his conscious intention. Iago is given excess of motives, and one may counteract the other, so that no one appears quite credible. When Hamlet spares the King at prayer he is thought to be deceiving himself: but in Elizabethan times great importance was attached to a persons's last actions before his death. This pivot of the action appears in Marston's *Antonio's Revenge*, where no one will suppose the behaviour to be the effect of subtle mental undercurrents. Prince Henry's monologue, 'I know you all . . .', if literally true, would stamp him as a hypocrite; but it is not from the depths of his character.

It belongs to the exposition, it is a kind of chorus. The rejection of Falstaff makes him appear a positively wicked hypocrite; but he is not meant to act reprehensibly. He is expressing Shakespeare's loyalty for the idea of kingship: the king's annointed person towers high above people like Falstaff, with whose soul his has nothing in common.

Shakespeare often gives no motives, e.g. Hamlet's assumption of madness, and his treatment of Ophelia, or Cleopatra's flight from Actium. Critics have differed, but the reason is the author cannot imagine the events should be understood except literally, i.e. Lady Macbeth's fainting fit. It has been ably disputed whether her unique strength of will and brutality and depravity are compatible with subsequent disintegration from forcibly restrained conscience. Also Shakespeare depicts remorse somewhat naïvely—Richard III, Claudius, Enobarbus. Yet he did seem to show that Lady Macbeth had to overcome inner resistance—unlike Richard III or Iago. If, then, her fainting fit was assumed, he would have told the audience, in accordance with his art-form. The tendency is to interpret primitive elements in Shakespeare from the standpoint of modern thought: and it helps the subjective method that Shakespeare often assigns no motive. He was probably too absorbed in his work to imagine any difficulty, and had ceased to exist outside his creations. He embodies individual personalities so fully and intensely that the whole is recognizable in the expression. Hence delicate shades of difference; and also—thanks to his romantic temperament and vast imagination—he appreciates and assimilates what is curious, fantastic, and exceptional. It may be due to his rapid thinking that he fails to see motives not readily intelligible. His mind rushes on, especially when he follows a ready-made action. But he never intended anything to be obscure, and the fewer unexpressed ideas we introduce the more likely we shall be to interpret truly. In many cases the solution lies in his materials; and thus to understand his train of thought we must explore his sources.

Shakespeare's characters are manifestly realistic; and the *Tempest* holds a distinctive place. Yet Prospero is unlike the other heroes, lacking the infinite wealth of human traits and interplay of qualities. He has a certain dryness, his mysterious art is not allied with corresponding mysterious depths of his nature. He is something of a schoolmaster—but Shakespeare did not intend this. Miranda is a child of nature, yet conscious of her innocence, and therefore artificial. The truth is that Shakespeare exceeds the limits of realism in self-characterization. Perhaps the play lacks Shakespeare's usual skill in character-drawing because it treats the supernatural—and the solemn atmosphere causes an abstract style of expression. In Miranda he glorifies innocence resting on *naïveté* due to lack of experience. He appears as member

of an artistic school, like that of Beaumont and Fletcher. It is characteristic of a conventional and artificial society to find virtue only outside
its own realm. Shakespeare betrays his own best traditions where the
most noble and refined righteousness shines brightest amid life's
tempests. Ariel's unwillingness to serve is transformed into longing
for freedom. His figure charms to-day because based on sense of
freedom and sense of nature—two romantic traits which then began
to gain enormous influence over the thoughts of modern men. Caliban
has the deeply rooted opposition of the mean and base to the noble:
hence he is psychologically probable, and has more specific personal
attraction than the most finished Shakespearian villains. With consummate skill Shakespeare has added the peculiar sadness which
accompanies spiritual deformity.

Prospero is said to be Shakespeare—but if his last speech is intended
allegorically the meaning is made needlessly difficult: and it was only
natural that he should dismiss his spirits. Shakespeare never wholly
enters into his characters, and the irony is that the world's greatest
humourist should be identified with that one of his creations who
has the least humour. We reject the various allegorical interpretations
of the play that have been suggested. Nineteenth-century speculations
on the nature and soul of the artist were unknown at the beginning
of the seventeenth century. Caliban is a fish-man, not a native: the
spectator saw him merely as a monster. Shakespeare may have used
the new information about men and conditions in the colonies as
additional material. Of the evolution theory (missing link) we find
no trace in Shakespeare's reflections; nor of political conception—
that Caliban was the soul of the masses. One cannot tear away traits
of the individual to make character a type. As well regard Shylock as
representative of Jews, and Falstaff of poor noblemen. Shakespeare's
art was individualistic, and Caliban's most effective side was the comic.
Shakespeare did not write for the small audiences that alone could
understand such allegories. He was no dramatic innovator, but
developed and made original contributions to what existed. . . .

A book like Professor Schücking's has its uses, though it has been
described as the historical method run mad. It is well to know how
Shakespeare appeared to his contemporaries, though the historical
may be but a minor branch of criticism. We persist in thinking that
the true method is the romantic, as Professor Schücking calls it—
that a work of art endures because it can stimulate the minds of
succeeding ages to think and record thoughts that bear the impress of
such stimulation. But the basis of art, of all that is most ideal and
imaginative, is reality—that is, something related to man's earthly
hopes and fears: and in this the historical method can help us. Rousseau's *Nouvelle Heloïse* was based entirely on imagination, and though
it conquered a contemporary world, it has proved fairy gold, and we of

the morrow are left with withered leaves. Virgil's imagination
refined out of reality the forest and river and branched road of Avernus;
and familiar Bedfordshire supplied Bunyan with the awful lanes and
by-paths and wicket-gates of the *Pilgrim's Progress*. It cannot be
said that Professor Schücking's book helps us to appreciate Shakespeare,
but we admit that after reading it our feelings for Shakespeare are
slightly changed. These changes operate when he deals with the
reality that underlies a character's spiritual life. We hardly know
whether to accept or reject his saying that if Hamlet was shattered by
his mother's marriage it does not prove his noble nature; but it is
partly true that ingratitude was not a wholly worthy cause of Lear's
passion; and also that Miranda should not have been conscious of her
innocence. Prince Henry's first soliloquy is well explained as chorus or
exposition; but in the rejection of Falstaff the critic touched absurdity.
Similarly with the character of Caesar, with Macbeth's 'irritable
nervous system', Hamlet's 'neurasthenia', Lear's 'breakdown rather
than development', he is outside poetry—his standard is the external
one of many preceding German critics. His account of Cleopatra
witnesses that he looks upon the human soul like a piece of machinery
or mechanical toy wound up to run a limited course, with no hidden
depths or unexploited resources. If he recognizes Shakespeare's true
greatness—his imagination, his character-drawing, his verse—it is in
a parenthetical manner exceeding that of Professor Creizenach's—
as if he were repeating something learned by rote, or that had no bearing on the present subject. Nowadays we do think of Shakespeare as
hampered by popular demands—as emitting his liquid melodies
through the bars of an art-form imposed from without. Professor
Schücking celebrates the temporal rather than the eternal; but now
and then, at those points where temporal and eternal converge, he
meets us, book in hand, with the timely reminder not to admire too
uncritically.

VIII

FRIEDRICH GUNDOLF [1] looks back to the turn of the sixteenth
and seventeenth centuries when Shakespeare was introduced to the
Germans by English players. There was a dull seriousness and bigoted
narrowness in the German of the period; and the English drama, that
represented men of action and passionate feelings, became pantomime
on the German stage, with loss of all rhetorical, poetic, spiritual, and
cultural elements. *Titus* was the favourite play: that corresponded best
to the taste of the German public. But it was simply a theatre piece,
whereas *Hamlet* and *R. and J.* were pure creations of the absolute
poet. In these the central fire overpowered the raw material and the
apparatus of the theatre; and we see that though he may have been

[1] *Sh. and the German Spirit*, 1920.

conscious of the stage and his audience, the inward poetic compulsion was stronger than his theatrical intentions. This appears specially in *Hamlet*—while *R. and J.* is a song of songs of the Renaissance.

There is much of the Renaissance in *Hamlet*, but it belongs essentially to the unfathomable and individual spirit. The problem before us on the stage is only a pretext for the spiritual—the struggle between the necessary limited act and unlimited thought, between life and knowledge. Hamlet the active man must have no conscience—but as contemplative man he has too much. His duty is to do a determined action, but he is lamed by his recognition of the world as a whole. He sees the deed not as something isolated, but in connexion with the whole world. This problem was Shakespeare's sole property, and he represented it in Renaissance fashion as two living forces working against one another. He wrote this particular Hamlet for himself alone; but the frontal mask sufficed the playgoers. Even in England the audience would prefer action to soliloquy. The tension here consists less in the development of fate than its concealment, less in unfolding than coiling, less in colour than dread, less in illuminating outspokenness than curious silences, less in powerful outline than ambiguous veiling in gloom; in glaring, sudden, restless lights and shades. No other work has such a profound depth of space, nor discovers such peculiar qualities in space and time. No doubt all this strangeness attracted an English audience, besides the fact that it presented for the first time the English national disease of spleen. For the German public it was too delicately shaded.

Such humour and irony were new to the Germans—the thought that any one could experience the world as a compassionate human being and overlooking god: as a present from which there is no escape, and as an arbitrary vision. Hamlet's jokes and cynicism are the result of too great a suffering in the face of the world, and too clear a vision of its distortion—of knowledge of things as a whole and trouble at their disfigurement. The garden and balcony scenes of *R. and J.* are alive with Shakespeare's glowing breath, and they contain the whole essence of the play. The rest is action or fate; for, with Shakespeare, the enmity of the houses only exists that Romeo and Juliet may find themselves in the garden scene. The death of Tybalt and its consequences are only ways and means for the balcony scene, to give full effect to union and separation, inner conquest and outer ruin. From these two scenes his creative power has extracted their utmost meaning.

Shakespeare recognized three worlds: the spirit world, void of space, time, and responsibility, where caprice and vision are the only realities; the noble human world which creates illusion out of its passionate reality; and the ordinary human world which out of its illusion creates a grotesque reality. He thus gains spaciousness, and creates new dimensions and changing perspectives. For the air-perspective of the artist, the dramatist gives degrees of reality—difference in intensity of his numerous characters or groups. This difference separates the popular from the heroes, not difference of disposition. When his works are called 'profound', it is not so much on account of his philosophy as because he creates a deeper spiritual atmosphere. He does not practise on the surface, but his figures are three-dimensional, and every fact is placed in a higher or measured by a lower, and each of his figures or groups modelled out of the light and shade of the remainder. He is therefore not only a creator but a judge of reality —not in the sense of good and bad, but actuality or appearance, self-sufficing or conditioned, fate-full or fate-poor, tragic or comic. His fools and citizens exist that his heroes may be better modelled from them: they exist only as shadows, corporeal from the bodies beside which they work. These three worlds cross and intermingle in *M.N.D.*, and out of graceful play and overbrimming laughter is created this symbolic work for the imagination as a power of life.

The whole air and landscape are part of his characters: in the first scene, before there is any development of plot or character, fate and being shine out of them. He thinks in atmosphere as well as character —the heath in *Lear*, the summer night in *R. and J.* are features of character. *J.C.* has the walls, towers, chimneys, with their rabble; *A. and C.* has the vessel on the Cydnus; to the English peers belongs the blood-stained field of battle. The woods, moonshine, flowers, wind, of the fairy tales almost embody the human souls. Everything in the elements reflects more gloomily or happily the spiritual. Costume, place, historical setting, are never matters of chance. If Macbeth had not been of the north,[1] Romeo of the south, and Brutus no Roman, the plays would have lacked meaning.

Shakespeare's sentences are atmospheric, rhythmic, architectonic; his verse originates in what is vital; in it speak the powers laden with things and men, or embodied through them. Their speech presses from within outwards, from the will, the impulse, the sense, to take colour and form. In Shakespeare's pictorial speech we must distinguish between similes and actual pictures—two mental actions of different origin. The first is the Renaissance habit; the pictures are forms of his thought, not means but substance of his poetic conception. Pictures replaced similes more and more as his work ripened, and they help to decide the chronology of plays, e.g. contrast Juliet's monologue (simile) with Othello's pictorial speech.

By nature we understand the sum of all whereby man lives and has being; by fate the sum of all whereby he acts and suffers. Shakespeare has united the two by the principle of creation. Creation belongs equally to nature and fate, to freedom and necessity, to

[1] Cf. Montégut.

becoming and doing; and Shakespeare's men face fate as nature, or
are placed in nature as the bearers of fate. Nature and fate are not
opposed for Shakespeare; and in his work, like creation itself, he exposes
the contradictions which the beholder or artist or hypocrite find in
them, and among which they must choose, if a world picture is to be
created. He creates both world and reality, while others give only
pictures of the world. Still others take up a definite standpoint
within or without the world: the standpoint with Shakespeare is as
wide as the world itself.

His beings are creatures of reality who come into conflict with
other parts of reality: a conflict that determines their fate, and is their
fate. He did not lack morality in its wider sense—i.e. the value of
reality—but he used reality as his measuring rod, and it is more
dynamic than actually moral. He saw no judgement in destruction,
and knew no absolute good or bad. His misdoers do not fail because
they have erred in the choice between good and evil, but because they
have conflicted with a greater power—a stronger reality. Morality
for Shakespeare is one of the realities of the world, like others, and it
does not always prevail. Stupidity, wickedness, genius, beauty, power,
may be as strong or stronger. *M.N.D.* has no more morality than
a dream; in *M. for M.* no mention is made of it; and characters like
Falstaff and Autolycus scoff at it. Moral laws are not for Shakespeare
immanent as they were for Schiller.

Like no one else, Shakespeare has expressed the incalculable in man
and nature. He has revealed the hidden kingdom of the spirit, and by
animating dead nature has revealed her secrets—the powers, impulses,
riddles, latent in the atmosphere. He is master of the vagaries of the
will, he is the great ironist, the supreme humourist, who can joke
beside the most shattering tragedy. He has made the tragic Danish
prince a cynical world-fool. He is an unequalled master of language
—and of romanticism in three respects: universal fantasy, universal
thought and irony, and in power of speech. . . .

It is hard to think that this abstract work could ever be popular
in England as it has been in Germany, but it is to be reckoned with in
the study of its subject, because it deepens the Shakespearian mystery.
To understand it, we may recall two popular sayings: that Shakespeare
is nature—and that this world may be imperfect because it is part of
a larger scheme. If we reconcile these we gain some light on Shakespeare's moral system, and the rewards and punishments which he
deals to his characters. What helps to overcome the abstractions is
the comparisons between Shakespeare and other poets, and those
between his own characters. They impress according to their degree
of reality—and the fools are shadows of the heroes. But the tragic
Hamlet is also a cynical world-fool—Cleopatra's nature is linked to
the Cydnus, Lear's to the heath, and Macbeth's to the north. Dis-

joined from these they would lose some reality: but no poet has united like Shakespeare the opposites of living and dead nature, natural and spiritual things—or shown that if morality is a force in the world, so is stupidity. All art is symbolic, but Gundolf succeeds in conveying that there may be more things in Shakespeare than are yet dreamt of in our philosophy.

IX

HELÈNE RICHTER[1] finds that Shakespeare laughs gladly and heartily, and this delightful carelessness gives him mastery over life. He is not occupied by the problem of the division of soul and body, but the straightforward, wholesome, positive, character of the whole human being, which stands in no antagonism to the world. He wrote primarily for the stage, and left much for the actor to interpret. It does not seem probable to the reader that the ardent Romeo should hear of Juliet's death and remain master of himself. Trusting in the actor, without being rhetorical, he can by a word or two show the condition of a man's spirit. When Lady Macbeth dies, Macbeth speaks a few seemingly cold words—but here is scope for the actor's craft.

Shakespeare, while fully individualizing a character, nearly always has in view a typical fundamental quality. In several plays the same type appears variously specialized: Cressida and Helena are both heartless and faithless, and awaken violent passions, yet each is an individual. And so Margaret and Elinor are both ambitious for power. These differentiations make the typical more impressive. But even more frequently are characters opposed, and this serves the same purpose of linking individual examples by general representation. Alcibiades and Timon are absolutely distinct, but are linked by the common fate of exile. One becomes lonely and resentful; the other spends his time in dissipation, and then marches against his native town. Brothers are often paired, as hero and villain—Edgar and Edmund, Prospero and Antonio, the elder Hamlet and Claudius. Or an ideal may light up a character and transmute it from individual to type—Othello, Shylock—neither of whom are created to exemplify any race problem. The more salient the typical idea in a character, the more careful is Shakespeare to add individual traits, to satisfy reality, and not condemn under one ethical heading any living organism.

Perfect characterization is mingling justly the personal and universal. The marvel of Shakespeare is that he mingles individual qualities which correspond with nature, and excludes anything abnormal. The most excellent has his less worthy side, the unworthiest some better trait. Characters possess the defects of their quality and the advantages of their crimes. As mentioned above, the individual struggles and frees himself from the general and typical. As Shake-

[1] *Sh. the Man* (Leipzig, 1923).

speare increases his mastery, both type and individual are finely and with discrimination raised to the point where the struggle begins between them, and the sternest human conflict follows. Thus national custom and contemporary morals urge Hamlet to revenge, but nature swerves him from the task.

The plays usually contain a fundamental idea like a musical theme —or nerve of the play—to which all the persons are related: ambition (*Macbeth*), credulity (*Othello*), jealousy (*W. Tale*). This makes Shakespeare's dramas pictures of the world, humanity, and fate. Credulity crosses *Othello* like a diagonal line. Iago shows it when he suspects Othello and his wife, and Desdemona does penance for lack of cunning. Men at their highest shake off the individual qualities of chance, and show nearer to type. Shakespeare towards the close of his career preferred such characters: Prospero, Hermione, Queen Katharine.

The fate of Shakespeare's heroes is the inevitable result of their behaviour: even Romeo and Juliet are self-determined by their passion. Othello's fate was the blind trust of a strong nature in an unworthy one. The finer a character is organized, the more he pays for the least failing. Hamlet and Timon succumb to the exaggerated cult of an idea: with Hamlet it is the ideal of personal perfection, with Timon human brotherhood. At first Desdemona seems only to want tact; but, looking closer, we see the want of control of the patrician's daughter accustomed to a life of pleasure. Fate is the reparation demanded by a moral world order. Edgar expresses it when he says that our pleasant sins are the instruments to punish us. With Shakespeare, the normal, healthy, and natural is the measure of all things.

Macbeth, with his vital imagination, might have become a great poet, in more favourable circumstances. Visions are more real to him than facts, and he is a slave to impulse. The wish becomes an imperative imagination from which he cannot free himself. The idea once conceived that Duncan may die, he has already made the leap into evil. Nerves and imagination explain his passage from innocence to guilt, and the upturning of his whole inner nature. His outcry when Duncan's death is discovered is genuine, but the cause is not: for he despairs because he has killed the King, not because the King is dead. He laments because he cannot now die guiltless; the elementary power in him is conscience. His better nature is torn to pieces by consciousness of guilt and takes its revenge.

Lady Macbeth is without personal ambition, but has womanly cunning and readiness of tongue, and is inclined to exaggerate. We must accept conditionally her reproach to Macbeth that he is too gentle, and also her own inhuman bursts of speech. Her soliloquies betray some hysteria—another womanly trait, and perhaps the germ of her later collapse. Her appeal to demonic powers is unconscious confession of weakness, and her shrinking from actually killing Duncan herself shows something other than a fury. Macbeth knew her tenderly strung nature, and tried to spare her knowledge of Banquo's murder. She earned the ingratitude of many self-sacrificing women: she disappears in the third act—her part in his life is over. He has separated himself more and more from his fellow-creatures; and the crime they have shared stands between them like a ghost. Arrogant Macbeth endures no contradiction, and no longer requires his former counsellor. . . .

There is much that is conventional in this essay, especially what relates to *Macbeth*; and the analysis of Desdemona is hardly convincing. But there is a creative touch in the handling of the character theme of type and individual; and also in the revival of the 'fundamental idea', and the larger conception of the moral order of the world. The writer is able to use, without obtruding, her own experience of life.

X

JULIUS BAB [1] says of *J.C.* that it is the first tragedy since *R. and J.*, that it precedes *Hamlet* and introduces Shakespeare's darker period. Brutus is the forerunner of Hamlet and even the progenitor of Troilus. Like Troilus he stands, a noble man of highest moral character and earnestness, in a world of fools and egoists; and he even recalls Hamlet's great cousin Don Quixote. It is true that he does do the deed; but through the whole play Shakespeare shows how hopeless was his struggle, and how senseless in its true nature was his heroic deed. Yet hardly has he drawn any character with so much love, tenderness, and power. Though taken from Plutarch, all that is human and animating, all that decides the man, is in the imperceptible turns that set Shakespeare's figures in motion, and the sound of their words. He is neither good politician nor great general, but it is always his nobler qualities that urge: and therein the tragic bitterness of the play. In depicting Caesar as a charlatan, Shakespeare has made exceptional use of Plutarch's details. It was his duty as an artist to belittle Caesar, and place Brutus's tragic folly in the clearest light.

Hamlet's task was not insuperable—as we see when Laertes quickly carries out his revenge—nor were deep thoughts the wanderings of a lunatic. Equally false is the interpretation that he was the higher type of modern man who cannot shed blood. The murder of Polonius, dispatch of Rosencrantz and Guildenstern, struggle at the grave, and killing of the King, are part of the whole great picture, not alien elements.[2] He is neither over-tender, nor an ethical genius, nor sick in mind—but richly gifted, strong in mind and body, with

[1] *Sh. Wesen und Werke,* 1925.   [2] Cf. J. M. Robertson.

imagination, feeling, and spirit—with passionate blood in his veins and a strong joyful will towards life. When the blow falls his balance is overthrown, consciousness becomes overwhelming, and instead of yielding naturally to his feelings he meets each experience with a bitter question. It is not an insoluble task that overthrows his nature— but he cannot perform the task because his nature is overthrown. When he spares the king and lets himself be sent to England, the cause is said to be self-deception, but the terrible truth is that his sinews of action have been destroyed. Plunged into awakened knowledge of the world, steeped in disgust of reality—all action, all idea of wishing to change the world as it is, appears to him stale and unprofitable. Consciousness, not conscience, makes cowards of us all; but the latent vitality in these superior natures works furiously when they lose control over the enforcedly passive spirit. There is 'something dangerous' in him, as he confesses.

The spiritual centre of nature has died in which the vital spirit guides and ennobles the sensual instincts and actions. No moral consciousness, but a vital obstacle, only giving way at moments, separates him from action. Between the first scene and the churchyard scene Hamlet scarcely develops: the fate in his inner being merely unfolds. He thinks to play with madness, but madness plays with him. Every man who separates his fate from that of mankind, who loses the feeling of self-understanding, through which alone life is bearable, totters on the verge of madness: as we see from Cassandra to Nietzsche. Here, as with Lear, Shakespeare shows his mastery, and reveals the full richness of a soul through the process of its dissolution. All that Ophelia saw in him was true; but his greatness and nobleness, like Lear's, show clearest in the bitter passion with which his spirit resists destruction. He struggles to deliver his soul, he condemns violently his own inaction. This noble truth and goodness finally enabled him to effect a kind of reconciliation with fate.

The secret of *Lear*, as of every work of art, is in the innermost retreats of life. The kernel of Shakespeare's plays is always the man himself; and he had no greater or keener vision of a man than in Lear. With Lear it is not the exaggeration of this or that quality, as with the other heroes, but the whole man is exaggerated—too strong to heed or suffer the limitations of the world. The first scene gives far more than the wild moods of an old man: according to the law of nature he meets his own being in his daughters. Cordelia is so entirely the offspring of her unbending, passionate father that she cannot speak a gentle word: she, too, is 'every inch a king'. Her sisters have inherited the strength without the noble disposition. In the end Cordelia incurs the fate which her own nature helped to let loose.

Macbeth at first soliloquizes like Hamlet, but, unlike him, he listens to his blood. Once the hindrance of consciousness overcome, he is caught in the whirlpool. In a more frightful way his world becomes unhinged; but while Hamlet's world is mentally clear Macbeth's is dull and murky, filled with a dark power. The criminal desire is in him—and also in the mist over the heath, the moist air in the walls of his castle. But the power of fate is not outside him: the man and his fate are one. He is not made of the hard stuff of the great criminals —Richard III, Edmund, Iago. He loves his wife, he fears loneliness, he has imagination and feeling. To perform a criminal act is therefore alien to his nature, and when he succumbs to passion he falls into hell, helpless under the weight of facts.

We therefore retain a human feeling for him that his cruel deeds cannot wholly crush. In his power to dream, see, fear there lies a soul; and as we realize how his soul, under the weight of the world and conscience, grows benumbed, we grow benumbed with him. There is nothing more shattering in literature than his speech after his wife's death —the passing of the only being that clings to him. Shakespeare aims always to awaken our soul's compassion, not shock our nerves. In this play, as in *Hamlet* and *Lear*, there is a contrasting upward movement— a powerful moral counter-voice. In all three there are good powers to deliver, and carry on the wholesome power of life over all past suffering and death. Here the part is filled by the younger Malcolm and Macduff. . . .

At this late hour it may seem strange that we are still concerned with criticism that deals with old problems and seems to offer no new solution. Thus when Brutus is placed absolutely in the front line of Shakespearian characters, we are reminded of those German critics who judged Shakespeare as philosopher rather than poet; and when Hamlet's violent deeds are included in one grand picture with his soliloquies, our minds return to nineteenth-century criticism and the ages of faith. However, if the writer makes these his centre, his mind continues to work outwards, so that he comes within sight of the mysteries. We feel the salt of modern inquiry in the air when he finds the tragic bitterness of *J.C.* in Brutus's nobler qualities—or decides that Macbeth has a soul. Comparisons between Macbeth and Hamlet in the past have not been happy, yet he says well that Hamlet's world is clear while Macbeth's is dull and murky. No doubt other explanations of Hamlet are to be preferred to his, but he has well defined the intermediary state—the illness of the soul— between the originating cause and its outer consequences.

XI

ON the subject of morals critics are not unanimous, though most incline to the moral side, including Bab. Wolff calls Shakespeare's work a moral organism; Kohler and Hélène Richter say that he recognizes a moral world-order; Mauerhof remarks that he stresses conscience. Schücking finds that in his world evil effects spiritual self-destruction; and he makes the point of some other modern critics, that the social sense was little developed in Shakespeare. Creizenach denies there is proof that he believed in a moral force controlling the universe; and Gundolf says that he looked upon morality as one of the world's realities, among others that may be as strong.

In religion Wolff denies to him other-worldliness, but calls him a great reader of the universal in man's soul. Kohler speaks of his infallible insight into spiritual conditions. Creizenach says he had no religious dogma, but was probably anti-Catholic. To Gundolf his standpoint was wide as the world itself. Leschtsch alludes to his knowledge of the Bible.

Wolff calls his characters individuals, not types; with Helène Richter the individual and type are justly mingled; and Creizenach also says the characters are both individual and typical. Schücking concentrates on his intense conception of delicately graded individual character.

Wolff credits him with unequalled art, but says that action most imports with him. Schücking agrees that at times he followed action too closely, at the expense of psychology—and his plot was made up of alien elements often unfused: that sometimes he is a careful artist, and at others impulsive and sketchy. Creizenach continually emphasizes his deep artistic wisdom. It seems to Gundulf that the inward compulsion of poetic power prevailed over the needs of the theatre and audience. For Helène Richter, the fundamental idea makes his plays pictures of the world, humanity, and fate. Against Schücking Bab praises his psychology—and also his art.

Wolff mentions his unconscious universality, and calls him the unattainable poet of all time: high development inclined him to pessimism, which he overcame. Creizenach celebrates his mighty power over words, his overflowing wealth of passion, his sunny humour, and penetrating knowledge of human nature. He had an independent and lofty conception of life and raised all that was base and mean in his model to the level of pure poetry. Creizenach also alludes to the creative might of his all-compelling intuition—and thinks he was of aristocratic temper. Schücking denies much free play in his work to his individuality, but considers him a fervent royalist, and one who shows exquisite feeling for human dignity: from his romantic temperament and vast imagination he deduces an emotional life hard to order, and an inclination to the strange and fantastic. Gundolf calls him absolute poet—one whose creative power extracts the utmost from scenes—who produces a symbolic atmosphere: great ironist, supreme humorist, romantic master of speech. . . .

At the risk of the charge of prejudice we cannot help chronicling a feeling of disappointment at these final generalizations of contemporary German critics. Now that the metapysical shadow has lifted they seem to be merely overtaking the work of their fellows in England and France. The works of Creizenach and Schücking outstand, but in them historical criticism predominates over aesthetic. If it is possible to apply a single generalization to the entire company of German critics, it is that they lack the lightning touch of imagination.

Chapter XLII

ENGLAND 1924–1925

I. A. M. MACKENZIE.   II. MACNEILE DIXON.   III. WINSTANLEY
IV. TUCKER.   V.'CHAMBERS.   VI. J. M. ROBERTSON.   VII. PRIESTLY.
VIII. GRANVILLE-BARKER.   IX. ABERCROMBIE.   X. CONCLUSION.

I

MISS AGNES MURE MACKENZIE [1] says that as a man of the pre-Puritan Renaissance Shakespeare saw women sharing as fully as men in the life about him. The women of the earliest plays interest him less in themselves than for the emotions they arouse. Those of the narrative poems are boring, while Tamora, Lavinia, Margaret, Eleanor are simply effective on the stage—forces that move the action, not motive-power of other forces. Margaret has little subtlety, if much force—is Marlovian, and her courage is that of the virago type of great Renaissance lady. Shakespeare always saw women as human, but human in another way than men—a way that made life more complex and therefore more dangerous.

The women of *L.L.L.* and *Verona* do not interest greatly as women, but the whole of *L.L.L.* is the relationship between the men and women —a study of theory and reality in the relations of conventionally bred man and woman. Biron's speech is the core—that love gives the knowledge of life. *Verona* takes the same theme, but here the obligation is to honour. The new love of Proteus lacks strength of honour as its base. Motives are still more than dynamic personages, but the latter are not lay figures. Silvia is more of an individual than Julia, if not modern at least human, and she makes Julia seem a piece of sentimental romance. Adriana (*Errors*) is a tiny but curiously poignant sketch. She and Katharine (*Shrew*) are *révoltées*, but Shakespeare tried to humanize the *Shrew* and transformed the termagant of farce into a figure who invites uneasy pity. Adriana is a dramatic blemish, for she steps out of farce and breaks into bitter reality

The treatment of the women throughout the next seven plays is experimental rather than always successful. They begin to acquire real personalities, but are less individuals than brilliantly rendered types. Those of *M.N.D.* have a streak of unintentional vulgarity; [2] but perhaps Shakespeare as yet had few opportunities of intercourse with ladies. [3] However, they are little more than puppets, elements in the fantastic pattern of a dream. Shakespeare was using his people as vehicles for situation or witty or poetic language. The plot of *All's Well* should either have been handled as a farce or with the savage

[1] *The Women in Sh.'s Plays* (Heinemann, 1924).
[2] Cf. Furnivall.   [3] Cf. Wells.

irony of *T. and C.* or *M. for M.* Bertram's snobbery *may* be a desperate clutching at his only possible defence. After having done the forcing, Helena becomes sleekly submissive like one who can afford to wait. For once Shakespeare falls below his sources. That Helena should so dupe Bertram as to make him thoroughly ridiculous to his intended mistress is hardly the way to win anything more like love from him. *R. and J.* first gives the perfect balance between dramatically patterned action and the persons who carry it out, especially the women. Juliet is a triumph and dominates the play as a person. Death is not waste, but life's consummation. Shakespeare converts a piteous incident into a facet of the terrible warfare between age and youth. Juliet's passion, expressed in her soliloquy, is clean as fire. The pain of parting at dawn makes even danger seem unreal. Juliet has a quality of her own that saves her from being overshadowed even by Lady Macbeth or Cleopatra. In outlines she is the conventional heroine of romance; all her actions or situations are in the orthodox tradition. But she has been conceived with the vital intensity of Shakespeare's young imagination at white heat dreaming nobly and reverently of love. The Nurse is a notable dramatic audacity, showing the commonplace prose-current that surrounds the tragic pair, and making them part of life instead of a remote dream-world.

The women of *Richard II* merely throw light on the men; the Duchess of York pleading for her son is like any terror-stricken mother. *Richard III* is a Marlovian type of play, though there is nothing of Marlowe in the almost artificially symmetrical arrangement of the complex action. The women have no dynamic part in the action. They reflect the realities behind it—the women's side of civil war—the ruin and sorrow that are the issue of successful hatreds. *John* is a picture of England coming to her feet in strength, and the women help to project the characters that express its theme. Constance is vehement rather than forceful, and helpless against Elinor's cold power and the men's chilly selfishness.

The characters of the *Merchant* are so developed that they mar the plot: a defect of Shakespeare's qualities, for puppets will do as they are told, but not living persons. The women are dynamic elements in the scheme of action, and also human. They teach us intellectually so that we are interested in them, and emotionally so that we like them. Portia is a little generalized and made upon a formula, not born, like Juliet, of the clear passion of the imagination. She is sententious and therefore less loved than Rosalind or Imogen, and she had no right to admire Bassanio—who was rather a housemaid's hero—though she might love him.

Between 1596 and 1600 Shakespeare was fully master of his tools. His women become marvellous artistic creations and delightful people. Those of *Henry IV* and *Henry V* only 'feed' the other characters, or play 'reflector' parts to cast light on Falstaff, Hotspur, Henry V—for Shakespeare knew that one of the main keys to a man's nature is his fundamental attitude to women. Note the personal nature of Lady Percy's appeal after her husband's death; she thinks of all in terms of her own Harry. *Henry V* is a *tour de force*, and the King is hardly Shakespeare's ideal man, but he is thoroughly able, and can gauge his own effects, and combines self-restraint and calculated frankness, like the born manipulator of men as distinct from the born leader. The wooing scene shows his talent for 'managing' people; the Princess becomes the seal upon a treaty. Mrs. Quickly's kinship is with Dickens, and she is never really sorry for herself.

A.Y.L. is simply the personality and fortunes of Rosalind. She is intensely alive and adorable, but not drawn in subtle or complex fashion—except for the mystery that underlies all great melody. Akin to Portia and Silvia, she is more perfect as art and has a more delightful personality. Till now love at first sight had been a common thing, but *M. Ado* brings a different type of love—something that threatens the virginity of spirit in which a character like Beatrice took pride, and out of the seeming ruin produces a deeper reintegration. Neither Benedict nor Beatrice stop to consider if they love; but each considers how to shield the other from pain. Hero lives so completely that we realize with a shock hers is but a passive part. There is some passivity in the main figures of *Twelfth-Night*. Circumstance and impulse guide Orsino and Olivia rather than will; and Viola's will is enduring rather than active. One is made to feel Olivia's appreciation of Viola's *personality*—her real nature under her disguise.

Twelfth-Night had prepared the way for tragedy by hinting at the fate of dreamers in a practical world. Shakespeare was now inclined to find tragedy congenial, though he handles it in a detached manner. In every one of the following ten plays the woman is disastrous more or less. Though Shakespeare's arraignment of life is followed by a vindication, one of the strongest counts is his indictment of women's share in men's life. No anti-feminist has written such terrible things of women, and no feminist has so vindicated them. From Julia and Silvia onwards, pluck and initiative distinguished Shakespeare's women, but *J.C.* first denounces weak women; though already in *Twelfth-Night* Olivia had failed to see clearly the actualities of any issue and to act on it promptly. Perhaps women were only introduced into *J.C.* to make room for the two clever boys of the company; but Shakespeare had the skill to make integral this incidental element forced into the play by irrelevant necessity. Portia shows us the private emotions of Brutus beneath the political; while the Calpurnia scene adds a few sardonic touches to the unflattering portrait of the living Caesar, to be contrasted later with the enormous power of his spirit. And yet each is a study of a personality. Portia is subtle, and she is also the first

woman in Shakespeare to belittle her sex to gain man's approval.
She does not steel her will like Lady Macbeth, but excuses her weakness by imputing it to her womanhood, and counts her virtues self-
achieved. She kills herself to prove to herself that she is not weak,
and Brutus takes her at her own valuation, and never feels that she
has failed him.

Both layers of the action of *T. and C.*—Shakespeare's bitterest
work—depend on the women. The war focusses the values—a ten
years' war for such another woman. These two women live and
flourish, while men die for them or become foul and false. Every line
of the play is pitilessly relevant to its theme, but it remains unsatisfying for lack of the driving power of complete intellectual and
emotional conviction. Shakespeare's inmost soul believed in his good
characters as much as his bad, and only when his spirit is sick with
a new bruise, or wearied out after his supreme tragedies, does he
blaspheme life. The play was probably written immediately before
Hamlet, for its whole stuff—which is but one element in *Hamlet*—
is disgusted disillusionment with life in general and above all with sex.
Sex causes the dreamer's tragedy in both plays, as it does in a different
manner in *J.C.* and the sub-plot of *Twelfth-Night*. The important
objective point of Shakespeare's private grief is what he tells us himself
—that it related to a woman. Probably the discipline of shaping his
torment in writing prevented collapse and saved Shakespeare from
going mad. He will never be light-hearted again, but he has gained
the secure vision that is faith.

The women of *Hamlet* are drawn more temperately and therefore more terribly. The root of the tragedy is the weakness, not the
wickedness, of Gertrude. Ophelia not only strengthens Hamlet's
torment, but the state of mind that makes it possible for him to be set
free from it. But the true evil was his placid, kindly mother. In his
view she had committed incest; but she is unconscious of having done
anything to be ashamed of. Ophelia's truth and purity might have
meant much to him, but he now doubts her. Is she like his mother
who, until lately, had always seemed chaste to him?[1] She should have
been big enough to think first of his trouble and attempt to help him:
but she is simply frightened—as much by his dishevelment as his
passion. The Queen is like a pleasant animal—docile, kindly, loving
her offspring, brave to defend her mate. The two Hamlets believe in
her, so she ruins them and herself: but it is they who suffer. She has
no ill will, but causes all the deaths, and is simply stupid, coarse, and
shallow. Ophelia is not unlike, though not coarse, only obvious—and
both unconsciously sow ruin all about them.

The good and evil women alike become ruinous now—and the
good are really and nobly good. Shakespeare knew goodness to be

[1] Cf. Clutton Brock.

more complex than evil and therefore more artistically interesting. *M. for M.* is dull and boring, and two-thirds of the people, including the heroine, are not alive. The main driving-power is perception of the loathsome possibilities of sex. Angelo's fall is the central thing, and women are incidental to him. Shakespeare was tired of the feeble heroine, but could not love Isabella like Beatrice or Viola, so never gives her of his life. Cordelia, Lady Macbeth, Volumnia are like Isabella in type, but each has a poignant beauty of her own. If Shakespeare saw them mercilessly he also saw them with infinite pity. But at the time of writing *M. for M.* his pity was swallowed up in weary nausea. After the prison scene Shakespeare tires of Isabella and no longer tries to make her live, and he has not attempted it with the other women. Two fine scenes—the pleading and prison scenes—do not make a fine five-act play, but Shakespeare was exhausted after *Hamlet.*

Othello once more is the study of a man whose whole-souled faith in a woman he has loved and trusted is suddenly proved baseless. The play has a transitionary quality that appears in the type of heroine. Desdemona is not strong, and in a way fails like Ophelia, because she fails to enter Othello's mind and share his trouble. But Ophelia fails because she is stupid, self-centred, and a coward: whereas Desdemona's lack of comprehension is pardonable, and he never *asks* for help. She is too clean to imagine foulness, and when she hears is too paralysed with horror. Time would have fused Othello and Desdemona, but Iago acts when they are still separated by race, speech, thought—and this circumstance ruins them. The play shows Shakespeare's strength recovered; he has mastered himself and again exults in life. Desdemona's suffering expiates Cressida, Gertrude, and Ophelia. Shakespeare arraigns not women as such, but the relation between men and women. Each ruins the other: but she suffers as much. His actions belie her faith, but he is the man who won it.

A great work of art means a wholesale squandering of vitality, and after *Othello*, as after *Hamlet*, Shakespeare was bound to be Titanically weary.[1] *Timon* was the result, to be succeeded by *Lear*. Shakespeare opens the latter with a scene which shows how utterly the two generations misunderstand one another: Gloster ignores his son's presence and feelings. Then Lear would bribe Cordelia to outgo a couple of greedy liars: and the whole Court look on at her humiliation. She, on the other hand, is too engrossed by her own judgement of the situation, and though she pities his future with Goneril and Regan, she does not perceive the horrible sense of being no longer effectual that is one of the tragedies of old age. Goneril is absolutely sure both of her rightness and power, and quite stupid—the most distressing type for the sensitive to deal with. Regan is smaller and shriller, and

[1] Cf. Dyboski.

less self-possessed. When Cordelia reappears in the fourth act we have forgotten her hardness, and have long ago forgiven Lear. The women singly are simple enough characters, but subtly drawn as a group. They are sisters, and akin to each other and to their father. Goneril has deadly power because she is sure of herself. The same thing applied with absolute honesty and unselfishness makes Cordelia ruin herself and Lear. For though the evil is Goneril's, the blame is Cordelia's and Lear's. Regan is smaller, and more to be despised, as a coward—one of Shakespeare's most horrible figures. Cordelia and Goneril differ less in nature than direction of nature. Cordelia acts on reverse principles from Goneril's, but in the same way.

Shakespeare was now interested in the strong and forceful type —the woman who is fiercely loyal to a person or principle, and who brings ruin in her wake because she is too single-minded to perceive the general values of conduct. Lady Macbeth is Shakespeare's most fully drawn woman, almost his greatest, and the most misunderstood. The central things in the play are Macbeth's relation to his crime and to his wife. The two are indivisible: but for her he would never have murdered Duncan and become the man he does become. There is not a word to suggest that she ever wished for the crown. She is feminine, plucky, and rather stupid,[1] and sees nobody in the world but her husband, like the ideal Victorian wife. The result is that she plunges the soul of a brave and noble man into blackest ruin. She has a false idea of greatness; to her it consists in external power. She is enormously brave, but also in material fashion—because she ignores spiritual risks. She understands her husband up to a point—but she can only see what she thinks he ought to feel. To 'smear the grooms' is a childish expedient, but she is not very intelligent, and also under the influence of wine and overstrain. After the crime she can help him no more, so they drift apart. The sleep-walking scene reveals the quality of her horror: she sees the facts that have happened, never consequences or possibilities. Even now her restraint is terrible, for there is no emotional outburst, and she speaks bare memories and nothing more.

With *A. and C.* Shakespeare returns to the old pain that had nearly wrecked him in the days of *T. and C.* and *Hamlet*, and now finds life splendid because of it. The theme becomes not what the woman has done to him but what he has had of her: and he thanks her for her royalty—for the shame and agony as well as the glory. It is hard to analyse Cleopatra's spell, for the whole of her is so much greater than the mere sum of her parts. She does not hold Antony through his senses; she is not particularly intelligent. Her secret is akin to Falstaff's: she is great by the sheer life in her. Antony has it too, and for this reason, though a ruined wastrel, he excels the respectable Octavius.

[1] Professor Bradley says Lady Macbeth has no remarkable intellect.

Octavia can give her strength *for* Antony, as Fulvia does, but not *to*
him. Cleopatra gives something of her quality to Charmian and
Iras.

In four of the last plays, after the old scores are cleared, a new and
finer life comes through a woman of a younger generation. Marina
(*Pericles*) is a first sketch for Perdita and Miranda. Imogen (*Cymbeline*)
has something of Cleopatra's swift life, with the courage and clear
honour, the pride and gentleness and wifely loyalty, of Juliet or
Beatrice or Desdemona. Shakespeare had her in his mind so clearly
that even in the wager scene he does not spoil her. Save Imogen, the
play has little to recommend it, and it is difficult to say where her
charm lies. Perhaps her image quickened Shakespeare's tired spirit, so
that she and little else awakes for us and casts round her her own
atmosphere of beauty. What concerns Shakespeare in the *W. Tale* is
the eventual destiny of his people—the issue of the endeavour from
storm to calm. He overlooks Leontes' experience of jealousy to define
the situation to which it is a means—above all, Hermione's side of it.
One ceases to know his characters so well; they are alive but less
studied and lived into: more like symbols seen in relation to something
that matters more than themselves. Prospero is the *Tempest*, and
Prospero is Shakespeare's soul. Ferdinand and Miranda, like Florizel
and Perdita, make a fresh beginning in the abundance of new life inherited from all sorrow transmuted. The man of forty-eight who could
describe the love scene between them, ten years after *T. and C.*, had
come through life victoriously enough. The artist writes less to express
his soul than discover it, and the author of the *Tempest* had done that.
His was the serene forgiving wisdom of those who have mastered
suffering and drawn more than royal power from it. . . .

A stimulating book like this naturally invites oppostion. In dealing
with the women of the tragedies Miss Mackenzie reverts to the
school of Leslie Stephen—a criticism admirable in its day, and
useful—like Huxley's Biblical criticism—but not the last word. She
calls Goneril and Lady Macbeth stupid—forgetting the saying of
Coleridge that the great passions are atheists and believe in no future; [1]
and she compares Goneril and Cordelia. Surely the critic should
not use the reason too exclusively, should not pause to take up the pen
until every echo of the divine music has ceased. We ask that the critic
should convey to us something of the rhythm of his subject, intellectualized and hall-marked by his own nature. When Arnold discusses the
problem of translating Homer, his prose has a movement lacking to
the verse of F. W. Newman—the translator from whom he dissents.
When Professor Bradley describes Othello's previous romantic career,
on which marriage with Desdemona was about to be placed like a

[1] Leslie Stephen suggested 'stupidity' as a key to the character of Dorothea
Casaubon in George Eliot's *Middlemarch*.

crown, we almost see the heavens open, as we do indeed when Othello himself proffers his dying words.[1]

Having made this protest we can whole-heartedly admire the rest of Miss Mackenzie's work. We feel her undivided nature—not merely her reason—behind her judgement in *R. and J.*—that death is not waste, but life's consummation—or on Olivia's appreciation of Viola's personality beneath her disguise. The latter, and her saying that Rosalind is adorable but not complex, and her qualified praise of Portia (*Merchant*), show her individual critical gift at its best: she sees women as much as they appear to each other as to men. This, and her distinctions of cleverness in some and stupidity in others, has led her reviewers to call her 'modern' and 'Meredithian', and to suppose that she discovered these qualities in Shakespeare. We would disclaim for Shakespeare anything of a limiting nature, and suggest that consciously or the reverse Miss Mackenzie is proving his mind to be universal. Also by concentrating on the women's parts she can show us a play from a new angle—notable the *Merchant* and *Henry V.* But she is modern in her power to subdivide emotions finely—the power to recollect imaginatively and dispassionately the pains or pleasures from a complex nervous system, e.g. her criticism of Helena (*All's Well*)—of Ophelia—of Mrs. Quickly who is never really sorry for herself—and of Romeo and Juliet to whom the pain of parting makes danger seem unreal.

II

PROFESSOR W. MACNEILE DIXON[2] is perplexed by the riddle of tragedy. He notices that the tragedian offers grief as a means to happiness, and the strange fact that suffering promotes delight. Shakespeare's achievement is more remarkable in one way than that of Aeschylus, because he rose to an equal height in stories that had not the Greek solemnity of religious tradition. He made life seem vaster and more mysterious to the Elizabethans. Marlowe avoided realism, the ruin of tragedy, and achieved magnificent melodrama. Shakespeare also declined to represent actual life, but preserved the noble earnestness which is the real foundation of tragedy. Nature was a living unity to Aeschylus; Shakespeare sees our earth without attachments—a peopled but lonely planet in empty space. The Greeks looked on man as built into the structure of the world, with nothing in him that was not there before him: if he loved, Aphrodite constrained him, &c.[3]

Modern tragedy avoids fate and concentrates upon character, e.g. a saner Lear might have done better. But if the fault were always the victim's it would become a morality. Tragedy to deserve its name must refuse to make all things plain, and must prostrate itself

[1] Leslie Stephen did achieve this rhythm in certain essays, e.g. on Wordsworth and De Quincey.   [2] *Tragedy* (Arnold, 1924).   [3] Cf. Stapfer.

before the unknown. Its roots are in the incalculable, and Euripides is to be blamed for transferring attention to character alone and testing all by intellect.[1] It is humanity's experience that chance and accident take a hand in the game and often play a dishonest and determining card. From the dawn of tragedy the influence of the unseen upon the seen was never lost sight of by the Greeks. The fundamental problem of all religions, that of evil, is likewise embedded in tragedy, ancient and modern. Aeschylus exposes the foundations of human society and examines unsparingly man's place in the universe. What laws should he obey, and what affections and sympathies should guide him? Beyond all other dramatists he was a theologian. We only approach tragedy when we reflect and our reflection fails us—when we become aware of that Necessity which brought us into being, governs us, and removes us from the scene.

There is evil not of man's making in the world, so tragedy cannot be limited to the commerce of men with men. It is what Nietzsche called the deeper conflict, the antagonism at the heart of the world. Aeschylus fell back on time and considered the words and wisdom of Zeus not final, as he was young in time, but moving on with the world of men and gaining in wisdom. The foundation of his drama was consciousness of man's partnership with nature, and the generations with each other—the solidarity of things. Man is a fated sufferer, and only becomes noble by struggling.

The earliest Greek myths reveal a malignant deity. Then came Nemesis, the transition from the spiteful to the retributive god. There is a limiting barrier to man—Adam, Prometheus, Faust. To the gods and Destiny succeeds Fortune—a pathetic testimony to the mystery of our human state. The history of a tragic hero is that of a man like Oedipus or Othello, at home in and apparent master of his world, on whom another and unseen world begins to encroach. Character is only a factor in tragedy; the differences of men, enormous and vital, dwindle to a cipher when set against their resemblances and common destiny. The essence of true tragedy is that such things happened to a human being like ourselves.

The accident of birth entangles Hamlet against his will; whereas critics have decided that he is the victim of his own irresolution. Natural aversion is constructed as shortcoming. His mind was ill at ease in such a detestable society, and his repugnance was no fault of character; but to Fate belongs the blame. Aristotle's 'catharsis' does not represent the processes of the mind at a performance of *Hamlet*. The interest is more intellectual than emotional, but Aristotle's measure was that of sheer emotional poignancy. Tragedy transcends sensation drama; its peculiar nature is that it strives after more than it expresses, its religious and philosophic attachments.

[1] Cf. Stapfer.

Its function is to exalt, not to cure, us. The mysteries which Aristotle explains away return to haunt us. His 'catharsis' is a charmingly vague word, and it is unknown if the error is moral or intellectual. What should Orestes, Hippolytus, Hamlet have done? There is no truth in the doctrine that the afflictions of the good are necessarily the fruits of their own acts. Nature and society do not deal with individuals according to their deserts. Lear was not justly served for his impatience, or Hamlet for his irresolution. Tragedy awakes in us just bewilderment at life and the ways of Heaven, and arouses our pity for unmerited suffering. Aristotle disregards the moral perplexities of life, which the poets reveal. Tragedy exalts its hero, but he would put him in the wrong. Oedipus did not deserve his fate, and Lear was not appropriately punished. The moral offensiveness we meet with in the world is the tragic problem. The tragedians face it: we revolt, and the intensity of revolt is the measure of our souls. The paradox of tragedy, which escaped Aristotle, is that it meets the darkest aspects of the world to our comfort and delight. It produces a transformed and reborn vision, a higher scale of values, a new and vaster perspective, cosmic rather than earthly consciousness.[1]

Magic, or earliest religion, is the ritual out of which tragedy arose —primitive man's acknowledgement of a transcendental world. It is a plausible conjecture that in some fields of knowledge the heated mood reveals a vital truth hidden to logic. Poetry, music, beauty are nature in us, and are to be reckoned with, unless there is some monstrous flaw in the constitution of things. The central issue is that Nature does seem to have a purpose, though it may not be ours. Her aims do not include human happiness, nor does she seem to watch over the good and just. This is the great divide, the extreme of all perplexity—a world that satisfies one part of our being and disgusts another. It is an icy consolation that what happens to Antigone, Hamlet, Cordelia does not matter—but only what they are.[2] The tragic poets have raised no false alarm, and evil is no illusion. The individual is the Absolute of poetry and our concern is not for the universe but for ourselves. The heroes of tragedy are as unwilling to part with life as the rest of us. Neither Athenians nor Elizabethans were pessimists, but delighted in life. Tragedy achieves its end when it makes us feel that we are greater than we know. Its peculiarity is to

---

[1] Mr. John Galsworthy writes: 'The cosmic sense is rare. We are most of us too definitely anthropomorphic to have it; we see even the Deity from the human point of view; have little of the old Greek sense of our position in the scheme of things. *L'état c'est nous.* We *are* the scheme and working thereof. This may be natural, but from the point of view of Father Time, who for some billions of years looked on a world untenanted by human beings, it is rather a parvenu conviction. Mystery enwraps the cause, the origin, the end of life, yea, even of human life. And acceptance of that mystery brings a certain dignity to existence. . . .' *Castles in Spain* (1927), p. 161.   [2] Cf. Bradley on Cordelia.

pluck this conviction from the heart of failure. Struggle with misfortune provides an incomparable exhilaration. We desire for ourselves the strength, courage, will, imagination of Clytemnestra and Macbeth. *R. and J.* expresses a passion of fulfilment rather than an image of despair, and raises us above ourselves. Tragedy is the art of metaphysical comfort, a metaphysical supplement to the reality of nature. The doctrines of Schopenhauer and Nietzsche, that existence is rooted in suffering, do not account for man's passion for life and love of it and reluctance to part with it.

The conclusion is that tragedy leans on our mysterious preference for the best. Surrender to the downfall of Oedipus, the sufferings of Cordelia, is the great betrayal. The tragedians do not tell us that men obtain what they merit, or merit what they obtain, that innocence is a protection against suffering, or calamity a proof of folly or sin. They teach that the history of humanity is that of painful effort, and struggle with nature and itself. The wonder is that our nature should harbour ideals far beyond the lessons of practical circumstance. Tragedy leads to discoveries within ourselves and guesses regarding the larger nature which has given birth to us. It reveals in us an inborn passion for justice that cannot be an illusion. . . .

Although Shakespeare is not the direct subject of this book, it cannot be omitted from a history of Shakespearian criticism because of the light it throws on tragedy. It impressively brings home to us the fact of a vast and mysterious world interpenetrating our own. It is full of learning, intellectual honesty, and optimism of the best kind. Man clings to life, yet we accept with a kind of joy the ending of *Lear* and *Othello*. Professor Macneile Dixon says truly that realism is the ruin of tragedy, that Lear and Othello were not treated according to their deserts; yet in his partial repudiation of Aristotle's 'catharsis' we discern something of a gap. To fill it we would turn back to the tragic hero as defined by Professor Bradley—the man who is no eccentric but possesses in a heightened degree the qualities of ordinary men—Othello, Macbeth, Antony. Professor Macneile Dixon says that the essence of true tragedy is that such things happened to a human being like ourselves, and also that the individual is the Absolute of poetry; but we think he neglects the individual nature of the advanced man that alone can conduct the lightning. Neither Benedict nor Malvolio could do it, neither could Shylock because of his comical outcry about money. Hamlet's recoil may be natural, but we cannot associate the catastrophes that ensue with any mind but his. He indeed is a man of genius, not the heightened ordinary man, but his fate and Lear's and Othello's and Macbeth's and Antony's survive as warnings and portents because they were kings in the true sense of the word on this lower earth. The book's final message is hope and reverence for man, and wonder at the strange world in which he plays his part, and the unknown forces that surround him. We turn back to Stapfer and contrast his gentle positivism with the believing-agnosticism here eloquently expressed. The writer feels that a divine explanation of the mystery does exist, though the small finite human mind may be unable to grasp this largest of infinites.

III

THE key-note of Miss Lilian Winstanley's latest book,[1] as of her previous ones, is that the men of Shakespeare's era habitually thought and wrote in symbolism. Thus Spenser's *Faerie Queene* is really an epic of the religious wars in Europe. All French poets and historians use this method, and so in an Italian author of Shakespeare's day we find the story of Othello. His race have terrific passions, unrestrained by laws of God or man; and he, the soldier of fortune, is jealous and suspicious. She has the fatal gift of appreciating strangers more than her own people. This story was nearer to *Othello* than Cinthio's novel, and it is by Alessandro Tassoni, and describes the tragedy of Italy in the grip of Spain. Shakespeare has it, but not Cinthio, that Desdemona's father repudiated her before the Doge, that the senate decided on the possibility of her marriage to Othello and journey to Cyprus, that her nuptials should be celebrated at Cyprus, that the State of Venice should be present *officially* at all her great crises. *Othello* was produced in 1604, the year when the Pope, who was 'father' of Venice, quarrelled with Venice, with the result that Venice was isolated and delivered to Spain. The Venetian senate had to ratify the formal treaty with Spain in 1571, and these alliances were termed marriages. Loss of Cyprus to the Turks caused the treaty, and Spain came to the rescue. It is the Cyprus question that exalts Othello with the Venetian senate and makes them ratify his marriage. Don John of Austria commanded the united Venetian and Spanish fleets at Lepanto which redeemed Cyprus, and soon after he lost the favour of Philip II who was jealous of him, and suspected he desired to make for himself an independent kingdom of Italy. It was suspected that Philip had murdered his French wife, Elizabeth of Valois. A handkerchief, which the King saw in the gallant's hands, plays a part in the tale—a tale told by Antonio Perez, Philip's ex-minister and chief enemy, who had been in England as protégé of Essex.

The impression remained that this murder led to the overthrow of Italian liberties. Shakespeare's story is a human story of human interest, but it is also the symbol of a national destiny. Both tragedies, national and individual, turn on the same personality and traits— jealousy, suspicion, evil counsel. All poets of the day, and most historians, drew on this common stock of European mythology. Thus

---

[1] *'Othello' as the Tragedy of Italy* (Fisher Unwin, 1924).

Spenser makes Gloriana and Belphoebe stand for Elizabeth, the Red Cross Knight for England, Orgoglio and Mammon for Spain, &c. It is to be noted that Orgoglio and Mammon are both Philip II and Spain itself. We find this mythology alike in State documents, proclamations, private letters, political tracts. Knox calls Mary Queen of Scots a mermaid enticing men by her beauty and flattering tongue —and Elizabeth was the subject of a vast mythology. James I is compared with Merlin, ruling a fairy race in an enchanted isle. Drake, to the Spaniards, is a dragon, wizard, devil; to the English a magic being, a spirit all of air and fire.

Political pamphlets appealed to emotion, and told, by means of certain traditional forms, some highly dramatic story. Some compare the Spaniards to Moors and Jews, and accuse Philip of wife-murder. They call the Spaniards a 'black' race, and describe the white race in their power as a bride wooed and enticed, to be destroyed later. It was a regular custom to personify countries and cities as individuals. In reading the panegyrics of Elizabeth it would be hard to say where the Queen's personality ends and that of England begins. Ben Jonson's comedy of humours is one of types, and Shakespeare starts from type. Othello incarnates the 'idea' of Spain. Shakespeare's great figures are human, but also more than human. To start from type, not individual, marks an important difference in literary psychology: and the aim was universal truth. Catholicism stood for Spain and Protestantism for England. Shakespeare was not indifferent to religion, but, being an impassioned English nationalist, he was also an impassioned Protestant. It is explicit in *Richard III* that he regarded human history as progressive revelation of God's judgements on human kind. *Othello* is a study of divine retribution on Philip II and Spain itself, and of the retribution that will follow the political murder of Italy. The poet does not invent his material; Homer, Dante, Shakespeare were less men than eras of the human spirit. The whole of the sixteenth century and every country in Europe helped Shakespeare to write his plays.[1]

That the Spaniards were of Moorish blood and that Philip II murdered his wife were commonplaces of anti-Spanish tracts. Tassoni's notorious tract was an impassioned plea to the princes of Italy to unite and save their country from Spain. All the tracts describe Spain as a desert sun-baked country. One distinguishes between the incompatible Spanish and Venetian natures. The Spaniard is passionate, rebellious, new to power, strange to law and civilization;

[1] Carlyle in *Historical Sketches* says that our ancestors regarded Spain with horror, as a rich and wondrous country, with its huge empire, but of infernal nature. James I solicited an alliance with Spain, thinking even to *convert* the Devil. It was the beginning of a breach between King and Parliament. In August 1623 joy-bells rang all over England at the Prince's home-coming without the 'thick-lipped' Infanta.

yet he believes in destiny and loves glory. Spain is warned she may undertake too much, and that to murder Italy may mean her own suicide. Compare Othello's pride and wanderings, his violent temper that may turn to savagery despite the master-impulses of love and fame. Much of Spain was once subject to the Moors, and Spain smote the Turk at Lepanto, as Othello did in Aleppo. Desdemona is like Venice, and the writer of the tract deplores that Italy's imagination is stirred by strangers, and she will leave her own people to ally herself with warlike strangers. The Venetian Senate required Othello because the Turks captured Cyprus. Hence the Treaty of Alliance on one hand, and the nuptials at Cyprus on the other. Venice is modest, tranquil, quiet, chaste, pure, loving to all men, like Desdemona. Brabantio describes his daughter as opposed to marriage.

In Cinthio the ensign who plays Iago helps to kill her. The Moor does not kill himself, and Desdemona's father does not repudiate her. We hear nothing about the diverse natures of Othello and Desdemona; neither is she described as quiet and modest, loving to all men, chaste and pure, inclined to desert her own for strangers. Shakespeare took the story from Cinthio and made plain its relation to history. Cinthio's characters are not great, nor is his conception tragic, and his book was not translated till 1795. The *Filippiche* tracts to which Tassoni contributed were published about 1615.

Philip II was married to a wife much younger than himself, whom he loved with a mad passion. The Marquis del Pozzo visited one of her ladies by night and picked up a handkerchief which the Queen had dropped. She was unintentionally compromised, and, like Desdemona, gave way to mournful forebodings. The King's suspicions were excited, and he first ordered a servant to poison her, as Othello ordered Iago—and when this failed, stifled her in the bed she had polluted. Cinthio has it that a child stole the handkerchief, and the murder was done with a sandbag. European tradition seized on the tale and on the parallel. Phillip's act was symbolic; he stifled his wife as he stifled freedom of thought and political liberty in every country that he ruled.

Antonio Perez hated Philip and knew all his secrets of state. He stands for Iago, for, even in that age of terrific crimes, the more than mortal hate between Philip and Perez was the wonder and horror of Europe. More than all it destroyed Philip's reputation and lowered Spain's prestige. Perez had been Philip's most trusted servant, but he abused this confidence to excite the King's jealousy against his brother Don John of Austria, and to impel him to commit certain murders, and to attempt to murder his brother. When Philip found he had been deceived he imprisoned and tortured Perez. The latter escaped, fled to England, and became one of Spain's most dangerous enemies. Europe regarded him with disgust and horror because he had been

Philip's trusted servant, and a Spaniard who would ruin Spain. Many pamphlets had been written alluding to Philip's moral denseness in letting a mere servant influence him.

The two motives in *Othello* are Othello's jealousy and his subservience to Iago. The latter name is Spanish and typical of Spain—as St. George of England. Iago's intrigue against Cassio resembles that of Perez against Don John. Perez excited horror not only by treachery, but by desire to ruin his own country. He possessed one of the acutest intellects of his age—he was cunning, far-sighted, unscrupulous, and unrivalled in combining utter villainy with cold intellectual skill. It is likely that Shakespeare knew him and was impressed by him. All Europe regarded his concentrated hate and cold intellectual power, and his master's helpless subjection, as an almost supernatural example of the power of evil. Perez professed to be Don John's friend, intoxicated him with the idea of power, betrayed him to Philip, and made Philip frenziedly jealous of him. He caused his disgrace, but Philip afterwards learnt his mistake and bitterly repented of his jealousy and credulity.

When Shakespeare wrote *Othello*, about 1604, the burning European question was Spain's attempt to subjugate Venice and the latter's quarrel with the Pope. Shakespeare as an ardent nationalist would sympathize with Italy's struggle. *Othello* is the epic tragedy of Italy: on that awful bed lay stifled the glory and genius of the most gifted race in the world. Tho pro-Spanish tendencies of James I would alarm the nationalist party, and they would use the drama to warn him against a nation alien to the true genius of Europe and destructive to those united with it. If Shakespeare chose an obscure and savage story, glorified it, and had it played before his King, it was because Cinthio's novel resembles Venetian-Spanish history. The motives embodied are the murder of the innocent and beloved wife through jealousy, the attempted murder of Don John through jealousy, the blind moral slavery to the brilliantly intellectual but insanely wicked Perez, who tricked Philip into crimes of which he repented in vain. It is all symbolic of Spanish temper and history, and the tragedy is both personal and epic.

Othello is ruined by moral blindness, and Desdemona's love and trust for the Moor is so unnatural that even Othello feels it. Tassoni says that Italy is bewitched by Spain, and he acknowledges Spain's valour, chivalry, lofty spirit of adventure, and love of renown. Modern critics ignore the intense moral and physical repugnance of Shakespeare's age for Moors. The black colour implied one who was devil-possessed. The Moor to Shakespeare's England was like the negro to southern-state Americans to-day. Shakespeare tells us that Othello had a fearsome aspect—and Iago stresses his lustful love. Only Desdemona fails to recognize the disproportion between them. Othello has an

element of evil, of lust and horror and frenzy and sheer downright
cruelty—yet also marvellous fascination, romance, valour. When
excited he shows intense and lascivious jealousy—and when angry,
horrible blood-lust. He wishes to torture those whom he hates.
That he should be noble though repulsive is explained if we see him
as the power of Spain. The Spanish veterans were the finest infantry
in Europe, and they fought to the drum and fife which Othello
recalls. They were used to live in the field and take their wives
—as Othello claims the right to do. Othello is as much sailor as
soldier; he draws his metaphors from the sea; and his adventures
repeat the most remarkable incidents in Spanish history. Like Spain
he was in barbarous captivity—like Spain he smote the Turk—on
behalf of Venice.

The most crucial passages between Othello and Desdemona take
place in the presence of the official representatives of Venice. Othello's
first overt breach with Desdemona is before Ludovico, and in the
same scene he is told of his recall. Personal and official alienation
proceed side by side—as the marriage coincided with the opening of
the official employment. After her death the Venetian ambassador
appears and judges Othello. Shakespeare's Venetian lady and Tassoni's
are the same; but Cinthio has no one of these episodes. Desdemona's
State is officially present at her marriage, officially protests against the
insults offered to her, is officially present at her death. The same
bonfires celebrate Othello's nuptial and the destruction of the Turkish
fleet. Like Don John Cassio is disgraced soon after.

The personal tragedy of *Othello* is based on a terrible and gloomy
episode of Spanish history; the epic tragedy is that of Italy and Spain.
Shakespeare's personal motive was to protect England—lest England
should be the 'tragic loading' of Othello's marriage bed. . . .

Assuming what has been said about Miss Winstanley's previous
books to stand for the present one—that she transfers the interest from
Shakespeare to history—but that a certain amount of interest recoils
upon Shakespeare—we will note that in the present case the interest
of the recoil is connected with Othello's inner nature. Though she
admits his fascination, his great deeds, his love of fame, she exposes
what is bad in him when passion-stirred by her device of historical
parallels. We are accustomed to think of him as more sinned against
than sinning, and to dismiss his colour as an accident, but Miss
Winstanley conveys to us that the central fire in him, of which his
lightest word gives some hint, was terrible as well as glorious, and that
his black colour may have a meaning. We feel something of the horror
that Desdemona expressed when she saw him rolling his eyes and
gnawing his lip on the fatal night. We cannot wholly agree with
Miss Winstanley's theories, but it would be foolish to dismiss them as
a fantasy, in the presence of the political pamphlets which she quotes,

and, above all, the great instance of the *Faerie Queene*. But we must always bear in mind that even if Shakespeare consciously strove to teach political lessons, his business was with the individual, and that when his mind was well started on its adventure he was not concerned with politics. Granting, therefore, that every word written by Miss Winstanley were true, her treatise would remain once removed from the highest critical truth, for it would not necessarily enable us to read the play with added zest.

IV

PROFESSOR T. G. TUCKER, writing about the Sonnets,[1] approaches them as simply artistic creations of the same mind which produced the dramas. In none of Shakespeare's writings, he says, is it more important to have mastered the various meanings which are possible to his mere words, and to select the one most appropriate to its setting. He discusses the question whether they are autobiographical or dramatic, and remarks that sincerity differs from spontaneity. Even in those that are painfully laboured, there is nothing incompatible with a fundamental reality of the poet's sentiments. Neither is there anything to disprove that they were addressed to a real person. In this case he would endeavour to poetize every aspect of the connexion, and inequality would result from ebb and flow of inspiration. There are contradictions—such as the convention of disparaging and glorifying his own verse.

To imagine that if an emotion is real it must keep aloof from art would make the sonnet itself impossible. We should have to say that a feeling which seeks to express itself in fourteen lines, with a certain placing of the rhymes, cannot be sincere because it is thinking of something besides its own sincerity. The natural impression is that the poems are from Shakespeare's experience. The person addressed by most sonnets of the first series becomes to the mind a real contemporary of Shakespeare. Their 'argument' befits a distinct individual and no mere type or lay figure. Who can doubt but that 29, 30, 31, 32, 49, 57, 66, 73, 120, and, above all, 90[2] are genuine? Sidney's sonnets were genuine, so why not Shakespeare's? Such revelation would cause no surprise to the reader of the plays: he must have known the feelings which he describes vicariously. To unlock the heart in drama is a sin against art: but the sonnet is the true vehicle for personal emotion. An ambitious poet would not find in the young man and

[1] *The Sonnets of Sh.*, 1924 (Cambridge University Press).
[2] George Wyndham writes of Sonnet 90: 'I doubt if in all recorded speech such faultless perfection may be found, so sustained through 14 consecutive lines. That perfection . . . arises from perfect verbal execution. . . .' *The Times Lit. Sup.* (11 Dec. 1924) says Sonnet 90 'more and more asserts itself as the greatest of them all'.

the dark woman the most suitable lay figures for his verse. The situations are often peculiar, and the expression takes for granted too intimate an understanding of special circumstances. The suggestion of the particular situation is ever present, but less unveiled than the inventor of such a situation would think necessary. There are bare hints and allusions to which we often miss the key, e.g. 90, 111, 77, 86, 107, 124, 125. Best conclude that we should not treat every piece alike as concerned with one and the same object of affection, or regard the whole series as an equally spontaneous and emotionally consistent record of Shakespeare's relations with that object.

The dedication disproves that W.H. borrowed Shakespeare's pen. How could he be wished immortality for his verses, while it is admitted that the verses are not his? Circumstances often indicated are Shakespeare's own, not those of a patron. The most likely theory is that W.H. was Herbert, but it is neither proved nor provable.

The allusions to the dark woman are so individual that we conclude that she was real. The ethical standards of writing have advanced, for the 'dark woman' sonnets would discredit a writer of to-day. She was probably a married woman of no high position who entangled the poet's unwilling affections for a time.

The sonnets are amazingly unequal, with some frigid artificiality and even verbal weakness: but as a whole they rank with the highest creations of their kind. The best poetry contains a 'breath and finer spirit' which informs, but it is no component of the artistry which can be analysed. As regards artistry we find examples in every kind— the sonnet of passion, of serious reflection, of fancy, of occasion, &c. Often the finer spirit is omitted in favour of conscious ingenuity— and there are worse things. Shakespeare achieves his effect, by alliteration, assonance, strong vowels, weighty monosyllables, and, above all, by antithesis, to which the final couplet specially lends itself. . . .

Professor Tucker uses the weapons of learning, common sense, and fine critical distinctions, with great effect in examining an old problem. The first two qualities help him to decide as he does the questions of the patron and the dark lady, and they also appear in his general view of the sonnets as mainly autobiographical. He then subtly analyses the poems, dividing them into classes, and we feel that he tells us something both about the poet and the man. Surely the right method is to judge Shakespeare before all else as a poet, and through word-movements to guess at spiritual rhythms. It is no longer the fashion to separate the aesthetic from the natural man, or to doubt that Beauty is Truth. The pens of all worthy modern critics who discuss old problems are steadied by time; they keep a middle course; and this moderation gives to their remarks a further meaning.

V

WE are already familiar with the work of Sir E. K. Chambers, but we must include his present pamphlet[1] because it deals with the burning question of the integrity of the Folio. After touching on the earliest 'disintegrators' he says that modern criticism of the canon really began with Fleay—and he calls Fleay inaccurate, irresponsible, changeable, and over-confident. He then turns to Mr. J. M. Robertson, with whom he disagrees, though he admits that Mr. Robertson aims to exalt, not depreciate, Shakespeare. He says that Mr. Robertson looks for a Shakespeare always at the top of his achievement, and this is an arbitrary process. Shakespeare has moments of artistic oblivion or carelessness, where the brain flags or the insight fails; he has trivial scenes where quibble speaks to the boxes or horseplay to the pit; he has exasperating scenes where psychological realism makes ugly nonsense of a romantic convention; he has perfunctory scenes which amount to no more than commonplace Elizabethan carpentry. If we omit these we may get an ideal, but we lose Shakespeare. He was an experimentalist in style, receptive as well as creative, and no doubt he experimented in the manner of Marlowe, Greene, or Chapman.

Metrical tests may be useful in determining the chronology of plays—and at one time Shakespeare certainly used rhyme and later emphasized the verse paragraph rather than the individual line; but they only indicate a trend of development, and this may be diverted in any play by accidents of subject-matter, such as refractory personal names which have to be coerced into the metre—or because certain rhythms suit certain scenes—above all, because Shakespeare experimented in rhythm. He might easily use double-endings freely in early plays, then restrict them, and increase them later, instead of working on a smoothly progressive curve. Percentages to have value must be worked on enough lines to allow a fair average. A single speech or scene leads to nothing; indeed, single passages are more often governed by the adaptation of rhythm to subject-matter which may qualify the general trend of metric development in a whole play. Thus the first scene of *John* requires the emphatic use of 'father', 'mother', 'brother' at the ends of the lines.

As to the search for alien hands, surely Shakespeare and his predecessors used a common poetic diction that may be traced to Spenser and Sidney. Shakespeare and Chapman innovated freely, and Shakespeare might borrow words as he did plots; and the oftener Chapman used a word the more likely it was to stick in Shakespeare's memory. That Chapman was employed by Shakespeare's company is outside the probabilities of literary history. The Folio was not undiscriminating,

[1] *The Disintegration of Sh.*, Annual Sh. Lecture, 1924 (pub. for Brit. Acad. by H. Milford).

but left out nine plays already printed under Shakespeare's name or initials. . . .

We will not follow Sir E. Chambers in his advance into the territory of Messrs. Pollard and Dover Wilson, as the matter there treated is bibliographical rather than aesthetic. We have endeavoured to summarize fairly his attack on Mr. Robertson, and the student has ample material on which to judge between them. We ourselves do not agree with the critic who says that Mr. Robertson, though a skilled writer, who can be trusted to make the best of his case, must surpass himself if he succeeds in rehabilitating it in the face of Sir E. Chambers's attack.[1] The gist of Mr. Robertson's theory is that Shakespeare's verse is unequalled, that *M.N.D.* proves that he had formed an early style of his own, and was therefore not likely to compose whole plays or even interpolated passages in the manner of others. Surely Sir E. Chambers exaggerates his experimental habit, and surely the verse of every great poet is an individual thing—from the thunder-roll of Homer to the violin-note of Mr. de la Mare. Even in the fixed traditions of the eighteenth century, how wide is the gulf between the writers of the heroic couplet—e.g. Pope and Crabbe! Also is it a fact that Shakespeare and his predecessors wrote a common style derived from Spenser and Sidney? Mr. Robertson does not contend that Shakespeare was always at the top of his achievement, but that he always wrote characteristically. *Timon* is a composite play, but the following lines spoken by Flavius (II. ii) seem to us typical of Shakespeare, though not Shakespeare at his highest:

> So the gods bless me,
> When all our offices have been oppress'd
> With riotous feeders, when our vaults have wept
> With drunken spilth of wine, when every room
> Hath blazed with lights and bray'd with minstrelsy,
> I have retired me to a wasteful cock,
> And set mine eyes at flow.

Lastly, we will succumb to an argument like Matthew Arnold's, 'Wragg is in custody'; though we remember how sternly Herbert Spencer denounced as unphilosophical the method of using one extreme exception against a whole theory. However, as Herbert Spencer's reputation has lapsed, we will venture upon it. When Bolingbroke hears that Mowbray is dead, he exclaims,

> Sweet peace conduct his sweet soul to the bosom
> Of good old Abraham![2]

Can any one believe that these are the words of Shakespeare's Bolingbroke?

[1] *Times Lit. Sup.*, 11 Sept. 1924.   [2] *Richard II*, IV. i.

VI

MR. J. M. ROBERTSON starts his new book[1] by asserting that orthodoxy is always fertile in ill-based theories, and goes hand in hand with heedless guess-work in the ultimate tasks of literary judgement. He aims to trace the Master by his style, and reach a final vision of him, if at all, only when his real work is made fairly sure. He retorts to the traditionists that they in turn eliminate from *Pericles* and *Timon* sections which clash with *their* sentimental taste. By what right do they decide that parts of those plays are too poor to be Shakespeare's work? When all the technical data have been really studied, it is our sentiment that finally pronounces critically on Shakespeare as man and dramatist. The disintegrators find that repellent action exhibited as if it were sympathetic is always associated with alien features of style, diction, and verse. Automatic acceptance more destroys critical efficiency than reckless scepticism. Professor Herford writes on 'Shakespeare's Treatment of Love and Marriage' with the idea of divining his outlook on life from his choice of subjects. He decides that Shakespeare preferred the normal, yet from paradox loved to take up outrageous situations. Constraint of the arbitrary presuppositions of traditionism prevents the skilled critic from seeing that Shakespeare will take up any plot and has no 'chosen field'. The orthodox school is anchored to theories with no basis of fact.

All's Well is a bad play from the standpoint of world-literature. Parolles is arbitrarily imposed on the play and is outside the plot, unlike Touchstone and Falstaff. It lacks the great poetry of *M. for M.* and the dramatic force of its main action. There are frequent though scattered traces of Greene, but the play as a whole does not suggest him. 'They say miracles are past . . .', recalls Chapman; and the dialogue between Lafeu and Parolles is a feeble essay at the irrelevant realism of idle dialogue which Chapman uses in the *Usher* and *D'Olive* and *Goosecap*. Scene ii is monotonous Chapman verse. 'You know my father left me some prescriptions' is absolutely Chapman. *Languishings* is a Chapmanese noun nowhere else in the Folio. 'Rendred lost' is an idiom of Chapman's, and he also has 'render cheered', 'render slain', and others. Surely upholders of the Imitation Theory will hardly maintain that the master-poet wrote down to every passing fashion of bad style. The blank verse of the opening scene section of Act II hints at revision by Shakespeare, but the dialogue between the King and Helena shows no sign of rehandling. The nearly 40 per cent. of double-endings is a Chapmanese rate, and the couplets are no less un-Shakespearian. Helena's speech, 'Ere twice the horses...', has a pre-Shakespearian note, though the last two lines are Chapman. Cf. Greene's *Alphoneus* (IV. i.): 'Thrice ten times Phoebus with his

[1] *Sh. Canon*, Part III, 1925 (Routledge).

golden beams . . .', and in the next scene, 'Thrice Hesperus . . .'. It is likely, but unproved, that Greene introduced from Cinthio the main plot of *All's Well*, and the clown scenes savour of Greene—but every scene supports the Chapman theory. The slabs of couplets are like neither early nor late Shakespeare, but are solely like Chapman. After Bertram dismisses Helena Shakespeare resumes revision—into III. i, though there are traces of Chapman. After the clown section comes revision again, but not drafting—as Helena's soliloquy shows, viz. the Chapmanese verb 'consolate'. At most Shakespeare curbed Chapmanese tedious volubility, and we infer his hand in the rhythm of the King's lines, 'For we are old, and on our quick'st decrees . . .', but only as heightening or controlling another's work.

It would be strange for the mature Shakespeare to resort to couplets in the middle of blank-verse dialogue, but it is a special habit of Chapman's. He switches from rhyme to blank verse and prose to rhyme. Another clue is reversion to chorused speeches—a pre-Shakespearian trait, that occurs in *Titus*, never in *M.N.D.*, once in *John*. Chapman abounds in 'omnes' and 'ambo' speeches, and they occur here (II. i. 3, III. v). There is an all-pervading Chapman atmosphere—in the 'serious' commentary on affairs in the dialogue—and in the idea of securing life-like effect by making every character in some way peculiar. Parolles, D'Olive, Cortezza, Poggio, Bassido are blatant and ridiculous figures made prominent. On the Imitation Theory, Parolles is Shakespeare's deliberate attempt to create and handle such a Chapman figure; yet Parolles is less vigorously sketched than D'Olive. The medical element finds a parallel in the *Usher*.

Was Shakespeare likely to renounce his unmatched faculty for verse to copy every charmless verse-style that came in his way? The 42 per cent. of double-endings would class the play among his later works; it would therefore be a work of artistic and intellectual decadence. The Imitation Theory would further make him a copyist of other men's tags and phrases. '. . . many coloured Iris', '. . . common and an *outward* man', 'impression of mine eye infixing', are all Chapman formulas. 'Embossed' (III. vi. 107) for Shakespeare has always the huntsman's meaning of foam-spotted' or swollen—and he was at home in the language of hunting. Here it has Chapman's meaning of 'ambushed' or 'surrounded'. Chapman uses the following words, including usual and unusual terms—Allurement, Applications, Barricado, Boggle, Capriccio, Congied, Fisnomy, Hawking, Misprision, Prejudicates, Recantation, Ruttish. That Shakespeare should use all these Chapman words in one play only is an unlikely thing. The argument of Sir E. K. Chambers, that the oftener Chapman used a word the more likely it was to stick in Shakespeare's memory, is a hand-to-mouth treatment of a complicated question. Some of the *once-used* words in *All's Well* appear in Chapman only *after* the date assigned by Sir E. K. Chambers to the play.

Hitherto there has lacked a simple notation of differences of versification, style, diction—and a comparison of styles in the Folio with those of contemporary dramatists. The Imitation Theory would have it that Shakespeare laboriously imitated Peele, Marlowe, Greene, and Kyd in *Titus*, Greene in *Verona*, Marlowe and Kyd in *Richard III*, Marlowe in *Richard II*, *Henry V*, and *Errors*, and now Chapman in 'A Lover's Complaint', *M. for M.*, and *Wives*. He even sinks below their higher plane since some of the comic work in *All's Well* is poorer than that of the *Usher* and coheres less with the plot. Yet now and then in these plays he inserts a scene or speech that belongs to another aesthetic world, besides the whole of *M.N.D.* Where else in the history of literary progress is there a precedent for such a zigzag of slavish mimicry and artistic mastery? How account for the iteration of hackneyed tags and use of poorest rhythms by the master of the best? Chapman's plays were handicapped by his turgid and contorted style: and Shakespeare would not imitate this. *M. for M.* presents in great Shakespearian verse the didactic equivalents of certain philosophemes which Chapman ill-expressed. 'Spirits are not finely touched . . .' is as a crystal fused from the quartz of Chapman's diction. What interested him he made his own, and thus lent the play goodness and greatness in detail, since nothing could save it as a whole. *All's Well* belongs to the same period, and to assume that Shakespeare deliberately experimented in bad writing is a fantasy of perverse apologetics. It is more likely that he did not feel it worth while to rewrite, though he had to prune and curtail: and the result is a certain balance of effect which Chapman never attained. The parts of Helena and the King seem actual, though the plot stultifies Helena's part; and the Countess and Lafeu are above Chapman's characters. Sir E. K. Chambers dates this play after *J.C.* and much of *Hamlet*. He implies that Shakespeare, after emerging from the chrysalis of an abject imitator, now returns to the cast-off husk. The great majority of the plays were not drafted by Shakespeare, and the object of these inquiries is to *integrate* the true Shakespeare, to trace his handiwork through all the poorer matter framed by other hands.

The 'Phoenix', despite Mr. J. Middleton Murry, is Chapmanese in form, theme, diction, vocabulary, crudity, convulsive infelicity, alternate terseness and circumlocution, force and feebleness. A rhetorical collapse is in nearly every quatrain, and the final rhyme is a flat makeshift, like many of Chapman's. He introduces the philosopheme of two-in-one into his plays and poetry at least ten times. *Andromeda* shows the same ringing of quibbling changes on one pseudo-poetic thesis.

R. and J. is based upon an old play. Save Greene none of the pre-Shakespearians has movingly presented a true love-theme in drama. Even Shakespeare could not have drafted so moving a drama without Brook's poem and Painter's prose to found upon. This was the vital factor—the opportunity given by a great *story*. The laments in the Second Quarto have proved a stumbling-block to orthodox critics. It is to be inferred that there was a prior play-structure in which some of Peele's work is overlaid by work of Kyd. The laments in the First Quarto are by Peele, whose serious work often produces a burlesque effect. The play is composite, and we see the hands of Peele and Kyd at different stages. The First Quarto has much of Shakespeare's verse and diction, although in the Second there is much non-Shakespearian matter of later date. Both contain much that is neither by Shakespeare, Peele, nor Kyd. An old curtailed text has been used, probably modified in parts: and this explains the phenomena. Many omissions from Quarto I tell of deliberate elision from an acting text; while from Quarto I the owners or printers had *a* manuscript deriving from the theatre. An old German *R. and J.* was played in Germany in 1626. The first three scenes differ absolutely, yet we may infer a pre-Shakespearian form of our play. It stages the history of a family feud, with a didactic purpose. Though without prologue, the first scene, which presents Montagu and Capulet, who do not meet in our play, explains the first chorus of our play. There would be no gain in superimposing details of a feud scheme on a play that begins like ours. The German piece also abandons the schematic method in favour of the Tybalt action. The English adapters in the second stage saw this, re-began with the serio-comic fray, and reduced the 'State' episode to the Prince's verdict after the fray. Both German and English plays move towards realism and effective action, as against didactic exposition. There are suggestions of Peele, but it is impossible that the German version preserves the old play mentioned by Brooke in 1562. We have proved the habit of collaboration among writers, also the practice of chronic emendation and recasting; and so *R. and J.*, founded on the archaic play, would be the more adapted because of its possibilities.

Shakespeare cannot have written certain portions of both Quartos, and besides the whole plot, two-thirds of the whole drama, including the main features of Capulet, Tybalt, Romeo, Benvolio, Mercutio, and the Nurse, appear in the German play. The verse of the Friar's speeches in the First Quarto was certainly revised, if not largely drafted, by Shakespeare; but we do not know who drafted his speeches in rhyme and blank verse, and at what period. Juliet's speech, 'Gallop apace . . .', suggests Marlowe's 'Gallop apace, bright Phoebus, through the sky' (*Edward II*, IV. iii. 45), and there are many more Marlowe clues, and his spirit is in the Mercutio-Tybalt fight. It recalls the Bastard in the old *John* play, and the Roses scene in *1 Henry VI*. Shakespeare's touch has absolutely transfigured Juliet, yet her rapturous soliloquy was more probably drafted by Peele or Marlowe. It has Peelean touches such as 'love-performing Night'; and even before 1595 Shakespeare might have framed something more subtly psychic. Helena's and Hermia's voices are true trebles, real girl-voices—but in this scene Juliet's is not a girl-voice, though it is in other scenes. Aged fourteen, she generalizes knowingly and rhetorically on what married lovers do, from the point of view of the average man. Peele and Marlowe often psychologize thus non-dramatically. But Shakespeare had to leave standing what had served the stage, and the speech is good stage rhetoric. Also his real women are more of the Lucrece than the Venus type. Finally, she is an ideal lover without it, and is glorified not by this, but by what precedes and follows.

The First Quarto retains traces of an early version, and has parallels in sentiment and dialogue with the German play. As the play proceeds both Quartos reveal more un-Shakespearian matter, but give a general impression of his revision. Apart from Peele and Kyd, we discern Marlowe. Cf. 'But soft! what light . . .' with 'But stay, what star shines yonder in the east?' (*Jew*, II. i). Also '. . . death lain with thy wife' is a variant of a common Marlowe trope. Cf. '. . . death-darting eye of cockatrice' with *Richard III* (IV. i. 55) and the pre-Shakespearians. In *M.N.D.* and *John*, dated immediately before and after *R. and J.*, there are no such reduplications of Marlowe phrases. *R. and J.* seldom varies rhythmically from the iambic norm, as *M.N.D.* does from the outset. These and other contrasts are explained if we regard *R. and J.* as a composite play, drafted before Shakespeare by several hands, revised and expanded by him in the First Quarto version, and further modified by his hand and others in the Second Quarto. If he did no more it was because Marlovian rhetoric was good acting matter.

There is no doubt of Marlowe's hand. Mercutio and Romeo suited an evolving art grown tired of the Superman. The old story delineated Juliet more movingly than Abigail in the *Jew* is delineated. Marlowe, with his Abigail of fourteen, was likely to reduce the age of Juliet from sixteen of the actual tale to fourteen. He was also likely to disregard time and force the pace of the action. Thus Juliet's family storm at her for 'evermore' weeping for her cousin who was killed yesterday. Juliet's quibbles, such as *aye* and *eye*, are in Marlowe's manner of inserting bad puns in serious matter. The vigorous phrasing and the verse movement of the dialogue of Romeo, Benvolio, and Mercutio are characteristic of Marlowe. The play on 'banished' points to *Edward II*, and the whole scene has pre-Shakespearian colouring. Perhaps *R. and J.* led Marlowe to write on Hero and Leander—as the poem often recalls the play. The storming scenes of Capulet's are Marlowe's, and also Juliet's 'Ancient damnation' speech.

Juliet praises Romeo like Marlowe praises Leander, and her speech contains Marlowe's mannerism 'cònjure' and 'conjurèd'. Cf. his 'sèpulchre' and 'sepùlchre', 'hòrizon' and 'horìzon'. To Marlowe we assign the draft of the bulk of the dramatic as distinguished from the narrative portions of Act V, but Shakespeare's control appears over the diction. Cf. 'There is thy gold . . .' and *Jew* (I. ii). The Prince's speech has the note of stateliness often lent by Shakespeare to kings.

The Friar is sympathetically handled, whereas Marlowe and Peele always treat Catholic priests coarsely. His sententious couplets recall Greene in *James IV*. They are too neat for Kyd, too didactic for Marlowe, too concise for Peele. The couplets in Lady Capulet's praise of Paris are like Greene in phrasing and iambic stress. Romeo's first speech to Juliet opens with rapture, but after 'Ethiope's ear' descends to Greene's plane. His share may belong to an early stage, with Peele's—to be revised later by Kyd as well as Shakespeare. The Friar's exhortation to Romeo unmanned is long, out of proportion to the need, and in Greene's later iambic manner.

Kyd's work on *Arden* connects him with *R. and J.* There is no doubt of him in the Second Quarto. *R. and J.* differs from all pre-Shakespearians but Kyd in realism of detail. The newer art substituted for 'comic relief' servants and musicians who spoke in character. *Arden* reveals Kyd's true power of plotting realistic plays with a character interest. One of the special difficulties is how far Shakespeare developed the Nurse?

These tests are subjective, but the above criticism proceeds on connotation of all the data. The simple historic fact is that Shakespeare belonged to a company of players who lived by stage plays; that he took plots much as he found them, and revised other men's plays to make them serve the company's ends. . . .

It is natural that Mr. Robertson's theories should have created a stir in the world of letters. The two camps are known respectively as 'Accepters' and 'Disintegrators', and the issue is described as follows: The accepters start to investigate from the apparently valid premise that the plays were published as Shakespeare's work. The disintegrators, of whom Mr. Robertson is chief, start from a premise of their own, that a great many of the plays were other men's work.[1] This is fairly stated, but it is less fair to say that Mr. Robertson considers his method alone to be 'scientific'. He is the first to admit that the final test is subjective, and we think it is a matter that every reader must decide for himself. Let him recall his impressions after reading certain plays which are usually accepted as Shakespeare's, viz. *Richard II*, *Henry V*, *J.C.*, parts of *R. and J.* and *M. for M.*, and decide whether or not the verse seemed to him inelastic and the characters less 'universal' than those of the true Shakespeare. If he is satisfied, and

[1] *Times Lit. Sup.*, 11 June 1925.

feels no inarticulate regret for the true Shakespeare, let him become an accepter. If not, let him join the disintegrators, and he will find no surer guide than Mr. Robertson, no one better versed in the Elizabethan dramatists.

Among the impressions left by the present volume two stand out clearly: Chapman's presence is declared beyond all doubt in *All's Well*; and Shakespeare's radiant spirit never more outshone his contemporaries than in his rehandling of *R. and J*. Specially convincing among single points is Mr. Robertson's refusal to accept Juliet's quibbles on 'aye' and 'eye'. The 'inhuman want of humour' would alone exclude the passage from Shakespeare. As this is the last of Mr. Robertson's books that falls within our period we will make one concluding remark. In a former work he said that Shakespeare's power to adapt himself to the circumstances of his age was a kind of personal trait. In the present he says that Shakespeare had a sane and sure vision of life and man, and we may therefore question as his any matter in the plays which lacks this suggestion. Surely these two comments bring Shakespeare the man slightly nearer to us! We speak with diffidence, for we still think that the best reply to those who ask where Shakespeare dwells is that of Musaeus to the Sibyl, 'Nulli certa domus'.

VII

MR. J. B. PRIESTLEY,[1] writing of the comic figures, reveals further treasures in the inexhaustible well of Shakespeare's mind, and by a subtle reminder that it is the 'midsummer moon' which calls out the poet and humorist in Bottom, discovers one of the inner harmonies and deeper unities of the play. He discriminates Bottom once for all by saying that he was the only one of his associates fit to be 'translated'. Otherwise he is a large, heavy-faced, somewhat vain and patronizing man, with some humour and imagination, who induces in women either irritation or adoration. A trades-unionist among butterflies, a rate-payer in Elf-land—yet among his group the romantic, poetical, imaginative man, who naturally takes command. Conceited but an artist, he is keen on the drama, while the others only wish to please the Duke. Because he has imagination and spirit he would play every part. To the gods he is no more ridiculous than Wagner at Bayreuth. If ignorant and vulgar, it is in a superficial way. He is Shakespeare's most insular figure, and such men are to be found all over England, chiefly in hostelries. Is he laughing at us, as we laugh at him?[2]

Of Touchstone, Mr. Priestley says that he has no unconscious absurdities, and is only droll by vocation, not laughable in himself. He then skilfully describes the effect of his humour on the other

---

[1] *The English Comic Characters*, 1925 (Lane).   [2] Cf. Maginn.

characters and the economy of the play. If his humour disquiets
Rosalind and Celia, it is because he reduces everything to one grotesque
level; and the feminine mind has hallowed chambers that must be
spared the jangle of motley's bells. Yet—and here is Mr. Priestley's
great point—which a German critic would have mangled—they reveal
his quality as a man, for they pay him the compliment of selecting him
as the companion of their flight to Arden. Once in Arden he resumes
his own business of parody and mockery; his whimsicalities are
a distorted reflection of what passes elsewhere in the drama. As he
stays outside the pastoral and remains in this world, he has to be content
with marrying an Audrey—the kind of damsel really to be found in
the countryside.

Mr. Priestley's estimate of Malvolio is startling and original, but,
we think, slightly too temperamental to be the whole truth. He says
truly that he is outside the real comic tradition, and that Shakespeare
contrives that he shall be covered with ridicule but never regards him
as a comic figure. But he over-insists on Shakespeare's personal
dislike for Puritans—for hard, unsympathetic, intolerant persons, over-
ambitious climbers, who have will and intellect divorced from tolerance,
charity, and love of the good things of this world. Mr. Priestley sees
in Malvolio a figure not untouched by pathos, and thinks it not
entirely preposterous that Olivia should return his passion. So far so
good, but he proceeds to say that Sir Tobies are now discredited, and
Shakespeare's villains are becoming our heroes: in fine, Malvolio the
pushing Puritan is the hero of half the American novels ever written.
Lastly, he detects a shade of Iago in Malvolio, and concludes that
his imprisonment was his purgation—for Shakespeare saw his soul
was in danger.

Mr. Priestley describes Sir Toby as a Falstaff without genius—
witty but not the cause of wit in others—an elderly schoolboy, whose
one problem is how to pass the time pleasantly. He makes no complaint
when hurt, and though fear of ridicule may explain this, it does
argue a stout nature. The last sentence hints at the seriousness
which always underlies Mr. Priestley's criticism, but we think it
excessive to speak of Sir Toby's marriage with Maria as his doom.[1]
Mr. Priestley foresees imaginatively that Maria with a husband to
reform will be a different thing—an effective schemer to restrain his
freedom. Was this present to Shakespeare's vision, and does it consort
with the most joyous of the comedies? Yet Mr. Priestley concludes
succinctly that we have caught Sir Toby's days at their highest point.

Mr. Priestley analyses Sir Andrew with deep penetration, and we
think his seriousness here is well timed. He shows how the world can
be centred in a poor human being. Every speech, he says, has a certain
Aguecheek flavour, and his childlike capacity for enjoyment is born

[1] Cf. Boas and Stopford Brooke (1913).

of a sense of wonder—a sense that experience destroys in all but the extremes of human kind—simpletons and geniuses. He cannot conceal what he thinks and feels. Like the sight of a monkey—a parody of life—he diverts but leaves us shamefaced. We see things done openly that we do in secret, and we blush for the monkey and for self.

We will pass over Falstaff's circle, as Mr. Priestley says truly that they are foils to Falstaff, merely noting that he has excellent things about Pistol and Mrs. Quickly, and calls Shallow a poor cinder in the darkness, whose silly talk with Silence can yet light up for a moment the whole strange business of this life. Falstaff, he says, as a literary figure, has no rival in his own sphere of the comic. Alluding to the criticism that Shakespeare worked too well and that the character exceeded the plot, and that either Falstaff should have been less fascinating or Henry should have acted differently, he rejects it because it assumes that Shakespeare expected us to 'take sides'—instead of which he simply showed us what does happen in the world. Henry had the ruthless fervour of the converted, and if you are to be King Falstaff must go. As we see from Falstaff's speech on honour, he was the avowed enemy of all responsibilities. In the light of responsibilities he appears so monstrous that we even drive him away resentfully. Shakespeare does not blacken him in Part II, for his worst offence was the robbery [1]—but he emphasizes the fact that he was an impossible companion for a ruler. Henry as a converted rake, conscious of improvement, naturally talks like a prig: and he was never a gentleman. The Falstaff of the stage was more the bloated buffoon than the subtle character that engages the philosopher. Morgann concentrates on Falstaff's incongruities, and tells us what he is—Professor Bradley tells us what he does. The two together—incongruity and freedom—give us Falstaff's secret, and that of the whole comic world. Falstaff embodies masculine comradeship, ease, and merriment. He is the supreme example of the clubbable man—and women, who suspect he would undermine their good work, do not like him. He appeals to us all the more by his naturalness, against his background of statesmen and stiff-armoured warriors. Compared with him we are slaves with our laws and restraints. He collapses in the end because he has done something he had no right to do—he has loved Henry, and cannot laugh it away.[2] It is the last stroke of irony and incongruity that the comic hero should be betrayed by his heart. . . .

We must admit that here again it seems to us Mr. Priestley over-emphasizes the shadows that must fall even on a comic landscape. His criticism is delicate and poetic, but to him, as to all sensitive persons, contact with the real world is something of a shock. No one can enjoy Falstaff's humour more; but his immediate thought which comes from the impression has been trebly distilled by meditation, and he

[1] Cf. Middleton Murry.   [2] Cf. Rötscher, Boas, Marriott.

has added to it his own experience of life. Whether this experience is
close enough akin to that of which such figures as Falstaff and Malvolio
were wrought is a question that we will raise, but not answer. There
is a lyric note in Mr. Priestley's criticism; he emits some unrivalled
flashes of insight, but we think his system-building to be slightly out
of perspective. At the same time his criticism is of the carefully
finished kind; while dealing with the separate part of the play the
whole of it is imaginatively present to him. Let it be added that
Professor Bradley's statement that the conclusion of *Henry IV* leaves
an unsatisfactory impression which was not intended has not been
disproved.

VIII

MR. HARLEY GRANVILLE-BARKER [1] reminds us that Shakespeare was not only a dramatist, but an Elizabethan dramatist—
a topical wit. Finally, perhaps he tried to do more with the theatre
than its nature allowed—and failed. What gave the theatre its sudden
direct hold on the people was the newly arisen art of emotional acting,
lacking to the older plays. Burbage and Alleyn gave their audience
music and poetry and popular oratory in one. Shakespeare like all
artists had both a complaisant and a demonic side. He gave his
audience what it wanted, but was also bent on having his own way.
The idea to him was more than the thing, the character more than
the plot. Even *L.L.L.* survives dramatically through its ideas.
Costard's apology for Sir Nathaniel, 'There, an't shall please you . . .',
does not belong to the plot or fun-making scheme—has been inspired
by no fashion or learnt in any school of play-writing. Already (1591)
Shakespeare is having his way—the Shakespeare who was to lodge
Shylock in a fairy tale and create Falstaff. The demonic genius had
always to strike a bargain with the popular playwright—but he went
from success to success. We measure his progress by those suddenly
illuminating things that light up not one dramatic moment, but a man's
whole nature or even the background of his life, e.g. the hostess's
tale of Falstaff's death—or Bardolph's 'Would I were with him . . .'.
    When Shakespeare wrote *Henry V* he was master of his craft, and
had a spacious subject: yet he disappoints. To complete Henry he
must sacrifice Falstaff, for the newly dignified king could never
survive the old ruffian's ironic comments—but is he rewarded? The
play is one of action—yet all the while Shakespeare is apologizing that
he cannot make it effective. Henry is the perfect man of action,
neither ill drawn nor uninteresting, but we only come near him
on the night before Agincourt when he searches his soul. Yet this
is not new, as we saw in the scenes with his father and Hotspur—and

[1] *From Henry V to Hamlet*, 1925 (Brit. Acad. Annual Sh. Lecture. New
York: Oxford University Press).

soul-searching is not his strong suit. One can detect Shakespeare's disappointment with his hero, and disillusion with his art and his ambitious self. Yet he had learnt that to present the external pageantry of great events his theatre availed as little as a puppet-show—and that the successful man of action did not make the most interesting hero. There must be an idea to give life to the action.

In the comedies that follow he creates and reveals character; in *J.C.* he chooses for his hero not Caesar, but Brutus the philosopher, the wise man who does the wrong thing. He is unsatisfactory for drama because unemotional. Now Cassius runs away with the play, now Mark Antony: for when a character springs to life Shakespeare will nor refuse him his chance. Yet he returns to Brutus, for to Shakespeare the essential thing now is not what a character does, but what he *is*. If *Henry V* was the danger-point, *J.C.* is the turning-point of his career. It was the prelude to *Hamlet*, which, according to foot-rule criticism, has every fault. Yet it succeeded, because he made comprehensible man's passionate spiritual struggles. *Hamlet* is the triumph of dramatic idea over dramatic action, of character over plot. The play that follows—*M. for M.*—has beauty and ruthless wisdom, but Shakespeare is not working happily. That he may do his duty to the plot his characters must suffer violence at the end. The plot of *Othello* is made impossible by the compressions of the second act. There was no moment when Desdemona could have sinned with Cassio. But Shakespeare knew that intensity of experiences counts above arithmetical process. Drama henceforth lay only formally in external action, and really in revelation of character, in clashes between men's natures, and the struggles in a man's own nature.

Shakespeare had only the spoken word to interpret his idea, and after *Othello* he uses the soliloquy sparingly and falls back on hard-hitting dialogue. His problem was to hold his audience in the bonds of illusion, and how he solved it remains his secret. There is no explaining the marvel of the sleep-walking scene. *Lear* has a double plot, and he saved himself from writing a longer play than *Hamlet* by heroic measures. No character more runs away with him than Lear. To develop Lear he accumulates every stage device, and, through the storm, he relates him to the rigours of this world as they fall on rich and poor alike. The storm also reflects the greater storm in Lear's mind, and it is the really dramatic thing.

It has been said that Shakespeare's plays suffered because they were written for the theatre, but perhaps the Elizabethans responded more to the art of personal expression than we who live in a scientific age. We ask whether, in his greatest work, he enlarged or shattered his medium? But his greater plays have hardly yet been put to full theatrical proof, and the theatre was changing before he ceased to write for it. However, it is but common sense to judge him before all as an

Elizabethan playwright. We know the Elizabethan stage, but only experiment will show us the effect it can produce. Shakespeare depended on an art that is irrevocably wedded to the playwright's, but largely in this case his own incidental creation—the art of interpretative acting. His art has not yet been truly studied in this respect—of the demands which his greatest work makes upon acting according to the privileges which the technique he evolved bestowed on it. Much should be handed down from master to pupil in the traditional way; but we neglect our theatre's traditions.

The crowning moment is when actors and singers lose themselves in their art. This is nothing so finite as perfection; but perfection is surpassed and something of the quality of life itself assumed. Because the interpretation is done in terms of life itself, through the medium of living men and women, it is done more fitly. No other art can make the world of the imagination so real to us and the immaterial so actual. It is foolish to transport Shakespeare from the world of the theatre into a vacuum of scholarship. It may be possible to bring such a theatre as Shakespeare's into being, for he was always the practical playwright. His was the art of speech made eloquent by rhythm and memorable by harmony of sense and sound; and he sought to pour his vision into the crucible of human nature and let it abide there as a living symbol. . . .

These are certainly fruitful ideas, and they proceed from the mind of one who, to the accomplishments of the actor, has added much of the critic and something of the poet. It has been usual to think that Shakespeare is better appreciated in the study than on the stage. If Mr. Granville-Barker does not disprove this, he at least makes us doubt, and it might be well to turn back to Lamb's famous essay. What he does is to convince that it is humanly possible to present the whole of Shakespeare's thought by means of acting: but whether it has ever been presented, or ever will be, is another question. He at least explains to us that there is an upper region where all the arts mingle, and he points to the ladder whereby the dramatist, and Shakespeare in particular, mounts towards it. Among lesser matters we may mention that he makes plain that Shakespeare used his form merely as a vehicle to express his idea; and by another road he joins with those critics who have remarked that *Hamlet* pleases a popular audience despite its unsolved mystery.

IX

MR. LASCELLES ABERCROMBIE [1] has some pregnant thoughts on the balance of good and evil in Shakespeare's tragic art, that might be fitly compared to those of Professor Bradley on the effect of evil in Shakespeare's world, and to Professor Macneile Dixon's belief that

[1] *The Idea of Great Poetry*, 1925 (Secker).

character is only a factor in tragedy. Mr. Abercrombie says that we are to look for the final harmony of good and evil precisely in the character which creates and endures the evil. He is the evil he endures, and also the good which exists by reason of his endurance of that evil. In a personality's assertion of itself against the hostility it has provoked —in the vigour by which a man is *himself against the world*—Shakespeare places the good his tragedy requires. Thus he turned sordid motive and habitual crime into the tragedy of Macbeth.

Macbeth commits crime upon crime till life ceases to have any meaning: such is the process of evil, and it is wholly in Macbeth. The murders are evil in themselves, but the tragedy is concerned with the evil that they are to Macbeth. The unimaginative Lady Macbeth succumbs to the strain, but he, sensitive and highly strung, endures to the last, and grandly looks despair in the face. The more he suffers the more capable of suffering he becomes. He has staked all and lost, and damned himself for nothing—yet he masters this appalling moment because he *knows* it, and with his unquenchable mind makes the evil live before him. There is no depth below the conviction that life is an affair of absolute inconsequence. Misfortune and personality now unite, and the whole tragic action is incarnate in the life of Macbeth. We see not only what he feels, but the personality that feels it, and because he proclaims that life signifies nothing, personal life does *signify itself*.[1] The unity of the poem's total impression is Macbeth himself. His quality as an individual, that cannot be analysed, is a symbol of life itself, creating, enduring, and relishing its own tragic destiny.

Hamlet, Mr. Abercrombie says, has been taken at his own valuation by critics, but has not impressed the world as a contemptible figure. Because he has the inexplicable individual force which is the essence of personality, his contradictions of thought and action always seem to be *in character*. The Ghost and play scene can be explained away, but he is finally convinced by intuition that Claudius has killed his father. He delays because the delay exists in his own mind. He himself is the reason why his desire remains unacted. We see exposed the trapped anguish of human nature found weaker than events—and his weakness is involved with human nature's finest strength. The events are tragic because transformed into the very stuff of the personal life around which they organize themselves. The evil of Hamlet's tragedy is that he must express bitter self-contempt: but the harmony proceeds from his concentration of the whole order of the poem into himself. Harmony cannot exist unless there is good to match evil: but no one can miss the good in Hamlet's character. . . .

Mr. Abercrombie is a critic of strong convictions, absolute sincerity,

---

[1] Mr. Middleton Murry considers that Macbeth's 'To-morrow . . .' speech overcharges the play, and that it belongs to Shakespeare, not Macbeth. Cf. also Figgis.

and forcible utterance. He is swayed by no opinions of others, but looks fixedly at his subject and then records his vision. Unlike the Germans he can pursue a thought to its logical conclusion and yet retain its poetry. He locates in the individual that force which, according to Professor Macneile Dixon, exceeds the individual. It might be objected that Macbeth does not become more capable of suffering as he plunges into crime, and that his final despair is more negative than positive: but we prefer to submit our minds to be stimulated by the main argument. That all things are finally to be referred to man—and that good is present in one who does bad actions—these, we think, are thoughts that count in any estimate of man's destiny and place in the universe. This best kind of modern criticism, like Mr. Granville-Barker's, helps us to realize that the object of art is to guide us ever a few steps onward into the endless labyrinth of the soul.

X

WE will first deal with general remarks on Shakespeare's religion. To Miss Mackenzie the tragedies are a prouder confession of faith in God and man than anything that has been written since the Gospels. To Professor Macneile Dixon, Shakespeare, compared with Aeschylus, to the wonder of succeeding generations appears himself without religion, blind or indifferent to the larger questions and issues, the continuity and the whole of things. Miss Winstanley, on the other hand, says that his great tragedies are as religious as those of Aeschylus or Sophocles; and that it was impossible for Shakespeare, who was a strong nationalist, to be indifferent to religion. Mr. Priestley finds him interested in this world to the exclusion of more distant and nebulous realms.

Of moral and philosophical comments we present the following: Professor Macneile Dixon compares him with Sophocles, in that he will not support the moral order of the world by suppressing the facts. Miss Winstanley says that he excelled in the universal truth at which the men of the sixteenth and seventeenth centuries aimed. He had a questing philosophy, according to Sir E. K. Chambers—a firm hold on the ultimate values of life. Mr. J. M. Robertson thinks that he was not bent to reshape the world, but sought to live in it as best he could; neither was he preoccupied about moral lessons, though well enough able to moralize; but he had a sane and sure vision of life and man, and besides being a great poet had a great perception of Reality. Mr. Granville-Barker's opinion is that he had what is now called a social conscience, since pity is the basis of genius; and that his drama brings us into immediate and intimate contact with man as he essentially *is*, in an *ever present tense*. Mr. Abercrombie considers that his method of deriving good from evil enabled him to be supreme in greatness of achievement above all other tragic poets.

We get but two political comments: Miss Winstanley's, that he was an impassioned English nationalist; and Miss Mackenzie's, that he would have agreed with Burke that the most important thing for any nation is the personal character of the men who rule it.

Miss Mackenzie describes his characters as real people, whose emotional experiences of events are also real. To Miss Winstanley his great figures are superhuman as the sibyls and prophets of Michael Angelo: all the elements are human, but there is something in the total effect above humanity. Sir E. K. Chambers alludes to his intuition of character; and Mr. Granville-Barker says that he cared much for character and little for plot.

Miss Mackenzie finds in his plays a strong skeletal structure of idea. He mastered his rebellious medium, she says, by nothing so easy as 'inspiration', but by the sheer desperate labour of a mighty personality, driven and guided by the tremendous uses of the will. He achieved the balance between creative and constructive power that is the hall-mark of the greatest artists; and he was creative as no man else, though not inventive. Sir E. K. Chambers speaks of his magic of phrase, lyrical impulse, and clash of drama. Mr. Robertson gives him unmatched verse faculty; and calls it his supreme achievement that he could mediate between the soul of the multitude and his own, and lay great bases for eternity in popular works which yet contained his utmost power. The idea was more than the thing to Shakespeare, in Mr. Granville-Barker's opinion; and the vital quality in his art was the principle behind the plot by which it seems to move of itself—less in writing great dramatic poetry than the power to project character in action.

The following unclassified general remarks remain: Mr. Robertson's, that his life was an evolution, like that of all men; and Miss Mackenzie's, that he had no sex-obsession, but saw all sides of it as an affair of the whole self, of will and brain no less than impulse of soul or body. . . .

A few positive statements about Shakespeare's religion and politics still linger on, but we put these aside as we attempt to form an image of him through the means of his latest critics. That image is of a man like us but beyond us. He uses religion, philosophy, morals, politics, human characters, drama, verse in such a way as to exceed our power of generalization. The best way to read him is to bring to him in absolute sincerity our whole experience and feel the mystery when the mind-abyss into which it plunges returns no echo. These latest critics also bring to the work of interpretation not only special gifts of intellect, but of heart also—even personal idiosyncrasies—and they do not bring them in vain: yet Shakespeare remains aloof, all-absorbing—he remains Shakespeare.

ALPHABETICAL LIST OF CRITICS

ABERCROMBIE, Lascelles
Addison, Joseph
Alden, R. Macdonald
Allen, J. W.
BAB, Julius
Baculard d'Arnaud, F. Th.
Bagehot, Walter
Bailey, John
Baker, G. P.
Barante
Baretti, G.
Baynes, T. S.
Beeching, H. C.
Benedix, R.
Benson, John
Birch, W. J.
Blair, Hugh
Boas, F. S.
Bodenstedt, F.
Boerne, Ludwig
Bowden, H. S.
Bowdler, Thomas
Boyle, R.
Bradley, A. C.
Brandes, G.
Bridges, Robert
Brooke, Stopford
Brown, C. Armitage
Brown, Henry
Brown, Jane
Bucknill, J. C.
Bulthaupt, H.
CAIRD, Edward
Campbell, Thomas
Canning, A. S. G.
Capell, E.
Carlyle, Thomas

Cartwright, William
Case, R. H.
Cavendish, Margaret
Chambers, E. K.
Chasles, P.
Chateaubriand
Chedworth, Lord (John Howe)
Chevrillon, André
Clarke, Charles Cowden
Clarke, Mary Cowden
Clutton-Brock, A.
Coleridge, Hartley
Coleridge, S. T.
Collins, J. Churton
Corbin, John
Corson, H.
Courtenay, T. Peregrine
Courthope, W. J.
Cowl, R. P.
Cowley, Abraham
Creizenach, W.
Croce, Benedetto
Cuningham, H.
Cunliffe, J. W.
DAVIES, T.
Dawson, George
Deighton, K.
De La Roche
Delius, N.
Denham, Sir John
Dennis, John
De Quincey, Thomas
Deschamps, E.
Diderot, Denis
Digges, Leonard
Dixon, W. Macneile

Doering, A.
Dowden, Edward
Drake (1699)
Drake, Nathan
Dryden, John
Duport, Paul
Dyboski, R.
ECCLES, I. A.
Edwards, Thomas
Eliot, T. S.
Elze, Karl
Emerson, R. W.
Eschenburg, J. J.
Evelyn, John
FARMER, R.
Faucit, Helen
Feis, J.
Felton, S.
Figgis, Darrell
Fischer, Kuno
Flathe, J. L. F.
Fleay, F. G.
Flecknoe, Richard
Fletcher, George
Friesen, H. F. von
Fuller, Thomas
Furnivall, F. J.
GANS, E.
Garve, C.
Geoffroy, J. L.
Gerstenberg, H. W. von
Gervinus, G. G.
Gessner, Th.
Gildon, Charles
Giles, H.
Girardin, Saint-Marc
Goethe, J. W. von
Granville-Barker, H.

Renan, E.
Riccoboni, Louis
Richardson, William
Richter, Helene
Ritson, J.
Robertson, J. M.
Robertson, Thomas
Rohrbach, Carl
Rose, Edward
Rötscher, H. T.
Rowe, Nicholas
Rümelin, G.
Rymer, Thomas
SAINTSBURY, George
St. John, Spencer
Schelling, F. E.
Schlegel, A. W.
Schlegel, F.
Schmidt, J.
Schücking, L. L.
Seccombe, T.
Sedley, Sir Charles
Sélincourt, E. de
Seymour, E. H.
Sharpe, Henry
Shephard, Samuel
Sherlock, M.
Sievers, E.
Simpson, R.
Sisson, C. J.

Skottowe, A.
Snider, D. J.
Spalding, William
Spedding, J.
Staël, Madame de
Stapfer, P.
Steevens, George
Stendhal, De (Henry Beyle)
Stephen, Leslie
Stoll, E. E.
Strachey, Lytton
Swinburne, A. C.
Symonds, J. A.
Symons, Arthur
TAINE, H. A.
Talbot, B.
Tate, Nahum
Taylor, E.
Temple, Sir William
Ten Brink, B.
Theobald, Lewis
Thompson, A. Hamilton
Thorndike, A. H.
Thümmel, J.
Tieck, Ludwig
Traumann, E.
Trench, W. F.
Tucker, T. G.

Türck, H.
Tyler, Thomas
ULRICI, H.
VERPLANCK, G.
Viehoff, H.
Vigny, A. de
Villemain
Vischer, F. Th.
Voltaire
WARBURTON, W.
Ward, A. W.
Warton, T.
Wells, William
Wendell, Barrett
Wendlandt, W.
Werder, Karl
Werner, H. A.
Wetz, W.
Whalley, Peter
Whateley, Thomas
White, R. Grant
Wild, Robert
Wilson, John ('Christopher North')
Winstanley, Lilian
Wolff, M. J.
Wordsworth, Charles
Wyndham, George
YEATS, W. B.
ZIEGLER, F. W.

INDEX